Architecture and the Landscape of Modernity in China before 1949

This book explores China's encounter with architecture and modernity in the tumultuous epoch before Communism – an encounter that was mediated not by a singular notion of modernism emanating from the west, but that was uniquely multifarious, deriving from a variety of sources both from the west and, importantly, from the east. The heterogeneous origins of modernity in China are what make its experience distinctive and its architectural encounters exceptional.

These experiences are investigated through a re-evaluation of established knowledge of the subject within the wider landscape of modern art practices in China. The study draws on original archival and photographic material from different artistic genres and, architecturally, concentrates on China's engagement with the west through the treaty ports and leased territories, the emergence of architecture as a profession in China, and Japan's omnipresence, not least in Manchuria, which reached its apogee in the puppet state of Manchukuo.

The study's geographically, temporally, and architecturally inclusive approach framed by the concept of multiple modernities questions the application of conventional theories of modernity or post-colonialism to the Chinese situation. By challenging conventional modernist historiography that has marginalised the experiences of the west's *other* for much of the last century, this book proposes different ways of grappling with and comprehending the distinction and complexity of China's experiences and its encounter with architectural modernity.

Edward Denison is an architectural historian and lecturer at the Bartlett School of Architecture, University College London. His previous publications include *Ultra-Modernism: Architecture and Modernity in Manchuria* (2017), *Luke Him Sau, Architect: China's Missing Modern* (2014), *The Life of the British Home: An Architectural History* (2012), *McMorran & Whitby* (2009), *Modernism in China: Architectural Visions and Revolutions* (2008), *Building Shanghai: The Story of China's Gateway* (2006), and *Asmara: Africa's Secret Modernist City* (2003).

Architecture and the Landscape of Modernity in China before 1949

Edward Denison

LONDON AND NEW YORK

First published 2017
by Routledge
2 Park Square, Milton Park, Abingdon, Oxon OX14 4RN

and by Routledge
711 Third Avenue, New York, NY 10017

Routledge is an imprint of the Taylor & Francis Group, an informa business

© 2017 Edward Denison

The right of Edward Denison to be identified as author of this work has been asserted by him in accordance with sections 77 and 78 of the Copyright, Designs and Patents Act 1988.

All rights reserved. No part of this book may be reprinted or reproduced or utilised in any form or by any electronic, mechanical, or other means, now known or hereafter invented, including photocopying and recording, or in any information storage or retrieval system, without permission in writing from the publishers.

Trademark notice: Product or corporate names may be trademarks or registered trademarks, and are used only for identification and explanation without intent to infringe.

British Library Cataloguing-in-Publication Data
A catalogue record for this book is available from the British Library

Library of Congress Cataloging-in-Publication Data
Names: Denison, Edward, author.
Title: Architecture and the landscape of modernity in China before 1949/ Edward Denison.
Description: New York: Routledge, 2017. | Includes bibliographical references and index.
Identifiers: LCCN 2016036629| ISBN 9781472431684 (hardback) | ISBN9781315567686 (ebook)
Subjects: LCSH: Modern movement (Architecture) – China. | Architecture and society – China – History – 20th century.
Classification: LCC NA1545.5.M63 D46 2017 | DDC 720.1/03 – dc23
LC record available at https://lccn.loc.gov/2016036629

ISBN: 9781472431684 (hbk)
ISBN: 9781315567686 (ebk)

Typeset in Sabon
by Florence Production Ltd, Stoodleigh, Devon, UK

Through the great Gate
Along the towered Wall
By banks where ducks preened in the winter sun
We rode.

You lifted the reins.
Swiftly you drew away.
Your cry came back in the wind.

That Gate, that Wall are levelled.
Wind stirs the dust.
Wind whispers the echo
of you to me
of me to you.

(Poem by Wilma Fairbank to Phyllis Liang (Lin Huiyin) *c.*1958, Peabody Essex Museum, Salem, Massachusetts)

To others

Contents

List of illustrations ix
Preface xv
Acknowledgements xvii

PART I
China and the meaning of modernity 1

1 Introduction 3

2 Intellectual orientations: the unavoidable burden of context 11

3 China's multiple modernities 27

4 Chinese art and its multiple modernities 67

PART II
Architecture and modernity 89

5 The advent of architecture 91

6 Foreign settlements before 1912 100

7 Modernism and nationalism 136

8 Japan: China's mirror to modernism 200

9 Shanghai: multiple modernities' exemplar 257

10 Curtailed modernities 292

Bibliography 311
Index 329

Illustrations

Figures

1.1	Shanghai's Joint Savings Society Building containing the Park Hotel (1934)	5
1.2	Modern industrial buildings at Anshan steel foundry, near Fushun	6
1.3	The monumental headquarters of the Hong Kong Shanghai Banking Corporation (1935)	6
1.4	The quasi-Japanese design of the Department of Communications, Hsinking (Changchun), Manchukuo	7
1.5	The Zhong Hua bookstore (1936), Guangzhou	7
1.6	The shops and multicultural shoppers on Harbin's Kitaiskaya Street in the mid-1930s	7
1.7	The potential to convert Nanjing's ancient city walls into a highway for motorcars	8
1.8	Model of the Mayor's Office (1934), one of the principal modern buildings in Shanghai's Civic Centre	8
1.9	Plan of Dalian (1903), laid out by the Russians	9
1.10	Map of the centre of Hsinking, the capital of Manchukuo, planned by the Japanese	10
2.1	'Progress', by a western cartoonist in China	18
3.1	Advertisement and still from the film *San Ge Mo Deng Nü Xing* (*Three Modern Women*) by Tian Han	52
3.2	Advertisement for Aspirin, employing temporal references and imagery	58
3.3	Speed defined the spirit of the age as this 1935 advertisement from Shanghai attests	58
3.4	Cartoon from Shanghai in 1924 emphasising temporal progress depicted in various every day scenes	59
6.1	Trinity Cathedral (1866)	105
6.2	The first Hong Kong and Shanghai Banking Corporation (HSBC) offices in Shanghai (1877)	105
6.3	The Public Market (1899) on Shanghai's Nanjing Road	106
6.4	The Palace Hotel (1907) on Shanghai's Bund	106
6.5	The Club Concordia (1907), Shanghai	108
6.6	Arthur Adamson and Poy Gum Lee photographed in 1928 on the terrace of the Foreign YMCA, Shanghai	110
6.7	The Russo-Chinese bank (1902) in Shanghai	114

x   *Illustrations*

6.8	Shanghai skyline depicted in a Christmas greeting published in 1933	114
6.9	Architectural drawing of one of Harbin's many residences for the staff of Russia's China Eastern Railway	120
6.10	Harbin's hotel 'Moderne' (1914)	121
6.11	Russian plan of Dalian showing the 'European City' centre	123
6.12	Russian Dalian in 1903 showing the public parks, paved roads and many buildings under construction	124
6.13	The SMR zone of Changchun designed by Katō Yonokichi in 1907	130
7.1	Lü Yanzhi (1894–1929), graduate of Cornell University	141
7.2	Fan Wenzhao (aka Robert Fan) (1899–1973), graduate of the University of Pennsylvania	141
7.3	Yang Tingbao (1901–1982), graduate of the University of Pennsylvania	145
7.4	Zhao Shen (1898–1978), graduate of the University of Pennsylvania	145
7.5	Chen Zhi with Liang Sicheng before studying architecture at the University of Pennsylvania in the mid-1920s	147
7.6	Liang Sicheng and Lin Huiyin with their friend Wilma Fairbank	148
7.7	Dong Dayou (1899–1973), graduate of the University of Minnesota and Columbia University	152
7.8	Liu Jipiao (1900–1992), graduate of the Université de Paris, Sorbonne, and L'École Nationale des Beaux-Arts	152
7.9	The China section at the Exposition Internationale des Arts Décoratifs et Industriels Modernes in Paris, 1925	154
7.10	Liu Jipiao's design for the China section at the Exposition Internationale des Arts Décoratifs et Industriels Modernes in Paris, 1925	154
7.11	Some of Liu Jipiao's designs for the West Lake Expo (1929)	155
7.12	Luke Him Sau with his colleagues at the Architectural Association, London, between 1927 and 1930	157
7.13	Concept drawing in 1935 of the Bank of China headquarters	158
7.14	The Bank of China headquarters (1935–9), Shanghai, designed by Luke Him Sau and Palmer & Turner	159
7.15	The Lester Institute of Technical Education (1934), Shanghai	160
7.16	Huang Zuoshen with Le Corbusier, after graduating from the Architectural Association in 1939	161
7.17	Five United Architects	161
7.18	The front entrance and lighting design of Paramount Ballroom (1934), Shanghai	163
7.19	Advertisement for Modern Home, a modern interior design firm established by Richard Paulick	163
7.20	Concept design for Pére Robert Apartment, Shanghai, by H.J. Hajek (1933)	164
7.21	Beijing Union Medical College (1917), Beijing	167
7.22	Henry Killam Murphy, senior partner of Murphy & Dana (later Murphy, McGill & Hamlin)	168

7.23	Design for the Yale in China campus, Changsha, by Murphy & Dana (1916)	169
7.24	The Sun Yat Sen Mausoleum (1925), designed by Lü Yanzhi	171
7.25	Liu Jipiao's concept designs for the Nationalist government's headquarters in Nanjing	174
7.26	Sketch by Huang Yüyü illustrating the national style for the Plan of the Capital	176
7.27	The Central Agricultural Laboratory (1934), Nanjing	177
7.28	The National Central Museum (1935), Nanjing, designed by Xu Jinzhi	178
7.29	The plan for Greater Shanghai (1931) showing the cruciform Civic Centre	181
7.30	Designs for the library and museum in the Shanghai Civic Centre (1935) by Dong Dayou	183
7.31	Artist's impression of the China Aviation Association building (1935), Shanghai and plans	183
7.32	The Chinese Society of Architects, 1933	187
8.1	The Japanese garden in Shanghai's northern district of Hongkou	210
8.2	Cover of 'Manchoukuo-German Trade and Goodwill Number' of the journal *Manchuria* (1937)	213
8.3	A front cover from the Manchurian Architectural Association (*Manshu Kenchiku Kyoukai*) journal	214
8.4	Advertisement for the state-sponsored Yamato Hotel chain	219
8.5	Advertisement for the South Manchuria Railway's Asia Express, and the Asia and the Tabusa	220
8.6	The plan of Harbin showing the three settlements created by the railway	224
8.7	A scene from Harbin's thriving Kitaiskaya Street	225
8.8	Plan of Dalian from the early 1920s	227
8.9	The 'ultra-modern' JQAK radio station (1936), Dalian	228
8.10	The Tokiwa Cinema (1928–1931)	230
8.11	Dalian Railway Station (1937), designed by Takaoka Building Contractors	231
8.12	Plan of Hsinking, dominated by the Tatung Circle	235
8.13	The Kotoku Kaikan and the Nikke Gallery on Hsinking's Chuo-dori	237
8.14	The Feng Le Cinema (1936), Hsinking	238
8.15	The massive Tatung Circle forming the heart of Hsinking's new plan	238
8.16	Plan of the centre of Hsinking showing the Tatung Circle and surrounding city blocks	239
8.17	Residence of the President of the Central Bank of Manchu designed by Arata Endo	240
8.18	The Manchoukuo Mixed Court (1939), Hsinking	242
8.19	Plan for the South Lake Complex (1939), designed by Junzo Sakakura	243
8.20	Fast-ism is characterised in this cartoon titled 'Speed Crisis' by Shinkyo Comics	246

xii *Illustrations*

9.1	Paul Veysseyre (1896–1963), graduate of the École Nationale des Beaux-Arts in Paris	260
9.2	Josef Alois Hammerschmidt (1891–?), graduate of Vienna's Polytechnic University	260
9.3	René Minutti (1887–?), graduate of the Polytechnic School of Zurich	261
9.4	Bright Fraser (1894–?), graduate of Liverpool University	261
9.5	Broadway Mansions (1934), Shanghai, designed by Bright Fraser and Palmer & Turner	262
9.6	George Leopold Wilson (1880–1967), Head of Palmer & Turner's Shanghai office	263
9.7	Chinese-style interior of the Shanghai home of George Wilson, Head of Palmer & Turner's Shanghai office	263
9.8	Designs from advertisements for the Shanghai Power Company	265
9.9	Advertisement for the Shanghai Power Company	266
9.10	Montage titled 'The Future Shanghai Race Course' showing the march of modernity	267
9.11	Advertisements for Andersen, Meyer & Co. drawing on the theme of modernity	269
9.12	Cartoon by the famous Shanghai artist, Sapajou, in 1937 following the Japanese invasion of China	270
9.13	Aerial photograph of Shanghai in the 1930s showing dense urban grain	271
9.14	The 21-storey extension to Wing On department store (1934)	277
9.15	Sun Sun department store (1926), designed by Charles Gonda	278
9.16	The illuminated tower of the Grand Theatre (1933) designed by László Hudec	281
9.17	Advertisement (1937) for Ford by Chang Ching-huei	282
9.18	Proposal for the headquarters of the China Merchants Steam Navigation Company (1939)	284
9.19	The 'Ultra-Modern' suite inside the Cathay Hotel	286
9.20	The devastating scenes outside Shanghai's Great World on 14 August 1937	287
10.1	Liang Sicheng with other members of the UN Permanent Headquarters Committee	298
10.2	Liang Sicheng is the only non-westerner among an all-star cast of western professionals attending the bicentennial conference titled Planning Man's Built Environment	299

Plates

1. Two covers from 1932 of the magazine *Xian Dai (Les Contemporains)* by Shi Zhecun
2. Front cover of the 1931 edition of *Xian Dai Xue Sheng (Modern Student)*
3. The eroticism of this scantily clad Chinese woman conveys one version of modernity by breaking with artistic and moral convention

Illustrations xiii

4   The cover of the magazine *Shi Dai*, which employs a variety of imagery and devices to denote modernity
5   Advertisement of Shanghai's Grand Theatre, designed by László Hudec (1933)
6   Detail of Nanjing's Da Hua Theatre, designed by Yang Tingbao (1934)
7   The foyer of the Nan Ping Theatre in Kunming, designed by Allied Architects (1939)
8   The Asahiza Cinema (1936), Changchun
9   The Continental Theatre (1938), Shenyang
10 The Tokiwa Cinema (1932), Dalian, designed by Munakata Architectural Office
11 Concept drawing of Shanghai's Metropol Theatre (1934), designed by Zhao Shen of Allied Architects
12 St Francis Xavier Cathedral (1849) designed by Father Nicholas Massa
13 The Union Assurance Company of Canton (1916), designed by Palmer & Turner
14 One of the residences for the staff of Russia's China Eastern Railway in an art nouveau style
15 The entrance of West Lake Expo (1929), Hangzhou, designed by Liu Jipiao
16 St John's University, Shanghai, designed by Atkinson & Dallas
17 Former Memorial Building (1917) of the West China Union University, Chengdu, designed by Frederick Rountree
18 Sun Yat Sen Memorial Auditorium and Monument (1926), Guangzhou, designed by Lü Yanzhi
19 The National Stadium (1931), Nanjing, designed by Kwan, Chu & Yang
20 The Mayor's Office (1934), Shanghai, designed by Dong Dayou
21 The China Aviation Association Building (1935), Shanghai
22 The main entrance to the Shanghai Stadium (1935), Shanghai, designed by Dong Dayou
23 Cover of *The Builder* from June 1936 with an artist's impression of Bank of China headquarters
24 Front cover of a special edition of the *Journal of Manchurian Architectural Association* (July 1933)
25 The State Council (1936), Hsinking, designed by Ishi Tatzuro
26 Advertisement for the South Manchuria Railway Company with its conspicuously colonial message
27 Grosvenor House apartments (1934), Shanghai, designed by Albert Edmund Algar and Palmer & Turner
28 Bank of China Headquarters (1935–9), Shanghai, designed by Luke Him Sau and Palmer & Turner
29 Illustration of a locomotive by the architect-artist Liu Ji Piao for the cover of *Gong Xian*
30 Shanghai's industrial and architectural eminence combine in this advertisement for coal

31	The former Sun department store (1933), Shanghai, designed by Kwan, Chu & Yang
32	The Transport Bank (1937–1946), Shanghai, designed by Charles Gonda
33	Magy Apartments (1936), Shanghai, designed by Léonard, Veysseyre & Kruze
34	The Joint Savings Society Building (1934), Shanghai, designed by László Hudec
35	The China Baptist Publishing Society (1930), Shanghai, designed by László Hudec
36	Cover of *Man Hua Jie* encapsulating Shanghai's decadance and modernity
37	Cartoon of Shanghai's intoxicating nightlife
38	The gaudy interior of the Grand Theatre, designed by László Hudec
39	Cigarette advertisement employing various modern devices
40	The science-fiction image of urban modernity depicted on the front cover of *Zhong Guo Man Hua*
41	A dystopian future illustrated on the front cover of *Zhong Guo Man Hua* from December 1936
42	The carefully choreographed skyline of Pudong provides a fittingly future-facing backdrop to historic Shanghai on the opposite side of the river
43	Map of China showing the principal cities, treaty ports and foreign settlements
44	Map of Manchuria, showing the principal railway lines and settlements

Preface

History is a record of power. The writing of history is a privilege of life's winners and denied its losers. The twentieth century – modernism's century – was dominated by 'the west' and its 'official' history bears testimony to its dominance. For scholarship generally and architectural history specifically, the consequence is a picture constructed in the west's image and constricted by its partial gaze; the richness of a global landscape reduced to familiar terrain. It is a fact that sites outside the west are disproportionately under-represented in modernist historiography compared with those in or of the west. Despite modernism's international pretensions, implicit in its original vision and its subsequent historiography is the assumption of inferiority of subjects beyond the west, a postulation asserted through inauthenticity, belatedness, diluteness and remoteness, geographically, intellectually and even racially. This artificial edifice, constructed collectively and often unconsciously over the course of acentury, is at last crumbling to reveal a more multifaceted image of the global encounter with architectural modernity that more accurately reflects the profound experiences that have led to the urbanisation of our species and the dawn of the Anthropocene. The emerging historical landscape, as with the balance of political power internationally, is shifting from a singular concept of modernism observed through a western lens, to a more complete and complex picture of constantly changing and multiple modernities that have transformed our planet in less than a century.

A multiple modernities approach is as vital to understanding the past as it is to planning for the future. It is especially pertinent to the Chinese context because it not only questions the application of conventional theories of modernity, development and post-colonialism, but also offers a more effective way of comprehending the unique multifariousness of China's encounter with architectural modernity. Furthermore, it resolves the inherent paradox in examining China using non-Chinese criteria.

Situated firmly in this new landscape, this book sets out to explore and better understand the exceptional example of China's encounter with architecture and modernity throughout the first half of the twentieth century. 1949 is by no means intended to be decisive, as there were obviously examples of architectural continuity after the Communist victory that year, but the date offers a manageable point to take stock before the next chapter of China's history unfolded. Three key themes dominate this study: *architecture*, *modernity* and *China*. In the context of architecture, it seeks to contribute to current knowledge of the practice in pre-Communist China. In terms of the study of modernity, it addresses the uniqueness of China's encounter with modernity through the concept of multiple modernities. In the context of China studies, it aims to contribute to redressing the current under-representation of architecture within studies of the modern arts.

The premise of this study proposes that China's encounter with architectural modernity was mediated multifariously, constantly negotiated by internal political conditions and by contact not only with western powers but also with an eastern power, Japan. The heterogeneous origin of modernity in China is what makes its experience unique and its architectural encounters distinctive, from the dominant presence of western nations in China's treaty ports and leased territories, through the emergence of architecture as a profession in China, to Japan's imperial activities in Manchuria.

To cope with the unique multiplicity of China's experience, the methodological approach is geographically, temporally and architecturally inclusive. It is geographically broad within the bounds of China, seeking insight from the collective experience rather than individual sites in isolation. Temporally, while focusing on the early twentieth century, it acknowledges China's incomparably long building traditions and recent urban development. Architecturally, it considers contributions of Chinese and foreign architects as integral rather than separate.

Acknowledgements

This book is the culmination of nearly two decades of collaboration with so many people around the world it is almost impossible to recall everyone who has offered me their support. I am indebted to you all: Guang Yu, Ella, and George, Eleanor and John, Hou and Ren, and Alexa, John, Henry, Zoe, and William, and Nancy Berliner, Ed Bottoms, Lily Brett, Lin Ci Brown, Helen Castle, Judith Cligman, Patrick Cranley, Kerri Culhane, Ding Feng, Carma Elliot, Holly Fairbank, Fan Li, Adrian Forty, Murray Fraser, Paul French, Michelle Garnaut, Cathy Giangrande, Susie Gordon, the Hansons, Lenore Heitkamp, Peter Hibbard, Alan Hollinghurst, Tess Johnston, Tina Kanagaratnam, Dr Luk Shing Chark, Men-Ching Luk, Men-Chong Luk, Henry Ng, Lynn Pan, Karolina Pawlik, David Rankin, Peg Rawes, Margaret Richardson, Valerie Rose, Prof. Ruan Yisan, Daphne Skillen, Shinnosuke Takayanagi, John Stubbs, Tom Weaver, Wang Haoyu, Anne Witchard, Jennifer Wong, Frances Wood, Shixuan Ying, Prof. Zheng Shiling, countless libraries and librarians throughout China, the Arts and Humanities Research Council, The British Council, The Peabody Essex Museum, The Royal Asiatic Society, The World Monuments Fund, and last but by no means least all my students and colleagues at The Bartlett School of Architecture (UCL), for challenging and supporting my research.

The author owns the copyright of the maps (Plates 43 and 44) and all contemporary photography, except for Plate 21, which has been granted with kind permission from David Thompson. The author wishes also to thank the following families for giving permission to publish materials associated with: Liu Jipiao (Plates 15 and 29, and Figures 7.8–7.11 and 7.25); Yang Tingbao (Figure 7.3); Liang Sicheng, Lin Huiyin and Wilma Fairbank (Figure 7.6); Luke Him Sau (Figures 7.12 and 7.17); and Poy Gum Lee (Figure 7.24).

Part I
China and the meaning of modernity

1 Introduction

The two principal aims of this book are to contribute to restoring the discursive connections linking China's modern architectural past with the present, connections that were damaged and often broken during the second half of the twentieth century, and to advance understanding of China's encounter with architecture as a distinct modern art practice. To achieve these aims, this encounter is situated in the broader landscape of modernity in China as it took shape in the first half of the twentieth century by adopting two concurrent perspectives. One looks forwards and backwards chronologically at the history of building in China in an attempt to understand better the interconnections between its ancient and recent past. The other looks around from a specific moment in time before the Second World War at other cultural expressions of modernity in an attempt to locate architecture among other art practices and encounters with modernity.

Architecture, modernity and China

While the subject of *architecture*, the notion of *modernity* and the context of *China* pose no exceptional analytical problems individually, the same cannot be said when considered collectively. Further complicating this problem is the temporal context in which these themes first coalesced: the first half of the twentieth century, a medial epoch bridging the ancient and the modern. Framed by China's uniquely enduring civilisation, modernity presents some very particular questions, as Jonathan Spence observed: 'The incredible complexity and durability of Chinese culture pose a challenge to the historian who is seeking elements of the new.'[1]

With continuous building traditions spanning four millennia, the transition effected by the advent of the architectural profession and its outputs in China from the mid-nineteenth century was more momentous in terms of its impact on established practices and physical forms in the built environment than that which occurred anywhere else in the world. Despite the extent of this transformation in the early twentieth century and the scale of urbanisation in the early twenty-first century, China's initial encounters with architectural modernity remain relatively obscured. Owing to its particular circumstances – internally and externally – these earlier events and cross-disciplinary discourses have either been overlooked or entirely erased from the historical record.

In an attempt to address such deficiency, this interdisciplinary study is located at the confluence of *architecture*, *modernity* and *China*. Architecturally, the aim is to expand current knowledge about the evolution of the profession in China up to 1949 and thus to contribute to improving China's comparative under-representation in the historiography of modern architecture globally. In terms of modernity, this exploration aligns itself with recent trends in social theory that have made the case for multiple modernities, and sets China's architectural experience within these nascent theories, proffering a different way of understanding this experience. In the context of China studies, it aims to contribute to elevating architecture from relative obscurity and to a position of parity with other cultural and artistic practices.

As a conceptual grouping *architecture*, *modernity* and *China* pose and expose particular questions that will be explored throughout the course of the book. However, one particularly dominant problem shadowing this trilogy is the western, or more specifically European, origins of modernity and architecture. The inauthenticity of these two concepts in the Chinese context complicates subsequent analyses and presents a paradox – is it right to examine China using non-Chinese criteria? The answer to this determines the nature of supplementary questions such as whether modernism existed in China and, if not, why not or, if so, what form did it take? Was it a singular hybridised modernism forged from the unique context of China or did this context cultivate multiple forms of modernity? Was it merely a surrogate of western modernism that, once severed from its source, could not survive, or did it assume a genuinely indigenous character that, after 1949, either self-destructed or was reconstituted?

Recognition of the paradox is an essential precondition to exploring China's encounter with modernity and architecture in the first half of the twentieth century and consequently determines this study's structure, which forms two parts. The first part focuses on *modernity* and the second on *architecture*. *China* is the overarching context for both. Part I develops a critical discussion of modernity through five analytical themes that approach the subject from different perspectives that consequently inform and contextualise Part II, which concentrates on *architecture* and, cumulatively, the development of the built environment throughout China which today has more city dwellers than any other country on earth.

Space, time and architecture

The inclusive methodological approach of this study is determined by a number of factors. These include China's uniquely complicated architectural condition up to the second half of the twentieth century, a response to existing studies in this field, as well as current related theories. Comparative studies tend to focus on individual elements of architectural history in isolation, disconnected from external events and conditions. A lack of thematic inclusivity whether from within or without the field of architecture in China evades the types of questions that make the study of architecture in China distinctive and uniquely challenging.

Methodological inclusivity can be defined three ways: *geographically*, *temporally* and *architecturally*. These criteria were acknowledged by Murphey in his prophetic and aptly titled paper, 'What Remains to be Done?' published in 1985 following a conference on the rise and growth of south east Asian port cities. Scholarship in this field has advanced significantly, though less so in the context of architecture. Murphey noted a number of methodological shortcomings including neglect of the 'comparative and cross-cultural dimension'; the 'essential [need to] examine Japanese colonialism in Asia, comparatively with the dominantly British scene'; and the need to be less 'temporally as well as locally specific'.[2] These observations are as pertinent in the twenty-first century as they were in the late twentieth century. They also resonate with the scholarly shortcomings identified by Wittrock in *Early Modernities,* where a better understanding of modernity demands addressing practices 'not only from outside the European and American sphere but also over long periods of time'.[3]

Satisfying just one or, as occurs in rare cases, two of these three methodological criteria is unlikely to lead to meaningful or particularly insightful conclusions. For example, in the case of geographic scale, analyses of modern architecture in China that focus solely on treaty ports while overlooking developments in Manchuria are undermined by what they ignore. The same would be true in the case of temporal scale, where attention cast only on the 1930s would be at the expense of preceding or succeeding periods that were informed or were a consequence of this critical decade. And in the case of architectural scale, examining the architecture of either Chinese or western architects separately reveals only fragments of a much richer picture that emerges when they are treated as integral parts of a whole.

The particularity of China's modern architectural condition calls for an inclusive approach precisely because nowhere else on earth possesses such multiple architectural experiences today. To make sense of China's unprecedentedly diverse architectural condition demands an equally plural method of analysis. In no other country did architectural modernity assume such heterogeneity. It was manifest in Asia's tallest skyscraper, the Joint Savings Society Building (1934), built in Shanghai, designed by a Hungarian–Slovak architect, and funded by a Chinese client (see Figure 1.1). It emerged in the proliferation of modern industrial facilities, such as factories, ware-

Figure 1.1 Shanghai's Joint Savings Society Building containing the Park Hotel (1934), the tallest building in China until the 1980s, designed by a Hungarian–Slovak architect, László Hudec, for a Chinese client, the Joint Savings Society.

Figure 1.2 Modern industrial buildings at Anshan steel foundry, near Fushun, showing the 350-tonne steel furnace (*left*) and blowers (*right*).

Figure 1.3 The monumental headquarters of the Hong Kong Shanghai Banking Corporation (1935), Hong Kong, designed by George Wilson of Palmer & Turner in a progressive classical style befitting colonial Hong Kong.

Figure 1.4
The quasi-Japanese design of the Department of Communications, Hsinking (Changchun), Manchukuo.

Figure 1.5
The Zhong Hua bookstore (1936), Guangzhou, designed by the University of Pennsylvania graduate, Fan Wenzhao.

Figure 1.6 The shops and multicultural shoppers on Harbin's Kitaiskaya Street in the mid-1930s.

8 *China and the meaning of modernity*

Figure 1.7 Illustration by Huang Yuyü c.1929 portraying the potential to convert Nanjing's ancient city walls into a highway for motorcars as part of the city's modernisation programme.

Figure 1.8 Model of the Mayor's Office (1934), one of the principal modern buildings in Shanghai's Civic Centre, designed by Dong Dayou.

houses, breweries, power stations and steelworks from Fushun to Fuzhou (see Figure 1.2). It was conspicuous in the staid national styles of the colonial and quasi-colonial territories skirting China's periphery from Dalian to Hong Kong (see Figure 1.3 and Figure 1.4). It could be encountered in the novel commercial enterprises and entertainment facilities, such as department stores, shops, bars and cinemas from Kunming to Harbin that fuelled a budding consumer society, which in larger cities like Shanghai were popular literary settings for China's modernist writers (see Figure 1.5 and Figure 1.6). It appeared in the new public buildings and infrastructure designed by Chinese and foreign architects in Nanjing and Shanghai and dominated their search for a modern Chinese architectural vernacular (see Figure 1.7 and Figure 1.8). It saturated the modern town plans across Japanese-occupied Manchuria where it reached its apogee in the 'ultra-modern' urban planning and architecture of Hsinking, the new capital of Manchukuo (see Figure 1.9 and Figure 1.10).

Given China's architectural range this study asserts that only by acknowledging all three criteria can a full picture be constructed of China's modern architectural encounter. Collectively, therefore, the triumvirate of *geography*, *temporality* and *architecture* determine the contextual parameters of this study and provide the basis of its methodological framework – a structure within which the 'missing links' in the existing understanding of China's modern architectural history (in relation to ancient and contemporary building), as well as its place among proximate professional disciplines and regional experiences will be explored. Intellectual contributions are drawn not only from the examination of many original or previously unpublished materials but also from the re-examination of existing material under a new light cast by this inclusive approach.

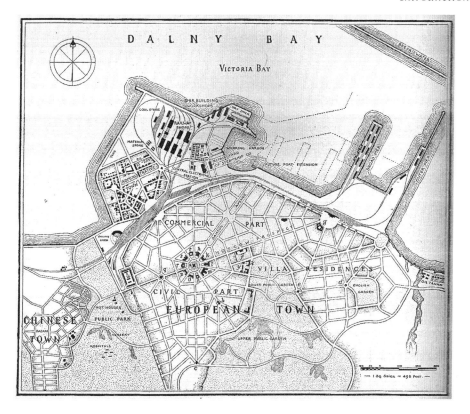

Figure 1.9 Plan of Dalian (1903), laid out by the Russians and characterised by the radial system with streets converging at large circuses and based around modern requirements such as railways, industrial docks and motorised transport.

Previous studies

This study builds on four previous publications: *Building Shanghai – The Story of China's Gateway* (Wiley, 2006), *Modernism in China – Architectural Visions and Revolutions* (Wiley, 2008), *Luke Him Sau, Architect – China's Missing Modern* (Wiley, 2014) and *Ultra-Modernism – Architecture and Modernity in Manchuria* (HKUP, 2017). To avoid undue repetition and duplication, some of the details, facts, descriptions and representations (particularly of specific buildings) have been omitted and can be found in these other publications.

To adopt a phrase from one of China's early architects, Liang Sicheng (1901–72), who used it in reference to the publication of his own work internationally, elements of these earlier publications were 'an attempt at popularization, not scholarship'.[4] As a consolidation of over a decade of research and writing aimed at exposing China's early modern architecture to new audiences, this study adopts a more critical and systemic approach that places the examination of China's modern architectural development within the wider landscape of modernity in China in the first half of the twentieth century. As any scholar of China or more specifically of architectural history in China will recognise, the research landscape is fraught with difficulties, obstacles and omissions. Much work remains to be done and this study aims only to make a meaningful contribution to the task.

10 *China and the meaning of modernity*

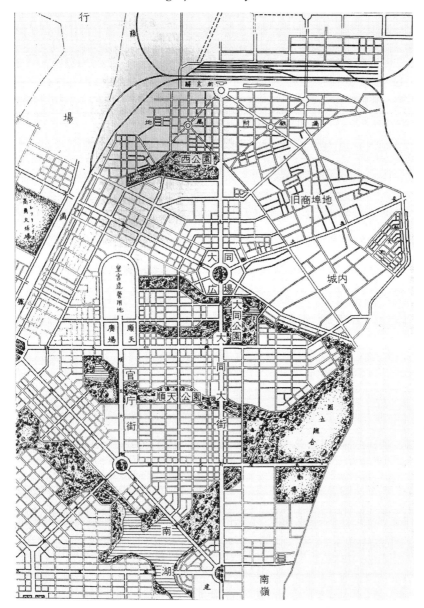

Figure 1.10 Map of the centre of Hsinking, the capital of Manchukuo, planned by the Japanese on a vast scale and employing some of the principles established by the Russians in Dalian and Harbin.

Notes

1 Spence, 1998, p. 10.
2 Murphey, 1985, p. 288.
3 Wittrock, 1998, p. 21.
4 Letter from Liang Sicheng to Wilma and John Fairbank, 21 November 1940, Peabody Essex Museum, Salem, Massachusetts.

2 Intellectual orientations
The unavoidable burden of context

Locating the study

One of the characteristics of studying subjects outside familiar territories is the need to provide sufficient context, both of the subject itself and its relationship with established areas of knowledge for it to be legible to new audiences. It is a fact, as Shmuel Eisenstadt points out in *Early Modernities*, that 'Asia, like Africa and Latin America, figures less in major scholarly tomes than do either Europe or North America'.[1] This chapter seeks to address such relative deficiency by examining the ways in which *architecture* and *modernity* in the context of *China* have been treated by other studies.

Architectural analyses

Misleading though chronological classifications often are, this summary proposes the division of the international historiography of building in China into four phases: pre-twentieth century; the first half of the twentieth century; before the open-door policy; and anything since. Within these four groupings there are further subdivisions along thematic and linguistic lines. Thematically, publications can be subdivided three ways: those that focus on foreign buildings in China, those that focus on Chinese buildings and those that focus on both. Linguistic subdivisions occur along similar lines: those written by non-Chinese for an international audience, those written by Chinese for an international audience and those written by Chinese for a domestic audience. The following four subheadings explore these different categories and their subthemes in relation to their contribution at the time of publication and to their significance in this study.

Pre-twentieth century

Pre-twentieth-century studies of Chinese building are dominated by foreign writers. The earliest include *Letter from a French Missionary in China* (1743) by the French Jesuit monk Father Jean Denis Attiret, which describes in detail Beijing's Forbidden City; the earliest attempt at compiling a comprehensive account of China by another Jesuit, S.J. Du Halde, *The General History of China* (1736); William Halfpenny's *New Designs for Chinese Temples, Triumphal Arches, Garden Seats, Palings, etc* (1750); Paul Decker's illustrations in *Chinese Architecture, Civil and Ornamental* (1759); and Sir William Chambers's *Designs of Chinese Buildings, Furniture, Dresses, Machines, and Utensils* (1757) and *A Dissertation on Oriental Gardening* (1772).

Numerous observational and often derogatory accounts by foreign merchants and travellers appeared in general writings on China thereafter, until the late nineteenth century, when more learned accounts started to appear and the first significant thematic division occurred. Some writers concentrated on Chinese buildings and proto-urban settings (Joseph Edkins, *Chinese Architecture*, 1890; and the unauthored, *General Description of Shanghae and its Environs*, 1850), some focused on foreign developments in the Treaty Ports (J.W. Maclellan, *The Story of Shanghai from the Opening of the Port to Foreign Trade*, 1889) and others wrote about both (J.D. Clark, *Sketches in and around Shanghai, etc.*, 1894).

Edkins's book is notable as an early demonstration of a growing desire among foreign scholars to understand Chinese building techniques. For example, he refutes the hitherto common assumption made by foreigners that Chinese buildings merely replicated tents ('Chinese architecture then had nothing to do at first with the imitation of tent forms'[2]). However, his observations are often misguided, a fault derived primarily from a chronological approach governed by stylistic considerations. Interestingly, though, the last of these architectural phases is described as the 'Modern Style',[3] not of the nineteenth or twentieth centuries as one might expect, but of the Song Dynasty (960–1279) and caused by the spread of Taoism. Whatever shortcomings these early critical accounts had, they laid the foundation for a more scholarly approach to the study of the history of building in China which blossomed in the first decades of the twentieth century.

Early twentieth century

The beginning of the twentieth century saw a marked increase in the number of publications on methods of building and various styles owing to both a growing interest among foreigners and the development of the domestic publishing industry. The first significant contribution of this period was Stephen Bushell's *Chinese Art* (1904), the third chapter of which was devoted to architecture and noted all the familiar landmarks, but is most interesting for its inclusion of building as an art form in China, something that counters the customary Chinese view. The most comprehensive account of China's modern urbanisation was Arnold Wright's *Twentieth Century Impressions of Hong Kong, Shanghai and other Treaty Ports of China* (1908). The definitive titles of this period focus on Chinese buildings: Ernst Boerschmann's *Chinese Architecture and its Relation to Chinese Culture* (1912) and Osvald Sirén's *A History of Early Chinese Art* (1929).

Boerschmann's work was the result of a three-year journey around 14 of China's 18 provinces in what was then the most extensive exploration of ancient Chinese buildings. The result, however, was a 28-page document that could do little more than provide a glimpse of what a country 'covering an area seven times greater than Germany, and with exactly seven times its population' possessed in the way of ancient buildings.[4] Another shortcoming, despite his extensive travels, is that he, like so many foreigners, cannot avoid taking for granted the pre-eminence of Beijing, a site that he claims would 'serve as typical for all China'.[5]

In contrast, Sirén's weighty study of Chinese art from the prehistoric period onwards was printed in four volumes, two of which are devoted to art, one to sculpture and one to architecture. Despite its size, the written content is brief and based on empirical observations. The book's strength lies in the 120 plates illustrating ancient structures and ruins.

Concluding this period in terms of foreign accounts of ancient Chinese building are Perceval Yetts's *A Chinese Treatise on Architecture* and *Writings on Chinese Architecture* (both 1927) and D.G. Mirams's *A Brief History of Chinese Architecture* (1940), which, as the title suggests, is rather summary, but is notable for being the first foreign account of the history of Chinese building to include the 'modern' period (Chinese structures built after 1911) albeit only in three pages.

Another important development of this period is the first publication of writings by China's first architects, made possible by the growth of China's publishing industry, based in Shanghai. Rather than exploring China's ancient buildings, these writings tend to tackle issues concerning theory and continuity in response to the onset of modern construction techniques and materials. The first is William Chaund's *Architectural Effort and Chinese Nationalism – Being a Radical Interpretation of Modern Architecture as a Potent Factor in Civilisation* (1919) published in the *Far Eastern Review*.[6] This periodical embodies the heterogeneity of western and non-western engagements in China throughout the early twentieth century. Established by an American journalist and engineer, George Bronson Rea (1869–1936), in American-occupied Manila in 1904, the publication moved to Shanghai in 1912, where it became the pre-eminent journal concerned with engineering, finance and commerce in Asia. Having been anti-Japanese in his early career, Rea did a volte-face and later became vigorously pro-Japanese,[7] causing the *Far Eastern Review* to become an important mouthpiece for Japan's increasingly aggressive propaganda machine. From 1920 the monthly journal was subsidised by the Japanese government, and in 1932 Rea became adviser to the Ministry of Foreign Affairs of the Japanese-controlled Manchukuo government, writing *The Case for Manchoukuo* in 1935.

A hiatus in architectural writing by Chinese professionals followed Chaund's article in the *Far Eastern Review* until the launch of the two major Chinese architectural journals, *Jian Zhu Yue Kan* (*The Builder*, 1932–7) and *Zhong Guo Jian Zhu* (*The Chinese Architect*, 1933–7), both of which provided a crucial outlet for the opinions of critics and the works of architects. Other publications included the journal *T'ien Hsia*, where the architects Dong Dayou (1899–1973) and Tong Jun (1900–83) wrote for the column *Architecture Chronicle*. Tong Jun became a prolific architectural writer, his domestically published books including European and Russian architecture and English-language articles such as 'Foreign Influence in Chinese Architecture',[8] 'Chinese Gardens' and 'Glimpses of Gardens in Eastern China'.

The period concluded with members of China's by now more experienced architectural community publishing their work in international journals. Pre-eminent among these examples are Liang Sicheng's 'Open Spandrel Bridges of Ancient China (Parts I and II)'[9] in *Pencil Points* and 'China's Oldest Wooden Structure'[10] and 'Five Early Chinese Pagodas'[11] (both 1941), in *Asia* magazine; and Chen's *Recent Architecture in China*[12] and *Chinese Architectural Theory*[13] (both 1947) in *Architectural Review*.

Early Communist period

Following the founding of the People's Republic of China in 1949, a flurry of publications emerged that demonstrated a consolidation of academic enquiry into the history of building in China and the presentation of this subject to a more general audience internationally. First was Laurence Sickman and Alexander Soper's *The Art and Architecture of China* (1956), only the second part of which, by Soper, concentrated on architecture. Like most before it, its chronological extent covered everything from 'the earliest times' to 1912 and makes no mention of foreign or Chinese architecture in China during the succeeding period.

Far more insightful and consequently one of the most important books of its time on the subject of Chinese architecture is Xu Jinzhi's (1906–1983) *Chinese Architecture – Past and Contemporary* (1964). Xu was a renowned architect in China before the Second World War, and his book, written from a position of exile in Hong Kong in the 1960s, provides an important and critical perspective on the subject at a time when such views were not permissible from his contemporaries in China. Xu's work is the first to acknowledge the continuity that existed between China's ancient buildings and nascent architectural profession in the first half of the twentieth century. 'Chinese Architecture is deeply rooted in the distant past', wrote Xu, and 'for this reason, any attempt at a thorough understanding of contemporary Chinese Architecture and its future trends will of necessity involve a study of its historical background'.[14] From his privileged position among those Chinese architects practising before the war, the book offers a rare and valuable insight into China's architectural history and theory at this critical period. While he can be criticised for not giving attention to the work of foreign architects in China, he does nevertheless acknowledge that it was in their offices that 'Chinese draftsmen and superintendents were trained'.[15]

Andrew Boyd's *Chinese Architecture and Town Planning: 1500B.C. – A.D.1911* (1962) is an ambitious attempt to summarise three and a half millennia of building and urban history. He opens with an admission that 'A very small book on a very large subject, the architecture of a subcontinent, must have drastic limitations',[16] but his ambition to liberate the study of architectural history from 'an excessive pre-occupation with "our own" traditions' is laudable.[17] Although he too chooses not to enter the twentieth century, Boyd acknowledges in a postscript that architectural traditions did not stop at 1911, conceding that foreign influences were 'naturally quite disruptive of Chinese traditions both of building and planning'.[18]

Much of Boyd's material appears to draw from the pioneering research conducted by Chinese scholars under the auspices of the Institute for Research in Chinese Architecture between 1931 and 1946. How Boyd had access to the information is unclear as it was not published in full until the posthumous publication of Liang's seminal *A Pictorial History of Chinese Architecture* (1984). Liang's work was nearly lost in its entirety in the decades after 1949, but through the efforts of his friend and sinologist, Wilma Fairbank, was finally published in 1984. Before its international release, Liang's friend and fellow architect, Chen Zhi (1902–2002), wrote to Fairbank with the hopeful assertion that Liang's book 'will far surpass the ones by Boerschmann and Sirén. Being the first one of its kind written by a Chinese architect it deserves widespread recognition'.[19]

Liang's book is chronologically difficult to locate, being the result of what was indisputably the most extensive and original studies in the emergent field of architectural history in China. Written during the Second World War and expected to be published soon after it, it has been included here in the post-1949 category, though it might just as appropriately be in an earlier or later category. It precedes and surpasses any other publication on the subject by a Chinese or foreign author and consequently Liang's name and reputation still dominates this professional field. His analysis and reinterpretation of the ancient Chinese building manual, the *Ying Zao Fa Shi*, together with the prolific and pioneering fieldwork represent the first scientific approach to the study of the history of building in China and can justly be recognised as making a greater contribution to improving the understanding of this subject than any other single work.

Following the resumption of university education after the Cultural Revolution, architectural studies in China increased considerably. There are now too many domestic research outputs to summarise; however, generally speaking, the period leading up to 1949 has remained until very recently something of a taboo in official or institutional circles. Academics have therefore tended to focus on either ancient or recent (post-1949) history, overlooking the intervening period that is the focus of this book. Only very recently has this changed and a greater degree of objectivity been embraced in historical research, though political compliance and a deferential culture in Chinese academia remain critical factors that persistently threaten greater impartiality.[20]

The late 1970s to the twenty-first century

Despite political sensitivities, the generally more receptive intellectual scene surrounding China studies since the open-door policy has seen the research and publication of one of the most comprehensive collective biographical works in this period, *Who's Who in Modern Chinese Architecture*, edited by Lai Delin.[21] Another much larger collective survey of historical architecture is the superlative series on modern Chinese architecture (1840s–1949) in sixteen Chinese cities, sponsored by Toyota and edited by Wang Tan and Terunobu Fujimori, which remains the most comprehensive survey of individual buildings of this period in China ever undertaken.[22]

The period also displays a proliferation of work by Japanese scholars, though this remains largely confined to local or regional discourses. The translation of these works into Chinese, English and Russian would make a major contribution to scholarship internationally. Of the many Japanese scholars who have pioneered the exploration of their comparatively recent and undeniably sensitive imperial past through the built environment are Shin Muramatsu and Akira Koshizawa. Shin's investigations of Chinese urban history and architecture reveal fresh insights and Akira's pioneering work on Manchuria's urban planning and Changchun are more advanced than anything by any scholar outside Japan, whether Chinese or western.

The first internationally available illustrated publication of this period was Laurence Liu's voluminous *Chinese Architecture* (1989), which attempted to chart the nation's building traditions throughout time, stopping short of the twentieth century. Liu's book was followed over a decade later by a comparable volume, paralleling its contents and even adopting its title. *Chinese Architecture* (Nancy Steinhardt (ed.), 2002) begins by acknowledging that 'Chinese architecture has been studied less than the architecture of almost any other great civilization on the globe', and attempts to redress this shortcoming by examining the subject from 2070BC to AD1911.[23] Like Liu, Steinhardt is concerned with what she describes as 'traditional Chinese architecture', terminating the analysis over four millennia at 1911, which she justifies by claiming that 'many Chinese architects and architectural historians believe that a clear separation exists between pre-twentieth century and twentieth century buildings'.[24] While this may hold some truth in the writing of architectural history, it applies less to the history of building itself. The year 1911 may have been politically momentous for China, but it was not so architecturally.

16   *China and the meaning of modernity*

Pre-dating these two publications and surpassing them in ambition is the *History and Development of Ancient Chinese Architecture* (1986), compiled by researchers at the Institute of the History of Natural Sciences, Chinese Academy of Sciences.[25] Reprinted in several versions, the initial publication appeared as a special edition in 1959, but further work to complete it was interrupted by the Cultural Revolution. It has therefore been placed among contemporary writing, although it is not internationally available. It builds on the corpus of material gathered by the Institute for Research in Chinese Architecture. The Chinese architect from this period, Chen Zhi, rightly describes it as a 'monumental work',[26] though it examines only Chinese building and does not elaborate on foreign architecture in China from the nineteenth century.

The start of the twenty-first century has witnessed a major escalation in scholarly and general writing on different aspects of Chinese architectural history. This reflects a growing interest not only in China generally as it has emerged from relative international obscurity, but also more specifically in architecture as the country has undergone the most substantial process of urbanisation in human history. The broader process of China's development in the twenty-first century, of which urbanisation is just a part, has fundamentally altered the international relations and is changing the balance of power globally. As the balance of power shifts, so too, inevitably, will the writing of history.

This resurgent interest in architecture in China can be seen in a plethora of publications in the early twenty-first century. Guo Qinghua's *Chinese Architecture and Planning: Ideas, Methods, Techniques* (2005) stops short of analysing twentieth-century architecture, except for its pioneering chapter on Changchun, Japan's imperial capital in Manchuria. Jeffrey Cody's brilliant *Building in China: Henry Murphy's "Adaptive Architecture" 1914–1935* (2001) was among the first international publications to exploit the rich mine of original documentation in Chinese archives as they opened up to the general public for the first time in decades. It will thus likely remain the definitive title in this specific genre of studies of foreign architects working in China attempting to combine ancient Chinese building with modern construction. Peter Rowe and Seng Kuan's engaging and informative *Architectural Encounters with Essence and Form in Modern China* (2002) represents the most recent attempt to tackle the slippery subject of tradition and modernity, and from this perspective it succeeds in advancing the discourse that Xu Jinzhi began in 1964. Zhu Jianfei's *Architecture of Modern China: A Historical Critique* (2009) adopts a broad historical narrative (1729–2008)[27] identifying that existing studies rarely traverse established historical periods. The main focus is in its account of architectural events after 1949.

Before turning attention to modernity, in the context of architecture it is important to highlight Joseph Esherick's *Remaking the Chinese City: Modernity and National Identity, 1900–1950* (2000), whose intellectual origins lie in a conference in San Diego in 1996 titled *Beyond Shanghai: Imagining the City in Republican China*. Choosing to pay scholarly attention to encounters between modernity and the urban realm beyond the overwhelmingly dominant shadow cast by Shanghai represents an endeavour whose progressiveness in the context of the 1990s should not be understated. Shanghai's pre-eminence in so many aspects of China's encounters with modernity has resulted in privileging the story of one metropolis over the rest of China. However, even though it was the purpose of this publication to redress the imbalance, its authors had their doubts as to the appropriateness of doing so. Esherick concedes that 'going beyond Shanghai cannot mean ignoring Shanghai' because 'only Shanghai was a proper standard of modernity. There was hardly a city that was not linked in some way to Shanghai'.[28] In the final chapter Strand admits that 'no Chinese city with progressive or modern aspirations or institutions could ever really escape the influence of Shanghai'.[29] The importance of this publication lies in the thematic and geographical scope of the contributions, which were unsurpassed in their time for geographical inclusivity. Although architecture is not examined separately, notable chapters include Buck's 'Railway City and National Capital: Two Faces of the Modern in Changchun', and Musgrove's 'Building a Dream: Constructing a National Capital in Nanjing, 1927–1937'. The relative novelty of these studies is evident in their sources, Buck drawing most of his evidence from the seminal work of the Japanese historian, Koshizawa Akira, and Musgrove relying on Xu's *Chinese Architecture – Past and Contemporary* and an article in *National Geographic* from 1938: 'The Rise and Fall of Nanjing'.[30] These articles and the others in this publication are significant and comparatively rare for demonstrating the type of contextual inclusivity essential for dealing with a subject as geographically, temporally and architecturally broad as China.

Measuring modernity

Modernity is a vast subject that is constrained here by its relationship with and interconnections between *architecture* and *China*. The following survey concentrates on three interrelated approaches to *modernity* that provide context to the discussion of modernism outside the west. The first approach examines contemporary theories of modernity and how these impact on the Chinese focus of this study. The second is a comparative assessment of studies concerning modernity and the built environment in other regional or cultural contexts. And the last explores modernity's appraisal in relation to other art practices in China.

Contemporary theories of modernity and their impact on China studies

Modernity, a manifestation and an abstract expression of the European Renaissance notion of *modern* as well as the theoretical basis for the appearance of the twentieth-century idea of *modernism*, is part of a conceptual coterie that has underpinned western thought for centuries. These notions have accompanied, prefigured even, events and processes that have fundamentally influenced the course of global developments and their interpretation since industrialisation, the emergence of nationalism, the rise and fall of colonialism, and the spread of capitalism. It is through modernity that the west's hegemonic aspirations have dominated subsequent philosophical and intellectual discourse. From Hegel, Comte, Marx, Tönnies, Weber and Durkheim to Foucault, Wallerstein, Habermas and Fukuyama, a western conception of modernity remained central throughout.

Although this study is grounded in the intellectual terrain prepared by these thinkers, it does not entirely share their views on modernity. Rather than seeing modernity as a singular westerncentric and homogenising (and threatening, according to Berman's account) process, this study regards modernity as a perpetually reconstituting global phenomenon (albeit with European origins), with multiple manifestations producing heterogeneous outcomes. The theoretical affiliation of this study lies in the emerging sociological paradigm of *multiple modernities* and follows a small number of architectural studies to make this association explicitly.

18 *China and the meaning of modernity*

The notion of multiple modernities emerged out of a growing regard for precisely those milieus that had until recently (and certainly throughout the twentieth century) been sited on the periphery of perceived centres of modernity. It refutes the 'cultural program of modernity' proposed by Marx *et al.* and the homogenising theories of post-war 'theories of modernization',[31] and assumes what Eisenstadt refers to as 'the existence of culturally specific forms of modernity shaped by distinct cultural heritages and sociopolitical conditions'.[32]

This study's concurrence with multiple modernities occurs out of the particularities of the three principal themes: *architecture*, *modernity* and *China*. Whether studied independently, or in pairs, and certainly collectively, these themes do not fit within established social theories that assume the homogenising and hegemonic impact of western cultural agency and the inevitability of the 'global village', 'clash of civilizations' or 'end of history'.[33] Such themes, as will be revealed throughout this study, demonstrate the fallibility of conventional theories of modernity in dealing with subjects outside established centres of modernism. More precisely, China's encounter with architectural modernity provides an example that demands and supports the conceptual framework proffered by multiple modernities.

The principal architect of multiple modernities is Shmuel Eisenstadt (for a collection of his works, see *Comparative Civilizations and Multiple Modernities*, 2003), and the value of his work to this study exists in his refutation of modernity's equation to westernisation and the consequent assumption that this trajectory of progress leads to homogenisation, and in questioning the narrowness of many of our perspectives on the past. China's absence from publications on modernism or architecture, or both, exemplifies this experience (see Figure 2.1).

THE TURK, THE AFGHAN, PERSIAN AND CHINEE, WERE PICTURESQUE AND VIVID AS COULD BE

BUT PROGRESS WAVES ITS WAND AND NOW WE SEE THE TURK, THE AFGHAN, PERSIAN AND CHINEE
PROGRESS

Figure 2.1 'Progress', by a western cartoonist in China illustrating the homogenisation of 'picturesque' foreigners in the west's image.

Despite modernism's international claim, its outward march beyond Europe and North America took the form of a crusade that resulted in architectural theories and practices retaining the hallmarks of its geographic, intellectual and cultural origins, however inapt in their new setting. As Astradur Eysteinsson argued in *The Concept of Modernism* (1990) in a manner that anticipated the emergence of multiple modernities:

> While everyone seems to agree that as a phenomenon modernism is radically 'international' (although only in the limited western sense of the word), constantly cutting across national boundaries, this quality is certainly not reflected in the majority of critical studies of modernism. Such studies are mostly restricted to the very national categories modernism is calling into question, or they are confined to the (only slightly wider) Anglo-American sphere.[34]

When framed in the context of China, Eysteinsson's views resonate with Christopher Bush's efforts to restore its presence in the history of literary modernism (*Ideographic Modernism: China, Writing, Media*, 2010):

> for all its talk of globalization and transnationalism, contemporary modernist studies know less and care less about China than did many writers and thinkers in the modernist era itself. As a result, the extensive traces of China in the text of literary modernity have largely been read over or read out of the history of modernism.[35]

Malcolm Bradbury and James McFarlane's *Modernism* (1976) makes no mention of China or, for that matter, any sites outside the west. More recently, as attitudes have changed and research methodologies become more inclusive, intellectual attentions have turned increasingly to the role of the west's *other*. However, as William Curtis's encyclopaedic *Modern Architecture Since 1900* shows in relation to architecture, despite attempts made by scholars to achieve a wider perspective and a greater degree of objectivity, China remains overlooked as a result of its complicated history. Concordant with the critical approach of multiple modernities, Curtis recognises that 'Modernism needs to be examined in relation to a variety of world views and social projects.'[36] However, even his tour de force in which the 'net was cast wide' and drew examples 'from places as diverse as Spain and India, Finland and Australia, France and Mexico, and the United States, Switzerland and Japan', and later 'Finland and Britain, Brazil and South Africa, Mexico and Japan', as well as recognising 'new "strains" of modernism in diverse national cultures (e.g. Spain, Australia, India, Japan)', China remained entirely absent from the global narrative prior to the onset of Communism in 1949.[37] China's uniquely extended distance from modernism's core for structural, geographical, intellectual and cultural reasons has caused it to be overlooked more than most *others*. This oversight has in turn weakened China's claim to possess what Lee called its own particular 'brand of "modernism"'.[38]

The occlusion of modernity in areas outside the west, and in China in particular, reverberates with Edward Said's seminal thesis, *Orientalism*, the first critical examination of cultural transactions between the west and other parts of the world. Although Said's Orient is not China, the asymmetrical relations and interpretations between China and the west possess many parallels with his analysis. Both are

20 *China and the meaning of modernity*

constructed by and in relation to the west: distant, exotic and, importantly, unmodern. But China's case complicates even this standpoint. From a western perspective during the Enlightenment, China received the approbation of leading thinkers such as Christian Wolff (1679–1754), François Quesnay (1694–1774) '*le Confucius européen*', and Charles de Montesquieu (1689–1755) and Voltaire, all of whom claimed its cultural parity with or even superiority over the west.[39] China's belief in its own superiority or, as Edward Graham describes, 'distinctive self view and world view', meant that by assuming a Chinese perspective 'when you get to China, Said's analytical apparatus can about as well be applied one way as the other'.[40]

Arriving in succession to Europe's philosophical admiration for China was an emergent aesthetic curiosity manifested chiefly through the idiom of the exotic with the introduction into the decorative arts of chinoiserie from the eighteenth century, following the publication of first-hand accounts of Chinese design by Europeans such as Father Jean Denis Attiret (1702–68), Jean-Baptiste Du Halde (1674–1743) and Sir William Chambers (1723–96). Having designed London's Kew Gardens (1757–62) and some of its early buildings, including the Great Pagoda (1759), Chambers claimed 'no nation ever equalled the Chinese in the splendour and number of Garden structures'.[41] Eighteenth-century Britain was bewitched by a fashion for fantastic architectural curiosities inspired by China that embellished aristocratic gardens and, occasionally, new public spaces. Beyond Kew Gardens, there was Ranelagh House and Gardens in Chelsea with its Chinese pavilion and gardens, and the famous Vauxhall Gardens with various structures inspired by chinoiserie.

Critical reaction against China's European aficionados was swift and lasting. Horace Walpole (1717–97), who considered *Chambers's Dissertation* 'more extravagant than the worst Chinese paper',[42] was elated when William Mason (1725–97) wrote his scathing rebuttal of Chambers's work, *Heroic Epistle to Sir William Chambers* (1773), a 'bona fide abhorrence of Sir William Chambers' architectural essays on Chinoiserie'.[43] Walpole wrote to Mason claiming to have 'laughed till I cried, and the oftener I read it, the better I liked it'.[44] Two years earlier James Cawthorn had published *On Taste*, his own pointed riposte to chinoiserie, which mocked:

> *Of late, 'tis true, quite sick of Rome and Greece,*
> *We fetch our models from the wise Chinese,*
> *European artists are too cool and chaste,*
> *For Mand'rin only is the man of taste . . .*[45]

These derisory responses can be seen as the beginnings of a negative portrayal of China that accompanied western imperialism and its consequent commercial dominance that, by the end of the nineteenth century, saw China labelled 'The Sick Man of Asia', placing it firmly within Said's conceptual framework of power relations in which the west exerted a dominance that lasted throughout the twentieth century.

A key element of this framework from the perspective of modernism was the presumption of the one-directionality of its influence: from the modern and civilised west to the unmodern and uncivilised Orient. Vital to deconstructing the illusory line that separates as well as defines the west and its *other* is the multidirectionality of cultural transactions that occurred between the two. Critical studies of China's influence on western modernists are still undeveloped and have received attention largely in artistic and literary fields: Bush, Hayot, Shih, Huang, and Qian,[46] all of whom lay some claim towards China being 'one of the major "influences" on western modernisms',[47] and for 'the great Modernists – Yeats, Pound, Eliot, Williams, Stevens, and Moore – it was the Far East rather than the Near East that was a richer source of literary models'.[48] The Nobel Laureate for Literature, Saint-John Perse (1887–1975), used China as a theoretical setting for his book *Anabase* written in 1924 after spending five years in Beijing. In art there is the singular example of Mark Tobey, a founder of American abstract art, who was deeply influenced by Chinese brushwork.[49]

As more evidence emerges, the true nature and complexity of the landscape around China's encounter with modernity becomes clearer. As Patricia Ondek Laurence argues, modernism 'constructs itself not only from European sources, but a greater range of cultural phenomena including Chinese art, literature, and culture at the forefront of change',[50] further reinforcing the fact that modernism in China cannot be conceived as a single entity but one of multiple entities.

The first published statement proposing the 'multiple modernities' thesis was in 1998 in *Dædalus* (*The Journal of the American Academy of Arts and Sciences*), where it appeared under the precursory heading *Early Modernities*. The edition sought to:

> avoid three fallacies: first, that there is only one modernity; second, that looking from the west to the east legitimates the concept of 'Orientalism'; and finally, that globalization and multiculturalism ought to be regarded as indications that a new axial principle has in fact emerged, which goes under the name of post-modernity.[51]

Although the only concentrated discussion on China was in Frederick Wakeman's 'Boundaries of the Public Sphere in Ming and Qing China'[52] (other essays focused on south Asia, India, Japan and Spain), there is considerable resonance with China's encounter with architectural modernity in the overall hypothesis:

> While European (and American) historians have collaborated successfully to analyze the most minute aspects of European life during these centuries ... there have been no comparable in-depth analyses of how civilizations of the east during these same centuries and how they changed.

Such an imbalance is both intellectually undesirable and historically unsustainable. Eisenstadt concurs when claiming 'social scientific studies of the future [are] likely to take into greater account societies and religions, traditions and practices still too little known today, concealed from the west by many factors'.[53]

Two years after the publication of *Early Modernities* the concept was developed further in an edition titled *Multiple Modernities*,[54] which set out to challenge 'many of the conventional notions of how the world has changed ... in this century predominantly'.[55] *Multiple Modernities* was part of an expanding intellectual domain critical of 'many of the prevailing theories about the character of contemporary society while questioning whether traits commonly described as "modern" do in fact accurately and fully render the complexity of the contemporary world'.[56] It has subsequently attracted widespread intellectual attention, criticism and approbation, and 'spread rapidly in social sciences',[57] with publications such as Dominic Sachsenmaier and Jens Riedel's *Reflections on Multiple Modernities: European, Chinese and Other Interpretations* (2002). Here, the most notable development is the reference to China in the title, though none of the essays explore architecture or the built environment. In Eisenstadt's earlier work it was Japan that he identified as being 'the most important test-case – and paradox' because of its unique example as a fully modernised non-western state.[58]

Multiple modernities has since been employed as a conceptual framework for examining a widening range of subjects, from feminist studies, cinema and popular media, to Muslim culture,[59] in which architectural reflections first emerged in *Multiple Modernities in Muslim Societies* edited by Modjtaba Sadria (2007), which received the Aga Khan Award for Architecture.

Multiple modernities resonates with other scholarly approaches to the question of modernity outside the west.[60] Common to all these perspectives is an elemental questioning of the west's ownership of the concept of modernity which has arisen both out of the dissonance between the multifaceted modernity that is familiar to those experiencing it and the uniformity of that which has been promoted by western academia for a century and the increasing exploration of encounters of modernity in settings outside the west. Writing about other cultural practices, Washburn, for example, cites the modernist Japanese writer, Yokomitsu Riichi, who was motivated:

> by an aspiration to create a culture that was modern and Asian, to somehow overcome the modernity of the west ... a culture that was at once parochial and universal – a culture that subsumed the west under an all but impossible synthesis of the national and the cosmopolitan.[61]

This desire for non-western expressions of modernity assumed important architectural implications in China under the guise of Japan's annexation of Manchuria, which is the subject of Chapter 8.

China, more so than Japan because of its position as a recipient of both western and Japanese versions of modernity, provides one of the most compelling examples of why experiences of modernity are distinct in different settings and would offer little insight if framed homogenously. China's example also challenges the often held assumption that multiple modernities only ever occur at cross-national or cross-civilisational levels and cannot occur within a single national or civilisational context.

Closely related to multiple modernities and in many ways a precursor to it is the growing body of literature concerned with encounters with modernity in regions of the world traditionally considered to be peripheral to the west. As scholarly attention has been trained increasingly on these underexplored sites, established perceptions have had to recast their worldview and the experience of modernity in different regions. There is not the space in this study to undertake comparative studies of encounters with modernity in different regions and across subjects in relation to China, but a number of works that focus on architecture and the urban realm stand out in highlighting useful and contrasting experiences.

Modernity and the built environment in other regional or cultural contexts

In terms of modernity's impact on architecture and the urban realm, analyses of regional comparisons reveal the relative belatedness of China as a subject of enquiry, nationally or geographically. Other regions, such as south east and Central Asia, South America, and, to a lesser extent, Africa have all received comparatively more scholarly attention and intellectual scrutiny. For example, Robert Ross and Gerald Telkamp's *Colonial Cities* (1985) gives many examples including Central America, (Zeelandia), Batavia, Calcutta, Cape Town, Rio de Janeiro, Kingston, Algiers, Saigon, Dakar, and Bombay, but overlooks China except for the recurrent influence of the Chinese diaspora and one essay on Taiwan.

Terry McGee's *The Southeast Asian City* (1967) pioneered the study of modernity in the south east Asian context and was a critical response to the region's rapid urban development, political independence, nationalism, industrialisation and economic reform. Anthony King's *Colonial Urban Development* (1976) furthered this line of enquiry by bringing India and other sites of British colonial rule into a common frame of reference that assisted subsequent investigations of colonial urban contexts. China was absent from most of these studies despite its historical pre-eminence and its close relationship with the British Empire. Acknowledging the enduring continuity of urban settlements in India, King concedes 'the exception of China, [which was] not subject to the same kind of western imperial experience'.[62] The work of Rhoads Murphey (*Shanghai: Key to Modern China*, 1953 and *The Treaty Ports and China's Modernization: What Went Wrong?*, 1970) stands out as the one exception.

In China's absence, historical studies of urban development in Asia tend to concentrate on colonial, cultural or economic conditions in either India and the subcontinent,[63] south east Asia,[64] or both.[65] A recent and instructive work to emerge from the expanding intellectual landscape forged by Asia's encounter with modernity is Harry Harootunian's *History's Disquiet* (2000), which explores the historical question of modernity from the perspective of those outside Europe and America, and concentrates on Japan to expose the 'fiction that modernity was solely a western idea'.[66] Here, questions of modernity in an Asian context converge with multiple modernities in demanding a broader and more inclusive understanding of modernity.

Another more recent publication and further proof of the growing need for and approbation of a multiple modernities perspective is William Lim and Jiat-Hwee Chang's *Non-West Modernist Past: On Architecture and Modernities* (2012). Representing the published proceedings of an eponymously titled international conference held in Singapore in 2011, this book is methodologically and thematically more closely aligned with this study than any other publication. In his barn-storming opening speech, the book's editor, William Lim, pronounced: 'Global power shift towards the New World Order has subverted the long dominance of the entire centre-periphery structure. Now is the time for the non-west to reset the global historiography on a broad front for all disciplines.'[67] Although the selected essays focus on sites from around the non-West, China is conspicuous in its inclusion – a situation that until comparatively recently would have been unlikely at best. The critical position and the range of theoretical themes it engages with represent the strength and originality of this publication in relation to the study of architectural modernity in China. Questioning modernism's singularity, acknowledging its complexity and interrogating its plurality are characteristics of the common ground shared with this study.

Modernity's appraisal in other art practices in China

The two earliest and most prolific cultural manifestations of modernity in China in the early twentieth century occurred in art and literature, the two fields that have dominated studies of China's first encounter with modernity since China emerged from its relative global isolation in the late 1970s.

In art, attention has concentrated on the painters and movements whose reputations and contributions have been obscured by decades of political partiality. Among the most significant contributions that have helped to redress this is Jo-Ann Birnie Danzker, Ken Lum and Zheng Shengtian's *Shanghai Modern 1919–1945* (2004) and Julia Andrews and Shen Kuiyi's *A Century in Crisis* (1998), which both explore various different artistic movements and genres. Another is Pang Laikwan's *The Distorting Mirror* (2007), which explores modernity's manifestation in visual culture in China before 1949.

More developed than the discussion of visual arts are literary critiques of modernism in China, which have received widespread scholarly attention since the 1980s. Shih Shu-Mei's *The Lure of the Modern* (2001) is among the most comprehensive, highlighting the manifold trajectories of and intersections between literary modernism in China and contemporary discourses of colonialism and modernism. Intellectual concurrence with multiple modernities is evident in Shih's suggestion that there exists a 'more complex circulation and articulation of Chinese agency than previously assumed', placing Shih's work as an important comparative reference to this architectural study.[68]

Another work of critical importance to this study is Patricia Ondek Laurence's *Lily Briscoe's Chinese Eyes: Bloomsbury, Modernism and China* (2003), which is not only an exemplary account of literary modernism in China before 1949, but also charts the complex web of interrelations between various protagonists. Laurence's exposure of the international scope of modernist influences that informed and were informed by Chinese examples provides ample evidence to support the multiple modernities thesis, which is implicit in her argument 'for the existence of multiple aesthetic, cultural, political, and economic discourses in a nation and against a monolithic notion of modernity or movement of modernism'.[69]

Eric Hayot's *Chinese Dreams: Pound, Brecht, Tel quel* (2004) and Christopher Bush's *Ideographic Modernism: China, Writing, Media* (2010) are important contributions to the understanding of the west's literary appropriation and approbation of China in the twentieth century, with Bush's work attempting to 'restore the lost historical and interpretive significance of [China's] presence' in the text of literary modernity.[70] Other literary studies include Huang Guiyou's *Whitmanism, Imagism, and Modernism in China and America* (1997), and Qian Zhaoming's *Orientalism and Modernism* (1995) and *Ezra Pound and China* (2006).

Bridging art and literature by concentrating on modernism's manifestation in the minutiae of the everyday is the extensive and pioneering work of Lee, which began in the literary field[71] but has expanded to include cultural explorations of Shanghai.[72] Lee's work is an example of the advantage held by overseas Chinese scholars in being uniquely positioned to examine China's encounter with modernity. Unlike their contemporaries in China, they are unconstrained by political allegiance and institutional orthodoxy (e.g. Ping, 2002[73]) and, unlike most of their contemporaries outside China, they are unconstrained by cultural and linguistic obstacles. This architectural study willingly follows in the footsteps of Lee's literary and cultural work, and in so doing attempts to broaden the understanding of the contribution of architecture and the built environment to China's encounter with modernity before 1949 as part of a wider contribution to challenging modernist hegemony. As Hosagrahar asserts in *Indigenous Modernities*: 'The project here is not merely to celebrate and give voice to minority discourses and knowledges in order to include them in their subordinate positions into existing privileged accounts of modernity, but to question the master narrative.'[74]

Notes

1 *Dædalus*, Summer 1998, pp. v–vi.
2 Edkins, 1890, p. 6.
3 Edkins, 1890, pp. 27–36.
4 Boerschmann, 1912, p. 539.
5 Boerschmann, 1912, p. 540.
6 Chaund, 1919, pp. 533–6.
7 The politically influential Australian journalist, William Henry Donald (1875–1946), editor of the *Far Eastern Review* from 1911, later resigned in protest to Rea's pro-Japanese stance.
8 Tong, 1938, p. 410.
9 Liang Sicheng, 1938, pp. 155–60.
10 Liang Sicheng, 1941, pp. 387–90.
11 Liang Sicheng, 1941, pp. 450–5.
12 Chen, 1947, pp. 26–8.
13 Chen, 1947, pp. 19–25.
14 Su, 1964, p. 1. At the time of publication in 1964 his name was spelt 'Su Gin-Djih', but using the contemporary system of pinyin, it is 'Xu Jinzhi'. While his book will be referenced under Su, his name throughout the text will be referred to using the pinyin format.
15 Su, 1964, p. 133.
16 Boyd, 1962, p. 1.
17 Boyd, 1962, p. 1.
18 Boyd, 1962, p. 157.
19 Letter from Chen Zhi to Wilma Fairbank, 8 January 1984, Peabody Essex Museum, Salem, Massachusetts.
20 It is notable that a six-part documentary about Liang Sicheng and his wife, Lin Huiyin (1904–55), due to air on China's state television (CCTV) in late 2010 did not go on general release as anticipated owing to the subject's continued sensitivity and the producer's refusal to accept further editorial censorship.
21 Lai, 2006.
22 *Zhong Guo Jin Dai Jian Zhu Zong Lan* (*Overview of Modern (pre-1949) Architecture in China*), 1992.
23 Steinhardt, 2002, p. 1. It is one in a series on The Culture and Civilization of China.
24 Steinhardt, 2002, p. 3.
25 This is an English translation of the Chinese book (*Zhong Guo gu dai jian zhu ji shu shi*) by the same Institute (Zhong Guo ke xue yuan, zi ran ke xue shi yan jiu suo) and published the previous year (1985) the same publisher.
26 Letter from Chen Zhi to Wilma Fairbank, May 1985, Peabody Essex Museum, Salem, Massachusetts.
27 'From when European perspective and formal geometry were introduced into China, to the present time when China assumes a new position in nation building and international relations' (Zhu, 2009, p. xv).
28 Esherick, 2000, pp. 12–13.
29 Strand, 2000, p. 213.
30 Eigner, 1938, pp. 189–224.

26 China and the meaning of modernity

31 *Dædalus*, Winter 2000, p. vi.
32 Eisenstadt, 2002, p. 1.
33 *Dædalus*, Winter 2000, p. v.
34 Eysteinsson, 1990, p. 89.
35 Bush, 2010, pp. xiv–xv.
36 Curtis, 1996, p. 10.
37 Curtis, 1996, pp. 16–17.
38 Lee, 1999, p. xiii.
39 'Many of the learned of our northern climes have felt confounded at the antiquity claimed by the Chinese. . . . There is no house in Europe, the antiquity of which is so well proved as that of the Empire of China . . . the Chinese, for four thousand years, when we were unable even to read, knew everything essentially useful of which we boast at the present day'. Voltaire, *Philosophical Dictionary*, Section 1, 'China', 1764.
40 Graham, 1983, p. 31.
41 Chambers, 1772, p. 35.
42 Walpole, 1937, p. 34.
43 Vines, 1934, p. 28.
44 Walpole, 1937, p. 101.
45 Cawthorn, 1771, p. 198.
46 Bush, 2010; Hayot, 2004; Shih, 2001, p. 4; Huang, 1997, p. 15; and Qian, 1995, p. 1.
47 Shih, 2001, p. 4.
48 Qian, 1995, p. 1.
49 Tobey's example is elaborated in the final theme.
50 Laurence, 2003, p. 326.
51 Eisenstadt and Schluchter, 1998, p. 2.
52 Wakeman, 1998, pp. 167–89.
53 *Dædalus*, Summer 1998, p. vi.
54 *Dædalus*, Winter 2000.
55 *Dædalus*, Winter 2000, p. vii.
56 *Dædalus*, Winter 2000, p. vii.
57 Sachsenmaier and Riedel, 2002, p. 1.
58 Eisenstadt, 2003, p. 435.
59 Harding, 2008; Lau, 2003; and Sadria, 2007.
60 Herz, 2015; Lim and Chang, 2012; Hosagrahar, 2005; Scriver and Prakash, 2007; Gaonkar, 2001; Chakrabarty, 2000.
61 Washburn, 2001, p. 222.
62 King, 1976, p. 182.
63 King, 1976; Appadurai, 1996; Chakrabarty, 2000 and 2002; Hosagrahar, 2005; and Scriver and Prakash, 2007.
64 Yueng and Lo, 1976; O'Connor, 1983; Forbes, 1996; Kim *et al.*, 1997; Evers and Korff, 2000; and Yeoh, 2003.
65 Basu, 1985; Breckenridge and van der Veer, 1993; and Lim and Chang, 2012.
66 Harootunian, 2000, p. 63.
67 Lim and Chang, 2012, p. 2.
68 Shih, 2001, p. xi.
69 Laurence, 2003, p. 390.
70 Bush, 2010, pp. xiv–xv.
71 Lee, 1973. Průšek and Lee, 1980; Lau *et al.*, 1981; Lee, 1985, 1987; Arkush and Lee, 1989; and Goldman and Lee, 2001.
72 Lee, 1999 and Lee, 2000.
73 He Ping is Professor of History at Sichuan University and author of *China's Search for Modernity: Cultural Discourses in the late 20th Century*, in which the 'launch' of China's 'modernization project' is suggested to have begun after 1949 and consequently is attributed to the Communist Party (2002, p. 4).
74 Hosagrahar, 2005, p. 6.

3 China's multiple modernities

Many factors problematise analyses of the west's *other*,[1] not least the western origins of the theories upon which such analyses are founded. Theoretical and perceptual westerncentricities distort understanding and subsequent examinations. Explanations that focus on difference ('non-west', 'east', 'Orient', 'Third World', 'Underdeveloped', 'Developing World' and 'Global South') have privileged the rhetoric of opposition, rather than an alternative complementarity. In China's case, combative or dualistic interpretations of its relationship with the west are typical (e.g. 'east/west' or 'Occident/Orient') and although they may indicate a different relationship with the west to alternative types of *other*, they too retain a problematical simplicity that disregards the particularities of local and regional experiences akin to the crude generalisations that permit the construction of the clash of civilisations thesis.[2]

The particularities of China's encounter with modernity, especially architectural modernity, demand specific analysis, not only because of China's distinction from other *others*, but also because a multiple modernities perspective requires the understanding of the distinctly Chinese characteristics through which modernity was confronted and mediated, rather than treating the results as inferior versions of an idealised western type. For example, in the Chinese context, the concepts of colonialism, nationhood, language, and time cannot be treated on western terms alone. Furthermore, architectural modernity outside the west is commonly associated with post-colonialism and independence movements after the Second World War. In China these encounters occurred earlier in connection with political and cultural reform movements and were also negotiated through mediatory third parties such as Japan and foreign communities with vested interests in China.

Japan was the first non-western power to consciously modernise. Its dominant presence in China, culturally, commercially and, later, imperially, complicates China's case, just as the influence of the many virtually autonomous foreign settlements within China do. Other complicating factors arise out of China's regional disparities, the differences between Shanghai and Beijing, and the political divisions that reached their apogee in the civil war between Communists and Nationalists. The uniquely 'local and global contexts of Chinese modernism',[3] as Shih describes it, therefore fall outside most of the recent discussion about modernity beyond the west and obliges the adoption of a different approach.

So as to contextualise the subsequent architectural analysis, this chapter explores these connections through five themes that reveal the distinctiveness of China's encounter with modernity and that set its experience apart from the west's other *others*: Japan as modernity's mediator; the imperial, the colonial and the quasi-colonial; nation-building and nationalism; the etymology of modernity; and modernity and time.

Japan as modernity's mediator

Encounters with modernity outside the west are, by their very nature, multifaceted. For China, however, an added dimension has been the unique factor of its relationship with Japan. A central tenet of modernisation theory has been the presumption of westernisation and modernisation's conflation. The history of Japan, the first country outside the west to become fully modernised, challenges this supposition. In *Non-West Modernist Past: On Architecture and Modernities* (2012) Lim places Japan in 'the west' on account of it not being part of the 'non-west'.[4] Little attention has been paid to Japan's role in China's early modernisation and in its architectural development in particular, a process that Christiane Reinhold broadly describes as a 'journey of self-discovery through the intellectual "encounter" with the "enemy"'.[5] This encounter 'not only refracts the China–west binary model of confrontation, but sometimes displaces the role of western modernism entirely'[6] in ways that have rarely occurred elsewhere.

Until the late-nineteenth century, China had always viewed Japan as a subaltern neighbour and cultural underling. Conversely, the Japanese, as the British poet and scholar, Laurence Binyon (1869–1943), noted, 'look to China as we look to Italy and Greece, for them it is the classic land'.[7] 'The China Factor', as Lincoln Li describes it, was embedded in Japanese traditions not only as a 'cultural element', but also 'often [as] a source for cultural renewal'.[8] For Japanese scholars, tenth-century China was a 'modern age',[9] and succeeded a period from the seventh century where 'Japanese architecture drew heavily on Chinese precedent'.[10] The historical relationship between China and Japan is a critical factor in determining China's modernisation from the late nineteenth century and presents some difficulties for established discourses of modernism within which China has been largely overlooked, and Japan framed as something of an aberration.

China's relationship with Japan was upended in the nineteenth century. Each country's response to encroachment by western powers would change the subsequent course and nature of their relationship with each other. Both countries sought to contain foreign intervention by limiting trade to specific ports: Guangzhou in China[11] and Nagasaki in Japan, but the first Opium War between Britain and China and the concluding Treaty of Nanjing (1842)[12] turned foreign influence from an external nuisance to an internal crisis. Japan faced no such official indignities. Although the arrival of the *US Mississippi* in Eto (Tokyo) Bay led to the signing of the Convention of Kanagawa (1854), opening Shimoda and Hakodate to foreign trade, the crucial difference from China concerned foreign settlement, which was permitted in China but not in Japan.

China and Japan's consequently divergent paths are commonly attributed to the Meiji Restoration, marking the start of Japan's rapid modernisation following the fall of the Tokugawa Shogunate and the reinstatement of the emperor in 1868. With its programme of westernisation, the Meiji Restoration paved the way for Japan's passage from its Oriental origins to a new, modern future. But this should not be seen in isolation from China's parallel decline, which was well underway by the 1860s. China's example was a catalyst for change within Japan. The reformist intellectual, Fukuzawa Yukichi (1835–1901), wrote in 1899: 'we came to dislike everything that had any connection with Chinese culture. Our general opinion was that we should rid our country of the influences of the Chinese altogether'.[13] Fukuzawa had already made a small but significant contribution to this campaign in 1869 when he produced a world atlas that became a school textbook, in which China was portrayed as a weak, lethargic and a retrogressive empire. Written in a poetic style, it became a favourite among women and children and, according to Yukichi, 'served as a popular lullaby and many children were put to sleep every night with their nursemaid reciting this book from memory'.[14] The new Meiji generation were thus nurtured on a negative picture of China imprinted on their minds from a tender age.[15]

China's capitulation to western powers sent a powerful message to other non-western countries. For Japan it stimulated a double-sided impulse: the 'desire for conquest intersecting with anxiety about the self-same Other'.[16] The threat of colonisation, whether 'imagined or real,' became a key influence in Japan's choosing 'to become a "civilised" nation in the image of the west'.[17] As this newly stratified relationship evolved, the interconnections between Japan and China further complicated the negotiation of modernity during the early twentieth century. Chinese and western values represented two polarities for Japan: the past and the future. According to the reformist politician, Sakuma Shōzan (1811–64), they were still 'both foreign', just as 'China was neither Japanese nor western'.[18] Japan's strategy for maintaining this political and cultural autonomy as it sought to modernise relied on *wakon yōsai* (Japanese spirit [and] western techniques), which safeguarded the essential cultural characteristics or 'spirit', while adopting western utility; in China, a similar contemporaneous westernisation Movement or Self-Strengthening Movement was much less successful.

Japan's distinctive modus operandi in pursuit of modernisation in response to western and Chinese alterities helped to forge and subsequently reinforce Japan's medial position between the west and China, and would, in part, define their triangular relationship from the mid-nineteenth century onwards. Japan's selective severance of its Asian roots embodied in the successful political and cultural reforms brought it closer to the west while retaining its uniquely medial position. Epitomising the tenor of the time, Fukuzawa's editorial piece, *Datsuaron* (*Departing Asia*), published in the Japanese newspaper *Jiji Shimpo* in 1885, acknowledged the irresistible 'winds' from the west and declared the need for Japan to set sail and leave Asia and its uncivilised neighbours behind.[19]

Fukuzawa's predictions proved accurate. The apogee of China and Japan's new and increasingly complicated relationship was the Sino-Japanese War (1894–5), 'the darkest hour in China's "century of humiliation" '.[20] For China, defeat was unexpected and devastating. A 'thunderbolt in a dream' was how the Chinese reformer, Liang Qichao (1873–1929) described it.[21] For Japan, victory cemented its ascendant position over its cultural antecedent. Shortly afterwards, Fukuzawa delivered a speech on the modernisation of Japan in which he claimed Chinese studies 'contribute nothing new – and nothing to true learning. Therefore, Chinese studies, along with the Chinese scholars, ought to be dispensed with!'[22] Accompanying the inevitable cultural and geopolitical consequences was an outcome whose significance was under-appreciated at the time. A supplementary treaty of commerce and navigation attached to the Treaty of Shimonoseki (1895) signed by China, Japan and Britain granted Japanese subjects the right to 'carry on trade, industry and manufactures' at any of the treaty ports, a right extended to other nations through the 'Most Favoured Nation' clause.[23] Officially, it was thus Japan's interventions, not those of the west that initiated foreign industrial development in China, and 'eventually led to an industrial revolution in

China'.[24] For China, the doors to modern industrial production – a hallmark of modernity – were unlocked not from the west but from the east.

China's defeat by Japan vindicated the increasingly desperate demands of China's reformers, as China's former subordinate was seen by many politicians and intellectuals as the model for political reform and modernisation. The consequent triangular relationship forged between China, Japan and the west challenges the dualistic and westerncentric notion of modernity's arrival from the west as Japan assumed the role of a 'mediating transmitter of western culture and a potent force in the formation of Chinese modernism'.[25] For China, there emerged what Jacques describes as 'the world's first example of reactive modernization: of a negotiated modernity in the context of western power and pre-eminence [that] deliberately and self-consciously walked the tightrope between westernization and Japanization'.[26]

So successful was Japan's modernisation that it matched and in some cases usurped western hegemony in the region. Japan was the only non-western nation to possess settlements in China's treaty ports, and its colonial ventures in China were larger, more ambitious and more complete than that of any western power. Even as early as 1905, it was in possession of Taiwan, Korea and parts of north-eastern China. By the early 1930s it had occupied the whole of north-eastern China known as Manchuria and rebranded it a new state called Manchukuo, which became the site of some of the most intense and concentrated modern architectural production in the world before the Second World War.

Once underway, Japan's colonial policy, manifested not only militarily and politically but also culturally and intellectually, was presented as saving Asia from the scourge of western imperialism. Although Japanese scholars 'found the real China to be a poor shadow of what they were familiar with',[27] China was more studied by Japanese than by westerners in the late nineteenth century. Japan's literary China hands, or *Zhinatong*, 'wrote books on the Chinese national character, describing it as antimodern, antirational, and antimoral'.[28] Frequent references by these writers to China as *Zhina*, *Shina* or even *China* were further evidence of Japan's new contempt for its once superior neighbour, since all were a departure from the formerly reverential term *Zhong Guo* or *Chugoku* (*Middle Kingdom* in Chinese and Japanese respectively).

The *Zhinatong* writers were among the first generation to present a view of Japan that 'saw itself not simply as modernizing, but as modern'.[29] They included Yokomitsu Riichi (1898–1947), who wrote *Shina*, and Akutagawa Ryūnosuke (1892–1927) 'an early modernist and writer for the Osaka Daily', whose celebrated China travelogue, *Travels in China,* is used by Shih as an example of a Japanese writer's 'propensity to celebrate their superiority, and the Chinese intellectuals' surprisingly uncritical reception of such views'.[30] Their often demeaning tone is exemplified by Riichi's portrayal of Shanghai as a city of 'decay and decomposition ... a center of moral, spiritual, and physical degradation, a vast "waste dump of Asia" filled with all the forms of filth by then familiar to readers of Japanese accounts of China'[31] – far removed from the vibrant, pulsating, inspiring and profoundly modern city that many of their Chinese contemporaries wrote about. Nevertheless, Chinese writers were often inspired by their *Zhinatong* counterparts. Intellectuals such as Xia Mianzun (1886–1946) famously claimed that the Chinese should use Akutagawa's observations 'as a bright mirror to look at our own ugly faces!'[32] It is no surprise, then, that Xia, when translating Akutagawa's *Travels in China*, used the word *Zhina* rather than

Zhong Guo, a perfidious gesture that highlighted the prevailing paradoxes within Chinese intellectual discourses.

The empathy that Chinese intellectuals had for Japan was the result of two particular conditions: the political refuge Japan afforded dissident Chinese reformers and the comparatively inexpensive international education that Japan offered. Most Chinese intellectuals and scholars that benefited from either of these retained close ties with Japan despite its increasing belligerence. Shih cites the example of the writer Zhou Zuoren (1885–1967), who frequently sought to distinguish 'metropolitan Japan and colonial Japan', insisting that 'the former produced an admirable culture while the latter produced imperialists and barbaric bigots'.[33] *Xian Dai* (*Les Contemporains*), the literary journal edited by Shi Zhecun (1905–2003), often emphasised the alliance between Chinese and Japanese leftist writers against Japanese imperialism. Its launch in May 1932, months after Japan's infamous bombing of Shanghai, was described by Shih as 'the most memorable event after the bombing in terms of Chinese modernism'.[34]

China's Japanese education

The impact of Japan's system of education on China's encounter with modernity has, for historical reasons, been largely overlooked. As China's nemesis, followed by the atrocities committed following the 1937 invasion, Japan's intellectual contributions to China have been comparatively overlooked. Conversely, and in part consequently, America's educational contributions have been elevated. This imbalance in the historical record is particularly pertinent in architecture and will be examined later.

Privately, Chinese students had travelled to Japan for education long before their country's defeat in the Sino-Japanese War. China's once inferior neighbour was increasingly seen as a place to gain a modern education, particularly in the sciences. After the war this view gained official sanction. In 1896, thirteen students from Hong Wen College[35] travelled to Japan accompanied by China's ambassador. Such initiatives were pushed by a generation of reformers that, according to Reinhold, 'without exception, felt friendly towards Japan. They all shared a high opinion about the Meiji Restoration ... It was with these men that the modern Japan discourse in China began'.[36] Japan proved to subsequent generations of Chinese intellectuals that modernism was not merely desirable and attainable, but with the right conditions it could be achieved on their terms – not dictated by the west.

Among this group was the Qing official, Zhang Zhidong (1837–1909), who wrote *Quan Xue Pian* (*Exhortation to Learning*, 1898), in which the merits of a Japanese education in comparison to other overseas destinations was explained: a year spent in Europe was better than five years reading western books, and attending a foreign school for a year was better than spending three years at a Chinese school. Japan, however, was the best place for Chinese to study overseas because of its geographical, cultural and linguistic proximity, all of which made it economically, educationally and administratively practical. Zhang observed how the Japanese had already selected and translated key western materials, which assisted Chinese scholars. Japan, in Zhang's eyes, was therefore both a legitimate and trusted filter of western knowledge, making Europe somewhere Chinese only needed to go if seeking specialised skills or qualifications.

32 *China and the meaning of modernity*

A Japanese education was also relatively expeditious. In order to attract Chinese students, the Japanese government introduced a fast-track system for those attending Chinese colleges in Japan and engaged in teacher-training, politics or law, subjects that attracted most Chinese students.[37] The majority of China's teachers, junior politicians and military graduates in the early twentieth century were Japanese-trained fast-track students.[38]

The first Sino-Japanese college to assist Chinese students to learn Japanese language and subjects was established in 1898. When every Chinese province was invited by the Japanese government to select and send students to Japan, the official, Yang Shenxiu, declared:

> If China wants to make a success of studying overseas then we must start from Japan. I hear Japan has opened the door to help us, to enlighten us, to take our students, to pay for our fees; then we must take such an opportunity.[39]

When the Chinese government established a nationwide programme of sending students to Japan, limiting applications to 200 per year from 1902 to 1908, actual numbers far exceeded expectations. Wang claims the total number of Chinese students in Japan rose from 280 in 1901 to 15,000 by 1906, of which 8,000 were recipients of provincial government scholarships on fast-track courses – more overseas students than at any other time or to any other country.[40] By 1908, there were over 10,000 Chinese students in Japan. Even by 1912, when the Qing programme was past its peak, 1,100 students travelled to Japan.[41]

China's 'Japan hands'

Paralleling the growing number of Chinese with educational experience of Japan was the steady rise in China's 'Japan hands', among the most renowned and ultimately influential of whom were the reformers Liang Qichao and his mentor Kang Youwei (1858–1927). Both lived in Tokyo for over a decade following their involvement in a failed attempt to instigate institutional reforms known as the 'One Hundred Day Reform' under the auspices of the young Emperor Guangxu.[42] The primary consequence, rather than delivering educational, constitutional, military and economic reforms, was a conservative backlash and *coup d'état* by the Empress Dowager Ci Xi (1835–1908). Six of the reformers, including Kang's brother, were executed.[43] In exile, Liang and Kang established the *Bao Huang Hui (Protect the Emperor Society)*[44] and petitioned for the reinstatement of the emperor under a constitutional monarchy.[45]

Chinese reformers flourished in their Japanese sanctuary. Liang published two radical journals, *Qing Yi Bao (Honest Criticism)* and *Xin Min Cong Bao (A New People)*, which he 'smuggled back into China through the Treaty Ports' and in so doing 'had China's reading public virtually to himself'.[46] After the fall of the Qing Dynasty in 1911 the pair returned to China, Kang continuing his crusade to reinstate the emperor and Liang pursuing a career in political and educational reform, becoming a revered reformer and statesman.

Other key individuals whose personal debt to Japan demonstrates China and Japan's concord include Jiang Jieshi (Chiang Kai Shek) (1887–1975), who received his military education at the Rikugun Shikan Gakkō (the Imperial Japanese Army

Academy) from 1907 and served two years in the Japanese Imperial Army before returning to China in 1911. From the opposite side of the political spectrum were Li Dazhao (1888–1927) and Chen Duxiu (1879–1942), future founders of China's Communist Party, who both studied in Japan. Chen fled there in 1913 following his involvement in the failed 'Second Revolution', though he had previously visited in 1901 and 1905 when he enrolled briefly at Wasedu University (the first Japanese university to accept Chinese students).[47] Li studied there too, from 1913 to 1917, after which he returned to China and worked with Chen as editor of the influential journal, *New Youth* (*Xin Qing Nian*), and Head Librarian at Peking University where he employed an impoverished Mao Zedong as library assistant.[48] Reinhold argues that it was Li (and Li Fanfu) 'not Mao Zedong', who 'represented the Japan view of the Chinese Communist Party, which was highly critical of Japanese imperialism on the basis of Lenin's discourse on imperialism'.[49] No 'Japan hand' became more influential than the leader of the *Tong Meng Hui*, Sun Yat Sen, who went on to play an integral role in the 1911 Revolution and sealing his reputation as the founder of the Republic of China.[50]

Outside politics, 'Japan hands' included many of China's leading modernist writers and poets. Guo Moruo (1892–1978), the co-founder of the modern literary society, *The Creation Society* (*Chuang Zao She*), studied medicine and lived in Japan from 1914 to 1923, married a Japanese woman, Tomiko Satō. Yu Dafu (1896–1945), the 'anointed "Father of modern Chinese literature"'[51] and fellow co-founder of *The Creation Society*, studied economics at Tokyo Imperial University from 1913 to 1922. Tian Han (1898–1968), also a co-founder of *The Creation Society*, as well as poet, playwright and a leading authority in modern Chinese cinema and theatre, was educated in Japan and returned to China in 1921.[52] Lu Xun (Zhou Shuren 1881–1936), widely regarded as China's pre-eminent modern literary figure and symbolic figurehead of the May Fourth Movement owing, in part, to his story *The Diary of a Madman*, a metaphorical tale railing against Chinese tradition, was awarded a government scholarship to study medicine in Japan from 1902. After a brief language course followed by two years at medical college in Sendai, he famously quit in order to seek a cure for his country's spiritual ills.

Lu Xun was among a group of privileged Japanese-educated Chinese writers who found themselves in a unique professional, political and cultural position. As messengers of modernity they were viewed by compatriots as professionally and culturally advantaged because of their exposure to and intellectual engagement with Japan. They also possessed the linguistic skills that made them gatekeepers of prized modernist texts hitherto only available in Japanese. Many of these writers translated these materials, making the work of Japanese modernists and Japanese interpretations of western modernism accessible to a Chinese audience for the first time. Shi Zhecun, in conversation with Shih, estimated that 'between the late-Qing and the May Fourth period, 80 per cent of all translations of western literature were retranslations from the Japanese'.[53] From this corpus of material, many new Chinese words and ideas associated with modernity were formed.

It was through literature that the language China had once exported to Japan was being reconstituted and imported back as a means of expressing modernity. Chinese writers always wrote in their native language, but if a certain meaning did not exist in Chinese, they would often adopt western and Japanese terms to express modern concepts. Japanese thus became a linguistic medium through which the Chinese were

34 *China and the meaning of modernity*

exposed to and articulated modern ideas, regardless of whether those ideas originated in the west. For example, a Chinese translation of a Japanese essay on Futurism in 1914 employed the words *xiandai shenghuo* (modern life) and *xiandai wenming* (modern civilisation) to describe the changes brought about by Marinetti's ideas. According to Shih 'Modernism' in the form *'modanpai'* (*sic*)[54] (lit. 'modern school') derived from a translation of an article by the well-known Japanese literary historian, Noboru Shōmu (1878–1958). Other examples include the term 'avant-garde', the Chinese origins of which Lee accredits to Shi Zhecun who claimed it appeared in Chinese (*qianwei*) around 1926–8 and was derived 'from Japanese sources on Soviet literature'.[55]

The imperial, the colonial and the quasi-colonial

In 1920, Liang Qichao invited the British philosopher and social critic Bertrand Russell (1872–1970) to teach at Peking University. After a year in China, he wrote *The Problem of China*, an excerpt from which reads:

> Apart from war, the impact of European civilization upon the traditional life of China takes two forms, one commercial, the other intellectual. Both depend upon the prestige of armaments; the Chinese would never have opened either their ports to our trade or their minds to our ideas if we had not defeated them in war. But the military beginning of our intercourse with the Middle Kingdom has now receded into the background. . . . The Chinese have a very strong instinct for trade, and a considerable intellectual curiosity, to both of which we appeal.[56]

Russell's observations demonstrate the apparent inseparability of modernity in China from the imperial or colonial experience whether direct (e.g. militarily) or indirect (e.g. commercially or otherwise). China's encounter with modernity cannot be understood without reference to external pressures. But was it, as Russell suggests, driven by intellectual and commercial interests or was modernity, as is commonly suggested, 'often experienced most forcibly through the encounter with expanding European empires'[57] and thus 'produced and experienced in the historical context of imperialism and colonialism'?[58] In other words, was China's encounter with modernity because of or in spite of aggressive foreign influence? Moving beyond the extensive field of post-colonial studies in non-western contexts, the aim of this exploration is to understand how China – an essentially non-colonial context – experienced and responded to foreign intervention, whether fuelled by intellectual, commercial, colonial or imperial interests, and the consequences this had for architecture.

From the mid-nineteenth century, China's encounters with the west were more varied and more complex than that of any other country outside the west. Owing, in part, to the country's size, the variety of administrative systems operating within its borders was unparalleled. Academic attempts to describe China's unique condition have resulted in the employment of the generic label *semi-colonial* (e.g. Murphey, 1985; Lee, 1999; Harootunian: 2000, Jacques, 2009) and for this reason China has largely been interpreted through post-colonial discourse.

Offering a slightly different approach, Shih draws more useful comparisons with continents rather than with individual nation-states, wherein China can be viewed as 'an Africa of multiple imperialisms struggling over spheres of influence'.[59] This study proposes a different perspective from that of *semi-colonialism* and consequent post-colonial approaches on the grounds that China was a civilisational state composed of multiple entities that cannot be subsumed into the singular unit of a nation-state.

Assorted foreign settlements

In the century prior to 1949, China possessed approximately five different foreign settlements types. The distinctions between them were often imprecise and the regulations governing their jurisdiction were vaguer still. Since most physical foreign interventions in China were centred on or focused around urban areas, what happened in these settlements determined the subsequent development of the built environment, not only within these sites, but also affected architectural development throughout the rest of China. To understand China's multiple modernities demands an acknowledgement of the distinction between these sites and the consequent architectural and urban heterogeneity.

The settlements over which China had least control were the colonies which foreign powers acquired with indefinite rights, such as Hong Kong (British, 1842), Macau (Portugal, 1887) and Taiwan (Japan, 1895).

Rather different from these colonial settlements was the annexation of Manchuria by Japan in 1931, comprising the provinces of Guandong, Liaoning, Jiling and Hailongjiang.[60] Manchuria, despite being declared a separate state with a puppet government headed by the former Chinese emperor, Pu Yi, was effectively a Japanese imperial territory.

Next were the leased territories, loaned on a fixed term determined by treaty, such as the Kwantung (Guandong) Territory (Russia 1898–1905, Japan 1905–45), Lantau and the New Territories (Britain 1898–1997), Weihaiwei (Britain 1898–1930) and Jiaozhou Bay (part of Shandong Province, Germany 1897–1914).

Then there were the foreign concessions granted to specific nations and governed by representatives of that nation or shared between nations (e.g. British and American Settlements in Shanghai were amalgamated in 1863 to become the International Settlement). Legal jurisdiction inside the concessions was vague and initially rested with the Consul of the foreign nation owning the concession; evolving later as the settlements grew to a complex series of regulations formulated by elected (often contentiously) municipal councils. Extraterritoriality ensured foreign nationals inside the concessions enjoyed legal immunity from Chinese law. America, Austria and Hungary, Belgium, Britain, France, Germany, Italy, Japan, Portugal, Russia, Spain and the Netherlands all possessed concessions in China at some point in the century leading up to the Second World War.

Foreign concessions usually comprised a portion of another settlement type: the treaty port, which emerged in 1842 following the signing of the Treaty of Nanjing.[61] Jurisdiction of treaty ports, which numbered over 60 at their height, lay with the Chinese and access to them was granted to a particular foreign power usually under the 'most favoured nation' clause. Many treaty ports were divided into separate foreign concessions or settlements often surrounded by Chinese-administered areas, forming a series of settlements within a city. The largest number of foreign settlements in a treaty port was Tianjin, which had up to nine separately administered areas. A further exception was the Foreign Legation in Beijing (1861–1959), where the foreign embassies and their personnel were permitted to reside.[62]

Questioning 'colonial'

The incompleteness of China's colonial experience has led many scholars to treat foreign settlements homogeneously as *colonial*. Isaacs, for example, refers to the Chinese as 'in effect a colonial population, the "natives" of a regime complete with all the trappings of the European colonial system.... Society in Shanghai was made up of the familiar colonial pieces'.[63] However, if colonial discourses are concerned with 'colonized peoples and, by extension, of oppressed others more generally',[64] this definition does not fit China, for the vast majority of its population did not live under colonial rule and many of those living or working in the foreign settlements could be seen as 'the chief actors in the treaty-port trade'.[65] Notions of colonialism with all its iniquitous connotations and accountability to distant centres of power are therefore inadequate in describing China, and make the application of recent theories of post-colonialism to the Chinese situation questionable, if not entirely inappropriate.

Politically, treaty ports could not be considered colonial entities since they were neither directly accountable to a single foreign government, nor were they the outcome of singular purposeful colonial adventures. Occasionally, these composite foreign entities relied for their survival on the presence of foreign troops,[66] but treaty ports were essentially a commercial response to trade that had grown too large to be managed effectively by the merchants whose activities had spurred the growth.

Some scholars, such as Lee, attempt to resolve China's particular experience by employing the prefix *semi*. The 'semi-colony' suggests a 'hybrid sense of a mixture of colonial and Chinese elements'.[67] In Chinese scholarship, *semi* is attached to *colonial* and *feudal* to describe the country's debased condition before 1949. Shih employs the term in the form *semi-colonialism* 'to describe the specific effects of multiple imperialist presences in China and their fragmentary colonial geography (largely confined to coastal cities) and control, as well as the resulting social and cultural formations'.[68] Defending its use, Shih explains that *semi* implies the 'fractured, informal, and indirect character of colonialism, as well as its multi-layeredness' (as opposed to implying a '"half" of something').[69]

Shih is right to stress 'the term's inability to describe the rivalry among foreign powers, and the multiple layers of domination among the foreign powers and China [and] its inadequacy in reflecting the relations of cooperation among the foreign powers in China',[70] however, the degree to which exploitation was a result of a concerted and coordinated effort among the foreign communities remains questionable. Competition among these *others* was equally divisive. In one of the first internationally available books about Shanghai by a Chinese author, written in 1929, Hsia prefigures Shih's bi-polar model: 'The greatest stumbling block to that spirit of unity in Shanghai is the constant friction between the Chinese and the foreign communities which divide themselves perpetually into two camps.' However, he goes further, observing how 'each national group builds a wall round itself; group and national interests usually come before the community interest'.[71] Not simply a case of 'them and us', this was a deeply divided community within which different groups exploited each other as much as the Chinese.

Just as fractious as the relations among and between foreign communities were the relations between Chinese groups residing in these cities. The ways these divisions occurred depended on the city and the nature of the groups. Chinese intellectuals often highlighted how Chinese communities coalesced into groups of individuals with shared experiences or vested interests. Shi Zhecun and Shu Xincheng both cite education as a basis for this division. Lee highlights how Shi divided Shanghai's writers into three main groups along linguistic lines: 'the English language group (those educated in England, America, or the prestigious missionary universities of Yenching, Tsinghua, or St John's); the French-German language group (those, like Shi himself, educated at Catholic universities such as Aurora in Shanghai – or those who had studied or wandered around Europe); and the Japanese-language group (who had studied in Japan)'.[72] This view is corroborated by Shu Xincheng in *The Modern History of Chinese Overseas Study* (1927), which observes that returning Chinese students would congregate in their own small communities and rarely mix with those from other backgrounds.

Given the heterogeneousness of China's urban settlements and the undeniable impact of settled (but not colonial) foreign communities, the prefix *quasi* would be more appropriate than *semi*. Although the two prefixes share the same oblique and stratified characteristics, *semi* implies a partial relationship to a virtually non-existent colonialism, whereas *quasi* suggests resemblance. *Quasi-colonial* thus describes any of the different administrative conditions directly imposed by or indirectly influenced by multiple foreign powers in China while not implying any explicitly colonial relationship.

A key feature of China's quasi-colonial settings was the contribution they made to political and social change, particularly in the early twentieth century. These settlements constituted islands of extraterritoriality whose provision of relative security and virtual legal immunity for foreigners and Chinese alike, provided fertile ground for the cultivation of political agitation and intercultural experimentation. Unlike many colonial experiences where domestic hostility was aimed squarely at the colonisers, the hostility aimed at the diverse foreign contingent in China's quasi-colonial settlements was often no less strong than that between different Chinese factions, particularly tensions that came to define and reinforce what would become the catastrophic schism between Nationalists and Communists.

Another facet of China's quasi-colonial condition emphasised by its foreign residents was its distinction from residents in other formal colonial settings. Foreigners in quasi-colonial settings would often distance themselves from the morally indefensible relationship that separated the coloniser and the colonised in official colonies. Representing to a lesser extent the excesses of power and authority that true colonialism wielded, foreigners in China's quasi-colonial settlements attempted to project a more palatable alternative to colonialism that emphasised the positive role they played in China's modernisation. The *quasi* complicated resistance too. Shih argues that the 'insufficiently formalised colonial structure, lacking systematic institutional infrastructure, did not overtly position the colonial powers as the unequivocal targets of cultural resistance',[73] contrasting China with India's 'formal colonialism' to support this argument. Although this interpretation is valid, it would be mistaken to assume that the foreign administrators of China's quasi-colonial settlements were not the explicit targets of Chinese dissent. The threat of Chinese insurrection was present both inside and outside such settlements, and, although usually political in origin, it permeated most cultural, religious and economic activities. Boycotts against foreign nations were frequent, sometimes violent and often extremely effective.[74] Foreign settlements both stimulated and harboured malcontent, as Ransome (1884–1967) noted after a trip to China in 1927:

38 *China and the meaning of modernity*

> Foreign settlements and concessions have come to play a very important part in Chinese politics. A politician can at any moment assume a cap of invisibility by crossing a street. He is close at hand, surrounded by Chinese territory, can keep in close touch with events, and yet be inviolate. The unequal treaties have thus built up a system of political sanctuary from one end of China to the other.... The foreign banks, like the concessions, contribute largely to the amenity of Chinese civil war and political strife. Once loot is turned into money and deposited with them by the looter it is sacred and beyond public recovery.[75]

A key weapon in China's armoury of resistance to foreign influence was what Rey Chow describes as its 'linguistic integrity'.[76] The extent to which China was able to maintain its language in spite of growing foreign interventions set it apart from colonial experiences elsewhere. The fractured nature of foreign presence made it impossible for a single power to assert linguistic authority. Linguistic integrity also played a major role in Chinese literature, which underpinned patriotic fervour throughout this tumultuous period, most explicitly during the May Fourth Movement. Shih quotes Shi Zhecun as saying: 'There is no such thing as importation in literature. Everything that is written in Chinese by the Chinese is Chinese literature. Even when it is about foreigners it is Chinese literature.'[77] Some of China's first architects later assumed a similar self-assuredness in the context of their own art form.

Maintaining the native language was critical to China's particular articulation of modernity and to maintaining a sense of identity. Lee asserts that 'in spite of their reading knowledge of foreign literatures, modern Chinese writers did not use any foreign languages to write their work and continued to use the Chinese language as their *only* language',[78] allowing Chinese writers 'to embrace western modernity openly, without fear of colonization'.[79]

Another feature of China's complex cultural relationship with the west emanating from the diversity of foreign settlements was its position as a destination for western modernists, 'diplomats, luminaries, and pleasure-seekers ... gathering Chinese cultural materials',[80] or, as Said describes, individuals engaged in the 'struggle over geography', not as representations of the military such as 'soldiers and canons', but as the guardians of ideas, forms, images and imaginings.[81] In China, these figures include Bertrand Russell, John Dewey, Alexis Léger, Goldsworthy Dickinson, Harold Acton, Christopher Isherwood, Wystan Hugh Auden, Mark Tobey, and even Noël Coward. Virginia Woolf's nephew, Julian Bell, whose journey to China was a 'cultural combination of curiosity, ignorance, enthusiasm, stereotypes, and sympathy',[82] is another example. Laurence, like Said, draws a distinction between these agents of cultural modernity and the iniquities and aggression associated with colonialism by equating their search 'for inspiration [and] not to exploit, do trade and for gain' with the 'materials and perspectives of African art [that] inspired the cubists in France'.[83]

Imperialism from the east

Further challenging China's 'colonised' designation is the distinction between 'colonialism' and 'imperialism'. Said claims the former, 'almost always the consequence of imperialism, is the implanting of settlements on distant territory' while the latter is 'the practice, the theory and the attitudes of a dominating metropolitan centre ruling a distant territory'.[84] Citing Doyle's *Empires*, Said further describes empire as 'a relationship in which one state controls the effective political sovereignty of another political society'.[85] The multifariousness of China's infiltration by foreign powers challenges these definitions, which are better suited to unambiguous cases where the political or cultural sovereignty of one nation over another was absolute.

Taking Said and Doyle's definitions, only the Japanese case (in Manchuria and throughout eastern China during the Second World War) comes close to an imperial venture, though the territory it sought to rule was not, as Said suggested, 'distant', but culturally and geographically proximate. It is worth pointing out that Said excluded Japan from his account of imperialism as a 'complicated exception',[86] just as it does not fit within modernisation theories. China, despite having been subjected to various forms of foreign domination, remains outside almost all imperialist discourses.

China's principal encounter with imperialism therefore came from the east, not from the west. Its political sovereignty was frequently weak, but even during the warlord period China never submitted to any single foreign power. Only after 1937, when Japan conquered the capital, Nanjing, and occupied much of northern, eastern and southern China was political sovereignty largely surrendered, but even then it occurred in a manner that challenges common western interpretations of international dominance and subjugation. Despite the uniquely varied nature of direct foreign influence in China from the mid-nineteenth century to the mid-twentieth century, it was Japanese imperialism that terminated the west's relationship with China and brought an end to the heterogeneous treaty port settlements.

Nation-building and nationalism

Benedict Anderson claims 'nation, nationality and nationalism all have proved notoriously difficult to define, let alone to analyse',[87] so this study makes no attempt to do so. Instead, it focuses on China's encounter with these concepts which, like modernity, with its western origins, pose and expose equivalent analytical problems.

Most discourses associated with the abstract notion of nationhood and its relationship with modernity outside the west are intertwined with colonial or imperial experiences, wherein native autonomy and foreign exploitation represented constant and uncomfortable polarities, between which an effective, if unstable, compromise was mediated until independence. Paradoxically, the construct of nationhood was often contingent upon and invariably a reaction to aggressive interaction with and partial dependence on other nations, as well as the conscious construction and promotion of a collective *national* identity.

China's first conscious encounter with the notion of nation-building in a western sense was its response to western incursion, echoing Japan's Meiji Restoration, but preceding it by several years. Known as the Self-Strengthening Movement or westernisation Movement (*Yang Wu Yun Dong*) it lasted from the early 1860s until the close of the century. Sun calls it the 'advent of modernity' in China.[88]

Prominent officials and industrialists[89] who played leading roles in the reforms associated with the Self-Strengthening Movement proclaimed that the way to strengthen China was to combine western efficacy with Chinese ideology; a belief founded on the idea that ancient Chinese teaching was most suitable for moral and ethical instruction, while western knowledge was most suited to scientific and technological practice. Zhang Zhidong later encapsulated this in the famous phrase: 'Chinese learning for essence, western knowledge for practical application' (*zhong xue wei ti, xi xue wei yong*).[90] Implemented initially for military purposes, the projects carried out under the aegis of the Self-Strengthening Movement quickly evolved to reforms of the civil service, industry, commerce and diplomacy.

The significance of the Self-Strengthening Movement on architectural modernity in China lies not in its characteristics or achievements per se, an analysis of which there is not space for, but in its relationship with the onset of a national (rather than civilisational) consciousness, which preceded the type of nationalism that dominated China during the first half of the twentieth century and was manifest in architecture and urban planning. The Self-Strengthening Movement was, according to reformers like Liang Qichao, the first phase in China's evolution towards a modern national consciousness, brought about by China's feelings of inadequacy over the west's material superiority exemplified by armaments, ships, canons, and scientific instruments.[91] The second phase of this process began after China's defeat to Japan in 1895, by which time the Self-Strengthening Movement and its outcomes were exhausted.

For China, nationhood represents a preoccupation that was complicated by its cultural diversity and civilisational longevity. The type of statal cohesion that China had mastered since antiquity provided it with a form of self-identity akin to nationhood but born out of the notion of civilisation. In 1899, Liang Qichao explained in an essay:

> The Chinese do not comprehend that people of a nation exist; for thousands of years the only two comparable words in Chinese are *guo* (kingdom) and *jia* (family) . . . *Guo jia* is to see the kingdom as a family's assets. . . . When one family loses power, another will take over; brutal power will replace brutal power, endlessly.[92]

China's ancient sage, Confucius, lived through the worst of these power struggles and consequently defined the essence of Chinese civilisation. The exceptional scholar, Gu Hongming (1857–1928),[93] likened Confucius to an architect in a speech given to the Oriental Society of Beijing in 1915. At that time, there were no qualified Chinese architects and it would be another three years before Gu invited Frank Lloyd Wright to China for his first and only visit. In response to the question after his presentation, 'What did Confucius do when he saw that he could not prevent the destruction of the Chinese civilization?' Gu replied:

> Well, as an architect who sees his house on fire, burning and falling over his head, and is convinced that he cannot possibly save the building, he knows that the only thing for him to do is to save the drawings and plans of the building so that it may afterwards be built again; so Confucius, seeing the inevitable destruction of the building of the Chinese civilisation which he could not prevent, thought he would save the drawings and plans, which are now preserved in the Old Testament of the Chinese Bible: the five Canonical Books known as the Wu Ching (Five Canons). . . . The greatest service which Confucius has done for the Chinese nation was that, in saving the drawings and plans of their civilisation, he made a new synthesis, a new interpretation of the plans of that

civilisation, and in that new synthesis he gave the Chinese people the true idea of a State – a true, rational, permanent, absolute basis of a State.[94]

In his book *Chun Qiu* (*Spring and Autumn*), Confucius claimed that orthodox Chinese culture was based on a perception of *zun wang rang yi* (respect the emperor and repel the barbarians).[95] The term *hua yi zhi bian* epitomises this perception, where *hua*[96] refers to Chinese culture or people, *yi* refers to barbarians and *bian* refers to the distinction between the two. The basis of this distinction is the idea of civilisation and ritual, not race or ethnicity, which generally define western notions of nationhood. Anyone willing to adopt Chinese culture could become Chinese, while those who rejected it remained barbarians. Consequently, China's history possesses abundant examples of different kingdoms accepting or rejecting the rituals of Xia.

Qualitatively, then, *civilisation-state* rather than *nation-state* more aptly conveys China's condition, but not in the manner of Huntington's crude 'civilisation identity' where religions (e.g. Islam/Hindu) and nebulous geographic entities (e.g. the west/Latin America) are combined to create problematic abstractions. Instructively, in evidence of his westerncentric perspective, Huntington does not include the Chinese among his list of civilisations, while he does include Japan.[97]

Quantitively, China's cultural weight and temporal scope were matched by other exceptional characteristics that made it proportionally unique and further destabilise prescribed nation-based categorisations. Comprising the world's third largest geographical area, possessing the greatest ethnic diversity, and accommodating the largest population, China, on the point of scale, scarcely conforms to the usual categorisations applicable to most other nations. Irrespective of ethnic diversity, 90 per cent of the world's nations are less than 10 per cent of China's size and only 4 per cent have a population greater than 10 per cent of China's. China's continental size highlights the problems of analysing China using a national yardstick. Just as *nation-state* is inadequate to describe China qualitatively, *continent-state* more aptly conveys China's condition quantitatively, introducing the notion of *intranationalism* to describe its true state.

China's intranationalism also challenges its place in post-colonial studies. It has no primary city or any obvious preeminent dualistic urban pair distinguished by old and new, such as New Delhi/Mumbai; Yangon/Mandalay; Jakarta/Jogjakarta; Manila/Cebu; or Singapore/Kuala Lumpur. Shanghai and Beijing are often combined for this purpose, but this overlooks their distinct approaches to modernity, as well as interrelations with other major cities such as Guangzhou, Tianjin and Hong Kong. Ginsberg highlights the contrast between old and new towns in China as being 'usually between an old Chinese and a modern foreign city,'[98] which was invariably a construct of foreign projection more than a true reflection of reality. The Russians and Japanese in Manchuria and other foreign powers in the larger treaty ports often emphasised the antiquity and shabbiness of the old Chinese settlement to accentuate the contrast with their newer yet often equally untidy creations.

However, foreign cities in China were often anything but foreign, whether in appearance or population. Behind the formal façades that fronted main roads, railway stations or riverfronts could invariably be found a mass of residential and commercial properties built by Chinese for Chinese, who, whether in Russian Harbin or British Hong Kong, were always the dominant population. Herein lies another characteristic peculiar to China emanating from its unique size and civilisational stature. Just as the comparatively large Chinese populations of foreign settlements in China denied the very existence of a 'foreign' city in China, the Chinese were unique in exporting on such a scale urban forms and modes of living overseas. The global phenomenon of Chinatowns is evidence that Chinese settlements are not confined to China, but the same might also be said of 'Chinese' cities. In Borneo, for example, Lee points out that port towns were 'entirely devoid of indigenous features, being largely Chinese in material form and atmosphere ... the ubiquitous Chinese shop-house gives all the towns a Chinese atmosphere'.[99]

China's cultural dominance throughout the region complicates conventional theories of modernisation and post-colonialism which commonly frame China as a singular entity on the periphery of a western worldview. Domestically, China's multidimensionality and the conscious rivalry that existed between elements of the whole, historically and in the period in which nationalism flourished in the early twentieth century, ensured that the divergent expressions of modernity within China could be just as great as those between China and the west or other places outside the west. Under the ambit of one civilisation, this intranational composition challenges western concepts of nationhood and modernity and, like multiple modernities, demands a reconceptualisation of these ideas to accommodate examples that, owing to their qualitative and quantitative uniqueness, are located outside established methodological parameters.

For Sun Yat Sen, the founder of the Republic of China and 'chief apostle of its modern nationalism',[100] the resolution of the unique problems surrounding nation-building in the Chinese context was to subsume it within his Principles of the People (*San Min Zhu Yi*): Nationalism, Democracy and Livelihood (*Min zhu, Min quan,* and *Min sheng*).[101] Echoing Abraham Lincoln's dictum at Gettysburg,[102] Sun was careful to claim a greater debt to the wisdom of Confucius. Adopting Confucius's term *ge ming* to describe revolution, Sun's revolutionary political philosophy was based on Confucian ideals amalgamated with European and modern philosophical theory:

> The principles which I have held in promoting the Chinese revolution were in some cases copied from our traditional ideals, in other cases modelled on European theory and experience and in still others formulated according to original and self-developed theories.[103]

By linking the two potentially incompatible concepts of modern nationalism with China's ancient understanding of civilisation, Sun was able to wed nationalism to the idea of civilisation, but with modern and radical political overtones.

As he saw it, Sun's revolution was therefore not a historical aberration but was part of an ancient continuum that inevitably and necessarily summoned China's patriotic spirit to overthrow foreign rule. By employing historical example and linking classical ideas with the Three Principles of the new Republic, China's political transition was no paradigm shift, but instead the rearticulation of China's ancient political attributes. Through an attempt to achieve an indigenous modernity by association with civilisation, the idea of modern nationhood became a palatable and uniquely Chinese alternative in a modern age. Henceforth, the nation-building project continued to preoccupy China as the country sought, from Sun's perspective, to maintain its independence in a global family of nations.

Nation-building and a modern education system

Nation-building relied on a modern system of education that, according to Wang, was not designed 'to enlighten the individual', but was the principal 'device to strengthen China'.[104] The results, however, seldom achieved either. By the end of the nineteenth century, of the three main areas of reform China confronted – the constitution, the military, and education – Wang argues that

> the educational reforms were probably the most fundamental, since they were intended in part to develop a new kind of civil servant to implement future reforms [and] were endorsed by both the radicals and the conservatives at court and consequently enjoyed much more support than the other reforms.[105]

Established under the aegis of the Self-Strengthening Movement, China's first modern educational establishments outside missionary institutions were linked to newly created manufacturing facilities. These nascent industries provided the physical and institutional basis for the subsequent development of educational establishments that taught modern subjects and in some cases primed students for study overseas – a radical strategy that did not come naturally to a culture based on Confucian education and filial responsibility. Examples include Shanghai's Jiangnan Arsenal, which by the late nineteenth century was said to be 'the highest development of Chinese technical industry'[106] and later became one of the largest arms manufacturing facilities in the world; Fuzhou's famous shipyard founded by Zuo Zongtang; and the arsenals at Nanjing and Tianjin founded by Li Hongzhang.

Initially, China's modern educational establishments, materials and teachers were too few to compete with the west, so a programme of overseas education was a necessary and superior alternative that later had important architectural implications. At this time Chinese students could be separated into four broad groups: those affiliated to semi-governmental programmes; those on government scholarships; those under the auspices of missionary schools; and those who were privately funded.

Students from the first group included those attending China's industry-affiliated institutions initiated with government support but operated with virtual independence under the supervision of influential officials.[107] A prominent example from this group is Yan Fu (1854–1921),[108] who was one of China's most eminent translators and philosophers of his generation and former associate of the Fuzhou shipyard. His case also demonstrated the common experience that, despite the programme's military orientation, the benefits were often outside the military.

Government scholarships and religious missions are often affiliated, as in the case of China's first overseas student, Yung Wing (Rong Hong, 1828–1912) who became the first Asian to successfully enrol at Yale University and the first Chinese to graduate from an American university.[109] In 1870, Yung proposed to the imperial court to send young boys to America for education, a gesture that coincided with Li Hongzhang and Zeng Guofan's direct communications with the emperor in 1871 outlining the practicalities of sending children overseas. A year later, 30 boys aged 9–15 were sent from Shanghai to San Francisco on a programme nicknamed the 'Yung Wing Mission'. Over the next four years 120 children travelled overseas under the programme and went into various universities including Yale, but by 1878 the programme was prematurely terminated and all the children were recalled. For the next decade at least, prospective students had to personally arrange and finance overseas studies.

A lack of coordination between private, missionary and semi-governmental initiatives and the arbitrary nature of their selection processes undermined China's early efforts to institute a modern education system. In 1890 the government established an organised system for facilitating, if not directly supporting, overseas education by sending two students overseas for up to three years accompanied by China's ambassadors to Britain, Russia, France, Germany and America. Following defeat in the Sino-Japanese War, the programme was extended to Japan, which in educational terms dominated the subsequent two decades of China's modern education and was the font of China's architectural education.

A few years later, after the Boxer Uprising, the popularity of a western education increased.[110] The compulsory signing of the Boxer Protocol on 7 September 1901, a politically humiliating and financially punishing consequence of the Boxer Uprising for China, demanded the payment of reparations worth 450 million taels ($333m.). Calculated at 1 tael per head of Chinese population to be paid over 39 years, the scheme became known as the Boxer Indemnity. This settlement contained educational programmes that permanently linked China with the west, connecting the causes and effects of the Boxer incident with modern education in China and its encounter with modernity more broadly.[111]

In 1908, America was the first western power to commit repayments to educational schemes by remitting half the payments and committing the balance into a programme that became known as the Boxer Indemnity Fund and offered scholarships to Chinese students to study at some of America's foremost universities.[112] In 1911, a preparatory college in Beijing, Tsinghua Xue Tang, was established under the new scheme. It accepted children from the age of 15 with the intention of sending them to America (100 for the first four years and 50 per year thereafter).[113] Tsinghua was run entirely along American lines, with an American curriculum and employing only American teachers. Critics of the American system highlighted the paradox whereby America was busy Americanising foreigners while China was busy westernising the Chinese.

America's educational appeal stemmed from the perception that it was the quickest and easiest place to get a degree. It was regarded as the destination of choice for over 49 per cent of all China's self-funded students. From America's perspective, Chinese students represented over 20 per cent of the overseas student population, higher than any other of the 97 countries with a student representation. From 1911 to 1928, a total of 1,031 Chinese students travelled to America through the Boxer Indemnity scheme. With an annual budget of $1.5m., the average cost per student was nearly $25,000, a figure that drew much criticism. Another criticism of Tsinghua Xue Tang, whose pupils entered the school under the age of 15 and would not return to China as graduates for up to a decade or even more, was that students had insufficient experience of China, culturally or educationally, and there was no guarantee that the subject they had set out to learn was going to be needed when they returned many years later.

In 1911, students started to be sent to France. In contrast to the American system and not as methodical, it represented more closely the revolutionary and even socialist tenor of the time. As Levine claims, 'The ideals enunciated in the *New Culture Movement* were nowhere better actualized than in the movement to work and study in France'.[114] Initiated by Cai Yuanpei (1868–1940), the Republic of China's first Minister of Education, prospective students bound for France were assisted not financially, but by an educational association, and some attended preparatory schools in Sichuan, Shanghai and Beijing.[115] However, with the advent of the First World War engaging much of France's workforce, Chinese student workers provided an expedient solution, undermining the programme's educational purpose. By 1919 many of the students sent to France went not into universities but into factories. The following year, according to the *China Students' Monthly*, there were 6,000 Chinese students in France (compared with less than 3,000 in America), of which 1,700 were work–study Chinese students.[116] Unlike their Tsinghua Xue Tang counterparts or the wealthy privately funded students predominantly from the affluent eastern provinces, these student labourers were mainly from China's poorer provinces, such as Hunan and Sichuan.[117] By 1921, after the end of the First World War, there were nearly 2,000 Chinese students in France, mostly unemployed and impoverished. A dispute arose between the French and Chinese governments over a plan to repatriate them and Cai Yuanpei had to travel to France to resolve the matter. By 1925 virtually all the Chinese students had left.

The programme was predicated on *qing gong jian xue* (hard work and frugal living to support study) and owing to some renowned left-wing alumni, including Deng Xiaoping (1904–97), Zhou Enlai (1898–1976), Zhao Shiyan (1901–27), Nie Rongzhen (1899–1992) and Li Weihan (1896–1984),[118] has been lauded above other overseas study programmes in Communist historiography and received wider attention in western scholarship. Levine's claims that it was 'France, rather than Great Britain, Germany, or the United States, which was perceived as the best place for sojourning Chinese'[119] overlooks, for example, the far greater number of Chinese students educated in Japan. Caution is therefore needed when assessing the relative impact and importance of the French programme, since the subject is loaded with political and historical subjectivity, in a way that mirrors the manner in which the American programme has more recently experienced greater recognition since China began warming to the west. Both the Tsinghua and French programmes were significant in their own way, but neither ever matched Japan in terms of student numbers.

A persistent criticism of China's overseas education programme was that students acquired inappropriate skills. The country desperately needed specialists in agriculture, mining, transportation, not a surplus of lawyers, linguists or political philosophers.[120] In response, the Boxer Indemnity stipulated that 80 per cent of students had to study practical subjects, a policy that the Republican government inherited and was pursued throughout the Nationalist government's tenure. Self-funded students, for example, received no assistance unless they were studying practical subjects.[121] The shift in emphasis from theoretical to practical subjects was ultimately successful, at least in purely statistically terms. According to Shu, by 1916, 83 per cent of China's overseas students were studying applied sciences and practical subjects.[122]

These figures mask another problem whereby graduates failed to pursue a career in their specialist field. Returning students tended to congregate in social and professional circles, often in China's emerging universities where they sought security in academic positions. Shu claims that of 58 engineering graduates, only 29 became engineers; of 25 mining graduates just 2 went into mining; of 10 agricultural graduates just 1 pursued a career in agriculture; and despite 101 people working in banks, hongs and companies, only 16 had studied business.[123] A missionary educator from the University of Nanking, J.H. Reisner, is quoted by Wang as saying in 1926: 'I don't know of a single graduate of an American college of agriculture who has returned to a strictly rural community and made himself an important factor in the life of that community'.[124] Wang makes a further point that had parallels in architecture:

> The proportion of unemployed and of those employed by foreigners was higher among engineers than among any other group ... engineers had to depend on industrial and construction activities that did not generally flourish in China during the 1920s. As a consequence a number of them accepted foreign employment and some even became unemployed.[125]

Further criticisms can be levelled at the educationally and geographically disproportionate intake of students. Although there were nine times as many students in state schools in China (34,880) as in missionary schools (3,901) from 1922 to 1925, over 89 per cent of privately funded Chinese students in America were from missionary schools. The majority of overseas students were from the more modernised eastern provinces. Jiangsu Province around Shanghai comprised 18.6 per cent of all Chinese students sent to Europe and America (221 students) in the same period.[126]

For China, the period between the end of Yung Wing's missions in 1881 and the establishment of foreign educational programmes was one characterised by political turmoil and cultural fracture. The transition from dynastic rule to a democratic Republic in 1912 presented a major challenge in maintaining China's structural integrity. China was increasingly framed as one element in a new world order rather than the traditional idea of being the centre of the world surrounded by disorder. Education was critical to safeguarding its integrity physically and conceptually throughout the period of political change that began in the nineteenth century with the Self-Strengthening Movement, accelerated towards the end of the century through the efforts of reformers such as Yan Fu, Kang Youwei and Liang Qichao, and culminated in Cai Yuanpei's New Culture Movement. Such an evolution cannot escape the fundamental irony that a programme of nation-building should, as a survey conducted by Southeastern University in Nanjing and Beijing Normal University in 1925 revealed, produce a generation of graduates, 90 per cent of whom were foreign educated.[127]

National salvation: the new culture movement and the May Fourth Movement

In 1916, amid growing disenchantment with the new Republic, the New Culture Movement emerged from Peking University (where Cai Yuanpei had recently become Chancellor) in protest against China's continued debility. Where earlier reformers raised on Confucianism had based their ideas on that custom, the New Culture Movement viewed Confucianism as culpable for China's sorry condition and the reason for its failure to modernise. While it did not advocate outright Occidentalism, there was a growing conviction that salvation would come from western pedagogy.

Propelled by a heightened sense of nationalism following the widespread anger caused by Yuan Shikai's acceptance of Japan's Twenty One Demands[128] issued in 1915, the New Culture Movement sought to improve China by promoting modern scientific thought and democratic ideals. The New Culture Movement's impact peaked in the late 1910s and early 1920s when the country faced cultural decay, economic ruin, political infighting and a descent into warlordism.

Crucial to China's modernisation, the movement's opening salvo was aimed squarely at the ancient and prejudicious system of writing, or Classical Chinese (*gu wen*) and its literary formulae (*ba gu wen*), which excluded all but the educated from reaching the highest echelons of society and had come under increasing pressure to reform since the late nineteenth century. Literary and linguistic reforms accompanying the New Culture Movement were dominated by the scholar Hu Shih (1891–1962), himself a Boxer Indemnity student educated at Cornell and Columbia Universities under the American philosopher, John Dewey (1859–1952).[129] These reforms coincided with and to some extent precipitated a publishing revolution that not only mirrored what occurred in eighteenth-century Europe, but also, through the proliferation of newspapers, journals and novels, facilitated what Anderson describes as the 'birth of the imagined community [and] provided the technical means for "re-presenting" the *kind* of imagined community that is the nation'.[130]

For the Chinese language to be accessible to the uneducated masses required its simplification and transliteration into Vernacular Chinese (*bai hua*).[131] Vernacular Chinese not only reinvigorated the Chinese language, but also produced a broad-based literary revolution. It is hard to overstate the role this linguistic transformation had in facilitating modernity's penetration of China, with the introduction of modern words and meanings such as individualism, self-awareness, democracy, social justice, intellectual freedom and modernity itself. As John Fairbank put it: 'The tyranny of the classics had been broken' and in a period of revolutionary fervour and universal turmoil following the First World War, 'China's scholar-elite, still a tiny top crust of their ancient society, instinctively took on the task of understanding and evaluating this revolutionary outside world at the same time that it struggled to reevaluate China's inherited culture.'[132]

The publication of works by leading writers of the age, exemplified by Lu Xun and his *The True Story of Ah Q* and *Diary of a Madman*, both of which were written in Vernacular Chinese and appeared in a collection of his work, *Call to Arms*[133] (1923), were integral to China's nation-building project. More importantly, *Diary of a Madman* appeared in the May edition of *New Youth* in 1918 and became the literary standard for the May Fourth Movement, whose title was inspired by the single most important date associated with the New Culture Movement.

Having outraged Chinese opinion four years earlier with the Twenty One Demands, Japan was again the focus of China's indignation when its demands for possession of Germany's former territories in China were approved at Versailles. On 4 May 1919, thousands of students congregated in Beijing's Tiananmen Square to protest, spawning a movement whose roots went far deeper than the immediate events at Versailles. Paradoxically, although the May Fourth Movement was precipitated by the west's presence in China, its central premise was that China's salvation (*jiu wang* or *jiu guo*) lay in westernisation. Reacting against Chinese paternalistic tradition, the May Fourth Movement was China's first mass intellectual movement. Benefiting from youth and from an international education, the May Fourth Movement represented the flowering of a new consciousness derived from the chaos of preceding decades. Intellectuals associated with the movement believed China had arrived in the modern world, and with international experience they were obsessed by the objectivity of logical and scientific thought as the precondition of modernity. For May Fourth intellectuals, modernisation was the objective, westernisation was the method and nationalism cemented the two.

After 1919, two rival factions struggled to control the course of China's modernisation. Many believed that China's very existence was at stake and the optimistic and idealistic enlightenment (*qi meng*) ideals that succeeded the 1911 Revolution were a distraction from the pursuit of national salvation (*jiu guo*). Modernity was caught in the middle. Schwarcz describes this contest as 'the conflict between nationalism and the cultural critique – or, in Chinese terms, between the external imperatives of *jiu guo* and the internal prerequisites of *qi meng*'.[134] For many intellectuals, nationalism, rather than invigorating China's cultural and political revival, was seen as the death knell for its enlightenment.

As nationalism struggled with cultural enlightenment in the post-May Fourth era, one of the most explicit manifestations was the retreat of individualism in relation to the collective or the nation. Individualism in intellectual discourses or self-expression in artistic media were key attributes of the modernist agenda in China, as elsewhere, and were keenly embraced by Chinese scholars, writers and artists, not least because they opposed the collectivist and paternal precepts passed down from Confucius. The essayist Xiao Qian (1910–99), who grew up in Japan and later graduated from Cambridge University, explained that China had 'quite imperceptibly' experienced 'an immense transformation [wherein] the individual replaced the family, just as industry is taking the place of craftsmanship and agriculture'.[135] The contest between individualism and nationalism culminated in the latter's victory and the suppression of the former by the Nationalist government's New Life Movement launched in 1934, the architectural implications of which will be discussed later.

On 18 March 1926, protestors once again gathered in Tiananmen Square to remonstrate against the government's failure to oppose the unequal foreign treaties. The response from the once all-powerful warlord Duan Qirui (1865–1936) was to order troops to open fire, killing 47 protestors and injuring over 150. Lu Xun responded mournfully: 'where we live is not the human world'.[136] Later that year, in a desperate effort to quell further dissent and hold the organisers to account, Duan ordered the arrest of 50 leading intellectuals, including the brothers Lu Xun and Zhou Zuoren, precipitating the flight from Beijing of China's cultural establishment.

Most fled to Shanghai, which, despite its hedonistic, commercial and international spirit, eclipsed Beijing as China's cultural hub. Though Beijing's cultural and political influence was never extinguished, its decline was hastened further the following year with the establishment of the new capital in Nanjing by Chiang Kai Shek, following the Kuomintang's relatively successful military campaign to unite China. In 1927, as one important chapter in China's nation-building project was coming to a close, another was opening. For the first time since the fall of the Qing Dynasty in 1911, China was united under a single albeit fragile government that would survive for little more than two decades. During this time the nation-building project and nationalism dominated the domestic agenda in the face of increasing foreign intervention and Japan's occupation of China from 1937 to 1945.

The degree to which the nation-building project advanced or hindered modernity in China from the late nineteenth century up to the mid-twentieth century depends on political interpretation. The Nationalist Party's victories over the warlords and the Communists were seen by many as key victories, but for most artistic and intellectual pursuits, nationalism was more of a constraint than a liberating force. While pursuing western methods acquired from their educational experiences, Chinese scholars and professionals, especially architects, were invariably compelled to imbue their work with an element of 'Chineseness', though precisely how this was defined remained ambiguous.

The rigid and often superficial prescription of 'Chineseness' as a means of claiming or projecting cultural or national authenticity intensified with China's increasing politicisation following the May Fourth Movement. At its most extreme, the cost of pursuing an independent or strongly partisan vision of modernisation and nationalism was death. Three of Shanghai's most prominent literary figures, Mu Shiying (1912–40), Liu Na'ou (1900–39) and Yu Dafu (1896–1945),[137] were assassinated during this period, and before the close of the 1940s, many others fled the country. While nation-building had at first been closely associated with the concept of China as a civilisation and was palatable to most Chinese, it later became one point of fracture between the Nationalist and Communist movements and marked the division between their respective strategies for the country's future.

The etymology of modernity

Another theme that exposes the distinctiveness of China's encounter with modernity and highlights its plurality is the language of modernity, etymologically and connotatively. Almost two millennia separate the early Latin word *modus* from the early twentieth-century Chinese word *modeng* – a timespan constituting less than half of China's cultural lineage. By the time the Romans had invented the root of *modern*, Chinese civilisation had already passed middle age. Of concern here is not the definition of *modern*, over which western scholars have struggled to reach consensus, but rather with how the Chinese language accommodated the western concepts of *modern* and *modernity*, a process that has received surprisingly little analysis in either western or Chinese scholarship.

Baudelaire defined modernity as 'the ephemeral, the fugitive, the contingent, the half of art whose other half is eternal and the immutable'.[138] Architecturally, Heynen identifies 'three basic levels of meaning' depending on which historical period is taken as the point of reference: the current (from before the late sixteenth century, its opposite being the past), the new (from the seventeenth century, its opposite being the old) and the transient (from the nineteenth century, its opposite being an indeterminate entity).[139] Departing from this historical method of classification, she goes on to suggest that *modernity* is 'what gives the present the specific quality that makes it different from the past and points the way toward the future ... [it] is also described as being a break with tradition, and as typifying everything that rejects the inheritance of the past'.[140]

Continuity and fracture are constantly contested by those seeking to define modernity. Habermas's project of modernity emphasises continuity where:

> 'modernity' repeatedly articulates the consciousness of an era that refers back to the past of classical antiquity precisely in order to comprehend itself as the result of a transition from the old to the new. This is not merely true for the Renaissance, with which the 'modern age' begins for us; people also considered themselves as 'modern' in the age of Charlemagne, in the twelfth century, and in the Enlightenment.[141]

These observations, broad and inconclusive though they are, correspond to the two principal interpretations of *modern* in relation to *architecture* as perceived in the west. Buildings are 'modern' in the post-Renaissance era when they deviate from the classical and seek to improve upon the ancient; or, alternatively, buildings are modern when they seek to break from all previous precedents, as implied by the twentieth century's self-declared Modern Movement, where, as Colquhoun explains, it refers to 'all buildings of the modern period regardless of their ideological basis, or an architecture conscious of its own modernity and striving for change'.[142]

It was the latter version that appropriated and popularised Jonathan Swift's term *modernism*, which Heynen defines as 'the body of artistic and intellectual ideas and movements that deal with the process of modernisation and with the experience of modernity'.[143] For Habermas *modernism* represents a 'radicalized consciousness of modernity that detached itself from all previous historical connection and understood itself solely in abstract opposition to tradition and history as a whole',[144] an interpretation which has dominated the creative arts since the late nineteenth century. It was this version that predominated when the notion of modernity was exported from the west to, among other places, China, rather than the earlier less radical versions. In its capitalised form, *Modernism* illustrates not only the apogee of a modern consciousness, or state of *modernity*, but also the formal expression of a range of artistic genre, including architecture, that were exported and in turn were reconfigured, reconstituted and reclaimed outside the west.

Modern and China

Few examples better support Eisenstadt's notion of multiple modernities than China's linguistic engagement with the term *modern* and its multiple meanings. Historically, no word existed for *modern* in the Chinese language. By the twentieth century there were several. Words such as *xin* (new) had increasingly appeared in literature and in the popular press, but the New Culture Movement precipitated a variety of entirely new words. Chen Duxiu, editor of the journal *New Youth*, coined the phrase *jinshi* to describe *modern*. Others included *jindai* (modern time: lit. 'near generation'), *xiandai* (modern: lit. 'now generation'), *xiandai zhuyi* (modernism), *shimao* (fashionable/in vogue) and *shidai* (era/epoch),[145] which Lee suggests is derived from the Japanese *jidai*,[146] and *modeng*, a transliteration of *modern* favoured by metropolitan writers, particularly in Shanghai.

The prefixes *xiandai*, *jindai* and *modeng* were used interchangeably with the suffixes *xing* and *pai* to imply modernity and modernist respectively (e.g. *xiandai xing*, *xiandai pai*, *jindai xing*, *jindai pai*, *modeng xing* or *modeng pai*). *Xiandai hua* means *modernisation*. Modernism was constructed by applying the suffix *zhuyi* to *jindai* or *xiandai* (e.g. *jindai zhuyi* or *xiandai zhuyi*). It is interesting to note that the third prefix, *modeng*, was never used in conjunction with *zhuyi* to imply *modernism*, a fact that might be evidence of the growing hostility by the literary elite towards *modeng* and their discrimination against the term. The abundance of different meanings stemming from these three prefixes reflects subtle nuances in meaning and application depending on the user and the context, nuances that will be referred to throughout this study and which demonstrates modernity's plurality in the Chinese context.

Modeng and *xiandai* were the two words most commonly used to describe modernity in early twentieth-century China, with *jindai* a third, rarer, alternative. The three words, in addition to serving as prefixes to describe types of *modern*, illustrate the complexity and multifaceted nature of *modern* in China: *modeng* is a westward-facing transliteration created by the Chinese; *xiandai* is a Chinese translation of a Japanese word (*gendai*) for *modern*; and *jindai* is an ancient Chinese word that referred to a period close to the present (much like *modern* did in Europe up to the late sixteenth century), and was commonly used by the Japanese to describe *modern* in the context of world history.

The fate of these terms says a great deal about how the Chinese perceived modernity. It is no coincidence that the transliteration (*modeng*) from the capitalist west became associated with decadence and fell out of favour, eventually becoming a derogatory term, while the translation of the Japanese term (*xiandai*) endured and proved to be the most popular term, and the term that descended from ancient Chinese (*jindai*) fell into obscurity, though, curiously, it was revived in the late twentieth century to describe 'modern history' (*jindai lishi*), referring to the period from the mid-nineteenth to the mid-twentieth centuries, as well as its various constituents, e.g. modern writer (*jindai zuojia*) or modern architecture (*jindai jianzhu*).

Xian Dai was used in an essay by Zhou Zuoren in 1918 when, in discussing the work of Dostoevsky, he employed it in the sense of *modern*, as well as *xiandai xing* (modernity). *Xian Dai* came to be used in magazine titles such as *Xian Dai Ping Lun* (*Contemporary Review*), founded by a literary association in Beijing in 1921, and in 1932 in isolation, *Xian Dai* (*Les Contemporains*), by Shi Zhecun, which was published by *Xian Dai Shu Ju* (*The Modern Book Company*) (see Plate 1).

Modeng is said to have been conceived in Shanghai in 1928,[147] succeeding *xiandai* by at least a decade but sharing, initially, a similar meaning. Before the advent of *modeng*, there had been two ways to perceive *modern* in China. One was stylistic, aimed at ephemeral pleasures such as clothing, appearance, food, leisure and entertainment, while the other was more essential and concerned with social customs. *Modeng*'s unique social and geographical origins played a large part in determining its evolution, away from the latter meaning toward the former, unlike *xiandai*, which always remained true to the latter and, due in part to the fate of *modeng*, willingly surrendered any association to the former. When the two terms diverged, *xiandai* remained the pre-eminent term to describe *modern*. Conversely, *modeng*, which implied more than others a break with the past, came to refer to the faddish, assuming a trendy, almost decadent connotation, owing in part to its place of origin, which in turn contributed to its rebuttal by left-wing writers.

Modeng's adoption and espousal was rapid. In the June 1928 edition of *Woman Today*, one of the many Shanghai-based lifestyle magazines of the 1920s and 1930s, the editor explained that the magazine calls itself ' "*modeng, modern*", but one cannot judge from the appearance that it is *modeng* or not. It is sometimes "*shimao*" (fashionable), sometimes "*fugu*" (retro) ... We as editors wish for the magazine's thoughts and words to be "*modeng*" '.[148] By 1934, *modeng*'s widespread use attracted attention in the monthly magazine *Shen Bao Yue Kan*, the monthly magazine of the popular newspaper *Shen Bao*:[149]

> there are three meanings to the word of *modeng* ... 3. is the translation of the English word *modern* by Mr. Tian Han ... at present, those who try to explain

the word mostly refer to this last meaning ... in French it is *Moderne* and in Latin *Moderno* ... all with the meaning of *xiandai* (current generation) and *zuixin* (the newest) ... put simply, *modeng* is the newest and least out of date.[150]

As a product of Shanghai's nefarious culture, *modeng* possessed a unique specificity to this exceptional metropolitan setting and became associated with its fashionable and profligate foreign pleasures. In the Chinese *Dictionary of New Vocabulary* (1934), *modeng* is described as meaning '"*xiandai de*", "*jindai de*", commonly meaning fashionable (*shimao*)', embracing all three possibilities. *Shimao*, a reincarnation of a traditional Chinese term principally associated with fashion, was much older than *modeng* and although they both implied a sense of being fashionable, *modeng*'s almost obsessive imitation of the west is what principally separated it from *shimao*. In associating itself with the material aspects of modernity the emergence of *modeng* also relieved *xiandai* of such seemingly frivolous implications, allowing it to assume a weightier connotation.

While *modeng*'s reverence of materialism and the west was one way of viewing its meaning, there had been an attempt by left-wing writers to claim the word. Tian Han is said to have defended his choice of *modeng* in the context of his film *San Ge Mo Deng Nü Xing* (*Three Modern Women*), claiming that *modeng* meant more than the comparatively vacuous *shimao* (see Figure 3.1). *Modeng* implied a progressivism that transcended mere fashion, clothing and accessories and embraced also political thought and even revolutionary activities. He closed scornfully by declaring: 'I pity these empty headed women and treasure the word *modeng*.'[151]

Modeng, in the context of architecture (*jianzhu*), was relieved of its decadent attribution and acquired the subtle implication of breaking with the past. Its earlier espousal by Shanghai radicals made it the more popular prefix to 'architecture' than *xiandai* when implying 'modern architecture'. Qiu Tongyi, in the official publication of the 1935 architectural student exhibition at Xiang Qin University, Guangdong Province, offered this explanation: 'From the point of modern society, *modeng* jianzhu (architecture) is the progressive form of *xiandai* jianzhu (architecture)',[152] the nearest

Figure 3.1 Advertisement and still from the film *San Ge Mo Deng Nu Xing* (*Three Modern Women*) by Tian Han who deliberately chose modern's Chinese transliteration *modeng* for the title.

comparison in a western context perhaps to the distinction between *Modernism* and *modernism*.

Such architectural assertions, however, were not sufficient to detach *modeng* from its materialistic connotations. After losing the battle, left-wing writers such as Zhang Tianyi and Mao Dun turned on the word. In *Chun Lai Le* (*Spring Has Come*, 1933), Mao Dun reiterated the association, exclaiming pitifully 'those *modeng* men and women pursuing decadent pleasures',[153] anticipating the Nationalist government's anti-materialist and anti-individualist New Life Movement launched the following February. Among its many social stipulations was the call for men and women not to pursue fashion, drawing specific attention to the example of permed hair, which had been one of the ultimate expressions of *modeng*.

In the interim, one article voiced the angry opinions of one writer, Quan Ren:

> Those Yang Jin Bang scholars[154] think *xiandai* is not *modeng* enough, so abandoned *xiandai* and only use *modeng* ... these ignorant people ... calling everything strange, extraordinary and romantic *modeng* ... shops named *modeng*, magazines called *modeng*, is this really the meaning of *modeng*?[155]

Weeks later a group in Hangzhou, the capital of Zhejiang Province neighbouring Shanghai, called *Modeng Po Huai Tuan* (*The Group to Destroy Modeng*) in a bid to promote Chinese products launched scissor and chemical attacks on fashionably attired women. Such incidents reflected the political tensions in China during the 1930s, tensions that originated in issues of national salvation but reverberated in words and their meanings. By the late 1930s, *modeng*'s descent was all but complete as it became a form of insult used to deride fashionable (*shimao*) girls. In such a climate, quite unlike a decade earlier, it became vital to distinguish *modeng* from *xiandai*. When referencing 'modern beauty', the cartoonist Guo Jian Ying, who had often used *modeng* to describe the beauty of the epoch ten years earlier, wrote: '*Xiandai mei* (modern beauty) is not something simply produced by adding *modeng* decoration on the surface.'[156]

Another method of conveying modernity literally was to employ English words in the Chinese text. In late 1928, the Shanghai-based writers Chen Baichen and Zhao Minyi established a literary association called *Modeng She* and the following June launched the associated monthly journal *Modeng*, which appeared on the front cover alongside the English word *Modern*, just as the supplement to Tian Han's *Zhong Yang Ri Bao* (*Central Daily Newspaper*) had done the previous year and *Xian Dai Xue Sheng* (*Modern Student*) did from 1931 (see Plate 2). The concurrent use of Chinese and English both clarified any ambiguity over Chinese interpretations as well as reaffirmed the sense of modernity through explicit association with and reference of the foreign (in this case Latin) script. Guo Jian Ying adopted this approach in a caption for his cartoon *In the Swimming Pool*: 'Do you know the beauty of 1929? In the eyes of the MODERN boy that is baptized by the time.' The author, Liu Na'ou, when translating the work by the Japanese writer Kawasaki Choutarou, *The Woman Later On*, wrote: 'the police searched for the MODERN girl, MODERN boy'.[157] The Shanghai writer Mu Shiyin (1912–40) also used this technique in his 1931 novel, *The Shanghai Foxtrot* (*Shanghai De Hu Bu Wu*), where no equivalent Chinese word or phrase existed, such as 'chicken à la king', or where a translation would not sufficiently convey the right meaning, such as 'afternoon tea',[158] and even used it to describe a typical modern Shanghainese woman: 'What a girl who lives on excitement and speed! Jazz, machines, speed, urban culture, American, MODERN beauty... the combination of all these products'.[159]

English words appear in the celebrated example of Mao Dun's *Zi Ye* (*Midnight*), when he describes the dizzying scenes of Shanghai, China's ultimate landscape of modernity, as experienced by a newcomer:

> From the [Garden] bridge looking east, foreign warehouses are visible like huge monsters, sitting low in the dark, thousands of lights like small eyes, looking west. Suddenly startled by a neon advertisement high up on top of a villa and extraordinarily large, emitting a fiery red light and scales like green flames: LIGHT, HEAT, POWER![160]

The transliteration and adoption of foreign words by the Chinese was not confined only to western languages. Many more modern words and terms arrived from Japan in a process that paralleled linguistically China's rapidly shifting relationship with its neighbour during the late nineteenth century and provides further evidence that Japan was a primary mediator of modernity for China. Before the modern era, China's significant influence on the Japanese language was not reciprocal. It was a one-directional process in which Japan received from China, but the unequal cultural relations between the two countries prevented the reverse. Like so many other cultural norms between China and Japan, this linguistic certainty was upended after the Meiji Restoration when many western ideas were incorporated into the Japanese language and from there, for the very first time, exported to China. What makes this linguistic milestone all the more notable is that among the various ways Japanese language made its way into Chinese, the most common was *wasei-kengo*, where new or modern words such as *ke xue* (science), *ge ming* (revolution), *min zhu* (democracy), *jin hua* (evolution) and even *Gong Chan Dang* (Communist Party) were composed from the Chinese derivative *kanji*, not from the Japanese *kana*. The familiarity of the characters and the practicality of the translation made these terms and their wider meaning palatable to the Chinese. Although there was some resistance from the Chinese in adopting these constructed terms from abroad written in their characters from a formerly subservient neighbour, many such terms were eventually subsumed into Chinese and consequently provided the vocabulary that allowed China to articulate its encounter with modernity. Modernity had not only found new means of expression; it was the very basis of the process by which this expression became manifest.

Multiple moderns

More remarkable than the wide range of Chinese terms and methods for describing *modern* and its associated concepts, a range which exceeded that in the west, was the speed and extent of their proliferation. In the space of three decades, there entered into the Chinese language an assortment of terms relating to *modern* that altered the potentialities of Chinese vocabulary.

China's linguistic encounter with the notion of *modern* not only provides compelling evidence in support of the multiple modernities paradigm but it also pre-dates by nearly a century Jacques's observation that 'rather than there being a single way of being modern, we are witnessing the birth of a world of multiple and competing modernities'.[161] By tracing the etymological root of *modern*, it is clear that while it is originally western, or more specifically, European, its multiple translations into Chinese gave it different inflections, which in turn changed through subsequent translation and retranslation. The process mirrored that highlighted by Vitruvius (6.7.5) when alluding to the technical difficulty faced by early Roman writers in developing Latin equivalents for Greek architectural terms.

One of the few definitive conclusions that can be drawn from China's unique linguistic experience of confronting modernity is the confusion and contradiction felt by those attempting to express or describe it. As Zhang Tianyi playfully wrote in Shanghai in 1937, 'there is only contradiction and dilemma in *xiandai* (modern). I say "*modern*" should be translated into "*maodun*"',[162] which can be translated as 'dilemma' or 'contradiction'.

Modernity and time

The final theme through which China's encounter with modernity will be examined is that of time – as a concept, as a depiction of progress, and its linguistic importance. Without the adoption of western temporality, modernity in China would have been meaningless. China's customary methods of time-keeping were more advanced, enduring and more societally pervasive than anywhere else outside the west, yet China's encounter with modernity required a fundamental reconceptualisation of time along western lines. The relationship between modernity and time in China occupies two distinct domains: the first and temporally broader territory concerns the relationship between time and China's spatial, philosophical and historical outlooks; the second concerns the encounter between western and Chinese interpretations of time.

The relationship between time and space

China's traditional view of time was so elementary and all-encompassing that the official adoption of the Gregorian calendar in 1912 precipitated structural changes that were so socially and culturally profound that many argue they are, as Wakeman suggests, 'an essential part of the Chinese identity crisis that still persists'.[163] Before this cataclysmic temporal incident, China's understanding of the world spiritually, culturally and historically had always been entwined with a cyclical temporal awareness; an awareness forged by an amalgam of religious beliefs, philosophical doctrines and time-honoured customs – notably Confucianism, Taoism and Buddhism. Common to each of these is a conviction in cyclical time.[164]

Cyclicality is essential also to China's spatial understanding of the world, which has always been defined concentrically, with China at the centre surrounded by peripheral states – a spatial conceptualisation with fundamental resonance in Chinese planning and building. In contrast to western notions of lineal progress[165] that relied on constant expansion, China's relations with peripheral states were defined more by the Confucian ideals of morality and sound governance, more akin to a concentric model of expansion and contraction around a constant core. The lineal and the cyclical can thus be seen as the key distinctions between western and Chinese spatio-temporal perspectives.

56 *China and the meaning of modernity*

China's concentric view veils a self-confidence that is manifest not only culturally and philosophically, but also linguistically. *Tian Xia*, literally 'all that is under heaven', describes China's worldview cosmologically. China's self-ascribed title, *Zhong Guo* (Middle Kingdom), leaves little doubt as to its position under heaven. China's primacy was guaranteed not only by its centrality within a concentrically arranged scheme but also by its physical proximity to heaven that this centrality guaranteed.

China first encountered western temporality in the seventeenth century through the Jesuit missionaries. Matteo Ricci, the first foreign missionary to reside in Beijing, claimed that his 'admission to the Ming Court' was because he presented 'a clock and repeating watch to the emperor'.[166] The Jesuits' temporal influence in China was felt in two particular areas. The first and most critical was in improving the accuracy of the infamously inaccurate annual calendar – fundamental to organising social and political life in China. Ricci's intervention was so important that the survival of the Jesuit mission in China would eventually depend on it.[167] The second, less important impact was the Jesuits' role in China's adoption and subsequent manufacture of timepieces.

Western scientific methods, particularly in relation to astrology and mathematics, challenged conventional Chinese perceptions of time and implanted the western concept of lineal temporality that permitted a chronological perspective. The elementary link between these developments and the subsequent cultivation of modern consciousness in China cause many scholars to conclude that time and lineal means of marking time to be the basis for China's adoption of modernity (e.g. Lee: 'time – and the system of calendrical dating – is the foundation on which modernity is constructed';[168] Shih: 'time was the crucial category in the radical rethinking of Chinese culture and literature during the May Fourth era'[169]).

Kang Youwei was among the first Chinese intellectuals to posit a Chinese version of linear time. Derived from, of all places, Confucius's *Chun Qiu* (*Spring and Autumn*), his 'unilinear, irreversible process of evolutionary development'[170] was framed as *Three Ages* (*san shih*): 'disorder', 'increasing peace', and 'universal peace'. Sharing Kang's 'almost mystical faith in progress'[171] was Yan Fu, who possessed a different but nevertheless perspicacious perspective conveyed in his famous statement in 1895:

> The greatest and most irreconcilable difference between Chinese and western thinking is that the Chinese love the past and neglect the present, while the westerners strive in the present to surpass the past. The Chinese believe that to revolve from order to disorder, from ascension to decline, is the natural way of heaven and of human affairs. The westerners believe, as the ultimate principle of all learning and government, in infinite, daily progress, in advance that will not sink into decline, in order that will not revert to disorder.[172]

Yan and Kang, as well as Liang Qichao, more than being representatives of a unique generation of Chinese reformers raised on Confucian teachings and exposed to western scientific texts, were key protagonists in championing the notion of progress in China. Yan translated Darwin's *Origin of Species* and published *Tian Yan Lun* (*The Theory of Evolution*) in 1898, which introduced Darwinian Theory to the Chinese for the first time. He also translated the works of Thomas Huxley's *Evolution and Ethics*, Herbert Spencer's *Study of Sociology*, John Stuart Mill's *On*

Liberty and Adam Smith's *Wealth of Nations*, works that were not only vital in laying the ground for a complete reconceptualisation of China's philosophical, political, economic and historical understanding, but also essential prerequisites to realising the New Culture Movement and May Fourth Movement that depended on and advocated the notion of progress.

Without lineal time, the May Fourth Movement would have had no rational ideological basis. It was Yan who managed to convince a generation of Chinese reformers that 'the westerners' secret was belief in progress. Chinese believed in cycles and got nowhere. Westerners believed in progress and progressed.'[173] As Shih explains:

> the quintessential embodiment of the May Fourth zeitgeist was the desire to leap into the time of the modern.... But for the magical leap to be possible, modern time had to be a concrete and measurable entity with a universal standard that could be accessed with due effort. This measurable time was the Darwinian time of linear development, the Hegelian time of World History and modern western calendrical time that allowed the emergence of a global consciousness.[174]

Darwin had been an important figure in China's Reform Movement in the late nineteenth century and earned a reputation among Chinese for being a pro-reformist. According to Pusey, Liang Qichao 'more than any other individual, called over and over again on the powerful authority of Charles Darwin',[175] and even chose to invoke the spirit of survival of the fittest in the anti-Manchu question before the end of the Qing Dynasty. Pusey claims that Liang's

> attack on the monarchy was often Darwinian [and] in the long run, the most important of all the specific cultural revolutions that he led himself – certainly the one in which he most relied on the help of Darwin – was in the study and writing of history [which] laid the absolutely necessary groundwork for Chinese Marxism and the Thought of Mao Tse-tung.[176]

Time manifested

The efforts of reformers such as Yan, Kang and Liang to instil in China a new understanding of temporality and progress both caused and witnessed China's rapidly changing sociopolitical environment from the late nineteenth century. Written and spoken language as well as products such as calendars, clocks and other devices whose function and symbolism went beyond merely marking time, guaranteed temporality's increasing articulation through popular cultural devices.

Western temporality became manifest in artefacts for popular consumption, none more so than the calendar poster, published in the leading Chinese language newspaper *Shen Bao*, where the Gregorian calendar appeared alongside the Chinese calendar and proved so popular that by the early 1890s they were illustrated. By the 1920s, the calendar poster and other forms of posters were commercial devices par excellence bearing illustrations of modern merchandise accompanied invariably by architectural representations and prurient depictions of scantily clad or seductively posed modern Chinese women whose very appearance in advertising can be seen as part of modernity's manifestation conforming to Harootunian's 'exteriorizing' of women (see Plate 3).[177]

58 *China and the meaning of modernity*

Figure 3.2
Advertisement for Aspirin, employing temporal references and imagery, including architecture in the skyline backdrop, to emphasise modernity.

Figure 3.3
Speed defined the spirit of the age, from architecture to dry cleaning, as this 1935 advertisement from Shanghai attests.

Clocks and time were often employed by Chinese writers as popular depictions or symbolic evocations of western modernity, especially in the urban milieu. The speed of the city, the passing of time, the measurement of days, weeks, months or years, were common attributes of the modern literary style, particularly in Shanghai (see Figure 3.2, Figure 3.3 and Figure 3.4 and Plate 4). Time also provided a means of measuring the urgency with which modernity could be realised: the avant-garde tended to emphasise accelerated time, while the conservatives emphasised restraint.

An obsession with temporal linearity and fracture were literary devices employed by Chinese writers, such as Mu Shiying, Mao Dun, Shi Zhecun and Liu Na'ou who frequently referred to the inalterability and rapidity of time's lineal march in deliberately urban surroundings that relied on architectural settings. Shi Zhecun writes in *Zai Ba Li Da Xi Yuan* (*In the Paris Theatre*): 'What is the time? 11.40. My watch is ten minutes fast. It is only 11.30, early. I should invite her for a night snack.'[178] In *Shi Zi Zuo Liu Xing* (*Shooting Star of Leo*) he writes: 'she heard the clock downstairs strike 10 times, 11 times, but not 12 times'.[179] In *Mo Dao* (*The Devil's Way*), the character's hurried journey to the cinema calls on various temporal cues: 'something nearby should be Odeon ... it is still early, 8.20 ... what happened? The clock has stopped? Where is the watch?... 8.25 ... Is this already W-Café?'[180] And the two characters in Liu Na'ou's *Liang Ge Shi Jian De Bu Gan Zheng Zhe*

Figure 3.4 Cartoon by Sapajou from Shanghai in 1924 emphasising temporal progress depicted in various every day scenes.

60 *China and the meaning of modernity*

(*Two Who Do Not Feel The Time*), dash 'from the racecourse to the coffee shop from the coffee shop to the busy street . . . Encouraging the tired body with the strong black coffee'.[181]

The terminology of time

China's espousal of temporal linearity had a profound impact on the Chinese language. Just as China's encounter with modernity demanded the fabrication of new words, so too did the concept of lineal time. China's temporal transformation appears in words such as *jindai, xiandai* and *dangdai*, (near, now and current generation) and through characters such as *xin*, 'new', which, as a prefix, became a critical linguistic device to imply modernity in various fields (e.g. *xin xue* (new knowledge), *xin zheng* (new politics), *xin min* (new people), *wei xin yun dong* (Westernisation Movement), *xin wen hua* (new culture), *xin wen xue* (new literature)). Names and titles of periodicals, books and political writings, particularly during the May Fourth era, clearly indicated the altered perspective: *Xin Qin Nian* (New Youth), *Xin Min* (New People), *Xin Chao* (New Tide), *Xin She Hui* (New Society), *Xin Sheng Huo* (New Life), *Xin Wen Yi* (New Literature and Art) and *Xin Shi Dai* (New Epoch).

While *xin* was used to evoke modernity, the increasingly acute awareness of time among Chinese intellectuals was expressed by the characters *shidai* (time or epoch). *Shidai* is said to have originated in Japan and made its way to China along with various other terms associated with the modern that, since the nineteenth century, the Chinese vocabulary had struggled to articulate. As precursors to China's multiple expressions of modernity, *shidai* and *xin* were exemplars of the 'breathlessly rapid changes and incessant innovation'[182] that epitomised the post-Qing era (see Plate 4).

Encapsulating China's metropolitan May Fourth mindset with its obsession on temporal linearity and newness is Chen Duxiu's essay *The Year 1916*:

> The epoch that all of you are born into, what kind of epoch is it? It is the beginning of the sixteenth year of the twentieth century. Changes of the world are evolutionary, every month is different and every year is different, the grand human civilization is evolving faster and faster . . . Twentieth century civilization has only just started and cannot yet be judged, but people who are born into the time must lift your head and consider yourself a man of the twentieth century and create a new civilization of the twentieth century . . . To create the twentieth century's new civilization (we) must disregard the inheritance of previous civilizations as an achievement. . . . In this time of dispensing with the old and planning the new . . . we shall renew our effort, to achieve new personality, new country, new society, new family, new nation.[183]

Chen's futurist rhetoric reinforces the complexity and interconnectedness of modernity, westernisation, colonialism, nationalism and temporality. The essential relationship between temporality and nationalism that dominates Anderson's *Imagined Communities* is unambiguous in the Chinese context and delivered in unequivocally Darwinian tones. Earlier alarmist writings such as those by Liang Qichao had underlined the reality of China's struggle for survival: 'Day by day, month by month, they will slowly be eaten away until there are no more of them left, and their race no longer lives on the earth.'[184] The adoption of lineal temporality dominated Chinese thought during the early Republican periods and Darwin, more than anyone else, influenced China's interpretation of progress. Liang's obsession with Darwin, according to Pusey, even implicates him for setting 'in motion the intellectual currents that would lead not only to the May Fourth Movement, but to the "Great Cultural Revolution" of Mao Tse-tung'.[185]

Such is the interconnectedness of these previous five themes and their engagement with and cultivation of modernity, the impact of the modern landscape they helped create in China from the late nineteenth century continues to dominate Chinese society today. In the next chapter these various encounters with modernity will be used to explore art as a comparative analysis to architecture in Part II.

Notes

1 This study recognises the inherent problem of the term 'the west' and acknowledges that within this homogenised label there are multiple expressions of modernity. These cannot be explored here, so references to 'the west' in this study assume the geopolitical entities of Europe, North America and Australasia.
2 Huntington's seven civilisations (western, Confucian, Japanese, Islamic, Hindu, Slavic–Orthodox, Latin American) disregard religious, cultural and geographic distinctions and include 'possibly African civilization'. Huntington, 1993, p. 25.
3 Shih, 2001, p. x.
4 Lim and Chang, 2012, p. 2.
5 Reinhold, 2001, p. xiii.
6 Shih, 2001, p. 4.
7 Binyon, 1908, p. 6.
8 Li, 1996, p. 2.
9 He Ping, 2002, p. 8.
10 Stipe, 1999, p. 31.
11 Macau, Xiamen and Taiwan were at different times exceptions to the general rule.
12 Five of China's southern ports, Canton (Guangzhou), Amoy (Xiamen), Fuzhou, Ningbo and Shanghai, were opened to foreign trade and settlement, and the island of Hong Kong was ceded to Britain.
13 Yukichi, 1981, p. 91.
14 Yukichi, 1981, Appendix, p. 53, n. 9.
15 Narsimhan, 1999, p. 170.
16 Shih, 2001, p. 28.
17 Pincus, 1996, p. 239.
18 Li, 1996, pp. 2–3.
19 Fukuzawa was referring to Korea and China.
20 Jacques, 2009, p. 306.
21 Liang, 1923 (unpaginated).
22 The speech was delivered on 12 December 1895. The translated version appears in Oxford, 1973, p. 91.
23 The supplementary treaty was signed in Beijing on 21 July 1896 (see *Manchuria: Treaties and Agreements*, 1921, p. 3).
24 Kuonin, 1938, p. 144.
25 Shih, 2001, p. 4.
26 Jacques, 2009, p. 55.
27 Li, 1996, p. 1.
28 Shih, 2001, p. 21.
29 Washburn, 2001, p. 219.
30 Shih, 2001, p. 22.
31 Shih, 2001, pp. 28–9.
32 Translation of Xia Mianzun's words in Shih, 2001, p. 22.

33 Shih, 2001, p. 18.
34 Shih, 2001, p. 249.
35 Hong Wen College was established by the Imperial Court specifically to prepare students for Japanese study.
36 Reinhold, 2001, p. 45.
37 In 1905, of the 1,300 Chinese students in Japan, 1,100 were studying one of these three subjects (Shu, 1927, p. 25).
38 Up to 90 per cent of China's senior military figures throughout the first decades of the twentieth century were Japanese-trained (Shu, 1927, p. 64).
39 Shu, 1927, p. 23.
40 Wang, 1966, p. 59.
41 Educational links were sustained in other ways too. Shu (1927, p. 65) explains that an agreement was reached in 1909 between the Chinese government and five Japanese universities to each accept up to 165 Chinese students a year, funded by their native province. By 1923, of the 73 universities and colleges in Japan, 50 accepted Chinese students, whose numbers exceeded 11,750, with an estimated 10,071 students affiliated elsewhere.
42 11 June to 21 September 1898.
43 Guangxu was placed under house arrest in the Forbidden City until his death in 1908.
44 In Vancouver, Canada, in 1899.
45 The *Baohuang Hui* had milder objectives than the more radical and republican, *Tongmeng Hui*, the forerunner to the Kuomintang.
46 Pusey, 1983, p. 179.
47 The Second Revolution was aimed against the first Provisional President of the Republic of China and, briefly, self-declared Emperor, Yuan Shikai.
48 In 1927 Li was captured by the Kuomintang and executed.
49 Reinhold, 2001, p. 55.
50 Sun was educated in Hawaii and Hong Kong, and, like Kang and Liang, he travelled the world to raise support for political reform in China. Also like Kang and Liang, Sun relied on the sanctuary that Japan provided, living there intermittently for over a decade.
51 Shih, 2001, p. 56.
52 Tian penned the words of the Chinese National Anthem, *March of the Volunteers*, the original version of which first appeared in one of his films before eventually being adopted as the national anthem for the People's Republic of China after 1949.
53 *Interview with Shi Zhecun*, 22–24 October 1990, in Shih, 2001, p. 16.
54 Shih, 2001, p. 56. Other references to *modanpai* have not been found, leaving the author to assume, perhaps incorrectly, that this is a misspelling of *modengpai*.
55 Lee, 1999, p. 134.
56 Russell, 1922, pp. 73–4.
57 Bayly, 1989, in Daruvala, 2000, p. 14.
58 Daruvala, 2000, p. 14.
59 Shih, 2001, p. 32.
60 Later, a special district of Jehol and part of Mongolia were added, the whole becoming the 'Northeastern Federation' or Manchukuo ('Manchu Land').
61 The first five ports were Shanghai, Ningbo, Xiamen, Fuzhou and Guangzhou.
62 Following the Boxer Rebellion in 1900, during which the Legation Quarter became a focus of violent anti-foreign demonstrations, the foreign powers built a wall around the settlement, barring access to the Chinese.
63 Isaacs, 1985, pp. 5–6.
64 Breckenridge and van der Veer, 1993, p. 5.
65 Fairbank and Twitchett, 1983, p. 23.
66 E.g. Shanghai during the Small Swords, Taiping Rebellion and the Boxer Rebellion, and Tianjin during the Boxer Rebellion.
67 Lee, 1999, p. 309.
68 Shih, 2001, p. 31.
69 Shih, 2001, p. 34.
70 Shih, 2001, p. 32.

71 Hsia, 1929, p. 138.
72 Lee, 1999, p. 129.
73 Shih, 2001, p. 373.
74 E.g. anti-American 1905, anti-British 1920 and 1925, and anti-Japanese 1908, 1915, 1920, 1925, 1929 and 1931, but for a detailed account of Chinese boycotts against foreign powers see Remer, 1933. An Anti-Japanese Association was established by the Chinese in 1928, which called upon Chinese workers to take industrial action and Chinese consumers to boycott Japanese products, as they had done following the May Fourth protests in 1919.
75 Ransome, 1927, p. 123.
76 Chow, 1995, pp. 61–2.
77 Shih, 2001, p. 345.
78 Lee, 1999, p. 310.
79 Lee, 1999, p. 312.
80 Shih, 2001, p. 8.
81 Said, 1993, p. 6.
82 Laurence, 2003, p. 7.
83 Laurence, 2003, p. 10.
84 Said, 1993, p. 8.
85 Doyle, 1986, p. 45, in Said, 1993, p. 8.
86 Said, 1993, p. 350.
87 Anderson, 1983, p. 12.
88 Sun Lung-kee, 1986/87, p. 44.
89 E.g. Zeng Guofan (1811–72), Zhang Zhidong (1837–1909), Zuo Zongtang (1812–85) and Li Hongzhang (1823–1901).
90 *Zhong Xue Wei Ti, Xi Xue Wei Yong.*
91 Liang Qichao, 1923 (unpaginated).
92 Liang Qichao, 1899 (unpaginated).
93 Gu Hongming was born on a British-owned rubber plantation in Malaysia in 1857. His father, the plantation manager, was Chinese and spoke Mandarin, Malay and English. His Portuguese mother spoke English and Portuguese. At the age of 10, the multilingual Gu was sent to England for schooling, where he studied Classics and went on to attend Edinburgh University. In 1877 he went to Leipzig to read Philosophy and Literature before taking on Classical Chinese. In his lifetime, he spoke nine languages fluently and gained 13 PhDs. Gu translated many Chinese classics into English and German, and was instrumental in advancing the west's knowledge of and appreciation for Chinese civilisation.
94 Gu, 1915.
95 Gongyang Gao, *Gong Yang Zhuan*, (date unknown; attributed to Warring State period, 475–221BC).
96 *Hua* is an abbreviation of *hua xia*, owing to its origins in the Xia Dynasty.
97 Huntington, 1993, p. 25.
98 Ginsberg, p. 4, in Yueng and Lo, 1976.
99 Lee Y.L., in Yueng and Lo, 1976, pp. 87–9.
100 Fairbank and Twitchett, 1983, p. 23.
101 Livelihood is often interpreted as *socialism*, emphasised by public welfare as distinct from forms of Marxism.
102 Government of the people, by the people and for the people.
103 Sun Yat Sen, 1953, pp. 76–7.
104 Wang, 1966, p. 50.
105 Wang, 1966, p. 52.
106 Thomson, 1875, p. 407.
107 In 1877 a group of ministers and high officials, including Li Hongzhang, who were associated with these semi-governmental institutions arranged for seven students to travel to Germany and twelve to travel to England to study a range of practical, mainly military, subjects. The programme was stopped in 1882, a year in which a further ten students had been sent to England and France. It did not resume until 1891.

108 Yan Fu began his career as a trainee in the new naval academy attached to Fuzhou's shipyard from where he was sent in 1877 to England to continue his naval training, first in Portsmouth then at the naval academy in Greenwich, London. Yan's chief interest was political thought, which he exercised through his translations of modern western scientific texts. Yan is responsible for introducing the Chinese to some of the most important western social and political theory, particularly social Darwinism.

109 Yung Wing's unique experiences and knowledge of the west served him throughout his illustrious career working for the Qing government, where his role was pivotal in the advancement of China's pursuit of an overseas education programme.

110 In 1900, the Boxers, a group of discontented Chinese railing at China's increasing subjugation at the hands of foreign nations, successfully, albeit temporarily, laid siege to the Foreign Legation in Beijing. Consequently, the foreign powers (Japanese, Russians, British, American, French, German, Italian and Austrian) assembled an army of 49,000 troops in the northern port of Tianjing, 20,000 of whom went on to march on Beijing on 14 August and liberate the besieged foreigners within days.

111 The idea to send Chinese students to America had been mooted by the Ministry of Foreign Affairs to the emperor Guangxu in June 1908, shortly before his death in November. With the change of emperor from Guangxu to Puyi, China's last emperor, the Ministry of Foreign Affairs broached the subject again in May 1909; their appeals coincided with America's plan to establish formal educational links with China.

112 On 26 May 1924 the Senate passed a resolution remitting all further payments.

113 The predecessor of China's celebrated university, Tsinghua.

114 Levine, 1993, pp. 21 and 28. The precursor to the Work–Study programme was the Frugal Study Society (*Jianxuehui*), established in 1912 by Li Shizeng (1881–1973), entrepreneur, anarchist and privileged son of a Qing high-official, Li Hongzao. Abstemiousness and diligence were encouraged as endorsing the new values defining the modern age: moral, intellectual and logical enlightenment. Engaging in paid work to fund educational development in France was to provide the means to achieve this. A similar programme was intended for study in England, but was never realised.

115 The Beijing school was established by the anti-royalist and nationalist, Wang Jingwei (1883–1944), who controversially became head of state during the period of Japanese occupation throughout the Second World War.

116 Wang, 1966, p. 110.

117 These provinces provided more labourers than any other province.

118 Levine, 1993, pp. 21 and 28. Levine makes the case that China's Communist groups in Europe contained many of the leading figures of both the earliest and the subsequent incarnations of the Chinese Communist Party. For a full list of names, see Levine, 1993, p. 4.

119 Levine, 1993, p. 27.

120 Shu, 1927, p. 260, claims that 61 per cent of all returned overseas students were engaged in political occupations.

121 Other efforts were more direct, such as the Department of Transport's programme to send over 600 individuals (mostly railway specialists) to Europe from 1909 to 1925. By country this was divided accordingly: America: 235; Britain: 180; Japan: 119; Belgium: 52; Austria: 41; Germany: 37; France: 23; USSR: 6; and Switzerland 3. Shu, 1927, p. 107.

122 Shu, 1927, p. 258.

123 Shu, 1927, p. 256.

124 Wang, 1966, p. 170.

125 Wang, 1966, pp. 170–71.

126 Shu, 1927, p. 230.

127 Shu, 1927, p. 212.

128 The Twenty One Demands were a series of secret ultimatums made by Japan that sought to secure its regional dominance over China. The demands included China ceding control of the former German territory of Shandong; extensive rights for Japan in Manchuria, including the construction of railways, leasing of ports, and the right of Japanese citizens to erect buildings and carry out industrial and commercial activities, and an obligation on the Chinese government to engage Japanese advisers.

129 Hu used the literary journal edited by Chen Duxiu, *New Youth*, to promote his revolutionary views.
130 Anderson, 1983, p. 30.
131 An attempt to make the language more accessible was first made nearly 2,000 years earlier, when the Buddhist monks Lin Ji and De Shan used the vernacular language to record their masters' teachings (Pu Ji, *Wu Deng Hui Yuan*, Vol. 7, 1252). Their efforts initially flourished but were quickly discredited by a conservative movement which reinstated Classical Chinese. Initial attempts to transliterate Chinese had been made by Indian scholars, whose efforts preceded those by European scholars from the seventeenth century to Romanise different Chinese dialects phonetically so that they could evangelise without having to learn the language.
132 Fairbank and Goldman, 2006, pp. 266–7.
133 Na Han.
134 Schwarcz, 1986, p. 1.
135 Xiao, 1944, p. 61.
136 Lu Xun, 1956, p. 251.
137 Liu Na'ou grew up in Japan and Yu Dafu was educated there and killed while in exile in Sumatra in 1945.
138 Baudelaire, 1964, p. 13.
139 Heynen, 1999, p. 8.
140 Heynen, 1999, p. 8.
141 Habermas, 1996, p. 39. Although this attempt to reconcile historical differences permits the existence of modernity as far back as the twelfth century, the first written record of *modernity* was by the author George Hakewill in 1635. 'Yea but I vilifie the present times, you say, whiles I expect a more flourishing state to succeed; bee it so, yet this is not to vilifie modernitie, as you pretend' in Hakewill, 1635, p. 192.
142 Colquhoun, 2002, p. 9.
143 Heynen, 1999, p. 3.
144 Habermas, 1996, p. 39.
145 Although *Shidai* means 'the times', it was invariably employed to imply modern times.
146 Lee, 1999, p. 44, and repeated in Lee, 2000, p. 32.
147 It is commonly accepted that the first person to use *modeng* was Tian Han. Though it has never been proven unequivocally, this attribution is likely to have stemmed from the fact that in February 1928, when Tian was Chief Editor of the *Zhong Yang Ri Bao* (*Central Daily Newspaper*), the paper published a supplement titled *Mo Deng*, where the English word *modern* appeared next to its Chinese transliteration. Four years later, Tian wrote the script of the famous Chinese film *San Ge Mo Deng Nu Xing* (*Three Modern Women*), by which time *modeng* was widely used, especially in Shanghai.
148 'The Editor', *Jin Dai Nu Xin* (*The Modern Lady*), Vol. 1, Shanghai, June 1928, Preface.
149 *Shen Bao* was established in 1872 in Shanghai by two British entrepreneurs, Frederick and Ernest Major.
150 'Xin Ci Yuan' ('New Vocabulary'), *Shen Bao Yue Kan*, Vol. 3, No. 3, Shanghai, 1934.
151 Tian, 1984, p. 464.
152 Qiu Tongyi, *Guang Dong Sheng Li Xiang Qin Da Xue Gong Xue Yuan Jian Zhu Tu An She Ji Zhan Lan Hui Te Kan* (Special Publication for the Architectural Design Exhibition of the Guangdong Provincial Xiang Qin University Engineering Department), Xiang Qin University, Guangdong, 1935, p. 4.
153 Mao Dun, 1933, p. 24.
154 The Yang Jin Bang was one of several creeks that defined the boundary of Shanghai's International Settlement. Over time, it assumed a meaning greater than that of a physical appellation, describing the characteristics of life inside the settlement.
155 Quan Ren, 1933 (unpaginated).
156 Guo Jianyin, 1934 (unpaginated).
157 Kang and Xu (eds), 2001, p. 365.
158 Mu, 2004, p. 11.
159 Mu, 2004, p. 17.
160 Mao Dun, 1977, p. 1.

161 Jacques, 2009, p. 11.
162 Zhang Tianyi, 1937, p. 75.
163 Wakeman in Sachsenmaier and Riedel, 2002, p. 15.
164 E.g. Confucius's principle of dynastic growth and decline and Mencius's repeated cycles of order and chaos (*yi zhi yi luan*), Zhou Yi's alternating 'Five Virtues' or 'Five Elements' (金, 木, 水, 火, 土) metal, wood, water, fire, earth), or Buddhism's cycles of life through reincarnation.
165 Though western concepts of time evolved from similarly cyclical notions in antiquity, such as the Classical 'Eternal Return', the pre-eminent view since the Renaissance has depended on linear notions of time that gave rise to the concept of progress, which was in turn critical to the cultivation of modernity.
166 Elman, 2006, p. 70.
167 In a letter to his colleagues in Europe, sent in 1621, Ricci's former student, Terrentius, sought 'a calculation of the eclipses, especially solar, according to the new observations', which he stressed was 'supremely necessary for the correction of the calendar. And if there is any means by which we may escape expulsion from the empire it is this' (quoted in the online Catholic Encyclopaedia (www.newadvent.org).
168 Lee, 1999, p. 79.
169 Shih, 2001, p. 49.
170 Chang Hao, 1987, p. 52.
171 Pusey, 1983, p. 15.
172 Pusey, 1983, p. 51.
173 Pusey, 1983, p. 51.
174 Shih, 2001, p. 49.
175 Pusey, 1983, p. 181.
176 Pusey, 1983, p. 193.
177 Harootunian, 2000, p. 116.
178 Shi Zhecun, '*Zai Ba Li Da Xi Yuan*' ('In the Paris Theatre'), *Xiao Shuo Yue Bao* (*Literary Monthly*), Shanghai, Vol. 22, No. 8, 10 August 1931, p. 1009.
179 Shi Zhecun, '*Shi Zi Zuo Liu Xing*' ('Shooting Star of Leo'), *Shan Nü Ren Xing Pin* (*Shanghai Liang You Tu Shu Yin Shua Gong Si* (Shanghai Liang You Book Publishing Company), Shanghai, November 1933, p. 4.
180 Shi Zhecun, '*Mo Dao*' ('Devil's Way'), *Xiao Shuo Yue Bao* (*Literary Monthly*), Shanghai, Vol. 22, No. 9, 20 October 1931, p. 1139.
181 Liu Na'ou, '*Liang Ge Shi Jian De Bu Gan Zheng Zhe*' ('Two Who Do Not Feel The Time'), *Jin Dai Fu Nü*, Shanghai, No. 11, 1929, p. 7.
182 Sun Lung-kee, 1986/87, p. 44.
183 Chen Duxiu, 'Year 1916', 15 January 1916, in *Duxiu Wen Cun* (*Collection of Duxiu's Works*), *Ya Dong Tu Shu Guan*, Shanghai, Vol. 1, 1922, p. 41.
184 Liang Qichao, 1898, pp. 7–8.
185 Pusey, 1983, p. 180.

4 Chinese art and its multiple modernities

In the 1930s, a talented artist and one of China's most renowned cartoonists of the twentieth century, Feng Zikai (1898–1975), wrote an essay titled *Yi Shu De Yuan Di* (*The Garden of Art*). In this piece he used the garden as a metaphor to describe China's eight different artistic pursuits: painting, sculpture, architecture, decorative art, music, literature, dance and theatre. As China encountered modernity in the early twentieth century, its art practices were forced to negotiate, 'in the name of modernity, a series of shocks and transformations that may be unprecedented in its history'.[1] To better understand the triangular relationship between *architecture*, *modernity* and *China*, this chapter explores the impact of modernity on China's visual and literary arts by means of a comparative analysis before focusing on architecture in Part II.

Members of these artistic groups in China helped to inflict as much as to parry the shocks and transformations described by Andrews and Shen. This was most conspicuous in visual art, the scope of which ranged from fine art, through propagandist art, to commercial art, and appealed to everyone from the wealthiest tycoon commissioning a portrait to the rickshaw driver collecting cigarette cards. Among the most entertaining were the performing artists who, throughout this period, made the successful transition from stage to screen and cultivated one of the world's most prolific and productive film industries in the process. Some of the most influential artists were the writers whose work, written in Bai Hua (Vernacular Chinese), was more widely disseminated and digested than other art forms. Collectively, the analysis of these artistic outputs not merely presents an opportunity to summarise or record modernity's impact on their respective practices, but provides by way of comparison the necessary historical perspective and thematic insight for the forthcoming investigation of architecture.

Modernity and the visual artist in China

Visual art in the Chinese context, like building, has no accurate western equivalent. The encounter with modernity in the twentieth century, therefore, provides a useful parallel to the study of architecture's arrival in China during the same period. The distinctions that separate Chinese and western art forms, along with their respective encounters with modernity, cast a tangential light on one of this study's principal questions – how to examine China through western usages. Corresponding with the notion of multiple modernities, it also urges the adoption of a non-western perspective if the process by which an indigenous art practice was encountered and mediated by a foreign *other* is to be fully understood.

Chinese art, unlike in the west, comprised the assimilation of the 'three perfect things': painting, calligraphy and poetry. Increasing commercialisation combined with the abolition of the literati system in the early twentieth century undermined longstanding artistic conventions and forced artists to become more commercially minded and exposed their work to a wider audience. China's educational and social reforms augmented these changes when art was included in a nascent national curriculum along with the adoption of western teaching methods. The early twentieth century saw Chinese art practice revolutionised with the wholesale change of the artist's role, their subjects, their styles and their techniques.

Before encountering the modern, the traditional Chinese artist's work, uncontaminated by western ideas and possessing the three vital qualities, was often misinterpreted and misunderstood by foreigners. Such cultural misreadings were common and often found willing expression in China's building practices. The essential art practices of calligraphy and carving of stone seals have no equivalent in western art. It is understandable, therefore, that the writer and architect Lin Huiyin implored her American friends, the renowned Sinologists John and Wilma Fairbank, 'to be a little "brush-stroke-minded" and Chinese-minded'[2] when visiting the International Exhibition of Chinese Art at London's Royal Academy in 1936, which had been opened weeks earlier amid 'astonishing scenes of enthusiasm' that '[drew] unprecedented crowds and [broke] all records for attendance'.[3]

As Chinese art encountered modernity, the quintessentially Chinese art forms of calligraphy and seal-carving were surrendered by China's modern artists. To understand this process of attrition, it is helpful to return to Feng Zikai's garden:

> Calligraphy is in the depths of the eastern part of the garden, up on the highest hill where it enjoys the most beautiful scenery. Visitors are almost all Chinese; occasionally some Japanese. Westerners do not come at all. Although visitors are mainly Chinese, most stop at the bottom of the hill. Very few climb the hill and reach the top. That is why this is the quietest part of the garden and a lot of people do not even know it exists ... Calligraphy as an art is particular to China. ... westerners do not know such art. ... In China, it has always been said since ancient times that '*shu hua tong yuan*' (calligraphy and painting are from the same origin). Painting must take the strokes of calligraphy to reach the real spirit. That is why most Chinese painters can do calligraphy and most calligraphers paint. Painting takes examples from calligraphy but not vice versa. ... Qualitatively, calligraphy is higher than painting, but quantitively, painting is greater than calligraphy. ... Seal carving is the smallest and most delicate part of the eastern part of the garden. Although small, it is very high up. It receives very few visitors and even fewer reach the top. Masters of carving are mostly masters of calligraphy and painting (e.g. Li Shutong). Very few people appreciate it and so it is the quietest of all parts of the garden.[4]

Such weight of tradition inevitably parried modernity's impact. Unlike its western equivalent, modern Chinese art was not measured by its originality. In China, tradition was modernity's reliable companion and consequently a creative condition. As Sullivan states, 'even the works of the most daring individualists were daring only in their technique, never in expressing unfamiliar or disconcerting ideas'.[5] The same was true of traditional building techniques where approbation derived from emulation not innovation.

The westerncentric view of China's encounter with modernity in art is similar to that held in building: in the process of becoming modern an imperfect Chinese practice was enhanced and evaluated through contact with a superior (western) alterity. The unevenness of this encounter echoes Hosagrahar's proposition that Europe, by 'appropriating history and historiography' was able to 'construct itself as the prototypical "modern" subject [and] claimed the right to define its meaning and assert its forms'.[6] A more inclusive perspective reveals a more complex discourse wherein Chinese educators, artists and curators in the early twentieth century were making 'a conscious challenge to European "metropolitan" modernism and were insisting upon a non-western modernity'.[7]

The first artistic encounters between China and the west occurred in the seventeenth century when Jesuit missionaries brought western painting techniques to the Imperial Court.[8] These famously included the introduction into Chinese art of new methods and techniques such as vanishing perspective, shading and shadow, which were commonly ascribed to Giuseppe Castiglione (1688–1766), who devised 'a cunning synthesis of Chinese technique and western realism'.[9] It is tempting to conclude from his example that western techniques had a lasting impact on Chinese art, but the Jesuits' influence should not be overplayed. European painting was, after all, 'considered by scholars as an expensive exotic luxury of the emperor [whose] influence did not extend beyond the walls of the Palace'.[10] As Sullivan observes, 'if, around 1900, one had entered the studio of a Chinese artist, one would have discovered no hint of foreign influence in his painting'.[11]

However, the inclusion of Castiglione's work in the catalogue of a travelling exhibition of contemporary Chinese art at the Musée du Jeu de Paume, Paris, in the summer of 1933 (*Exposition de la Peinture Chinoise*) demonstrates that for the Chinese organisers the scope of Chinese art, from a twentieth-century standpoint, should be considered more broadly. Castiglione's inclusion represented the durability of a two-way discourse between Chinese and western art extending from the seventeenth century. The French modernist poet and writer, Paul Valéry, further enriched this artistic exchange when writing the preface to the exhibition catalogue described eastern and western art as 'the resolution of a profound dissonance rather than the result of difference, nothing less than two ways of seeing'.[12]

Valéry's observations point towards the conciliatory 'Middle Way' promoted by moderate Chinese artists and educators, such as Cai Yuanpei, who proposed that Chinese and western art were engaged in a more complex discourse than westerncentric perspectives suggested. In the preface of the catalogue accompanying the *Exposition Chinoise d'Art Ancien et Moderne* at the Palais du Rhin in Strasbourg in 1924 that he organised, Cai wrote: 'Ever since the Renaissance and particularly in our day, Chinese style has inspired European art.'[13]

China's influence on western art and, later, modernism, shares similar experiences to other sites outside the west as well as other Chinese art forms, notably literature. Often ignored, invariably underplayed and sometimes denied, these interconnections prove the complexity of certain cultural exchanges and how their interpretation has been corrupted over time. Danzker cites the example of Chinese and Japanese *Bildsprache*, or visual language, which was absorbed by 'nineteenth century Euro-American art ... and modulated for its own (local purposes)'[14] and highlights 'tantalising hints that Chinese Literati painting may have had more impact on European painting at the beginning of the twentieth century than has previously been realised'.[15]

The most striking case of the influence of Chinese art on western modernism is that of Mark Tobey, whose debt to Chinese brushwork is little known but whose work reveals unequivocal connections between China's painting traditions and American abstract art, manifested '(pre-eminently) in the work of Jackson Pollock'.[16]

Tobey's connection with China started at the University of Washington in Seattle, where, from 1927 to 1928, he was taught calligraphy by Teng Baiye (1900–90), the first Chinese artist to teach in a western university.[17] The effect that Teng's lessons in Chinese brushwork had on Tobey 'was so great because Tobey was imbibing not just a technique or a style but a way of looking at the world'.[18] Having had an 'early interest in pursuing a career in architecture', Teng enrolled at Harvard where he designed the 'Chinese Room' in the University of Pittsburgh's Cathedral of Learning,[19] but he never completed his studies. In 1931, he was appointed Head of the Department of Fine Arts at Yenching University, Beijing, although Japan's invasion of Manchuria later that year caused him to move to Shanghai where he established his own studio and taught at the Shanghai Art School and the University of Shanghai. He broke his journey from America to China with a trip to Europe, becoming a Fellow of the Royal Society of Arts (RSA, 1929–35) in the United Kingdom. Teng's experiences are worth highlighting because they are representative of many Chinese artists in the early 1930s, including numerous architects, whose cultural encounters in America and Europe were critical to their subsequent engagement in their chosen profession in China.

Teng's experiences gave him a cultural and linguistic proficiency that placed him in the privileged position of having access to the cultural life of both Chinese and foreign communities in China. In 1934, he delivered two lectures to the foreign community in Shanghai[20] in which he demonstrated his understanding of western modernism and developed the theme in his writing the previous year for the American arts journal *The Open Court*. Titled 'Art in Modern China', the article highlighted the link between Chinese art and modern art in the west:

> Not very unlike the Futurists in the west, Chinese artists paint the flight instead of the birds only. Like the Impressionists, Chinese artists paint the atmospheric effects of rain, mist, storm, and sunset in the landscape, instead of the landscape as it usually appears to most eyes.[21]

In their unique position bridging China and the west, Teng and his colleagues in other artistic disciplines embody the multiple modernities that characterised cultural engagements in early twentieth-century China. Their experience is encapsulated once again by the architect Lin Huiyin in her correspondence with Wilma and John Fairbank:

> You see I was bi-culturally brought up, and there is no denying that, the bi-cultural contact and activity is essential to me. Before you two really came into our lives I was always somewhat lost and had a sense of lack somewhere, a certain spiritual poverty or loneliness which need nourishing.[22]

Owing to their cross-cultural experiences and proficiencies, many members of this group have subsequently been overlooked or erased from China's historical record, victims of a politically motivated omission that only recently started being redressed.

Teng and Tobey were reunited in Shanghai in 1934 when Tobey visited China and resided at Teng's house.[23] The impact that Shanghai had on Tobey was, according to Clarke, crucial to his later work. Here was an Asian metropolis, both quintessentially and uniquely modern, effecting the development of this particular genre of western modern art:

> it was actually whilst he was in Shanghai that Tobey began to discover an alternative kind of subject matter, one which would allow him to express in his art the new understanding of the world in terms of process or dynamic interconnectedness that he was coming to favour. This subject matter was both drawn from his Chinese experience and at the same time without precedent in Chinese art. The new subject matter I am referring to is the dynamism of the modern city. Such subject matter appears in a number of Tobey's paintings but it is first seen in Broadway Norm of 1935, a work completed soon after his trip to China and Japan. In this abstracted image all solidity of form, all sense of mass is abolished in favour of an imagery of flux. . . . It can be argued that the imagery of urban dynamism which Tobey develops is a direct response to his experience of the bustling street life of Shanghai.[24]

In a tone evoking Shanghai's *modeng* writers of the 1930s, Tobey later published his recollections of Shanghai and the city's impact on his understanding of Chinese painting in the *Magazine of Art*. In so doing, Tobey elevated Shanghai's distinctive form of modernity above that of its American rival, New York:

> England is small, and America large. . . . England collapses, turns Chinese with English and American thoughts. Thousands of characters are twisting and turning. In every door is a shop. The rickshaws jostle the vendors, their backs hung with incredible loads. The whole scene is alive in a way Broadway isn't alive . . . the human energy spills itself into multiple forms, writhes, sweats, and strains every muscle towards the day's bowl of rice. The din is terrific. All is in motion now. A design of flames encircles the quiet Buddha. One step backward into the past and the tree in front of my studio in Seattle is all rhythm, lifting, springing upward. I have just had my first lesson in Chinese brush from my friend and artist Teng Kwei. The tree is no more a solid in the earth, breaking into lesser solids bathed in chiaroscuro.[25]

The encounter with modernity in Chinese art

This study is concerned principally with those elements of Chinese art that inform the wider examination of China's encounter with modernity and, specifically, where through comparison they inform the arrival and development of the architectural profession in China. The most conspicuous observation drawn from this summary account is the evidence of multiple modernities, through interactions with Europe and America, the pervasive influence of Japan, institutional developments, and the experiences of prominent individuals.

China's modern system of art education extends back to the mid-nineteenth century with technical and missionary schools teaching art and drawing. Its subsequent development was, as Sullivan puts it, 'slow, cautious and severely practical'.[26]

By 1902, China's dearth of art teachers hastened the establishment of the first teacher-training college in China.[27] Modelled on the Japanese system of art education, Japan also provided qualified teachers as well as the institutional and curricula framework (which in turn had been taken from western (especially French) systems). Furthermore, Japan's cultural and geographic proximity to China made it the destination of choice for ardent art students who, in Tokyo, 'could experience for themselves the pulse of European art'.[28] Thus, 'the Japanese became the first agents of western art in China'.[29] The first Chinese artists to study there were Li Shutong (1880–1942) and Zeng Yannian (1873–1936),[30] who both attended the Tokyo School of Fine Arts and graduated in 1911.

Throughout the 1910s and 1920s, many more art students followed the first wave of Chinese students graduating from Japan's art schools. The debt of many of these individuals to Japan is often underplayed, especially in subsequent Chinese historiography. Lum asserts that Ni Yide (1901–1970), the founder of the radical *Storm Society*, 'received his formation in progressive ideas about art in Japan'.[31] The organisers of the Chinese art exhibitions that toured Europe, Xu Beihong and Liu Haisu, both had experience of Japan: Xu was introduced to western-style painting when he travelled to Tokyo in 1917, and Liu visited Japan for a year from 1918 and again from 1927 to 1928. Their experiences further highlight the unique multiplicity of modernity's negotiation in and between China and Japan throughout the early twentieth century, and mirror architecture's contemporaneous experience.

Not only did figures such as Liu and Xu 'personally observe the emergence of a complex, intercultural Modernism resulting from close contacts between the Japanese and European avantgarde',[32] they were also able to make important contacts with leading figures in the Japanese art world, including Fujishima Takeji (1867–1943), Ishii Hakutei (1882–1958), Fujita Tsuguharu (1886–1968) (aka Léonard Foujita),[33] and Mitsutani Kunishirō (1874–1936).[34]

One personality who has been largely written out of subsequent Chinese accounts of art history yet represents the triangular link between China, Japan and the west, was the Sichuanese painter, Chang Yu (1901–66).[35] After his initial art training in China, he exhibited work in Japan where he was exposed to 'virtually all up-to-date modernist styles'.[36] Having lived in Paris and Berlin, he married a Frenchwoman in 1923 and, according to Pang Xunqin (1906–85), befriended Picasso.[37] Although Chang Yu's international life was plagued by personal and professional misfortune and financial hardship, he, like the writer and architect Lin Huiyin, was one of those few true Chinese cosmopolitans.[38]

The most popular overseas destination for art education was France (Paris in particular), where, according to Shen, Chinese artists could find 'the most direct and respected source of modernist styles'.[39] The first Chinese students to attend the École des Beaux-Arts left China in 1912–13,[40] but it was those who arrived after the First World War that would make the biggest impression on Chinese art in the interwar years. Eminent among this generation were Xu Beihong and Lin Fengmian, who both arrived in France in 1919.[41] In 1923, Xu travelled to Germany, returning to China in 1927. Lin studied at the École des Beaux-Arts, first in Dijon then Paris, and, like Xu, travelled to Berlin in 1923 to complete his studies. He returned to China in 1926 and became Director of Beijing Institute of Fine Arts before co-founding (together with Cai Yuanpei) the National Academy of Art.

In the 1930s, a 'short-lived love affair' occurred between Europe and China in art, with two travelling exhibitions appearing at least seventeen times in fourteen cities[42] in eight different countries throughout Europe from 1931 to 1934. The influence of these exhibitions extended beyond painting and touched many modernist figures in Europe. When one of the exhibitions reached the New Burlington Galleries in London in early 1935, the modernist writer and member of the Bloomsbury Group, Vanessa Bell, wrote to her son Julian (who was then teaching in China) exclaiming how 'All London had gone Chinese . . . no one talks of anything but Chinese art'.[43]

Consistent with China's multiple modernities, Laurence frames Bell's perceptions as part of a broader picture that represented the restoration of chinoiserie in twentieth-century Britain and 'shaped the way the British thought about Chinese culture' at the height of the modernist period.[44] Just as had occurred in the eighteenth century, increasing numbers of travellers and adventurers returning from China brought with them 'products and ideas [that] contributed to the construction of British tastes, and consequently, modernist perspectives'.[45] Further concurrence with multiple modernities occurs in Laurence's assertion that the degree to which 'Chinese art and decoration in England intertwined in the development of British modernism'[46] has not received sufficient recognition and intellectual scrutiny.

When foreign-trained Chinese artists returned to China in the 1920s and 1930s the indisputable artistic hub was Shanghai, where they formed groups forged along political, educational or professional lines. The French-trained students created the *Dong Fang Hua Hui* (*Oriental Painting Society*) and the *Tian Ma Hui* (*Heavenly Horse Society*), which assembled around the French Concession schools such as the Shanghai Art Academy and Xinhua College of Art, while the Japanese-trained students created the *Bai'e Hua Hui* (*White Goose Painting Society*) and the *Shi Dai Mei Shu She* (*Times Society of Arts*) congregating in and around the Japanese areas of Hongkou.[47] Together the French Concession and Hongkou cultivated the so-called 'French School' and 'Japanese School' and 'constituted the major centres in Shanghai where events associated with western painting took place'.[48]

Artistic societies were based also on professional outlook or personal conviction. In 1931, Japanese and French-trained students came together to form what Shen describes as 'the first modern art society in China', the *Jue Lan She* (*Storm Society*), originally the *Société des Deux Mondes* (1930). Founded in Shanghai by 'one of modernism's most effective advocates',[49] Pang Xunqin[50] and Ni Yide,[51] the Storm Society advocated a more rigorous and radical approach to modernity and was active in hosting four major exhibitions from 1932 to 1935. Sullivan describes their Manifesto as 'a cry of despair about the present state of art, and of hope for the future'. Part of it reads: 'Whither has gone our ancient creative talent, our glorious history? Our whole art world today is decrepit and feeble. . . . We hate the old forms, the old colours! We want to use the new art to express the spirit of a new era'.[52] The Storm Society's ambitions were ultimately never realised and, having represented little more than the middle way, they disbanded in 1935.

Outside Shanghai, the pre-eminent modern art movement was the Guangzhou-based Lingnan School, founded by the brothers Gao Jianfu and Gao Qifeng. Their Japanese experience had convinced them that China's artistic salvation lay in embracing a liberal internationalism, much like Japan had achieved through the *nihonga* style since the Meiji Restoration. Typifying China's intranational character, this 'southern' school was seen by its critics to have little influence beyond Guangdong Province.

Commercial art

Near the entrance of Feng Zekai's *Garden of Art* was the new branch of painting concerned with the advertising of products. Sullivan claims Li Shutong was the first to 'stress the importance of teaching advertising and commercial art in the art schools',[53] a professional plea and personal campaign he started when working as the art and literature editor at the Shanghai-based *Tai Ping Yang Bao* (*Pacific Monthly*). Unillustrated when he joined, Li set about drawing his own illustrations and subsequently pioneered the use of commercial art in newspapers and journals that reached its cultural and commercial apogee in Shanghai, the centre of China's publishing industry.

Commercial art was critical to China's commoditisation as capitalism took hold in the early twentieth century. Advertising reinforced consumption, newness, fashion and its attendant temporal cycles, all of which were integral to works of modernist writers, sociologists and philosophers that focus on the everyday machinations of urban life – Baudelaire, Joyce, Kracauer and Benjamin, or, in the context of Japan, Yasunosuke Gonda, Tosaka Jun and Wajirō Kon.

In Shanghai, the Chinese entrepreneur, pioneer of the Chinese pharmaceutical industry, Huang Chujiu (1872–1931), owner of the city's famous entertainment complex, The Great World, famously nurtured the Hangzhou artist Zheng Mantuo (1888–1961), promoting his work and helping him to establish 'a new tradition of commercial art that combined traditional Chinese painting techniques with modern design (they were sometimes framed with decorative patterns now regarded as Art Deco) and utility'.[54] Chen Zhifo (1895–1962), also from Hangzhou and a graduate of Tokyo School of Fine Arts (1919–23) where he was 'the first foreign student of design', wrote 'what is believed to be China's first graphic design textbook': *Tu'an fa ABC* (*ABC of Design Method*, 1930).[55] Andrews claims that Chen and his younger colleague Qian Juntao (1907–1998) designed many book covers in a very graphic style that 'cultivated a simplicity associated with Japanese design and later with European modernist design' that came to epitomise the modernist graphic styles typical of Shanghai throughout the 1930s.[56]

Lee often emphasises Shanghai's graphic artists' proclivity for 'Art Deco', attributing it to the influence of American lifestyle magazines such as the *New Yorker* and *Vanity Fair*. Far from taking these magazines lightly, they provided 'Chinese readers in Shanghai in the 1930s . . . a window on western literature, art design, and a sophisticated urban lifestyle'.[57] Entwined with the cinematic aura of Hollywood, these publications were exemplars of an international modernity that fuelled Shanghai's image of modern metropolitan cosmopolitanism and cultivated an artistic genre in the form of commercial art that was unparalleled in China.

Li Shutong was responsible not only for initiating commercial art in China but also the woodcut, an art form inexplicably absent from Feng's *Garden of Art*. The woodcut's popularity lay chiefly, but by no means exclusively, in its appeal to the propagandist, and to groups such as the *Pu Luo Yi Shu Yun Dong* (*Proletarian Art Movement*). For politically engaged artists who embraced the May Fourth Movement and believed that art should serve social ends, the woodcut was an ideal medium. Its keen political adoption has caused it to be relatively overlooked in subsequent accounts of twentieth-century Chinese art.

From its inception in the late 1920s, China's modern woodcut movement assumed a comfortable position between other visual arts and China's modern literary movement, owing in part to its support from Lu Xun. An avid and learned investor in both Chinese and western art and one of China's foremost art collectors, Lu Xun recognised the woodcut's potential to disseminate an ideological message in much the same way he intended his writing to do. He also collected Soviet art, which gave him an appreciation of the woodcut beyond its merely propagandist potential, often using samples from his collection to illustrate his literary journals such as *Ben Liu (Torrent)*[58] and the published works of the *Zhao Hua She (Morning Flower Society)*, which he formed in December 1928 with five literary friends to promote foreign literature and different woodcut styles, 'from Aubrey Beardsley to Russian Constructivism'.[59] Sullivan highlights a further dimension to the internationality of this particular modern art movement, citing attempts by Rou Shi (1902–1931), Lu Xun's 'devoted follower', to write to Robert Gibbings in England and Käthe Kollwitz in Berlin 'begging for examples of their work'.[60]

In 1927, Lu Xun moved to Shanghai and settled in the Japanese quarter where he remained until his death in 1936. His experience of Japan and the Japanese language made him very much at home in this cosmopolitan corner of China. He befriended the owner of the famous Japanese Uchiyama Bookstore, Uchiyama Kanzō, and between them they were integral to the success of the woodcut as a modern art form in China, organising exhibitions of foreign woodcuts in Shanghai and, later, conducting training courses.[61]

More than any other art form from this highly volatile period before the Second World War, the woodcut became bound to radical politics, attracting persecution from the Nationalist Party. The woodcut story is fascinating, complex and tragic, its brief history, according to Sullivan, making 'shocking reading'.[62] Radicalised groups of artists dissatisfied with China's liberal art institutions formed splinter groups and pursued an ideological course that positioned art as a form of salvation for China's deep social, moral and political ills. A number of students in the art academies of Shanghai and Hangzhou who were affiliated to the League of Left-wing Writers, formed the League of Left-wing Artists. Though they had left-wing affiliations, this was not the grass-roots Communist movement depicted by subsequent historiography. Staunch nationalism and patriotism were the common attributes among the woodcut movement's various groups.

Fearful of political opposition, the Kuomintang pursued a policy of cautious vigilance. Members of different woodcut groups were arrested and in January 1931, three of the founding members of Lu Xun's Morning Flower Society, though not strictly a woodcut group, were arrested for attending a clandestine meeting of Communist writers, artists, students and workers in Shanghai's International Settlement. The three, including Ruo Shi, who had earlier appealed to Gibbings and Kollwitz, along with twenty-three other young men and women, were murdered by the Kuomintang. Only China's intranationalism permitted the movement to continue elsewhere; the impetus shifting to Guangzhou,[63] away from the political spotlight around Nanjing, and other groups forming in Beijing[64] and Tianjin.[65] All art practices, including architecture, were deeply affected by politics in 1930s China, but the woodcut movement proved more than any other that the unity and stability provided by nationalism came at the expense of creative freedom.

Chinese artists had demonstrated that they were neither immune to modernity nor reluctant to experiment with it, but unlike their Japanese mentors they nevertheless revealed a resistance to it. In defending this resistance, Sullivan highlights the paradox that Chinese artists, including architects, were 'conscious all the time that while they were trying heroically to revive Chinese culture they were being widely accused of destroying it'.[66]

The persistence of Japan's central role as a model and a mirror emerges not only in its capacity as vanguard of modern art in Asia but also as an exemplar in the system and method of education. Although Chinese artists fought vigorously to counter Japan's impact at home and abroad, in Europe, the exhibitions of Chinese art confronted a public perception that Japanese art was modern compared to China, 'a nation whose cultural achievements belong to the past'.[67] China's reluctance to forego its artistic conventions, combined with the increasing pervasiveness of western techniques and theories ensured that the overall experience of modernity for Chinese artists was one neither of westernisation nor was it indebted primarily to Japan, but rather, as with so many things in China during this period, it was marked by a combination of radical experimentation, fear of separation from the past, anxiety about which course to take and a certain exhilaration in the unknown possibilities of the future.

Literary modernity in China

Returning to Feng's *Garden of Art*, the largest site on the western side is occupied by literature, below music and dance, and is equivalent to painting on the eastern side. Owing to its extent, literature was not commonly considered part of the garden and, according to Feng, those who do visit have little energy left for anything else because it is so extensive. When viewed from the early twenty-first century, this interpretation appears prophetic since China's early twentieth-century literary scene has received considerably more scholarly attention internationally than any other art practice. It is not the objective of this study to provide a summary, but in the interests of drawing insights from comparisons with architecture it is worth highlighting the commonalities and critical intersections between literary encounters with modernity and those in other artistic fields.

Once again, the problem that immediately confronts attempts to examine China's encounter with modernity in a specific art practice lies in what Shih highlights as 'the deployment of western critical terminology in the analysis of non-western writing [which] can readily unsettle Eurocentric paradigms of cultural discourse'.[68] Resonating with notions of multiple modernities, Shih adds: 'This is particularly the case when we use the term modernism, which has been invested with decades of scholarly attention and has acquired a kind of hegemonic cultural value in the west.'[69] China's encounter with literary modernity complicates westerncentric perspectives of modernity's espousal and dissemination in the same ways that occur in studies of architecture and the built environment. In both cases they prove that the interconnections between China, the west and other sites outside the west are not one-way or top-down, but multidirectional, multidimensional and multifaceted precisely because by the time western modernism arrived in China 'its point of origin was already ambiguous'.[70] China's experience rebuts assumptions of modernity's diffusion based on centre-periphery and is better understood as a complex web or constellation of relations spanning the globe.

Literature and China's multiple modern movements

China's literary scene in the early twentieth century enjoyed a central position in the country's complex encounter with modernity. It not only provided the primary means of articulating modernity both in intellectual and public domains, but also was the artistic medium most closely associated with modernity. It was through literature that notions of nation-building and national identity, time and debates about the espousal of western ideas, etymology, language and the mediating role of Japan were most clearly articulated and widely disseminated.

China's writers tended towards one of two literary positions: the uncompromisingly modern which, disillusioned with Chinese tradition, rejected cultural precedent in favour of western models, and a hybrid view, which accommodated tradition. Both sides accepted that change was inevitable and essential. Among the first group were those associated with the May Fourth Movement, while those generally sympathetic to the latter were the late-Qing reformers and post-May Fourth 'neotraditionalist' intellectuals. A detailed literary study would necessarily explore the many intermediate positions between these polarities, but this study is concerned only with how China's literary encounters with modernity might inform contemporaneous architectural experiences.

China's reformers from the late nineteenth century, such as Liang Qichao and Yan Fu, questioned the primacy of the west as a model for outright emulation. Adding weight to this conviction was the ordeal of the First World War, which was interpreted by many as proof of western civilisation's bankruptcy. Disillusioned with the west, Chinese writers found themselves 'groping toward a moderate position by mediating and seeking compromises between western modernity and Chinese tradition'[71] in the same manner as their counterparts in painting. Parallels can also be drawn with European Enlightenment philosophers two centuries earlier, who were disillusioned with western society and looked east for salvation and whose ideas coincided with – and in part stimulated – equivalent approbation in art and architecture that spawned chinoiserie. These sentiments enjoyed a spirited, albeit brief, revival in the twentieth century making a considerable impact on British art and literature before the Second World War, which is the focus of Witchard's notable work *Modernism and British Chinoiserie* (2014). Twentieth-century writers such as John Dewey, Bertrand Russell, Goldsworthy Dickinson, Roger Fry, Harold Acton, Arthur Waley, Christopher Isherwood and Wystan Hugh Auden can be considered early ambassadors of the notion of multiple modernities by arguing that culturally, east and west 'should not be hierarchized and should instead be given equal respect and combined to produce a higher form of culture than what the world has known'.[72]

As had occurred in painting, May Fourth writers and critics were preoccupied by the question of whether or not the development of modernism in their artistic domain 'was a continuation of past literary practices or the interjection of western thinking and practices'.[73] The May Fourth Movement, as has already been emphasised, was intimately bound to concepts of time and linear progress. The espousal of linear temporality, in sanctioning the notion of modernity and emphasising the present, set the respective literary traditions of China and the west against one another: the modern, forward-looking, individualistic, material, industrial, optimistic west versus the old, backward-looking, collective, spiritual, artisan, pessimistic Chinese. Shih explains this stance clearly:

Many Chinese writers valorized western modernism as the signifier for the modern and the tool to delegitimize traditional Chinese culture, binding modernism to a kind of masochistic denial ... [justifying] their appropriation of modernism as a counter discourse to Chinese tradition (however problematic that may be), as a means to accelerate the arrival of modernity, and as a mark of their cultural power as iconoclasts.[74]

May Fourth writers were united in being pro-western and pro-modern, but the alliance was complicated and sometimes fractured by its members' views on nationhood. On one side were the metropolitan writers, to whom the urban environment *was* modernity and *was* the locus for the nation's spiritual and intellectual enlightenment. These were largely cosmopolitans who favoured and thrived on the multiculturalism and internationalism that existed in China's larger cities, particularly Shanghai. For the others, their cause was rooted in a traditional and rural alterity. Loyalists sided with the left-wing, providing the basis for the League of Left-wing Writers, established by a group of authors including Tian Han, Yu Dafu and Lu Xun on 2 March 1930. They were later embraced by an embryonic Communist Party, though it would be erroneous to suggest that they were all communists; their position merely proved that literary conservatism was not incompatible with a radical, progressive political position.

With the claims for literary modernity drawn along political battle lines, a question remained over the location of the theatre of conflict. In the aftermath of the May Fourth Movement, Beijing was considered China's cultural and literary heart, but the city's social and political instability throughout much of the 1920s caused the cultural establishment to decamp to Shanghai, altering the situation completely. The nation's cultural centre of gravity shifted on its axis and Shanghai, China's commercial hub and moral sink became the literary frontline until the late 1930s.

For the League of Left-wing Writers, literary modernity was a mass movement, but for China's metropolitan writers such as Mu Shiying, Liu Na'ou, Dai Wangshu or Shi Zhecun, modernism was 'indisputably urban'[75] and modernity's ideological home was Shanghai. Shih describes the city's version of modernism as being 'intently interested in the erotic, exotic, urban, material, and decadent, and often approximated in content mass cultural forms such as cinema and popular magazines'.[76] All such themes were scorned by left-wing intellectuals. The products of this very particular cultural milieu frequently featured in the stories, poems and essays of Shanghai writers: prostitutes, automobiles, neon lights, advertising, gadgets, music and architecture, all of which became 'fetishized as embodiments of exoticism and providers of "carnal intoxication"'.[77]

A figure to whom Shanghai represented the beginning and end of the quest for modernity was Shao Xunmei (1906–68), 'poet, essayist, translator, publisher, and flamboyant dandy' who Lee describes as 'the least suited to the May Fourth prototype of a writer of social conscience'.[78] Shao was educated at Cambridge University and mixed in European cultural circles as a member of China's cultural elite. His extensive experience of the west was manifest in various interests and pursuits, including his literary journal *Jin Wu* (*Golden House Monthly*) based on Aubrey Beardsley's *The Yellow Book* and his sexual appetite for western women. Although married into a wealthy family, on his return to Shanghai, Shao engaged in a long-term affair with

Emily Hahn (1905–97), the *New Yorker*'s reporter in Shanghai and author of *China to Me* (1944).

Other writers to whom 'the city was the only world of their existence and the key source of their creative imagination'[79] included Liu Na'ou and his friend Mu Shiying. Both were educated in Japan where modernist encounters occurred almost exclusively in the urban realm. Inspired by the Japanese Shinkankakuha they were instrumental in the formation of Chinese New Sensationism and founded the modern literary group, the X*in Gan Jue Pai* (*New Sensationists*). Born in Taiwan, educated with private resources in Japan and at the Jesuit's Aurora University in Shanghai's French Concession, Liu's financial and cultural independence afforded him unique freedom in the search for modernity. He revealed his professional position in a letter to Dai Wangshu in 1926 in which he 'established the connection between the city, urban sensations, and modernism'[80] in the manner of Italian Futurists:

> To us moderns, Romance cannot but be distant.... The streetcars are too noisy, the sky that was once blue is blackened by factory soot, and the songs of the skylarks are mute. Muses, their harp strings broken, have flown away to who knows where. Does this mean that there is no beauty in modern life? No, there is, except its form has changed. We don't have Romance, no trumpets sounding from castles, but we have thrill and carnal intoxication. This is what I mean by modernism [*jindai zhuyi*].[81]

The primitive thrill that inspired Shanghai's writers was animated by its vigorous publishing industry, the largest in Asia. Though this modern industry was not the reason why China's literary establishment congregated in Shanghai, it was undoubtedly a major advantage to them, offering relatively cheap and efficient means to produce and distribute work. From the 1920s there emerged a variety of literary magazines. Over one hundred journals were published by various literary groups, with temporal titles explicitly evoking the tenor of the age: *Xin Qing Nian* (*New Youth*), *Xin Ren* (*New People*), *Xin Shi Dai* (*New Epoch*), *Xin Chao* (*New Tide*), *Les Contemporains* (*Xian Dai Za Zhi*), *Jin Dai Fu Nü* (*Modern Woman*), *Xin She Hui* (*New Society*), *Xin Sheng Huo* (*New Life*), *Xin Wen Yi* (*New Literature and Art*), *Chuangzao* (*Creation*) and *Shu Guang* (*The Dawn*).

Shanghai's publishing industry was bound up with a collection of cultural pursuits that were prominent features of the city: advertising, graphic design, commercial art, bookstores and coffee shops. More than just selling books or coffee, many of these venues became important sites for social and professional interaction. Lee cites the example of Zeng Pu's bookstore on 115 Rye Massenett in the French Concession, which was frequented by his friends such as Shao Xun Mei, Xu Zhi Mo, Tian Han and Yu Da Fu,[82] a list that reflects the interdisciplinarity of China's artistic community. Lee further claims that by the 1930s, Shanghai was 'caught in a "coffee-house craze"',[83] citing the writer and 'avid Francophile', Zhang Ruo Gu,[84] that the coffee-house was 'one of the crucial symbols of modernity, together with the cinema and the automobile; and more than the latter two, it had an enormous impact on modern literature'.[85] Given Shanghai's multicultural population and large French Concession, it is not surprising that a café culture, centred round a rich blend of private and public space, played such an important role in the city's social and intellectual life.

The café frequently appears in the stories of Shanghai writers, including *Zhang Cha, kafei, maijiu (Tea, coffee, ale)*[86] and *Xian Dai Du Hui Sheng Huo Xiang Zheng (The symbol of modern urban life)*,[87] Tian Han, *Ka Fei Guan De Yi Ye (One night in a café)* and Yu Dafu's translations.

Other venues for the kinds of informal associations and collective experiences essential to the engagement with and articulation of modernity by Shanghai's modern writers and artists included cinemas, a vital building type within the *oeuvre* of architectural modernity. Feng's *Garden of Art* possesses a cinema, but rather than being a place, it is represented in much the same way as Kracauer does in *Little Shop Girls Go to the Movies* (1927)[88] as a huge mirror on the west side of the garden, reflecting all the other art forms. Parallels with Kracauer, himself a student of architecture, are instructive. His writings on urban life in pre-war Berlin bear a strong resemblance to Shanghai, where life for the masses was experienced through distraction 'because things are so miserable at home and they want to get a bit of glamour'.[89] Cinema was one such distraction whose popularity attracted many visitors in Feng's *Garden*. For the architect in China, the proliferation of cinemas provided an unprecedented opportunity and building type that became a prominent feature of their work throughout the 1920s and 1930s. Along with clubs, theatres, dance halls and department stores, foreign and Chinese architects designed some of the most flamboyant and modern cinemas in Asia, including Shanghai's Grand (1933), Lyric (1934) and Metropol (1934), Nanjing's Da Hua (1934), Kunming's Nan Ping (1939), Dalian's Tokiwa (1931), Shenyang's Continental (1938) and Changchun's Feng Le (1936) and Asahiza (1936), reflecting the commercialisation and commoditisation of the urban realm that reached its height in Shanghai and which will be later examined in detail architecturally (see Plates 5–11).

Opposing May Fourth's Occidentalism and Shanghai's assorted metropolitan modernisms, literary or otherwise, was a small group of writers and theorists united by their determination to resist the outright westernisation of Chinese literature. Centred in Beijing, this group became known as the Beijing School, or *Jingpai*. Although termed 'neotraditionalist', their interests were not in yearning for the past but rather integrating it with the present and future.[90] Laurence describes *Jingpai* as 'a more academic modernist movement' whereas *Haipai* represented the 'glitter of the cosmopolitan trends in Shanghai'.[91] Furthermore, *Jingpai* was more of a group of individuals, in the literal sense, than *Haipai*, which collectively described a group of groups. The dichotomous relationship between these schools is further evidence of China's intranational condition and multifaceted modernity.

In many ways the two cities represented two separate worlds, but not in a postcolonial sense of primate cities. Beijing, an ancient city and an imperial capital, was steeped in political, cultural and intellectual tradition. Shanghai, conversely, was a comparatively young city: commercial, materialistic and modern. The politician and intellectual defined Beijing, and the merchant and urban dandy defined Shanghai. Historically, few figures were vilified more by China's literati than the pitiable merchant. Little had changed by the early twentieth century – Beijing's intelligentsia scorned Shanghai's apparent boorishness as much as Shanghai's glamorous internationalists despised Beijing's apparent conservatism.

Ideologically, both schools regarded themselves as modern. Often from privileged backgrounds and assuming the intellectual high-ground, Beijing intellectuals, unlike their Shanghai colleagues, rejected the idea that to be modern required the disavowal of Chinese tradition. They believed their aims could be achieved by expanding 'the notion of global modernity to include aspects of Chinese culture'.[92] Such attempts at assimilation were common in architecture in China and on a global platform literally and figuratively can be likened to the international design for the United Nations Headquarters in New York after the Second World War. Liang Sicheng, the Chinese representative in the architectural team that included Le Corbusier and Niemeyer, proposed that the plan should be square with a Chinese garden in the centre and each building should be oriented on an east–west axis, in keeping with Chinese tradition.[93]

Prominent among *Jingpai* personalities were the female writers Lin Huiyin (the wife of Liang Sicheng) and Ling Shuhua (1904–90). Both are important for representing the multifacetedness of modernity in China before the Second World War, but Lin in particular represents the constellation of modernity's interconnections across art practices and underlines the importance of adopting a wider view of architecture when examining China's encounter with modernity. Symptomatic of China's partial historiographical treatment, which has seen the country's history written from a westerncentric perspective by those outside and from a left-wing perspective from those inside, Shih observes that Lin and Ling have been 'largely ignored in standard literary histories in China and the US'.[94]

Similar treatments, by both western and Chinese scholars, have occurred with other *Jingpai* scholars, such as Julian Bell, nephew of Virginia Woolf and among the second generation of the Bloomsbury Group, and the poet and writer Xu Zhimo (1897–1931), a flamboyant character and cultural celebrity. Xu's example is instructive not only because he represents another case of China's multiple modernities, but also because he was tutored by and devoted to Liang Qichao, the father-in-law of Lin Huiyin. Completing and complicating this small but influential circle was Xu's infatuation with Lin, with whom he had an affair when Lin attended secondary school in the UK.[95]

Xu studied at Clark (1918) and Columbia (1919) universities before travelling to the UK where he acquired his appreciation for modern English poetry. He enrolled at King's College, Cambridge, during which time he met and sometimes befriended leading British scholars and writers such as Goldsworthy Dickinson, H.G. Wells, I.A. Richards, Roger Fry, Arthur Waley, John Middleton Murray and Katherine Mansfield. It was at Cambridge that Xu claimed his 'eyes were opened, [his] appetite for knowledge was stimulated [and his] concept of "self" was nursed',[96] and it was through his time in England that he became 'the great link with Bloomsbury'.[97] When he returned to China in late 1922, Xu founded the literary group *Xin Yue She* (*Crescent Moon Society*), whose title derived from a poem by Nobel Laureate Rabindranath Tagore (1861–1941).

Tagore travelled to China for two weeks in 1924 and both Xu and Lin acted as his interpreters. The day he gave a lecture at Peking University is described by Shih as 'a day of fated encounters and celebrations',[98] not only because of Xu and Lin's dual role, but also because it was the day that Ling Shuhua met her future husband, Chen Yuan (1896–1970). A decade later, Ling strengthened the bond that Xu had established between China's modern writers and Britain's Bloomsbury Group by having an affair with Julian Bell, who had been appointed Professor of English in Wuhan University's School of Humanities from 1935 to 1937 by none other than Chen. Bell's residency in the relative isolation of Hubei Province was described by

Laurence as part of 'a web of relationships between two literary and intellectual communities'[99] in China and the west that, through his affair with Ling, introduced one of China's leading literary figures to Virginia Woolf.

The affairs that Lin and Ling had had with Xu reflected the small and incestuous circle of friends that constituted China's literary establishment and the embracing of a very unChinese sexual freedom in the Bloomsbury vein. In 1931, when Xu died in a plane crash, he was having an affair with the esteemed American writer, Pulitzer Prize winner and Nobel Laureate for Literature, Pearl Buck (1892–1973).[100]

The analogous trajectories of Ling and Lin's lives demonstrate the limited extent of China's exposure to international modernism, however multifaceted it might have been. Both were from similarly advantaged, respected and cultured backgrounds[101] and shared similar educational and early professional experiences in China as well as overseas.[102] Both led similarly isolated and lonely lives as refugees in remote Sichuan during the Second World War, throughout which, both attempted to retain fragments from former lives as international ambassadors of modern Chinese culture. Lin maintained her link principally through John and Wilma Fairbank, and Ling through her correspondence with Virginia Woolf.[103] Later in their lives, Lin and Ling would also come to share similar positions in relation to their experience of different cultures, experiences that, like other artists such as Teng Baiye, would come to symbolise the tensions among China's intelligentsia as their country was exposed to the outside world. Laurence describes Ling as 'a cosmopolitan Chinese artist who identified deeply with the nation of China, but who was in love, whose imagination freely connected with different people and different parts of the world'.[104] Fairbank describes Lin as:

> an artist by nature, an architect by training, and a poet by vocation ... exceptionally pretty, vivacious and quick-witted, fluent in English, and by nature deeply responsive to her surroundings ... her popularity among both sexes was intoxicating. She had left her family and the constraints of her culture and conquered in this new world.[105]

Ling's relationship with Woolf and the Bloomsbury Group is expertly examined by Laurence in *Lily Briscoe's Chinese Eyes: Bloomsbury, Modernism and China* (2003), which supports the multiple modernities paradigm. Some scholars have framed Woolf and Ling's relationship from a position of inequality, in a way that evokes post-colonial asymmetry. Shih, for example, suggests that 'the imbalance of their correspondence also probably explains why Ling did not attempt to clarify how her name should be spelled and allowed Woolf to mistakenly call her Sue Ling again and again; Woolf did not at all understand the conventions of Chinese names, nor did she try to understand them'.[106] Laurence, however, rejects the post-colonial view of master/servant, insisting that correspondence between the two does 'not adopt the tone, stance, or vocabulary of "domination" and "subordination" or "master" and "oppressed"'.[107] What their relationship 'does most though is underline the complexity of the matter and that an all-embracing notion of "east" or "colonised" is inadequate'.[108] Ling remained in contact with Woolf until her suicide in 1941, seeking advice about writing, including the production of an autobiography, which Woolf urged should be written in English and eventually was, titled *Ancient Melodies* (Hogarth Press, 1953) with a preface by Vita Sackville-West (1892–1962).

Recent scholarship has done much to expose the close if small bond between China's literary elite and leading modernist writers in the west, strengthening the emergent intellectual position that modernity's encounter outside the west and particularly in China was more complex than the one- or even two-way process that has been portrayed until recently.[109] In studying the modern movement's[110] influences, Qian Zhaoming highlights how the Orient 'has been underemphasised', revealing instead 'a far more penetrating influence of the Far East'.[111] Such studies have caused Qian and other scholars (Shih Shu-Mei in particular) to conclude that 'Historical interactions between the west and China in the cultural arena in general, and in the writing of western modernism in particular, have shown China to be an important part of the non-western alterity that constituted western modernism'.[112]

Lin and Ling were among a wider group of Chinese literary modernists that helped to produce a body of literary and artistic experiences that for China and the west cannot be omitted from the modernist record. These include Bertrand Russell and John Dewey (invited to teach at Peking University by Liang Qichao); two Bloomsbury affiliates, Goldsworthy Dickinson (1862–1932), who travelled to China in 1912, and Roger Fry (1866–1934);[113] Harold Acton who lived in China from 1932 to 1939; Christopher Isherwood (1904–86) and Wystan Hugh Auden (1907–73) who travelled to China and later co-wrote *A Journey to a War* (1939) about their experiences as witnesses to the Sino-Japanese War; and even Noël Coward who spent four days recovering from illness cooped up in Shanghai's pre-eminent Cathay Hotel writing *Private Lives*. After his stay, the hotel, which boasted 'ultra-modern' suites designed in minimalist modernist styles by the Bauhaus graduate Richard Paulick, renamed his room 'The Coward Suite'.

Other manifestations of modernist encounters include those where 'British modernists presented literary and cultural challenges to the Chinese literary critics of the 1920s and 1930s',[114] such as the friendship between the Cambridge graduate Xiao Qian (1910–99)[115] and Edward Morgan Forster. Another example, which is often overlooked in the experiences of Japonism and chinoiserie, is the circular assimilation of artistic precedent, where modern western practitioners sought inspiration from the ancient east only for modern-seeking eastern practitioners to later draw from the assimilated western ideas. Shih argues that Hu Shi's (1891–1962) famous *Ba Bu Zhu Yi* (*Eight Don'ts*), which 'heralded a new literature in the beginning of the May Fourth era',[116] were 'partially taken from the Imagist manifesto, which in turn had earlier been influenced by the tenets of classical Japanese and Chinese poetry'.[117]

The round trip of Oriental ideas, exported to the US before being imported back into China, is evidenced in the work of Ezra Pound,[118] described by T.S. Eliot as 'the inventor of Chinese poetry for our time'.[119] Pound was introduced to Chinese literature through art, much of which he saw first-hand in his native Philadelphia, 'one of the earliest repositories of Chinese art and decorative objects, the bounty of traders, collectors, and importers'.[120] He is often cited because he represents 'the most prominent example of how Chinese materials were used in western modernism',[121] particularly in his *Cantos* and his earlier poetic translations published in *Cathay* (1915) which, not speaking Chinese himself, he undertook with the aid of Ernest Fenollosa's notes. Pound's Imagist poetry drew inspiration from earlier Chinese translations by Orientalist scholars such as Fenollosa and Waley. Of interest to this study is not so much the material content of western modernist writers inspired by China, directly or indirectly, or the impact it had on western modernist literature and literary criticism, the vast subject of which lies beyond the bounds of this study and is expertly dealt with by the likes of Bush, Hayot and Qian, but instead how increasing scrutiny paid to the original sources of literary works indicates a shifting stance in scholarship that is causing the west to surrender absolute ownership of modernity's intellectual territory. This repositioning is part of a wider interest in international scholarship to examine China's early modernists and to reveal 'the significance of their contribution to Chinese literature – particularly to the development of literary modernism – after more than half a century of scholarly oblivion'.[122]

Conclusion

The purpose of this exploration into how China's various encounters with modernity distinguished itself from the west's other *others* has been to prepare the ground for the examination of China's architectural encounter with modernity. In extracting conclusions from these preceding explorations, the following points stand out.

Modernity's interconnectedness across thematic boundaries is one of the most conspicuous observations and supports this study's view of architectural modernity in China more broadly: Japan's constant but often veiled presence; the indirectness and multifacetedness of western influence; the weight of tradition and rise of nationalism as motivating and impeding forces in its search for modernity; and the necessary reconceptualisation of ancient precepts such as time and language.

China's experiences demonstrate not only the complexity and multifariousness of modernity's encounter outside the west, but also the need for contemporary scholarship to reconstitute existing notions of modernity to accommodate contexts formerly regarded as peripheral. Individuals such as Teng Baiye, Chang Yu, Lin Huiyin and Ling Shuhua attest to this both in their respective artistic outputs and in the impact they and other Chinese artists from previous generations had on the work of western modernists. This constellation of modernist influences challenges the inadequate notion of centre-periphery and proposes instead that Chinese modernism 'both challenges the constructed history of modernism as primarily a Euro-American event, and destabilizes western modernism's claim to ontological primacy and aesthetic uniqueness'.[123]

A final observation concerns modernity's incompleteness throughout the first half of the twentieth century. Modernity's global encounters outside the west, particularly in architecture, were predominantly a phenomenon of the second half of the twentieth century. For China, as these themes demonstrate, modernism, the notion of modernity and nationalism, though very much confined to a growing metropolitan and intellectual class, occurred earlier and were well underway before the Second World War. Even in the context of global conflict, China displays a distinction from regional or international *others*. For China, the Second World War started earlier than it did throughout much of the rest of the world, and its conclusion was followed almost immediately with civil war and complete structural change that caused equally dramatic transformations in the cultural realm that still reverberate. China's first encounter with modernity was not only characterised by extreme diversity, but it remained unfinished and incomplete – experiences that were as evident in conventional art practices as they were in architecture, the focus of Part II of this study.

Notes

1. Andrews and Shen, 1998, p. 2.
2. Letter from Lin Huiyin to Wilma and John Fairbank, 29 January 1936, Peabody Essex Museum, Salem, Massachusetts.
3. 'Chinese Art Exhibition in London', *The China Journal*, Vol. 23, No. 6, Shanghai, December 1935, pp. 323 and 360.
4. Translated from the original Chinese in Feng Zikai, 1990, p. 36.
5. Sullivan, 1996, p. 6.
6. Hosagrahar, 2005, p. 1.
7. Danzker *et al.* (eds), 2004, p. 62.
8. Seven monks in particular are said to be responsible for introducing European painting techniques into the Imperial Palace: Attiret, Castiglione, Sickelpart, Damascene, Panzi, Belleville (who was also a sculptor and architect) and Gerardino ('the first who introduced the art of painting in oil to China') in John Ferguson, 'Painters Among Catholic Missionaries and their Helpers in Peking', *Journal of the North China Branch of the Royal Asiatic Society*, Vol. LXV, 1934, p. 25. Interestingly, Ferguson chooses to add to this list the early pioneers Ricci and Benoist, 'for both of them did almost as much as any of the painters themselves to bring European painting to the attention of China's rulers'.
9. Sullivan, 1996, p. 6.
10. Ferguson, 1934, p. 35.
11. Sullivan, 1996, p. 5.
12. *Exposition de la Peinture Chinoise*, catalogue, May–June 1933, in Danzker *et al.*, 2004, p. 32.
13. Exhibition Catalogue, Palais du Rhin, Strasbourg, 1924, in Danzker *et al.*, 2004, p. 23.
14. Danzker *et al.*, 2004, p. 31.
15. Notes, Danzker *et al.*, 2004, p. 411.
16. Clarke, 2004, p. 98.
17. Teng was born and educated in the famously cultured city of Suzhou, from where he travelled to America in 1924. As a student at the University of Washington, Teng was among the first Chinese artists to study sculpture overseas and went on to complete his Master's and study for a PhD at Harvard, which he never completed. Clarke, 2004, p. 86.
18. Clarke, 2004, p. 95.
19. Clarke, 2004, pp. 89–90.
20. The first was in January to the Shanghai Art Club titled *Expressionism in Chinese Art* (the lecture was published in *The North China Herald*, Shanghai, 31 January 1934, p. 172), and the second was in May to the Royal Asiatic Society, titled *Bamboo and Bamboo Painting*.
21. T'eng Kwei, 'Art in Modern China', *The Open Court, December* 1933, pp. 488–9.
22. Letter from Lin Huiyin to Wilma and John Fairbank, 4 January 1936, Peabody Essex Museum, Salem, Massachusetts.
23. Teng's house was on Rue Lafayette in the French Concession (Clarke, 2004, p. 95), now Fuxing Lu, from where Tobey wrote of his experiences to Dorothy Elmhirst (1887–1968), co-founder of the Dartington Hall Trust in Devon, England.
24. Clarke, 2004, pp. 97–8.
25. Tobey, 1951, p. 230.
26. Sullivan, 1996, p. 27.
27. Nanjing's *Liang Jiang Shi Fan Xue Tang* (together with Beijing's *Bei Yang Shi Fan Xue Tang*) were China's first two institutions to train the country's first generation of art teachers.
28. Zheng in Danzker *et al.*, 2004, p. 193.
29. Shen in Andrews and Shen, 1998, p. 92.
30. There is some dispute over the year of his death, with Japanese sources citing 1921 and Chinese sources citing 1936 or 1937.
31. Lum in Danzker *et al.*, 2004, p. 218.

86 *China and the meaning of modernity*

32 Danzker *et al.*, 2004, p. 25.
33 Fujita Tsuguharu was a graduate of the Tokyo School of Fine Arts, friend of the Montparnasse artists and member of the 'Paris School' (see Birnbaum, 2006).
34 Mitsutani Kunishirō had travelled to Paris and from 1911 to 1914 studied at the Académie Julian, where he became heavily influenced by Matisse (see Sullivan, 1996, pp. 59 and 73).
35 Also known as Sanyu in French.
36 Andrews, 2004 (unpaginated).
37 Shen, 1998, p. 177.
38 Wong (2001) states that one of Chang Yu's works appeared in Xu Beihong's 1933 exhibition in Paris.
39 Andrews and Shen, 1998, p. 176.
40 Wu Fading (1883–1924) and Li Chaoshi (1894–1971), Kao, 1983, pp. 15–16.
41 Having already experienced Japan, Xu studied at l'Académie Julian in Paris then the École Nationale Supérieure des Beaux-Arts.
42 Cities included Paris, Berlin, London, Milan, Geneva, Bern, Heidelberg, Frankfurt, Düsseldorf, Amsterdam, The Hague, Moscow, Leningrad.
43 Letter from Vanessa Bell to Julian Bell, 7 December 1935 in Laurence, 2003, p. 335.
44 Laurence, 2003, p. 336.
45 Laurence, 2003, p. 224.
46 Laurence, 2003, p. 327.
47 Zheng, 2004, p. 179.
48 Zheng, 2004, p. 179.
49 Shen, 1998, p. 176.
50 Pang Xunqin had studied oil painting at l'Académie Julian in Paris for five years.
51 Ni Yide had studied at Tokyo's Kawabata Academy from 1927 to 1928.
52 Sullivan, 1996, p. 62.
53 Sullivan, 1996, p. 29.
54 Lee, 1999, p. 76.
55 Andrews and Shen, 1998, p. 186.
56 Andrews and Shen, 1998, p. 189.
57 Lee, 1999, p. 126.
58 Lu Xun founded *Benliu* with the writer, Yu Dafu, in June 1928 (Sullivan, 1996, p. 80).
59 Shen, 2004, p. 267.
60 Sullivan, 1996, p. 80.
61 According to Shen (2004, p. 267) the first exhibition, containing Russian, French and German woodblocks, was held on October 1930 at the Japanese Union Hall near the Uchiyama Bookstore, followed the next year by another in the Shanghai German Bookstore (Yinhuan Bookstore) in July 1931.
62 Sullivan, 1996, p. 83.
63 At the Guangzhou Art School, the Modern Woodcut Society (*Xiandai muke hui*) was established in June 1934 by the Japanese-trained Cantonese artist, Li Hua as well as the Wild Grain Woodcut Society, established by Chen Tiegeng, Chen Yanqiao (1911–70) and He Baitao (1913–39) (Shen, 2004, p. 262).
64 Wild Fire Woodcut Society (Shen, 2004, p. 262).
65 Pingjin Woodcut Research Society (Shen, 2004, p. 262).
66 Sullivan, 1996, p. 30.
67 Danzker *et al.*, 2004, p. 30.
68 Shih, 2001, p. 1.
69 Shih, 2001, p. 1.
70 Shih, 2001, p. 10.
71 Lee, 1999, p. 47.
72 Shih, 2001, p. 164.
73 Laurence, 2003, p. 292.
74 Shih, 2001, pp. 14–15.
75 Lee, 1999, p. 142.

Chinese art and its multiple modernities 87

76 Shih, 2001, p. 268.
77 Shih, 2001, p. 262.
78 Lee, 1999, p. 241.
79 Lee, 1999, p. 190.
80 Shih, 2001, p. 262.
81 Liu Na'ou letter to Dai Wangshu, 10 November 1926, collected in Kong Lingjing (ed.), *Xian Dai Zhong Guo Zuo Jia Shu Xin (Letters of Modern Chinese Writers)*, Yixin Shudian, Hong Kong, 1971, pp. 266–7, quoted in Shih, 2001, p. 262.
82 Lee, 1999, p. 20.
83 Lee, 2001, p. 99.
84 Lee, 2001, p. 98.
85 Lee, 1999, p. 22 and 2001, p. 99.
86 In *Fu Ren Hua Bao (Women's Pictorial)*, 1935, pp. 9–11.
87 In *Ka Fei Zuo Tan (Café Forum)*, Zhen Mei Shan Shu Dian, Shanghai, 1929, pp. 3–11.
88 In 'Little Shop Girls Go to the Movies' (1927), Kracauer describes films as 'the mirror of the prevailing society' in Kracauer, 1995, p. 291.
89 Kracauer, 1998, p. 88.
90 The Creative Review group affiliated to the Southeastern University in Nanjing were also seen as similarly traditionalist.
91 Laurence, 2003, p. 4.
92 Shih, 2001, p. 16.
93 Newhouse, 1989, pp. 117–20.
94 Shih (2001, p. 188) includes also Fei Ming in this list.
95 Xu had been living in Sawston outside Cambridge and Lin in London with her father, Lin Changmin.
96 Hsu, 1963, p. 67.
97 Laurence, 2003, p. 129.
98 Shih, 2001, p. 207.
99 Laurence, 2003, p. 3.
100 Laurence, 2003, p. 146.
101 Lin's father was a high official in the Beiyang government; Ling's father, the former Mayor of Beijing and Governor of Hebei Province and her grandfather, Xie Lansheng (1760–1831), was an eminent painter-calligrapher.
102 Lin first travelled to the UK with her father in 1920 (Wilma Fairbank, 1994, p. 11), while Ling was sent to Japan to study for three years with her sister in 1911.
103 Letter dated 5 April 1938, in Nicolson and Trautmann, 1980.
104 Laurence, 2003, p. 249.
105 Wilma Fairbank, 1994, pp. 10 and 24–5.
106 Shih, 2001, p. 217.
107 Laurence, 2003, p. 249.
108 Laurence, 2003, p. 249.
109 In Asia more broadly, this imbalance is being redressed with various literatures written about western modernist writers including P.S. Sri: *T.S.Eliot, Vedanta, and Buddhism*; Amar Kumar Singh: *T.S.Eliot and Indian Philosophy*; Masaru Sekine: *Yeats and the Noh: A Comparative Study*; and Shiro Naito: *Yeats and Zen: A Study of the Transformation of his Mask*, but it has been less explored in relation to China.
110 Qian's use of the Modernist Movement refers specifically to the Anglo-American poetic revolution of the 1910s and 1920s.
111 Qian, 1995, p. 2.
112 Shih, 2001, p. 4.
113 Laurence (2003, p. 370) describes Fry as an 'Avatar of modernism, [who] sees "modernity" in Chinese in Song landscapes [consisting of] a "passionate and disinterested contemplation of nature"'.
114 Laurence, 2003, p. 202.
115 Xiao Qian studied at Cambridge University from 1941 to 1944.
116 Shih, 2001, p. 10.

117 Shih, 2001, p. 10.
118 And to a lesser extent William Carlos Williams.
119 Pound, 1928, p. xvi.
120 Ira Nadel, 'Constructing the Orient: Pound's American Vision' in Qian, 2006, p. 12.
121 Shih, 2001, p. 8.
122 Lee, 1999, p. 190.
123 Shih, 2001, p. 5.

Part II
Architecture and modernity

5 The advent of architecture

Feng Zikai deliberately and symbolically placed architecture near the entrance of the *Garden of Art*. Architecture's novelty in the Chinese context and its affiliation with industry meant that it was considered the most practical and prosperous of the arts. The association with the applied rather than the artistic within this allegorical Chinese landscape acknowledges architecture's craft origins, questions architecture's artistic credentials and challenges its creative spirit, so much so that Feng Zikai claimed that many visitors to the garden avoided this section altogether.

One might even venture to suggest that architecture is fortunate to have had a place in the garden. Traditionally, architecture was never considered an art form in China. 'Architecture as an art, not as a trade, came to China at the moment, and as a part, of foreignization', wrote the Chinese architect Chen Zhanxiang in 1947.[1] Its admission in Feng's garden is a reflection of his twentieth-century perspective but its specific location in relation to other art practices indicates a prevailing ambivalence about its artistic credentials when compared with China's other art practices.

It is no coincidence, therefore, that Feng Zikai drew attention, derisively, to architecture's close affiliation with the materialistic pursuits of commerce and industry rather than emphasising its artistic or intellectual merit. 'The barrier between scholar and builder', noted Chen, 'was practically insurmountable',[2] which explains why one of his contemporaries, Dong Dayou, claimed that

> China never achieved what the Greeks and Romans did in the art of building. Chinese art has always found its favourite expression in painting and calligraphy. ... Chinese people revelled in the beauty of nature and had little interest for material beauty such as is found in architecture which they considered as something subservient to daily needs.[3]

In setting out to explore the landscape of architectural modernity in China in the first half of the twentieth century, this study acknowledges that the framing of *modernity* and *architecture* within the context of China poses a problem when both are western imports. In Part II, the multiple modernities paradigm is employed as an *architectural* concern to examine the impact of the importation of western concepts and meanings, and to assess how far these represented a domination of or assimilation with local theories and practices.

Another aim of this investigation is to contribute to the irresistible shift in architectural history specifically and in academia more broadly from an accepted position of westerncentricty to a truly global perspective. Studies of architectural modernity outside the west are scant in comparison to the scholarly investment over the last century in analysing Europe (particularly western Europe) and North America. Although this imbalance is beginning to be redressed, there remains a chronic paucity of scholarly attention paid both to the 'non-west' and to the interrelations between architectural modernity and the contexts in which it occurred outside the west. Throughout the twentieth century there was a certainty in the west's dominance that does not exist in the twenty-first century.

For architectural historians, the twentieth century is especially significant for three reasons. The first is that this century was, more than any other before it, the century of modernity – modernism flourished, modernist ideas and principles were enshrined, and modernist history was written. The second is an outcome of the first and concerns the structural inequality derived from the west's claim over modernity as theory and as architectural expression, the consequence of which accentuates a restricted view of history at the expense of wider perspectives – thematically, geographically, temporally and socioculturally. This partiality impoverishes our knowledge of the past because architecture situated in or derived from the non-west is overlooked and undervalued and studies of the 'non-west' are framed by methodologies that support values and approaches ascribed by the west, sustaining the west's dominance over others. Architecture's history is an Orientalist vision of building – a western mode of 'dominating, restructuring and having authority' over others.[4] The third reason is more general and poses existential questions for our species. The twentieth century witnessed the dawn of the Anthropocene, an epochal shift closely associated with humanity's unprecedented move from a rural to an urban habitat. Fuelled by modernity's commencement and entrenchment, this transition has a profound impact not just on our species, but also on the systems that sustain life on earth. It is therefore inadequate, fruitless and fallacious to understand modernity on anything other than global terms, consigning to history architectural analyses and designations based largely on political power supported by arbitrary abstractions such as nationhood or absurd assumptions founded on the existence of a unitary Modern Movement or International Style. For architectural history, the twenty-first century will be defined by the wider appreciation and deeper understanding of this epochal era, enriching and correcting a truly global historical landscape characterised not by a singular modernity but by multiple, competing and constantly contested modernities.

Understanding the true nature of architecture's encounter with modernity globally throughout the twentieth century requires much work by scholars situated in or focused on sites once regarded as geographically and intellectually remote from the west. This work is already well underway, with scholars of the Middle East, Asia and South America reclaiming the intellectual territory subsumed by the high tide of western imperialism. Africa's comparatively conspicuous absence cannot be separated from the uniquely savage experience of colonialism inflicted on the continent. Nevertheless, the historical landscape revealed by a global viewpoint presents a much richer and more intricate picture of what actually occurred than modernist historiography was ever able or willing to paint. The result is a deeper understanding of sites and regions that, despite representing the vast majority of the world's population, landmass and built environments, have been concealed for too long from intellectual attention.

Towards a Chinese architecture

At the start of the twentieth century there were no Chinese architects and there was no consensus on a Chinese title for their profession. According to Chen, 'the conception of architecture as an art in the western sense followed on the introduction of occidental styles into the cities about the time of the 1914–18 war'.[5] Before then, building in China was not a documented process but an applied one with practical skills and techniques passed down from master to apprentice over millennia. The same had been true in Europe until the Renaissance when the printing press permitted the unlimited duplication of prints and drawings, which Leon Battista Alberti (1404–72) exploited with his publication of the *Ten Books of Architecture* (1452), precipitating a long tradition of architectural and historical discourse.

Half a millennium separated the formulation of an architectural history and the advent of modernism in Europe. In China these occurred simultaneously. The concurrence of these experiences raised important questions and major challenges for China's first architects, as the Foreword to the first edition of *Jian Zhu Yue Kan* (*The Builder*), a Chinese architectural journal published from 1932 to 1937, passionately exposed. The author used the opportunity to rail at the debilitating consequences of China's cultural attitudes to building and to highlight the key factors that defined the country's encounter with modernity – a lack of precedence, the absence of documented history, deference to the past and intellectual arrogance:

> Society has never paid attention to architecture . . . there are no professional books to study. . . . Society does not seek progress and improvement, it follows tradition. One or two talented inventors are considered aliens. This makes intelligent people reluctant and talented craftsmen abandon their tools. . . . Our country has always considered the gentry as important and looked down upon builders and craftsmen. . . . Society does not see building techniques as a science.[6]

For China, the simultaneousness of its encounter with architectural history and modernity was emblematic of the temporal compression that characterised China's wider experience of modernity. The novel concept of lineal time and the associated combination of time and speed were exploited by China's modern writers, painters and sculptors, but they uniquely challenged architects. In a Confucian society, a cyclical view of history privileged stasis over progress, placing a primacy on the past and maintaining the status quo. 'If traditionalism and resistance to change have been prime characteristics of the Chinese way of life from beginning to end,' argued Soper, 'there is no more vivid illustration of their working than that given by the history of architecture'.[7] For China's building traditions to be recast and the concept of architectural modernity to emerge, lineal temporality had to replace cyclical. Such a transition was not without its serious professional and societal dilemmas. Not only did their chosen profession represent the slowest of the arts, but they were also simultaneously engaged in constructing, architecturally at least, China's future and its past.

Modernity, by definition, demanded a history and the responsibility for creating this fell on the shoulders of China's first architects, none more so than Liang Sicheng who decoded and rewrote in Vernacular Chinese the *Ying Zao Fa Shi* (1103), China's first publication on building standards.[8] The *Ying Zao Fa Shi* was not an architectural treatise but an attempt to eliminate profligacy and waste by producing a comprehensive set of building regulations, codifying the individual elements of a building to a degree of extraordinary detail. With a focus mainly on large-scale, governmental or imperial buildings, the *Ying Zao Fa Shi*'s most immediate practical contribution was the way it regulated building materials and labour costs, significantly reducing waste and corruption in government construction. Of the 34 volumes, 13 explained the quantity of building material used so as to determine the time used on labour, transport and production.

Ying Zao Fa Shi was also a magnum opus in standardisation.[9] In prescribing all the parts of a building and the way to put them together, it also defined China's social organisation, since the size and scale of a building directly reflected the social standing of its owner. In China, buildings enforced and guaranteed social order and rank by upholding *li* (礼), the rituals enshrined in a system of social regulation and moral codes that support the indisputability of the deferential relationship (e.g. between master and servant, husband and wife, and father and son). *Ying Zao Fa Shi* did not invent the modular system of building or define complex social hierarchies, but did synchronise past practices and codify the rational system of construction on which these things depended.[10]

Standardisation became the means by which the imposition of social order through the built environment became most fully articulated. The impact of standardisation on China's built environment is generally under-appreciated, but its centrality in the evolution of construction methods and the way in which buildings were perceived in society makes it essential in the analysis of China's twentieth-century encounter with modernity and architecture.

Standardisation appeared in *chi*, the unit of measurement that defined the relation between the physical dimensions of a building and the status of its occupant. No building, for example, could be wider than nine *chi*, which was reserved for the emperor. Standardisation also appeared in the building unit, *jian*, the square unit defined in plan by four columns. The number of *jian* in a building was also determined by social rank. The extent of standardisation in structural and decorative features according to social rank was such that the status of a building's owner could be deduced from the appearance of a building. Standardisation was therefore manifest in the societal impact of a building's structural characteristics and decorative features such as height, width, breadth, function, location, colour, decoration and material, all of which were consequent on the inhabitant's social position.[11]

Building made visible the logic and order of Chinese society. Despite shifting attitudes and tastes over centuries and throughout different regions, the fundamentals remained constant – every unit of development from the city to the smallest room was treated as a microcosm of the universe individually and in relation to the environment around it. Harmony and hierarchy remained paramount. Beauty was dependent on achieving harmony and respecting hierarchy, and embodied in the structure, not the appearance, of a Chinese building. Symmetry was one outcome of this complex web of interrelated conditions and appeared at multiple levels, from the arrangement of objects in a room, through city planning, to one's position in the universe – architecture and the cosmos were combined.[12] It is no coincidence that China, to the Chinese, is referred to as *Zhong Guo* or *Middle Kingdom*. Under these conditions, the relationships between the universe, the country, the city, the building, the room and the objects within it were not only plausible, they were essential.

The corporeal construal of heaven as a roof over the earth and the vital connection between the two were essential concepts that became manifest in building practices, structural elements and their arrangement. Buildings represented and thus facilitated the organisation of everything, from the position of the cosmos to an artefact on a table. As Boerschmann observed:

> Only in China and in no other country one sees a world conception, a philosophy, embodied in visible form. One sees an architecture that is a direct expression of this conception, a conception formed of the universe and its moving forces.[13]

Only in China does the strength of the relationship between the built environment and the universe, and the concept of cyclical temporality bring new meaning to the modernist idiom: space, time and architecture.

While the *Ying Zao Fa Shi* established the basis of the standardisation of building practices and, by extension, society, the different trades engaged in building were defined with equal exactitude. One of the craftsmen with a claim to being the architect's antecedent was the *Jiang Ren* (匠人), who was responsible for constructing ancestral temples and the *Ming Tang* (Bright Hall, 明堂) in the emperor's palace compound. The role of the *Jiang Ren* was buried in an intricate hierarchy of trades, each stratum of which had the same social standing. According to the *Record of Trades* in the *Rites of Zhou*, there were six types of crafts and three types of work. One of these was woodwork (*Mu Gong* 木工) in which *Jiang Ren* was one of seven categories of craftsmen.[14]

The structures fabricated by *Jiang Ren* played a critical role not only in representing social order, but also in their role preserving this strict order through the way they regulated the etiquette of the user and the impression of the viewer. If these characteristics resemble certain traditions in the west, their scale and scope in China sets them apart. Magnificent buildings – palaces, halls and temples – rather than being the product of an artistic process to signify pomp and power of their patron, were essential to the establishment of social order and the representation of one's position not only in the community, or even just on earth, but in the entire universe.

Nevertheless, despite the size, scale and social significance of their work, the *Jiang Ren*'s skills were equivalent, socially at least, to those of the *Lun Ren* (轮人) who made carriage awnings, the *Lu Ren* (卢人) who made weapon handles, and even the *Zi Ren* (梓人) who made frames for hanging instruments.[15] Traditionally, therefore, the social eminence attached to constructing buildings in China was no different from that of any other object fashioned by carpenters, whether a filing cabinet or cooking utensil. Until the twentieth century and the advent of architecture, building in China was incomparable to the higher arts of poetry, painting or music and could never constitute art or be accepted into its canon.

Despite its artistic exclusion, building did enjoy a prominent position within the impressionistic landscape created by China's literati. By the Song Dynasty (960–1127), people were growing weary of the rigid regulations governing the physical environment and the literati became aware that the design of houses and gardens could be pleasurable places that influenced their well-being. Gardens played a particularly important role as a place of artistic contemplation and inspiration, and over time were increasingly populated by buildings in the form of pavilions and other structures. However, the refinement of the Chinese garden, which specialised in manipulating artificial space, still failed to raise the *Jiang Ren*'s status to that of the artist.

The role of the *Jiang Ren* was concerned chiefly with repairing or modifying existing wooden structures. 'Unlike the Egyptians,' wrote the architect Dong Dayou, the 'Chinese cared little for permanence'[16] or, as Confucius put it, 'the impermanence of permanence haunts us every single day'. The skills of the master craftsman were sustained through a system of apprenticeship. Because these skills were inferior to the much larger philosophical and cosmological significance of building in a wider cultural context, the means of construction changed very little over time. The impermanence of buildings in China belied the permanence of their construction methods. Historical precedent set the standard a newly commissioned building. Under such circumscribed conditions, as occurred in traditional Chinese art, innovation was subordinate to the preservation of customs and creativity was considered neither important nor necessary.

For centuries, individual creativity remained repressed, professionally and socially, until the twentieth century and particularly so in the anonymous practices associated with building. As Chen explained, 'the imposition of the individual on a tradition which was essentially anonymous, governed by principles which offered no scope for the individual and to which the self-assertiveness of the architect could only have been abhorrent'.[17] Individualism was a facet of modernity, as China experienced it, that permitted the alien conduct of personal expression, which for Chinese architects possessed a particular significance and meaning because there were no artistic conventions to which practitioners of this new art practice were bound or which they had to discard.

China's encounter with modernity was not only negotiated internally with the transition from ancient modes and methods of building to the modern practice of architecture, but it also underwent a protracted interpretation externally. In the wake of China's encounter with the west, China's ancient building traditions were translated by foreign observers through their own architectural and cultural language and communicated to audiences at home as primitive or exotic.

The case for primitivism was constructed on the claim by western commentators that the basic concept of building in China was founded on the tent. 'The Chinese have made the tent the elementary feature of their architecture',[18] wrote Bigelow in 1831. Five years later, Ljungstedt claimed that for the Chinese 'the tent was the only model before them; and that they imitated it, their houses and temples and pagodas, built at the present day, afford abundant proof'.[19] By the mid-nineteenth century, the primitive narrative had become official history. 'The type of all Chinese buildings,' asserted Bury in *Rudimentary Architecture: For the Use of Beginners and Students* (1853), 'whether they are used for the purposes of religion or as residences, is undoubtedly a tent.'[20]

The case for exotic was founded in the early eighteenth century with the first documented accounts of Chinese building by missionaries leading to the propagation of chinoiserie in Europe. Its persuasive rhetoric and partial gaze caused it to persist deep into the twentieth century. 'Chinese architects could design ornament which was as good as Roman ornament for interior decorations', wrote the historian Peter Collins in the first edition of *Changing Ideas in Modern Architecture* (1965).[21] His use of European precedents as a comparison echoed the debate among Enlightenment philosophers over the superiority of Chinese or classical civilisation, but it also highlighted the west's proclivity for ornamental novelty that emphasised the picturesqueness of Chinese design over other more fundamental characteristics. Exoticism and ornament were ways the west, consciously or not, prevented China from being, to use Said's terminology, 'a free subject of thought or action'.[22] Architecturally, Collins concurs,

Exotic influences have usually been confined either to the borrowing of such ornamental motifs as could satisfy the current desire for novelty, or to the imitation of forms and dispositions which western architects were already prone to adopt for reasons ignored by the oriental originators.[23]

One of the greatest monuments to this Orientalist tradition is the Great Pagoda in Kew Gardens, London. This atypical example of a Chinese-style structure in Europe features in an interesting and rare literary outing that upends the west's architectural misinterpretation and challenges its cultural domination and authority. The Chinese modernist writer Lao She (1899–1966), who lived in London between 1924 and 1929, wrote a novel *Er Ma*[24] as a critical reflection of his experiences as a young Chinaman in the heart of the British Empire. From a Chinese perspective, the author's depiction of the Great Pagoda possesses no exoticism but instead represents cultural assimilation for a wistful Chinaman cast adrift overseas. In a moment of melancholy the main character, Mr Ma, visits Kew and upon seeing the Great Pagoda he 'grows more cheerful [as] he stood there in a daze for ages, all his thoughts led by that pagoda-spire back to China'.[25] *Er Ma* offers a unique Chinese perspective of London at this critical moment in the development of literary modernism. However, more importantly, it offers a rare and important insight into the complexity of cultural interrelations manifest in this instance through the east's impression of the west's architectural interpretation of the east located in the west. At Kew, Mr Ma's marvelling at the bamboo garden can be read as a prescient premonition of Said's Orientalist treatise:

> This empire-building isn't just stupid self-aggrandisement. . . . They don't just seize other lands and destroy other nations: They also make a proper business of bringing back things from other lands and studying them. . . . Yes, knowledge and military strength. . . . Yes, they are a terrible lot, the English, but, at the same time, so admirable!

When architectural modernism with its disavowal of decorative ornament emerged in the west and was encountered outside the west, China's contributions were already cast as unoriginal, traditional and ornamental, despite having been a source of inspiration for emerging modernists in a variety of art practices. Western modernism defaulted on the debt it owed to China and invested it in a supposedly new aesthetic it claimed its own. As Laurence explains:

> It is this multiplicity of scenes, views, perspectives, and surprises in the [Chinese] garden as well as painting and poetry that drew European modernists, sometimes unwittingly, to the Chinese aesthetic [which in turn] filtered into British perception and practice and influenced the developing British modernist aesthetic.[26]

In architecture, even where Chinese characteristics such as rational and modular modes of construction and systemic standardisation mirrored those of modernism, as they did in Japan, China's building traditions were overlooked by architectural modernists in the west. Consequently, China's built environment encountered western forms to a far greater extent than can be said of the reverse. The Chinese architect Tong Jun highlighted this fact in 1938: 'From India and the west, China has received

98 *Architecture and modernity*

much architecturally but given little.'[27] Tong's inclusion of India with the west is telling, since it ignores China's position as architectural progenitor to Korea or Japan.

Architecture's inclusion in Feng's *Garden of Art* places it firmly in the twentieth century and provides the setting for the subsequent exploration of China's encounter with architectural modernity, an encounter that was unique for the complexity of its global interrelations, the multifariousness of its constituents and the variety of its manifestations.

Notes

1   Chen Zhanxiang, 1947b, p. 27.
2   Chen Zhanxiang, 1947a, p. 19.
3   Dong Dayou, 1936, p. 358.
4   Said, 1978, p. 3.
5   Chen Zhanxiang, 1947b, p. 27.
6   'Foreword', *The Builder*, No. 1, Shanghai, 1932.
7   Sickman and Soper, 1956, p. 205.
8   As with Alberti's treatise nearly half a millennium later, the *Ying Zao Fa Shi* relied on the advent of printing, which occurred in China around 1040 with the invention of movable wooden blocks that were later superseded by more efficient clay printing blocks that allowed the printing of large quantities of Chinese letters. The *Ying Zao Fa Shi* comprised 34 volumes in five sections, 357 chapters and 3,555 items. It regulated the construction methods of all wooden structures, including the design, materials, structure and scale.
9   For example, based on the Cai Fen system, the *Ying Zao Fa Shi* lists eight grades of timber determined by size. The choice of size from the outset determines everything about the building thereafter; once the grade of timber is determined (according to the rank in society of the prospective owner) the building's size, volume, shape of the roof, proportion, details and construction techniques are all set.
10 The *Ying Zao Fa Shi* was out of circulation around 1103 and reprinted in 1145 but did not remain in circulation. Many hand-copied versions were handed down through generations. The version commonly used contemporarily is a copy discovered by Zhu Qiqin in 1919 in Nanjing Library. In 1734, the *Gong Cheng Zuo Fa Ze Li* (*Methods and Examples of Construction*) was published, though this was more of a case study of buildings, comprising 27 building types, and was not an attempt to propagate the study of building theory.
11 An example is the *mo shu* (模数 module), which governed every element of scale in building and city planning. Similar to the Golden Mean in Classical European architecture, the Chinese version applies not to the elevation, but to the plan, which defines the elevation and every other elemental unit upwards therefrom: the *mo shu* governs the size and scale of everything.
12 Axial planning first appeared in China in the Zhou Dynasty (1066–221BC); (see Song and Cai, 2004, pp. 54 and 139).
13 Boerschmann, 1925, p. 547.
14 'Kao Gong Ji' ('Record of Trades'), in *Dong Gong* (*Office of Winter*), *Zhou Li* (*Rites of Zhou*), 200–300BC in Zhou and Zheng, 2001, pp. 1311–72.
15 'Kao Gong Ji' ('Record of Trades'), in *Dong Gong* (*Office of Winter*), *Zhou Li* (*Rites of Zhou*), 200–300BC in Zhou and Zheng, 2001, pp. 311–72.
16 Dong Dayou, 1936, p. 358.
17 Chen Zhanxiang, 1947b, p. 28.
18 Bigelow, 1831, p. 133.
19 Ljungstedt, 1836, p. 236.
20 Bury, 1853, p. 59.
21 Collins, 1965, p. 34.
22 Said, 1978, p. 3.

23 Collins, 1965, p. 34.
24 The Two Mas, or Mr Ma and Son.
25 Lao She, 'Er Ma', *Xiao Shuo Yue Bao* (*Novel Monthly*), Vol. 20, No. 10, 1929. The significance of Lao She's portrayal lies in its rarity. It was written in London in 1929 and published in monthly instalments between May and December that year.
26 Laurence, 2003, pp. 317–22.
27 Tong, 1938, p. 410.

6 Foreign settlements before 1912

China's encounter with architectural modernity was critically bound to the experience of engagement, invariably under duress, with foreign powers. Until relatively recently, China's twentieth-century architectural history has been approached and portrayed as two largely separate experiences: foreign and Chinese.[1] Occasionally, these are treated as isolable or, less frequently, as elements of a combined experience that informed subsequent architectural discourse in China.[2] In defining 'foreign', none look both west and east. To better understand the true nature of 'foreign' architecture and the contribution it made to the development of architecture and the architectural profession in China, this chapter adopts a wider perspective of what constitutes 'foreign' experiences up to the founding of the Republic of China in 1912 before focusing on China's experience in the succeeding chapter.

Two distinct theatres of architectural production and urban development provide the context for this chapter. Arranged in two acts, each comprising three scenes, the first focuses on the treaty ports established along China's coastline and major waterways, and the second is set in the territory of north-east China known internationally as Manchuria. The principal task is less concerned with *what* constituted architectural modernity in China and more with *how* to understand the experience so as to gain a more complete picture of this unique historical encounter, and to establish ways and methods of better understanding these encounters not just in China but elsewhere.

Act 1

Scene 1: The missionary and merchant

With several millennia of continuous constructional practices, it was only comparatively recently that China's building traditions were challenged. The exemplar of early foreign influence in Chinese building was the pagoda, imported from India in the first century AD. The pagoda helped to change China's construction techniques and standards, and was assimilated to a greater degree than any other non-indigenous building type such as churches,[3] synagogues and mosques built by Nestorians, Jews and Muslims throughout the first millennium AD. Following the pagoda, sustained construction and development of non-indigenous types anywhere other than on or around China's periphery occurred only from the late sixteenth century. In Beijing, foreign missionaries built churches, whose influences still persist despite successive waves of persecution. By the seventeenth century, foreign incursions broadened to commercial interests accompanying the arrival of traders in southern China. The genesis of China's architectural transformations can be attributed chiefly to religion and commerce.

The first church constructed by the Jesuits[4] on mainland China was Beijing's Church of the Immaculate Conception (1650) built by Schall von Bell. Macau's Church of Sao Paulo (1580), the earliest significant foreign building constructed by Europeans in China, was not technically on the mainland.[5] Adorning Sao Paulo's classical façade, constructed by Chinese and Japanese craftsmen, are details that evidence the first fusion of European and Chinese decorative motifs in architecture. On the top three tiers of the façade, above Ionic and Corinthian columns and tabernacles containing statues of Jesuit saints are ornate bas-reliefs depicting local designs, such as chrysanthemum, cherry, Chinese lions and Chinese inscriptions.

Architectural output by the Jesuits was not limited to religious structures. In the early eighteenth century the emperor invited Castiglione, Jean-Denis Attiret (1702–68) and Michel Benoist (1715–74) to design and build several major structures in European styles along the northern perimeter of the Chang Chun gardens inside the emperor's summer palace gardens of Yuan Ming Yuan outside Beijing. Set in extensive gardens in the style of Le Notre, containing a labyrinth, ponds and numerous fountains, the buildings were completed in a contemporaneous Baroque style. The Jesuits were competent designers and site managers, directing effectively the Chinese labour that constructed their churches and other structures. Although less attention has been paid to the Jesuits' building activities than to their other achievements in China, their architectural and constructional proficiency matched their scientific and artistic accomplishments.[6]

The stone and brick buildings constructed by the Jesuits in China possessed a physical permanence that endured long beyond the novel techniques and styles they employed, which had little lasting impact on Chinese building. At Yuan Ming Yuan, the Baroque structures in a private, royal setting were, as Tong Jun suggested two centuries later, 'executed for imperial pleasure', not an exercise in architectural education.[7] Although subsequently reproduced in some isolated cases by local artisans, Jesuit buildings could not represent any fundamental transition in building practices, just as the exotic amusements of Chambers's Pagoda at Kew and Nash's Royal Pavilion at Brighton affected no lasting impact in western architecture. Innovation in Chinese architecture, as occurred in Chinese painting, cannot therefore be attributed to the Jesuits.

Superseding religion as a catalyst for a more substantial and meaningful link between antiquity and modernity in China's built environment was commerce. Initial foreign encounters occurred at Macau in the early sixteenth century, whose physical disconnectedness from the mainland was significant for China's imperial court, which was ambivalent about European merchants within their sphere of influence. Forbidden from permanently residing in China, foreign merchants rented accommodation in or nearby China's maritime settlements. Needing storage facilities, the simple and architecturally innocuous warehouses on the island of Macau were the first structures to be built by Europeans in China. Before the conclusion of the first Opium War in 1842, Macau possessed the two archetypal foreign architectural typologies in China: religious and commercial.[8]

In 1757, Guangzhou (Canton) became the only Chinese port at which foreigners could conduct trade. Here the dominant dwelling type among foreigners was the

102 *Architecture and modernity*

factory, which occupied a strip of land along the riverfront outside the city wall.[9] For nearly two centuries on this 'microscopic space' was concentrated 'the greater portion of the trade, and almost all the diplomacy then current between China and the west'.[10] Like most structures built by foreign merchants in China before the establishment of permanent settlements, the physical character of the early factories was basic: 'flimsy structures of almost prehistoric simplicity and absolutely devoid of anything approaching grace or beauty'.[11]

Improvements in trade generated improvements in the quality of foreign buildings. By the nineteenth century, most of the factories were of a style termed locally and derisorily as 'compradoric', an expression derived from the fact that 'there were no foreign architects [so] the plans had to be drawn by the merchants themselves, with the assistance presumably of the Chinese architect or contractor. Probably the whole thing was managed by the compradore'.[12]

The compradoric style, like its namesake, was a product of Guangzhou, and represents an important milestone in the development of architecture and construction in China. Thomas Kingsmill (1837–1910), one of Shanghai's early foreign architects, first coined the phrase when he claimed that a contractor named Chop Dollar 'developed a style of compradoric architecture peculiar to the place'.[13] Evocative of the British colonial style or potentially linked to Portugal via Macau, the key characteristics of the compradoric style were a one- or two-storey building with a veranda on at least three sides of the building. Most buildings were constructed in wood and, later (or if the budget permitted), stone. Considered 'simple in the extreme'[14] to some and creating a 'grand and imposing appearance'[15] to others, the style divided opinion. Despite its inappropriateness in colder climes, it was taken north by foreign merchants as more ports were opened to foreign trade after the Treaty of Nanjing in 1842. Even in the twentieth century in Beijing it was noted that 'there had been a mushroom crop of foreign built houses, mostly in the compradoric style, which have not added either to the beauty or to the dignity of the Capital'.[16]

More important than taste was the impact of this building type on the development of the building industry and its functionality. Construction was undertaken by Cantonese contractors using local techniques, and the design and materials suited Guangzhou's sultry climate. Guangzhou's waterfront factories therefore represented not only the first collection of buildings on mainland China in a western style of architecture (some buildings 'retained marks of native origin'[17]) but also the first significant synthesis of Chinese building and construction methods with a foreign *other*.

Scene 2: The amateur and professional

The first architects to practise in China were from Europe (overwhelmingly from Britain) and untrained. Herein lies an important distinction between China's quasi-colonial contexts and formal colonial contexts. India and Singapore, for example, were assigned governors who not only governed new colonial territories, but also, as patrons of architecture, governed aesthetic taste in those territories and were careful to employ architects who were well established in the west. The Irish Palladian architect George Coleman (1796–1844), for example, was Singapore's first Government Superintendent of Public Works from 1833. Coleman's death in 1844, contemporaneous with the Treaty of Nanjing and the opening up of China's first treaty ports, marked what Stewart described as:

the end of a colonialized architecture secure in the basic elements of the Anglo-Palladian legacy ... the men to follow Coleman lacked the fixed support of any established architectural tradition. They would be surveyors and no longer 'architects' in the older sense of the word.[18]

In China's quasi-colonial context, the officially sanctioned architectural input found in the colonies – whether in a firmly established tradition or not – was even further removed from its foreign source and therefore lacked the uniformity or formality of colonial settlements. Nevertheless, although buildings in Guangzhou and Macau 'were run up rather than built',[19] even these architecturally rudimentary settings in the Chinese context was where 'ideas for architectural styles were borrowed' and where 'the best specimens of architectural talent [were] available'.[20] This changed when Hong Kong was established as a colony and it became a regional base for the construction industry. From the 1840s, Hong Kong provided China's mainland treaty ports with their 'architectural aid'.[21]

Mutual distrust and antipathy between the foreign and Chinese communities meant that most treaty ports were established outside the walls of existing Chinese settlements. Urban growth was unplanned until the Russians arrived in the last years of the nineteenth century and the Japanese literally built on their example and in so doing created some of the largest planned cities in the world at the time. Initially, however, foreign merchants were neither interested in nor experienced at laying the foundation of future cities. The spatial configuration of most foreign settlements emerged from ad hoc developments over protracted timeframes that are now sewn into the urban fabric of many modern Chinese cities. The origins of major roads and street networks often began with random or chance occurrences – the route of a dyke, a towpath or animal track. In China's case, since nearly all foreign settlements were the result of trade, the origins of these settlements were influenced by the construction of the first warehouses, which in turn were connected to the veins of trade by nearby wharves and jetties. Goods were transported from the hinterland along China's network of creeks, dykes and canals to storage facilities, between which simple paths were trod. The routes of these ancient waterways and simple trails have left an indelible mark in many of China's cities, becoming major urban thoroughfares or administrative boundaries.

Buildings in early foreign settlements were of little architectural significance except to demonstrate the inadequacies that persisted for many years in the building industry. The crude collaboration between the architecturally inexperienced foreign merchants and the Chinese labourers using often novel materials and methods was an inconvenient marriage of convenience rather than a deliberate attempt to fashion a construction industry founded on the modern professions of architecture, engineering and planning. The foreigner was entirely reliant on the labour, practical expertise and negotiating skills of the Chinese craftsman, while the Chinese craftsman gained from the foreign client employment and exposure to new constructional techniques. As time passed, outcomes improved. In 1875 one British traveller to Shanghai noted the 'the avidity with which the native builders, carpenters, and mechanics of every sort, compete with each other to win the remunerative employment which those buildings afford' and the extent to which their work provided the 'elegance and perfection which the cultivated tastes of the foreign architect demand'.[22]

104 *Architecture and modernity*

Improved trade facilitated by military force allowed merchants to supervise their businesses all year round, increasing the demand for property ownership rather than tenancy. Magnificent residences were built with magnificent profits, stimulating a buoyant property market that further fuelled construction. As tiny settlements of just a few merchant buildings evolved into established communities, the necessary components of a civil society slowly emerged. Places of worship, administration, leisure, residence and business followed. Towns gradually turned into cities, pre-eminent among which was Shanghai, halfway down China's coast and at the mouth of the Yangtze River.

The first foreign-trained architect to reside in Shanghai was, according to Kingsmill, A.F. Strachan,[23] who arrived in 1849 and 'introduced a marked style of his own, a version of the so-called Greek at that period fashionable in England'.[24] It was under Strachan, claims Kingsmill, 'the art of building made considerable progress, and a school of workmen, mostly Ningbo men, were developed who did some really excellent work'.[25] Kingsmill himself amply demonstrates the relatively pliable definition of *architect* among foreigners in China in the nineteenth century. Often quoted as being an architect, Kingsmill is also credited for being an engineer and geologist.[26] Having arrived in Hong Kong as a geologist, in 1860 he left for Shanghai where he became an architect, completing his first building on the corner of Nanjing Road and Sichuan Road in 1862.[27]

By the late nineteenth century Hong Kong and Shanghai had superseded Macau and Guangzhou as centres of western architectural example in China. Trained architects were increasingly responsible for the design of prominent buildings. Kingsmill, for example, designed Shanghai's Central Police Station (1891–94), 'a dignified building of red brick in the Early Renaissance style erected during 1891–94 from competitive designs'[28] said to be 'the finest building in Shanghai'.[29] Outside Shanghai and Hong Kong, few foreign settlements had resident architects until the Treaty of Tientsin (1860) opened up trade to northern China and made Tianjin the biggest sphere of influence, architecturally, for foreign practitioners in northern China. Tianjin's proximity to Beijing had an impact on its subsequent development, since it provided a refuge away from the political intensity of the capital for both foreigners and Chinese.

The architectural competence of early foreign practitioners in China could be judged either by their work or by whatever professional recognition they brought with them from their country of origin. In the context of Britain, which dominated the architectural scene in China until the early twentieth century, membership to the Royal Institute of British Architects (RIBA) provided the principal measure. The first practising member of the RIBA in China was William Kidner (1841–1900), graduate of University College London (UCL) and apprentice to Sir George Gilbert Scott (1811–78).[30] Kidner arrived in Shanghai in 1864 to oversee the design modifications for the proposed Holy Trinity Church designed by Scott, and bearing a striking resemblance to his contemporaneous high-Gothic Midland Grand Hotel fronting London's St Pancras Station (see Figure 6.1). Scott's design was to replace the original church 'so unskillfully built that the roof fell in and the building showed general signs of approaching collapse'.[31] However, as with Scott's designs for Mumbai University, it was deemed too extravagant. Kidner was enlisted to make the necessary modifications and joining him in economising Scott's scheme was John Myrie Cory (1846–93), a graduate of Pembroke College, Cambridge, and assistant to Scott from

Figure 6.1
Trinity Cathedral (1866), designed by Sir George Gilbert Scott and William Kidner.

Figure 6.2
The first Hong Kong and Shanghai Banking Corporation (HSBC) offices in Shanghai (1877) designed by William Kidner.

1867 to 1869. Cory and Kidner had a successful architectural partnership in Shanghai from 1875 to 1879, when Kidner finally returned to England.[32] One of Kidner's most famous designs is the Shanghai offices of the Hong Kong and Shanghai Bank (HSBC, 1877), a classically styled three-storey symmetrical structure with a colonnade on the ground floor and a large semi-circular portico (see Figure 6.2).

A contemporary of Cory and Kidner based in Hong Kong was the British architect, William Salway (1844–1902), who arrived in 1865. Salway established an architectural practice that later hired Clement Palmer in 1883 and the following year, Arthur Turner, a structural engineer who became a partner in 1891. Under the new title, Palmer & Turner, the firm became one of the most prolific architectural and engineering firms in south east Asia, with work throughout India, Malaysia, the Philippines, Singapore and even Australia.[33] Another early Hong Kong-based practice was Danby & Leigh (later Danby, Leigh & Orange, then just Leigh & Orange), established in the 1870s.[34]

In nineteenth-century China it was common for foreign architectural and engineering services to be combined, but this synthesis acquired an added potency when China embarked on a programme of industrialisation and, after 1896, foreigners were permitted to engage in industry. Robert Moorhead, an engineer who came to China in the 1880s to work on the railways in Manchuria, eventually settled in Shanghai and in 1895 went into partnership with William MacDonnell Mitchell Dowdall (1843), FRIBA, an architect and resident of Shanghai since 1883. In 1907, after a period working independently, Moorhead formed a partnership with Sidney Halse, ARIBA, a graduate of London's Royal Academy. Moorhead & Halse designed many buildings in Shanghai, including the Burlington Hotel, the McBain Building (1916) and industrial facilities such as the Shi-Hui Cloth Mill 'said to be the first of its kind in China'.[35]

Also drawn to China by its industrial potential was Gabriel James Morrison, a 'skilled English engineer who came out for the special purpose of laying down the Shanghai railway'.[36] Settling in Shanghai, Morrison founded the architectural and engineering firm, Morrison & Gratton in 1885 with his partner Frederick Montague Gratton (1859–1918), FRIBA. Gratton graduated in engineering in 1875

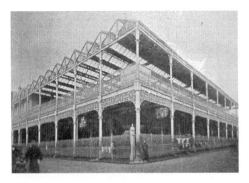

Figure 6.3
The Public Market (1899) on Shanghai's Nanjing Road, designed by Morrison & Gratton.

Figure 6.4
The Palace Hotel (1907) on Shanghai's Bund, designed by Scott & Carter.

and travelled to Shanghai in 1882 to manage the architectural element of Morrison's engineering firm. He designed Shanghai's Public Market on Nanjing Road, opened on 1 January 1899 (see Figure 6.3). In the same year, Morrison & Gratton hired UCL graduate Walter Scott (1860–1917), ARIBA, and became Morrison, Gratton & Scott from 1899 to 1902.

Scott was born in India and sent to England for his education, where he became a qualified architect in 1882 and continued his studies at UCL before arriving in Shanghai in 1889. Morrison, Gratton & Scott hired another British architecture graduate, James Christie (1877), ARIBA, a graduate of Glasgow School of Art. In 1902 Scott left Morrison & Gratton, taking Christie with him, to form his own firm with W.J.B. Carter, a partnership terminated by Carter's death in 1907. Despite their short existence, Scott & Carter designed many buildings in Shanghai, including, most famously, the Palace Hotel (1905–7) on Shanghai's Bund (see Figure 6.4).

Among the same generation was Gilbert Davies, who established a firm in Shanghai in 1896 before being joined by Thomas in 1899. Davies & Thomas designed many Shanghai residences and other larger buildings, including the offices of Butterfield and Swire, 'one of the most handsome structures on the French Bund',[37] and the Shanghai Mutual Telephone Company Ltd (1908).

By the twentieth century, the foreign architectural community was firmly established and its spiritual home was Shanghai. Although there were yet to be any trained Chinese architects and there was no way of acquiring a formal architectural education in China, a generation of home-grown architectural professionals was emerging among foreigners born in China to foreign or mixed heritage parents. Brenan Atkinson, son of the British manager of the Chinese powder mill at Lunghua, was a budding architect apprenticed to Thomas Kingsmill, with whom he worked for 14 years and designed the Central Police Station. He later established his own firm, Atkinson & Dallas, with Shanghai's former Assistant Municipal Engineer, Arthur Dallas, Vice-President of the Incorporated Institute of Architects in China and a member of the Shanghai Society of Engineers and Architects.[38] The establishment of professional associations, particularly the Shanghai Society of Engineers and Architects in 1901, were significant milestones in the formalisation of the architectural profession in China.

By 1909, the Society had 26 members and China's young engineers used it as a model when establishing their own society, the Chinese Society of Engineers, in 1912.

Atkinson & Dallas engaged in a variety of projects that evidenced the interconnectedness of foreign and Chinese architectural encounters. Atkinson's domicile status and his father's affinity with the Chinese likely played a part in securing several high-profile projects from Chinese clients, including the waterworks in the native city of Shanghai, the Chinese-owned Foo Fong Flour Mills, the first government paper mills in China at Lunghua, government buildings in Beijing, and the preparation of plans for the Chinese pavilion at the St Louis Exhibition in 1904. They also designed many residential buildings in Shanghai, including those for the Shanghai Land Investment Company, and many prominent buildings in the city, including Shanghai's Mixed Court (1899), the extension to the Astor House Hotel (1903), the Italian Consulate (1904), the China Mutual Life Assurance Company Building (1910), the Banque de l'Indo Chine (1914) and the New World (1914).

Another architect who resists the conventional categorisations of 'Chinese' or 'foreign' was Eric Cumine, born in Shanghai to a Scottish father and Chinese mother, whose interracial relationship would have been seen as taboo among the sanctimonious foreign communities cast adrift from distant homes. Cumine's father was an architect with his own firm, Cumine & Co, based at No. 7 Ningbo Road, Shanghai. In 1922, he sent Eric to the Architectural Association (AA) in London, where he proved to be an able student and keen sportsman, particularly in rugby, during his five-years study. Upon graduation in the summer of 1927, Eric received the Alec Stanhope Forbes Prize for the best colour work of the year and £50 for the Tite Prize. He returned to Shanghai in the 1930s and designed numerous buildings, including Dennis Apartments, a handsome nine-storey block on Bubbling Well Road.

It is insufficient to frame the experiences of Atkinson and Cumine as merely colonialism's inevitable consequence in the same way that so many whose privileged colonial upbringings helped catapult them on to a world stage. For a start, their home was not a colony, but more importantly, their experiences were born out of the early shoots of globalisation that operated outside the usual strictures of colonial rule and had given rise to cities like Shanghai – emergent global cities. Shanghai was the world of Ballard, not Kipling. Atkinson and Cumine's experiences can be likened to the renowned British modernist Wells Coates (1895–1958), whose upbringing in Tokyo and architectural tutelage by G.E.L. Gauntlett, an Englishman with a Japanese wife, would have a profound impact on his life and his architecture. Coates, like many other modernists, such as Frank Lloyd Wright, came close to witnessing China's tortuous struggle for artistic and political autonomy throughout the early twentieth century. In 1913 he left Japan for good, sailing to Vancouver via Qingdao with his father and in 1925 visited the seminal International Exposition of Modern Industrial and Decorative Arts in Paris where he would have witnessed Li Jipiao's design for the China pavilion (see Figure 7.9 and Figure 7.10).

Among the most prolific non-British architects practising in China at the turn of the century were the German architects Heinrich Becker and Carl Baedecker, the American architect Arthur Quintin Adamson, and the Japanese architect Yajo Hirano. Becker was originally from Munich and had spent five years in Cairo before arriving in Shanghai in 1898, whereupon he established a practice that later became a partnership with Baedecker, a friend from university in Munich. Becker & Baedecker were the preferred architects of the German community in China until Becker returned to Europe in 1911, having designed a variety of residences, offices and official buildings all over China. One of their most notable works, the Club Concordia (1907) in Shanghai, was designed in a Germanic style that drew heavily on the almost contemporaneous German Pavilion at the Paris Exposition of 1900 and was used again by Becker in his design for the Deutsch-Asiatische Bank in Beijing (1906–7) (see Figure 6.5). Adamson travelled to China in 1912 to oversee a radical programme of expansion of the YMCA in Asia, designing YMCAs in many of China's major cities from Shanghai to Kunming. Hirano was the most prominent among a growing community of Japanese architects in China, commissioned to design the Japanese Consulate (1911) in Shanghai.

Outside Shanghai, the only other treaty ports to possess sizeable architectural communities by the early twentieth century were Tianjin and Hankou. Tianjin's

Figure 6.5 The Club Concordia (1907), Shanghai, designed by Becker & Baedecker.

architectural practices and its architectural character reflected the settlement's multinational character. Administratively, no foreign settlement was more diverse than Tianjin. Nine foreign nations[39] possessed separate concessions in the city between its designation as a treaty port and the Second World War. The French firm Charrey & Conversy, founded in 1902, worked predominantly in the French Concession.[40] Loup & Young claimed to do anything 'from planning a palace or laying out of a township to selling or letting a house'[41] and prepared the master plans for the German and Belgian Concessions as well as municipal buildings for the Russians and a number of industrial buildings. The Hankou-based firm, Hemmings & Berkley, had an office in Tianjin, supervised by W.G. Parkin (ARIBA), a partner since 1922. Cook & Anderson, formed in 1913, designed a number of commercial and public buildings[42] and, like Loup & Young, conducted a lot of work in Beijing, including the buildings of the Dutch Legation, the YMCA, United Medical College and Hospital, and the Engineering College at Tongshan.[43]

Hankou, situated 600 miles up the Yangtze River, was the largest of China's river treaty ports. The settlement's most prolific architectural practice was Hemmings & Berkley, founded by R.E. Hemmings in 1909 and joined by Berkley soon after, until his death in 1917.[44] Between them they were responsible for 'most of the large structures'[45] in the city. Other firms included Nielsen & Malcolm, established in 1912 by H.R. Nielsen, a former member of Shanghai Municipal Council. He was joined in 1917 by a Scottish engineer D.A. Malcolm, who had arrived in China to work on the Taikoo Dock in Hong Kong. A British engineer, C.W. Burton, a Fellow of Royal Society of Arts and graduate of Glasgow's Royal Technical College, joined them in 1919, followed by R.N. Hewitt in 1920, who was in charge of the firm's architectural department.

The inseparability of western and Chinese architectural experiences applies not only to foreign buildings and their designers, but also to the impact that architecture had on those within and outside the profession.[46] Pang claims the great reformer, Kang Youwei, acquired his desire 'to pursue study (*sic*) of the west' after experiencing 'the grandeur of western architecture and the tidiness of the streets' in Hong Kong in the late nineteenth century.[47] The work of foreign architects had a similar impact on many aspiring Chinese students and influenced their decision to follow a career in architecture. On many occasions it also supported them through apprenticeships or employment. One prominent example was the American architectural practice, Murphy & Dana (Murphy, McGill & Hamlin from 1921), which opened a Shanghai office in 1918 and employed many returning Chinese graduates, including Fan Wenzhao, Zhuang Jun, Zhao Shen, Dong Dayou and, earliest of all, Lü Yanzhi (1894–1929) from Cornell University, who worked there until 1922.[48]

Scene 3: Experts and institutions

The first quarter of the twentieth century witnessed the foreign architectural community in China grow from a small and relatively informal professional group into a large and well-established institution. The period was characterised by a growing number and expansion of foreign settlements in China, which resulted in a growth in the size, quantity and sophistication of buildings.

Foreign architects increasingly worked in specialised teams with engineers, surveyors and contractors to complete larger and more complicated projects. Institutions such

110 *Architecture and modernity*

Figure 6.6 Arthur Adamson and Poy Gum Lee photographed in 1928 on the terrace of the Foreign YMCA, Shanghai.

as schools, universities and religious missions employed specialist subcontractors or established in-house teams of professional architects to undertake the complex jobs that only a few years earlier would have been carried out by untrained or relatively inexperienced foreign architects. The YMCA's China branch exemplified this process with its programme of expansion in Asia from 1910 and the formation of an architectural team under the supervision of Adamson who assumed the role of Director of YMCA's Building Bureau in China from 1912. One of his later appointments provides further evidence of the complex constellation of interrelationships in China's architectural community. Poy Gum Lee (1900–68) was born in New York's fledgling Chinatown in 1900 and attended the Pratt Institute in Brooklyn before studying architecture at Massachusetts Institute of Technology (MIT) and Columbia. From September 1921 to May 1922, Lee worked in the New York office of Murphy, McGill & Hamlin, where he gained valuable experience working on the firm's burgeoning China portfolio, including Beijing University. In 1923, he earned the opportunity to exercise this experience in China when appointed by the YMCA to run the China Building Bureau in Shanghai, which he did until 1927 when he formed his own practice (see Figure 6.6). Lee's experience as a Chinese New Yorker in China reflects just one of many personal and professional trajectories that challenge the binary relations that have framed China's architectural history until comparatively recently.[49]

The heterogeneity that characterised China's growing architectural community in the twentieth century could be read also in the architectural character of foreign settlements. It was possible to 'find a Greek temple, a Roman triumphal arch, a Gothic tower, a French palace, a Flemish gable, and several other types all grouped about the same square in a well known city'.[50] Architecture derived from assorted national sources that could be found throughout China and, collectively, often defined an urban ensemble: the curvaceousness of Orthodox churches and art nouveau in Harbin; the Teutonic character of Qingdao; the imposing 'neo-Renaissance' of commercial Shanghai; the tropical verandas of languid Guangzhou; and the sober neoclassicism of colonial Hong Kong. These varied urban entities physically reflected the diversity of foreign cultures with a presence in China and evidenced China's quasi-colonial condition. They also caused the evolution of these sites to be much less coherent and homogeneous than the more conventional colonial environments of India, south east Asia, Africa or South America. Furthermore, they were quite distinct from the Chinese-administered areas that invariably surrounded them, a disparity that Bertrand Russell noted:

> Often one passes through a gate, suddenly, from one to the other; after the cheerful disordered beauty of the old town, Europe's ugly cleanliness and Sunday-go-to-meeting decency make a strange complex impression, half-love and half-hate.[51]

Architecture was frequently used as an indication of a settlement's relative development. The varied descriptions in the local press depict both the prevailing architectural variety, as well as voicing doubts about its quality: German Renaissance, Tudor, Italian-style, Spanish revival, south Florentine, aristocrat Spanish-style, modern Greek Renaissance, English Renaissance, neo-Renaissance, free Renaissance, Early English were all used to describe different buildings throughout China from the early twentieth century. To the more critical eye such buildings were nothing more than 'atrocities perpetrated under the label "foreign-style buildings"',[52] or, as one architect wrote of Beijing's foreign legation in 1919, 'every variety of western hideousness can be studied in detail, from the simple biscuit box type to the economically pretentious'.[53]

The ambition and extent of the architectural development depended largely on the commercial stature of the settlement. The contrast between the largest and smallest treaty ports was extreme. Smaller ports, such as Jiujiang and Yingkou, displayed markedly less foreign character and their physical appearance remained relatively diminutive, with a small number of storehouses lining the riverbank to form a miniature 'bund' but with few structures of architectural significance. In larger ports such as Hankou, the architectural character of foreign settlements usually comprised a few houses on the riverbank 'each with its handsome columns, porticos, and verandas'.[54] In contrast to Russell's perspective, foreign impressions usually flattered their settlements at the expense of the Chinese surroundings: 'one's heart rises with pleasure at the sight – in juxtaposition with that obscene monster the native city – of our pretty little English concession with the charm of its soft turf, its neat gravel road, its park-like avenue, and its splendid houses!'.[55] Hankou's multinational character could be observed from its riverfront, where architecture defined the British, Russian, French, German and Japanese Concessions: the British had their 'five-storied mass of granite with a severity of outline [and] pillared and much architraved (*sic*) splendours of other buildings', the Russians had their 'Byzantine-like structures', and the French had their 'red-brick buildings in French style'.[56] The much larger Chinese settlement received no description whatsoever.

The pinnacle of foreign architectural production in China, and an exemplar of China's quasi-colonial settlements, was Shanghai, though 'it would always be a moot point whether in the eastern Hemisphere there might be a doubt as to whether Shanghai or Hong Kong had the honour of being the hub of that Hemisphere'.[57] Both foreign settlements were formally established upon the signing of the Treaty of Nanjing in 1842, but in 1857 one event 'immeasurably contributed to the future greatness and present preponderating influence of Shanghai over every other part of China at which Foreigners had touched'.[58] Lingering hostilities towards foreigners boiled over in Guangzhou where a number of British factories were razed, leading to the Second Opium War in 1860. The consequent signing of the Treaty of Tientsin opened up the 'Yangtze Ports' and Shanghai, at the river's mouth, was hit by 'a fever of speculation'.[59] Hong Kong's distinction as a colonial territory, like that of Taiwan, causes it to fall outside the scope of this study. Although distinct and yet inevitably interconnected with experiences in mainland China, Hong Kong and Taiwan were more akin to conventional colonies than any political or territorial context on the mainland and warrant separate studies that, over time, will form vital parts of the larger landscape created by China's architectural encounters with modernity. Their relative colonial detachment from events and architectural developments in China is exemplified by their experiences after 1949, when Hong Kong's almost entirely British architectural community was transformed by China's émigré architects with their kaleidoscopic national, cultural and professional backgrounds, and Taiwan became a place of exile for the ousted Nationalist Party.

Shanghai's first foreign settlement was defined on 20 September 1846 as a 'British Settlement' covering an area of 180 acres. In 1848 it was enlarged to 470 acres.[60] The boundaries of the adjacent American Settlement, on the opposite bank of Suzhou Creek, were not formally agreed until long after it had been merged with the British Settlement to form an amalgamated International Settlement in 1863 of over 1,000 acres.

To the south was the 'French Ground', initially a 164-acre site situated between the British Settlement and the walled Chinese city.[61] On 29 October 1861, when only four foreign buildings were said to have existed in the French area,[62] the French were granted a 23-acre extension to what was now termed a 'concession', lengthening the prized riverfront from 180 metres to 630 metres. The French Concession was small in comparison to the British Settlement, but although underdeveloped for many years and almost exclusively Chinese in appearance until well into the twentieth century, it remained strategically important. The greatest impact the French had on the built environment in the early years of settlement was through their religious missions, who built several churches in and around the French Concession, including the St Francis Xavier Cathedral (1849) designed by Father Nicholas Massa, the mission chapel (1847) and church (1851) in Xu Jia Wei, and St Joseph's designed by Father Hélot Louis (1862) (see Plate 12).

By the end of the nineteenth century, the British and French pressured the Chinese for large extensions to their settlements. In May 1899, the International Settlement grew by 1,908 to the west and by 1,896 acres to the east, making it 5,583 acres in total – the biggest it would ever be. On 27 January 1900, the French Concession was enlarged by 171 acres, almost doubling in size, but a further massive extension on 20 July 1914 resulted in it penetrating deep into the countryside as far as, but not including, the French Catholic Mission at Xu Jia Hui, which by now boasted the imposing St Ignatius Cathedral (1910), designed by MacDonnell Mitchell Dowdall.

Shanghai's settlement extensions were both the cause and effect of rapid improvement in trade conditions from the end of the nineteenth century. From 1895 to 1905, trade through Shanghai doubled, increasing by 30 per cent in just one year from 1904 to 1905. Shanghai alone accounted for more than half of foreign trade with China, which was then still dominated by British interests in shipping, banking, insurance, tea, cotton and silk. Economic growth stimulated building. The number of plans for new buildings submitted to Shanghai's Municipal Council rose dramatically during this period and especially after the settlement extension of 1899, from 5,672 in 1903 to 6,599 in 1904.[63] The Municipal Council blamed 'over building' in these years 'combined with depressed trade and the Revolutionary movement'[64] for the subsequent slump from 1907 to 1913, though in practice domestic strife in China always caused the foreign settlements to prosper.[65]

In 1916, when Shanghai was said to have 'made more material progress in the past three years than in any other six years of its history',[66] so great was:

> the demand for residence sites that many roads which were once dismissed as being too far out for such use now are fringed with handsome structures of brick, concrete and stucco, many of them surrounded by beautiful lawns and gardens where only two years ago the Chinese agriculturalist pursued the even tenor of his truck farming.[67]

Many of the sumptuous merchant villas that lined the International Settlement's Bubbling Well Road, noted one foreign observer, were 'founded on the remains of what was once a Chinese bourgeois home'.[68]

Improving trade was reflected in building statistics. Comparing the first quarters of two record-breaking years, 1906 and 1914, 1,350 and 2,394 houses were constructed respectively. In 1914–15, the Municipal Council issued over 23,000 building permits, causing 'former residents, returning, to say that they scarcely can believe that the city is that which they left only a few years ago'.[69]

Shanghai's development in the early twentieth century precipitated the formation of the most significant site of modernity in China before the Second World War. China's largest and most cosmopolitan city became the country's commercial and industrial centre. The importation or manufacture of modern materials, construction techniques and components caused it to be the site of all architectural innovations, whether in the use of new ideas or materials. Shanghai was the undisputed centre of China's Construction industry. The Shanghai Society of Engineers and Architects had 26 members in 1909 and by the late 1920s this had increased to 45.[70]

The Russo-Chinese bank (1902) by Becker and R. Steel of Yokohama on Shanghai's Bund was the first non-industrial building in China constructed in steel and concrete (see Figure 6.7). It was also the first in China to use elevators. Three years earlier, Shanghai's steel-framed Public Market designed by Gratton was built with 575 tons of steel and glass shipped from London (see Figure 6.3). In 1908, the Shanghai Mutual Telephone Company headquarters, designed by Davies & Thomas, was China's first office building constructed entirely from reinforced concrete. Eight years later, China's first office building constructed using a steel frame was the Union Assurance Company of Canton (1913–16), designed by Palmer & Turner (see Plate 13).

Globally, it had long been understood that the use of a frame, whether of steel or reinforced concrete, allowed for significant improvements in the form and function of

Figure 6.7 The Russo-Chinese bank (1902) in Shanghai designed by Becker and R. Steel of Yokohama.

Figure 6.8 Shanghai skyline depicted in a Christmas greeting published in 1933 by the Shanghai Builders' Association.

modern buildings, enabling the overall structure to be taller, lighter and spatially more flexible and efficient. Such developments were particularly beneficial in Shanghai, built on nothing but hundreds of metres of the Yangtze's soft alluvial deposits. Even in 1920, engineers claimed 'Shanghai can only stand six floors, London sixty floors, New York and Hong Kong any number'.[71] Within a decade, the high-rise would be one of the defining images of modern Shanghai, an extraordinary expression of metropolitan modernity that remains just as potent in the twenty-first century (see Figure 6.8).

Act 2

Scene 4: The Russians and Japanese

Manchuria was classic frontier territory – the contested no-man's land on colonialism's global chessboard. Cast adrift from China by the Great Wall, the Manchus finally breached this monument to engineered endurance to establish China's last imperial dynasty, the Qing (1644–1911). Britain was keen to open north-east China to international trade and the Treaty of Tientsin (1858) formally achieved this objective, establishing Yingkou (Newchwang) as a treaty port and the region's pre-eminent commercial port until the twentieth century. Over the next century, Manchuria would experience some of the most remarkable architectural encounters driven by a determined vision of modernity not from the west, but from the east.

Railways were an essential component in the machinery of modernity and in few places on earth were they as influential or ambitious as in Manchuria during the first half of the twentieth century. Their iron filaments extended deep into uncharted territories and extracted the resources demanded and devoured by modern industry. Fossil fuels, metal ores and agricultural produce depended on continuous columns of railway wagons shunting their cargoes to the nearest seaport and delivering them into new trade routes that spanned the globe. The British were the first to try to impose railways on China and succeeded in doing so in Manchuria in 1894, breaching the Great Wall at Shanhaiguan while laying the Beijing to Shenyang (Mukden) railway in an attempt to connect Tianjin and Yingkou along Manchuria's southern coastline. Skirting Manchuria's northern border was Russia's Trans-Siberian railway, the longest rail route in the world and the ultimate embodiment of modernity, linking Europe with the Far East for the first time. With construction starting in 1890, one witness marvelled a decade later: 'Since the Great Wall of China, the world has seen no material undertaking of equal magnitude.'[72]

For some eminent Chinese, the benefits of this new iron horse were clear, not least the government official and military general Li Hongzhang (1823–1901), who masterminded various modernisation programmes in China. Manchuria's fate would be decided by his diplomacy and defined by the railways he championed.

The laying of China's nascent railways coincided with China and Japan going to war over Korea. Japan's victory in 1895 and the subsequent Treaty of Shimonoseki permanently altered the course of China's modernisation by preparing the conditions for unprecedented construction and destruction – modernity's loyal bedfellows. Japan acquired parts of Manchuria's coastline on the Liaodong Peninsula, as well as several islands in the China Sea, including Taiwan (Formosa). The generous treaty terms not only disgraced China's ailing Qing government, but also rattled the western powers. France, Germany and Russia performed the 'Triple Intervention' that demanded

116 *Architecture and modernity*

Japan withdraw its claim on the Liaodong Peninsula and the port of Lüshun. On 5 May 1895, Japan bowed to the pressure in exchange for a larger indemnity. Japan's loss of face would be avenged, for which Russia would pay the heaviest price.

The following year, Li Hongzhang visited St Petersburg to attend the celebrations marking the Coronation of Emperor Nicholas II, Russia's last monarch. During the trip, Li negotiated the secret Li–Lobanov Treaty (June 1896), establishing a Sino-Russian alliance motivated principally by mutual antipathy toward Japan. The bonds of friendship between China and Russia were formed around a common enemy and strengthened by Russia's role in Japan's retrocession of the Liaodong Peninsula.

Li travelled to Russia with the draft of an unpublished accord dubbed The Cassini Convention.[73] Count Cassini understood Manchuria to be the key to Russian dominance in Asia and in the race to seize control of the region masterfully wrong-footed Britain. Russia's Trans-Siberian Railway had been forced to follow a wide arc that circumvented Manchuria – a costly detour that Cassini was determined to reduce and ultimately exploit. The Cassini Convention was therefore a blueprint for a shortcut that went through, rather than round, Manchuria, carving 500 miles off the journey from the newly established Pacific port of Vladivostok to St Petersburg. In an atmosphere of scheming, subterfuge and secrecy, the China Eastern Railway (CER), or *Kitaiskaya Vostochnaya Jeleznaya Doroga* (*Chinese Eastern Iron-road*)[74] was created following the signing of the Li–Lobanhov Treaty on 28 September 1896. With the help of Italian experts, Russian engineers constructed bridges and tunnels (the longest of which was over 3 kilometres) and nearly 100 stations in threading this vast line of communication across northern China.[75]

The Li–Lobanhov Treaty not only granted Russia the right to build their railway, it also allowed them to exploit the mining potential in the region and reserved their right to concentrate military forces in the port of Lüshun and the neighbouring settlement of Talienwan (Dalian Wan, Dalian Bay) in case she 'should find herself suddenly involved in a war'.[76] Construction of the CER began on 28 August 1897, marking the height of Russia's fleeting but fundamental involvement in Manchuria and the first episode in half a century of foreign meddling that culminated in Manchuria's severance from China and Japan's attempt to fashion it into a uniquely modern independent state.

The success of the Li–Lobanhov Treaty whetted Russia's appetite for control of the region. With Russia's Far Eastern Fleet paralysed in the frozen port of Vladivostok during the winter, it needed a warm water alternative. The obvious candidate was Lüshun, a natural deep-water port at the tip of the Liaodong Peninsula, which the Japanese wrested from China after their victory in the Sino-Japanese War, only for it to be humiliatingly returned following the Triple Intervention.

Two and half years after pressuring Japan to surrender its claim on the Liaodong Peninsula, Russia's Pacific Fleet arrived off the coast of Lüshun in the prologue to a performance of two acts combining manipulative military coercion and deft diplomatic courting. The imposing presence of the Russian navy moored at Lüshun provided sufficient coercion, while Russia's diplomats courted Li Hongzhang and his aides. On 27 March 1898, Russia's nimble performance resulted in the Russo-China Convention that leased to Russia the ice-free ports of Lüshun and neighbouring Talienwan, and the surrounding sea and hinterland 'for such a distance as is necessary to secure proper defence of this area' for a period of 25 years with the option of further extensions.[77]

Russia renamed Lüshun Port Arthur, which became a naval port for exclusive use by Russian and Chinese vessels. The surrounding area was renamed the Kwantung Leased Territory. Talienwan became Dalny (Dalian), Russian for 'Far Place', a moniker that even the earliest visitors noted would 'lose [its] former significance in our easy, come-and-go modern methods of communication'.[78] Dalian would become a commercial port open to foreign trade.

However, the masterstroke that sealed Russia's grip on much of Manchuria was the clause permitting Russia to connect the China Eastern Railway (CER) with Dalian, thereby creating the basic structure of the railway network that would 'stagger the imagination in reach and potentiality' as it transformed the region over the next half a century.[79] The original railway network was shaped like the letter 'T', with the CER crossing Manchuria in an east–west direction connecting Europe and Asia and, from a point approximately midway along this line, a 943-mile track extending southwards to Dalian. The new line turned the Trans-Siberian Railway from an internal enterprise serving Russia's modernising programme into what contemporary commentators described as:

> One of the greatest arteries of traffic the world has ever seen [and] one of the chief factors in shifting the centre of gravity of the world's trade. . . . The eventual effect will be colossal, for the railway will open up enormous underdeveloped regions, and will facilitate the conveyance of passengers, correspondence, and the lighter class of goods; a most important matter when it is a question of connecting within a fortnight's time the capital of Europe with those of China, Japan and Corea (*sic*). A great portion of the eastern section of the line will pass through a splendid country, – Manchuria, – a white man's country, and full of valuable resources.[80]

On 11 April 1898, a Russian engineer named Shidrovski arrived at the junction of this triple spur with a group of 20 men. The only buildings of note nearby were a Chinese distillery on the banks of the Songhua River and approximately 20 huts centred around a wine shop, called the 'Hsiangfang' (frying pan), with other houses dotted along the river.[81] Shidrovski is said to have bought the wine shop and surrounding dwellings and established the headquarters of the CER's construction group. The arrival of the railway would transform the barren landscape into an entirely new settlement: Harbin, a name said to be from the Mongolian, Ha-la-bin. Within months of its official foundation on 28 May 1898, Harbin became a bustling garrison town populated by several thousand Russians associated with the construction and protection of the railway under the leadership of Duke Hilkov and Chief Engineer Ignace. It would soon become one of the largest cities in Manchuria and among the first in China to be subject to modern urban planning.

At the other end of the line, on the coast, Russian railway engineers disembarked not at Dalian, which was surrounded by hills that would take months for the new railway line to traverse, but at a site on the Liao River upstream from Yingkou and almost half way between the ancient capital of Shenyang and Dalian. From this point it was easier and quicker to import all the necessary materials for the construction of the railway in both directions (north and south), while at the same time preparing Dalian. By 1899, the Russians had built a 14-mile branch line linking the river port to the main line at Dashiqiao (near Yingkuo), through which a 'huge quantity of rails,

118 *Architecture and modernity*

sleepers and other materials for the construction of the main line was rushed'.[82] 'Never, perhaps, in the whole history of colonization,' claimed one writer, 'has so much money been so recklessly squandered as in Manchuria'.[83] The iron rails were not like those on the Trans-Siberian route that weighed 48 pounds per yard, but much heavier, sturdier and costlier 65 pounders that would support the anticipated speed and weight of the massive American locomotives that were expected to race from Harbin to Dalian in 15 hours. The cost of the railway was estimated at £30,000 per mile, three times the average price of railway construction. Over 100,000 Chinese workers found employment on the CER, desperate to flee the poverty in their homeland and indulge in 'the golden shower of Russian roubles' emanating from the 'vast stream of gold that poured into North Manchuria from Europe'.[84]

Scene 5: Architecture and planning

In 1901 it had taken 17 days to travel from Yingkou to St Petersburg on an unreliable and uncomfortable railway. On 1 July 1903, the first trains started running along the shortened Trans-Siberian Railway, reducing the journey to 13 days on 'one of the most luxurious trains in the world'.[85] Passengers could travel from London to Shanghai via the CER in 18 days compared with the sea route, which took 31 days and was as much as double the price.

The new route to Europe accelerated the development of Dalian and Harbin. Unlike the unplanned, cosmopolitan and commercial treaty ports throughout China, Dalian and Harbin were the first sites in China to experience the implementation of modern urban planning. The same military engineers assigned to the railway were called upon to make plans for these cities. These early skeletal plans were swiftly furnished with architectural solutions to problems of a uniquely modern kind – factories, railway stations, telephone and telegraph facilities, radio stations, hotels and international ports.

Observing Harbin's development in 1904, one visitor noted:

> An Englishman or American would immediately have his commercial imagination stimulated by the position of the town. 'Here,' he would say, 'is the very place for a big city; let us make haste and build it.' The Russian says: 'We have plenty of space to fill up before we get to Kharbin. If Kharbin is to be a great place, it will become so all in good time.'[86]

And so it was that despite the considerable fortune spent on Harbin's early planning, the town grew somewhat haphazardly into a city over subsequent decades.

The initial plan of Harbin was determined by a combination of natural and man-made features – the navigable Songhua River created the northern boundary, to the south of which the two railway lines converged in the form of a three-pointed star that stretched to the farthest corners of Manchuria in the direction of Europe, the Pacific and the China Sea.

Comparisons between Manchuria and America's Midwest were common, especially among western observers and it is easy to see why. The shared experience of vast exploitable, rich and fertile territories facilitated by the expansion of railways and shipping on navigable waterways was obvious. But, despite these similarities, Manchuria was not the Midwest. The region was dominated by Russia and for this reason, cautioned Whigham,

One remembers Kharbin (*sic*) is not in America.... These three lines of railway are Russian lines, which would never have been built save for strategic purposes. This wide navigable river leads, not to a Chicago nor to a St Louis, but to Khabarofsk, to the Amur, a Russian river and finally to the sea, but to the Sea of Okhotsk.[87]

The original town of Harbin, which soon became known as the Old (Starrie) Town, was planned by the engineer Obromievski and laid out on 4,000 hectares of raised ground to the south of the later settlement in 1898. However, within weeks of their arrival, these pioneers witnessed devastating summer floods that inundated vast swathes of land that was to accommodate their future city. The deluge was a timely occurrence that determined the early layout of Harbin.

By 1901, a New Town (Novui Gorod) was planned on 3,000 hectares of raised ground west of the Old Town adhering to modern urban planning principles emanating from Europe and North America. Mr Miller, a US Consul, later described these plans in a report to Washington as a 'record of the wonderful enterprise worth special mentioning in the history of modern town-building in the nineteenth century'.[88]

Streets were laid out in a regular and orderly pattern, with a combination of rectilinear, diagonal, and curved routes converging at, or radiating from, key sites, such as parks or civic buildings to create a grand and dignified appearance. A smattering of public gardens provided a 'few cherished trees and plots of grass [to] relieve the eye, and a military band sometimes played without positive offence to the ear'.[89] The result was a city with a variegated urban grain formed by a series of differently scaled open spaces and roads, from monumental boulevards to quiet backstreets.

By 1903, the town's evenly mixed civilian population of Russians and Chinese had reached 20,000 and, despite opposition from city planners, an additional 5,000 hectares of low-lying land was given over to development between the New Town and the river. Here emerged the commercial district, Pristan (quayside), populated by the town's growing army of merchants and industrialists, who shared this cheap but inauspicious floodplain with the thriving Chinese settlement of Fuchiatien.[90] These suburbs, connected flimsily to the New Town by a single road bridge over the railway line, were intended only to be temporary, but the early builders constructed their shops and homes with permanence in mind, creating Harbin's primary business district and Manchuria's liveliest commercial centre.

Harbin's rapid development coincided with the global proliferation of the biomorphic style of art nouveau, which furnished the town with the most concentrated collection of this contemporaneous global style anywhere in China and perhaps even the world. Less than a decade after the Belgian architect Victor Horta (1861–1947) had unveiled his flamboyant organic 'whiplash' style in his design for the Hôtel Tassel (1893) in Brussels, the seeds of this style travelled the length of the Trans-Siberian Railway and blossomed in the unlikely setting of Manchuria.

Hotels, shops, department stores, offices and residences built by the Russians in Harbin at the turn of the century adopted this ostentatious aesthetic, which became a signature of the CER in its early years. Some of the most expressive and original examples of art nouveau in Harbin include the city's railway station, the administrative buildings on Bolshoi Avenue designed by D.A. Kryzhanovsky from St Petersburg, and, earliest of all, the residences built for the railway's supervisors (see Figure 6.9 and Plate 14). Constructed in wood and plastered stone, the organic, irregular and

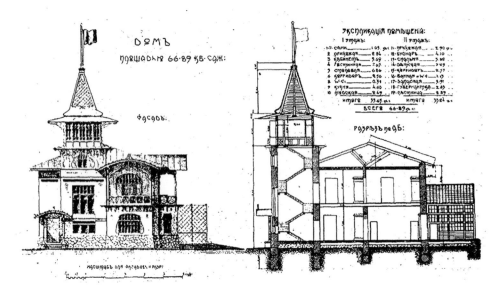

Figure 6.9 Architectural drawing of one of Harbin's many residences for the staff of Russia's China Eastern Railway, designed in the early 1900s in an art nouveau style.

playful character of some of these dwellings contrasts sharply with the pompous reserve projected by neoclassicism that proliferated in China's other foreign settlements from the same period.

By 1913, Harbin's population was 68,549, of which 34,313 were Russian. The city acquired a sense of identity forged by the vicissitudes of the CER's construction and the Boxer campaign. Just as had occurred in many of China's other treaty ports, such as Shanghai's Volunteer Corps, a mythology was constructed around the hardship and sacrifice of veterans that laid the foundation of Harbin's identity and vindicated Russia's claims to the city. By the 1910s, these pioneers had slowly helped to recast Harbin as a place of permanent abode rather than transient opportunity, as well as a place of emergent modernity. Around 1906, a Russian-Jewish merchant, Iosif Kaspe, commissioned the architect Sergei Vensan to design the city's most luxurious hotel 'Moderne', which opened for business in 1914 and even contained a cinema and theatre hall (see Figure 6.10). Harbin had become, as one Russian writer put it, a type of colony: 'If a colony implies a land remote from the metropolis, a land that represents a particle of fatherland transplanted to a foreign country, then, Harbin, with the Chinese Eastern Railway, is now the first and unique Russian colony.'[91]

This quasi-colony shared with many true colonies the common experience of having its fate decided not by events taking place around it, but by matters nearer to the heart of empire. Few events had a bigger impact on Harbin than the Russian Revolution. The exodus of hundreds of thousands of White Russians had a staggering affect on Harbin, particularly its cultural life, which was stimulated greatly by the wealth and expertise of these new arrivals. Many of these aristocratic refugees would later move south to Shanghai where they instigated an equally momentous conversion, transforming the physical, commercial and cultural character of the French Concession in the 1920s, and invigorated the social life of the entire city.

Foreign settlements before 1912 121

Figure 6.10 Harbin's hotel 'Moderne' (1914), designed by Sergei Vensan.

At the other end of the CER in Dalian, the Russians planned to 'build a modern city and port on gigantic scale [*sic*]'[92] that would be the only harbour north of Shanghai at which ocean-going liners could discharge their cargoes. Planned as a free port, the speed of Russia's progress not only 'startled the world' but, as one American writer explained, especially 'waked-up our British friends, as well as sorely depressed their spirits'.[93] Yingkou's commercial standing, like that of the foreign powers with vested interests in the treaty port and throughout Manchuria, was seriously undermined and never recovered.

Mr Kerbech, an engineer from the CER, planned Dalian with the assistance of the future Governor and Chief of Engineering Construction, Mr Saharoff, who had overseen the construction of the Egelsheld Wharf in Vladivostok.[94] Kerbech and Saharoff were responsible for introducing China to modern town planning. With a budget of 20 million roubles, their ambitious scheme covered an area of 100sq km, proving the Russian government was 'determined to build itself a metropolis complete in every detail. . . . Another power would have been content to build its railway and begin the harbour tentatively, and let trade do the rest. Not so Russia. Dalny is to spring into the world full grown.'[95]

'The manifold requirements of modern city construction,' observed the American writer Clarence Cary when visiting Dalian in 1903, were 'created at demand in double-quick order, by the exercise of an alert and intelligent foresight, backed with a generous purse'.[96] Attempting to make sense of the senseless, many commentators drew comparisons with the familiarity of western precedents. One American consul later described the scheme as 'a European city admitting a population of 40,000'[97] and another claimed it was modelled after Paris with 'the main streets radiating from several circles like the spokes of a wheel, and intersected by narrower streets'.[98] But Dalian cannot be seen as a western incarnation. To regard it as such is to misunderstand it.

As the journalist Whigham described:

> There is something splendid and Oriental and almost barbaric in [its] wholesale creation. . . . Even in its present embryo state Dalny is one of the marvels of the present age. For surely nowhere else in the world has a Government built a city and port of such dimensions on absolutely barren soil, hundreds of miles from its own borders, without a penny's worth of trade already in existence to justify the expense.[99]

The Russian plan was to create a complete and modern city on Chinese soil. Witnessing the nascent settlement in 1903, Whigham foresaw:

> a large seaport town with ample docks and wharves, with a splendid sea frontage and convenient railway depôt, with wide streets and boulevards and shady gardens, with a commercial quarter that will eclipse every foreign settlement in the East and a residential quarter which might grace Manchester or Philadelphia. . . . Those who love analogies see in Dalny the future New York of the East.[100]

However, unlike the great planned cities of Europe that had to contend with medieval foundations or the early urban plans of the United States of America that were devised in an era before railways, power stations, factories and unfurnished with electricity, gas and water supplies, Dalian, like Harbin, was a twentieth-century city and, as such, not only combined contemporary urban planning theory with the accoutrements of urban modernity, but was itself a product of modernity – the terminus 'of the greatest railway in the world'.[101]

Modernity's assimilation into contemporary urban planning was exemplified at Dalian by the railway and the vital link it had with the port. As the primary conduit for goods into and out of Manchuria through the city's wharfs, the railway was not a clumsy incision compromising an established urban plan but an essential part of an entirely new one. The completion in 1904 of the CER terminus made Dalian the gateway to Manchuria, placing the railway station as one of the principal architectural components of the urban and cultural landscape.

At Dalian the Russians planned and began to build Manchuria's first electrical power plant, the first waterworks and modern brick foundries that furnished the town with the building blocks of its first 'European-style' structures. The city's earliest significant buildings, including the town's first residential quarter, were constructed to the north of this railway line in a small area of land that jutted out into the bay and formed the initial phase of the Russian city plan.

Having erected a number of imposing edifices north of the railway, the Russians set about implementing the city plan to the south. The heart of Dalian's urban plan was an arterial circus in the city centre from which major roads radiated (see Figure 6.11). It was to be a modern and rational civic landscape that created a sense

Foreign settlements before 1912 123

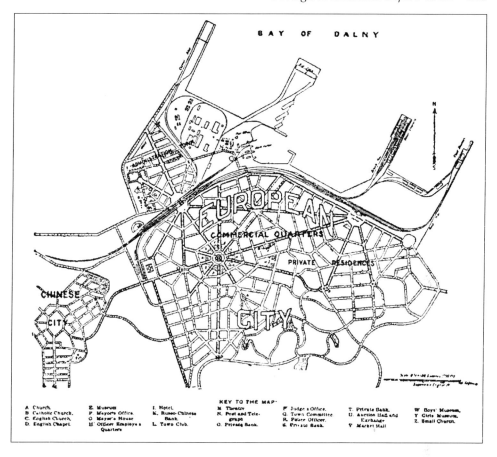

Figure 6.11 Russian plan of Dalian showing the 'European City' centre defined by the central circus surrounded by the railway and the port, and the separate 'Chinese city' to the west.

of formality and grandeur through the arrangement of broad boulevards connected at key nodes and junctions often landscaped as public parks, forming a more dense urban grain with minor streets serving residential or smaller commercial functions. Streets were sealed, guttered, paved on either side and electrically lit. Tramways, telegraph lines and a clean water supply were laid, and public parks were ample in size and number to accommodate the city's future growth (see Figure 6.12). Russia's bold ambitions at Dalian created the urban model for future modern planning through Manchuria, executed not by them, but by the Japanese.

Kerbech and Saharoff's plan was the subject of considerable professional approbation internationally. The British architect Inigo Triggs included it in his seminal book *Town Planning: Past, Present and Possible* (1909), where it features alongside Christopher Wren's plan for the rebuilding of London after the Great Fire in 1666. To Triggs, Dalian was:

> An interesting example of this type of the combined radial and chessboard system.... There are many diagonal arterial thoroughfares. The crossing points

124 *Architecture and modernity*

Figure 6.12 Russian Dalian in 1903 showing the public parks, paved roads and many buildings under construction.

of the different systems of radials create a number of local centres, the most important of which has been planned in front of the railway station. In the heart of the town a circular public space has been laid out, with ten long straight streets converging upon it. Built round this, with excellent effect, as may be imagined, there are ten structures, each in its separate block. The city is divided into various quarters, the Administration Town on the north, with three broad thoroughfares leading to the railway station; the commercial quarters in the centre of the city, radiating from one large rond-point round which are gathered the important public buildings; the private residences and parks, grouped together on the south-east, and the Chinese quarters in a separate city on the south-west.[102]

However, only a small proportion (around 8sq km) of Kerbech and Saharoff's plan was ever realised. The scene in August 1902 was of 'long empty roads, scaffolded buildings, and up-turned surfaces [that] had rather an air of inchoate desolation' and projected the 'somewhat melancholy expression which is a concomitant of dishevelled habitation-places wherever an appropriate sum of human life and endeavour is lacking, whether because this is yet to come, or has had its little day.'[103]

The Chinese settlement was less formal and, in a gesture that mirrored colonial settlements across the globe, was set 'aloof' from the Russian area by the large public park to ensure 'the multitudinous poorer classes of the indigenous folk [were] not to swarm among foreign residents as they have elsewhere been imprudently suffered to do' in their 'unpleasant and detrimental' manner in cities like Hong Kong and Shanghai.[104] 'Racial prejudice was a factor' in Russia's urban planning, where new towns were established away from existing Chinese settlements so that they did not have to 'mingle too closely with the natives'.[105]

In their planning of Dalian, Russia had visions of a fine modern city, but the reality was that Dalian was 'a "boom" town without any reason for a "boom"'.[106] Cary wrote:

> It is not a common thing in the line of human endeavour to evolve a sea-port, railway terminal city, with all the essential modern appliances, including ample provision for future residence, trading, and manufacturing facilities, before the advent of an expected population.[107]

There was something not only novel and audacious about Russia's ambitions but also chimerical. In the towns along the 943 miles of track that separated Dalian and Harbin it was claimed the Russians 'gave no thought to the construction of modern towns' and in the Chinese settlements 'not the slightest indication of modern town planning could be seen anywhere'.[108] Modernity had arrived in Manchuria but it was embryonic and unevenly distributed. A much larger and more immediate impact would be made by modernity's omnipresent companion: war.

In a state of growing unease at Russia's desirousness for neighbouring Korea, Japan proposed to Russia the establishment of a buffer zone between Manchuria and Korea. Russia's refusal to bow to Japanese pressure tested Japan's patience beyond breaking point. As occurred ten years earlier against China and would occur again four decades later at Pearl Harbor, they seized the initiative and launched a surprise pre-emptive attack on the Russian fleet at Port Arthur in the opening salvo of the first Russo-Japanese War (1904–5).

The long and costly war mobilised a million soldiers from each side on the Manchurian battlefield, but few had imagined the result. Japan paid a high price for the gamble. The 81,455 dead and 381,313 wounded Japanese soldiers[109] prepared the ground for future myth-making that would excuse far larger conflicts and much greater losses. Japan's victory avenged Russia's duplicity over the Liaodong Peninsula a decade earlier and seized back that very same asset from the Russians – it was, as one Japanese resident in Manchuria would later put it, 'territory *regained*'[110] – only in the meantime it had been richly furnished with the embryonic accoutrements of modernity – industry, manufacturing, mining, construction, ports, architecture, urban planning and, most importantly, railways.

On 5 September 1905, Russia and Japan signed the Treaty of Portsmouth which outlined the terms of peace and defined Japan's spoils of war. In principle, both powers were to leave Manchuria and the territory was to be returned to China, but there were two important exceptions. One was the Liaodong Peninsula, or Kwantung Leased Territory, the lease of which was to be transferred to Japan along with all public works and properties. The other was the railway. Russia had to:

> transfer and assign to the Imperial Government of Japan, without compensation and with the consent of the Chinese Government, the 520 mile stretch of railway between Chang-chun [Changchun] and Port Arthur and all its branches, together

126 *Architecture and modernity*

with all rights, privileges and properties appertaining hitherto in that region, as well as all coal mines in the said region belonging to or worked for the benefit of the railway.[111]

Russia retained the CER with its three-way junction at Harbin and the southbound track as far as Changchun.

The Russo-Japanese War marked the first time in the modern era that a western nation was defeated by an eastern counterpart. The consequences, for the title and tenure of modernity, were critical. As Harootunian put it, it was the moment 'the geopolitical monopoly of modernity was shattered' though this might be attributed to Italy's defeat to Ethiopia at the Battle of Adwa in 1896.[112] The war also signalled the completion of Japan's second vital step in its quest for empire. The balance of power in the region shifted dramatically and set a vital precedent for the next four decades.

Scene 6: Modernity from the east

Despite considerable efforts by western commentators to lay claim to modernity throughout the twentieth century (which was as strong in architecture as it was in any other field), Japan's experience, especially in the context of Manchuria, suggests that even from relatively early on modernity assumed many forms. The Russo-Japanese War dismantled modernity's western edifice and marked the point at which the subsequent bifurcation occurred – the dawn of an age of multiple modernities. Few, however, would accept it until a century later when the rise of China (which in 1905 was merely the muted and reluctant host to these global tensions) surpassed these competing powers to assume a position of genuine global authority.

By 1905, Japan was the first non-western nation to have successfully modernised. Western scholars have viewed Japan's indisputable state of modernity an anomaly in an otherwise entirely western encounter. As Kawakami put it in 1933:

> For the first time in history, a non-white race has undertaken to carry the white man's burden, and the white man, long accustomed to think the burden exclusively his own, is reluctant to commit it to the young shoulders of Japan, yellow and an upstart at that.[113]

In Manchuria, Japan's efforts to build an empire offers the earliest and one of the foremost examples of multiple modernities, where the experience and condition of modernity in the non-western host, China, was not imposed from the west, but arrived from the east and materialised largely in the absence of western participation.

With Japan in control of the spine of Manchuria's railway network, as well as key branch lines that plugged it into the region's natural resources, they set about creating a means of administering and exploiting these newfound gains. This task fell to one of Japan's most senior officials in Manchuria, Kodama Gentarō (1852–1906), the Imperial Army's Chief of General Staff and former Governor General of Taiwan.

In September 1905, Kodama invited his friend and former Head of Civilian Affairs in Taiwan, Gotō Shimpei (1857–1929), to Shenyang. Over the course of the previous decade, the pair had been instrumental in alleviating the fledgling colony of Taiwan from a state of relative destitution by introducing modern agricultural production, industry and railways. During their fleeting liaison in Shenyang, Kodama and Gotō hatched a plan that would similarly transform Manchuria from 'a tranquil and backward Oriental land without modern transportation facilities',[114] but on a larger scale and concentrated entirely on Japan's newly acquired railway network.[115]

At the time, China was as anxious to rid Manchuria of foreign forces as other foreign powers were to see Japan prevented from enjoying a monopoly in the region. Japan needed a solution that secured their control without aggravating an already tense diplomatic situation. The matter came to a head in Tokyo the following May after the Japanese Prime Minister Saionji Kinmochi (1849–1940) had paid a brief visit to Manchuria. Kodama presented the plan that he and Gotō had conceived the previous September. Kinmochi approved the plan and within weeks a special committee was established to decide how Japanese interests in Manchuria would be administered.

Kodama was appointed chairperson of the 77-member panel, but he died only days later. Gotō took the helm and the committee continued its mission, resulting on 11 August 1906 in the founding of Mantetsu – the South Manchuria Railway (SMR) – the physical and figurative backbone of Japanese-occupied Manchuria. By the end of the year, Gotō was appointed the company's first President.[116]

The SMR was a product of the early twentieth century and of modernity. The 'colonial policy' it embodied was, as Gotō emphasised, 'inescapable in our time'.[117] western powers had long jostled for positions of power in distant lands, but China was unique in the range and extent of its territorial partitioning. The SMR was both a cause and effect of the dysfunctional global puzzle that colonialism created. Not only was it a consequence of shifting power regionally and unique encounters with modernity in the early twentieth century, but it would also effect much more profound encounters in subsequent decades. The SMR continued the colonial tradition of utilising a combination of political and commercial interests to infiltrate and exploit a foreign domain. In this respect it bore similarities to Britain's East India Company, but it was also vitally different, not only for being based on land rather than sea, but also for carrying out research.

The Research Department (renamed the Research Section in 1908)[118] was born out of the SMR's organisational restructuring in 1907. The company was severed from direct political authority and began to function independently from the Kwantung Leased Territory, under the Governor General, Ōshima Yoshimasa, who reported directly to the Ministry of Foreign Affairs in Tokyo. Gotō appreciated the importance of research. 'I cannot exaggerate,' explained Gotō, 'the essentiality to the management of Manchuria of research into the economic conditions of Manchuria as well as study of popular and commercial customs'.[119] The activities of the Research Section were importantly linked to architectural production. Its work demanded the construction of libraries, workshops and laboratories, and staff studied and tested new building materials and technologies. It was through a vast and highly organised research apparatus that the SMR was able to furnish the Japanese authorities with the required information to administer and exploit their possessions in Manchuria and plan cities of the future. The Research Section helped define the SMR and there was nothing like it in the world. From its origins as a small office in Dalian in April 1907, the Research Section grew to a staff of 42 by 1909 and 2,354 at its peak in 1940.[120]

While the SMR followed similar western precedents, it was the first time that such an enterprise had originated outside the west. Furthermore, Japan's relationship with China was neither colonial nor distant. China was Japan's cultural progenitor and until the Sino-Japanese War had been revered by its neighbour. The SMR responded to this relationship in a way that western colonial ventures did not have to in their acquired and invariably culturally and geographically remote territories. It was subtle, sophisticated and scientific – learned even – and thus could be presented as a mutually beneficial enterprise that supported China's struggle against pernicious western interests and, eventually, the entire liberation of Asia.

The SMR became one of the essential cogs in the much larger geopolitical machine that was neither colonial nor imperial, not yet at least. Gotō knew that the SMR, if managed properly, could perform many of the functions of a colonial enterprise and guarantee Japanese control of the region by more subtle means: *bunsō teki bubi* 'military preparedness in civilian clothing'.

Japan's quasi-colonial campaign in Manchuria depended on the SMR. From humble origins, it grew into an enterprise of such immense power and influence that it became the very object through which Japan was able to realise its subsequent imperial ambitions. It controlled the trunk line between Changchun and Dalian, and numerous branch lines linking other towns and cities. It also owned the mining rights in the mineral-rich regions of Fushun and Yentai outside Shenyang, and the ports along the Kwantung coast.

The SMR was responsible for the planning, construction and public administration of the settlements along the railways, which were vigorously promoted as sites of metropolitan modernity. It also became a vital route for social and cultural engagements within Manchuria and throughout Asia more broadly. White Russians fleeing the Bolshevik Revolution, European émigrés, Chinese overseas students, warlords and legions of soldiers, merchants and adventurers relied on the SMR to gain access to or exit from China through the early decades of the twentieth century. It laid the very fabric of modernity in Manchuria and quickly became the region's primary asset.

From the outset, the SMR engaged in architectural production. Ports, mines and railway facilities all had to be developed swiftly for the company to be able to begin repaying its shareholders. Propelled by Japan's obsession with modernisation, Manchuria's built environment was swiftly transformed by the erection of entirely novel structures: wharfs, offices, stores, silos, factories, stations, warehouses, mines, workshops, hospitals, public libraries, town halls, fire stations and modern hotels.

In 1907 the Japanese established an SMR zone at Changchun one mile outside the old city's north gate, linked to the CER zone to the north. The urban plan was prepared by the civil engineer Katō Yonokichi (1867–1933), who implemented similar plans for Shenyang and oversaw the extensions to Dalian.[121] These plans were based on modern planning principles from Europe and North America, but they were also informed by Gotō's insistence that they should address the specific needs and incorporate the characteristics of Manchuria. Transplanted on to the once barren plains of Manchuria by a quasi-colonial enterprise, these modern schemes, reinterpreted, adapted and improved by the Japanese, were not western. Incorporating modern theories of zoning and replete with modern utilities, Japanese urban planning in Manchuria preceded by more than a decade Japan's first urban planning laws in 1919. By the Second World War, no other foreign power had embarked on such an ambitious programme of urban planning overseas before and, outside of wartime, none has tried since.

Katō's plan for Changchun was an organised and generous grid dissected by diagonal roads that radiated from two circuses and converged in front of the railway station (1914) (see Figure 6.13). Katō's urban plans were earnestly modern and, with the exceptions of Harbin and Dalian, were unlike anything seen before in China. Streets were wide, sealed, tree-lined and flanked by pavements. They formed regularly spaced city blocks served by modern utilities: water, drainage and electricity.

The buildings that populated these early Japanese settlements were predominantly designed in a western 'neo-Renaissance' style imported into Japan in the late nineteenth century with foreign architects and teachers before being exported to Manchuria by their graduated students. One such example is Matsumuro Shigemitsu (1873–1937), who worked for the Kyoto Prefecture and designed their offices in 1904 before travelling to Manchuria where he designed many of Changchun's early public buildings. Shigemitsu was encouraged to leave Japan for Manchuria by his former mentor, Kingo Tatsuno (1854–1919), who had studied at Tokyo's Imperial College of Engineering (ICE) under the British architect Josiah Conder (1852–1920), as well as University College London (UCL).

Matsumuro was among the first of many Japanese architects to seize the opportunity of empire. He became Head of the Construction Department in the Civil Affairs Bureau of the Kwantung Leased Territory and was their only architect until 1916. Other organisations, such as the SMR had their own architects, like University of Tokyo graduate, Ichida Kichijirō, who designed the three buildings around Changchun's new public square: the new railway station, the SMR offices (1910) and the Yamato Hotel (1909), the progressive art nouveau exterior of which boldly broke from the antiquated conventions of neo-Renaissance and neo-Gothic on which his generation had been raised.

Between Changchun and Dalian, the Japanese-controlled railway opened up the ancient city and regional capital of Shenyang. As in other towns and cities along the railway, Japan adopted the quasi-colonial approach of planning new settlements outside the 'native' area. The Japanese were quick to contrast the rectilinear pattern of modernity designed by Katō Yonokichi with the Chinese city, which guidebooks referred to derisorily as 'an unpolished bit of real "Old China"; dilapidated, time-soiled and worn down'.[122]. In Shenyang, visitors could find 'something new – yet ancient, a unique change from the "modern civilization series" of Europe and the Far West'.[123] An essential part of Japan's narrative of modernity and civilising endeavour was the casting of China as an outdated and barbarous alterity. 'The whistle of [SMR] trains on their way from Siberia to the Yellow Sea sounded the death knell of the old Manchuria,' lamented one writer looking back from the 1930s. The SMR's 'gleaming rails turned a land that three or four decades ago was almost a wilderness into the most easily accessible region in the Far East'.[124]

At Dalian, the Japanese had an opportunity to make a strong first impression in city planning outside Japan. Should they follow Russia's original and ambitious plan or should they erase the embryonic city and start again along more modest lines sympathetic to Japan's exhausted post-war condition and limited resources? The pragmatic consensus supported the latter, but Count Kodama, 'the very brains that had engineered the Russo-Japanese War, stoutly opposed the negative policy from an international standpoint'. Winning over 'one Minister after another of the Cabinet to his side, the Government at last decided to make the Civil Governor of Kwantung construct the City of Dairen according to the old Russian plan'.[125]

Some years later, the American Consul at Yingkou, Henry Miller, offered a similar, albeit romantic, interpretation of events, claiming that the Japanese, accustomed as

130 *Architecture and modernity*

Figure 6.13 The SMR zone of Changchun designed by Katō Yonokichi in 1907 showing the concentration of radial streets around the railway station.

they were 'to dainty landscape gardening', were swayed by their admiration for the 'fine specimens of western architecture' exhibited by 'the clusters of the Russian buildings [and] the extensive scale of the Russian plan'.[126] Kodama's decree resulted in the creation of what one writer later claimed was 'one of the leading modern cities [with a] city plan modelled after Paris [that] combines the best features of the radiating, square and circular system of modern city construction. . . . The streets radiating from the Central Circle in cobweb fashion' in particular 'symbolize the progressive freshness that is consistent with the colonial policy of present-day Japan'.[127]

Gotō Shimpei appointed Katō Yonokichi[128] to plan Dalian's expansion. Katō was responsible for the extensive grid system 'expanded on something like the American plan'[129] that stretched westwards from the Russian-planned core, anticipating the city's growth from an initial 200-acre site to 1,700 acres by 1919 and 5,270 by 1929.[130] The SMR bestowed on Dalian sewage works, waterworks, trams, hospitals, parks, schools, bridges, more railways and bigger harbours. By the early 1930s, nearly a quarter of a million Japanese lived in Dalian, most of whom were affiliated in some way to the SMR. The SMR was also responsible for introducing into China (and even Japan) the comparatively new theory of urban zoning, defining industrial, residential, mixed and commercial zones designed to aid the efficient functioning of the modern city.

The 'strictly modern plan, with many fine roadways radiating from centres where spacious circles provide public gardens surrounded by handsome buildings'[131] contained at its heart the original circus, around which the Japanese erected prominent buildings that appeared like the decorated figures on a carousel: Dalian City Hall,[132] Police Headquarters, Department of Communication, the Oriental Development Company, the British Consulate, the Yamato Hotel, the Yokohama Specie Bank and the Bank of Chosen. Separating these architectural ornaments were ten roads radiating outwards to every corner of the city. The largest, the Yamagata-dori, pointed northeast and led directly to the wharves. On the opposite side of the circus it became the Higashikoen-cho, which linked the city centre with new western suburbs. The Oyama-dori connected the city centre to the old Russian quarter and was the only road to cross the deep cut of the railway tracks. The rickety wooden bridge erected by the Russians for this purpose was replaced by 'a magnificent structure of three noble arches' and renamed the 'Bridge of Japan' or 'Nippon Bridge' (*Nihon Bashi*).[133] Like all great bridges, Dalian's 'Nippon Bridge' was more than a mere crossing. In Dalian the bridge became a potent symbol of Japan's power and presence.

Dalian was among the world's first examples of modern urban planning pursued by a non-western nation. The fledgling port, not yet a decade old, revealed modernity's increasingly complex condition at the beginning of the twentieth century – a unique product of its time and place. On China's coast, a resurgent non-western nation had seized from an ailing western empire a city designed according to the latest planning theories, and set about altering and enhancing this design according to its own particular interpretation. 'The desire to emulate and excel the west in the creations of the west is the strongest motive force in modern Japan,' concluded one observer in 1933, adding presciently, 'one wonders what will happen when the Chinese are seized with the same sort of ambition?'[134]

Echoing this sentiment, the writer and Japanese apologist, Henry Kinney, claimed Dalian demonstrated 'the seemingly anomalous condition where, Japan, herself an Oriental country, brought a thoroughly western civilization to Manchuria on a scale far more comprehensive than anything that has been accomplished in any other part of China'.[135] Dalian marked the moment when western modernity was first seized by the east. Japan never looked back.

Notes

1. E.g. Liu, 1989; Cody, 2001; Steinhardt, 2002; Guo, 2005.
2. E.g. Su, 1964; Esherick, 2000; Rowe and Kuan, 2002; Zhu, 2009.
3. The first Catholic church in China, for example, was, according to Davis (1836, p. 19), built in Beijing by John de Corvino, who was sent by Pope Nicholas IV in 1288 and permitted by the emperor 'to build a church, furnished with a steeple and bells', but nothing is known of how long it stood.
4. Matteo Ricci had built a chapel near Beijing's South Gate in 1605.
5. Constructed in 1580 the church was destroyed by fire in 1595 (some say 1601). In 1602, construction began on a new church which was completed in 1637 and became the largest Catholic church in Asia. Designed by Father Carlo Spinola, Sao Paolo mirrored the Jesuit's Mother Church of Gesù in Rome. In the mid-1830s fire again destroyed the church, but the granite façade survived.
6. See Elman, 2006, p. 70.
7. Tong, 1938, p. 410.
8. E.g. the churches of St Domingo, St Joseph and St Andrew; and merchants' dwellings and commercial facilities respectively. Public buildings such as Senate House (1784) were an exception, since no other foreign settlements in China possessed autonomous administrations demanding such official facilities.

132 *Architecture and modernity*

9 Factories were houses owned by the factor or commercial agent. There were 13 factories in total, occupying an area of land extending over 300m in length and 200m in depth. Three-fifths of this was occupied by buildings, the remainder being given over to spacious gardens.
10 Lanning and Couling, 1921, p. 94.
11 Lanning and Couling, 1921, p. 122.
12 Dyce, 1906, p. 34.
13 Kingsmill, 1911, pp. 76–7.
14 Dyce, 1906, p. 34.
15 Wright, 1908, p. 85.
16 King, 1919, p. 562.
17 Lanning and Couling, 1921, p. 122.
18 Stewart, 1987, p. 18.
19 Kingsmill, 1893, p. 24.
20 Kingsmill, 1893, p. 24.
21 Kingsmill, 1911, p. 75.
22 Thomson, 1875, p. 406.
23 Strachan is quoted in Lanning and Couling's *History of Shanghai* as being among the first British consular staff to arrive in Shanghai in 1843 as 'Clerk'. A 50th anniversary review of Shanghai published in 1893 claims he was responsible for overseeing the construction of the first British Consulate building in 1851 (*Shanghai – 1843–1893, The Model Settlement: its Birth, its Youth, its Jubilee*, Shanghai Mercury Office, Shanghai, 1893, p. 7).
24 Kingsmill, 1911, pp. 80–81.
25 Kingsmill, 1911, p. 81.
26 Kingsmill arrived in China through Hong Kong, where he conducted numerous geological studies, and after becoming a member of the Royal Asiatic Society (Rutt, 2002, pp. 74–5) sought to publish his geological findings with donations from Hong Kong's wealthy merchant members.
27 In 1870 he drafted plans for the new regional offices of the North China Branch of the Royal Asiatic Society (Rutt, 2002, p. 75).
28 Wright, 1908, p. 376.
29 Shanghai Municipal Council Report, 1935, p. 23.
30 Sir George Gilbert Scott was RIBA President from 1873 to 1875.
31 Kingsmill, 1893, p. 27.
32 On his return to the England, Kidner nominated Cory to become an Associate of the RIBA. In 1880 Cory's nomination was successful and six years later he became a Fellow and one of the most experienced architects in Shanghai at that time.
33 Salway worked in Hong Kong for 11 years, during which time he partnered Wilberforce Wilson, Hong Kong's Surveyor-General, and designed several prominent buildings in Hong Kong. After leaving for Australia in 1876, Godfrey Bird, an architect from Wilson's office, joined the firm before it became Palmer & Turner in 1891.
34 Long after the founding partners retired, the firm retained its name and included the architects William Laughton Leask who joined in 1904, Gerald George Wood who joined the following year, A.E. Griffin in 1908 and A.S. MacKichan in 1917 (Waters, 1990, p. 246).
35 Wright, 1908, p. 634.
36 Knollys, 1885, p. 129.
37 Wright, 1908, p. 632.
38 Frederick George Drewitt (1877–1958), ARIBA joined the practice from 1904 to 1909. In 1908, after Atkinson's death, the firm was joined by his brother, G.B. Atkinson.
39 Britain, France, America, Germany, Austro-Hungary, Russia, Japan, Italy and Belgium.
40 The partners were born in Annemasse and educated at the College d'Thonon, after which they attended the School of Art in Geneva (Wright, 1908, p. 744).
41 Macmillan, 1925, p. 143.
42 Cook & Anderson designed the Tudor-styled offices of the Tianjin Printing Press, established in 1894, where the *Jing Jin Times* (*Beijing Tianjin Times*) was first printed.

43 One partner, E. Cook, RIBA, trained in London and arrived in China in 1903. The other partner, H. McClure Anderson, FRIBA, qualified in Edinburgh and arrived in China in 1902 where he worked for Scottish and Irish Missions in Manchuria before settling in Tianjin and in 1912 became Municipal Assessor to the Russian Council (Macmillan, 1925, p. 147).
44 Hemmings retired in 1923, after which F.S. Reynolds became head of the firm and the following year took into partnership H.G. Turner, ARIBA and C. Hooper, ARIBA (Macmillan, 1925, p. 177).
45 Macmillan, 1925, p. 177.
46 Details of the prolific Shanghai-based architects appear in *Building Shanghai – The Story of China's Gateway*, Denison and Ren, 2006. Lai Delin's *Who's Who in Chinese Architecture* includes only Chinese architects.
47 Kang Youwei, *Kang Nan Hai Zi Bian Nian Pu*, 159, 163, quoted in Pang, 2007, p. 17.
48 The firm became Murphy, McGill & Hamlin after Richard Dana's departure in 1921.
49 Lee returned to New York at the end of the Second World War in 1945, where he established an architectural practice in Chinatown. For more information on Poy Gum Lee's life, see 'Chinese Style: Rediscovering the Architecture of Poy Gum Lee 1923–1968' (2015–16), Museum of Chinese in America and the work of Kerri Culhane.
50 Bergamini, 1924, p. 653.
51 Russell, 1922, p. 74.
52 Gunn, 1924, p. 645.
53 King, 1919, p. 562.
54 Knollys, 1885, p. 147.
55 Knollys, 1885, p. 147.
56 Macmillan, 1925, pp. 168–9.
57 Carles, 1916, p. 16.
58 *Shanghai – 1843–93, The Model Settlement: Its Birth, its Youth, its Jubilee*, Shanghai Mercury Office, Shanghai, 1893, p. 19.
59 Roberts, 1893, p. 13.
60 The extension, which was granted on 27 November 1848, caused the western boundary to move inland from the Huangpu River (*Feetham Report*, 1931).
61 The French were granted their settlement by the Chinese on 6 April 1849 (*Feetham Report*, 1931).
62 Two of these buildings belonged to American missionaries; the other two to a Parisian watchmaker and the French Consulate (Kuonin, 1938, p. 82).
63 The total number of permits is distinct from the number of permits for houses, the figures for which appear in each *Shanghai Municipal Council Annual Report*.
64 *Shanghai Municipal Council Annual Report*, 1911, p. 113.
65 Shanghai had always profited from China's woes. Destruction beyond its boundaries provoked refugee-fuelled development inside, from the Small Swords (1853), through the Taipings (1860–4), the Boxers (1900), the revolutionary movement in 1911 and the Kuomintang's northern march in 1927, up to the Japanese incident (1932) and eventual invasion in 1937.
66 *Far Eastern Review*, Vol. 13, No. 4, September 1916, p. 144.
67 *Far Eastern Review*, Vol. 13, No. 5, October 1916, p. 183.
68 Bland, 1909, p. 45.
69 *Far Eastern Review*, Vol. 13, No. 4, September 1916, p. 144.
70 AR Burkill & Sons; Dickeson, Jones & Co.; Brunner, Mond & Co.; Scott, Harding & Co.; Volkart Bros.; Denham & Rose; Atkinson & Dallas; Davies & Thomas; Albert Edmund Algar; Walter Scott; Moorhead & Halse; Yajo Hirano; Sander, Wieler & Co.; H.M. Schultz & Co.; Richard Haworth & Co.; Collins & Co.; Ebbeke & Co.; Tata, Sons & Co.; Dallas & Co.; Locksmith & Co.; Brighten, Malcom & Co.; Walter Nutter & Co.; Diederichsen, Jebsen & Co.; Telge & Schroeter; Wilhelm Klose & Co.; and Hillebrandt & Co.
71 Quoted in a pamphlet by Sidney J. Powell in Darwent, 1920.
72 Norman, 1902, p. 126.

73 The Cassini Convention was named after Russia's exceptional plenipotentiary to Beijing, Count Arthur Cassini (1836–1913).
74 Clarence Cary, 'Dalny – A Fiat City', *Scribner's Magazine*, Vol. 33, No. 4, April 1903, p. 485.
75 China consented to Russia building their railway on 8 September 1896 and ratified the Li–Lobanhov Treaty on 28 September 1896.
76 'The Cassini Convention,' *North China Herald*, 30 October 1896.
77 Article II, Russo-Chinese Convention, 27 March 1898.
78 Clarence Cary, 'Dalny – A Fiat City', *Scribner's Magazine*, Vol. 33, No. 4, April 1903, p. 485.
79 Clarence Cary, 'Dalny – A Fiat City', *Scribner's Magazine*, Vol. 33, No. 4, April 1903, p. 482.
80 Colquhoun, 1898, pp. 327–8.
81 Kaname Tahara, 'Harbin and Environs,' *Manchuria*, 1 August 1940, p. 350.
82 Kinnosuke, 1925, p. 57.
83 Whigham, 1904, p. 8.
84 Kinnosuke, 1925, p. 59.
85 Whigham, 1904, p. 50.
86 Whigham, 1904, p. 77.
87 Whigham, 1904, pp. 76–77.
88 'Official Report to DC by US Consul Miller in Manchuria in 20 years', *Far Eastern Review*, Vol. 22, 1926, p. 341.
89 Whigham, 1904, p. 79.
90 Fuchiatien derived its name from a woman named Fu who established a hostel outside the zone for the Chinese who were prohibited from residing in the CER zone.
91 A. Rykachev, 'Russkoe delo v Man'chzhurii', *Russkaia mysl*, Vol. 8, 1910, p. 122, in Olga Bakich, 'Emigré Identity: The Case of Harbin', *South Atlantic Quarterly*, Vol. 99, No. 1, 2000, p. 56.
92 *Far Eastern Review*, Vol. 24, February 1928, p. 78.
93 Clarence Cary, 'Dalny – A Fiat City', *Scribner's Magazine*, Vol. 33, No. 4, April 1903, p. 484.
94 *Dairen*, South Manchuria Railway Company, 1935, p. 3.
95 Whigham, 1904, p. 8.
96 Clarence Cary, 'Dalny – A Fiat City', *Scribner's Magazine*, Vol. 33, No. 4, April 1903, p. 489.
97 'Official Report to DC by US Consul Miller in Manchuria in 20 years', *Far Eastern Review*, Vol. 22, 1926, p. 344.
98 *Dairen*, South Manchuria Railway Company, 1935, p. 6.
99 Whigham, 1904, p. 8.
100 Whigham, 1904, pp. 8–11.
101 Whigham, 1904, p. 10.
102 Triggs, 1909, pp. 101–2.
103 Clarence Cary, 'Dalny – A Fiat City', *Scribner's Magazine*, Vol. 33, No. 4, April 1903, p. 493.
104 Clarence Cary, 'Dalny – A Fiat City', *Scribner's Magazine*, Vol. 33, No. 4, April 1903, p. 486.
105 'The Kwantung Government, Its Functions & Works'. *Manchuria Daily News*, Dairen, 1934, p. 137.
106 Whigham, 1904, p. 8.
107 Clarence Cary, 'Dalny – A Fiat City', *Scribner's Magazine*, Vol. 33, No. 4, April 1903, p. 482.
108 'Official Report to DC by US Consul Miller in Manchuria in 20 years,' *Far Eastern Review*, Vol. 22, 1926, p. 343.
109 Young, 1998, pp. 89–90.
110 Itō Takeo in Fogel, 1988, p. 5.
111 Article VI, The Treaty of Portsmouth, 1905.
112 Harootunian, 2000, p. 63.

113 Kawakami, 1933, p. vi.
114 SMR, *South Manchuria Railway: The Pioneer on the Continent*, 1939.
115 See Harada Katsumasa, *Mantetsu (South Manchuria Railway)*, 1981, p. 38 and Ramon H. Myers, 'Japanese Imperialism in Manchuria: The South Manchuria Railway Company, 1906–1933,' in Duus et al. (eds), 1989, p. 101.
116 Gotō was appointed President on 8 November 1906. Nakamura Zekō was Vice President.
117 Fogel, 1988, p. 14.
118 Gotō appointed as head Okamatsu Santarō (1871–1921), a law professor from Kyoto University whom he had previously hired in Taiwan. Okamatsu was replaced in 1908 by Kawamura Chūjirō, who remained head of research for a decade and later rose to become the head of the SMR. Fogel, 1988, p. 18.
119 Fogel, 1988, p. 16.
120 Employees were primarily from Japan (140,000 at their peak), China, Korea, Russia and Mongolia. Staff numbers were 51 by 1918; 167 by 1926, and from 1931 onwards rose dramatically.
121 Katō Yonokichi worked in the Civil Engineering Section of the Niigata Prefecture when he was appointed Manager of the SMR's Civil Engineering Department by Gotō Shimpei.
122 *Cook's Tourist's Handbook*, 1910, p. 75.
123 *Cook's Tourist's Handbook*, 1910, p. 7.
124 Scherer, 1933, p. 44.
125 Dr K. Uyeda, 'Manchuria in Twenty Years', *Far Eastern Review*, August 1926, p. 345.
126 'Official Report to DC by US Consul Miller in Manchuria in 20 years', *Far Eastern Review*, Vol. 22, 1926, p. 346.
127 'The Port of Dairen', *Far Eastern Review*, May 1940, p. 178.
128 Buck (2000, p. 68) cites Katō as being a public works specialist who designed the SMR settlements at Changchun and Shenyang and carried out the official survey of Changchun in 1907. He was also chief of SMR's Public Works Office from 1914 to 1923, after which he retired.
129 J.N. Penlington, 'Manchoukuo and Engineering Developments', *Far Eastern Review*, June 1933, p. 262.
130 'The Kwantung Government', 1934, p. 138.
131 *Cook's Tourist's Handbook*, 1910, p. 81.
132 Dalian City Hall (1917–19) was designed by Matsumuro Shigemitsu, Head of the Construction Department in the Civil Affairs Bureau of the Kwantung Leased Territory.
133 *Cook's Tourist's Handbook*, 1910, p. 82.
134 J.N. Penlington, 'Manchoukuo and Engineering Developments', *Far Eastern Review*, June 1933, p. 63.
135 Kinney, 1928, p. 44, and 1930, p. 48.

7 Modernism and nationalism

In 1927, the same year that the Nationalists united China, the British author and journalist, Arthur Ransome, observed: 'Every blow struck by foreigners in China is a blow in the welding of a nation.'[1] Unintentionally metaphorical, his words echo the relationship between building construction and nationalism in China. Whereas in many countries outside the west, nationalism became a potent force only after the Second World War, nationalism in China was fully developed much earlier, and significantly altered the nation's encounter with modernity and architecture.

Nationalism and national identity occupy a central position in studies of early twentieth-century architecture in China and are relatively well-researched topics that were acknowledged to be important to China's architects. However, consistent with this study's perspective, these familiar subject territories will be approached differently and with fresh evidence that challenges certain established perceptions. For example, the denotation of the ubiquitous term 'first generation of Chinese architects', referring to the American-trained Chinese architects of the 1920s is questioned, casting doubt on some of the other received ideas about China's encounter with modernity. Also challenged here is the privileged historical status given to architects that chose to remain in China after 1949; their careers have received disproportionate consideration in subsequent scholarship. Just as some painters and writers who fell out of favour during subsequent political currents have fallen into obscurity, so too have the work and careers of many architects associated with pre-1949 China been ignored, deliberately or otherwise. China's history is further complicated and distinguished from most countries outside the west by its partial colonisation. Notwithstanding Japanese imperialism and the quasi-colonial status of many of China's major cities, the integrity of China as a nation-state was seldom questioned, albeit frail and fragmented between the fall of the Qing dynasty in 1911 and the establishment of a Nationalist government, which was largely successful in securing a degree of sovereignty from 1927, even after the Japanese invasion of 1937 that forced the Chinese to retreat to the proxy capital of Chongqing. The greatest threat to national unity came not from any external pressure but from the internal struggle between the Nationalists and the Communists, a conflict that began in the 1920s and whose persistence into the twenty-first century continues to distort historical accounts.

Defining nationalism in the context of China is therefore complicated by both domestic and international circumstances. As discussed earlier, national unity derived less from notions of modern statehood than from a sense of China's enduring civilisation. Nationalist discourses were therefore invariably framed by the question of what it meant to be Chinese, rather than promoting the concept of China. For

China, *civilisationism*, rather than *nationalism*, might be a more appropriate term, though this awkward neologism will be acknowledged only in spirit when referring to nationalism here.

A national architecture

National identity has often been claimed through building. Observers interpret from architecture the features that they assert denote national characteristics. These are either accepted or rejected, but over time come to characterise and reinforce the world in ways that literature, poetry and painting do not and cannot. Nationalism therefore can be a cogent force in embodying the ideas or aesthetic values ascribed to a nation both actively, in the mind of the architect, and reactively, in the eyes of the viewer.

Architecture has by its very nature always been exposed to a wider and less select audience than the outputs of other art practices. Consequently, its potential to manipulate the cause of nationalism negatively or positively was often greater than that of any other form of art – a fact that did not go unnoticed among China's political elite. The paradox for China, as with many places outside the west, is that architecturally, nationalism and the study of the nation's built heritage that helped to define a national architectural style were contemporaneous with modernism, in contrast to the west where architectural historical research long pre-dated modernism, and where modernism was explicitly internationalist.

Before building as an art form could become an agency of nationalism in China it first had to move from a craft-based practice into one that could be manipulated by intellectuals to represent the modern state apparatus. Architecture – the means by which to achieve this – did not enter China until the twentieth century.

The development of a national style of architecture not only required trained architects, it also depended on a level of critical self-reflection found only in someone trained to think beyond traditional norms. Since no such professionals existed in China before the twentieth century, the only available point of reference as a national archetype was the comparatively recent palace structures in Beijing, which were the pre-eminent and most complete example of the Chinese vernacular at the point when China was exposed to the art of architecture. Since this first encounter, the palaces of Beijing have provided the quintessential reference for those seeking to emulate a Chinese 'style' of architecture, to the exclusion of other potential examples such as former palaces or temple compounds from other technically superior dynasties.

Not until the early twentieth century with the pioneering work of several Chinese architects and researchers, most of whom were trained in the west, did a more complete picture of China's history of building start to emerge. As previously stated, what makes China's case atypical is the simultaneousness of the advent of modernism and archaeological studies and building research that enabled the kinds of self-reflection critical to the development of a national architecture.

Leading this research was the University of Pennsylvania graduate, Liang Sicheng, son of the reformer, Liang Qichao. To this day, Liang's seminal work with the Institute for Research in Chinese Architecture remains the most complete and thorough investigation of Chinese building. Almost single-handedly, Liang brought this subject to an international audience by writing up research and tirelessly pursuing international publication. In the late 1940s, he had sent 'a rather rambling and random account' of his expeditions in north China to the *National Geographic*, revealing 'the "-ests" of Chinese architecture' – an effort that was, by his own admission, 'an attempt at popularization, not scholarship'.[2] Publication of the Institute's research only began in the late-1930s[3] (and in some cases was not resumed until the 1980s).[4]

Contemporaneous with the framing of Beijing's celebrated structures as *the* model of traditional Chinese architecture was the Boxer Uprising. For architecture, the Boxer Uprising was an event of considerable import, not for the destruction caused by foreign troops to the Baroque structures constructed by the Jesuits over a century earlier, or for excusing Germany's invasion of the port of Qingdao, or as a pretext for Russia to tighten its grip on Manchuria, but rather on account of the establishment by America of the Boxer Indemnity Fund for the education of Chinese scholars in America.[5]

China's 'first generation' of architects

The 'first generation' of Chinese architects is a label commonly assigned to architectural graduates of the Boxer Indemnity Fund. On returning to China, many of these became leading figures in various architecturally related pursuits, including professional practice for commercial and public clients, establishing educational curricula, building professional institutions and societies, and publishing.

However, there are sound reasons for questioning this definition of 'first generation' on the grounds that it does not distinguish the range and types of education that China's early architects received, and the diversity of their experiences upon returning to China. To be able to draw more meaningful insights from this founding period of architectural development in China, the common and generic interpretation of 'first generation' is divided in two, and defined by those who graduated before the mid-1920s and those who graduated afterwards.

The grounds for making this division are based on the contrast in the domestic conditions that confronted these two groups of students and their educational experience. The mid-1920s marked a critical change in China's educational, cultural and political conditions and, consequently, the professional setting in which returning architectural graduates operated. China's 'first generation' of architects, therefore, was not the non-specific collection of architects to leave China before the Second World War; it comprised a handful of individuals who were the first to be trained as architects or in fields closely related to architecture who returned to China before the mid-1920s. Though small, the group was professionally substantial, since they laid the foundations for a larger 'second generation', which began returning from the late 1920s.

The interconnections between these individuals' private, educational and professional experiences, and the wider context of China's encounter with modernity have never been fully elucidated. In order to explicate their role in contributing to China's multiple modernities, and to emphasise and validate some of the most significant aspects of these interconnections, it is vital therefore that the lives and careers of key individuals, and their influence collectively, are documented.

The scene into which those who had been trained abroad in the 1900s and 1910s returned was fundamentally different from that into which their successors returned in the 1930s. In the 1910s and 1920s, chaos reigned throughout much of China. Although overseas educational programmes had been established and students were going abroad in significant numbers, the institutions and professions they were expected to lead on their return were nascent and fragile.

In the tumultuous period around the 1910s characterised by Cai Yuanpei's New Culture Movement and the subsequent May Fourth Movement, the 'first generation' of Chinese architects were not sent overseas through a single government-sponsored initiative such as the Boxer Indemnity Fund and did not receive their training predominantly from a single institution such as the University of Pennsylvania, where many of their immediate successors trained. Theirs was a generation characterised by individual, disparate and often desperate attempts to receive a foreign education. Because almost every individual's experience was unique, it is harder to build up a general picture of their educational formation than it is for their successors.

A larger proportion of China's early architectural graduates were trained in Japan than occurred in the 'second generation'. As earlier chapters have shown, Japan's position as a primary educational destination for Chinese students had been secured since the late nineteenth century and provided the formation of many Chinese intellectuals and professionals. Until Europe and America became realistic destinations for significant numbers of Chinese students, which did not happen for architects until the 1920s, Japan was the obvious and only choice for most prospective students. Therefore, China's first taste of architectural education came from Japan, as an interpretation and adaptation of western teaching received second-hand.

Among the most important Chinese architects to have studied in Japan during this period was Liu Shiying (1893–1973), who left China in 1914 to study at the Tokyo Higher Technical School.[6] Having had six years experience in Japan, Liu returned to China to set up the country's first ever taught course for architecture. Before this, he engaged in private practice, initially with a Japanese architectural firm and then established his own firm, Hua Hai Architectural Practice, in Shanghai in 1923 with Liu Dunzhen (1897–1968), who travelled to Japan as a schoolboy in 1913 and attended the Tokyo Higher Technical School from where he graduated in 1921 before returning to China in 1922.

Technical rather than artistic competence was one distinguishing characteristic of the 'first generation' of Chinese architects. Initially, engineering commonly provided an introduction to architecture. Engineering graduates greatly outnumbered architects in China and had started travelling overseas for education long before their architectural colleagues. The first was Zhan Tianyou (1861–1919), a pupil on Yung Wing's first Mission in 1872 and who received a PhD in Civil Engineering from Yale.[7] In 1912, Zhan was instrumental in establishing the Chinese Society of Engineers, an institution that promoted the cause of engineering and preceded its architectural equivalent by fifteen years.

Although architecture and engineering were both novel professions in China, imported from the west, engineering's earlier emergence and the support it received through China's overseas educational policies meant architecture consistently lagged behind. Even in the 1910s, architecture was still too novel a concept for independent Chinese practitioners to earn a living from. The principal services offered by the very few Chinese firms established in or soon after the 1910s were founded on engineering.

One of the earliest engineer-turned-architects was Shen Liyuan (1890–1951). Originally from Hangzhou, Shen studied engineering at a technical school in Napoli in 1909 before switching to architecture. In 1915, he returned to China and founded his own firm in Tianjin, Hua Xing Architecture and Engineering, where he designed the Central Bank (1926), the French Club (1931), the Sin Hua Trust Savings Bank (1934), and the Jin Cheng Bank (1937).[8]

In 1921, the first Chinese architectural firm in Shanghai, the South-Eastern Architectural & Engineering Company, was established by the American-trained Lü Yanzhi and Guo Yangmo, and the British-trained Huang Xiling (1893–?). Lü was born in Tianjin, but moved to Paris aged eight with his sister following the death of his father (see Figure 7.1). From 1911, he studied engineering at the preparatory school, Tsinghua Xue Tang, before attending Cornell University for four years, after which he worked for the 'Oriental Division' of the American architectural firm Murphy & Dana, in their New York office at 331 Madison Avenue. Lü continued working for Murphy & Dana in their Shanghai office after his return to China in 1919.[9] Lü met fellow engineering graduate, Guo, at Cornell, but, like Shen Liyuan, he switched courses to architecture and went on to study at Harvard and MIT. Huang also studied engineering, but at University College London (UCL) after being schooled at Dulwich College in south London. Under the name Wong Sik Lam, UCL records show him to have started his studies in 1911. During his course he studied municipal, mechanical, civil and electrical engineering, as well as surveying and engineering drawing and design. There were no architectural elements except for building construction in his penultimate year.[10]

Another engineering student turned architect was Fan Wenzhao (aka Robert Fan) (1899–1973) (see Figure 7.2). A graduate of Civil Engineering from Shanghai's St John's University in 1917, Fan was the first of a group of Chinese architectural students to graduate from the University of Pennsylvania where he studied from 1919 to 1921. While in America, Fan worked for architectural practices, Day & Klauder and Ch. F. Durang, but reverted to engineering on returning in 1922 to his native Shanghai where he worked for Lam, Glines & Co before setting up his own firm and becoming 'one of the most distinguished architects in China'.[11]

In 1935, Fan was sent to London by the Chinese government to attend the 14th Assembly of the International City and Housing Design. He was the only representative from Asia and later wrote fondly of discussions he had with delegates on the eradication of slums, working-class housing and garden suburbs. After the symposium he toured Europe,[12] visiting Belgium, where he admired the steel and glass modernist buildings; Prague, where he attended a four-day seminar on the International Style; and Rome, where he attended the 13th International Architects Conference and met Mussolini during a visit to the new Mussolini Hospital and Rome University.

Another characteristic of China's 'first generation' of architects is the absence of state support they received in their search for a modern education, since such mechanisms were not yet established. The Boxer Indemnity-funded Tsinghua Xue Tang, the foremost preparatory institution for state-funded education overseas, was not created until 1911. Therefore, the likes of Guan Songsheng (1892–1960), one of the partners of Kwan, Chu & Yang which became one of the most reputed architectural firms in China before the Second World War, had to self-finance his studies at Andover Academy, Massachusetts, from 1907 to 1911. Only when he returned to America in 1914 to attend the University of Boston, followed by MIT in 1918, was he eligible for government support.[13]

Guan, like Shen, settled in Tianjin on his return from America and in 1920 set up private practice. In 1924 he was joined by his brother-in-law, Zhu Bin (1896–1971), and together they formed the firm Kwan, Chu & Associates, practising primarily in

Figure 7.1
Lü Yanzhi (1894–1929), graduate of Cornell University.

Figure 7.2
Fan Wenzhao (aka Robert Fan) (1899–1973), graduate of Civil Engineering from Shanghai's St John's University and the University of Pennsylvania.

Beijing and Tianjin. Zhu, being slightly younger than Guan, was eligible for Tsinghua Xue Tang, which he attended before becoming the first Chinese student to enrol in the University of Pennsylvania's School of Architecture. Zhu started his studies in Philadelphia in September 1918 and graduated in 1922, winning the Arthur Spayd Brooke Medal (Silver) and the A&A Medal (1922), before completing his Master's the following year.

Another prominent architect who benefited from Tsinghua was Zhuang Jun (1888–1990), a graduate of Architectural Engineering from Illinois University (1914). After returning to China, Zhuang worked with Murphy & Dana from 1918 in their Shanghai office and was engaged in the design and construction of Tsinghua Xue Tang under the firm's superintendent, Charles Lane. In 1923 Zhuang returned to America for postgraduate studies in architecture at Columbia University after which he established his own Shanghai-based firm, Zhuang Jun Architects, in 1925.[14]

Most of those students who travelled overseas before the 1920s went on to become important figures in their profession, which caused their names and biographies to be documented, albeit sometimes sketchily. One exception is William Chaund, whose only known work is a single published article in the August 1919 edition of the *Far Eastern Review*. What makes his case particularly tantalising is that this article, titled 'Architectural Effort and Chinese Nationalism – Being a Radical Interpretation of Modern Architecture as a Potent Factor in Civilisation', is the first critical piece by a Chinese architect to have been published in an international publication, and it reveals Chaund's extensive knowledge about and strong views on architecture, planning and development. Not for another decade were such views expressed by a Chinese architectural writer in the international media.[15]

Contemporaneous with the May Fourth Movement, Chaund's article is framed in a modern and westerncentric evolutionary discourse: 'To-day China must standardize itself anew. The motto of the twentieth century is EFFICIENCY ... [the architect] is thus considered – very justly so – an indispensable servant to human evolutionary progress.'[16] Like his contemporaries in other artistic pursuits, Chaund saw the architect's role in the rapidly changing environment that characterised China in the 1910s as one of utility over art; there was little room for the contemplative artist in the architect's persona dominated by the scientist and engineer:

> We have altogether overlooked the vital question of human efficiency, life standard and public safety; and have failed utterly in giving thought to the sanitary, hygienic and aesthetic possibilities of the environment in which we live – all of which from the architect's point of view, are problems affording particularly fascinating scope to his professional efforts and artistic skill ... for us to gain a proper understanding of the part that the architect is really playing in the civilisation of the world, we must evaluate architecture according to its various utilitarian aspects rather than the artistic. In other words, for us in China truly to appreciate the architect's proper place as a useful citizen whose work fills a place in the world's need, be it a necessity or a luxury, his profession must be presented and interpreted in terms expressive of utility, or industry, and science which we can grasp, and, which for the present at least, appeal to us, infinitely more than does the purely artistic consideration, as absolutely urgent for our national evolutionary progress.[17]

Chaund's observations highlight the important distinction between the years either side of the establishment of the Republic of China in 1912 and the comparatively settled years either side of the establishment of the Nationalist government in Nanjing in 1927. The former period was one characterised by social and political upheaval, radicalism and deep soul-searching among China's cultured elite, while the latter permitted deliberation, contemplation and engagement in the nation-building project. In this light, Chaund's article can be seen as a rallying cry for China's 'second generation' of architects.

China's 'second generation' of architects

In the first decades of the twentieth century the trajectories of the foreign architect in China and of the Chinese architect were separate. By the 1930s they had practically converged. The merging of the two (in so far as was possible in China's quasi-colonial context) is the clearest distinction between the first and second generations of Chinese architects.

As the Italian missionary architect Bergamini noted in 1924, 'the architecture of China [was] in a state of transition',[18] and transition was everywhere; for the foreign architect as much as for the Chinese. Transition was in the building industry and the techniques and materials they used; it was in the styles employed by architects; it was in the infrastructure developments taking place in China's larger cities; it was a feature of the shifting personnel within the architectural community; and, although Bergamini was almost certainly not alluding to this particular aspect of Chinese architecture, it was a key feature of the time. As the first wave of qualified Chinese architects were returning from overseas in the late 1910s and early 1920s and undertaking work with established firms or forming their own practices, a second wave was setting off abroad.

From 1918 to 1941, 25 Chinese students enrolled to study architecture at the University of Pennsylvania. Of these, 17 graduated with honours among which seven received a Master's. Collectively, they were the largest group of Chinese architectural graduates from a single overseas institution before the late twentieth century. Much attention has been paid to this group of students and the architectural bond they forged between China and America. No evidence has come to light to explain why the University of Pennsylvania proved so popular for aspiring young Chinese architects, leaving one to assume that it was a combination of word of mouth and the propitious conditions during the early 1920s. The establishment in 1915 of a University of Pennsylvania Club in Shanghai[19] may have influenced those living in or near Shanghai, such as Fan Wenzhao.[20] At the core of this group of alumni was a cluster of very close friends, including one engaged couple.

Attention has also been paid to the classical instruction that Chinese students received at the University of Pennsylvania, so much so that it is taken for granted that China's encounter with architectural modernity was experienced through the very unmodern lens of Beaux-Arts. However, a closer look at the evidence suggests this is more complicated than it appears.

The University of Pennsylvania's architectural programme was directed by Paul Philippe Cret (1876–1945) under the Dean, Warren Powers Laird (1861–1948). Between them, Cret and Laird dominated architectural teaching at the University of Pennsylvania for half a century. Laird was Professor of Architecture from 1881 to 1932 and Dean of the School of Fine Arts from 1920 to 1932, and appointed Cret as Assistant Professor of Design in the School of Architecture in 1903. Except for military service in France during the First World War, Cret remained at the University of Pennsylvania until his retirement in 1937.

The architectural course under Laird and Cret was firmly in the Beaux-Arts mould, but to assume that this dominated the Chinese students' professional outlook is misleading. Cret was born in Lyon and in 1893 started his architectural studies at the École Nationale des Beaux-Arts de Lyon.[21] In 1897 he won the Prix de Paris which helped finance his studies at the École des Beaux-Arts, Paris, where he excelled and was later articled to Atelier Pascal, under the supervision of Jean Louis Pascal.[22] At the École, Cret befriended a number of American students and used these contacts in 1902 when he first travelled to America in search of work. The following year, Paul Davis, a fellow alumnus of Atelier Pascal and graduate of the University of Pennsylvania, sought a qualified teacher for the School of Architecture and contacted Jean Louis Pascal, who suggested Cret. Davis consequently recommended Cret to Laird, who appointed him in the same year.

When Cret arrived in Philadelphia to take up his post at the University he established a private architectural practice and an atelier that students could attend for a nominal fee. Cret's chief professional legacy is the Beaux-Arts model he brought to architectural education in America and introduced to many of his students who, in some cases, worked for him. Among the staff assisting Cret were Harry Sternfeld and Jean Hebrard (Design), Herbert Everett (History of Art), and George Walter Dawson (drafting tutor) and Alfred Gumaer (architectural historian), an influential pair of bachelors who participated in Cret's atelier and toured Europe annually. Gumaer was highly regarded by the Chinese students and described by Yang Tingbao (1901–1982) as 'wonderful'.[23]

Cret's admiration for the Beaux-Arts tradition did not make him a traditionalist. He was acutely aware of the tension between tradition and modernity in architecture and while standing by the Beaux-Arts methods, he distanced himself from either extreme. His archive at the University of Pennsylvania reveals his determination to confront the subject objectively, promoting through lectures, writing and public speaking a 'new classicism'. He accepted the transitional period that architecture and architectural education was in and which coincided with the arrival in Philadelphia of China's first architectural students: 'there is more than one opinion in the teaching of an Art, where we are no longer standing on the firm, logical ground of an exact science'.[24] In a speech titled 'Modernists and Conservatives' delivered to the T Square Club, an architectural group in Philadelphia, he claimed that men were divided in two 'antagonistic' groups in society: those who are 'perfectly satisfied with things as they are and those who have this turn of mind which urge them to try if they could not be arranged in some other way . . . modernists and conservatives'.[25] By the 1930s, Cret was sympathetic towards modernism, acknowledging the:

> simplification of craftsmanship, the more quiet tone of appearance due to the casting overboard of most of our ornamental system, the emphasis on the constructivist system as a keynote of composition . . . 'a new classicism achieving beauty through good proportions rather than through picturesque' . . . all but this last result (and I am still hopeful), has been achieved by the modernists. The architecture of the XIXth and early XXth centuries was badly in need of pruning. . . . I hope that I have not given you the impression that I condemn the so-called 'modernist trend'. Those who have studied with me in our School, know that I am not afraid of experiments. I have always tried, however, to keep in my mind and yours, free from ready-made ideas or slavish acceptance of slogans even if they had the merit of being fashionable. Of the cocksuredness [sic] and the ballyhoo of many of the modernists, I was, and am, still distrustful.[26]

These opinions challenge the accepted view that Cret was responsible for turning out a generation of Chinese architects steeped in Beaux-Arts methods and modernist sceptics. His teaching shows that Chinese students learned much about each classicism and modernism and were made aware of the merits of both. In their attempt to reconcile their own traditions with western architectural theory and practice, they sought inspiration from each.

The only two Chinese students to enrol at the University of Pennsylvania in the 1910s were Zhu Bin (1918) and Fan Wenzhao (1919). None enrolled in 1920, followed in 1921 by Yang Tingbao and Zhao Shen (1898–1978) (see Figure 7.3 and Figure 7.4). The latter two would go on to be among the most eminent of China's early architects and partners in two of the most prolific private architectural practices before the Communist era, Kwan, Chu & Yang and Allied Architects, respectively.

Modernism and nationalism 145

Figure 7.3
Yang Tingbao (1901–1982), graduate of the University of Pennsylvania.

Figure 7.4
Zhao Shen (1898–1978), graduate of the University of Pennsylvania.

Yang and Shen were close friends and classmates from Tsinghua Xue Tang. In Philadelphia they became classmates of Louis Kahn. Yang, in particular, was a brilliant student, winning many university prizes, including the Emerson Prize, the Municipal Arts Society Prize and the Warren Prize. University records show that Yang received his Bachelor of Architecture in 1924 and his Master's in 1925. Shen received both in 1923[27] and stayed in America to work, participating in the design of a highrise building in the campus of the University of Chicago. Yang was a favourite of Cret's, who hired him and worked with him on the design of the Cleveland Museum of Art.[28] In 1926, Yang departed America to tour Europe for a year, a common pilgrimage for many Chinese architectural graduates from America. Shen later joined him and together they visited the buildings they had learned about during their studies.

Upon returning to China, Yang and Shen went separate ways. In 1927, Yang joined the Tianjin-based firm of Kwan, Chu & Associates, established by Guan Songsheng and fellow University of Pennsylvania alumnus, Zhu Bin. The firm became Kwan, Chu & Yang Architects and Engineers, and in 1933 took on another University of Pennsylvania graduate, Liang Yen (1908–?).[29] Liang is often overlooked in comparison to China's more prolific architects of his generation, but he is attributed with having designed the modernist International Club (1936) in Nanjing where, during the New Life Movement, 'the rule against public dancing helped make this modernistic center, fostered by the Government, a rendezvous of cosmopolitan society'.[30]

Before returning to China, Liang had been Frank Lloyd Wright's first Chinese assistant. He rekindled this association when he returned to America during the Second World War, working in Wright's office before joining the United Nations Planning

Office from 1946 to 1950, where he spent the rest of his career with Harrison & Abramovitz, who had been responsible for overseeing the design and planning of the United Nations Headquarters in New York. Liang spent three years as Harrison's assistant on the design of the modern Gothic First Presbyterian Church, Stamford, Connecticut, which Harrison later described as 'the most satisfying job I ever worked on'.[31]

Returning to Zhao Shen, he settled in Shanghai and began working for Fan Wenzhao until 1931, when he established his own practice. Shen was later joined by another University of Pennsylvania graduate, Chen Zhi, and together they formed Chao & Chen Architects, which evolved into Allied Architects in early 1933, when joined by a third University of Pennsylvania graduate, Tong Jun. The alliance between the three leading partners was an important one, not only because Allied Architects were the most prolific and receptive to modernist ideas in architecture (e.g. Metropolitan Hotel, Metropol Theatre (see Plate 11), Lyric Theatre, Sun Yat Sen Cultural Education Hall and Zhejiang No. 1 Commercial Bank), but also because it represented a professional nucleus around which much of China's pre-war architectural community revolved.

Chen Zhi (see Figure 7.5) started at the University of Pennsylvania in 1923, following a year in which only one Chinese student, Fang Lai,[32] had enrolled. Chen entered the School from Tsinghua Xue Tang, where he had shared a room with Liang Sicheng from 1915 to 1919 and the pair, along with Lin Huiyin, travelled to America together.[33] Chen arrived in Philadelphia with Liang and Lin Huiyin at the start of what was to be the heyday of Chinese students entering the School of Architecture. From 1923 to 1925, a total of 11 Chinese students enrolled on the architecture course and 8 graduated (6 with Master's).

Of the Chinese students, Chen Zhi (aka Benjamin) was the most at ease with assimilating to life in the west, except perhaps for the alluring and vivacious Lin Huiyin, Liang Sicheng's fiancée. Chen's classmate, Spencer Roach, described him as 'the most popular of the male students'.[34] Chen had an exuberant and outgoing character and joined a jazz band that performed in the Glee Club. By his own admission he was 'an architect of mediocre calibre'[35] and 'interested in too many things, particularly in concerts and operas and therefore was a lazy student'.[36] He was, in fact, an accomplished student, winning the Walter Cope Memorial Prize for Architecture in 1927, awarded by Philadelphia's T Square Club, worth $100 (Liang Sicheng received an Honourable Mention) and had a prolific career that started with a year apprenticeship in the New York office of Ely Kahn (1884–1972) from 1928 to 1929.

Allied Architects' third member, Tong Jun, entered the University of Pennsylvania from Tsinghua Xue Tang in 1925 and completed his Master's in June 1928. Tong was awarded runner-up in the Arthur Spayd Brooke Memorial Prize and, like Chen, also worked in Ely Kahn's office (1929–30), before travelling around Europe and returning to China to teach at the North-Eastern University. Chen later recalled that he and Tong 'much benefited by [their] experience and training'.[37] It is notable that Ely Kahn's approach to architecture, which began with a Beaux-Arts education and evolved to embrace progressive forms of experimentation, is now recognised as a major contribution in connecting Beaux-Arts with modernism.[38] In this respect, both stylistically and methodologically, Khan's work paralleled that of many foreign and Chinese architects in China (e.g. Chen Zhi, Tong Jun, Yang Tingbao and László Hudec). Tong had a sound architectural mind and no other Chinese architect pub-

Figure 7.5
Chen Zhi (*left*) with Liang Sicheng (*right*), room-mates at Tsinghua Xue Tang before studying architecture at the University of Pennsylvania in the mid-1920s.

lished so much written material, covering, as Chen described, 'a very wide field – architectural theory, foreign histories of architecture, modern architecture in Japan, architecture in Soviet Russia and Eastern Europe'.[39] As a corpus of work, Tong's published writing in English is one of the most significant sources for foreign researchers, casting an important light on the state of Chinese architecture from the first half of the twentieth century.[40]

Just 9 Chinese students enrolled in architecture at the University of Pennsylvania after 1926,[41] compared with the 16 from 1918 to 1925.[42] Of those in the earlier group, two warrant special attention. The lives and experiences of Liang Sicheng and Lin Huiyin represent so much more than architecture in China – they crystallise what it meant to be part of China's cultural vanguard and their careers epitomise the country's encounter with and articulation of multiple modernities in the early twentieth century.

Lin Huiyin and Liang Sicheng played a very particular role in the emergence of a modern architectural consciousness in China. These two characters were neither unique in having experienced life outside China at an early age, nor in having received a western education, or in being bilingual, or in being the favourite sibling within privileged and powerful families, or in being among China's cultural elite, but no one else combined all these characteristics. Furthermore, they were a couple (see Figure 7.6).

Their story is told comprehensively in Wilma Fairbank's enthralling *Liang and Lin: Partners in Exploring China's Architectural Past*. Fairbank's work on Lin and Liang during their 'most productive period' before 1949 is unrivalled and has provided the basis for various documentaries and articles internationally. As Chen Zhi said of Fairbank years later, 'no one else could claim himself (or herself) competent in

148 *Architecture and modernity*

Figure 7.6
Liang Sicheng (*left*) and Lin Huiyin (*middle*) with their friend Wilma Fairbank.

writing' about this subject with such 'knowledge and authority'.[43] Rather than duplicate Fairbank's work, this section draws on the original and often unpublished material that led to Fairbank's publication in an attempt to highlight the degree to which Lin and Liang found themselves positioned centrally within the development of architecture in China, and to reposition and reconnect their experiences with the wider architectural and artistic communities in China as they confronted modernity.

The pair's formidable contributions to architectural modernity in China had an unlikely origin. In 1920, when Lin Huiyin was living in London with her father, Lin Changmin (former Parliamentary Secretary General and Minister of Justice, and at the time serving as co-founder of China's delegation to the League of Nations), she attended St Mary's seminary school for girls. It was here that she:

> one day found a schoolmate leaning over a drawing board and asked her what she was doing. The girl replied, 'Drawing houses,' and told her briefly something about the profession of architecture. Miss Lin was immediately swept away by an enthusiasm; this was 'just what she wanted to learn'.[44]

Architecture, for Lin, satisfied her pursuit of a 'lifework that combined daily artistic creativity with immediate usefulness' and upon returning to China 'had no difficulty in leading Sicheng to the same decision. He had always loved drawing and had thought vaguely of a career as an artist. Architecture made sense to him and pursuing it together made sense to both.'[45]

To understand Lin's contribution to China's encounter with modern architecture and modernity more broadly, it is helpful to see her, as one friend described, as 'not one character, but a historical process'.[46] Born in 1904,[47] Lin was raised in Hangzhou by her mother, the first concubine to her father who had moved to Japan to study at Waseda University. Upon his return in 1909, the family moved to Shanghai, then to Beijing in 1912, where her father quickly rose in government circles and befriended Liang Qichao, the father of Liang Sicheng. By the 1920s, Lin and Liang (senior) had become influential figures in the Lecture Association of Peking which 'had sponsored

[Bertrand] Russell and others to bring to Chinese audiences the views of celebrated thinkers in the outside world'.[48]

Liang Sicheng was born in 1901 in Tokyo, where his father was exiled. The family moved several times, giving Sicheng a broad experience of Japan, before returning to China in 1912. Their home in China was a western-style mansion in Tianjin's Italian Concession.[49] In 1919, Lin and Liang (junior), favourite offspring in both families, were formally introduced – a modern alternative to the custom of arranged marriage.

The following year, Lin arrived in London and the heart of empire with her father where she was immersed in an influential international lifestyle. It was here that she first met the writer and poet Xu Zhimo, who Liang Qichao had introduced to Lin's father. It was through Lin's father that Xu was introduced to Goldsworthy Dickinson, who arranged for Xu to attend Kings College, Cambridge, as a special student in 1921. Xu became very fond of Lin's father but it was Lin that he would later fall in love with. Although this adoration could not be consummated, a friendship was forged around a mutual appreciation for modern literature, poetry and thought – one of the many strands of China's multiple modernities.[50] Over two decades later, when China faced war with Japan, Lin wrote to Fairbank in fond reference to Xu:

> I know everyone that I love among our friends all have moral guts, but we all lack the naive fervor, some blunt physical force that will push things somehow. I wish you knew my oldest and dearest friend (Hsu) Che-mo. . . . He *did* things, fought for things, more than he talked about them – and he talked a lot about that![51]

Lin's father extricated her from these complications in October 1921 by returning to China, where she was reacquainted with Liang Sicheng. In January 1923 they agreed to marry, but their intentions were not made public until 1927. The delay was a result of Liang Qichao's insistence that they complete their education before starting a family. Lin and Liang, with their friend Chen Zhi, left for America in July 1924 intent on starting at the University of Pennsylvania in the fall semester, in preparation for which they spent the summer at Cornell University.[52]

At this stage in their careers, Lin showed most promise and was most critically admired. Since returning from London, she had been an active member of the Crescent Moon Society, published her first work (a translation of Oscar Wilde's *The Nightingale and the Rose*), written her first poems and short stories, and had helped to arrange the first major concert of western classical music in Beijing, performed by the violinist Fritz Kreisler. Only weeks before her departure for America, she had been translator to Rabindranath Tagore on his tour of China. Her 'unfailing presence and youthful loveliness had gladdened his days' so much that Tagore penned a poem to her:

> The blue of the sky
> Fell in love with the green of the earth
> The breeze between them sighs
> 'Alas!'[53]

'Through the years when she was first establishing herself as a writer the idea of going to America to study architecture constantly persisted in her mind',[54] but on arriving at the University of Pennsylvania, Lin was devastated to discover that the architectural course, which she had convinced Liang and Chen to also join, was restricted to men. Consequently, she was forced to enrol at the School of Fine Arts, later working her way on to the part-time staff of the Architectural School. Lin and Chen, the most biculturally inclined of China's architectural students, embraced fully the freedoms associated with student life in America, described by Liang Qichao as a 'Buddhist Hell ... more frightening than the thirteen torture chambers of hell'.[55] His son was more inclined to his work.

Liang Sicheng's interest in architectural history was sparked in his first semester following a lecture by Professor of Architectural History, Alfred Gumaer. Asked by Gumaer about Chinese architectural history, Sicheng:

> thought there was nothing written on it; the Chinese had never considered architecture an art and had never paid much attention to it. ... At that time all the students were studying period architecture. Sicheng did a few problems in Chinese architecture based on Ernst Boerschmann's book of photographs of characteristic Chinese building types.[56]

Sicheng's mindfulness of the absence of any systematic discipline of Chinese architectural history combined with his professional training stimulated his desire to document China's architecture.

Lin and Liang completed their respective courses in February 1927. Lin received a high honours in Fine Arts and Liang a Bachelor of Architecture, during which he won the Arthur Spayd Brooke Memorial Gold Medal, the Pan American Architectural Exhibition Gold Medal and the John Stewardson Memorial Scholarship in Architecture (1926), for which his 'Treatment of a Façade' was produced in a modern idiom. For his Master's of Architecture he studied Italian Renaissance architecture.[57] Cret's invitation to them both to work in his office in the summer of 1927 provided useful practical experience before they parted company to continue their education.

Lin went to Yale to study stage design, while Liang was keen to find out what, if anything, was being written about ancient Chinese building in the west. He enrolled at Harvard Graduate School of Arts and Sciences with the aim of undertaking 'Research in Oriental architecture', his choice being inspired by 'the supreme importance of the study of the edifices and their preservation'.[58] It became apparent that there was virtually no material available and that 'as far as Chinese architectural history was concerned very little was known',[59] so by February 1928 he was ready to leave Harvard. He persuaded Lin to withdraw from her course at Yale so that they could be married in the Chinese Consulate in Ottowa, where Liang's brother-in-law was Consul General.[60]

Their honeymoon entailed touring Europe by car 'going from architectural monument to architectural monument'.[61] At home Liang Qichao took matters concerning their careers into his own hands. Having exercised his influence to 'lead Tsinghua University to consider (reluctantly) offering Sicheng a lectureship (in architecture?) and an opportunity to teach drafting',[62] another opportunity arose for Liang to establish an Architectural Department at the new North-Eastern University in Shenyang. Liang Qichao was 'very glad to hear of this opportunity'[63] and immediately set about planning his son's return. Tensions in Manchuria made Liang uneasy about sending his son to Shenyang,[64] but when faced with the choice between

Tsinghua and North-Eastern University, Liang Qichao confided in a letter to his eldest daughter that North-Eastern 'is the better because the prospect of launching an architectural career there is bright. He can organise a firm there and start in a small way, then gradually expand.'[65] The patriarch continued: 'Therefore before he answers, I have already made the decision for him, declined the offer from Tsinghua and accepted the Tung Pei [North-Eastern] position.'[66] Yang Tingbao later claimed that Liang Qichao contacted his son immediately and ordered him home, but communications were then slow and, with the honeymooners constantly on the move, it was impossible to keep them abreast of the rapidly changing situation. Liang and Lin, having planned an entire summer travelling around Europe, had to terminate their trip for what they assumed was the teaching post at Tsinghua, only for Liang Qichao to later explain to his son that he was destined for Shenyang.

To get home, Liang and Lin had to travel across what Liang Qichao described as 'barbarous and dilapidated Russia' via the Trans-Siberian Railway, China Eastern Railway and South Manchuria Railway. Having visited England, France, Switzerland, Italy, Spain and Germany, Liang and Lin travelled to Moscow and took the train to Dalian. Their journey would have been one of architectural discovery, not only in Europe, but also in Manchuria where they would have observed first-hand the recent architectural developments in the cities of Harbin, Changchun, Shenyang and Dalian.

Liang and Lin's reaction at being home and the numbing magnitude of the task ahead is conveyed by an American couple that they had befriended on their journey:

> The experience of friendship was strengthened and made memorable by long winding conversations midst the half-ruined glories of the Pei Hai, the Confucian Temple, and other haunting places, during which it gradually became apparent that coming back had been a shock and a let-down. It had become obvious, they said, that it was going to be extremely difficult – perhaps impossible – to find a way to be useful or to have any substantial influence, in spite of their training, on the chaotic and changing motherland of those years. The problems of melding the old with the new, both in the theatre world and in architecture seemed overwhelming. And yet 'Keep on! Keep on!' was the watchword.[67]

It was during his time in Shenyang that Liang 'became an ardent admirer of ancient Chinese architecture and decided to devote himself to the research in that field. Phyllis [Lin] too, showed her intense interest in the research work'.[68] Consequently, they contacted Zhu Qiqian, a friend of Liang's father who had established the Society (later Institute) for Research in Chinese Architecture in Beijing and funded privately by Zhu with a donation from the China Foundation for the Preservation of Culture. The aim of the Institute was, in Liang's words, 'the compilation of a history of Chinese architecture, a subject which has been virtually untouched by scholars in the past'.[69] As his friend Wilma Fairbank would later observe: 'the field of Chinese architecture has been so little explored that almost every find he makes is of primary importance to adding to the present knowledge'.[70] Zhu appointed Liang Head of the Department of Technical Studies with the Japanese-trained Liu Dunzhen Head of the Department of Documentary Research. It was in these posts that he and Liu conducted their monumental fieldwork and research until 1945.

The Chinese graduates from the University of Pennsylvania's School of Architecture formed the nucleus of China's early architectural talent in the first half of the

152 *Architecture and modernity*

Figure 7.7
Dong Dayou (1899–1973), graduate of the University of Minnesota and Columbia University.

Figure 7.8
Liu Jipiao (1900–1992), graduate of the Université de Paris, Sorbonne, and L'École Nationale des Beaux-Arts, where he studied architecture and interior design.

twentieth century, though many others came from a wide range of other institutions. Dong Dayou (1899–1973) went from Tsinghua Xue Tang to the University of Minnesota (1922–25) and worked in America for a further three years (see Figure 7.7). He was draughtsman in a number of architectural firms in St Paul, Chicago and, importantly, the New York offices of Murphy & Dana, after which he attended the Graduate School of Columbia University. Dong was from Hangzhou but spent much of his childhood in Japan and Rome where he 'received his first inspiration for choosing architecture as his future profession'.[71] He would draw on this valuable experience when supervising the architecture and planning of the Shanghai Civic Centre after his return to China in December 1928. Settling in Shanghai, he first worked with two fellow American graduates, Edward S.J. Phillips (in the architectural firm E. Suenson & Co in 1929) and Zhuang Jun, before establishing his own practice in 1930.

The rising popularity of America as a place of architectural education throughout the 1920s contrasted with Japan's experience. Although Japanese universities were still well attended by Chinese students throughout the 1920s and 1930s, numbers had dropped since earlier in the century. Of the few architectural students studying in Japan in the 1930s was the Cantonese Chen Bo Qi (1903–73). Chen enrolled at the Tokyo Higher Technical School in 1930 and later travelled to Germany to study at the Berlin University of Technology, from where he graduated in 1939 before returning to China in 1940.[72] Rising anti-Japanese sentiment, improved government funding and better relations with America and Europe all contributed to Japan's comparative lack of appeal.

In Europe there was no favoured institution or even a preferred country, which makes it harder to research the experiences of Chinese architecture students who were geographically scattered and educationally assorted. Europe, with its architectural traditions and burgeoning modernism, appealed to Chinese architectural students. Even those who studied in America often embarked on grand tours of Europe after graduation.

In 1924, Cai Yuanpei's *Exposition Chinoise d'Art Ancien et Moderne* in Strasbourg was the first exhibition of Chinese art in Europe, and provided an opportunity for China's artistic community in Europe (in the broadest sense) to congregate. Among this community was Liu Jipiao (1900–92), a student who bridged the worlds of art and architecture and east and west (see Figure 7.8). Born into a wealthy family in Meizhou, Guangdong province, Liu was sent to Paris in 1919 to study French before enrolling at the Université de Paris, Sorbonne, and then in 1922 L'École Nationale des Beaux-Arts to study architecture and interior design. In 1924, he and his friend and fellow artist, Lin Fengmian, travelled to Strasbourg to participate in Cai's exhibition. Lin Fengmian had travelled to France in 1918 under the work–study programme and enrolled in the École des Beaux-Arts in Dijon before moving to Paris in 1920.[73] The year after Cai's Strasbourg exhibition Liu designed the Chinese pavilion at the Exposition Internationale des Arts Décoratifs et Industriels Modernes in Paris from April to October 1925 (see Figure 7.9 and Figure 7.10).

Liu's design encapsulated his sensitivity to both eastern and western aesthetics and what would become his life-long ambition to combine the two. The China section employed a fusion of art nouveau and Chinese styles and motifs, with dragons, stalks and peacocks, cloud formations, banner calligraphy in a modern style, fan-shaped wall hangings, screens, carpets on marble flooring, hexagonal light shades and a semi-octagonal doorway with a semi-circular design above bearing the title: 'CHINE'.[74]

The Chinese section made little impact on this international stage.

> It received no press coverage at the time, nor has it received any attention since. It won none of the many prizes.... It aroused no great enthusiasm among even the intellectual public of China, and it was treated with indifference by the Chinese government. It failed to boost China's handicraft exports, or to alter the unfavourable view which western pundits held about contemporary China's art or politics.... [It] was in many ways a 'non-event', which struck no resonances at the time and left no visible effects behind it.[75]

The lukewarm reception belied the wider significance of the Chinese section in the Paris Exposition and the political and cultural setting in which it occurred. Throughout the 1920s and 1930s, a growing reverence for Chinese art, design and literature across Europe aroused a fleeting revival of chinoiserie in various art practices, though it made little if any impression on architecture.

For Liu, his experiences in Europe were decisive. In 1929, after returning to China, he was commissioned to design the West Lake Expo in Hangzhou (see Figure 7.11

Figure 7.9
The China section at the Exposition Internationale des Arts Décoratifs et Industriels Modernes in Paris, 1925, designed by Liu Jipiao.

Figure 7.10
(*below*) Liu Jipiao's design for the China section at the Exposition Internationale des Arts Décoratifs et Industriels Modernes in Paris, 1925.

Figure 7.11 Some of Liu Jipiao's designs for the West Lake Expo (1929).

and Plate 15). His designs were non-traditional and rendered in a bold geometric style with minimal detailing, similar to his proposals for the government offices in the new capital in Nanjing, which he produced in the same year (see Figure 7.25). Liu was appointed on to the staff of the National Academy of Art in Hangzhou, 'one of the most influential centres of French modernist styles',[76] which Cai Yuanpei had founded in 1928 with Lin Fengmian. At Hangzhou, Liu became head of department and together with Lin Fengmian established the avant-garde China Art Movement while also branching into construction. In 1929, he established a construction company, Da Fang, and his own architectural practice with the same title in 1932.[77]

Another French-trained Chinese student from the 1920s was Lin Kemin (1900–99), who attended Lyon Architectural Engineering School in 1926. Lin's experiences are noteworthy because he returned to China to assume a post in the Public Works Department of Shantou Municipality, Guangdong Province, where he was responsible for roads and urban planning, and became a prolific architect in southern China.

From Germany, one of the most renowned Chinese architecture students was Xi Fuquan, who graduated in Engineering at the Technische Universität in Dresden (1922–6). In 1929 he completed his PhD at the Technische Universität Berlin. Xi returned to China the following year via Britain, France, America and Japan, and worked for Palmer & Turner, who were then designing Shanghai's Metropole Hotel and Embankment Building, then the largest apartment block in Asia.[78]

Britain hosted a number of Chinese architecture students before the Second World War, one of whom, Luke Him Sau (Lu Qianshou, 1904–92), would become among the most prolific Chinese architects of the twentieth century.[79] Luke was born into a wealthy and learned family, and lived in the Wanchai district of Hong Kong. In 1927, he left the far eastern periphery of the British Empire and travelled to its heart to study at London's Architectural Association (AA) (see Figure 7.12). Having undertaken a four-year apprenticeship with the Hong Kong-based British firm of architects, civil engineers and surveyors, Denison, Ram & Gibbs, Luke was permitted to start his studies in the second year, one year behind J.B. Brandon-Jones and two years ahead of Eric de Mare. Luke did well in his first year, receiving mostly merits and winning second prize for the course to the value of 10 shillings in books, though his lecturer's notes at the end of the year recommend he 'do more sketching'.[80] He received a diploma and an honourable mention in the 'Henry Florence' Travelling Studentship in 1930, but his major breakthrough came a year earlier when he met Pei Zuyi (father of I.M. Pei), a senior official at the fledgling Bank of China. Pei was in London to open the bank's first overseas branch at Gracechurch Street in the City of London.

Pei met Luke and invited him to lead the bank's new Architecture Department. Luke accepted the offer and at the bank's expense embarked on a six-month tour of Europe and America to research bank architecture before settling in Shanghai, from where he designed offices, warehouses and residences for the bank all over China. Many of his buildings still remain in many cities including Shanghai, Nanjing, Qingdao, Chongqing and Hong Kong. Luke's most famous building is the bank's headquarters on Shanghai's Bund, which he designed in 1935 with the large Hong Kong-based firm, Palmer & Turner (see Figure 7.13 and Figure 7.14). The proud and tall Chinese structure cuts a lonely figure amid the line of 'neo-Renaissance' foreign banks and businesses that form Shanghai's world-famous riverfront, but it marks an important development in the size and character of architecture in China by the mid-1930s. At the start of the twentieth century, foreigners dominated the

Modernism and nationalism 157

Figure 7.12 Luke Him Sau (seated third form left) with his colleagues at the Architectural Association, London, between 1927 and 1930.

foreign settlements and the institutions they harboured. This was as true in the field of architecture as any other walk of life, but by the 1930s the prevailing imbalance had been redressed and was even turning in favour of the Chinese. The capacity of a Chinese institution such as the Bank of China to buy prime real estate and make its mark on the city through modern architecture was a characteristic of post-1927 China that was as evident in the urban plans for Shanghai Civic Centre and the new capital of Nanjing as it was in the towering Joint Savings Society Building in front of Shanghai's racecourse – the tallest building in China until the 1980s – financed by a Chinese consortium (see Figure 1.1 and Plate 34).

Other British graduates included Wang Dahong from Cambridge University, H.S. Chen and Huang Zuoshen from the AA and Chen Zhanxiang (1916–2001) from Liverpool University and UCL. One of the more notable features of China's British-trained architects was the formation in the 1940s of the architectural practice, Five United (Wu Lian), with Wang, Huang, Chen, Luke and the lesser known Zhen Guanxuan, for which no further record has yet been found.

Chen Zhanxiang, or 'Charles Chen' as he was popularly known, was born into an established family from Ningbo, a prosperous city near Shanghai and among the first five treaty ports prescribed in the Treaty of Nanking. His family had been friends with Chiang Kai-Shek's family who were also from Ningbo, forging an affiliation with the Nationalist Party that would cost him dearly in later life. Chen was educated in Shanghai at the private Lester Institute of Technical Education (built in Hongkou in 1934 and designed by Lester, Johnson & Morris), Shanghai's first school of architecture (see Figure 7.15).[81] Chen continued his architectural training at Liverpool University in 1938 under William Holford (1907–75), whom he befriended and lived with during his studies. Chen remained in Britain throughout the Second World War, moving to London in 1944 to undertake a British Council-sponsored doctorate in

158 *Architecture and modernity*

Figure 7.13 Concept drawing in 1935 of the Bank of China headquarters (1935–9), Shanghai, designed by Luke Him Sau and Palmer & Turner.

Planning at UCL under the supervision of Sir Patrick Abercrombie (1879–1957), who had been Professor of Civic Design at Liverpool and had also moved to UCL to become Professor of Town Planning. Chen's association with Abercrombie would prove vital not only for his own career, but also for Beijing's prospects of being preserved. In 1946 the Nationalist government invited Chen to return to China to take charge of Beijing's master plan. Abercrombie was thrilled for Chen, knowing that the role would be more than an adequate doctoral thesis. However, much to Chen's frustration, he was retained in Nanjing as Chief Engineer in the Department

Plate 1 Two covers from 1932 of the magazine *Xian Dai* (*Les Contemporains*) by Shi Zhecun, where '*xiandai*' 现代 was used in the title to convey 'modern'.

Plate 2
Front cover of the 1931 edition of *Xian Dai Xue Sheng* (*Modern Student*), which employed the modern device of using both the Chinese and Latin script.

Plate 3
The eroticism of this scantily clad Chinese woman with silk stockings, suspenders and a bare breast, as much as the unChinese interior and other objects, conveys one version of modernity by deliberately breaking with artistic and moral convention.

Plate 4
The cover of the magazine *Shi Dai*, which employs a variety of imagery and devices to denote modernity: the English language title *Modern Miscellany*; modern architecture (including the Metropole Hotel and Hamilton House); female with modern-style Chinese dress and hairstyle; and the clock (in this case from the Customs House that towered above Shanghai's riverfront and whose bell rang out across the city).

Plate 6 Detail of Nanjing's Da Hua Theatre, designed by Yang Tingbao (1934).

Plate 5 Advertisement of Shanghai's Grand Theatre, designed by László Hudec (1933).

Plate 7 The foyer of the Nan Ping Theatre in Kunming, designed by Allied Architects (1939).

Plate 8 The Asahiza Cinema (1936), Changchun.

Plate 9 The Continental Theatre (1938), Shenyang.

Plate 10 The Tokiwa Cinema (1932), Dalian, designed by Munakata Architectural Office.

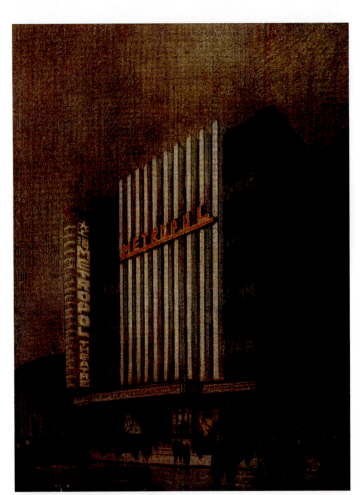

Plate 11
Concept drawing of Shanghai's Metropol Theatre (1934), designed by Zhao Shen of Allied Architects.

Plate 12
St Francis Xavier Cathedral (1849) designed by Father Nicholas Massa under the supervision of Father Hélot Louis.

Plate 13 The Union Assurance Company of Canton (1916), designed by Palmer & Turner.

Plate 14 One of the residences for the staff of Russia's China Eastern Railway, designed in an art nouveau style and completed in 1904.

Plate 15 The entrance of West Lake Expo (1929), Hangzhou, designed by Liu Jipiao.

Plate 16 St John's University, Shanghai, designed by Atkinson & Dallas.

Plate 17 Former Memorial Building (1917) of the West China Union University, Chengdu, designed by Frederick Rountree.

Plate 18 Sun Yat Sen Memorial Auditorium and Monument (1926), Guangzhou, designed by Lü Yanzhi.

Plate 19 The National Stadium (1931), Nanjing, designed by Kwan, Chu & Yang.

Plate 20 The Mayor's Office (1934), Shanghai, designed by Dong Dayou.

Plate 21 The China Aviation Association Building (1935), Shanghai.

Plate 22 The main entrance to the Shanghai Stadium (1935), Shanghai, designed by Dong Dayou.

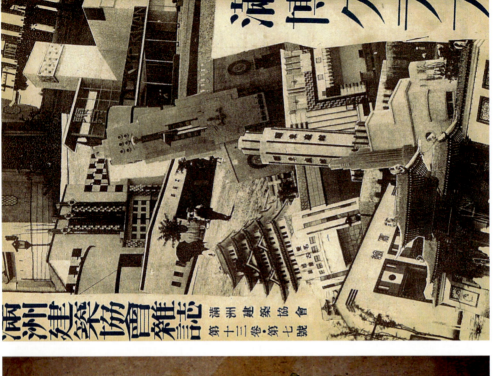

Plate 24 Front cover of a special edition of the *Journal of Manchurian Architectural Association* (July 1933) showing different designs of pavilions at the Manchuria Expo in Dalian.

Plate 23 Cover of *The Builder* from June 1936 with an artist's impression of Bank of China headquarters, Shanghai, designed by Luke Him Sau and Palmer & Turner.

Plate 25 The State Council (1936), Hsinking, designed by Ishi Tatzuro.

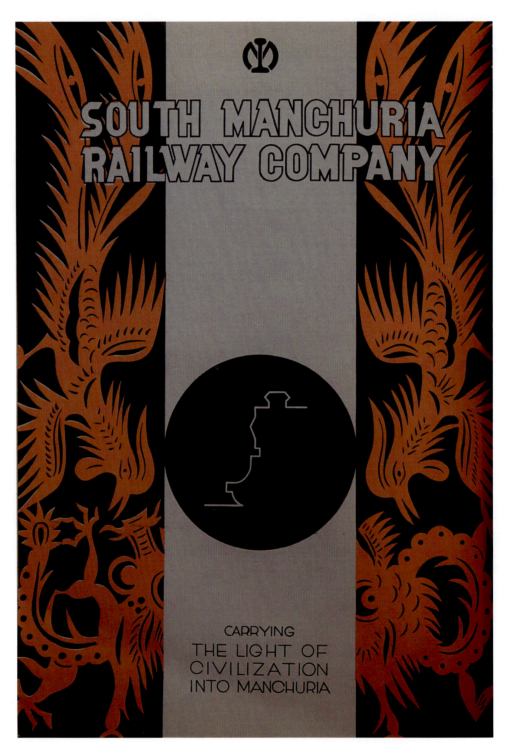

Plate 26 Advertisement for the South Manchuria Railway Company with its conspicuously colonial message.

Plate 27 Grosvenor House apartments (1934), Shanghai, designed by Albert Edmund Algar and Palmer & Turner.

Plate 28 Bank of China Headquarters (1935–9), Shanghai, designed by Luke Him Sau and Palmer & Turner.

Plate 29 Illustration of a locomotive by the architect-artist Liu Ji Piao, an essential facet of China's encounter with modernity, for the cover of the journal, *Gong Xian*.

Plate 30 Shanghai's industrial and architectural eminence combine in this advertisement for coal. Architectural imagery was often employed to convey a sense of modernity, here revealed in the layers of architecture with the older neo-classical structures in the foreground overshadowed by the taller newer buildings behind.

Plate 31 The former Sun department store (1933), Shanghai, designed by Kwan, Chu & Yang, which boasted the first escalators in China and decorative elements in a Chinese style.

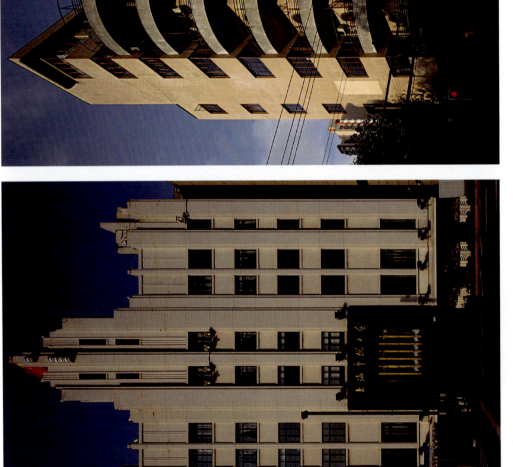

Plate 32 The Transport Bank (1937–1946), Shanghai, designed by Charles Gonda, showing evidence of a tendency towards vertical lines in Shanghai's architecture from the 1930s.

Plate 33 Magy Apartments (1936), Shanghai, designed by Léonard, Veysseyre & Kruze.

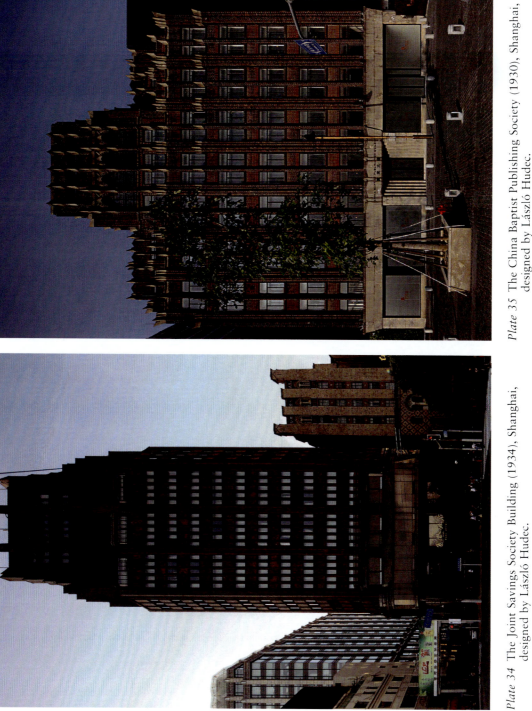

Plate 34 The Joint Savings Society Building (1934), Shanghai, designed by László Hudec.

Plate 35 The China Baptist Publishing Society (1930), Shanghai, designed by László Hudec.

Plate 36 Cover of *Man Hua Jie* (*The Comic*) encapsulating Shanghai's decadance and modernity, referencing the Hollywood star Charlie Chaplin and his film *City Lights*, Shanghai's notorious nightlife (bars, brothels, massage parlours, hotels and restaurants), high-rise architecture, clock towers and reference to the Nanking Theatre (1928), designed by Zhao Shen.

Plate 37 Cartoon of Shanghai's intoxicating nightlife, which was such a source of inspiration for modernist writers and artists.

Plate 38 The gaudy interior of the Grand Theatre, designed by László Hudec, used by Eileen Chang as a setting for a scene in her 1947 short story, *Duo Shao Hen* (*How Much Sorrow!*).

Plate 39 Cigarette advertisement employing various modern devices, including architecture, horse racing and the modern Chinese girl in a *qipao*, showing a bit of leg, of course, to reveal the absence of bound feet.

Plate 40 The science-fiction image of urban modernity forged by industry, architecture and war depicted on the front cover of *Zhong Guo Man Hua* (Chinese comic).

Plate 41 A dystopian future illustrated on the front cover of *Zhong Guo Man Hua* (*Chinese Comic*) from December 1936, predicting machines' conquest over man.

Plate 42 The carefully choreographed skyline of Pudong provides a fittingly future-facing backdrop to historic Shanghai on the opposite side of the river.

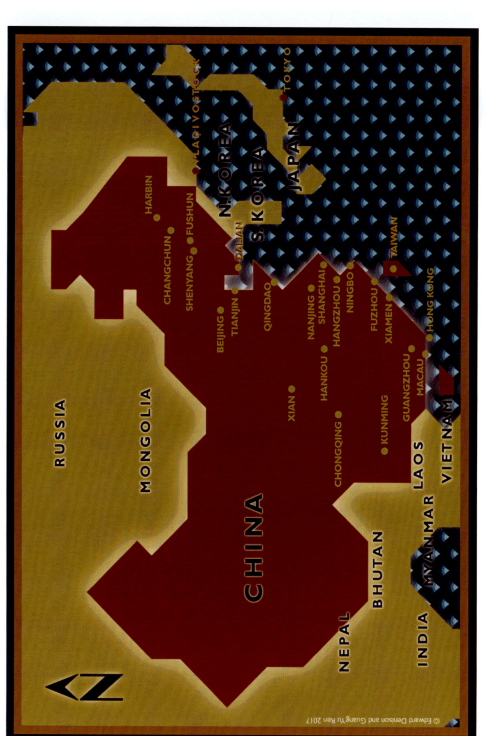

Plate 43 Map of China showing the principal cities, treaty ports and foreign settlements.

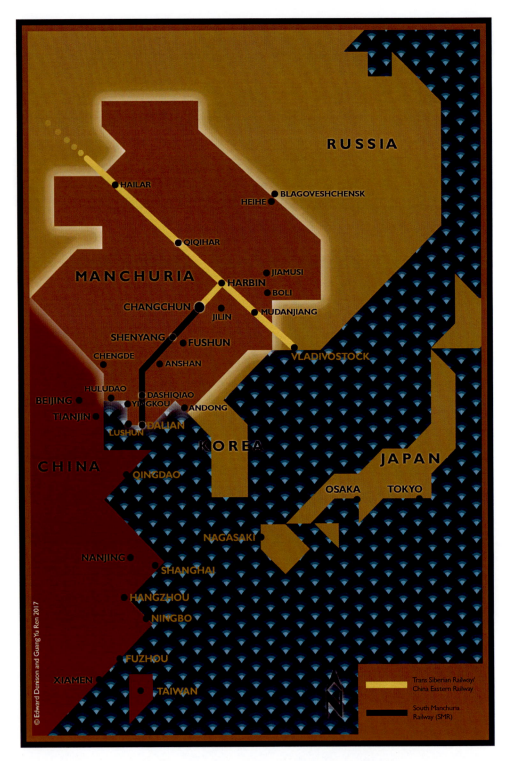

Plate 44 Map of Manchuria, showing the principal railway lines and settlements.

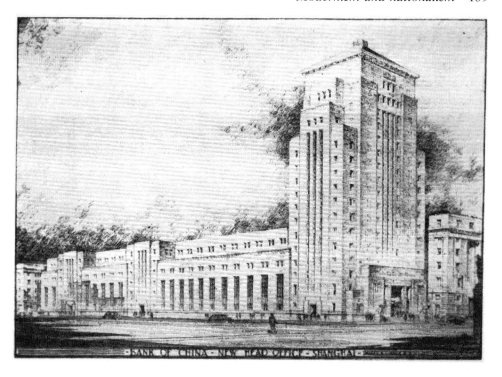

Figure 7.14 The Bank of China headquarters (1935–9), Shanghai, designed by Luke Him Sau and Palmer & Turner.

of Construction. In 1949, 'out of despair',[82] he wrote to Liang Sicheng, who by then was in charge of Beijing's new city plan, to explain his predicament and desire to work in China's restored capital. By October, Chen and his family moved to Beijing where he spent 'the most memorable time in [his] life working together with Liang'.[83]

Huang Zuoshen graduated from the AA in 1939 after the school had converted to modernism – a metamorphosis that was in its infancy when Chen and Luke studied there in the 1920s.[84] Huang was inspired by the small band of British Modernists such as Berthold Lubetkin (1899–1987), Maxwell Fry (1899–1987) and FRS Yorke (1906–1962), and later travelled to Paris and met Le Corbusier (see Figure 7.16). He was also an advocate of Walter Gropius, associating with him in Britain and following him to Harvard where at the Graduate School of Design, he became Gropius's first Chinese student and befriended the Hungarian-born Modernist Marcel Breuer (1902–1981). Huang returned to China in 1942 and later established a Bauhaus-inspired course at St John's University, one of China's most progressive architectural courses of the twentieth century.

The final member of Five United was Wang Dahong (1918–?), who was born in Beijing but grew up in Shanghai and neighbouring Suzhou (see Figure 7.17). His father, a prominent politician and diplomat, was assigned to The Hague in 1930, so Wang was sent to secondary school in Switzerland. In 1936 Wang studied Machine Engineering at Cambridge University before switching to Architecture. Following the outbreak of war in Europe, he was sent to America to enrol at Harvard's Graduate School of Design in 1940. Wang was taught by Walter Gropius and was briefly a

160 *Architecture and modernity*

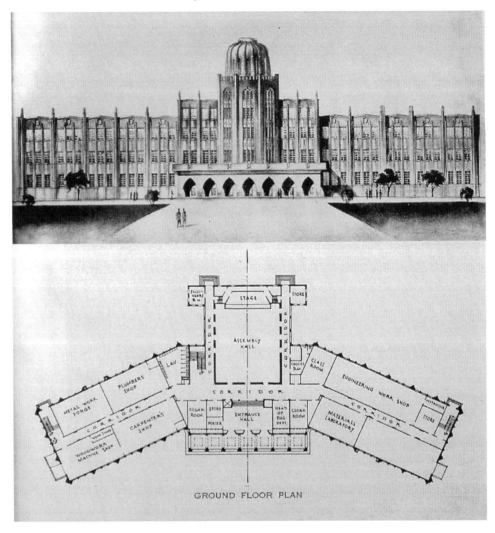

Figure 7.15 The Lester Institute of Technical Education (1934), Shanghai, designed by Lester, Johnson & Morris, Shanghai's first school of architecture and where Chen Zhanxiang trained before attending Liverpool University and University College London.

classmate of Huang Zuoshen (who left in 1941) and, later, I.M. Pei and Philip Johnson. He returned to Shanghai in 1947, shortly after which he was reunited with Huang when he joined Five United. The architectural output of Five United was limited owing to the short time the five members were together. In the dying years of the 1940s they designed a range of furniture, two projects in Taiwan – a residence for the Wei family and an office for the Taiwan Fisheries – and the Guangzhou branch of the Central Bank.

From the evidence of China's 'second generation' of foreign-trained architects, it is clear that of those who experimented with or were drawn to new ideas and practices in architecture, virtually all had experienced Europe first-hand either as graduates

Figure 7.16
Huang Zuoshen with Le Corbusier, after graduating from the Architectural Association in 1939.

Figure 7.17
Five United Architects (*clockwise from top left*): Chen Zhanxiang, Zhen Guanxuan, Luke Him Sau, Wang Dahong and Huang Zuoshen, photographed in Shanghai in the late 1940s.

from America on post-degree pilgrimages, or as students of European universities. When combined with the 'first generation', these two groups returned to China to not only become the only Chinese architects to practise in China before the Communist era, but also to lay the foundation of a domestic architectural education that survives to this day.

Architectural education in China

Of all art practices in China, architecture was the last to become subject to a systematic method of teaching in domestic educational institutions. Architectural education in China was, like other modern forms of art, dependent on returning overseas students. Architecture in China was therefore not only a foreign construct, but its teaching was dependent on foreign models. Too often overlooked – as with the experiences of China's overseas students – is the fact that the initial impetus for China's architectural education came not from the west, but from the east.

Systematic architectural education in China started in 1923 in the unlikely location of Suzhou, an ancient city in Jiangsu Province, near Shanghai, renowned for its exquisite gardens. The course was conducted by four graduates of the Tokyo Higher Technical School:[85] Liu Shiying, Liu Dunzhen, Zhu Shigui and Huang Zuomiao. In 1927, when the school was incorporated into the No. 4 Zhongshan University in Nanjing,[86] only Liu Dunzhen remained and so the course lost the Japanese emphasis on engineering and assumed instead a Beaux-Arts foundation to its teaching based on European and American traditions. The course's transition from Suzhou to Nanjing reflects also the shifting allegiance in architectural instruction in China. From this point, the Beaux-Arts became the model for the national curriculum, which was standardised by the Ministry of Education in 1928. In 1932, Liu Jipiao joined the teaching staff at the Central University, completing his move into the architectural community. In 1937, Central University was relocated to Chongqing, where it became the principal institution for architectural education and had on its staff Yang Tingbao, Tong Jun and Luke Him Sau.

162 *Architecture and modernity*

The principal legacy of Liu Dunzhen's involvement at the earliest stages of architectural practice and education in China was the technical expertise in these fields provided by schools in and around Jiangsu Province, which then contained Shanghai and bordered the affluent province of Zhejiang. These southern schools consequently offered a distinctly Japanese-oriented education compared with the later system adopted by the northern schools, typified by the North-Eastern University, which established its Architecture Department offering China's second architectural course in 1928.

In 1928, the Dean of the North-Eastern University's Engineering College, Gao Xibin, contacted Yang Tingbao, the most celebrated of the Chinese graduates from the University of Pennsylvania's School of Architecture, to offer him the job of establishing an Architecture Department. Yang claims he 'turned it down, because I was already tied up with the architectural office of S.S. Kwan and Pin Chu to which I became later a partner'.[87] Gao insisted Yang suggest a suitable alternative. Liang Sicheng had 'always considered Yang as his mentor in school days at Penn, as well as after',[88] so he recommended him for the role.

Liang Sicheng became 'Assistant Professor In Charge, Department of Architecture' at the nascent North-Eastern University in 1928 and the course that he and his wife Lin established was modelled on Cret and Laird's Beaux-Arts course they had received at the University of Pennsylvania. As the sole lecturers in the Architecture Department for the first year, Liang and his wife Lin did their best to instruct some of the first home-grown Chinese architects. Liang taught History of Architecture and Architectural Design and Lin taught Design.

In the summer of 1929, Tong Jun, Chen Zhi and Cai Fangyin joined the university.[89] Tong and Chen had graduated from the University of Pennsylvania the previous summer and returned to China to join their classmates in Shenyang, where they formed their own private practice, Liang, Chen, Tong & Cai Architects and Engineers. Lin's name was not in the firm's title, but Fairbank claims she was a 'full partner in the designing' and contributed to the planning of a park outside Shenyang, as well as 'designing private residences for wealthy [Shenyang] warlord families'.[90] Liang, Chen, Tong & Cai Architects and Engineers received several commissions, among which the only one to be realised was the new university campus (administration building, classrooms, and dormitories) for Kirin University,[91] completed in 1931.

The growing threat of war with Japan brought an early end to the aspirations of the North-Eastern University and those of its Architecture Department. Other factors also contributed. Lin was diagnosed with tuberculosis and returned to Beijing for treatment in late 1930. The following February, Chen left for Shanghai where he established a private practice with his friend and former classmate, Zhao Shen. Liang remained in Shenyang until the end of the academic year, when he handed over to Tong, a native of Shenyang.[92]

On 18 September, explosions on the South Manchuria Railway provided the pretext for Japan to occupy Manchuria in what western history calls the 'Mukden Incident'. For China, the orchestrated event is widely seen as the principal catalyst to the Second World War in Asia. Soon after, the North-Eastern University was closed and Tong made his way, via Beijing, to Shanghai, where he teamed up with Chen and Zhao to form Allied Architects in 1933.

The other educational establishments to offer architectural courses in China before the onset of Communism were Peiping Art College (Beijing), Xiang Qin University

(Guangzhou), Nanyang College (Shanghai) and St John's University (Shanghai). Peiping Art College established an Architecture Department in 1928,[93] and was unique in China for being the first architecture course to be based in an institution of art rather than engineering. However, the artistically led course taught by the French-trained Wang Shen and Hua Nangui did not last and was soon subsumed into the Engineering Department, which was closed by the Ministry of Education in 1933.

Xiang Qin University[94] established an Architecture Department in 1932, headed by Lin Kemin, the graduate of Lyon Architectural Engineering School. Xiang Qin University offered the first architectural course in southern China and advocated a modernist approach with a focus on engineering.[95] Staff members had diverse backgrounds and included the Tokyo-trained Yang Jin and Hu Deyuan and the Paris-trained Qiu Daiming, as well as other American-trained colleagues. Another important contribution to architectural modernism in China associated with Xiang Qin University was the establishment in 1936 of the journal *Xin Jian Zhu* (*New Architecture*) by two students, Zhen Zuliang and Li Lunjie, which promoted modernist architecture and published students' works that were carried out in a modernist idiom.

Nanyang College offered some engineering courses whose graduates produced architectural work.[96] An example is Yang Xiliu (1899–1978), who graduated in Civil Engineering, yet designed some of Shanghai's iconic modern buildings, including the Paramount Ballroom (1934) (see Figure 7.18) and the Nanjing Hotel (1933), and

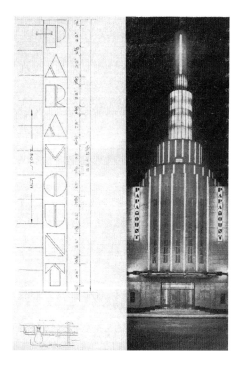

Figure 7.18
The front entrance and lighting design of Paramount Ballroom (1934), Shanghai, designed by Yang Xiliu.

Figure 7.19
Advertisement for Modern Home, a modern interior design firm established by Richard Paulick, a graduate of the Bauhaus.

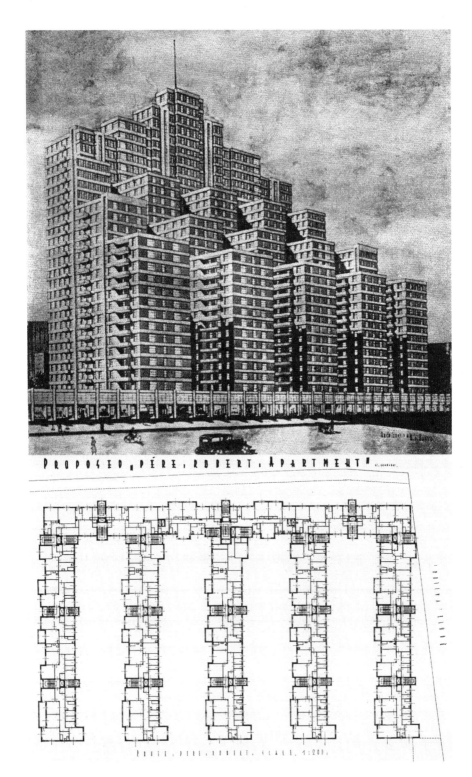

Figure 7.20 Concept design for Pére Robert Apartment, Shanghai, by H.J. Hajek (1933).

made a significant contribution to nurturing an architectural press in China. In 1934, Yang became chief architectural editor at the leading Shanghai-based Chinese newspaper *Shen Bao* and worked briefly on the Chinese architecture journal *Jian Zhu Yue Kan* (*The Builder*).

Finally, in 1942 the AA graduate Huang Zuoshen returned to China to establish the Department of Architecture at Shanghai's St John's University, which, like Xiang Qin University, established a course that embraced modernism and in so doing created another highlight in the constellation of modernist encounters in China. Huang gathered around him at St John's University a close coterie of architectural allies, including Luke, Zhen Guanxuan (of Five United), Richard Paulick from the Bauhaus, Eric Cumine and A.J. Brandt (both from the AA), and H.J. Hajek. Paulick taught urban planning and interior design and established the modernist interior design firm 'Modern Home' (see Figure 7.19). Hajek taught western architectural history and had drafted numerous ambitious and unrealised proposals for Shanghai in the 1930s, which he published in *The Builder* (see Figure 7.20).

Chinese revivalism

An inevitable outcome of China's encounter with architecture was critical self-reflection. For the first time, China's ancient buildings were observed in a new light: they were examined, studied and researched scientifically. Accompanying this new self-awareness was the threat of loss, as modern forms, techniques and materials proliferated in growing towns and cities. Reactions to these phenomena ranged from invigorated research into traditional building to new and progressive architectural approaches by both Chinese and foreign architects.

While assigning partial credit for this particular architectural development 'to the pioneering spirit of a few foreign educated architects', the architect Dong Dayou acknowledges that 'its origin must be traced to the earlier work of the missionaries who adapted Chinese style for their buildings'.[97] Although the sources of interest are connected, a distinction should be made between the motives of foreigners, for whom it was an aspect of the puzzle that was China and those of Chinese architects for whom it was a matter of the very survival of their building traditions. It was over the construction of mission schools that the question of an apposite architectural style and approach to a modern China arose for the first time, initiating a debate about modern Chinese architecture that continues to this day.

Colonial studies commonly refer to architecture as a means of fulfilling colonial policy, where the colonised environment is 'civilised' through physical order, planning and aesthetic reference. A familiar outcome, as the colonial environment evolves and the colonised assume a greater degree of participation, is the gradual assimilation of local styles, types and motifs. In the quasi-colonial setting of China's treaty ports and the non-colonial setting beyond their boundaries the situation was considerably more complex.

Missionaries and other western visitors seeking to indoctrinate the Chinese population were faced with the dilemma of how to assimilate with the Chinese in order to win their respect. Architecture and buildings were exploited to 'show a further attempt to develop Chinese relations'.[98] Missionary establishments flourished in China in the late nineteenth and early twentieth centuries. Medical, religious and educational institutions proliferated, and as their work expanded, the leaders of these

166   *Architecture and modernity*

institutions and their donors questioned what sort of physical appearance these places should assume. For the purely religious, they were confronted with the question: in what type of building should Chinese Christians worship? For those in education, as in the case of the high-profile Yale in China programme,[99] the problem was that 'for many years [they] were mistrusted'[100] by the local population. 'The ideal mission building,' claimed Bergamini, a foreign architect with experience of mission work in China, 'is one which is attractive, harmonizes with its surroundings and looks as little foreign as possible'.[101] The reason for this was simple. As another foreigner explained: 'It cannot be doubted that the great majority of Chinese view with apprehension buildings of foreign architecture.'[102] The architectural solution to emerge was one that advocated 'becoming as a Chinese to the Chinese that the Chinese may be gained'.[103]

The advantage of adapting western buildings to a Chinese aesthetic was recognised by those missionaries who understood enough about Chinese cultural sensibilities to appreciate that the alternative was ill-advised. Of the mock-Tudor or faux-Gothic campus, several of which were built in China, one writer commented that they all had:

> one characteristic in common, namely that they are utterly out of harmony with their environment. A Chinese city has a distinct architectural tone, and to plant a Mid-Victorian-Gothic chapel in the midst of it is as much out of place as for a group of people in the audience to begin singing a Moody-and-Sankey hymn during the interval of an oratorio by Handel. A glaring example of such discord is the spire with which we are so fond of finishing off a church.[104]

A church's spire is an exemplar of the inappropriateness of certain foreign building types that conflicted with the Chinese worldview, and the inviolable interconnectedness of heaven and earth. As the former British Consul of Shanghai, Walter Medhurst, remarked:

> These towers are apt to create ill-will in an entire population, the Chinese idea being that any erection pointing upwards unless it be done of their own propitiatory pagodas, is calculated to bring down evil influences productive of ill-fortune, disease, and death upon the entire neighbourhood.[105]

Learning from such advice or from others' mistakes, the missions increasingly employed architectural solutions that attempted to fuse western and Chinese architecture: the employment of western materials and techniques cloaked in a Chinese style or, as one commentator remarked, the 'battle between efficiency and beauty'.[106]

One of the first practices to experiment with this commixing of architectural types in the design of educational establishments was Atkinson & Dallas, whose leading partner, Brenan Atkinson, embodied, in part at least, the hybridising process, having been born and raised in China. Atkinson & Dallas designed the new buildings for the American Episcopal Mission in Shanghai in 1906 before it became St John's University. The college's originally modest two-storeyed Chinese buildings set around a quadrangle were razed in 1894 and replaced by the first 'modern buildings in the early twentieth century' (see Plate 16).[107] The style of the new buildings, which started with a Preparatory Department, and continued with a Science Building (1899), Dormitory (1904), Hall (1909), Library (1913) and Gymnasium

(1918), was 'wittily called "Eurasian"' on account of it being 'a combination of the European and Asiatic styles'.[108]

Atkinson & Dallas's solution was representative of what one western observer described as 'one of the most interesting and pertinent questions being discussed in foreign circles' – namely, 'the possibility and advisability of combining foreign construction and facilities with Chinese architectural style in modern buildings in China'.[109] In the case of the West China Union University (see Plate 17)[110] designed by the British architect Fred Rountree, it was acknowledged that 'not a few argued that we should present our best western styles and allow the Chinese to do their own adapting. But that we ourselves should make the attempt has prevailed.' With foreigners taking the lead, the college concluded that 'architecturally, or at least artistically, all are highly satisfied with the experiment'.[111] The speculative role cast 'the "mission architect"' as 'the "architectural missionary"'.[112]

By the late 1910s, the experimental marriage of Chinese styles with western scientific and technological methods of construction and design became ubiquitous among a certain type of foreign architect. In Guangzhou, it was employed by the Canton Christian College and the Southern Baptist Mission, for whom the Guangzhou-based architectural firm Purnell & Paget designed many buildings. In 1916, the Canadian architect, Harry Hussey (1880–?),[113] of the firm Hussey & Shattuck, began drafting plans for the Beijing Union Medical College, funded by the Rockefeller Foundation, 'designed to house the most modern hospital equipment and facilities' (see Figure 7.21).[114] One of Hussey's chief concerns was the need to build higher than the customary single storey. His model for attempting this fundamental modification was the Qian Men Gate in Beijing's city wall, which some claimed 'gives an idea of the robust ugliness of a Chinese building of several storeys'.[115]

Other concessions to modern requirements were the use of a concrete roof, which eliminated the professional work of carpenters formerly considered so integral to providing one of the essential characteristics of the structure. Hidden beneath a sea of glazed green tiles, this elemental amendment was a gesture believed to be one of several 'considerable concessions to art as against utility'[116] that the foundation made during the construction of a project that spiralled six times over the allocated budget and is said to have ruined Hussey's career.[117]

Figure 7.21 Beijing Union Medical College (1917), Beijing, designed by Harry Hussey.

168 *Architecture and modernity*

Figure 7.22
Henry Killam Murphy (1877–1954), senior partner of Murphy & Dana (later Murphy, McGill & Hamlin).

The foreign architect most closely associated with the quest for a modern Chinese architecture was Henry Killam Murphy (1877–1954), senior partner of Murphy & Dana (later Murphy, McGill & Hamlin) (see Figure 7.22), whose career is comprehensively documented in the excellent book by Jeffrey Cody *Building in China – Henry K Murphy's "Adaptive Architecture", 1914–1935* (2001). The basis of Murphy's 'life's work'[118] was 'his architectural theme of an "adaptive Chinese Renaissance"'.[119] Murphy was from New Haven, Connecticut, and had attended Yale from 1895 to 1899. He went into partnership with Richard Henry Dana, a graduate of Columbia University and the École des Beaux-Arts, from 1908 to 1921.[120]

Murphy & Dana's work in China began in 1911 with the Yale in China programme, but Murphy's first experience of Asia came in 1914 for the Episcopal Board of Missions in connection with a college in Tokyo and Korea. At the end of the trip he travelled to China with the Yale Foreign Missionary Society, during which he visited the Forbidden City and was so awed that he became committed to 'the revival of the ancient architecture of China into a living style by adapting it to meet the needs of modern scientific planning and construction'.[121] While in Beijing, Murphy had a chance meeting with the President of Tsinghua Xue Tang, Zhou Yichun, who, without having seen any of his work, invited him to undertake the design of the new college. Hereafter, 'he was engaged to design the Boxer Indemnity Fund College in Beijing'.[122]

By 1912, the local authorities in Changsha 'started a vigorous campaign to house Yale in China in a new group of buildings, scientifically planned and well built'.[123] A site for the campus was chosen less than one kilometre north of the city wall and construction began in 1914. Yale 'devoted . . . a great deal of study to the choice of

Modernism and nationalism 169

Figure 7.23 Design for the Yale in China campus, Changsha, by Murphy & Dana (1916).

a style; and the decision to use a modern adaptation of the traditional Chinese style of architecture was made only after most careful consideration of the objections raised to it in certain quarters'.[124] A Yale graduate from New York, James Gamble Rogers designed the hospital building, but most of the work was claimed by Murphy & Dana, whose design for the buildings was said to be 'an adaptation of the beautiful native architecture' (see Figure 7.23).[125]

Yale's vision and the role of architecture in achieving its objectives went beyond the purely stylistic and was among the first cases in China to openly claim to be preserving China's architectural traditions while embracing modernity:

> It was felt that in addition to the educational, medical, and religious objectives of the Yale movement there was also an opportunity for good in the buildings themselves, by showing the Chinese the possibilities of preserving their architectural heritage in a group of buildings embodying the most modern American ideas of planning and construction.[126]

Beijing's Qian Men Gate provided the inspiration for Murphy in his designs for the Library, though not as Hussey had done in his attempt to design more than one-storey, but in achieving an 'architectural climax' through stylistically emulating the massive solidity of masonry walls and their form.[127] For the first time in China, modern architecture was seen as having the potential to champion rather than counter the cause of preserving building traditions – a development later taken up and advanced by many Chinese architects (Liang Sicheng in particular) after sufficient research into ancient building practices had been conducted, and the fundamental principles identified and distilled so that they could be transposed into a modern architecture.

Much of Murphy's work in China in subsequent years fitted into this pattern, as he went on to receive many commissions for educational and missionary buildings throughout the 1910s and early 1920s.[128] Murphy also became adviser to Guangzhou Municipality's plan for a new civic centre and to the Nationalist government for the new capital in Nanjing.

The fusion of foreign and Chinese idioms is characteristic of a tendency found in colonial or quasi-colonial settings elsewhere for the more liberal or inquisitive architects to attempt to marry their own architectural position with native vernacular traditions. Whether motivated by religious or social appeasement or intellectual curiosity, this type of experimentation contrasted with the more customary attempts elsewhere to use architecture and planning to impose cultural ascendency over the colonised by means of a colonial version of 'civilised'. Interestingly, it was precisely because of China's unique political condition in the first decades of the twentieth century that the fusion of foreign and local vernacular architecture occurred away from the concentrations of foreign settlements, such as treaty ports. (This was not the case in Japanese-occupied Manchuria, where the one strand of modern architectural production proposed by the state advocated the incorporation of vernacular building styles and forms.) Commenting on the alternative world of the foreign treaty port, one foreign observer wrote:

> Treaty ports may be disregarded, because as long as they exist their architecture will be deliberately foreign, and they will be relatively less influential as Chinese cities take on their own metropolitan aspects. The treaty ports will not be expected to make any definite contributions to the development of the future Chinese styles, and the foreigners will continue to try to do buildings in the classic Greek or Italian Renaissance manner, as designed by North European or American architects who have never seen China, and executed in Japanese stucco by Chinese craftsmen.... The real field of development will be in the Chinese residence, government and institutional buildings, with foreign mission and mission architects either leading the way or retarding the natural development.[129]

Foreign architects' attempts to develop a hybrid style had much in common with the later efforts of Chinese architects, but their motives were different. It was left, ultimately, to China's young architectural community to take up the experiment, not as an architectural conundrum but as a national imperative, and, as Taylor predicted, the best lay in the design of government and institutional buildings.

National projects

By the late 1920s, the opportunities for China's young architects were greatly enhanced by a host of national projects promoted by the newly established Nationalist government. These have been well documented in previous studies and therefore feature here only in relation to the notion of multiple modernities as an important facet of China's modern architectural landscape.

The first public commission of Nationalist China was Sun Yat Sen's Mausoleum – the tomb for the Republic of China's founder – on Purple Hill overlooking Nanjing

Figure 7.24
The Sun Yat Sen Mausoleum (1925), designed by Lü Yanzhi and completed under the supervisions of Poy Gum Lee (left), photographed by C.H. Wong in 1929.

(see Figure 7.24). No national project carried such weight and significance. In May 1925, designs were invited through a public competition open to both foreign and Chinese architects. Results were announced in September with Lü Yanzhi winning first place and Fan Wenzhao coming second,[130] both elder statesmen among China's young architectural community.

Consequently, Lü became the first Chinese architect to confront the question of how to articulate a modern Chinese architecture: one that employed modern materials and techniques, and could claim to be Chinese in its character. His experience working for Murphy would have helped him, especially on projects such as Ginling College for Girls in Nanjing, considered one of the most successful examples of Murphy's 'adaptive Chinese Renaissance'. Lü's design attempted to represent three qualities, one of which reflected the foremost dilemma in Chinese architecture at the time – how to place traditional Chinese architecture comfortably in modern times. Lü's attempt at reconciling this apparent contradiction was to reflect in 'spirit', rather than a 'slavish' adherence, the form and layout of a traditional Chinese temple while ensuring the whole stands out 'distinctively as a creative effort in monumental construction of modern times'.[131] More ambiguously, it also sought 'to express the character and ideals of Dr Sun'.

Construction of the vast complex began in January 1926, but was interrupted by the Nationalist's military campaign and resumed in 1928. Access to the site was served by a 400-metre paved causeway. The mausoleum was constructed using a reinforced concrete frame, in-filled with brick and stone, a method of construction that, although modern, was claimed at the time to be 'purely Chinese in idea ... very much similar to Chinese system of posts and beams'.[132] Financial constraints dogged the project throughout and, for some, undermined its integrity as a Chinese structure. Intended to be constructed in solid masonry, the dome of the tomb had to be fabricated in a double shell of reinforced concrete faced with granite, and the roof tiles, rather than solid bronze, had to be glazed ceramic. Reinforced concrete was felt to weaken the spirit of the structure and could be seen as one too many concessions to western methods.

Had the structure been built entirely in stone rather than being a subordination of Chinese architecture to western techniques, argued one writer, it would have 'become an adaptation of western construction to Chinese architecture', which would have been altogether 'more desirable from an architectural point of view'.[133] At the time, the media claimed the 'fundamental ideas are in accordance with Chinese traditions both in planning and in the form',[134] but after a few years it was assessed more critically. Liang Sicheng, while expressing respect for Lü's 'great industry and imagination', made the assessment that the 'design still shows some lack of understanding of Chinese architectural principles'. His colleague and friend, Chen Zhanxiang, assumed a more global perspective, pointing to the trees and 'vast flights of steps' and exclaiming 'surely they derive from occidental classical monumentality and are wholly alien to our traditional conception. . . . It is no more Chinese than a Gothic Revival church by Godwin or Barry is Gothic'.[135] What is evident from the contemporaneous discourse surrounding the mausoleum, however critical, is a desire among Chinese scholars and practitioners to seize ownership not only of their architectural past, but also of the present and future.

In 1926, Lü won another major state-sponsored architectural commission: the Sun Yat Sen Memorial Auditorium and Monument in Guangzhou (see Plate 18).[136] Intended to be the largest hall in Asia, the Memorial Auditorium measured 70 metres by 80 metres in plan, rising to a height of 50 metres, and accommodated 5,000 people. Like the Mausoleum in Nanjing, the octagonal Memorial Auditorium (the number eight is auspicious in China) adopted a Chinese style in its detailing (e.g. roof line and eaves, internal balustrades, exterior columns and decoration), but its steel and concrete frame was entirely designed, detailed and fabricated by Andersen, Meyer & Co. Ltd, who boasted 'the interesting combination of most modern style of design with typical Chinese architectural features'.[137]

Although the Sun Yat Sen's Mausoleum and the Memorial Auditorium and Monument were considered to have failed to sufficiently capture the essence of Chinese building, they mark important milestones in the development of modern architecture for Chinese architects. They were forced to confront issues that prevented traditional constructional values from being reproduced in the modern world. For some, like Lü, the attempt to overcome this insuperable problem was achieved through the 'designs [being] conceived in a Chinese style and worked out in modern methods' so as to develop China's architecture 'into a living style'.[138] The architectural approach was 'an attempt at translating or rather developing Chinese architecture from wood to stone and concrete', but to some people it resulted neither in 'the adapting of Chinese forms to modern construction nor vice versa'.[139]

Successful or not, these structures represent the first attempt by a Chinese architect to design 'modern Chinese' buildings and their significance therefore lies in the precedent they set. When one considers the task that Lü set himself, it is evident that it would have defeated almost any architect in any culture:

> To recreate in the medium of architecture that character which is Dr Sun Yat Sen and to interpret in architectural form the spirit and ideals of Dr. Sun which seeks to embody the highest of the philosophical thought of ancient China into the practical solution of life problems of the human race by methods developed through modern scientific researches.[140]

In 1932, a nine-storey Memorial Tower in the form of a pagoda, designed by Murphy, was completed in the Martyrs' Cemetery near the Mausoleum complex. It was one of Murphy's last major structures before leaving China and the one he was most proud of. In a speech he gave at his farewell gathering in Shanghai in July 1935, he claimed his mission in China was twofold – one was to carry out the professional duties of an architect, and the other was to 'study Chinese architecture'.[141] He went on to make special mention of this pagoda and how he often thought about it and was honoured to have participated in its design, which was based on Nanjing's famous fifteenth-century porcelain pagoda, one of the Seven Wonders of the World before it was destroyed in 1856 by the Taiping rebels. Both pagodas were octagonal and contained a central spiral staircase, but Murphy's, unlike its white porcelain predecessor, was constructed in reinforced concrete.

During his time in China, Murphy had positioned himself close to the heart of government and his own 'adaptive Chinese Renaissance' architecture appealed to their sensibilities. Whether Murphy's design played a proactive or reactive role in creating a suitable national style of architecture is an open question. What is certain is that his designs corresponded to the attitudes of a certain section of Chinese society reconciling the parallel objectives of understanding and preserving the past and embracing and fashioning the future. These concurrent experiences materialised in numerous architectural projects of varying size and location, but none were as large and complete as the plans for the new capital, Nanjing, and the new civic centre of Shanghai. These two landmark projects have been the focus of various studies and are detailed in *Modernism in China* (Denison and Ren, 2008), but their presence and significance here lies with their comparison to other modern urban plans throughout China and their role as productive sites of architectural experimentation.

Nanjing: the new capital

Nanjing was the capital of China from 1368 to 1421. The Nationalist government's decision to relocate the capital from Beijing in 1927 presented unparalleled opportunities for China's young architects and urban planners. In the 1920s, Nanjing's municipality established a City Planning Bureau and the South-Eastern University, based in the city, established a civil engineering course that included urban planning, architecture and infrastructure development. In July 1928, the London and Cambridge graduate, Liu Jiwen, became Mayor of Nanjing and immediately set about implementing programmes to improve the city's decaying and outdated infrastructure,

174   *Architecture and modernity*

Figure 7.25 Liu Jipiao's concept designs for the Nationalist government's headquarters in Nanjing (*top left and bottom*), Auditorium (*top right*) and Martyrs' Shrine (*middle right*).

including a competition for the city's urban plan and the design of its public buildings. Unlike the competition entry by the Paris-trained architect-artist, Liu Jipiao, comprising idiosyncratic stepped pyramid designs, the chosen plan claimed to possess a national aesthetic (see Figure 7.25).

Despite their intent to counter foreign authority in China, the Nationalists sought foreign advisers to assist in their plans that 'conceptualized [Nanjing] as the new Washington, D.C.'.[142] The sympathetic Murphy was hired as chief architectural adviser in October 1928, a choice that cannot be disassociated from his commission in 1922 to draft China's first modern urban plan for an implemented civic centre for Guangzhou.

In Nanjing, Murphy hired the American engineer Ernest Goodrich, who had worked on harbour developments in South America, south east Asia and America, and with whom he had worked in Guangzhou. Goodrich hired two more Americans, Colonel Irving Moller and Theodore McCroskey, to 'assist in solving cartographic and engineering problems'.[143] Lü Yanzhi was also hired as the only qualified Chinese architect in the group.

Before the Americans were appointed, the city's transformation was already underway. In January 1928, the National Capital Construction Committee was established and the first draft plan for Nanjing, 'The Great Plan of the Capital' by I. Jingqi, was prepared, based on the zoning of different activities: residential, governmental, educational, shipping and industrial. The plan incorporated urban planning principles from the American 'City Beautiful' school here implemented by the Chinese for the first time; its features were radial design, grid plan, ring roads, monumental avenues and city parks. It was also deferential to Sun Yat Sen's own 'industrial plan' for Nanjing that he had devised in 1919, placing industry on both sides of the Yangtze River, emphasising the importance of the port, while political, municipal, and commercial facilities were concentrated in and around the city centre.

At the heart of the plan was the 12-kilometre axial thoroughfare, Zhongshan Road, which set a precedent for the subsequent layout of the city. It also caused 'bitter resentment'[144] among the local population, who suffered appallingly through the 'indiscriminate destruction of houses with the object of widening roads' by the authorities who were 'paying owners next to nothing in the way of compensation'.[145] So hurried was the execution of Nanjing's plan that the writer, Guo Moruo, is said to have written derisorily: 'It is as if 10 generations have been reduced to one hour in this place.'[146]

After the appointment of Murphy and his American colleagues, a new plan was prepared under their direction with the support of their Chinese colleagues on the National Capital Construction Committee – Lin Yimin, Zhou Yue and Huang Yüyü. In December 1929, the government formally revealed the 'Plan of the Capital', which was said to be 'based on the European and American principles of science and the advantages of aesthetics of our country'. Like its predecessor, it advocated the zoning of different activities, with the town separated into eight districts, including three different classes of housing. For the first time in China's architectural history, the design of mass housing became a professional objective. Government officials and wealthy classes enjoyed a suburban setting in detached villas, of which nearly 2,000 were built, while those of lesser rank were housed in higher density accommodation.

The Nationalist government's haste in implementing the Plan of the Capital and erecting the various government buildings was seen by some to reflect their own sense of transience: 'There exists a certain amount of scepticism,' remarked one journalist, 'as to the permanence of the government which is putting them in hand'.[147] Nevertheless, the audaciousness of the project was applauded by optimists who saw that the 'reconstruction of Nanjing may seem the enterprise of madmen, but there's a certain nobility in such madness ... to be well dressed is a great incentive to virtue, and it is a common experience that handsome does as handsome is'.[148]

Another novel feature of the Plan of the Capital was the stipulation that architectural style be a constituent of planning, a legacy either of Murphy's commitment to Chinese characteristics in modern buildings or the perceived necessity of representing national identity, as stipulated by Sun Yat Sen's son, Sun Ke, in his capacity as the government's international emissary in seeking financial support for their ambitious plans. The Plan of the Capital stated that the Chinese style was considered the 'most beautiful in colour arrangement, provides the best light and air [was] easy to build in stages [and] broadcasts the culture of the country'. Buildings in the political zone had to adopt the Chinese style and in the commercial areas buildings had to have certain Chinese decorations (see Figure 7.26). The requirements went beyond superficial appearance and the choice of decoration so that each building had to contain an internal courtyard. These design principles were depicted in a concept sketch by Murphy's assistant, Huang Yüyü, that was later denigrated by Chen Zhanxiang for looking 'alarmingly like peacetime Piccadilly Circus dressed up in Chinese clothes as tawdry as a music hall mandarin's'.[149]

176 *Architecture and modernity*

Figure 7.26 Sketch by Huang Yüyü illustrating the national style stipulated in the design principles of the Plan of the Capital.

Among the most prominent structures was the Ministry of Foreign Affairs, designed by Allied Architects in a restrained classical style. Construction started in 1931 and after its completion *The Chinese Architect* claimed it to be 'practical rather than grand'[150] and 'the most modern building in the capital. It fully expressed the art of our architecture, but is also practical. It does not have any unnecessary decorations to undermine the simplicity and elegance of the building'.[151] The symmetrical façade comprised two wings that stood proud of a taller central body fronted by a bulky stone porte-cochère. The building was constructed in reinforced concrete and faced with tiles and a granite base, and crowned by a large cornice supported by large corbels evoking a Chinese-style eave.

Nearby was the Supreme Court, designed by Guo Yangmo, the Harvard and MIT graduate and former partner of Lü Yanzhi, with whom he had designed the neoclassical Shanghai Banker's Association Building in Shanghai. The monumental pretensions of the entrance contrasted with the otherwise modest appearance of the three-storeyed symmetrical structure, described in *The National Geographic* as resembling 'an American school-house of 25 years ago' and being 'western, even to the awnings and lampposts'.[152]

More progressive, aesthetically, was the Central Agricultural Laboratory (1934), one of the first commissions for the architectural firm Sü, Yang & Lei (see Figure 7.27). The structure's horizontality derived from its inventive treatment of fenestration; interconnecting planar elements beneath low-pitched roofs evoked Frank Lloyd Wright's work and presaged their later and less embellished design for Shanghai's new fish market (1935) that was part of the Civic Centre development. The building's architect, Xu Jinzhi, was a graduate of Michigan University (1927–31) and later studied at the Cranbrook Academy of Art where he was apprentice to Eliel Saarinen

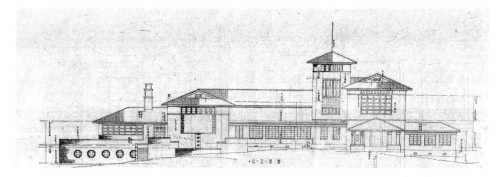

Figure 7.27 The Central Agricultural Laboratory (1934), Nanjing, designed by Sü, Yang & Lei.

during his work on the Kingswood School Cranbrook. Xu had also worked for Fan Wenzhao before establishing his own practice with colleagues Yang Runjun and Li Huibo in 1933.

The aesthetic variety of Xu's work, like that of many of his contemporaries, is revealed by contrasting contemporaneous designs for the Shanghai fish market and National Central Museum in Nanjing. His design for the latter comprised a central palace-style building in a Qing style sitting on a stone platform containing outbuildings. It was later amended in a Liao style, in line with the Nationalist government's refutation of the Qing and its Manchurian origins, which were considered un-Chinese (see Figure 7.28). The revision highlights another important component of China's complex circumstances in which intranational conditions complicated notions of architectural modernity and national style, and unsettled the dualistic discourse of nationalism and internationalism. The National Central Museum was one of many modern Chinese projects that exposed the tensions underlying the question of national style and the absence of a modern history of China's building traditions, which was little understood at the time by Chinese architects, let alone foreigners in China for whom Beijing's Forbidden City was the standard. It was Xu who, in exile in 1964, published the important architectural history book: *Chinese Architecture – Past and Contemporary*.[153]

One of the Nationalist government's more controversial projects was a national sports event to be held in 1931, an event that in its spectacle and lavish facilities reflects what Chakrabarty refers to as the 'carnivalesque aspects of democracy' through which nationalism and politics are 'performed'.[154] A site was chosen in the grounds of the Sun Yat Sen Mausoleum and Kwan, Chu & Yang were commissioned to prepare designs for a 60,000 seat stadium and additional facilities, including swimming pool, baseball, basketball, football, horseracing and martial arts. Ongoing conflict and natural disasters caused the event's cancellation, but construction continued hastily. Like so many modern buildings in China, preparing designs for entirely new typologies such as sports facilities which had no precedent in Chinese building and housed activities that Chinese viewed sceptically, posed an architectural conundrum. The structures had to satisfy a client that insisted public buildings display traditional characteristics, while at the same time ensuring they were in keeping with the surroundings of Sun Yat Sen's Mausoleum.

178 *Architecture and modernity*

Figure 7.28 The National Central Museum (1935), Nanjing, designed by Xu Jinzhi first in the Qing style (top) and amended in the Liao style (bottom).

The consequent compromises were a series of structures in reinforced concrete – durable, cheap and practical, but with Chinese motifs adorning certain elements such as doorways, window frames and entablatures. The main building of the open-air swimming pool was among the most traditional, said to be 'in a palace style [and] decorated with traditional elements inside and out'.[155] The main stadium's monumental entrance with its seven galleried bays flanked by two towers was an attempt to employ traditional elements in a new building type creatively, but the result appeared like an oversized traditional balustrade (see Plate 19). While it is difficult to judge these unprecedented structures aesthetically, functionally they were far from satisfactory. Poor planning resulted in some facilities being unsuited to their location and poor construction demanded continuous maintenance.

Responsibility for the physical representation of national identity and pride was (and to some extent still is) a burden that Chinese architects bore uncomfortably throughout the twentieth century. The city planning and individual structures in Nanjing between 1927 and 1937 represent the first large-scale attempt to address the question of reconciling China's ancient building practices and the potential of modern architecture, but hasty construction, an insufficient budget, a lack of experience and limited time prevented a satisfactory answer.

The Greater Shanghai Plan and Civic Centre

Challenging the power and authority of foreign settlements in China was one of the Nationalist government's immediate concerns upon taking office in 1927. This preoccupation assumed a significance in architecture and city planning that further destabilises established assumptions about prevailing power relations and challenges post-colonial assertions that, for example, 'from Rangoon to Cairo, Luanda to Singapore, cities were laid out by the rulers not the ruled'.[156] The Nationalist government declared the city a 'special district' and formed a City Government of Shanghai to administer the areas outside the foreign settlements, known as Greater Shanghai. A plan was devised to draw influence away from the foreign settlements by creating a new urban centre to the north, occupying a large area of land between the existing settlements and the mouth of the Huangpu River, where it joins the Yangtze River.

The Shanghai Plan has received more scholarly attention than Nanjing's, though, as MacPherson rightly stated, despite Shanghai's rank among the world's great cities before 1949 it was nevertheless 'ignored in the literature or dismissed as aberrant', and until comparatively recently treated by Chinese scholars as an 'ephemeral or aberrational phenomenon'.[157] Paralleling the fate of literary and artist endeavours during the Nationalist period, subsequent political attitudes have relegated the architectural contributions that furnished the Shanghai Civic Centre and the Greater Shanghai Plan.

The Civic Centre plan is an important episode in Shanghai's evolution. For the first time since the Treaty of Nanjing it represents China's will and ability to wrest control of its sovereign territory from foreigners, further layering its complex urban form and offering important insights into the sociopolitical conditions at that time. In the late nineteenth century, the Viceroy of Jiangsu Province, Liu Kunyi, had proposed a similar scheme, but it was never realised. The first Mayor of Shanghai,[158] Huang Fu, deserves 'due credit for reviving the idea',[159] though he was not able to see it through as his tenure lasted only from July to September 1927. The second Mayor (from 1927 to 1929), Chang Dingfan, kept the idea alive but nothing materialised until the third Mayor, Chang Chun, established a committee in July 1929 to oversee the implementation of the plan. In the same year, the Bureau of Public Construction:

> looking ahead to the day when the International and French Settlements will be surrendered to Chinese sovereignty and the whole city administered as a single Chinese municipal unit . . . invited architects to submit plans for a new civic centre and street system for the greater metropolis.[160]

Dong Dayou was appointed Chief Architect and Adviser and charged with creating 'a conveniently planned city with artistic thought on sound business lines'.[161]

The plan depended on and was a product of the more stable conditions following the establishment of a national government. Political stability fostered a heightened sense of national self-confidence that found expression architecturally, as in other art practices, in attempts to establish a national identity and project a sense of modernity. The judges of the Civic Centre plan, published in 1930, claimed that 'there was a lack of appreciation of the full possibilities of Chinese architecture and knowledge of how to adapt it to the practical requirements of modern city-planning and construction without sacrificing its essential aesthetic qualities'. It also claimed that 'the competition showed a distinct advance' over the Nanjing competition the previous year, 'but the competing architects had failed to appreciate the necessity for planning on a "monumental scale", such as the great future of the port called for'.[162] The initial observation reveals the prevalent predisposition in official circles for a modern *national* architecture. The perceived failure to adopt Chinese architecture to modern requirements is particularly revealing of a new attitude towards the significance of a national architectural tradition.

The list of prize-winners in the competition featured a number of foreign and foreign-trained Chinese architects, including the college friend and professional partner of Dong Dayou and former employee of Murphy, Edward Phillips, who came third, winning $750. The American architect Poy Gum Lee[163] (a former employee of the YMCA and Murphy) won $300 for first mention, while Shen Liyuan, the graduate of Napoli technical school and, by then, Professor of Architecture at the National Beijing University, won $100 for a mention. The winners were Zhao Shen (another former Murphy protégé) and Sun Ximing who won the $3,000.[164]

The winning design was used as the basis for the City Planning Commission, founded in 1929, to create the finished master plan for the entire development. The commission was headed by Dr Shen Yi, trained in Germany and supported by Dong Dayou. Later that year, a consulting engineer from San Francisco, C.E. Grunsky, studied the Chinese plans and made a few recommendations. In a memorandum, he suggested 'special study should be given to the location of parks, playgrounds, golf courses, a stadium, race course, etc'. Secondary mention was given to the location of 'schools and fire-engine houses'.[165]

The first plans produced by the City Planning Commission were published in 1931, after two years of consultation between other foreign advisers, including A.E. Philips from Washington, DC and Professor Hermann Jansen of Berlin University, and architects and engineers in the Greater Shanghai Municipal Government's City Planning Commission, including Dong (see Figure 7.29). Having established his own practice in 1930, Dong was largely responsible for the general layout of the streets, administrative buildings, public buildings and residential areas, which contained China's first modern social housing. Experience on a project of this scale served him well, as he became a prolific architect engaged with several major public commissions throughout the 1930s. He won fifth prize for the Sun Yat Sen Memorial Pagoda and subsequently participated in the planning of the capital cities of Jiangxi, Hubei and Guangdong provinces, and the city of Hankou.[166]

The plan for Greater Shanghai and the Civic Centre comprised new administrative and business districts, port and wharves, and railway terminuses. As with the plan for Nanjing, the different activities were to be arranged in zones around the Civic Centre, which occupied about 3 per cent of the 16,700-acre site. The different zones were to be connected to one another by a modern transport network, including a system of roads radiating from the centre, and an extension of the railway to link the port with the industrial areas and the wider railway network. The first bridge to span the Huangpu River was also proposed but never built. The plans for the road network combining grid and radial systems was made public in 1930 and revised in 1932.

The designs for rented housing and commercial buildings were open to competitions, won by Xu Ruifang and Poy Gum Lee respectively,[167] whose designs were predominantly variations on the *lilong* theme, the terraced dwelling that combined

Figure 7.29 The plan for Greater Shanghai (1931) showing the cruciform Civic Centre.

the Chinese courtyard house and the British terrace house, and was a distinctive architectural feature of Shanghai. No definite estimate of the cost of the scheme was given, but it was to be financed predominantly by the Nationalist government's policy of selling land in and around the scheme.

At the heart of the scheme was the Civic Centre, comprising monumental buildings, spacious parks and gardens, and a modern system of roads laid out in a grid ranging from 60-metre wide avenues to 25-metre wide streets. The layout of the Civic Centre was defined by the two primary avenues oriented in a north–south and east–west direction respectively. Along the southern avenue was planned a 2,500-foot long reflecting pool with two smaller pools along the eastern and western approaches. The cruciform plan containing ten government buildings covered approximately 330 acres. Its designers ascribed its axiality to traditional Chinese planning, but its monumentality might equally be attributed to contemporaneous planning principles in the west in the manner of the City Beautiful Movement. The location of the towering 200-foot pagoda at the central axis challenged convention, wherein pagodas were usually sited off-centre. Central public areas and gardens added 'breathing spaces' that covered 'no less than 15 per cent of the total area'.[168]

Like the City Beautiful Movement and Garden Cities, the plan for Shanghai, China's most industrialised city, was intended 'as an example for the encouragement of a general city-planning movement throughout the country'.[169] It is no coincidence that in the novel *Er Ma*, written in London in 1929 by Lao She, Welwyn Garden City was the site of an excursion by two leading characters who marvelled at its scientific planning – 'the use of electricity, the new forms of architecture, the ways of tending and protecting flowers and trees, the layout of the streets, all were scientific'.[170] The modernisation of China's ancient urban centres was regarded by many Chinese as vital to the nation's modernisation and pursued rigorously in the Chinese-controlled areas of several cities. In the 1920s, for example, Guangzhou was said to have 'forged ahead to convert the old city into a modern metropolis' and by 1930 was described as being 'progressive, modern, prosperous and rich [and] the only city with modern conveniences, entirely constructed and controlled by Chinese'.[171]

The persistent paradox confronting Chinese planners and architects was how to pursue modernity in an urban context while retaining Chinese characteristics. At Shanghai, the answer was sought not in the urban plan, but in the design and arrangement of individual buildings, the first of which, in Shanghai, was the Mayor's Office (1931–4), 'designed'[172] by Dong. After the plans for the Mayor's Office were revealed in 1931, the design was said to 'include all the Oriental beauty in architecture'[173] and became the benchmark for the generic term of ' "Chinese Renaissance" architecture'.[174] The term echoed Murphy's parlance and was liberally applied to any building constructed with modern materials, topped with a tiled Chinese-style roof and decorated internally and externally with Chinese motifs.

The four-storey Mayor's Office, constructed in reinforced concrete and steel, possessed all these characteristics and was said by one commentator to combine the 'colourful exterior of the Peiping Palaces with the requirements of a modern office building' (see Plate 20).[175] Attempts to retain key traditional features include the separation of the structure's base, middle and top, and the insertion of a ceremonial staircase leading to the first floor. The design of the Mayor's Office might not please the architectural purist, but as the first attempt to integrate traditional aesthetics with modern construction in an office building by Chinese architects and builders, it was an important milestone and an advancement of Lü Yanzhi's earlier efforts. More than Lü's work, however, it set the standard for many public buildings, such as museums and libraries designed by Chinese architects up to the late 1940s that was exported to Taiwan with the Nationalists after 1949.

Less stringent requirements to evince national characteristics were placed on buildings of lesser rank in Shanghai's Civic Centre, (e.g. museum, public library, hospital and sports centre). These reveal alternative but nonetheless equally interesting attempts to find solutions to the architectural dilemma of combing old and new. This can be seen in the library, the museum and the China Aviation Association building. The library and museum were two storeys high and constructed from reinforced concrete (see Figure 7.30).[176] As with some of Murphy and Hussey's earlier works, these structures sought inspiration from the traditional Chinese gate tower 'modelled after the Peiping style'[177] in the central portion of the building, flanked by wings containing ancillary rooms. The claim made by one commentator that these designs were 'simple and dignified'[178] is justified on the grounds that these solid and unembellished buildings were inspired by tall stone structures, unlike many other public buildings from the period, such as the Mayor's Office, that were based on wooden-frame structures.[179] In 1936, the museum hosted a major exhibition (the first outside Beijing) on the findings of the Institute for Research in Chinese Architecture led by Liang Sicheng comprising 300 large *'astonishingly impressive* [photographs] and *coloured renderings'* and scale models.[180] 'Too tired to take the trip down', Liang's wife, Lin Huiyin, 'had to cancel the trip to Shanghai and let [Liang] shine alone over our brilliant exhibition' that she had 'worked like a slave for two weeks' to prepare.[181] The rarity of the occasion and its specific setting belied its importance in demonstrating the fragile link between architectural theory and practice, where the historical and scholarly work by Liang and his colleagues in Beijing could be exhibited in an

Modernism and nationalism 183

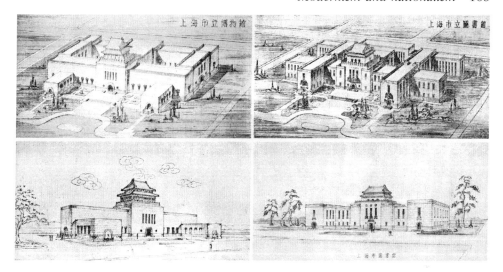

Figure 7.30 Designs for the library (*right*) and museum (*left*) in the Shanghai Civic Centre (1935) by Dong Dayou.

Figure 7.31 Artist's impression of the China Aviation Association building (1935), Shanghai and plans.

architectural space that was simultaneously modern, Chinese and located outside foreign-controlled Shanghai.

Breaking with historical convention, the China Aviation Association building was the most playful of the Civic Centre's otherwise rather sober structures. The design, in the shape of an aeroplane, might be seen as a rare Chinese tribute to Futurism, but it is more likely a literal representation of the building's client, designed to 'suit the environment and meaning of the aviation industry' (see Figure 7.31 and Plate 21).[182] In case this meaning was not conveyed explicitly enough in the building's form, the artist's impression further incorporates a model aircraft within a coronet of traditional balustrading on the roof above the main entrance.

Other features of the Shanghai plan included a recreation ground similar to that in Nanjing. Completed in autumn 1935 and costing $1,150,000 in a year that the municipality recorded a $3.5m. debt, the sports complex contained a gymnasium, swimming pool and athletics stadium, with additional land set aside for tennis courts and a baseball field. The massive stadium formed the centrepiece, seating 70,000 and with potential for further expansion to include an extra 30,000 seats. The unprecedented structure was built in reinforced concrete, red brick and artificial stone. By 1936, the media had settled on a generic response to these Chinese-style buildings, describing the stadium as 'Chinese in character but in line with modern construction' (see Plate 22).[183]

The Chinese architectural conundrum

While China's national projects are architectural curiosities, their greater significance is in the way they embody the dilemmas confronting China's young architects as they sought to reconcile a modern future with China's past. These dilemmas occurred in several phases and aroused numerous spirited debates invariably framed dichotomously: tradition versus modernity, nationalism versus 'foreignisation' and purity versus hybridity. They were also mediated by China's uniquely multifarious confrontations with Japan, foreign extraterritoriality, traditionalism, nationalism, intra- and internationalism, and colonialism's multiple manifestations.

The ultimate and unavoidable paradox facing Chinese architects was that the pursuit of 'Chineseness' was essentially incompatible with the entirely western origins of the practice in which they were engaged. Espousing the art of architecture (let alone the ideas, methods and materials that defined modern architecture) could alone be seen as an act of capitulation and subjugation. Although many of China's early architects recognised this paradox, they did not see it as irreconcilable. Their arrival into this novel profession coincided with China's wholesale exposure to modernity and their stance was no less contradictory than the strategies employed by other art practices. Unlike other arts, they had not been engaged in China's first encounters with modernism, but they, more than their artistic peers, carried a greater responsibility for literally and figuratively building a modern nation.

The arrival of modern construction methods and techniques, and the ideas of architectural modernism in China coincided with an existential crisis. As the imperial system of government, the classical language, the civil service examinations, and other customs deemed ancient and anachronistic were regarded by the new liberals as incompatible with modern China, so too was the 'heap of old rags' that constituted China's traditional buildings.[184]

The first phase of this shift away from a Chinese past was the espousal of western-style buildings, as had occurred in Japan years earlier. Prominent examples include private houses and late-Qing or post-Republican public buildings such as the Supreme Court of Justice (1914) designed by Atkinson & Dallas, and the new Parliament in Beijing (1910–11) and the Provisional Parliament (1912–13) designed by the Qingdao-based German architect Curt Rothkegel (1876–1946). The three-storey Supreme Court crowned with a clock tower and the four-storey Provisional Parliament crowned with three cupolas and reminiscent of the former Reichstag, were designed in western neoclassical styles, though the latter was never completed. Consequent on the prevailing architectural trend, in the generally conservative political and merchant communities that formed China's quasi-colonial settlements at that time, the Chinese perception of modern architecture was associated with western neoclassicism. The natural conclusion to this phase was that 'since the "new" must come from the west ... "modernization" [meant] "foreignization"',[185] a compelling and powerfully seductive assumption that has dominated and distorted modernist historiography ever since.

Architecturally, 'foreignization' was a trend noted by the Shanghai's Municipal Council as early as 1912, which reported that among the new Chinese houses 'a serious attempt [was] being made to provide a better house than has been the case in the past, and there [was] a strong tendency towards providing a "foreign air" to the structures'.[186] In 1914 the Municipal Report noted that 'there [was] still a growing tendency to embody features of a foreign-style house in those of Chinese construction ... the old fashioned dignified interior of a first class Chinese house [is] now very rarely met with in those of modern design'.[187]

The conflation of modern and foreign continued throughout the 1910s and up until the establishment of a national government in the mid-1920s. However, rather than espousing foreign styles and types outright, the period between the mid-1910s and mid-1920s was characterised by a general lack of architectural consensus. Dominated by the May Fourth Movement, the years of political disorder from 1911 to 1927 were a period of intense cultural and artistic activity. For Chinese architecture, however, it was a point of origin and the 'sad but inevitable consequences' were the unavoidable 'first outcome of a revolution'[188] where, as Dong Dayou later stated, 'the buildings put up were merely poor imitations of European models with the exteriors only a shade more hideous than the interior'.[189] The scene was aptly described by Gu Qiyi in his allegory published in *The Builder* in 1936:

> Someone asked: 'What style is this building?' to which the reply came, 'Italian Renaissance'. But that did not help. After a fuller explanation the person that posed the question understood what Italian Renaissance style was, but, still not completely satisfied, he asked, 'But the owner is Irish, the architect is German, the contractor is Danish, the materials are all made in the US, why do you call it Italian Renaissance?' The answer came: 'Because it is a beautiful style.' 'What is a beautiful style?!' he exclaimed. 'What you describe is like a book full of beautiful words that does not make sense!'[190]

Where the early Republican period and its attendant New Culture Movement had permitted a flurry of experimentation in Chinese art generally, it was to be more than a decade before architecture, which had no precedent in China, acquired any cultural recognition. 'The attainment of architectural consciousness,' explained Chen while drawing a parallel with China's political circumstances, 'had to be paid for as dearly as the birth of the nation'.[191] The chaotic scene in which China's first trained professionals found themselves immersed, is visible in the comparison between Lü's early private work and his design for Sun Yat Sen's Mausoleum. The contrast between the neoclassical Shanghai Bankers' Association Building designed in the early 1920s and the emerging 'Chinese Renaissance' style reveal the prevailing lack of consensus.

Nevertheless, it is through Lü that a foretaste of the next phase emerges. In his resignation letter to Murphy in 1922 he set out his career intent 'to combat the ever present "compradoric" architecture (some of which by foreigners calling themselves architects) which is disfiguring our bigger cities and countryside'.[192] Far from being a public call to arms aimed at Chinese architects, this very private statement and its criticism of foreign architecture in China anticipated the tenor of the next stage of architectural development in the country. Resonating with the comparative political stability of the late 1920s, this phase was characterised by a growing consensus around the professional and moral purpose of architecture. For China's architects, whose numbers, experience and organisation had by then matured markedly, the establishment of the Nationalist government, the Nanjing Plan and Shanghai's Civic Centre not only offered exceptional opportunities for building, but also created a political context within which architectural theory and a professional discourse could develop. These two landmark projects, along with notable earlier developments (e.g. Sun Yat Sen's Mausoleum in Nanjing and the Auditorium in Guangzhou), coincided with a growing national confidence and a heightened sense of nationhood, stimulated in part by opposition to Japanese imperialism and western ambitions for dominance.

In August 1932, at the height of the nationalist projects, the Chinese Society of Architects was formally established, the first professional body for Chinese architects. Its first incarnation, *Shanghai Jian Zhu Shi Xue Hui* (Shanghai Architects' Society),[193] was formed in October 1927, but a change in the law in 1931 prohibited skilled workers, including architects, from establishing groups engaged in scholarly activities.[194] The first President and first Vice-President were Fan Wenzhao and Lü Yanzhi respectively – both 'first generation' architects. Official sanction was not received until 1932 (see Figure 7.32). Concerned primarily with the architects' role within the wider building industry, their published objectives were 'to unite the architects of China so that they will combine their effort to uphold the dignity and standing of the profession and to render support to the public authorities in their civic developments and improvements'.[195] In November, they launched China's first domestic architectural journal, *Jian Zhu Yue Kan* (*The Builder*), the title, contents and scope of which reflected the society's international and cross-disciplinary stance (see Plate 23).[196]

Joining the society's membership that year were the group of architects from northern China associated with Beijing and the North-Eastern University in Shenyang.[197] Among this group were intellectuals, such as Liu Dunzhen, Liang Sicheng and Lin Huiyin, who remained architecturally removed from Shanghai's international and commercial setting and concentrated on historical research and architectural potentialities of a specifically Chinese nature. In July 1933, a new journal was launched that focused almost exclusively on Chinese architecture and whose title explicitly reflected this viewpoint: *Zhong Guo Jian Zhu* (*The Chinese Architect*). Both

Figure 7.32 The Chinese Society of Architects, 1933.

journals ended in early 1937, though a journal titled *The Chinese Architect* still exists today and would lay claim to a lineage originating in 1933. The ideological and thematic differences between these two journals reflect the persistence of *Jingpai* and *Haipai* in an architectural context, *The Builder* representing the commercial and international pragmatism of Shanghai and *The Chinese Architect* possessing the scholarly superiority associated with safeguarding cultural tradition.

In the early 1930s, members of China's increasingly formalised and united building trades issued a 'Manifesto' outlining the state of the industry, including architecture. The following excerpt offers an insight into the frustrations of China's architects and the paradox of which they were conscious:

> Architecture is the representation of a country's culture ... the old building techniques of our country have a playful design, rigorous structure, grand style and dignified and simple façade, it has been the model of the world for thousands of years.... When the barbarous countries were still drinking blood and eating raw animals, living in the caves in the wild, our country had already achieved the beauty of palaces and the pleasure of stages, the progress of the culture relied on the development of the architecture. Time has evolved.... The social structure and material system has changed in seconds and architecture has new ideas and creativity.... In our country, we are a nation that follows our ancestors.... For example in architecture, since we have inherited the skills from the past generation we have only been able to stick to a corner of the room with the old rules, we did not seek to enhance or improve it to suit the requirements of the time.[198]

Within the Chinese architects' response to modernity was a refusal to surrender tradition. They recognised that customs had to be adapted but at the same time were openly critical of earlier attempts by foreign architects to work with Chinese style. Murphy's design for Beijing University and Hussey's Beijing Union Medical College Hospital, argued Liang Sicheng, lacked 'the basic understanding of the proportion of Chinese architecture', claiming they focused only on copying the exterior while ignoring the structural differences between western and Chinese buildings. 'The Chinese roof on a modern building,' he explained, was 'structurally completely different';[199] they were nothing more than 'foreign buildings with curved roofs put on'.[200]

Tong Jun, who Chen Zhi described as 'unswerving when confronted with matters of principles and of professional ethics',[201] was similarly critical of crass attempts at Chinese revivalism. Referencing the source of inspiration for many foreign and Chinese architects, Tong pointed out that 'a heavy roof with wide projecting eaves is not the essence of Chinese architectural style, nor is the architecture of the Forbidden City the only possible precedent'.[202] Of buildings designed by foreign architects that incorporated Chinese elements, only the Beijing Library, designed by an American architect and completed in 1925, received approbation from a Chinese architect. In 1947, the Liverpool and UCL graduate Chen Zhanxiang claimed it 'shows a more sympathetic understanding of Chinese architecture',[203] though he did not qualify his assessment.

In the 1980s, Chen was described by Professor Marwyn Samuels of Syracuse University as 'one of the foremost architects and city planners in modern Chinese history'.[204] He was also one of the most vocal critics of China's early attempts at national planning and architectural design. Describing the Nanjing Plan, he wrote: 'spiritually and visually the idea of a pseudo-Chinese capital of China is most incongruous and depressing'.[205] Of the Shanghai's Civic Centre, designed by Dong Dayou, he wrote: 'its sources are obviously American' and the plans are 'nothing but abstract patterns devoid of any real meaning'.[206] But more than any other architect, Chen argued from a position of experience and knowledge for the essential and inviolable connection between Chinese planning and China's worldview in which the cosmos, philosophy, ceremony and social order were fundamental elements:

> The old Chinese planning patterns were arrived at by regarding buildings as an expression of a social order. For this reason, China's modern urban plans had nothing in common with the administrative centres in ancient cities which are based on their groupings of roads and buildings, on the ceremonies, rites and manners of the times responsible for them. . . . The new American pattern in China is only an empty shell, pretty though it may be.[207]

Criticising recent and current projects might have been one sign of China's growing architectural maturity, but a fundamental question articulated by Tong persisted as 'a problem taxing the brain of Chinese architects': 'How to create a building in China, planned and constructed in the foreign way, with a "native" appearance.'[208]

As occurred in other art practices, it was invariably framed as a reconciliation of opposites, 'the old and the new, the East and the West'.[209] Of the various professions seeking a resolution, one observer suggested that 'none is more interesting than the architect in the Orient who is beginning to rebel against the ugly, square, western boxes, that are making unsightly the ancient Oriental cities'.[210] These comments were written in the context of an appraisal of Tokyo's Kabukiza Theatre, one of the earliest major projects in Asia to fuse western construction techniques and eastern styles. The 'old wine of Japan, with all its old flavour, [had] been put into a strange new bottle'.[211]

In China, the reconciliation of old and new was first mediated by foreign architects at the turn of the century, but in a period of rising nationalism and cultural confidence it was Chinese architects who were expected to generate a genuinely national style of architecture by doing 'away with poor imitations of western architecture and to make Chinese architecture truly national'.[212] In 1947, when the political landscape in China had changed and foreign influence had diminished, Chen asserted: 'Only a style characteristic of the nation's character could inspire national spirit'[213] and as a corollary that 'buildings designed in European or American idioms could only do damage to national development'.[214] Chen's argument echoed the views expressed over a decade earlier in the architectural journal, *Zhong Guo Jian Zhu* (*The Chinese Architect*), in an article titled 'Some Advice to Chinese Architects':

> The Chinese imperial palace style occupies an important position in history. If we abandon it now, it is disrespectful to those who invented it; it is also surrendering what we have that is good in favour of something not so good, which is not wise. The answer is to modify imperial architecture to be practical and economical. Keeping the oriental elements is the priority of Chinese architects. If one wants to become a master, one should start from here. Following the old style with the new techniques is to make a Chinese architecture suited to the times that will not become outdated.[215]

The explanation by Dong Dayou of his most famous building, the Mayor's Office in Shanghai's Civic Centre, supports this 'advice': 'while the salient features of the old style are being followed faithfully, certain modifications are made to meet the requirements of modern planning and construction'.[216] He even went so far as to tacitly claim credit for the invention of this style: 'The distinction of the structure is achieved ... by the creation of a new style which not only retains the best features of Chinese architecture but also is in accordance with the principles of modern architectural design.'[217] Persistently undermining architects' attempts to resolve a modern Chinese style was the accusation of compromising constructional integrity, as referenced in this unauthored account of Murphy's Yenching University campus near Beijing:

> There will be, no doubt, protests from artist-builders here and there who insist that the first principle of building should be that each element in the structure should have its structural value, that beauty should be a matter of inspired utility. Such men will rail at the idea of rafters that do no 'rafting' and brackets that are cut across where they originally were meant to be strongest. But only in this way can anything of the old beauty of design of Chinese buildings be preserved in the present age of efficiency.[218]

Dong and others might have confidently believed they were producing 'old wine in new bottles', but many remained sceptical of this architectural approach. One contemporaneous architectural metaphor drew on the analogy of a modern Chinese woman who, in copying western beauty, could flaunt her shoulders and arms but made no attempt to alter her thought.[219] For many, the adoption of traditional characteristics was inauthentic and the greatest repeating offender was the Chinese roof. Tong believed that architects employed the Chinese roof as 'a handy crib [that] helped to give his design some sort of "face-lifting"'.[220] Tong employs the analogy of the pigtail, which Chinese males were forced to adopt under Manchu (Qing) rule up until 1911, in a critique that appears to be a deliberate response to an article Dong published in the same journal less than a year earlier in support of the Renaissance style where he claimed it was 'a great movement to bring back a dead architecture to life':[221]

> No less picturesque and just as antiquated is the Chinese temple roof, borrowed to cover a modern building: once a necessary evil, it later achieved the distinction of being the dominating feature in Chinese architecture. Its eminence was unquestioned until the advent of modern planning and modern methods of construction. The Chinese roof, when made to crown an up-to-date structure, looks not unlike the burdensome and superfluous pigtail, and it is strange that while the latter is now a sign of ridicule, the Chinese roof should still be admired. ... It would be at once an anachronism and a fallacy if the [Chinese] tile-roof is made to cover constructions of any size with modern interior arrangement ... much eloquence has been wasted in [its] cause. ... If this Renaissance is merely a matter of putting a temple roof over a factory, than adding a pigtail to a dead man ought to bring him back to life![222]

Concerns over cultural authenticity and structural integrity within the architectural profession tended to overshadow wider disputes about tradition and modernity. Since 'the enduring and sublime qualities in [Chinese] architecture rest with structural value alone'[223] (which, as Liang Sicheng so often stated in reference to the distinctive curve of the traditional roof, 'is a result of the structure'[224]), it was easy to anticipate, at least in the short term, the demise of China's building traditions and characteristic forms. As Tong explained:

> At present, classical Chinese architecture has nothing to offer to the modern building except surface ornamentation. ... It requires little imagination to foresee the rapid and universal adoption of the international (or modernistic) style in steel and concrete ... this style, in fact, has quickly become as common in this country as in any other.[225]

The pursuit of a modern Chinese architecture was complicated further and the search was made more difficult by the relative lack of knowledge of Chinese building practices. For many foreign and Chinese architects, the simulation of traditional Chinese buildings drew on the singular example of Beijing's palaces. Years later, Xu Jinzhi identified this in blaming foreign architects (because 'knowledge was pitifully lacking') for producing 'western looking building[s] wearing a Chinese roof as a hat'.[226] Such knowledge was largely impressionistic and it was not until a copy of the *Ying Zao Fa Shi* was unearthed in Nanjing's Provincial Library by the retired official Zhu Qiqian in the early 1920s that serious historical research started to develop.

Zhu had the fabled building manual faithfully reproduced and gave a copy to his contemporary, Liang Qichao. Before sending a copy to his son at the University of Pennsylvania, he read it and remarked, 'A thousand years ago to have a masterpiece like this . . . what a glory to the culture of our race!'[227] It turned out to be a discovery that would change Liang Sicheng's life forever and transform the scientific study of Chinese building. Liang spent years 'decoding' the ancient and, for many, unintelligible book and it became the basis of his lifetime's research. He was able to accurately and objectively build up the evidence of China's architectural traditions, evidence that would inform China's search for a modern architecture more than anything before or since and allowed him to command a more insightful and scientific approach, not one based purely on irrational nationalist sentiment or a superficial reading of style. He urged his fellow architects to 'refine the Chinese essence in old buildings [and] intelligently use the treasure of our own art' and not to 'alter life to suit the arrangement of European or American architecture. . . . We must produce buildings that suit us.'[228]

In 1950, long after his first findings, Liang explained: 'the characteristic of Chinese architecture, in terms of structure, is to build the frame first, then put up the walls and fix the windows'.[229] Liang's observations reveal one of the fundamental principles of Chinese building and, interestingly, showed that it was closer to the structural principles underpinning modernism than modernism was to the western architecture it supplanted. Among Chinese architects, Liang was a singular voice when drawing explicit attention to the proximity of China's building traditions to those of twentieth-century modernism: 'Every part of Chinese ancient buildings is the outcome of its structure, which is what people pursue in modern architecture design.'[230]

Xu Jinzhi was another to recognise this similarity between Chinese building and modernism, albeit some years later: 'Of the great styles of the world, Chinese architecture is the most remarkably functional in structure and logical planning.'[231] As early as 1919, a western observer also remarked that China's wooden frame was 'actually the precursor of modern building where the pillars are replaced by concrete or steel, and where the walls are screens and not supports',[232] but it remains a curiosity that the Chinese failed to explore this correlation more thoroughly and critically during this period. By the second half of the twentieth century, it was widely acknowledged, with Boyd writing in the 1960s about 'Chinese building [having] a refreshing directness and functional clarity which is stimulating to those who still value this aspect of the modern architectural movement'.[233]

Japan's experience did much to highlight the corresponding principles of the wooden frame and modernist architecture. Prefiguring Liang, Xu, Boyd and King was Professor Shozo Uchida of Tokyo Imperial University, cited by a colleague, Ino Dan, Assistant Professor of Tokyo University:

> The construction which is accomplished according to a principle which is nearest to that of the Japanese wooden structure is the iron skeleton concrete construction because both are erected on the basis of the skeleton frame. . . . Unfortunately the iron skeleton concrete structure had its development in the materialistic atmosphere of the commercial cities of America with the result that it has become a matter of course to assume such a form as it has today . . . If it had developed in Japan, it must have certainly been based on the style of wooden architecture, finding some artistic articulation in its form.[234]

'Any attempt', argued Dan, 'to restore the form of Japanese or Chinese architecture by means of iron and concrete should not be permitted under any circumstances'.[235] However, his caveat resonated with others and brought his argument back to where Uchida and, later (in the context of Chinese architecture), Liang stood: 'this does not mean a revival of the Japanese style of architecture in the modern city is hopeless ... a close scrutiny of the historic architecture of Japan reveals that there is something quite modern in its spirit'.[236] Dan's willingness to pair Japanese and Chinese architecture is also instructive, as no such affiliation would be made by a Chinese, for whom there was only one source of tradition.

It was through the prism of Japan that the functional affinity between the wooden frame and one of the central elements of modern architecture was acknowledged by prominent western architects. 'The Japanese tea room which has taught even as keen an architect as Le Corbusier,' argued Dan, 'has its beginning in the principle of functionalism'.[237] Bruno Taut (1880–1938), Richard Neutra (1892–1970) and Frank Lloyd Wright (1867–1959) are commonly referred to as enthusiasts for Japanese architecture on account of this association. Neutra and Wright visited China in 1930 and 1918 respectively, Wright at the invitation of the brilliant intellectual, Gu Hongming.[238]

Another important correlation between Chinese tradition and modernism was standardisation. Here, too, any sense of affiliation was recognised only through Japan's example, whose vaunted standardisation of tatami mats and paper screens reached their acme only in the seventeenth century, half a millennium after the *Ying Zao Fa Shi* and nearly a millennium after Japan's constructional precedents had arrived from China during the Tang Dynasty (618–907).

Despite these precedents, architectural discourse in China was neither in a position to defend its reputation. Tong Jun's optimistic yet intellectually hollow claim in 1937 reveals his profession's relative immaturity: 'Any attempt to give [the International Style] local "colour" will require study, research, and originality', and this would 'constitute China's contribution to world architecture'.[239] The Japanese, compared to the Chinese, were more ready to acknowledge that 'new architectural ideals [could] be found in the old architecture of Japan'.[240] It was an association that reflected the contentious relationship between China and Japan and their standing on the world stage. Major international architectural figures such as Wright became willing agents of Japan, asserting that the 'native home in Japan [was] the supreme study in elimination [and] a perfect example of the modern standardizing I had myself been working with'.[241]

The failure of Chinese architects to explore the potentialities in combining elements of traditional building such as the frame and standardisation and the possibilities of modernism is testament to the profession's relative immaturity and the unstable domestic conditions, especially when compared to their Japanese colleagues who not only embraced this link, but were joined by many leading foreign architects in doing so. Liang was the only Chinese architect to allude to the connection, but he did so only after the Second World War and only after he had been able to begin to formulate the basis of an architectural history from which such ideas could be drawn. By this time, however, Japan was firmly established as the pre-eminent Asian source in modernist architecture and China's engagement with the west was in sharp decline. Making a contribution to world architecture was not an objective of Chinese architects after 1949 nor was it palatable to foreigners. If there was any Asian contribution to the international modernist discourse in architecture in the twentieth century, it came from Japan, which in turn owed a considerable debt to China for the experience gained in Manchuria before 1945. This experience forms the dominant theme in the next chapter.

Notes

1. Ransome, 1927, p. 147.
2. Letter from Liang Sicheng to Wilma and John Fairbank, 21 November 1940, Peabody Essex Museum, Salem, Massachusetts.
3. Liang Sicheng, 19 January 1938, pp. 25–33 and March, 1938, pp. 155–60; July 1941, pp. 450–5; and pp. 387–90. Peabody Essex Museum, Salem, Massachusetts.
4. Liang Sicheng, 1984.
5. Other foreign powers also committed their repayments to educational initiatives, but none were as consequential to the development of architecture in China as the American scheme.
6. Now the Tokyo Institute of Technology.
7. In 1894, when employed in railway construction in northern China, Zhan became the first Chinese member of the English Institute of Civil Engineers and in 1909, became the first Chinese member of the American Society of Civil Engineers. Zhan's success in his field, particularly in the development of China's railways, helped to elevate the standing of the relatively unknown subject of engineering in Chinese society (Boorman, 1967, p. 15).
8. In 1930 Shen became Professor of Architecture at the National Beijing University, a post he held until 1934 (Lai, 2006, p. 123).
9. Lü Yanzhi was invited to become a member of the Commission on Art Education, established by Cai Yuanpei, which hosted its first meeting in Shanghai on 27 November 1927 at the residence of the poet, Li Jinfa, on Rue Massenet in Shanghai's French Concession. Other members included the French-trained oil painter Lin Fengmian and the Japanese and German-trained composer Xiao Youmei.
10. Although Huang successfully completed the course in 1915, his marks were invariably poor, being mostly third class.
11. *Men of Shanghai and North China* (2nd edn), 1935, p. 163.
12. Fan visited many cities, including Paris, Brussels, Amsterdam, Hamburg, Copenhagen, Stockholm, Berlin, Cologne, Frankfurt, Stuttgart, Munich, Prague, Bratislava, Budapest, Vienna, and Rome (*The Chinese Architect*, No. 24, 1936, p. 13).
13. Guan graduated with a BA in Architecture from MIT in 1919 (Lai, 2006, p. 39).
14. Zhuang Jun often worked in a neoclassical style, typified by the Jin Cheng bank (1925–7) on Jiang Xi Road and the later Bank of Communication in Qingdao.
15. Cody (2001) quotes from Chaund's article and claims he studied in America from 1913–17, but the biography in *Far Eastern Review* reveals only that he was enrolled in the Department of Architecture at the Armour Institute of Technology. The author's conversations with Cody have drawn no further clues.
16. Chaund, 1919, p. 533.
17. Chaund, 1919, p. 533.
18. Bergamini, 1924, p. 653.
19. Available at: www.archives.upenn.edu/histy/features/intrntnl/country/china.html, accessed 26 December 2010
20. The first Chinese graduate from the University of Pennsylvania was a dental student in 1899. In 1918, a former pupil of Tsinghua Xue Tang, Zhu Bin, was the first student to enrol at the University of Pennsylvania's School of Architecture, and others soon followed.
21. Cret started his education in 1892 at the Académie de Lyon. Following the death of his father, his mother's sister arranged for tuition fees to be paid by her husband, a businessman and younger brother of a Lyon-based architect, Joannes Bernard.
22. Thorne, 1999.

23 Wilma Fairbank interview notes with Yang Tingbao in Beijing, 16 October 1980, Fairbank family archive.
24 Cret, 1924, pp. 409–12.
25 Cret, 1927.
26 Cret, August 1933, pp. 91–4, and July 1933, pp. 483–91.
27 Shen received his Bachelor's in February and his Master's in June.
28 Wilma Fairbank interview notes with Yang Tingbao in Beijing, 16 October 1980, Fairbank family archive.
29 Liang completed just two semesters at the University of Pennsylvania (Autumn 1928 and Spring 1929) before studying at Yale, Cornell and Harvard.
30 Eigner, 1938, p. 208.
31 Newhouse, 1989, p. 172.
32 According to university records, Fang died in the spring of 1922.
33 Fairbank, 1994, p. 23.
34 Letter from Wilma Fairbank to Chen Zhi, 15 October 1979, Fairbank family archive.
35 Letter from Chen Zhi to Wilma Fairbank, 9 March 1990, Fairbank family archive.
36 Letter from Chen Zhi to Wilma Fairbank, 28 November 1979, Fairbank family archive.
37 Letter from Chen Zhi to Wilma Fairbank, 11 January 1981, Fairbank family archive.
38 See Stuart and Stern, 2006.
39 Letter from Chen Zhi to Wilma Fairbank, 10 November 1983, Fairbank family archive.
40 Besides numerous articles, he published several books including *Modern Architecture in Japan*, *Soviet Architecture – A Brief Description of Modern Architecture in Eastern Europe*, and *A Century of Western Architecture*.
41 The last two enrolled in 1935 and only five of these nine graduated.
42 Twelve of these sixteen graduated.
43 Letter from Chen Zhi to Wilma Fairbank, 30 July 1982, Fairbank family archive.
44 Wilma Fairbank written notes, Peabody Essex Museum, Salem, Massachusetts.
45 Fairbank, 1994, p. 18.
46 Letter from Y.L. Chin to John and Wilma Fairbank, January 1936, Peabody Essex Museum, Salem, Massachusetts.
47 Her University of Pennsylvania records state 19 October 1905.
48 Fairbank, 1994, p. 20.
49 Liang Qichao had had the house extended by building a larger white-stone three-storey villa designed by Italian architects.
50 Xu was already married, though he sought a divorce, and Lin's future had already been arranged and she could not have faced the responsibility of Xu's abandonment of his wife and child.
51 Letter from Lin Huiyin to Wilma Fairbank, November/December 1935, Peabody Essex Museum, Salem, Massachusetts.
52 Liang Sicheng had planned to start the year before, but a motorcycle accident in Beijing forced him to postpone his trip.
53 Fairbank, 1994, p. 22.
54 Wilma Fairbank written notes, Peabody Essex Museum, Salem, Massachusetts.
55 Ting, 1958, pp. 676–8.
56 Fairbank, 1994, p. 25.
57 Liang completed his Master's in June.
58 Fairbank, 1994, p. 28.
59 Fairbank, 1994, p. 30.
60 The wedding took place on 21 March 1928.
61 Letter from Wilma Fairbank to her family, 11 June 1933, Peabody Essex Museum, Salem, Massachusetts.
62 Fairbank, 1994, p. 33. Liang would eventually return to Tsinghua in 1946 to establish their architectural department.
63 Letter from Yang Tingbao to Wilma Fairbank, 6 December 1979, Fairbank family archive.
64 Manchuria had been controlled by the warlord Zhang Zuolin since 1918 and although officially part of China (Zhang was officially Governor-General), it had long been separated from China by the Great Wall. Stability was maintained by Zhang's vast

Fengtian Army, which tolerated the presence of Japanese soldiers of the Guandong Army in the extraterritorial zones adjacent to the South Manchuria Company's railway line. Zhang's ambitions to rule China and reinstate the Manchurian Qing Dynasty ultimately led to his downfall. Embarking on several offensives in an attempt to capture Beijing, which he did successfully in June 1926, Zhang was eventually defeated by Chiang Kai-Shek's Nationalist Army in June 1928. Incensed by Zhang's failure to resist the Nationalist Army, a Japanese officer planted a bomb beneath the railway tracks, killing Zhang as his train passed over it on his return to Shenyang on 4 June. Zhang's death precipitated a scramble for power in which his son, Zhang Xueliang, became the commander of the Fengtian Army and ruler of Manchuria, and swore his allegiance to Chiang Kai-Shek's Nationalist government. It would be Zhang, in December 1936, who kidnapped Chiang Kai-Shek in what was later dubbed the 'Xian Incident', in which Zhang and the general, Yang Hucheng, forced him to form a united front with the Communists against the Japanese.

65 Ting, 1958, p. 762.
66 Ting, 1958, p. 762.
67 Fairbank, 1994, p. 36.
68 Letter from Chen Zhi to Wilma Fairbank, 28 November 1979, Fairbank family archive.
69 Liang Sicheng, 1941, p. 387.
70 Wilma Fairbank, letter home to families, 11 June 1933, Peabody Essex Museum, Salem, Massachusetts.
71 *Who's Who in China – Biographies of Chinese*, 1933, p. 106.
72 During the Japanese occupation, Chen established the Architecture Department at the provisional capital's Chongqing University.
73 Lin Fengmian studied under the 75-year-old Fernand Piestre (1845–1924).
74 By 1937, Liu had established his own private practice in Guangzhou and in 1941 formed Da Di Architects in Shanghai. His chief legacy is his role nurturing a modern art movement in China.
75 Clunas, 1989, p. 100.
76 Shen in Andrews and Shen, 1998, p. 177.
77 For more information on the life and work of Liu Jipiao, go to: http://liujipiao.com. The website has been constructed by family members and friends, and in particular his granddaughter, Jennifer Wong.
78 Xi left Palmer & Turner in 1931 for Chiming & Partners Architects, where he worked for four years before establishing his own firm, Gong Li Architecture Engineering.
79 For a full account of Luke's life, see *Luke Him Sau, Architect – China's Missing Modern* (Denison and Ren, 2014).
80 In the second term of his second year (the fourth year of the course), Lu went straight to the fifth year, where his marks were either very good or poor; his designs of 'A Children's Fountain' and a 'Cinema Paybox' were among the lowest in the class and his 'Railway Waiting Room' and 'Construction' were among the highest. *List of AA Students: 1901–1951*, Accession Number 15845. 3rd Year Register A501.
81 Henry Lester, from whom the school derives its name, was a civil engineer and one of Shanghai's first philanthropists. He arrived in Shanghai in 1867 and worked for the Municipal Council before making his fortune in real estate. After his death in 1926 his fortune was divided between a Shanghai hospital and the establishment of the Lester School, which taught medical sciences, and the Lester Institute of Technical Education, which offered secondary and tertiary education in civil engineering, building and architecture. Three years before his retirement in 1916, Lester joined George A. Johnson and Gordon Morris to form Lester, Johnson & Morris.
82 Chen 198–?, p. 5 in the Fairbank family archive.
83 Chen 198–?, p. 5 in the Fairbank family archive.
84 H.S. Chen studied at the AA from 1925 to 1928 and Luke Him Sau from 1927 to 1930.
85 Lü Yanzhi was offered Head of the Architecture Department, but he turned it down because he was too busy, so Liu Shiying took up the post and together with Zhu Shigui founded the course. Liu Dunzhen arrived in Suzhou in 1926 and Huang Zuomiao after him.

86 The following year it changed its name to Central University.
87 Letter from Yang Tingbao to Wilma Fairbank, 6 December 1979, Fairbank family archive.
88 Letter from Chen Zhi to Wilma Fairbank, 2 February 1983, Fairbank family archive.
89 Wilma Fairbank states that all three were graduates from the University of Pennsylvania, but the university records show nothing of Cai.
90 Fairbank, 1994, pp. 42–3. In a letter to Chen Zhi dated 9 January 1980, she states that she received this information from Liang Sicheng 'in a long interview we did together in 1947', Fairbank family archive.
91 Letter from Chen Zhi to Wilma Fairbank, 28 November 1979, Fairbank family archive.
92 Liang and Tong had worked together under Harry Sternfeld in his atelier at the University of Pennsylvania.
93 *The Chinese Architect*, July 1933.
94 Now the South China University of Technology.
95 In 1938 Xiang Qin University was incorporated into Zhong Shan University.
96 Nanyang College was initially a public school established in the final years of the Qing Dynasty to train young Chinese students in modern subjects, such as engineering and communications, but by the 1930s, and after various incarnations, it was considered one of China's premier engineering schools.
97 Dong Dayou, 1936, p. 358.
98 Hume, 1914, p. 81.
99 Yale was invited to establish a school in Changsha, the provincial capital of Hunan, by the municipal government in 1903.
100 *Far Eastern Review*, Vol. 16, May 1920, p. 230.
101 Bergamini, 1924, p. 653.
102 Taylor, 1924, p. 660.
103 Throop, 1924, p. 57.
104 Throop, 1924, p. 57.
105 Medhurst, 1872, pp. 40–1.
106 'Concrete and Ideas Retain Old Beauty of Orient and Add Strength of West', *Far Eastern Review*, May 1926, p. 238.
107 *St John's 1879–1919 – A Booklet of Information about the University at the end of Forty Years*, Shanghai, 1919.
108 *The East of Asia Magazine*, 1904, p. 29.
109 Taylor, 1924, p. 657.
110 Part of the Canadian Methodist College.
111 Stewart, 1917, p. 605.
112 Taylor, 1924, pp. 660–1.
113 For an account of Hussey's life and work, see his autobiography: Hussey, 1968.
114 King, 1919, p. 562.
115 King, 1919, p. 562.
116 *Far Eastern Review*, Vol. 15, August 1919, p. 562.
117 Cody, 2001, pp. 82–3.
118 *The China Weekly Review*, 22 December 1928, p. 159.
119 Cody, 2001, p. 95.
120 Cody, 2001, p. 20.
121 *The China Weekly Review*, 22 December 1928, p. 159.
122 An Austrian builder, Emil Fischer, is said to have acted as contractor for the first educational buildings at Tsinghua in 1909 (in Lunt, 1927, p. 26).
123 *Far Eastern Review*, Vol. 16, May 1920, p. 230.
124 Hume, 1914, p. 82.
125 *Far Eastern Review*, Vol. 16, May 1920, p. 230.
126 Hume, 1914, p. 82.
127 Cody, 2001, p. 20.
128 Fujian Christian University (Fuzhou), Ginling College (Nanjing), Peking University (Beijing), Fudan University (Shanghai), Wayland Academy (Hangzhou) and the Anglo-Chinese College (Fuzhou). While the Wayland Academy and the Anglo-Chinese College

were completed in faux-Tudor styles, Fujian Christian University and the campuses in Nanjing, Beijing and Shanghai were in the same revivalist style as the Yale in China campus.
129 Taylor, 1924, p. 660.
130 When Lü won the competition, he had only recently moved from South-Eastern Architectural & Engineering Company and established his own studio, Yan Ji.
131 'Sun Yat-sen Memorial in Nanking and Canton by Y.C. Lu', *Far Eastern Review*, Vol. 25, March 1929, p. 97.
132 'Sun Yat-sen Memorial in Nanking and Canton by Y.C. Lu', *Far Eastern Review*, Vol. 25, March 1929, p. 97.
133 'Sun Yat-sen Memorial in Nanking and Canton by Y.C. Lu', *Far Eastern Review*, Vol. 25, March 1929, p. 97.
134 'Sun Yat-sen Memorial in Nanking and Canton by Y.C. Lu', *Far Eastern Review*, Vol. 25, March 1929, p. 97.
135 Chen Zhanxiang, 1947b, p. 28.
136 Fan Wenzhao came third in this competition. The complex surrounding the auditorium later incorporated a library, designed by Lu Shusen in a Chinese style.
137 *Andersen, Meyer & Co. Ltd of China*, 1931, p. 75.
138 *The China Weekly Review*, 22 December 1928, p. 159.
139 'Sun Yat-sen Memorial in Nanking and Canton by Y.C. Lu', *Far Eastern Review*, Vol. 25, March 1929, p. 98.
140 'Sun Yat-sen Memorial in Nanking and Canton by Y.C. Lu', *Far Eastern Review*, Vol. 25, March 1929, p. 97.
141 *The Builder*, Vol. 3, No. 5, 1935, p. 3.
142 Musgrove, 2000, p. 140.
143 *China Critic*, Vol. 2, July 1929, p. 517.
144 *North China Herald*, 25 May 1929, p. 305.
145 *North China Herald*, 5 January 1929, p. 15.
146 Guo Moruo, *Nanjing Yin Xiang (Impressions of Nanjing)* quoted in Musgrove, 2000, p. 149.
147 *North China Herald*, 18 May 1929, p. 265.
148 *North China Herald*, 18 May 1929, p. 263.
149 Chen, 1947, p. 28.
150 *The Chinese Architect*, Vol. 3, No. 3, August 1935, p. 5.
151 *The Chinese Architect*, Vol. 1, No. 1, July 1933, p. 11.
152 Eigner, 1938, p. 202.
153 Su, 1964.
154 Chakrabarty, 2000, p. 10.
155 *The Chinese Architect*, Vol. 1, No. 3, September 1933, p. 4.
156 King, 1976, p. xii.
157 MacPherson, 1990, p. 39.
158 This title refers only to the Chinese-controlled areas.
159 'Building a New Shanghai', *Far Eastern Review*, June 1931, p. 350.
160 'Greater Shanghai – Building a New Port and City', *Far Eastern Review*, June 1930, p. 296.
161 *The China Quarterly*, December 1935, p. 87.
162 'Greater Shanghai – Building a New Port and City', *Far Eastern Review*, June 1930, p. 296.
163 Lee was born in New York in 1900 and studied architecture at the Pratt Institute. He moved to China in 1923, when he started working for the China branch of the YMCA's Building Bureau.
164 'Greater Shanghai – Building a New Port and City', *Far Eastern Review*, June 1930, p. 296.
165 'Greater Shanghai – Building a New Port and City', *Far Eastern Review*, June 1930, p. 296.
166 In 1937, Dong established Dong & Zhang Architects with Zhang Guangqi.

198 Architecture and modernity

167 *Shanghai Special City Public Works Department*, Tender Document for the Designs of Buildings, June, Year 18.
168 'Growth of Greater Shanghai', *Far Eastern Review*, December 1936, p. 521.
169 *Far Eastern Review*, Vol. 27, No. 6, June 1931, p. 366.
170 Lao, 1929 (unpaginated).
171 *Far Eastern Review*, Vol. 26, No. 5, May 1930, p. 217.
172 *Who's Who in China – Biographies of Chinese*, 1933, p. 107. The foundation stone was laid on 7 July 1931, the anniversary of the City Government of Shanghai's formation and was completed in 1934.
173 *Far Eastern Review*, Vol. 27, No. 6, June 1931, p. 350.
174 *Far Eastern Review*, Vol. 27, No. 6, June 1931, p. 350.
175 'Growth of Greater Shanghai', *Far Eastern Review*, December 1936, p. 521.
176 The foundation stones for the Library and Museum were laid by the Mayor in December 1934.
177 'Growth of Greater Shanghai', *Far Eastern Review*, December 1936, p. 521.
178 'Growth of Greater Shanghai', *Far Eastern Review*, December 1936, p. 521.
179 It is curious that they used yellow roof tiles, which is a colour traditionally reserved only for the emperor.
180 Letter from Lin Huiyin to Wilma and John Fairbank, 22 April 1936, Peabody Essex Museum, Salem, Massachusetts.
181 Letter from Lin Huiyin to Wilma and John Fairbank, 22 April 1936, Peabody Essex Museum, Salem, Massachusetts.
182 *The Chinese Architect*, Vol. 3, No. 2, 1935, p. 5. Behind the Aviation Association building was the Hospital, a large complex of nine buildings arranged so that eight buildings containing different departments radiated around a central building in a semi-circular plan.
183 'Growth of Greater Shanghai', *Far Eastern Review*, December 1936, p. 523.
184 Chen Zhanxiang, 1947b, p. 27.
185 Chen Zhanxiang, 1947b, p. 27.
186 *Shanghai Municipal Council Report*, 1912, p. 17.
187 *Shanghai Municipal Council Report*, 1914, p. 2.
188 Chen Zhanxiang, 1947b, p. 27.
189 Dong Dayou, 1936, p. 358.
190 *The Builder*, Vol. 4, No. 7, Shanghai, 1936, p. 32.
191 Chen, 1947, p. 27.
192 Cody, 2001, p. 148 and p. 167n.
193 To reflect their nationwide scope, the title changed in 1928 to the Chinese Society of Architects.
194 The term *Xue Hui* (Society) carries an academic connotation.
195 *The China Journal*, 10 August 1928, p. 107. In this same article, further plans were to 'obtain a club house for its use for the benefit of students and draughtsmen who desire to learn architecture but who cannot obtain proper training, the society plans to include in the club house an atelier to give such students an opportunity to study architectural design'.
196 The first architectural journal in China was published by the Manchurian Architectural Association (*Manshu Kenchiku Kyoukai*) from 1924, a publication produced by and for a professional Japanese audience.
197 These included Liu Dunzhen, Yang Tingbao, Liang Sicheng, Lin Huiyin, Tong Jun and Chen Zhi.
198 'Manifesto', Special Edition for the establishment of the Shanghai Architects' Society, February 1931, p. 41.
199 Liang Sicheng, '*Jian Zhu She Ji Can Kao Tu Ji Xu*,' 1984, p. 221.
200 Chen Zhanxiang, 1947b, p. 27.
201 Letter from Chen Zhi to Wilma Fairbank, 31 March 1983, Fairbank family archive.
202 Taylor, 1924, p. 660.
203 Chen Zhanxiang, 1947b, p. 27. Zhu claims this was built in 1931 by V. Leth-Moller (Zhu, 2009, p. 35).

204 Letter from Professor Marwyn Samuels to Professor Michael Tomlan, Cornell University, 8 January 1988, Fairbank family archive.
205 Chen Zhanxiang, 1947b, p. 28.
206 Chen Zhanxiang, 1947b, p. 28.
207 Chen Zhanxiang, 1947b, p. 28.
208 Tong, 1937, p. 308.
209 *Far Eastern Review*, May 1926, p. 238.
210 *Far Eastern Review*, May 1926, p. 238.
211 *Far Eastern Review*, May 1926, p. 238.
212 Dong Dayou, 1936, p. 358.
213 Chen Zhanxiang, 1947b, p. 28.
214 Chen Zhanxiang, 1947b, p. 28.
215 'Some Advice to Chinese Architects', *The Chinese Architect*, Vol. 2, Nos 11 and 12, 1934, p. 1.
216 Dong Dayou, 1935, p. 89.
217 Dong Dayou, 1935, p. 89.
218 *Far Eastern Review*, May 1926, p. 240.
219 Tang, 1931, p. 49.
220 Tong, 1937, p. 308.
221 Dong Dayou, 1936, p. 358.
222 Tong, 1937, p. 308.
223 Tong, 1937, p. 308.
224 Liang Sicheng, 1986, p. 1.
225 Tong, 1937, p. 308.
226 Su, 1964, p. 135.
227 Liang Sicheng, 1947, cited in Fairbank, 1994, p. 29.
228 Liang Sicheng, 1944, p. 2.
229 Liang Sicheng, 1986, p. 1.
230 Liang Sicheng, 1944, p. 2.
231 Su, 1964, p. 1.
232 King, 1919, p. 562.
233 Boyd, 1962, p. 48.
234 Ino, 1932, p. 46.
235 Ino, 1932, pp. 39–43.
236 Ino, 1932, p. 43.
237 Ino, 1932, p. 43.
238 Gu showed Wright a selection of the country's historic sites and cultural relics, though nothing is known as to what impression this made on him.
239 Tong, 1937, p. 308.
240 Ino, 1932, p. 39.
241 Wright, 1932, p. 196.

8 Japan
China's mirror to modernism

If Harootunian is right to argue that 'among the development of Modernities, few examples offer historians a spectacle of greater ambiguity and certainty than Japan's experience in the twentieth century',[1] then China's experience must be even more complex, given that its encounter with modernity was partly refracted through and constructed by Japan. This chapter concentrates on Japan's role in cultivating a modern architecture in China.

Japan's presence in China's encounter with architectural modernity is omnipresent. Historically, its own architectural heritage cannot be uncoupled from China's. Japan shared with the rest of the non-west the experience of possessing building traditions entirely removed from the origins of modernity. With China, though, it shared an exclusive and common origin, since it was from China during the Tang Dynasty (618–906) that the dominant strain of Japanese architecture derived. Furthermore, Japan's cultural and geographical proximity to China generated shared encounters that inevitably impacted upon their respective paths towards modernisation and the development of modern architecture. China's position as Japan's architectural progenitor permeates all conversations concerning the architectural character of both nations. Until the mid-nineteenth century, China assumed the senior position in this relationship, but this was turned on its head following Japan's response to western interference, placing Japan on a path towards modernisation that transformed all aspects of life, including architecture. China's subsequent subordination has lasted one and a half centuries. With the advent of modern architecture, there remains the question as to whether China first looked to the east or to the west for inspiration and guidance both practically, in receiving materials and techniques to produce modern architecture, and theoretically, in the necessarily self-reflective critical analysis of its building traditions.

A second facet of Japan's role in China's encounter with architectural modernity was its annexation of Chinese territories including Manchuria, culminating in the partial occupation of the whole country during the Second World War. Japan's growing authority and presence in China during this period contributed to important industrial developments which in turn stimulated architectural production. Japan was responsible not only for China's dishonour, but also for the unprecedented scope of architectural and urban developments in Manchuria from 1905, which reached their apogee after the creation of the new state of Manchukuo in 1932. Nowhere in the world had an imperial power embarked on such swift, widespread and ambitious plans for construction and never had such plans been driven by such a conscious pursuit of modernity – Japanese 'ultra-modernism'.

Shared building traditions

China's unrivalled cultural lineage has dominated neighbouring regions and countries for millennia. The espousal and reinterpretation of Chinese traditions have had a profound impact on Japan. Its dominant religion, Buddhism (originally from India), was a Chinese export, as was its language, and its methods of building.

Impermanence, site, function, standardisation, and the absence of the architect and the inviolability of the craftsman were all attributes of building traditions shared by China and Japan before their respective encounters with modernity. The history of Japanese and Chinese building also offers a rare opportunity to consider an alternative, possibly even oppositional, stance to dominant westerncentric architectural historiography. Coming from the same source, these two traditions remained importantly and unavoidably interconnected, yet their separate and protracted maturity caused them to arrive at, encounter and respond to modernity in different and often distinct ways.

Comprehending Chinese and Japanese building and the relationship between them in this context requires us, as Arata Isozaki puts it, 'to remove our eyeglasses fitted with the western concept of "architecture" '.[2] The liberation of architecture from its western definition is frequently stressed by non-western practitioners and theorists as a vital prerequisite to historical studies of buildings, especially in relation to modernity, which is loaded with western meaning. When the Japanese architectural historian Hiroshi Adachi writes that 'the west discovered the quality of space in traditional Japanese architecture through the filter of western architectural tradition',[3] the difficulty for the non-western critic is to find any alternative criteria through which to recognise the properties of Japanese, or any other, non-western building tradition.

Seminal architectural texts published in the west in recent centuries have cemented and sustained this westerncentric paradigm, none more so than Banister Fletcher's *A History of Architecture on the Comparative Method* (1896), the 'tree of architecture' in which embodies the grounds for Isozaki's protest that Japan was 'posited as just an exotic peripheral, in company with India and China – a land where no proper concept of architecture existed'.[4] Isozaki explains that in Japan – as in China – 'there was no word "architecture," nor were there architects as we recognize them today'.[5] However, Isozaki's observation that 'buildings were undeniably made in which unique characteristics might be discovered'[6] echoes Hosagrahar's frustrations at westerncentricism that, in the context of Delhi, motivated her ambition to 'reclaim a history of a city that has been denied modernity'.[7] Reclaiming history, whether architectural or modern or both, is a fundamental tenet of this exercise.

Japan became consciously self-reflective of its own building traditions following its exposure to the west in the mid-nineteenth century. Previously, isolated and impervious, Japan had had no cause to analyse its building traditions since there was nothing to compare them with. The same could be said of China, though here the absence of critical self-reflection was less the result of a lack of an *other* and more about the consequence of cultural superiority and integrity which had caused building practices to remain constant for millennia. Architectural introspection for both Japan and China occurred early in the process of modernisation, albeit for different reasons, and, as with practically all experiences of modernity, in Japan before China.

In both countries there was a range of responses to modernity: apprehension, confusion and a search for origins and originality. Eminent examples of authentic

Japanese architecture that Japanese architects and scholars cite invariably include the Ise Jingū (Ise Shrine) (690) and the Katsura Imperial Villa (1615). Isozaki adds to these the Great South Gate at Tōdai-ji in Nara,[8] which he claims is 'an example of the Chinese style called *daibutsu-yō*, yet slightly inflected with Japanese taste (*wayō*)'. The relative impermanence of these definitive structures, especially Ise which is routinely rebuilt every 20 years, not only 'presents a notion of construction totally at odds with the western one that relies on enduring materiality',[9] but it also provides opportunities for frequent reinterpretation, adaptation and modification that permit the imposition of national identity on a formerly imported architectural type.

What had been a relatively slow and unarticulated process of architectural evolution over centuries became in the early twentieth century rapid and highly conscious. By this time, the quest for national authenticity assumed a political dimension. Nationalism and national identity were critical factors of modernity that demanded an architectural response. Much like their Chinese counterparts, Japanese architects were 'caught on the horns of a dilemma: how could they continue to ply their trade – a trade so closely tied to the west – and yet respond in a convincing fashion to the growing demand to affirm [Japanese] identity through their designs?'[10] Each country began this search at different times, the Japanese starting theirs in the late nineteenth century and before any other non-western country. The Chinese began theirs in the mid-1920s. Interestingly, both reached their zenith concurrently in the 1930s, by which time Japan's imperial adventures in Asia were well underway and in China the Nationalist government was established in Nanjing. Bisecting these two geopolitical episodes was Manchuria, where imperial Japan sought to carve a new state out of north-east China and which became one of the most concentrated and prolific theatres of modern architectural and urban production of the twentieth century.

Another facet of the architectural relationship between China and Japan architecturally related to authenticity concerns national pride. Authenticity and originality provoke strong emotions in promoting a national type, so it is unsurprising that Japanese architectural scholars such as Isozaki speak of 'beginnings' rather than 'origins' when discussing their nation's architecture, while the Chinese, who readily boast of several millennia of constructional constancy, do not hesitate to draw attention to Japan's architectural debt to China. In 1938, with Japan's invasion of China well underway, Tong Jun described Tang Dynasty architecture as 'Japan's source of inspiration'.[11] Though seemingly trivial, these subtly divergent perspectives duly play their respective roles in the bitter rivalries between these two countries and weigh heavily on those asserting that such a thing as an authentic national style exists.

In the eighteenth century, for example, the vogue for chinoiserie was not merely a distorted interpretation of Chinese design by western observers, but once in existence was responded to by Chinese artists and craftsmen who exploited their wares to satisfy this newfound demand. Chinese-ness, rather than a measure of authenticity prescribed by the Chinese, became, in part, a standard prescribed from outside – a reactive invented tradition. Orientalism incarnate. The west's perception became a mirror distorting what the Chinese saw, reflecting back for the first time an alternative version of themselves and precipitating a re-evaluation of perceived authenticity. For Japan, a similar process occurred in the nineteenth century when the western gaze fashioned japonoiserie (or japonism), a style unrecognised in Japan until the west had drawn attention to it. Both examples exemplify the power of the external gaze to motivate self-definition.

In the context of Japan and modern architecture, one of the foremost examples of the west's role as a distorting mirror to the non-west is Bruno Taut's famous appraisals of the Katsura Imperial Villa and Ise Jingū. Of Ise, he made the loftiest comparisons, claiming it would become, like the Acropolis, an essential destination on the global architectural pilgrimage trail. Taut's remarks are important not for their ambitious claims, but for what they effected. Isozaki points out, 'like Katsura, Ise Jingū had been little appreciated in the context of Japanese architectural history' and so 'it was dizzying that this globetrotting figure had affirmed the Katsura Imperial Villa, to which Japanese architectural historians had paid scant attention, as a masterpiece according to the measure of modern architecture'.[12]

Frank Lloyd Wright was another influential figure to interpret and distort Japanese design internationally. His experiences ran deeper than Taut's, who Isozaki claims knew 'almost nothing' about Japanese architecture when he arrived in 1933.[13] Wright's first encounter with Japanese architecture was in 1893 when he witnessed the replica of Kyoto's Hō-ō-dō (Pheonix Hall) of Byōdō-in (1053) at the World's Columbian Exposition in Chicago designed by the Japanese architect, Masamichi Kuru. The extent of Wright's debt to Japanese design is hotly contested. Described by Meech as 'a modernist inspired by Japanese graphic design',[14] there is little doubt about his admiration for Japanese woodblock prints, *ukiyo-e*, but as Stewart warns, we cannot assume that his affection for Japanese prints meant that Japanese building traditions influenced his own 'revolutionary proposals'.[15]

Having first visited Japan in 1905, Wright returned in 1913 when he won the commission to design the Imperial Hotel, 'the first Japanese building erected by a western architect of repute and talent'.[16] The Japanese-sponsored media claimed the hotel would 'typify the new spirit in world architecture [and] help teach Japan a new lesson in western civilization'.[17] Wright opened an office in Tokyo to oversee the completion of the hotel and other smaller projects.[18] He employed Endo Arata (1889–1951), an architecture graduate from Tokyo's Imperial University, to work on the Imperial Hotel. Having worked in Taliesin from 1917 to 1918, Arata became the office's senior draftsman and is jointly credited for the designs of the Jiyu Gakuen School and the Yamamura House.

Wright last visited Japan in 1922. Despite his admiration for Japanese design and architecture and his success in Japan, he is claimed to have said: '"You are all wrong ... I'm not indebted to the Japanese – the Japanese are indebted to me"',[19] though Meech warns that 'his protests must be taken with a grain of salt – he was never one to give credit to others'.[20] Irrespective of creative debt and its legitimacy, the greatest legacy of Wright's association with Japan was the impact it had in raising awareness of and appreciation for Japanese art and design in the west (much like Chambers had done for China 150 years earlier), particularly in the way it stimulated modernism.

Another prominent foreign interpreter of Japanese design was Antonin Raymond (1888–1976), Wright's former assistant on the Imperial Hotel. Raymond's credentials are interesting because they comprise experience of all three continents included in the triangular relationship concerned with modernity in this study. Born in Kladno, Czechoslovakia, he studied in Prague at the Technical University. After graduating in 1909, he travelled to America the following year and worked with Cass Gilbert (1859–1934), then designed the Woolworth Building (1913) in New York.[21] Raymond worked with Wright in Taliesin in 1916 and 1919, having spent the intervening years in Europe. He accepted an invitation to work with Wright on Tokyo's Imperial Hotel.

After a year, Raymond grew bored of the project, which he saw as a monument to Wright and which had 'nothing in common with Japan'.[22] He left Wright's office to establish his own firm, which he ran successfully until the outbreak of war in 1937.[23] During this time Raymond produced many notable buildings including the Reinanzaka House (1923–4), one of the earliest examples in Japan of the type of architecture that would come to typify the modern movement and, in his own words (conveying an immodesty that matched Wright), 'perhaps the first in this respect anywhere ... a milestone in the history of modern architecture'.[24]

Reynolds credits Raymond as having 'a strong (if selective) appreciation for Japanese architecture.... It is no accident that the particular "Japanese principles" on which Raymond focused closely coincided with his European modernist sensibilities',[25] which could also be said for Richard Neutra, whose 'love for the ancient, timeless, tea-house vernacular', permitted him to champion 'the modernist legacies of that tradition that had come forward to clasp hands with the modern movement in the west'.[26] As occurred with Wright, Taut, Raymond and japonoiserie, Neutra's Japanese association provided yet another version of the distorting mirror that became another example along with 'the eighteenth century picturesque's assimilation of chinoiserie and cubist reference to African artefacts [that] hardly accounted for more than another shelf in the cabinet of the west's exoticist collection'.[27]

The encounter between the west and its *other* in the east 'is not the simple model of the pioneers of modern architecture turning to Japan in search of inspiration', argues McNeil; 'in many cases, they knew exactly what they wished to find'.[28] The west discovered in Japanese traditions certain qualities it was looking for in constructing a western modernism and used it to define its own modern architecture, or, as Stewart put it:

> Neither the parents or forebears [of modernism] were Japanese, but the father, so to speak, ran off with the [Japanese] midwife. She, in turn, nourished the child, who learned to utter a few words of Japanese while the midwife, though retaining certain Japanese habits and her domestic accessories, never looked back.[29]

Identifying connections between modernism and Japanese design, Isozaki highlights these common attributes: 'simplicity, humility, purity, lightness, and *shibu-sa* (sophisticated austerity)'.[30] Two decades earlier, Reyner Banham used the words 'spare, slender, light, and open'.[31] Five decades before Banham, Taut wrote of 'cleanliness, clarity, simplicity, cheerfulness and faithfulness to the materials of nature'.[32] Preceding all these descriptions, Ino Dan argued 'a close scrutiny of the historic architecture of Japan reveals that there is something quite modern in its spirit'.[33] The union of domestic tradition and global modernity were emphasised by advocates of a new Japanese architecture, who in turn played down incompatible characteristics. It was, as Isozaki asserted, a conscious attempt to show that '"pure" Japanese elements and rationalist (or, to them, functionalist) modern architecture could coexist under one and the same aegis ... if only they could isolate the key compositional elements common to traditional Japanese architecture and modern design'.[34] In the context of Chinese architecture, the same wish had been expressed decades earlier by Liang Sicheng, but it was never realised.

An emerging architectural profession in Japan

Western encroachment into Japan's sphere of influence from the mid-nineteenth century did more to architecture than create an opportunity for Japanese critical self-reflection; it precipitated Japan's rapid architectural development. In China, the establishment of a professional architectural community dominated by western architects was the precursor to the formation of a domestic architectural community. In Japan, these occurred almost concurrently. For China, eight decades separated the Treaty of Nanjing and the formation of an organised domestic architectural profession. For Japan, the equivalent process took just two decades (from the Treaty of Kanagawa). 'Trained in the latest construction methods and in western styles', Reynolds claims the works of Japan's first architects 'housed the private and public institutions that drove the process forward, and they invented symbols of power and status that affirmed the newly emerging social order'.[35]

A critical discourse in Japanese architecture over the problem of how to safeguard national identity in the face of modernisation and westernisation emerged in the 1890s, over two decades before any equivalent in China. This discourse acquired a legal dimension when in 1897 public funds for the conservation of the nation's architectural treasures (the Koshaji Hozon Hō) were guaranteed by the Law for the Protection of Ancient Shrines and Temples.[36] The measures reveal not only the efficiency of a government administration (contrasting with China, where the following year the Empress Dowager carried out her coup against Emperor Guangxu's attempted reforms), but also the swiftness with which traditional building had become part of the nation's identity.

A key figure in the establishment of an architecture profession in Japan was the English architect Josiah Conder (1852–1920, ARIBA and FRIBA), referred to as the 'Father of modern Japanese architecture',[37] though Stewart cautions 'it is not easy to praise much of what [he] built'.[38] Conder arrived in Japan in 1877 having been awarded the Soane Prize the previous year and was an outstanding student under William Burges (1827–81). He was one of many foreign advisers from a range of technical disciplines invited by the Japanese government to help establish modern institutions based on western models following the Meiji Restoration. Conder was posted to Tokyo's Imperial College of Engineering (ICE), founded by the Ministry of Works in 1873 under the supervision of the Scottish engineer Henry Dyer (1848–1918).[39]

Conder's mentor, Burges, is credited with establishing architectural history education in Japan because of his professional relationship with Kingo Tatsuno (1854–1919), who had studied at University College London (1880–2) and worked in Burges's office before returning to Japan to become Head of the Department of Architecture at Imperial University, Tokyo. Drawing parallels with other western figures who have appeared in this study and who contributed to Japanese self-reflection, Wendelken argues that Burges's alleged impact on Tatsuno:

> constitutes yet another myth of origins in the reevaluation of Japanese tradition. A conservative revision could be received as progress because the interest of the foreign expert constituted a kind of mandate. In that anecdote, Burges parallels the role attributed to Ernest Fenollosa (1853–1908) in the appreciation of Japanese art, and later to Bruno Taut in the appreciation of modernity in Japanese architecture.[40]

Reynolds describes Tatsuno as 'a Japanese Inigo Jones: the native apologist for a foreign style imbibed at source [and] Japan's first fully-fledged professional architect'.[41] He established his own architectural practice in 1903, where he designed most of his celebrated works, including the West Japan Industrial Club (1909), the Manseibashi Station in Tokyo (1912), and the massive Tokyo Station (1914).[42]

The international experiences, educationally and professionally, of Japan's first generation of architects preceded their Chinese colleagues by at least three decades. It is true that China's first engineering students to travel overseas did so considerably earlier than their architectural counterparts, but these were engineers and none could claim to have ever practised architecture in the manner that Japan's early ICE graduates did, such as Tatsuno, or other members of Japan's first generation of architects such as Yamaguchi Hanroku (1858–1900) and Tsumaki Yorinaka (1859–1916).[43]

Japan's first generation of architects established the *Zōka Gakkai* (Building Institute) in 1886. Modelled on Britain's RIBA it sponsored lectures and published Japan's first architectural journal *Kenchiku zasshi* (*Architectural Journal*). The *Zōka Gakkai* was the forerunner to the *Nihon Kenchiku Gakkai* (Architectural Institute of Japan), founded in 1897,[44] four years before the establishment in China of the entirely foreign Shanghai Society of Engineers and Architects.

In May 1910, the *Nihon Kenchiku Gakkai* held a symposium to discuss the future direction of a national style of architecture, prompted by the pressing need to choose a suitable style for the National Diet Building. Two sides emerged in the ensuing debate: one, that a western style was most appropriate in representing Japan as a modern international nation, and the other was that Japan's traditional architecture must be incorporated. As was the case in China over a decade later, it was the latter position that provoked the most debate. The question, as will be seen later, was even more complicated in the third dimension of Manchuria.

One solution was Kikutaro Shimoda's (1866–1931), *teikan-yōshiki*,[45] or 'crown-topped', style, which became 'the recognised emblem of Japanese nationalism and, later, expansionism'.[46] The style was the closest Japanese equivalent to China's 'Renaissance' style and the most conspicuous representation of a national vernacular, or invented tradition. Following the competition for the design of the National Diet Building in 1918, Shimoda initiated a high-profile professional battle over the most suitable style for the building.[47] Criticising the short-listed designs (among which his was not included) for not adequately reflecting Japan's traditional architecture, he argued strongly and directly with the Diet for his mixed-style. The Diet remained unconvinced, critical even, as were his colleagues. Itō Chūta, another proponent of combining eastern and western styles, claimed in an unpublished paper written in 1921 that Shimoda's design 'violated the structural logic of building materials and undermined the spirit of both the European classical and Japanese styles', going so far 'as to declare [it] a "national disgrace"'.[48]

Itō, a former student of Kigo Kiyoyoshi (1845–1907),[49] was among a new generation of Japanese architects at the turn of the century contesting the pro-western stance of their predecessors and looking instead to their own traditions for inspiration, arguing that it 'could not move forward until it got back in touch with its own artistic and spiritual roots'.[50] It was a position that mirrored Liang Sicheng's after he began decoding the *Ying Zao Fa Shi* in the 1920s and, like Liang in the Chinese context, Itō undertook extensive surveys of traditional Japanese buildings, for which he developed a strong appreciation and made their study part of the curriculum at Imperial University.

Whereas the first generation of Japanese architects had received a western education and were taught to favour western classicism, the 'second generation' were the beneficiaries of an indigenous system of architectural education within which there was an appreciation for the nation's building traditions on account of the presence of figures such as Kigo and Itō, and because Japan's academic institutions increasingly had Japanese, rather than western, architects and scholars in senior positions. It was under their auspices that China's first architects would be trained.

Differences between these two generations underpinned professional debates throughout the 1920s and 1930s. Design competitions for public buildings demanded that entries should reflect *Nihon shumi* (Japanese taste), just as the Nanjing and Shanghai competitions had done in China. But unlike the Chinese context, the response of a group of young European- and American-trained Japanese architects to this doctrinaire and inward-looking approach was to look outward to the international architectural scene. Borrowing heavily from international parlance, they claimed their work to be 'new architecture' (*shinkenchiku*), 'international architecture' (*kokusai kenchiku*) and 'modern architecture' (*gendai kenchiku*).[51] There was no equivalent in China to this tendency.

In finding an explanation for this difference, the impact of the massive Tokyo earthquake cannot be overlooked, as the reinforced concrete structures such as Wright's Imperial Hotel remained standing while nearly half a million traditionally constructed wooden homes were destroyed. The earthquake caused the writer and professor at Waseda University, Kon Wajirō, to coin the phrase *modernology* – after the archaeology of the modern – and write the book *Modernologio* (1930).

Other reasons include the fact that, compared to China, Japan's architectural community was larger, more mature and more ideologically heterogeneous. The first established group of modern architects was the *Bunriha Kenchikukai* (*Secession Group*), formed in 1920 by six Imperial University graduates, including Kikuji Ishimoto (1894–1963), Sutemi Horiguchi (1895–1984) and Mamoru Yamada (1894–1966).[52] Influenced by German Expressionism, the Vienna Secession and De Stijl, they promoted their cause by hosting exhibitions and lectures, and publishing material. Despite lasting only eight years,[53] they played a key role in instilling a modernist sensibility among Japan's architects by advocating an 'iconoclastic newness and opposition to all prevailing tendencies'.[54] Some of the later work by their members achieves a remarkably high standard of structural and functional expression[55] that, as Stewart suggests 'would make some of the intervening work of the International Style look shoddily unsubstantial in comparison'.[56]

In 1923, another architectural group with modernist pretensions emerged from the Ministry of Communication, 'which took great pride in the image of speed and efficiency created throughout the nation – and, indeed, the Empire'.[57] Bruno Taut, with characteristic exaggeration, described the Ministry's Osaka Higashi Post Office (1931), designed by Tetsuro Yoshida (1894–1956), as 'the most modern in the world'.[58] The Ministry's architectural stance at a time when prevailing official architectural tastes distanced themselves from modernism and privileged nationalism is often cited as one of the anomalies of the period.

A third group, though less influential than either the *Bunriha Kenchikukai* or the Ministry of Communication, was the *Nihon Intānashonaru Kenchikukai* (International Architectural Association of Japan), which was responsible for bringing Taut to Japan in 1933.[59]

Many Japanese architects, like their Chinese counterparts, had conducted architectural pilgrimages to Europe, visiting iconic buildings and sometimes working with renowned architects. Ishimoto travelled to Germany in 1922 and worked with Gropius, as did Isaburō Ueno (1900–65), Bunzō Yamaguchi (1902–78), Iwao Yamawaki (1898–1987) and Chikatada Kurata (1895–1966). Kunio Maekawa (1901–86), Junzo Sakakura (1901–69) and Takamasa Yoshizaka (1917–80) all travelled to Paris and worked for Le Corbusier, and Junpei Nakamura studied at the École des Beaux-Arts in Paris. In 1929 Yamada travelled to Europe to attend the Congrès Internationaux d'Architecture Moderne (CIAM).

Horiguchi's seminal fusion of modernism and Japanese vernacular, Shien-sō (House of Purple Haze, 1926), was designed after a year touring Europe. His earlier Memorial Tower at the Ueno Peace Exhibition (1922) inspired Maekawa to become an architect. Maekawa was the most famous of Le Corbusier's Japanese draughtsmen. Faced with severe economic problems in Japan, Maekawa travelled overland to France in early 1928 from the Japanese-controlled port of Dalian in Manchuria across the Trans-Siberian railway, a trip partly facilitated by relatives working for the South Manchuria Railway. Maekawa's Trans-Siberian journey coincided with Liang Sicheng and Lin Huiyin's in the opposite direction, before launching their architecture course in Shenyang's North-Eastern University.[60] Maekawa was among a group of architects from various cultural and national backgrounds that, while crossing continents in either direction along the Trans-Siberian Railway, witnessed the rapidly evolving political and urban environments from Europe through Manchuria to Asia.

Maekawa's design for the Tokyo Imperial Household Museum (1931) stylistically and historically recalled Le Corbusier's unsuccessful design for the League of Nations (1928). In failing to win the competition owing to prevailing aesthetic prejudices favouring the *teikan-yōshiki* style, Maekawa's defeat symbolised the institutional struggle in which Japan's modern architects were engaged in pursuit of 'domestication of rationalism'.[61] Seen broadly as a struggle between modernists and traditionalists, Maekawa's supporting letter for his competition entry highlights the fractiousness of the debate:

> I must state that to construct *kara-hafu* [compressed arched gable] and imitate *chidori-hafu* [concave triangular gable] in reinforced concrete in this 2,591th year since the founding of the nation is a great blasphemy against the splendour of the last several thousand years of Japan's artistic past. . . . It is precisely because we [I and my colleagues] respect Japan's ancient art that we raise objection to this brazenly false Japanese architecture.[62]

The design of the Tokyo Imperial Household Museum, like the National Diet Building before it (and comparable national projects in China), crystallised architectural opinion for and against the invention of tradition and the employment of architectural motifs as aesthetic appendages in modern design.

Modernists were losing the argument for a rational interrogation and reinterpretation of the nation's vernacular. As occurred with modernism in the Soviet Union and Nazi Germany, its association with the western avant-garde invited suspicion and censure. In China, though, no equivalent political backlash against modernism occurred until the Communist era, and even then its condemnation was largely a proxy for Soviet sentiment. Political censorship of the avant-garde occurred only in fine art, notably with the brutal repression of elements of the woodcut movement, but not in architecture. 'Chinese Renaissance' was the style of choice for China's Nationalist government not to subvert modernism or its international ideological aspirations, but to promote nationalism and bolster the nation-building project. Architecture in China by the 1930s, unlike in Japan, had not evolved to a stage where it exerted political influence or posed a threat. Beyond the set-piece national projects, China's architecture was not a concern of the Nationalist government and even if the suppression of modernist architecture had been a political objective, China's quasi-colonial condition would have made it impossible to pursue outside Chinese-controlled areas.

In 1930, Japanese police disbanded the second meeting of the left-wing *Shinkōkenchikuka Renmei* (New Architects' League). According to Reynolds, from this point onwards 'modernists were constantly looking over their shoulders'.[63] In a repressive domestic political climate many Japanese architects went overseas to territories where Japan's expansionist Pan-Asia policy offered new and ample opportunities. Nowhere offered a more attractive environment for architects than Manchuria, soon to become Manchukuo, which became the primary locus for some of the most ambitious and experimental developments in Japanese architecture of the period.

Japanese architecture in China

If we are to adopt the schema of multiple modernities, then Japan's role in China, especially in Manchuria, is an example that warrants closer scrutiny. Japan's architectural activities in China before the Second World War were concentrated in Manchuria, but while focusing on this north-eastern corner of China, developments elsewhere should not be ignored. Beyond Manchuria, the Japanese enjoyed newfound authority from the late nineteenth century in other foreign settlements such as the island of Kulangsu off Xiamen and Shanghai. At Kulangsu the Japanese built a consulate only months after winning the Sino-Japanese War, placing them physically and geopolitically among the western powers who had hitherto enjoyed exclusive dominance in China's foreign settlements. Japan's presence among western nations in China played an important part in forging relations and framing perceptions between eastern and western powers over the succeeding decades, leading ultimately and irreversibly towards regional and global conflict. In no other treaty port were these tensions more acutely felt than Shanghai.

Politically and architecturally, Shanghai had been dominated by Britain until the turn of the century, when the balance of power shifted towards Japan. In the city's census of 1910, there were 4,465 British and 3,361 Japanese. By 1915, the Japanese had become the largest foreign population and by 1930 it was nearly three times the size of the British.[64] The Japanese congregated in the northern suburb of Hongkou, dubbed 'Little Tokyo', which became a thriving cultural hub, particularly in art and literature. The focal point of Shanghai's Japanese community was its Club, founded in 1906. A clubhouse was opened in 1914, located near the Japanese Temple (1908) and a Japanese garden (see Figure 8.1). Japanese housing in Hongkou reflected distinct cultural characteristics, with apartments, including the *lilong* terrace houses so particular to Shanghai, possessing lower ceilings and altered proportions to accommodate the tatami mat.

210 *Architecture and modernity*

Figure 8.1 The Japanese garden in Shanghai's northern district of Hongkou.

Symbolic of Japan's position on the world stage was the position of the Japanese Consulate (1909) on Hongkou's riverfront, the last and only non-western example in a row with three other foreign consulates: Russia, Germany and America. Designed in a 'European renaissance-style according to English standards' by the Japanese architect and University of California graduate, Yajo Hirano, the building reflected the multinational character of Shanghai, as well as the state of Japanese architecture at the time: a European-style building designed by an American-trained Japanese architect fitted with Bangkok teak and Singapore hardwoods treated with French polish and Ningbo varnish, with rooms finished with English wallpaper and a roof garden lined with French tiles.

As one of several Japanese architects practising in Shanghai, Hirano established his own firm in 1904 and designed various offices for Japanese companies and the Japanese Consulate in Hangzhou, as well as being among the first architects to design foreign-owned cotton mills.[65] Succeeding Hirano's generation and its use of the European idiom was the generation experimenting with modern interpretations of national characteristics. Yoshikazu Uchida (1885–1972) is one such example, whose take on Expressionism that became dubbed 'Uchida-gothic' characterised many of the buildings he designed for Tokyo's Imperial University after the earthquake of 1923, including the famous Yasuda Lecture Hall (1925) designed with Kishida Hideto (1899–1966).[66] Shanghai is the only Chinese city to possess examples of work from this phase of both Hirano and Uchida's careers. Uchida's Tong Wen College (1937)[67] bears a strong resemblance to Yasuda Lecture Hall, with its jagged profiles, slender verticals, pointed arches and the rich textural quality of bare brickwork.

The expressive style that characterises Uchida's buildings is compatible with his dislike of the explicit use of Japanese motifs in modern architecture, a view that was shared by Kishida. In 1950, Kishida's student and former resident of Shanghai, Kenzo Tange (1913–2005), would go on to design one of the most successful schemes to synthesise western and eastern design: the Hiroshima Genbaku Kinen Kōen (Atomic Bomb Memorial Park). Tange, who had lived in the Chinese Treaty Port of Hankou, was a graduate of Tokyo University's Department of Engineering and worked in Maekawa's studio from 1939, which had an office in Shanghai until 1943 and designed housing for employees of the Kakō Commercial Bank.

Ultra-modernism in Manchuria

If the encounter between Japan and China over Manchuria has been a historical taboo in post-1949 China,[68] then the region's architecture and urban planning can be viewed as illegitimate offspring – the bastard outcomes of a forced and brutal liaison. Chinese historians have not been alone in their comparative neglect of Japan's architectural activities in Manchuria. Western and Japanese scholars are equally culpable of overlooking the topic. Shame and a desire to conceal abortive colonial ventures have discouraged a closer and wider scrutiny of Japanese overseas architecture among Japanese scholars, as much as political difficulties have obstructed research. For western scholars, there has been the further obstacle of having to negotiate not one but two 'non-western' languages and cultures.[69] The study of architecture in Manchuria throughout the first half of the twentieth century therefore demands more work and international discourse, which was the primary motive for *Ultra-Modernism – Architecture and Modernity in Manchuria* (Denison and Ren, 2017). Taiwan, by contrast, has been more thoroughly researched, since its subsequent historiography has been less controversial in relation both to Japan's imperial past and within domestic scholarship compared with mainland China.[70]

At the heart of Japan's imperial project in Manchuria was the state-sponsored enterprise, the South Manchuria Railway (SMR), whose branch lines spread like iron tentacles into Manchuria and Korea. However, after the 'Mukden Incident' in 1931, Japan seized control of Manchuria. Their prize was a greatly expanded empire renamed Manchukuo (Manchuland), a new state concocted and, for all intents and purposes, administered by the Japanese.[71] Since 1905 Manchuria had been an expedient quasi-colonial adventure for Japan offering substantial economic and political dividends. Manchukuo, however, was an idea born out of imperialistic ambitions within the military in collusion with right-wing sympathisers in Tokyo.

On 23 February 1932, the former Chief of Intelligence of the Guandong Army who had helped to mastermind the 'Mukden Incident', Seishirō Itagaki (1885–1948), invited the former Chinese Emperor, Pu Yi, to become the Head of State of the new nation, comprising five races (*gozoku kyōwa*): Japanese, Manchus, Hans, Mongols and Koreans. According to Young, the builders of this new state were 'a motley crew' of right-wing pan-Asianists, left-wing revolutionaries and militarists.[72]

The Mukden Incident was a turning point for the SMR, for Manchuria and for the relationship between Japan and its new imperial realm. The SMR was stripped of its many commercial enterprises and reorganised as a railway company in service to a much larger militaristic machine. When the SMR President, Uchida Kōsai, switched allegiances in support of Manchurian independence, his resigning vice-

President, Eguchi Teijō pointedly remarked: 'This is Napoleon's Moscow. It will end in dismal failure.'[73] His cautionary words would take over a decade and another world war to prove accurate.

Before 1931 Manchuria had been a site of quasi-colonial exploitation from the motherland. After 1931, with the effects of the Great Depression undermining economic confidence, Manchuria was recast as Japan's future and its lifeline, protected in self-defence and preserved at all costs – the motherland and progeny connected by the fragile chord of the SMR. The inviolability of this vital connection caused Japan to sever its relationship with the League of Nations and to stand alone on the world stage. Within two years, Fascist Italy, the first country to officially acknowledge Manchukuo,[74] would be invoking Japan's treatment of Manchuria to legitimise its invasion of Abyssinia (Ethiopia) from neighbouring Eritrea, where it too was busy designing the built fabric of empire on modernist lines (see Figure 8.2). Two years later, Japan would in turn cite Italy's assault on Ethiopia to justify the wholesale invasion of China. Amid this new and precarious geopolitical landscape dominated by territorial expansion, Manchukuo became the site of some of the most concentrated architectural encounters with modernity during the twentieth century – encounters that were promoted by and in pursuit of a determinedly Japanese modernist agenda termed 'ultra-modernism' – an exaggerated neologism that deliberately distinguished it from its western alterity.

The assertion that Japan would perish without Manchukuo upended the conventional relationship between imperialism and modernity. The promise of modernity was a central facet of twentieth-century imperialism and much energy was expended and lives extinguished marching to modernity's tune. After the creation of Manchukuo, however, modernity's magic began to work not only in the conventional direction of metropolitan centre to imperial periphery, but also in the other direction. Manchukuo's claims to modernity were so compelling that, directly and indirectly, they effected the modernisation of the motherland and of Japanese society.[75]

Manchuria was seen by the Japanese as a component in the larger structure of empire, but Manchukuo was empire-defined. For architects and city planners motivated by the possibility of designing the future and the irresistible thrill of having these designs built, Manchukuo bristled with opportunity. The new state was 'a new country with no cultural legacy needing to be preserved and a mixed race country requiring a new architectural style'.[76] It was painted as a blank canvas on to which they could realise their vision of a brighter future, though the task proved very much more complex and confused than the state or the media would ever admit. Nevertheless, the vision was sufficiently alluring as to reflect an alternative image of modernity back to Japan, whose architects, planners and engineers flocked to Manchukuo to bask in imperial opportunity.

The construction boom that followed Manchukuo's creation not only attracted men of vision (and they were almost entirely men), but also huge numbers of skilled and semi-skilled workers to construct these visions. An army of construction workers, which doubled throughout the 1930s and included in its ranks over half a million Chinese migrants, was vital to Manchukuo's physical transformation.

The funding of this boom fell to the Japanese taxpayer. Large institutions such as the Bureau of Public Works, Central Bank of Manchu, General Directorate of State Railways, the Guandong Office's Public Works Department, and municipal offices collectively spent over 100 million yen annually on construction. The Bureau of Public

Japan: China's mirror to modernism 213

Figure 8.2
Cover of 'Manchoukuo-German Trade and Goodwill Number' of the journal *Manchuria* (1937), celebrating Japan's growing relations with Fascist Germany and Italy.

Works was responsible for the construction industry and 'looked after the drafting of plans, unification of construction, and the supply of materials for governmental construction'.[77] Railway expansion driven by the Guandong Army encouraged new urban plans for 104 towns and cities, 44 of which were implemented by 1940 and the other 60 remained at the planning stage.[78]

New architecture for a new state

The question of what form architectural modernity in Manchukuo should take posed a dilemma for the Japanese. It was difficult enough in Japan, but in Japan's imperial realm in China the issue was complicated further. The crown-topped style popularised by Kikutaro Shimoda had found favour among nationalists and imperialists. The Gothic style popularised by Yoshikazu Uchida was attributed to an emergent form of Japanese expressionism. And the rationalist concrete frames produced by Japan's growing band of young European-trained architects were international at best, but their association with the west invited censure from the right-wing. Japanese architects that either migrated to empire or engaged in it from a distance exported these

214 *Architecture and modernity*

domestic experiences and squabbles to Manchukuo, where the colourful language of Japanese architectural modernity acquired a distinctly Manchurian inflection.

From 1932, Japanese architects found themselves in the frontline of Japanese efforts to create and assert a new identity for Manchukuo. The new state represented a new territory, physically and figuratively, for Japan's architects to explore and realise their dreams of architectural modernity – a utopian setting that, it was hoped, would allow them to 'contribute some new theory and style to the architecture of the world'.[79] The Japanese committed huge resources to architectural theory and practice in Manchukuo, which was carried out under the auspices of architectural departments in state institutions and professional bodies such as the Manchurian Architectural Association (*Manshu Kenchiku Kyoukai*), which published its own journal from 1924 (see Figure 8.3 and Plate 24). Japanese researchers examined every detail of traditional building and its response to local conditions, building materials, climate, ecology and customs. The lack of earthquakes, a drier climate and extreme temperature variations throughout the year were features of Manchuria that distinguished it from Japan and contributed to its built form. For Japanese architects embracing imperial opportunity, these dissimilarities presented a major challenge that was not always successfully met but nevertheless was felt to have contributed to the development of Japanese architecture.[80]

Figure 8.3
A front cover from the Manchurian Architectural Association (*Manshu Kenchiku Kyoukai*) journal.

Timber – the elemental material for Japanese architects – was substituted by locally manufactured bricks (*peitzu*) comprising dried blocks of rammed earth that for millennia had risen out of the Manchurian plains in the form of city walls, forts, ramparts, temples and the humble dwelling of the peasant farmer. Solid walls of *peitzu*, topped with straw-covered timber roofs, created an impermeable barrier to the elements, quite unlike Japan's raised timber-framed homes with flexible and permeable screen walls. In towns and cities, *peitzu* were substituted by a more permanent fired brick, which became a characteristic feature of Japanese architecture in Manchukuo. Over 150 million bricks were used each year, 120 million of which were manufactured locally.

To combat the extreme winters, with temperatures below –40°C, Japanese architects experimented with 'the tatami-less house' and adopted domestic interiors that used tables and chairs.[81] Such foreign devices had become the norm in offices, schools and shops in Japan throughout the Meiji era, but less so in the domestic environment, where the tatami reigned. Homes were kept warm by a primitive form of central heating known as a *kang* (Russians called them *pechka*) – a raised platform projecting from the wall about 70cm high with a fire inside that warmed the walls and floor of the house.[82] The extreme summer heat was dry and therefore less of a concern for architects accustomed to resolving ways of cooling interiors. Other local conditions besides the continental climate included wartime preparedness, such as bomb-proofing and anti-air raid design. 'All of these things,' noted one commentator, 'contributed to the rise of a new, and different type of construction and architecture that had never existed before'.[83]

While practical considerations concentrated on construction techniques, materials, customs and local conditions (notably the disparity between Japan's temperate climate and Manchuria's continental climate, as well as wartime preparedness, including bomb-proofing and anti-air raid design), theoretical concerns focused on the question of architectural modernity in Manchukuo and what form this should take. The result was not an encounter with architectural modernity from the west, but a multifaceted modernity from the east. Initially, as one observer put it, 'a new type of construction was introduced by the Japanese, which was neither purely Japanese nor purely foreign ... the buildings put up by the Japanese were a compromise between western and Japanese types of construction'.[84] Later, with the advent of Manchukuo, architects were conscious that 'Manchurian architecture needed to be unique'.[85] The 'concrete massive walls and phantastic (*sic*) roofs' of Manchukuo's new buildings sought inspiration from 'the style of the "potala's" and the "p'ai-lou's" of Mongol monasteries'.[86]

In the domestic realm, the combination of 'native Manchus [taking] in the modern facilities' and the Japanese adopting aspects of Manchurian dwellings produced 'a new type of residential building'.[87] As the approach was steadily refined, some believed the result was that 'Manchurian construction came to possess qualities and characteristics peculiar to the country' and a mode of building 'that represented Manchuria finally emerged'.[88]

Architecture in Manchukuo was a predominantly metropolitan undertaking engaged in two main spheres of activity: architecture of the state (e.g. government offices, schools, hospitals, fire stations, railway buildings, industrial facilities and public housing) and private practice (e.g. department stores, shops, cinemas, hotels, factories and private housing). The architectural departments of state organisations were largely responsible for public schemes funded by private capital and commissioned by state organs such as the Kwantung Army, the SMR and municipal departments, while some public commissions were open to competition or subcontracted to independent architects whose work was otherwise principally engaged with private clients.

The distinction between these two spheres assumed an aesthetic connotation with the imposition by the state of stylistic censorship, especially after the foundation of Manchukuo. The charged political atmosphere and the desire for buildings to represent a fledgling nation under the patronage of an expanding empire imposed a loose set of stylistic conditions on design. With the benefit of hindsight, many architects were critical of this initial phase, where the explicit incorporation of Asian-style roofs and decoration on modern buildings driven by political expedience were seen as lazy, uninventive and even embarrassing.[89] Amid a political landscape rife with rivalries, the Japanese found themselves supervising the creation of a new style that was neither Chinese nor Japanese, but attempted to embody the solidarity between Japan and Manchukuo and reflect the utopian idea of the new state: a modern 'Manchu' style.

The keenest advocates of empire believed the path of progress led from the imperial centre to the periphery. 'New construction features were introduced by the Japanese heretofor unseen in Manchuria,' boasted Shinsaku Tsutsui, 'and Manchu people assimilated the gift of their better trained and better informed Japanese "instructors"'.[90] Japan saw it as a civilising duty to export to Manchuria all the facets of modernity – international standards of lighting, materials, ventilation, sound absorption, heating and cooling, and sanitation. However, Manchukuo also pointed Japanese architects towards a future for their own society in which everything from the domestic environment to urban planning was reorganised along modern lines. This was not merely an example of the dualistic relationship between colonised and coloniser, but the upending of the conventional centre-periphery model of empire entirely. Manchuria was a vast laboratory in which a new generation of Japanese architects and planners gained unprecedented experience and opportunity, the fruits of which would materialise much later. It would take nearly two decades and one world war before such futures were realised, but Manchukuo's role in Japan's post-war developments, whether acknowledged or not, are indisputable.

A modern Utopia

There was no stronger guiding principle for Japanese engaged in the design of the Manchukuo state, its cities or its buildings, than the pursuit of the modern. Modernity was omnipresent in Japan's quest for industrial expansion, military strength, technological development, and various forms of cultural and artistic expression. Manchukuo's programme of modernity was rooted firmly in the metropolitan realm, though unlike encounters with modernity elsewhere it did not place rural settlement in opposition to it. Japan's imperial policy promised progress and opportunity in rural and metropolitan contexts in equal measure, though it was in the cities that it flourished most fully. Modernity defined the means by which Manchukuo was presented to the Japanese and international public and sold to prospective migrants.

Architects and planners had to respond swiftly to the immigration boom that accompanied the founding of the new state. Migration programmes that promised millions would make the journey from Japan to Manchuria before 1930 never exceeded 10,000. After the establishment of Manchukuo, average annual migration peaked at nearly 100,000 a year.[91] In 1937, over 80 per cent of the 1,349,920 Japanese had arrived since 1931.[92] This was still some way short of expectations, as successive schemes aimed at boosting migration failed to meet targets. In July 1936, a plan was announced to send one million mostly low-income or unemployed households (5 million people) to Manchukuo for permanent settlement over 20 years.[93] Migration became a national obsession both domestically and in its creation of the new state. As one journalist put it, 'The final culmination of complete Manchu–Japanese solidarity will be achieved when the current mass immigration program from Nippon has been realized'.[94] Manchukuo became a concept – an ideal – that state-sponsored programmes aggressively promoted at home.

However, the vast majority of migrants who made the journey across the sea were skilled and semi-skilled workers destined for the cities.[95] Manchukuo's metropolitan focus contrasted sharply with Japan's imperial programmes in neighbouring Korea, where almost all the loans issued to settlers by the government-backed Oriental Development Company targeted agricultural schemes. In Manchuria half the loans were for urban projects and the rest were for manufacturing and transportation programmes.[96] Despite the government's best efforts at promoting rural policies and presenting a shared experience of modernity, immigration in Manchukuo turned out to be a predominately elitist, skilled and metropolitan phenomenon.

Rapidly expanding cities were served by ultra-modern transportation and communication networks connected to burgeoning industrial facilities. Urban electrical supply was as high as 95 per cent compared with an average of 5.4 per cent across Manchuria.[97] Even radio broadcasting, that 'aerial bond of unity for the toiling millions', remained an extravagance, beyond the means of most rural workers.[98] Film and drama too were played out only in the new and invariably glitzy cinemas and theatres in new cities.[99] Despite utopian ideas to the contrary, modernity in Manchukuo was an inescapably metropolitan affair.

The struggle to cultivate modernity in the countryside was compounded by the persistent and associated problem of local opposition (branded banditry by the Japanese) and mass migration from China. Fear of the natives – that perennial colonial dilemma – was no less of an issue for the Japanese resettling among their Asian cousins than it was for the thousands of Italian farmers Mussolini sent to Libya, Somalia and Eritrea at the same time and for the same reasons. The 14 million native 'Manchu' farmers who resisted the appropriation of their land was a constant concern, sapping Japanese resources and undermining confidence. For the 300,000 rural Japanese migrants marooned in small settlements in an alien and hostile landscape, their numbers would always remain a mere drop in an ocean of Chinese labourers.

Japan tried strenuously to appease the rural communities and counter the urban exclusivity of cultural production and engagement. The Comfort Train, which travelled along the myriad arteries of Manchukuo's many branch lines, delivered state-sponsored culture to the far-flung corners of the empire. Performing troupes and an on-board cinema entertained the rural masses with film shows, phonograph and dramatic performances. A basic medical service was also provided free of charge. As tension with China escalated, the Japanese recognised that arts and culture were effective antidotes to military machinations, and they went to great lengths to emphasise the 'even more vital task [of] collaboration in modern drama, music, filmplay, journalism and radio broadcasting between the two nations'.[100]

Cultural appeasement and propaganda worked in both directions. The information sections of the Manchukuo government and the film industry in Japan had helped spawn a thriving tourist sector that targeted the country's growing middle classes. The publication of brochures, maps, pamphlets, posters and books, and the production of feature films and documentaries were framed as helping 'foreign people gain a correct understanding of ever-developing Manchuria', but it was much more than that.[101]

Manchukuo became a film set on which the drama of Japan's imperial project was played out in glorious detail and projected back to a thirsty public at home and overseas. Films were made to convey every aspect of Manchukuo's path to modernity and played heavily on modern themes and imagery, including architecture and planning. *Honeymoon Express* was set on board the ultra-modern locomotive, the Asia Express. *Sora No Tabi* (Aeroplane Trip) was a story about a honeymooning couple on a journey around Manchuria by aeroplane. *Nobiyuku Kokuto* (Growing Capital of Manchukuo), commissioned by the Capital Construction Bureau, contrasted Manchukuo's new capital of Hsinking with its former incarnation, Changchun,[102] and *Kokuto Sai* (Capital Construction Festival), commissioned by the State Council's Bureau of Information, celebrated the completion of the first Five-Year Capital Construction Plan in 1937. In a quadrangular romance titled *Chi Chiao Tu* the lead protagonist was cast as an architect.

Manchukuo was billed as a place to experience the future – a land of modernity fashioned by Japan's benevolent and guiding hand – and became the ultimate destination for the discerning Japanese tourist. The route was well established, comfortable, imbued with cultural and imperial significance and, most importantly, increasingly affordable to Japan's growing middle classes. The first generation of Yamato Hotels in the larger cities were expanded, modernised and augmented by local branches in more remote areas, such as Chengde, Jilin, Jingyuetan and Qiqihar (see Figure 8.4).[103] The number of guests visiting SMR hotels rose from 21,865 in 1932 to 58,207 by 1939.[104]

Tourism was founded on the cult of the modern. It relied on modern technology, new buildings, novel facilities, and mass communication with all their comforts and gizmos: pneumatic suspension, air-conditioning, elevators, refrigerators, telegraphy, telephones[105] and radios. Manchukuo possessed luxury hotels; glamorous passenger steamers with the latest interior designs; a network of highways plied by inter-city buses, chauffeur-driven motor cars and 'motor omnibuses'; a state of the art railway boasting 'ultra-modern' high-speed trains and new airports that plugged it into an expanding web of international air travel. The elements were indivisible, each one a vital cog in the imperial machinery of modernity.

No single object epitomised this encounter more vividly and embodied its modernist urge more succinctly than the Asia Express, 'the last word in modern steam railway transportation' (see Figure 8.5).[106] This ultra-modern high-speed train was the pride of the SMR's empire and the prototype for Japan's subsequent world famous bullet trains.[107] The Asia Express was capable of travelling at 140km per hour – comparable to the fastest trains in America and 15km per hour faster than the fastest train in Japan. The streamlined locomotive embodied modern luxury travel. Its sleek elegance

Japan: China's mirror to modernism 219

Figure 8.4 Advertisement for the state-sponsored Yamato Hotel chain.

was more at home on a science fiction set than on Manchuria's vast plains and was constantly celebrated in the Japanese media:

> Since the recent inception of stream-lining, this technique and appearance has become the fad in modern railway design, as well as in the ships, planes and even bicycles throughout the world ... giving a pleasing appearance in design, and is especially befitting the elongated body of a fast express train. Not to be left behind, Manchuria did not hesitate to be in vogue, and embodied this quality in the construction of the Asia.[108]

In 1935, following Stalin's surrendering of the former CER, the incorporation into the SMR of the 240km line from Changchun to Harbin allowed the Asia Express to run between Dalian and Harbin for the first time without having to switch trains and gauges at Changchun, cutting 5 hours off the 18.5-hour journey.[109]

220 *Architecture and modernity*

Figure 8.5 Advertisement for the South Manchuria Railway's Asia Express, and the Asia (*bottom left*) and the Tabusa (*bottom right*).

The consolidation of both lines made it possible to depart Dalian at 9am on a Saturday morning and arrive in Berlin at 6.42am on the Wednesday eleven days later – a favourable alternative to the fastest sea route, which took 35 days. This extraordinary train upended the notion of centre-periphery on which modernism relied: new to old, progressive to backward, west to east. The Asia linked east to west; Empire to Motherland. It was not alone either. Another modernistic train, the 'Tabusa' with its distinctive streamlined white hood, joined the Asia in the late 1930s, and in the skies the 'Super Air Express' offered daily flights between Manchukuo's capital with Tokyo.[110]

The Asia became the symbol of what the Japanese regarded as the SMR's civilising mission (see Plate 25): part of the wider imperial aim of 'indicating to the Chinese a path toward modernity',[111] as one journalist wrote in 1936:

> The traveller in these old Manchu provinces of China, that used to be regarded as the Forbidden Land infested with bandits finds express streamlined trains, with solid Pullman cars rivalling the luxury of the "Twentieth Century Limited," towns

with palatial hotels and contiental [sic] service, travel buruaux [sic] and clubs where he is made welcome – Occidental civilisation transplanted to an Oriental setting.... So modern cultural and educational equipment is nearly complete and there remains very little to be added in these towns in respect of modern conveniences.[112]

City planning

The constellation of towns and cities scattered across Manchukuo relied on and owed their existence to the railways. For most metropolitan centres, this sprawling network of iron filaments determined not only their encounter with modernity but also their physical form. In the plan of Dalian, the Japanese retained the Russian 'spider-web' system, whereas the 'square system' predominated in the earlier railway zones planned by SMR, and in the larger cities 'both systems [were] blended'.[113] Modern city planning arrived on the back of Russia's railways and thrived in Japanese-controlled Manchukuo, reaching its apogee in the state's new capital, Hsinking (formerly Changchun).

In October 1933, the Town Planning Section was established in the Public Works Bureau of the Department of People's Welfare 'to direct and supervise town planning ... on modern lines. The Town Planning Section subsequently was transferred to the Department of Communications and expanded as the Town Planning Bureau',[114] which was instrumental in drafting the Town Planning Act of 1937.[115] Town planning in Manchukuo was carried out in conjunction with land improvement so that the municipal authority was able to make a profit from the sale of the land improved by the accoutrements of modernity: water and electrical supplies, waste systems, telephone and telegraph lines, recreational parks, wide and sealed roads, and abundant public amenities.[116]

Under the new regime, the ancient capital of Shenyang became the industrial and commercial centre – 'the Osaka of Manchukuo'[117] or the 'Manchester of Manchukuo',[118] depending on one's cultural predispositions. The ancient Manchu capital with its dilapidated 10-metre high crenellated wall was surrounded not only by the region's mineral wealth sprouting chimneys, mine shafts and electricity pylons, but also various foreign settlements with all their modern accoutrements.[119]

These started to change rapidly after 1931, when new architectural forms began to emerge. The General Directorate of State Railways spent 6 million yen on its brand new headquarters.[120] In the city centre, 'the scaffolded iron-concrete mass of the new Mitsui office' rubbed shoulders with 'big department stores and apartment houses, busy streets and overcrowded shopping districts glittering with innumerable neon-light signs'.[121] 'Instead of dirty, impassable, loamy streets,' the new city plan proposed 'excellent avenues, macadamized and asphalt roads'.[122] In five years from 1933, the Japanese population rose from 47,567 to 163,591, their world revolving around the Yamato Hotel, the 'centre of the settlement's social and business life'.[123] The small European and American community revolved around whichever social hub suited their particular taste. For the colonials there was the Mukden Club. For the missionaries there were the Irish, Scottish and French Missions. If you were a Nazi there was the Deutscher Klub, possessing beautiful gardens and home to the Charter of the Nazi Party. For the thousand White Russians stranded in Shenyang there was the Russian Orthodox Church, 'representing one of the best specimens of Russian architecture',[124] or the middle school, library and various sports clubs. The city even boasted Asia's largest 18-hole golf course. The urban plan divided Shenyang into five zones: residential (40 per cent), manufacturing (20 per cent), commercial (10 per cent), green zones (14 per cent) and reserved district (6 per cent) with the remainder unreserved.

All across Manchukuo, urban planners followed in the wake of railway engineers. Mudanjiang, once a small settlement around a railway station on the eastern section of the former CER near the Korean border, had become a large town of 46,000 with a Japanese population of 7,000. Around 80 per cent of the new buildings were said to 'have a strong Korean flavour', though they 'apparently lacked solidity, being ill-adapted to keep off the severe wintry cold'.[125] Nevertheless, urban planners were confident they could transform the city into one that accommodated 300,000 residents. Over 100,000 were expected to arrive within a year, 'attracted by the glamour of bustling boom that they fancied enveloping the rising town'.[126]

In nearby Jiamusi, exposed by the completion of the Tumen-Jiamusi line in 1937, urban planners anticipated a city of 300,000 in 30 years replete with all modern services, facilities and infrastructure. Despite a 'painful shortage of timber . . . a lively building boom [was] expected to set in as soon as the weather permitted'.[127] The same railway line opened up the rural settlement of Boli, where urban planners drafted ambitious plans to convert 'wild tracts stretching beyond the existing small town in front of the railway station into a modern city of decent size'.[128] Despite 'all its crudity', observed one journalist, Boli was 'lit with electricity since the beginning of the year as if to herald the influx of modernity'.[129]

On the other side of Manchukuo, Qiqihar, encountered a similar experience.[130] Urban planners immediately began making provision for a city of 600,000 within 10–20 years. By 1935 there were 6,623 Japanese residents (2,236 households) and a modern system of water supply was under construction. A network of sealed roads was laid out along with the spacious Lungsha Park, which contained a library, tower and small zoo.[131] In the centre of the town stood the 70-metre high reinforced concrete memorial to the Japanese soldiers killed in 1931, constructed in 1935. 'In several years,' the press boasted, 'the city [had] modernized with all facilities inseparable from modern life'.[132] A familiar story unfolded in Hailar, near Manchukuo's western border with Russia. Despite the formidable construction effort since 1931, 'the increase of buildings in number [was] still disproportionate to the rapid growth of the population'.[133] The formerly sleepy town was transformed by macadamised streets, parks, a sports stadium, 'houses of modern type, schools, hospitals, bridges, and roads; sawmills worked by electric power; telegraph and telephone lines' and regauged and repaired railways.[134] With the help of the railways, some of the remotest parts of Manchukuo encountered modernity and experienced its novel offerings, albeit fleetingly before debts had to be paid and scores settled.

Harbin

Harbin was as much a product of Manchukuo's short history as it was a victim of its fortunes. Few cities were as severely buffeted by the political storms that swept from Europe to Asia and back again. The settlement had grown from a garrison town blending rampant mercantilism and paranoid militarism in the late nineteenth century into one of Asia's liveliest and most cosmopolitan cities in just three decades.

By 1931, Harbin was the embodiment of China's unique and complex condition caused by its multifarious encounters with modernity. As the reporter James Scherer suggested, the city was 'a symbol' of a global dilemma: 'Lodged in the very heart of Manchukuo, it posits the Manchurian problem, which comprises three factors: the west, the east and Russia.'[135]

The city's development was always capricious, heavily dependent on international events unfolding far beyond its boundaries. Harbin had a troubled upbringing and throughout the early years remained something of an outsider. The settlement emerged from 'a desert wilderness'[136] in 1898 plagued by disease and deprivation to become a thriving town dominated by Russians and Chinese by the time of the Russo-Japanese War. The Great War and the Bolshevik Revolution further stimulated the city's growth, sending waves of White Russian migrants into China via the Trans-Siberian railway and CER. In Harbin these itinerant aristocrats were forced to rub shoulders with hundreds of displaced European and tens of thousands of Chinese residents. Of all the cities in China, only Shanghai had a greater ethnic diversity.[137]

In 1920 the wave of Russian migrants created a vast reservoir of stateless people in Harbin as the Chinese government ceased to recognise Tsarist Russia and rescinded all extraterritorial rights. The Whites came under pressure not only from the Chinese, but also from their Red counterparts. Soviet agreements with China signed in 1924 to co-administer the CER forced Russian workers to adopt Soviet identities. Patriots willingly obliged. Pragmatists chose between becoming Harbin radishes (red on the outside and white within) or Chinese citizens, their passports stamped with Russian émigré (*rossiiskii emigrant*). The diehard Whites sacrificed their jobs and remained stateless.[138] For the Russian population, Harbin throughout the 1920s was politically polarised: a tale of two cities – red and white, Communist and monarchist, Soviet and Russian. Members of both camps vigorously promoted their worldview, though also shared the common nostalgia of the immigrant. Yearning for a home that was geographically or temporally remote generated customs, rituals, institutions and even architecture that was often more potent than the authenticity of the original.

The establishment of Manchukuo in 1932 saw the 50,000-strong Russian community subsumed into a uniquely diverse new state – creating a problem for Japan as it sought to construct the image of Pan-Asian ethnic harmony symbolised in the new flag.[139] The Russian community was too large to be overlooked and the institutions it had built were too well entrenched in the life of the largest city in northern Manchuria. Although Russians could be found in most cities in Manchukuo, their concentration and numbers in Harbin distinguished the city from all others.[140]

In 1932 Harbin was a vivacious, anarchic and nocturnal city 'jammed with cabarets, taxi dance hall cafés and Russian restaurants',[141] somewhat at odds with Japan's morally charged imperialist ambitions. It had a thriving sex trade and notorious criminal underworld that flourished in the narrow alleys of downtown Pristan with its assortment of gaily lit Russian bars and night clubs. (There were more electric lamps in Harbin per capita than in Japan and 16 times the average for Manchukuo.)[142] Petty crime was rife and kidnappings were a regular inconvenience that law breakers and law makers both entertained. Had it not been for the romance of Harbin's character, created largely by 'the renaissance style or "art nouveaux"' architecture, a complete reorganisation might have been implemented by the new Manchukuo administration.[143]

From 1932, Harbin's Japanese population grew from 4,151 to 53,295 by the end of the decade. Over 50 new Japanese businesses engaged in building trades and public works contractors found immediate business in the large-scale construction programmes aimed at accommodating the new arrivals.[144] The rise of the Japanese population was inversely proportional to their Russian counterparts, who moved south to China's treaty ports or overseas. Stalin's sale of the former CER forced Russian workers to return to the Soviet Union where they faced persecution and even death simply for being 'Harbin Russians' (*kharbintsy*). Some Russian architects and engineers remained in Harbin and even formed their own society in Manchukuo, among whose ranks included Mikhail Matveevich Oskolkov and Petr Sergeevich Sviridov, but life was hard and the glory days were never to return.[145]

Harbin's new municipality, inaugurated on 1 July 1933, initiated a new city plan that laid the foundations of a 'Greater Harbin'. This was further developed in a five-year plan launched two years later that proposed the future development of the city around the nucleus of Pristan and the New Town (formerly Novui Gorod), rebranded Nankang (Nan Gang) by the Japanese (see Figure 8.6). Harbin, under its new administration, became a more orderly, if less carefree, city with ten districts stretching in all directions from its bustling core.[146]

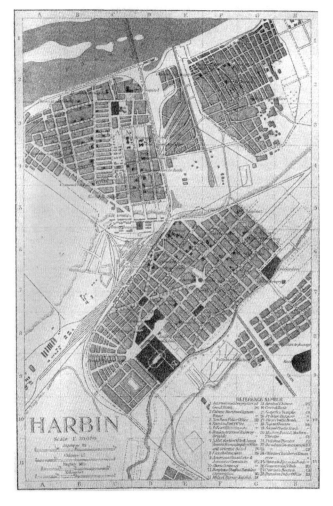

Figure 8.6
The plan of Harbin showing the three settlements created by the railway. *Clockwise from top left*: Pristan, Fuchiatien and the New Town (Novui Gorod).

Japan: China's mirror to modernism 225

In the heart of Pristan was Kitaiskaya Street, running from the Sungari River to the newly named Tatung Square. This thriving commercial thoroughfare lined with small Russian and Japanese shops and larger department stores was dubbed Harbin's Ginza, after Tokyo's pre-eminent shopping street, though the throngs of people 'sauntering down Kitaiskaya Street on a summer's evening [were] not exceeded by those in Ginza or in Shinjiku in Tokyo' (see Figure 8.7).[147] In the centre of Pristan the large Japanese department store, the Matsuura Yoko with its roof garden offering panoramic views of the city, competed for the skyline with the imposing St Sophia Church topped by its large bulbous dome.[148]

North of Pristan, along the banks of the Sungari River, was the district of Sungpu, forming Harbin's famous riverfront characterised by frosty scenes of ice-skating on the river in the winter and the languid atmosphere of cafés, bars and boating during the summer. Here the Yamato Hotel chain had a Yacht Club, an important social hub and summer annex. Harbin's Yamato Hotel opened on 1 October 1936 in the former CER's Board of Directors Hall. The conversion of this art nouveau-styled landmark designed by the Russians before the Russo-Japanese War[149] was proof of a general trend throughout the 1930s that saw Harbin's older streets becoming 'Japanified'.[150]

The Yamato Hotel was located in the tree-lined district of Nankang (Nan Gang), home to government offices and residences of wealthy merchants and officials. Principal buildings include the SMR's regional headquarters and the Japanese Consulate General 'the most colourful of consulate buildings in the whole of Manchoukuo [sic] ... in a Renaissance style according to plans designed by the famous Russian architect Jidanov'.[151] By the mid-1930s, Nankang was connected to the rapidly expanding residential district of Machia with its pretty homes, botanical gardens and schools

Figure 8.7 A scene from Harbin's thriving Kitaiskaya Street, dubbed Harbin's Ginza for being the city's busiest commercial thoroughfare.

that were home to many of Harbin's wealthier White Russian refugees. The White Russians referred to Machia as Tsarskoye Selo after the area outside St Petersburg that was home to the Imperial Russian family. The bucolic scene of 'private homes fenced in by wooden rails ... colourfully nestled in greenery' was noted as 'offering a delightful pastoral atmosphere which belies the fact that this is a part of a great metropolis'.[152]

A very different scene emerged in the former Chinese district of Fuchiatien (Fu Jia Dian) to the east of the city, which, having formerly been situated outside the railway zone in which Chinese were forbidden to live, was incorporated by the Japanese into the new municipal area. 'One step into this district,' alerted one journalist, Kaname Tahara, 'brings one into a totally different world from the rest of the Harbin'.[153] Under the new city plan, the rapidly expanding Fuchiatien, which had a population of nearly 200,000, was divided into Dong Fuchia (East Fuchia) and Xi Fuchia (West Fuchia) and acquired a new 1.5 square kilometre industrial zone. In 1936 it was keenly anticipated that Fuchiatien would 'soon be bristling with smokestacks and buildings for industrial purposes'.[154] Harbin had 53 modern oil mills compared to 23 flour mills and thousands of traditional mills – 'huge modern brick structures, with modern occidental equipments which make one's fancies travel back to Minneapolis'.[155]

As a Chinese enclave in a city dominated politically by Japanese and culturally by Russians, Fuchiatien's experience of modernity was unique. In this quaint corner of Harbin, a unique and particular form of modernity emerged that made the Chinese 'of Dairen and Mukden [look] no more than country yokels', wrote Tahara, invoking China's pre-eminent site of modernity, Shanghai: 'The Chinese culture of Shanghai has passed intact through South Manchuria directly into Harbin.'[156]

After a protracted and troubled upbringing, 1935 marked Harbin's maturity. With the population approaching half a million, a five-year plan was launched aimed at bringing order to the city.[157] The sale of the former CER permitted the first direct train service from Dalian, which arrived in Harbin's central station on 1 September 1935. The Badar swamp that had for decades been an incubator of disease was drained, with the intention of turning it into a park with 'shadowy walks, summer houses, fountains and grounds for sports' as well as tennis, football and baseball pitches.[158] The city's water supply was revolutionised, with the antiquated system of putrid and often poisonous wells[159] being replaced by a new municipal supply. Construction of a new dam on the Sungari River was designed to stop the devastating floods that frequently ravaged the city. A few years later, the Japanese built one of the world's largest hydro-electric projects boasting 'huge ultra modern turbines'.[160]

According to the Japanese, Harbin was 'fast approaching the level of a modern Japanese city, in name as well as in reality',[161] but the city would forever remain a victim of history and its origins. Its social, commercial and physical character had been defined by its position at the strategic junction not merely of the two of the most important railway lines in Asia, but also of two continents. Consequently, the Japanese invested less here than in other cities nearer to the commercial and political centres of Manchukuo. Harbin's strong international character made it a miniature Shanghai and shaped its multifarious encounter with modernity. Ultimately, its history and relative proximity to Russia encumbered Harbin's development, particularly in comparison to the other key cities along the SMR, notably Dalian and Hsinking, which enjoyed their status as Manchukuo's modernist gateway and its ultra-modern capital.

Dalian

Within two decades of its inception, Dalian was China's fourth biggest port,[162] but as Manchuria became Manchukuo, the city assumed an even greater importance as the gateway to a modern state and Japan's hard-won empire (see Figure 8.8). Since Russia had relinquished the city, its development 'had been phenomenal', with a fourteenfold increase in population, a tenfold increase in trade and a nearly threefold increase in size.[163] In 1930, new building regulations were established to anticipate a population of one million. By the mid-1930s, Dalian was second only to Shanghai, with which it shared many similarities in its dependence on and projection of a sophisticated and progressive urban modernity. But, unlike Shanghai, a consistent and essential facet of modernity in Manchukuo was the railway, whose network of tracks extended like veins across the hinterland from the main artery of the SMR. Dalian was at the heart of this vital imperial project.

'I wish I could show you the Darien [Dalian] of today,' wrote one American visitor in 1933. 'It is a city of telephones, electric lights and street cars, automobiles, broad, paved streets, and hard-surfaced roads leading out into the country.'[164] Dalian offered an experience of modernity that matched and often exceeded modern urban experiences in Japan. Modern communications such as wireless radio beamed programmes across the airwaves to Manchuria's first ever radio listeners. As an important mode

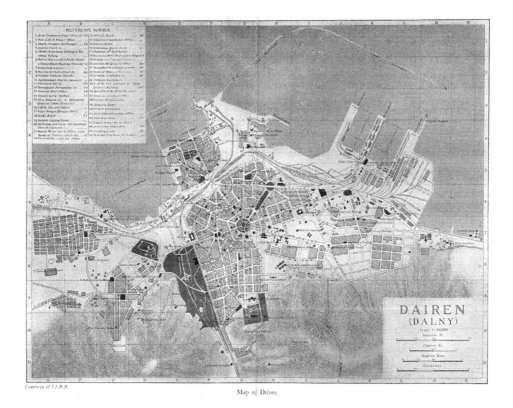

Figure 8.8 Plan of Dalian from the early 1920s showing the consolidation of the initial Russian plan and the beginning of westward expansion.

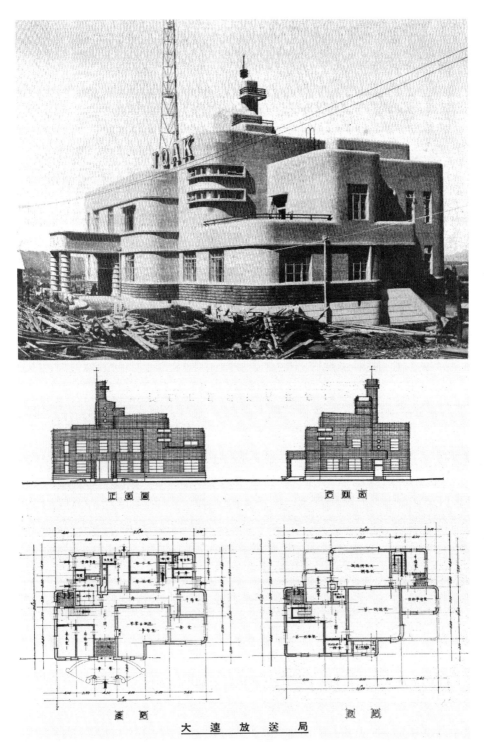

Figure 8.9 The 'ultra-modern' JQAK radio station (1936), Dalian, showing elevations (*middle*) and plans (*bottom*).

of propaganda, the Japanese went to considerable lengths to emphasise the egalitarianism of their imperial machine compared with western equivalents. Comparing the 93,000 listeners among the 37 million Chinese in Manchuria with just 40,000 among 350 million Indians in British India, the Japanese claimed such figures 'go to show that Manchoukuo is making tremendous progress as a modern civilized state in the Far East ... an unparalleled advancement in the history of modern civilization'.[165]

Modern communications demanded modern infrastructure, which in turn stimulated modern architecture. Japan's architects grappled with entirely novel building typologies: cinemas, railway termini, factories, workshops and radio stations, which were built all over Manchukuo. One of the most striking examples was the futuristic premises of the JQAK radio station built on Shotokugai Park in the western suburbs of Dalian to avoid interference from the concentration of wireless communications in the port (see Figure 8.9). Like a spaceship beaming its message to the stars, the 'modernistic studio standing on a low mound in the outskirts of Dairen, [called] forth nightly to its countless number of international radio fans throughout the world'.[166]

Dalian also bore early witness to the future potential of film. In February 1906, the first film ever aired in Manchuria was shown at a fundraiser for Dalian's Okayama Orphan Asylum. By 1910 the city boasted Manchuria's first motion picture theatre, 'Denki Yuen' (which became the Denki Kan), courtesy of the SMR who constructed it in a city park. From 1907, the Dalian branch of the YMCA hosted public screenings of short reels and in 1914 imported the first full feature-length film into Manchuria, *Quo Vadis?*, screened in Dalian's Kabuki-za theatre. This was followed in 1915 by *Les Miserables*, screened at the bastion of Japan's upper classes, the Yamato Hotel. The hotel's orchestra made this popular art form more palatable to the exclusive guests.

In 1928 Manchuria's movie scene was revolutionised by the screening of the first ever 'talkie'. Fox Movietone Party brought the film and equipment to Manchuria and played it at Dalian's portable Kyowakaikan, owned by Romoo Koizumi, proprietor of the Tokiwaza theatre. In 1930, Koizumi purchased modern equipment for talkies and screened Charlie Chaplin's *City Lights* at the Kyowakaikan before it had been aired in Japan (see Plate 40).[167] Manchuria fell in love with cinema. 'All the leading cinemas in Dairen installed modern sound equipment,' wrote one journalist in 1939, asserting that 'Manchuria was not a whit behind Japan'.[168]

In 1936, the municipality drafted plans for an expanded city to accommodate one million people, extending it over 16km to the west.[169] The ambitious plan aimed to relieve pressure on the old centre by planning new suburbs that were linked by new wide roads and a modern tram network. Main roads leading from the city were widened to 60 metres and modern trams wove their way to new residential districts and brought the 'scenic trio' of coastal resorts, Fukasho, Hoshigaura and Rokotan, within half an hour of the city.

From the centre of town, trams passed through Tokiwabashi to Fushimi Heights, a quiet district with a number of schools, including the Dalian Middle School (1935), notable for its emphatic form and spirited brickwork recalling the Dutch Expressionists of the Amsterdam School. Beyond Fushimi Heights trams travelled through Tankatun and the industrial zone of Taizantun before reaching Hoshigaura (Star Beach, Xing Pu), Dalian's premier summer resort with its golf course, tennis courts and beautiful sandy beach overlooked by a bronze statue of Gotō Shimpei. The final stop was the terminus at the resort of Rokotan ('Fierce Old Tiger'), named after the rocky promontory that appeared to be howling at the sea.[170]

230 *Architecture and modernity*

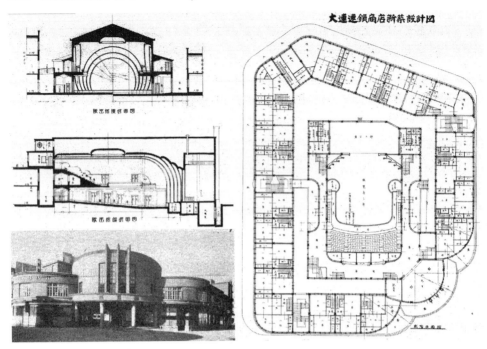

Figure 8.10 The Tokiwa Cinema (1928–1931), designed by the Munakata Architectural Office. *Clockwise from top left, sections*: first-floor plan showing the cinema surrounded by shops; the main entrance.

In the city centre, old markets were replaced by sanitary indoor facilities and fashionable department stores that matched those in Tokyo's famous Ginza district. Two million yen was spent constructing a 'Japanese version of a modern shopping quarter'[171] at Rensagai, opposite the railway station, known as the Tokiwabashi. 'The important civic centre of modernistic Tokiwabashi'[172] was designed by the Munakata Architectural Office and constructed between 1928 and 1931. Expressive architectural elements and sculpted concrete detailing that evoked Frank Lloyd Wright's recently completed Imperial Hotel (1923) in Tokyo adorned the scheme. In the middle was the famous Tokiwa cinema, a little gem from the golden age of cinema owned by Dalian's king of cinema (see Plate 10), Romoo Koizumi. Inside and out, the design was a modernist drama that was as progressive as the films it screened – the Tokiwa was among the first cinemas in Asia, let alone Manchuria, to air 'talkies' (see Figure 8.10).

Throughout the 1930s, Dalian's construction furnished the city with a new hospital and museum, and the largest public library in the Far East. Even the fire brigade underwent wholesale modernisation, with new stations designed and built throughout the 1930s in a style and manner that reflected the speed and efficiency of the modern service.[173] By 1938, one journalist boasted that 'the brigade is now run with military precision. Everywhere is orderliness, efficiency and speed'.[174] Nowhere were these hallmarks of modernity more explicitly sought than through the SMR and no building epitomised the company's progressive vision more than the ultra-modern railway station in Dalian, 'the finest in the whole of the Far East'.[175]

Dalian's railway station was literally and figuratively the gateway to Manchukuo (see Figure 8.11). Architecturally, it bore enormous weight and symbolism, and the SMR invested heavily in ensuring it met expectations. The origins of the design go back to 1924, when the SMR sought to simultaneously redevelop the harbour and the railway station. An architectural competition was held and won by Inoue Sontarou, but only the harbour was ever completed. The design was said to be similar to Tokyo's Ueno Station but with additional features – luxurious reception rooms, barber shops, public bathroom and a lunch room.

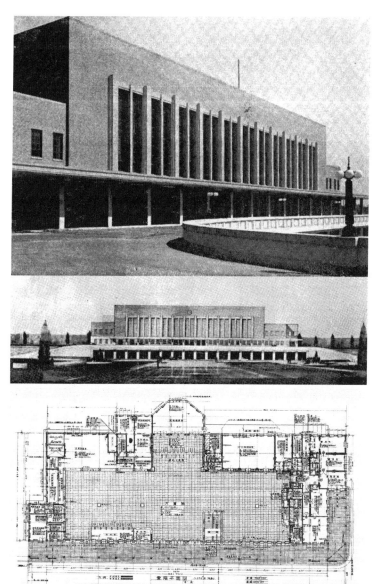

Figure 8.11 Dalian Railway Station (1937), designed by Takaoka Building Contractors.

Construction of the railway station eventually began in August 1935, under the supervision of Takaoka Building Contractors.[176] An army of 450 Chinese construction workers built the station, supervised by 20 Japanese technicians and foremen. The building's superstructure comprised a 'lofty and far-reaching steel framework'[177] 100m wide, 50m deep and 25m high – equivalent to five storeys. The station stood in an elevated position overlooking the square with approach roads giving access to the station's entrance on the first floor via ramps supported on plain concrete pillars. The price tag of 3 million yen made the station the costliest building in Dalian's history[178] and upon its inauguration a spokesman for the Takaoka Building Contractor claimed fittingly: 'The SMR has designed the building to be the largest and most stately station along its entire line, a building worthy of Dairen, the gateway to Manchuria.'[179]

Dalian received the majority share of Japan's capital investment in Manchuria of over 600m yen, and the property market boomed as Dalian became home to the largest concentration of Japanese outside Japan. New suburbs were planned and furnished with rows of houses built from modern non-combustible materials such as reinforced concrete and brick and connected by 'roads [that] were far better than roads in Japan'.[180] Development quickly consumed the remaining land within the urban plan that Russia had so generously laid out.

Dalian, because of its early urban form, was frequently likened to western precedents such as Paris, Boston, Washington or St Petersburg – even the 'rows of strongly built houses' in the city's sprawling western suburbs 'reminded one of Lancashire'.[181] However, beneath the thin veneer of architectural form and style was something more profound. 'These houses of solid brick and double windows [had] no likeness to an English or Russian house inside, for the interior is Japanese.'[182] Whatever might have seemed familiar to the outsider on the outside looking in was countered by the unfamiliarity of the inside. Japanese interiors and domestic habits were exported wholesale to Dalian where the relatively salubrious climate permitted the use of wooden floors, tatami matting and screen walls. In Dalian, 'the Japanese worker returning home at the end of the day will discard his foreign clothes and don the comfortable kimono, after the daily hot bath'.[183]

In 1938, the Chairman of the American delegation to the Fifth America–Japan Student Conference in Tokyo recognised that although to his eyes Dalian was 'very much a European city', he could see that it was 'different from Japan and the United States and the civilizations of Europe as well as some of the Far East and, represented something unusual'.[184] Dalian was indeed unusual – a model of Manchukuon modernism – but it was not the site of Manchukuo's ultimate encounter with modernity, the fledgling nation's newly prescribed capital, Hsinking (Changchun).

Changchun

Selecting a capital for Manchukuo was not straightforward. The string of major cities along the SMR all had their merits and shortcomings. The port of Dalian was the natural gateway to Manchukuo. It had the largest Japanese population[185] and was closest to Japan, but its coastal position isolated it from much of the country. Further north, the ancient regional capital of Shenyang was the largest city and well connected by road and rail, but its imperial associations and large Chinese population made it unattractive to those with grand visions of a modern metropolis befitting a new state. Next was Changchun, which, despite marking the union of the SMR and CER, was comparatively underdeveloped. Harbin, the most northerly city, was in the centre of Manchukuo, but its Russian origins and character were not the image Japan's empire builders wanted to project.

Within four days of announcing Manchukuo's establishment, Japan declared Changchun the new capital, citing its geographic, strategic and historic advantages and giving it a new title: Hsinking (New Capital).[186] Free from cultural precedent and unencumbered by large pre-existing urban areas and landownership issues, Changchun, more than any of the other cities, was a blank slate on which the Japanese could fashion their ideal city. Such an opportunity and undertaking on this scale had never occurred before, either in Japan or in China.

Hsinking, Manchukuo's 'ultra-modern' capital, was unprecedented. In the decades leading up to the city's construction, urban planning had emerged as a distinct profession, detached from the zealous visions of ambitious architects, engineers and cartographers. By the time the new capital was being conceived, the irresistibly rational logic of modernism was revolutionising the progressive professions of urban planning and architecture globally.

Modern city planners promised a better standard of living defined by space, light and efficiency. Completely new and consciously modern cities had been envisioned on paper by some of the most resolute modernists, such as Le Corbusier, but none had yet been built. The colonial capitals of Lutyens's Delhi and Burley Griffin's Canberra were of an earlier age. Hsinking was the first modern capital on this scale, but conventional history tells us that such utopian projects were only accomplished after the Second World War, in the post-colonial era with projects such as Niemeyer's Brasilia and Corbusier's Chandigarh. Modernist history equates modernisation and westernisation, and purports that a universal modernism found fertile ground in newly independent states. Hsinking does not fit into this narrative and thus has been written out entirely, an anomalous victim of historical circumstance defined by three combined and consequent conditions: the west's assumed ownership of modernism, Japan's dishonour and China's humiliation.

Nevertheless, in the fleeting period between Manchukuo's establishment in 1932 and Japan's wholesale invasion of China in 1937, conditions were right for the world's first non-western modernist capital: 'A splendid new capital for a new empire.'[187] For some, it was 'a "neo-Japanese" city, in which the ideas of Nippon and those of Europe have been ingeniously blended'.[188] 'The houses one sees are cubes with flat roofs, a few columns, strangely shaped turrets,' remarked another, drawing the conclusion that 'this seems indeed to be the town of which Le Corbusier, the famous French architect, was dreaming'.[189] But modernism in Hsinking was not that of Le Corbusier or other self-acclaimed modernists in the west. It was inevitably different and a distinctly eastern brand of modernism conceived and constructed in exceptional circumstances by the first non-western nation to have embraced and achieved a state of modernity. Hsinking was planned entirely by Japanese planners and all of its buildings were designed by Japanese architects, except the Foreign Affairs Bureau, designed by the French architect Brossard Mopin, which was described in *Architectural Forum* as 'Bumbling neo-Egyptian', with the added suggestion that Manchukuo had replaced the Soviet Union as having the world's worst architecture.[190]

Setting Hsinking apart from most colonial cities was its projection as being more modern than Japanese cities. The future could be experienced in Hsinking. Unlike in western colonies, where conventional dualistic relations based on 'centre-periphery' were dependent on an enduring state of inequality and subservience, the Japanese project in Manchukuo was driven by the pursuit of modernity and produced conditions that were comparable to, if not more modern than the motherland. Hsinking, more than any other city in Manchukuo, defined the aspiration to be ultra-modern. Even the name – Hsinking (New Capital) – emphasised modernity. Its built environment embodied Manchukuo's distinct and eclectic encounter with modernity. As one American visitor and war veteran, General J. Leslie Kincaid, wrote following his visit in 1938:

> Manchoukuo [sic] has dramatized modern empire-making more effectively than any other country in this world, and any intelligent observer who has travelled through the new empire and has seen the wonderful new capital of Hsinking must be convinced that Manchoukuo [sic] has been solidly built in the few short years, and built for all time.[191]

Within days of Manchukuo's creation, the new government established the Capital Construction Bureau (CCB) and launched a Five Year Capital Construction Plan, one of the most ambitious and consciously modern city plans ever undertaken at that time, not merely in Manchukuo, but throughout the world. The CCB was headed by Yūki Kiyotarō with an Architecture Department directed by Kensuke Aiga, who joined the CCB from the SMR. Kensuke designed the CCB offices in Hsinking in 1934, a white 'cathedral-like' building with a 'central skyscraper tower', which the CCB shared with the Ministry of Education.[192] Starting small, the Bureau grew rapidly to a large office with over 400 staff within two years.

The Guandong Army was the principal authority in commissioning Hsinking's urban plan and appointed Sano Toshikata (1880–1956) as chief adviser. Toshikata was an expert in seismic design and particularly concerned about public hygiene, declaring that all new buildings should be fitted with modern water closets. Toshikata was a student of Gotō Shimpei and had succeeded Kingo Tatsuno (1854–1919) as Head of Architecture at Tokyo Imperial University. In Manchukuo, he helped the Guandong authorities devise an urban planning policy and invited the CCB and the SMR to submit suitable designs. Although broadly similar in principle and configuration, the two proposed plans differed principally over the site and location of the emperor's palace, a highly emotive political issue. Pu Yi, the puppet emperor, insisted in vain that the palace should be located along the city's central axis, according to Chinese tradition. Although the appeals of a symbolic local figurehead could not be allowed to determine Japan's designs for their colonial capital, they could not be entirely ignored either for risk of stirring dissent among the native population. The issue was never fully resolved and as Hsinking rose all around him, the emperor was housed in temporary accommodation.

Despite uncertainty over the palace, the proposed master plan of 1932 was applauded by a partisan press as an example of 'modern city-planning, designed to transform Hsinking into a great metropolis [and] present a gorgeous modern European city'.[193] By any measure, the plan was ambitious, but it was not European, or even western. Hsinking's form and layout was characterised by axial roads linking circular nodes that permitted a modern 'rotary system' of traffic management and provided expansive open areas and monumental vistas that dissected a rectilinear grid-system of smaller roads. Such urban planning features had their precedents in the west, but the conditions under which Hsinking was being realised were wholly different from the likes of L'Enfant's Washington, DC, Haussmann's Paris, Prost's Casablanca, Burley Griffin's Canberra, or Lutyens's Delhi. Whether the desired state of 'ultra-modernity' was ever achieved or not in Hsinking is immaterial. Modernity was the driving force behind the city's total planning and design in a way that surpassed these antecedents and was not matched until after the Second World War with modernist urban reconstruction programmes and the advent of the post-colonial city.

Hsinking's plan was 'guided by the dual consideration of the traditional Oriental idea and traffic facilities have adopted in principle the checker-board system, blended, where permissible, with the wheel-spokes and the cobweb or loop systems' (see Figure 8.12).[194] The cost of the construction programme was to be covered by the sale of individual plots to private investors within a rectangular development area covering 200sq km, containing the old town and former CER and SMR zones (see Figure 6.13).

Development was planned in two phases, each encompassing 100sq km and accommodating half a million people. The first phase, which was later reduced to a

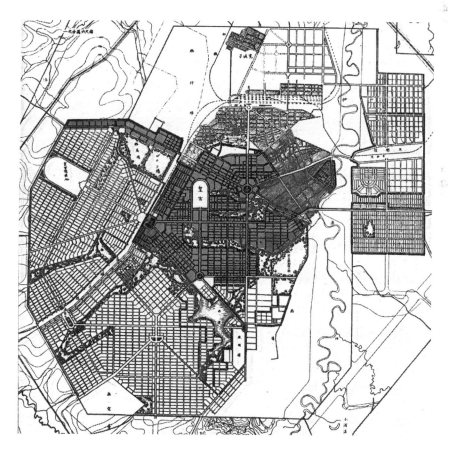

Figure 8.12 Plan of Hsinking, dominated by the Tatung Circle, with the old SMR zone to the north and the old Chinese city to the east, the new imperial compound to the west, and much of the new capital spreading out to the south and south-west.

more manageable area of 79sq km,[195] concentrated on the city centre, extending southwards from the railway station.[196] Densities were kept low by a generous allocation of public parks and open spaces which also served as 'excellent centres of refuge in times of emergency'.[197] Parks also played an important role in hosting cultural institutions such as museums, libraries, public halls, zoos and botanical gardens.[198]

Hsinking's modern roads were surfaced in either asphalt, stone or hard brick and lined with trees, and stratified in three main categories: trunk lines (26–60m-wide), branch lines (10–18m) and feeder roads (less than 10m). The 60m-wide highways exemplified Hsinking's progressive planning. The central section comprised a 16m-wide central promenade, flanked by 12m-wide carriageways for motor vehicles, then 10m-wide pavements on either side. These pavements not only served pedestrians, but were also easily accessible conduits for modern utilities: drainage, sewage pipes, power supply, telephone cables and telegraph lines.

Pre-eminent among Hsinking's new streets was the Chuo-dori (Central Thoroughfare), 'the most representative modern thoroughfare in the city'.[199] It formed the central section of the city's spine that extended in a straight line from the railway station in the north to the city's southern perimeter. The northern section comprised what was once the main section of the Japanese railway zone and started at the station, which had been so instrumental in the city's encounter with modernity. Assembled around the 'plaza' in front of the station were the Yamato Hotel, the police station, library, custom house and a large stone torii that marked the entrance to the shrine of the city's guardian deity: the sun goddess Amaterasu Okuninushino-mikoto and the spirit of the Emperor Meiji.[200]

From 1932, the central and southern section of the Chuo-dori was laid out across open fields and named the Tatung Boulevard. This main axis became a stage set on which the drama of this new city was dutifully choreographed. Architecture had a leading role in this performance, fashioning major public departments, offices and commercial venues along the road. The 'severely modern'[201] Guandong Army Headquarters (1934) contained the seat of the Japanese Legation. The eight-storey Hozan department store offered its guests a rooftop garden from which they could admire the attributes of the modern city: 'gaiety of colours … great cinemas, magasins, the glitter of plate-glass and of stainless steel'. Nearby were the Minakai department store and the Kotoku Kaikan, a large four-storey crenellated block with rounded corners and turret rising above the main entrance evoking the battlements of an old city wall and accommodating the offices of Mitsubishi and other large corporations. In contrast, next door, was the 'ultra-modern' Nikke Gallery, an affiliated concern of the Nippon Woollen Textile Company and the self-styled 'Oasis of the Capital City' (see Figure 8.13). With its roof terrace, *piloti*, glossy white walls and sleek *fenêtre en longueur* that wrapped around the façade, the Nikke Gallery was as close to the International Style as any building in China before the Second World War. A needle tower crowned the structure, with a light at the base faced in a series of glass panels stepping up in three vertical stages to a flagpole at the summit. Inside, on the ground floor, behind the rows of pillars, was a showroom, above which was the 'Nikke Parlour' that was, some claimed, 'certain to impress one as reminding one somehow of Tokyo in its atmosphere'.[202]

In the smaller streets behind the Nikke Gallery and Kotoku Kaikan were some of Manchukuo's most modern cinemas: the Asahiza (Morning Sun) (see Plate 8) and Feng Le, a striking brick structure evoking the expressionism of Northern Europe

Figure 8.13
The Kotoku Kaikan (*background*) and the Nikke Gallery (*foreground*) on Hsinking's Chuo-dori.

that was popular in Japan in the 1930s (see Figure 8.14). Hollywood was the staple supplier of films to Manchukuo until the Manchuria Motion Picture Producing and Distributing Corporation (*Manshu Eiga Kyokai*) banned American imports in 1939.[203] In the absence of Hollywood, the Corporation was tasked with creating Manchukuo's own silver screen. Furnished with studios in Hsinking that were 'the largest and best equipped in the Orient', it produced 'annually at least 60 "feature" plays and many more short news and educational pieces'.[204]

Nearby, and interrupting the straight line of the Tatung Boulevard about a third of the way down its length, was the annular form of the Tatung Circle, a vast circus and urban spectacle at the heart of the city plan (see Figure 8.15 and Figure 8.16). Japan had learned from the Russians at Dalian and amplified the circus form to fantastical proportions. Six roads radiated out from the Tatung Circle, between which were some of Hsinking's most important buildings: the headquarters of the Telephone and Telegraph Company (designed by the CCB's Kensuke Aiga, who also designed the Ministry of Education and CCB offices (1934)), the Police Headquarters, Hsinking Special City Hall, the Capital Construction Bureau, and the headquarters of the Central Bank of Manchu, designed by Kensuke Yokoi, situated on the northwest corner of the Tatung Boulevard.[205] Replete with modern conveniences, such as ventilation, lighting, air-conditioning, sanitation and heating, little

238 *Architecture and modernity*

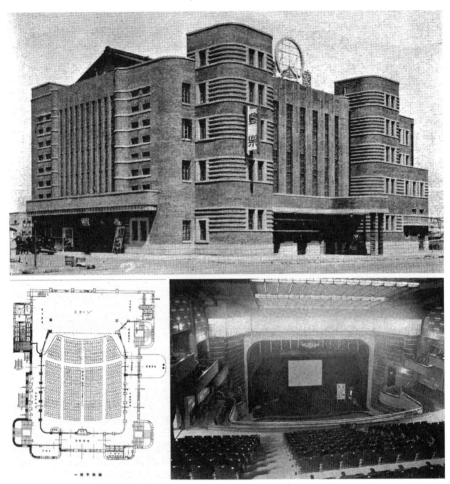

Figure 8.14 The Feng Le Cinema (1936), Hsinking. *Clockwise from top left*: exterior after completion; interior from upper gallery; first-floor plan.

Figure 8.15 The massive Tatung Circle forming the heart of Hsinking's new plan, showing the new buildings (Telephone and Telegraph Company, *left*, and Central Bank of Manchu, *right*) under construction and the Tatung Boulevard with its new department stores extending in the distance to the right.

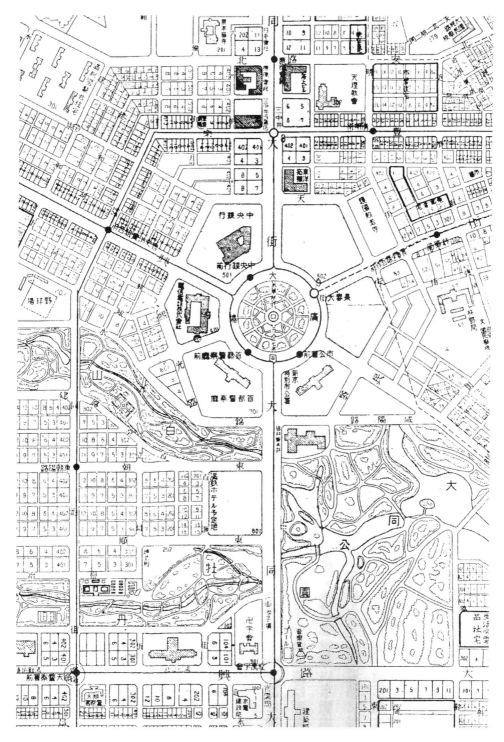

Figure 8.16 Plan of the centre of Hsinking showing the Tatung Circle and surrounding city blocks.

240 *Architecture and modernity*

expense was spared on the bank's interior finishings. Floors were lined with linoleum tile. Fascist Italy provided the marble for the bank counters and columns. Nazi Germany supplied the glass for the huge dome above the banking hall.[206] More than just 'one of the most beautiful and impressive structures that has been built in the city so far',[207] the press wilfully ignored its Grecian overtones and directly associated the building with Hsinking's encounter with modernity:

> The new building stands as a monument to the energy of the Japanese and Manchoukuo [sic] leaders, whose far-sighted policies have been instrumental in transforming the once characterless gloomy town of Changchun into a majestic new metropolis built along modern and dynamic lines – a city befitting the capital of a new and progressive state.[208]

In the late 1930s, the bank commissioned a senior draftsman from Frank Lloyd Wright's Tokyo studio, Arata Endo (1889–1951), to design staff residences and a club. Arata moved to Hsinking for the project, where his designs for the homes of the bank's head and high officials evoke Wright's prairie style with their horizontal arrangement of low, broad roofs, deep overhanging eaves and thick-set windows (see Figure 8.17).

In 1938, the French correspondent Jean Douyau remarked of the Tatung Circle:

> In the centre [of Hsinking] is what would correspond to the Étoile in Paris, all duly and properly proportioned. When certain glorious centuries have passed, I suppose that an 'arc de triomphe' will be erected in the middle of the town and

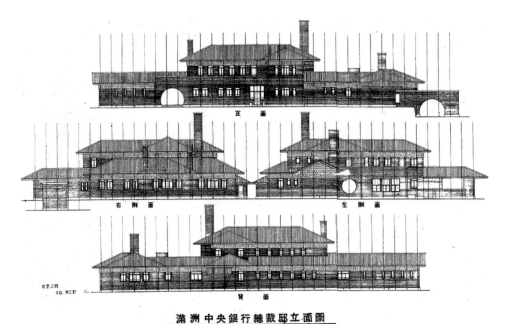

Figure 8.17 Residence of the President of the Central Bank of Manchu designed by Arata Endo, senior draftsman in Frank Lloyd Wright's Tokyo studio.

the avenues running to the four points of the compass will bear the names of its greatest men. At the moment it is a vast garden in the form of a circle, 'un grand round,' a great ring as one sees at Toulouse on which are being built the administrative buildings. The majority of these have been completed and they are of adequate size with great simplicity of line. The architects and engineers have looked well ahead and made plenty of opportunity for the future though the whole is well equilibrated. The Étoile of Hsinking will be most attractive.[209]

Directly west of Tatung Circle were the grounds of the Imperial Palace, not laid out until the late 1930s. Arranged longitudinally in a north–south orientation, the site (0.5sq km) with a 125,000sq m plaza in front, was semi-circular at its northern end to symbolise heaven and horizontal at the southern end to symbolise earth. The emperor, in accordance with Chinese tradition, occupied the space between the two, though in Changchun he never got that chance. The Japanese were in no hurry to expend valuable resources on architecture designed to placating the locals. A building committee was established in 1935 and dispatched to Beijing and India to research palace architecture.[210] Construction started on 10 September 1938, but was never completed. It was much easier for the media to promote the building than for the authorities to construct it.

The Shuntian Highway connected the Imperial Palace to the city's largest park, the South Lake Complex. Parallel to the southern stretch of the Tatung Boulevard, the Shuntian Highway hosted the highest concentration of Manchukuo's government offices, the 'oriental' roofs and decorative treatment on which contrasted with the pragmatic commercialism of the Tatung Boulevard. The 'curly roofs'[211] and Asian style of the Department of Justice's central tower was said to have 'surprised people' for its inventiveness,[212] but the massive State Council attracted most attention.

Located at the northern end of the Shuntian Highway, adjacent to the Imperial Palace compound, the State Council was the most important civic building in Manchukuo (see Plate 25). Completed in 1936, Ishi Tatzuro's design was based on the controversial National Diet Building (1918–36) in Tokyo, the origins of which gave rise to the *teikan-yōshiki* or 'crown-topped' style. Parallels between these two politically important buildings are obvious: the symmetrical plan and elevations, the monumental stepped tower set on a three-storey Doric portico supporting a smaller colonnade above and the extensive use of masonry. The New State Council is both more classical, in the western sense, and borrows more explicitly from Asian iconography in its roof design and stone detailing, than the National Diet Building. The latter is simpler in line and detail, and the crown of the tower is an abstracted stepped pyramid, whereas that at Hsinking is in the style of a traditional Japanese roof, said to represent 'the refreshing beauty, symbolic of the rising metropolis in this modern setting'.[213]

At the southern end of the Shuntian Highway, on the northern perimeter of the South Lake Complex, was the Manchukuo Mixed Court (1939), a monumental steel-framed structure clad in brick and topped with an 'oriental' roof (see Figure 8.18). The massing of geometric volumes in the main body of the building behind a huge porte-cochère evoked the gate towers that punctuated old forts or city walls. The tiered structure and plastic forms were more inventive and imaginative than most of the often simplistic attempts by Japanese or Chinese architects to 'orientalise' modern steel or reinforced-concrete frame structures in the period before the war.

242 *Architecture and modernity*

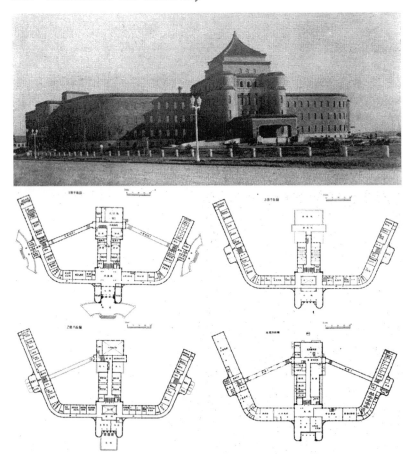

Figure 8.18 The Manchukuo Mixed Court (1939), Hsinking.

   The South Lake Complex was the site of a new suburban district for wealthy Japanese residents and businesses commissioned by the Japanese government in 1939 (see Figure 8.19). Junzo Sakakura (1901–69), who was working in Le Corbusier's office at the time, was invited to design the large mixed-use scheme of offices, apartments and villas. Sakakura's design, clearly inspired by his mentor's approach to planning and architecture, linked the natural and urban environments in a layered hierarchy from the water's edge to the urban grid. A network of meandering footpaths followed the lakeside, behind which a long circuitous road lined by detached villas wound its way from the main road to a club building on the banks of the lake. Behind this irregular landscape the planning changed completely into a rectilinear grid comprising twelve large squares formed by roads. The two squares near the southern end of the lake were further subdivided and contained smaller low-rise apartment blocks. A chain of much larger apartment buildings arranged in a perpendicular pattern linked the other squares together in an uninterrupted sequence across the entire site. These higher rise structures, raised on piloti to allow the free circulation of pedestrians and vehicles at ground level, can be likened to Le Corbusier's famous Unité d'Habitation apartments in Marseilles, but preceded this modernist exemplar

Japan: China's mirror to modernism 243

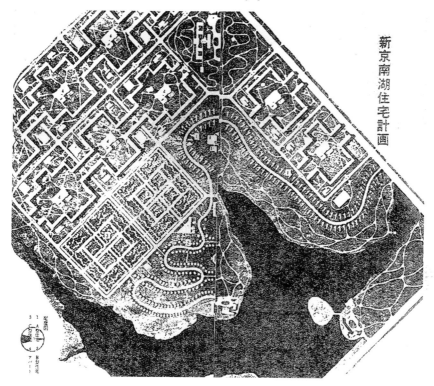

Figure 8.19 Plan for the South Lake Complex (1939), designed by Junzo Sakakura, an assistant of Le Corbusier.

by nearly a decade. However, such architectural aspiration proved too grandiose for wartime Japan. Sakakura's South Lake Complex was never built.

Nevertheless, the scheme's scale and ambition made a significant impact on a generation of young Japanese architects. Kenzo Tange (1913–2005), an employee of one of Le Corbusier's other Japanese apprentices, Kunio Maekawa (1905–86), travelled around Manchukuo and worked with Sakakura on the South Lake Complex. Tange would become one of Japan's most celebrated post-war architects and in 1960 drew on his experience in Hsinking to design the celebrated and influential plan for Tokyo Bay. Maekawa, like many Japanese architects in the 1930s, exploited Japan's invasion of China in 1937 by opening an office in Shanghai in 1939. There he designed a dormitory for employees of the Kakō Commercial Bank (1939–43) and sent 'some of the office staff to Manchuria to work for the Manchurian Aircraft Company – designing factory buildings in Shenyang'.[214]

Hsinking's construction plan also included a new airport, a meteorological observatory, a wireless station, an athletics stadium, an international racecourse and proposals for an underground railway – second only in Asia to Tokyo's, which had opened in 1927.[215] As with telephone and telegraph cables, subterranean railways were deemed preferable for maintaining the serenity of the urban environment, the same reason that in Hsinking noisy, disruptive and unsightly electric trams were banned in favour of motor buses and building heights could not exceed 20 metres, so as 'to eliminate the discomfort that may result from the construction of skyscrapers'.[216]

Japan's lust for modernity in Hsinking was unambiguously projected through monumental and efficient urban planning and state-of-the-art infrastructure, but it was harder to define architecturally. Kensuke Aiga, the prolific CCB architect, explained that his goal had been to create the official buildings in the capital of an ideal country. Evidently burdened by the weight of responsibility, a satisfactory architectural solution eluded him. Having explored various alternatives, a tolerable compromise was one that added a 'modern style' to a 'Chinese style exterior ... to create a new and modern overall form interwoven with a Japanese style interior'.[217]

Manchukuo's political condition, continental climate and the vernacular buildings of northern China (Manchuria and Inner Mongolia) – temples, fortifications, city walls and palaces – all played their part in constructing Manchukuon modernism, an architectural encounter with modernity too far removed from western precedents to be measured by the same standards. The experience and expression of modernity in Manchukuo was, by definition, exceptional, creating an entirely new architectural landscape that was one among multiple modernities globally.

Another condition of Manchukuo's architectural modernity was not simply its potential to inform architecture in Japan, but that Japanese architects in Manchukuo were conscious of this potential. Colonies throughout the world were abundant sources of inspiration for modernism in all its forms, but the western artists who commandeered such cultural cues seldom acknowledged their debt. Instead, they incorporated these ingredients into modernist recipes and exported them back to the colonies as innovation. In Manchukuo, Japanese architects were candid about the potential for the imperial realm to inform the motherland, reversing the conventional notion of centre-periphery and the one-directional exchange between coloniser and colonised. Manchuria's architecture was not only relevant to Japan, it was, like urban planning before it, deemed by many to be an essential factor in the advancement of the nation and the wider expansion of colonial territories. After 1937, Japanese officials increasingly saw Manchukuo as a model for subsequent imperial acquisitions under the umbrella of the Greater East Asia Co-Prosperity Sphere and capable of stimulating domestic reforms.

Another trait that the metropolitan modernism of Hsinking shared with many other global exemplars – Paris, Berlin, London, New York or Shanghai – was the often conscious distinction from tradition. Japanese architects in Manchukuo recognised the enduring conflict between old and new forms.[218] They acknowledged local traditions and were even critical of their often poor efforts to incorporate such traditions into a modern architectural language for Manchukuo, though were grateful for the experience.[219] Throughout the world, modernists of all varieties emphasised this binary relationship, even if it was seldom more than a charade, because it served their purpose and justified the progressiveness of their ideas. Architecture and planning were two effective and conspicuous means of reinforcing this dichotomy, which assumed many forms: rural–urban; old–new; past–future; tradition–modernity; rich–poor; dark–light; quiet–loud; dirty–clean; small–big; backwards–forwards; and fast–slow.

Duality was emphasised at a metropolitan and a global level. In the older quarter of the city one visitor claimed 'colourful Oriental charm abounds',[220] defining it in terms of 'curious shaped shop signs hanging from the eaves of dark, gloomy looking "Mud Huts" and clustered red, yellow and green lanterns festooning the narrow streets'.[221] In stark contrast was:

the remarkable modernization of Hsinking's city planning, with magnificent buildings and residential quarters, and the well mapped-out plan for further improvements ... a beautiful picture of a gorgeous modern capital with rows of ultra modern 'edifices' adorning the tree-lined thoroughfares, from which the ugliness of telephone wires and sewers is completely hidden.[222]

However, within this projection of ultra-modernity was a perennial and conscious attempt to accommodate tradition – something that Europe's early modernists went to great pains to deny. For Hsinking, an oppositional relationship with the old was used primarily as a device to distinguish it from western and Chinese precedents. Hsinking's modernity was presented as distancing itself from and accentuating the primitive and chaotic state of Chinese settlements, while at the same time making European cities, especially London, appear 'old-fashioned', 'dreary', 'dirty', and 'overcrowded'.[223]

Hsinking's 'ultra-modernity' was founded also on speed, both in the pace of life and the swiftness of the city's emergence (see Figure 8.20). Speed even acquired an architectural designation. Masami Makino, writing in the journal of the Manchurian Architectural Association, referred unfavourably to the first five years of Hsinking's development as 'fast-ism'.[224] The views of foreign visitors, and certainly those that the Japanese press were willing to publish, were often more favourable. A Canadian basketball player touring Manchukuo in 1939 'couldn't believe that the majority of buildings of Hsinking have been built within five years'.[225] Having been a native town dubbed the 'City of Beans' surrounded by fields in 1932, by 1940 Hsinking had become an 'ultra-modern metropolis' and the 'pride of Asia'.[226] 'On an unknown tract of farm fields and straggling huts', wrote another journalist, 'now stand rows of palatial government edifice's (*sic*) etc., lining broad, well-kept streets, stately residences, big stores and shops, all in the brief span of only four years or so'.[227] The transformation from old to new was both literal and figurative, as one Japanese visitor reminisced a few months later:

> Looking backward, with the muffled roar of this newest metropolis in my ears, I see once more the deserted streets of old Changchun and the people groping in darkness and uncertainty. And then, as by magic, there comes a light revealing as it grows brighter, a new vista of life, a city beautiful, with its many buildings and spacious gardens, with its throngs of happy men and women, labouring in peace and moving in harmony, under the five-coloured banner of Manchoukuo [*sic*].[228]

Hsinking's unique brand of ultra-modernity was fashioned by the Japanese and enthusiastically promoted to a largely ambivalent global audience. However, foreign visitors who did witness Manchukuo before the outbreak of the Second World War – and some were paid by the Japanese to do so – were invariably overawed by the experience. Writing in the journal *Manchuria* in 1939, Gilchrist eulogised about Hsinking's design:

> How magnificently planned are these streets with their side-alleys, their crossings, the huge squares from which radially new streets are streaming, rising and sinking with the undulating steppe.... No other city in the world compares, perhaps

246 *Architecture and modernity*

Figure 8.20 Fast-ism is characterised in this cartoon titled 'Speed Crisis' by Shinkyo Comics. The first person is saying 'Whoa! That was close again. I will be run down and killed any time soon,' to which the second replies, 'Speed crisis'.

for Ankara, though that 'lacks the "genuine" touch of Hsinking' because it was mostly designed by the German architect Holzmeister.... One seems to breathe freer in such an atmosphere of complete 'modernism'.... Here in the heart of the Asiatic continent a 'dream city' of modernism is growing ... surely more adapted for the requirements of the future times than many other towns.... Modernism in Asia![229]

Hsinking's frequent comparison to other modern foreign cities affirmed its modernist credentials by proxy and reinforced its distinction. It appeared just as 'modern and prosperous'[230] to American visitors as it did to a Polish journalist. The only difference being that the former might be reminded of Washington, DC or Midwest cities that sprang up along railroads and the latter might be 'reminded very much of the Baltic port of Gdynia, which is virtually a brand new city built in the modern style'.[231] Another American scholar visiting Hsinking in 1938 claimed the city's:

magnificent city planning and construction work literally took [his] breath away. ... The buildings along bold and impressive lines, compare most favourably with our finer government structures in the United States and the planning closely resembles that of our more modern American cities.[232]

For a Canadian, Hsinking was 'a tremendous model city' and could be 'compared with Vancouver with a history of fifty years of building behind it',[233] whereas to a Frenchman it recalled 'Casablanca on the Mediterranean', which 'showed the power of our construction work just as Hsinking indicates the same in the Orient'.[234]

All accounts were acts of cultural and intellectual appropriation in their shared attempt to contextualise the experience of modernity they had encountered by recalling foreign precedents, but none was truly comparable. Hsinking was unique and destined not to last. The experience and expression of modernity in Hsinking and throughout Manchukuo more widely was, by definition, exceptional and, consequently, the landscape of architectural modernity was unique – one strand of the global encounter with multiple modernities that was swiftly severed by global conflict.

Unfinished Utopia

Manchukuo's ultra-modernity, like so many modernist visions of Utopia, was encountered more fully on paper than in concrete reality. Despite the considerable efforts of the state-sponsored media and foreign journalists, the pan-Asian co-prosperity dream that the Japanese claimed the new state represented turned into a nightmare of global proportions. 'In Europe modernism expresses itself in slaughter and destruction', asserted one visitor in 1939; 'here it finds its expression in planned construction.'[235] On 7 July 1937 skirmishes between Japanese and Chinese troops at the Marco Polo Bridge (*Luguo Qiao*) sparked Japan's invasion of China and the Asian preface to the Second World War.

For Manchukuo, Japan's formerly concentrated interests and resources were dispersed across a much wider area. Construction peaked in 1937 and would never again return to the same feverish levels experienced in the preceding five years. In 1936, a visitor would have noted 'New houses going up and old ones being remodelled to take care of the ever rising tide of newcomers',[236] but it was never enough. Between 1937 and 1939 house building was sufficient for just 10,000 families (approximately 50,000 people), almost half of the actual demand generated by 95,000 arrivals in the same period. In 1938, only 727 residential houses (for 2,414 families) and 400 commercial properties accommodating residential units on the first floor were constructed. In 1942, a revised urban plan for Hsinking was published that was much less ambitious than its antecedent from 1932.

For the Japanese, the deteriorating economic situation in Manchukuo was amplified at home. For architects in Japan, work had been drying up throughout the late 1930s. By 1944, construction in Japan had fallen by 75 per cent since 1937.[237] Attracted to empire by the worsening conditions at home, this drought caused some of Japan's most important modernist architects – Sakakura, Maekawa, Arata and Tange – to experience Manchukuo. However, the militarisation of the state was simultaneously suffocating architecture, planning and the once-rich variety of research activities conducted by Japanese scholars and professionals. Collectively, these formerly worthy endeavours were victim to what one SMR researcher described as the 'fascist assault and repression by the military'.[238]

Despite worsening conditions, many professionals engaged in realising Manchukuo's modernist city remained in their posts at the SMR, the CCB or numerous municipal authorities throughout Manchukuo during the war. As the tide turned, they were left stranded and exposed, the incidental flotsam marking the high-water mark of empire.

248 *Architecture and modernity*

These individuals and their families, friends and colleagues would pay a terrible price for their involvement – for many, it cost them their lives.

Manchukuo epitomised the doomed alliance of construction and destruction. In 1937, the military's role in orchestrating Manchukuo's encounter with modernity reached its inevitable and horrifying conclusion. Having constructed so much, Japan's invasion of China precipitated total war, the scale of which was unprecedented in human history. Shortly after the invasion, the President of the SMR boasted:

> At last Nippon is in for the final, for a knock-out decision; a once-and-for-all house cleaning of all tortuous tangles in the Sino-Nippon relations which have been plaguing the East for ages. . . . We are free to admit that Nippon has been exceedingly annoying to her neighbour, China. Nippon is expanding. And what country in its expansion era has ever failed to be trying to its neighbour? Ask the American Indian or the Mexican how excruciatingly trying the young United States used to be once upon a time. But Nippon's expansion, like that of the United States, is as natural as the growth of a child. Only one thing stops a child growing: death . . . [Nippon] is fighting to keep Asia from becoming another Africa.[239]

Japan's warmongering was legitimised through Japan's ancient and inalienable bond with the Chinese and other Asian countries. Japan asserted that under its leadership Asia could fight the pernicious triumvirate of Soviet Communism, western capitalism and Chinese nationalism. In 1939, this myth was given the title of 'New East Asia':

> A new revitalized East Asia rising from the devastation. . . . A golden age of racial harmony and collaboration among the three great nations of the Far East, Japan, Manchoukuo [sic] and a resurgent China has been ushered in. . . . Nothing will sidetrack Japan from this mission of creating the new order for the permanent stability of east Asia.[240]

With a war on all fronts, Manchukuo's strategic importance increased. A Five Year Industrialisation Plan was launched by the Guandong Army in conjunction with the SMR's Research Department. The Japanese architect in Manchukuo was cast as a national hero when on 22 May 1940 a new law was passed declaring 'those engaged in public works and building construction are the pioneers in the establishment of a new order in east Asia [which] forms the basis for the construction of Manchoukuo [sic]'.[241] An ambitious migration programme was launched to deliver one million families (five million people) to Manchukuo before 1957. Iron and coal production was accelerated, as was electricity generation, with 15 new power plants planned and nine under construction. Manchukuo went from optimistic aspiration to suicidal ambition.

For architects, professional discourse between the Japanese in Manchuria and the Chinese throughout the rest of China was non-existent. Regardless of their cultural and historical associations, Manchukuo and China were, architecturally, entirely separate worlds, albeit orbiting in the same broader civilisational system. Personifying the anguish that Japan's occupation caused Chinese is the example of Liang Sicheng, architect and historian. Liang's father sought political refuge in Japan, causing Liang to spend the first eleven years of his life there. He never mentioned this to his close friend Wilma Fairbank, whom he first met in 1932, months after the Mukden Incident and shortly after leaving his post at the North-Eastern University in Shenyang. Fairbank later wrote of her discovery of Laing's Japan years as 'startling', not least because, she claimed, 'in the years I knew him I never heard [Sicheng] speak of Japan or Japanese with anything but outrage'.[242]

Sicheng's example is characteristic of many Chinese modernisers, whose inspiration and impetus derived from Japan, but were ultimately forced to conceal or rescind their debt. Fairbank reflects on this in a letter to the partner of Allied Architects, Chen Zhi, in 1979:

> [Liang] must have known the Japanese language well. Yet his career was for 20 years to be frustrated by Japanese aggression, his family nearly killed by their bomb in Changsha, and the long war against the Japanese enemy reducing them to sickness and poverty.... Did he at once turn anti-Japanese as he was when I knew him in Peking? It seems to have become so deep-rooted that he doesn't even acknowledge prior discoveries by Japanese scholars.[243]

Japan's rise and ultimately successful graduation into the west's colonial club posed a dilemma for western observers too. Japan's creation of empire was to some a sign of having achieved western status, as one commentator alluded to in drawing parallels between the 'French genius for the rehabilitation of the natives of Morocco and the application of Japanese genius for making the best of the bare lands of the far east'.[244] Even before Japan took control of what became Manchukuo, there were visible signs of western assimilation and modernist practices, as summarised by the Hawaiian teacher, journalist, SMR employee and 'one of the most effective propagandists for Japan',[245] Henry Kinney (1879–?), in 1929:

> the Japanese establishments in Manchuria are far more modern, in a western material sense, than are any parts of Japan itself, due largely to the fact that here was a clean slate on which to write, and also to the fact that the development was in the hands of a strongly centralized administrative machine, unhampered by traditions or politics, and this machine called into its service some of the best brains of Japan. Western writers visiting Manchuria, and more especially Dairen [Dalian], have claimed that here is found a picture of what Japan will be in future. Some regret the fact that the artistic and aesthetic factor is being subordinated to the material and concretely useful considerations, but the point remains that in Manchuria Japan has established a contribution to modern civilization.[246]

Japan's version of ultra-modernity in China under the guise of Manchukuo may not have been complete, but the intent, the application and the consequences demonstrate a unique example in which western architectural ideas were successfully assimilated by a non-western culture and executed elsewhere. As the author of *Manchoukuo: Jewel of Asia* observed, 'Not only are actual conditions [in the east] quite different from western conditions, but events seem to take place in an entirely different way.'[247] Few, if any, sites offers a more compelling case of multiple modernities than Manchuria. Only one other site in China could compete, albeit under very different conditions: Shanghai.

Notes

1. Harootunian, 2000, p. 59.
2. Isozaki, 2006, Preface.
3. Hiroshi Adachi, 'The Japanese House: Discovering Aesthetics and Space', in 'Japanese Aesthetics and Sense of Space – Another Aspect of Modern Japanese Design', Sezon Museum of Art, 1990, p. 297, quoted in McNeil, 1992, p. 282.
4. Isozaki, 2006, p. 27.
5. Isozaki, 2006, p. 27.
6. Isozaki, 2006, p. 27.
7. Hosagrahar, 2005, p. 1.
8. The Great South Gate was built in the eighth century and rebuilt in the twelfth century.
9. Isozaki, 2006, Preface.
10. Reynolds, 2001, p. 2.
11. Tong, 1938, p. 410.
12. Isozaki, 2006, pp. 12–13.
13. Isozaki, 2006, p. 9.
14. Meech, 2001, p. 17.
15. Stewart, 1987, p. 63.
16. Stewart, 1987, p. 77.
17. 'The World's Finest Hotel', *Far Eastern Review*, Vol. 17, January 1921, p. 57.
18. E.g. the Jiyu Gakuen School (1921) and the Yamamura House (1918–24).
19. Thomas E. Tallmadge, *The Story of Architecture in America* (rev. edn), New York, Norton, 1936, p. 229 in Meech, 2001, p. 19.
20. Meech, 2001, p. 21.
21. Raymond designed the building's terracotta cladding tiles.
22. Raymond, 1973, p. 71.
23. Raymond returned to Japan in 1948 and remained until 1973.
24. Raymond, 1973, pp. 101–2.
25. Reynolds, 2001, pp. 80–3.
26. Hines and Neutra, 1982, p. 94.
27. Isozaki, 2006, p. 3.
28. McNeil, 1992, p. 293.
29. Stewart, 1987, p. 64.
30. Isozaki, 2006, p. 4.
31. Banham, 'The Japonization of World Architecture', in Suzuki *et al.*, 1985, p. 16.
32. Taut, 1937, p. 9.
33. Ino, 1932, p. 43.
34. Isozaki, 2006, p. 10.
35. Reynolds, 2001, p. 2.
36. Wendelken, 1996, p. 34.
37. Title of Conference and Exhibition at the Japanese Embassy in London, 1 October 2009.
38. Stewart, 1987, p. 36.
39. As Head of the ICE until 1882, Dyer implemented a six-year course divided into three parts: the first two years were spent studying general and scientific subjects; the second two years were spent specialising in a specific technical field; and the final two years were spent in practice (Stewart, 1987, p. 33).
40. Wendelken, 1996, p. 30.
41. Reynolds, 1987, pp. 37–48.
42. Finn, 1995, p. 247.
43. Stewart cites Tokuma Katayama (1853–1917) as the 'other great architect of the Meiji period' (Stewart, 1987, p. 55) alongside Tatsuno, but like many of his contemporaries Katayama was not selected for overseas training. Yamaguchi studied in Paris until 1879 and returned to Japan to work as an architect for the Ministry of Education, designing many new educational establishments. The Number Four High School in the Ishikawa Prefecture, which he designed in 1891 with Masamichi Kuru (the architect responsible

for the Hō-ō-dō Temple at the World's Columbian Exposition in Chicago that is said to have inspired Frank Lloyd Wright), is said to be the oldest surviving example of a western-style building designed by a western-trained Japanese architect.

44 The change in title derived from the linguistic complication of adequately translating the word *architecture*. *Zōka*, literally meaning 'house-building', was deemed too technical and not representative of the art of architecture, so the architect and future Professor of Architecture at Imperial University, Itō Chūta (1867–1954), proposed *kenchiku*, whose two characters meant erect and build. Itō also proposed to replace the 'overly scientific' term for institute, *Gakkai*, with *Kyōkai* (Reynolds, 2001, p. 20).
45 Also referred to as *teikan-heigō*.
46 Stewart, 1987, p. 107.
47 Shimoda was engaged in another high-profile dispute over Frank Lloyd Wright's design for the Imperial Hotel, which he claimed Wright copied from one of his earlier designs.
48 Reynolds, 1996, p. 44.
49 Kigo was a master carpenter and an important but overlooked figure in the Imperial University's Department of Architecture because of his method of teaching traditional timber construction (*kiwarihō*).
50 Takeuchi, 2004, p. 197.
51 Reynolds, 2001, p. 2.
52 In 1932, Yamada's work (Electrical Laboratory, 1930) was to be the only Japanese representation in the International Style exhibition at New York's Museum of Modern Art.
53 They disbanded in 1928.
54 Stewart, 1987, p. 96.
55 E.g. Kamahara's Kosuge Prison (1929–30) and Horiguchi's Oshima weather station (1938).
56 Stewart, 1987, p. 99.
57 Stewart, 1987, p. 99.
58 Stewart, 1987, p. 115.
59 They had already invited Walter Gropius to be a member.
60 Maekawa's journey was assisted by his uncles in Dalian and Shenyang, one of whom worked for the South Manchuria Railway. While in his Paris atelier Maekawa worked, unpaid, on Moscow's Centrosoyuz and upon his return to Japan worked for five years in Raymond's office (Reynolds, 2001, p. 55).
61 Stewart, 1987, p. 113.
62 Reynolds, 2001, p. 97.
63 Reynolds, 2001, p. 77.
64 In the 1930 census, the British population had risen to 8,449 and the Japanese to 18,796 (Feetham, 1931, Table 2, Appendices (unpaginated).
65 These included Shanghai Cotton-Spinning Mills (1897) and the Chu Zung Cotton Mills (1907).
66 Kishida was a lecturer in the Architectural Department of Kyoto's Imperial University before moving to Tokyo Imperial University to become Assistant Professor in 1925 (Reynolds, 2001, p. 37).
67 Tong Wen College was a Japanese state-sponsored institute for educating Japanese students in Chinese language and culture. The building is now occupied by the Shanghai Institutes for Biological Sciences.
68 Buck (2000, p. 89) cites the example of the *Great Encyclopaedia of China* containing no reference to Changchun, Xijing or Manchukuo in the section on *Architecture, Parks and City Planning*.
69 Adding to this complicated mix is also the Russian factor in the context of Manchuria's northern cities and in particular Harbin.
70 For a more detailed account of architectural development in Manchuria, see *Ultra-Modernism – Architecture and Modernity in Manchuria* (Denison and Ren, 2016); Chapter 7 of *Modernism in China* (Denison and Ren, 2008) and William Sewell, 'Japanese Imperialism and Civic Construction in Manchuria: Changchun 1905–45' (PhD thesis), University of British Columbia, 2000. Buck's chapter 'Railway City and National Capital:

252 Architecture and modernity

Two Faces of the Modern in Changchun' in Esherick (2000) joins Guo's paper, *Changchun: Unfinished Capital Planning of Manzhouguo, 1932–42*) in being a focused study of Changchun, the capital of Japanese-occupied Manchuria (Guo, 2004; this article also appears as a chapter in his book published in 2005). Buck admits that his work is based on the work of the Japanese architectural historian, Koshizawa Akira. (Works include: 'City Planning in Colonial Manchuria', 1978; 'L'urbanisme en Mandchourie', *Urbi*, Vol. 6. No. 1, March, pp. 78–81; 'The Planning of Manchukuo Capital City: An Inquiry into Tokyo's Present and Future', 1988; 'City Planning in Harbin, 1898–1945', 1989). Beyond architectural matters, the work of Young makes a major contribution to the history of the Japanese development of Manchuria (Young, 1998; and 'Imagined Empire: The Cultural Construction of Manchukuo', pp. 71–96, in Duus *et al.*, 1989).

71 Manchukuo was formally established on 1 March 1932.
72 Young, 1998, p. 13.
73 Fogel, 1988, pp. xii and 123.
74 Italy formally recognised Manchukuo in November 1937. The only other countries to recognise Manchukuo's legitimacy were Japan, Nationalist Spain (1 December 1937), Germany (20 February 1938) and El Salvador.
75 For a thorough account of this particular aspect of Manchukuo's encounter with modernity, see Young (1998).
76 Masami, 1942, p. 19.
77 Shinsaku, 1938, pp. 46–7.
78 'Communications in Manchoukuo', *Far Eastern Review*, September 1940, p. 339.
79 Ino, 1932, p. 43.
80 Masami, 1942, p. 17.
81 Masami, 1942, p. 17.
82 Shinsaku, 1938, p. 46.
83 Shinsaku, 1938, p. 46.
84 Shinsaku, 1938, pp. 42–3.
85 Masami, 1942, p. 19.
86 Gilchrist, 1939, p. 1442.
87 Shinsaku, 1938, p. 45.
88 Shinsaku, 1938, pp. 43–5.
89 See Masami, 1942, pp. 15–24 and Hideo, 1942, pp. 35–44.
90 Shinsaku, 1938, p. 45.
91 Young quotes that 'before 1930 the Japanese population rose at an average of 9,350 per year, by the 1930s it was 83,132 per year', 1998, p. 257.
92 The total population was then 36,949,972. Up until Japan's surrender in 1945, a total of 321,882 Japanese emigrants had arrived in Manchuria.
93 A total of 400,000 of these households were to engage in agriculture.
94 Murotsu, 1939, p. 898.
95 The composition of Japanese immigrants remained consistent throughout the 1930s with the four main enterprises comprising commerce (25 per cent), the colonial administration (22 per cent), manufacturing (21 per cent), and shipping and railways (18 per cent).
96 These figures were for 1926, but they reflect the general trend since Manchuria became a field of operations for the Oriental Development Company in 1917. See Herbert Bratter, 'Japan's Colonizing Agency', *Far Eastern Review*, May 1930, p. 213. Similar comparisons can be seen in the overall investment in industry, manufacturing and agriculture in Manchukuo in the 1930s. From 1935 to 1937, total investment in industry and manufacturing rose from 707 million to 2.2 billion yen and from 363 million to 653 million yen respectively. Agriculture, in contrast, rose from 120 million to 300 million yen over the same period.
97 Household electrical supply was 97 per cent of Anshan, 95 per cent in Dalian, 67 per cent in Hsinking, 70 per cent in Fushun, 42 per cent in Harbin and 40 per cent in Shenyang. 'Electricity in Manchuria', *Far Eastern Review*, July 1937, p. 275.
98 Murotsu, p. 898.
99 Shenyang had 16 Japanese cinemas and 16 Manchu. Hsinking had 6 and 5 respectively, and Harbin 3 and 8 (and 6 foreign). In total, Manchukuo had 62 and 64 and 8 respectively.

Japan: China's mirror to modernism   253

100 Murotsu, 1939, p. 898.
101 'Railways in Manchuria', *Manchuria*, 1 July 1936, p. 52.
102 *Nobiyuku Kokuto* was filmed in two reels and subtitled in Japanese, Manchukukuo, German and Italian.
103 The Qiqihar branch was opened on 15 August 1936.
104 Young, 1998, p. 263.
105 From 1906 to 1932 the number of telegraph and telephone offices in Manchukou rose from 44 to 214 and from 21 to 254 respectively, and the number of long-distance calls rose from 17,000 to 1.25m. From 1906 to 1937 the number of telephone subscribers in Manchukou increased from 785 to 69,246, 42,446 of which were Japanese. This paled in comparison to Japan, where for every hundred people, telegraph use was 450 compared with 32 in Manchukuo and the number of telephone subscribers was 9.8 compared with 0.15 in Manchuria. 'Manchuria's Electrical Communications', *Far Eastern Review*, September 1938, p. 339.
106 *Manchuria*, 25 May 1938.
107 The cost was boasted as being cheaper than the $200k three-car express trains operated by the Union Pacific in the USA.
108 *Far Eastern Review*, Vol. 34, February 1938, p. 72.
109 The track was changed in the early morning of 31 August 1935 by groups of 15 workers each given short stretches.
110 Launched on 1 June 1937, this new service took 9 hours and 48 minutes, leaving Tokyo at 7.27am and arriving in Changchun (Hsinking) at 5.15pm. The aeroplanes used on this 233km service were Nakajima A.T. models. 'Air Services', *Manchuria*, 15 June 1937, p. 355.
111 'The Development of Manchuria,' *Far Eastern Review*, October 1927, p. 430.
112 'Survey of Kwantung Government', *Manchuria*, 1 October 1936, p. 224.
113 'The Kwantung Government, its Functions & Works', *Manchuria Daily News*, 1934, p. 138.
114 'Communications in Manchoukuo', *Far Eastern Review*, September 1940, p. 339.
115 In May 1940, the Manchoukuo Public Works and Building Association was established and geared towards military requirements such as national defence.
116 By 1940, 26 towns had a modern water supply and 30 others were under construction. 'Communications in Manchoukuo', *Far Eastern Review*, September 1940, p. 339.
117 Geo White, 'Construction Work in Mukden', *Far Eastern Review*, June 1938, p. 238.
118 Geo White, 'Rapid Development In City Of Mukden', *Manchuria*, 1 January 1937, p. 15.
119 In early 1935, the government launched a plan for city construction in six cities in Mukden Province: Taoan, Shanhaiguan, Jinzhou, Penchihu, Andong and Yingkou.
120 It also constructed dormitories and 1,430 houses along the railways, including 140 family houses in Shenyang.
121 Geo White, 'The Flourishing City Of Mukden', *Manchuria*, 15 December 1936, p. 391. Shenyang was electrified in 1910, among the first cities in China to have a municipal supply. In 1929 a new plant was erected by Andersen, Meyer & Co. and was one of the most modern in China.
122 These were arranged in four separate classes: first (50–60m), second (30–40m), third (22–27m) and auxiliary streets (4–8m). Geo White, 'The Flourishing City of Mukden', *Manchuria*, 15 December 1936, p. 390.
123 Geo White, 'The Flourishing City Of Mukden', *Manchuria*, 15 December 1936, p. 391.
124 Geo White, 'The Flourishing City Of Mukden', *Manchuria*, 15 December 1936, p. 391.
125 'Mutankiang Expands Rapidly', *Manchuria*, 1 August 1936, p. 104.
126 'Mutankiang Expands Rapidly', *Manchuria*, 1 August 1936, p. 104.
127 'Tumen-Chiamussu Railway Completed', *Manchuria*, 15 February 1937, p. 108.
128 'Tumen-Chiamussu Railway Completed', *Manchuria*, 15 February 1937, p. 109.
129 'Tumen-Chiamussu Railway Completed', *Manchuria*, 15 February 1937, p. 109.
130 Japanese troops occupied Qiqihar on 19 November 1931 when the resident Japanese population was just 123 and the town had no water supply.
131 The Japanese population of Qiqihar in 1932 was: 1,225 Japanese (522 households); 1933: 2,669 (1,176 households); 1934: 4,406 (1,749 households); and 1935: 6,623 (2,236 households).

254 *Architecture and modernity*

132 'Metropolis of Northwest Manchuria', *Manchuria*, 1 September 1936, pp. 171–6.
133 Kuklin, 1936, p. 322.
134 Kuklin, 1936, p. 322.
135 Scherer, 1933, p. 78.
136 North Manchuria and Chinese Eastern Railway, 1924, p. 270.
137 A census taken in Harbin in February 1913 revealed that the city's 68,459 residents comprised 53 nationalities and spoke 45 different languages, the most dominant being Russian, Chinese, Polish and Yiddish. Groups of nationals with over one hundred residents were: Russians (34,313), Chinese (23,537), Jews (5,032), Poles (2,556), Japanese (696), Germans (564), Tatars (234), Latvians (218), Georgians (183), Estonians (172), Lithuanians (142), and Armenians (124). In Bakich, 2000, p. 53.
138 See Bakich, 2000, p. 58.
139 Four stripes in the right-hand corner of the Manchukuo flag symbolised the different ethnic groups: red (Japanese), blue (Han Chinese), white (Mongolian) and black (Korean). The yellow background represented the Manchu. Official Manchukuo publications of later years stated that 'the five coloured stripes [*sic*: five colours] of the Manchoukuo flag signify the cooperative unity of five dominant racial groups in Manchuria, namely, the Manchus, the Hans [Chinese], the Mongols, the Japanese, and the Chosenese [Koreans]'. Bakich, 2000, p. 64.
140 By the mid-1930s the Japanese established the Bureau for the Affairs of Russian Émigrés, which registered 44,086 Russians in Manchukuo, 25,942 in Harbin and 16,192 in the rest of Manchukuo. Bakich, 2000, p. 62.
141 Tahara, 1940, p. 403.
142 Harbin had 109 electrical lamps per 100 people. Manchukuo had 6.7 and Japan had 59.4. 'Electricity in Manchuria', *Far Eastern Review*, July 1937, p. 276.
143 Tahara, 1940, p. 352.
144 'Harbin Conditions of Today', *Manchuria*, 15 August 1936, p. 141.
145 Note 31 in Victor Zatsepine, 'Russia, Railways, and Urban Development in Manchuria 1896–1930', Victoir and Zatsepine (eds), 2013, p. 35.
146 Pristan, Hsinyang, Nankang, New Town, Machia, Tungfuchia, Hsinfuchia, Kuching, Hsingfang, Taping and Sungpu.
147 Tahara, 1940, p. 403.
148 St Sophia was funded by the merchant prince Chisteyakov. Tahara, 1940, p. 404.
149 The building was not completed and after the war it became a hospital, army headquarters and a consulate.
150 Tahara, 1940, p. 353.
151 Tahara, 1940, p. 353.
152 Tahara, 1940, p. 401.
153 Tahara, 1940, p. 402.
154 Upshinsky, 1936, p. 19.
155 Kinnosuke, 1925, p. 71.
156 Tahara, 1940, p. 403.
157 The 1936 census put the population at 466,472.
158 Upshinsky, 1936, p. 20.
159 Harbin had 411 wells, 93 of which were not fit for drinking, 150 were only good for drinking after boiling and 51 were drinkable after filtering. Upshinsky, 1936, p. 20.
160 Taylor, 1940, p. 376.
161 'Harbin Conditions of Today', *Manchuria*, 15 August 1936, p. 141.
162 Only Shanghai, Hankou and Tianjin were bigger, with the once formidable Canton in fifth place.
163 'The Kwantung Government', 1934, p. 139.
164 Scherer, 1933, p. 41.
165 'Manchuria's Electrical Communications', *Far Eastern Review*, September 1938, p. 342.
166 'Manchuria's Electrical Communications', *Far Eastern Review*, September 1938, p. 342.
167 Liu, 1939, p. 3.
168 Liu, 1939, p. 3.
169 By July 1938 the city's population was 515,743.

170 'The Port of Dairen', *Far Eastern Review*, May 1940, p. 178.
171 'The Port of Dairen', *Far Eastern Review*, May 1940, p. 178.
172 'The Port of Dairen', *Far Eastern Review*, May 1940, p. 179.
173 In 1937, 224 fires caused over 1m. yen of damage in city.
174 'Fire Fighting in Dairen', *Manchuria*, 1 August 1938, p. 523.
175 'Developments in Dairen', *Manchuria*, June 1937, p. 371.
176 The cornerstone was laid on 22 August 1935.
177 'New Railway Station for Port of Dairen is Being Completed', *Far Eastern Review*, July 1936, p. 317.
178 Nevertheless, it was still a relative bargain compared with what an equivalent building in Tokyo would have cost owing to lower local wages, the absence of the need for earthquake-proofing and the extensive use of local materials. 'New Railway Station for Port of Dairen is being Completed', *Far Eastern Review*, July 1936, p. 317.
179 'New Railway Station for Port of Dairen is Being Completed', *Far Eastern Review*, July 1936, p. 317.
180 'Engineering Feats in Kwantung', *Far Eastern Review*, February 1927, p. 75.
181 Penlington, 1933, p. 261.
182 Penlington, 1933, p. 261.
183 Penlington, 1933, p. 261.
184 Schmidt, 1938, p. 583.
185 In 1931, the Japanese population of Dalian was 102,768. By 1941, it had nearly doubled to 192,059.
186 'The Birth of a New World Capital', *Far Eastern Review*, July 1936, p. 269.
187 'Manchoukuo News', *Manchuria*, 1 August 1938, p. 539.
188 *Contemporary Manchuria*, Vol. 2, No. 3, May 1938, p. 124.
189 Gilchrist, 1939, p. 1442.
190 'Japanese Architecture in Manchukuo', *Architectural Forum*, October 1937, p. 96. For more information on the work of Brossard Mopin, read David Tucker, 'France, Brossard Mopin, and Manchukuo', Victoir and Zatsepine (eds), 2013.
191 'Manchoukuo Built for all Time, Gen. Kincaid Declares', *Manchuria*, 1 December 1938, p. 796.
192 'Souvenir Enthronement Supplement', 1934, pp. 50 and 59.
193 Kwata, 1939–40, p. 7.
194 'Rapid Expansion of Hsinking', *Manchuria*, 1 September 1936, p. 165.
195 This included 6.5sq km for government offices, 21sq km for highways, 3.5sq km for public utilities, 7sq km for parks, 9sq km for military purposes and 53sq km for private purposes (including 27sq km residential, 8sq km commercial, 6sq km industrial, 10sq km undesignated and 2sq km for special purposes such as dairy farming).
196 In the first fiscal year, an area of 20sq km was prioritised for the urgent development of private residences (6.5sq km), government offices (2sq km), commercial areas (2sq km), highways (4.5sq km), public utilities, schools and museums (1.5sq km), industrial (1sq km), parks and recreation (2sq km) and agriculture (0.5sq km).
197 'The Birth of a New World Capital', *Far Eastern Review*, July 1936, p. 296.
198 Parks and open spaces, like the residential districts, were arranged into categories according to scale. Large and medium-sized parks contained recreational facilities such as golf courses, sports fields and race tracks, and were connected by main streets. Small parks were designed for residential areas with primary schools.
199 'Hsinking, Capital of Manchoukuo', *Far Eastern Review*, April 1940, p. 140.
200 'Hsinking, Capital of Manchoukuo', *Far Eastern Review*, April 1940, p. 140.
201 'Souvenir Enthronement Supplement,' 1934, p. 59.
202 Kwata (ed.), 1939–40, p. 15.
203 Construction of the Manchuria Motion Picture Producing and Distributing Corporation studios began in 1937 and they were completed in 1939.
204 Murotsu, 1939, p. 898.
205 The Central Bank of Manchu was established on 15 June 1932 and had 150 branches in Manchukuo and one in Tokyo.

206 The guest rooms and president's and vice-president's offices had mantelpieces of Italian marble and finished in hardwood. Guestroom walls were lined with Japanese marble and satin damask, and the president's and vice-president's offices were lined in teak veneer.
207 'Manchoukuo's New Bank', *Far Eastern Review*, September 1938, p. 344.
208 'Manchoukuo's New Bank', *Far Eastern Review*, September 1938, p. 344.
209 Douyau, 1938, pp. 124–5.
210 'Construction of Hsinking Palace Starts Sept. 10', *Manchuria*, 15 September 1938, p. 637.
211 'Souvenir Enthronement Supplement', 1934, p. 59.
212 Masami, 1942, p. 19.
213 'Hsinking, Capital of Manchoukuo', *Far Eastern Review*, April 1940, p. 140.
214 Reynolds, 2001, p. 97.
215 'The Birth of a New World Capital', *Far Eastern Review*, July 1936, p. 296.
216 'The Birth of a New World Capital', *Far Eastern Review*, July 1936, p. 296.
217 Kensuke, 1942. p. 8.
218 Kensuke, 1942, p. 8.
219 Masami, 1942, p. 17.
220 'Hsinking, Capital of Manchoukuo', *Far Eastern Review*, April 1940, p. 139.
221 'Hsinking, Capital of Manchoukuo', *Far Eastern Review*, April 1940, p. 139.
222 'Hsinking, Capital of Manchoukuo', *Far Eastern Review*, April 1940, p. 139.
223 Gilchrist, 1939, p. 1442.
224 Masami, 1942, p. 19.
225 Higashi, 1939, p. 1347.
226 The team's Asian tour included Japan, Korea, Manchuria and the Philippines. 'Hsinking, Capital of Manchoukuo', *Far Eastern Review*, April 1940, p. 139.
227 'Mutankiang Expands Rapidly', *Manchuria*, 1 August 1936, p. 104.
228 Dan, 1936, p. 410.
229 Gilchrist, 1939, p. 1442.
230 'Manchoukuo Built for all Time, Gen. Kincaid Declares', *Manchuria*, 1 December 1938, p. 796.
231 Roman Fajans was a Polish journalist working for two Warsaw dailies, Kurjer Warszawskl and Polska Zbrojn, and spent seven months touring Asia. He visited the Polish community in Harbin before travelling to Hsinking. 'Manchoukuo News', *Manchuria*, 1 August 1938, p. 539.
232 Schmidt, 1938, p. 571.
233 Higashi, 1939, p. 1347.
234 *Contemporary Manchuria*, Vol. 2, No. 3, May 1938, p. 124.
235 Gilchrist, 1939, p. 1442.
236 Dan, 1936, p. 408.
237 Reynolds, 2001, p. 97.
238 Itō Takeo, SMR researcher, cited in Fogel, 1988, p. 203.
239 Matsuoka, 1937, p. 701.
240 'Revitalised East Asia', *Manchuria*, 15 January 1939, pp. 934–5.
241 'New Building Law Announced', *Manchuria*, 1 June 1940, p. 262.
242 Letter from Wilma Fairbank to Chen Zhi, 27 August 1980, Fairbank family archive.
243 Letter from Wilma Fairbank to Chen Zhi, 15 October 1979, Fairbank family archive.
244 *Contemporary Manchuria*, Vol. 2, No. 3, May 1938, p. 124.
245 Powell, 1945, p. 309. In Kinney's book (1930, p. 18), the extent of his partisanship is revealed in his comment: 'Some foreign writers have a fondness of depicting Manchuria as "The Balkans of Asia" and as the field of another world war, but it would be difficult to find any intelligent resident in Manchuria who shares this fear'.
246 Kinney, 1929, p. 44; 1930, p. 48.
247 Collier, 1936, p. 248.

9 Shanghai
Multiple modernities' exemplar

Throughout this study China's negotiation of modernity has highlighted the problems of viewing western notions of cultural engagement in binary terms: west/east, developed/developing and modern/traditional. China's unique political, historical and cultural circumstances in recent centuries contribute to a far more nuanced and distinctively composite understanding, manifested in a wide range of cultural media wherein 'the values of modernity are separated from the motivation toward modernism'.[1] However, there was no place in China (and few places in the world) where a pluralistic and advanced modernity was so highly developed than Shanghai. China's largest city (and by 1929 the fifth largest in the world) offers an unrivalled viewpoint from which to draw together the themes of this study and a position from which to attempt to begin to draw conclusions about China's encounter with architectural modernity more broadly.[2]

Modernism frequently claimed to transcend nationality, but few places genuinely achieved an environment where this was possible. Those metropolitan centres that claimed international status were seldom truly places of unfettered internationalism. Shanghai, in contrast, was a place in which modernity was negotiated and refracted variously and was quite distinct from many western cities and other cities outside the west, whose exotic or traditional attributes tended to prevent them from being seen as 'modern'. Shanghai's modernity was uniquely multilayered: at a metropolitan level, Shanghai possessed its own distinct interpretation of modernity in the form of *Haipai* and spawned the unique modern axiom *modeng*; at a national level, Shanghai represented a version of modernity that was new and expediently removed from ancient precedents; and at an international level, Shanghai was a hub of migration globally at a unique point in history, where new ideas, new technologies and new opportunities penetrated China and were interconnected through a web of interrelations that, in terms of their impact and profundity, had never occurred before.

Shanghai – at least in a 'modern' sense – was a young city with a unique exposure to the world that generated a version of modernism that was not tied to any particular national identity or cultural agenda, but which also did not arise from an established state of modernity. Although Shanghai was a city ahead of its time in being both international and ruled by global capital, it was not an epicentre of artistic modernism. It was not Paris, Berlin or New York. Laurence argues that this situation, where expressions of modernism (here the preserve of a tiny minority and privileged class) exist in a wider context that is fundamentally 'unmodern', provided the conditions for the 'existence of multiple aesthetic, cultural, political, and economic discourses in a nation and against a monolithic notion of modernity or movement of modernism'.[3]

Throughout the 1920s and the 1930s Shanghai was possibly the best example in the world of a city where multiple modernities co-existed within a wider context that was anything but modern.

Shanghai, 'unmatched as far east as America and as far west as Europe',[4] was in China and a product of China's condition, but, just as it was not a colonial city, it could not be said to be wholly Chinese either. The peculiarity that Shanghai presents is often sidestepped by the suggestion it was not Chinese, a dismissal that frames it as a historical anomaly. 'Shanghai, despite all its influence', writes Esherick, 'was still not China'.[5] However, although its position literally and figuratively at the crossroads of global trade and politics might not make it entirely of China, Shanghai was unquestionably a Chinese city. The problem, especially for westerners, is the desire to circumscribe what constitutes Chinese and what constitutes modernity – if Shanghai's modernity cannot be denied, then according to conventional modernist historiography it must be stripped of its nationality, since the two cannot exist concurrently. This study proposes that they can, they did, and, if more proof was needed, they still do. In the twenty-first century, few cities on earth strive for modernity like Shanghai (nothing like it exists in the west) and no one can dispute its national or cultural context.

Shanghai was an exemplar of the treaty port's ambiguous qualities, a 'concrete example of the problem of China',[6] outgrowing the regional context in which it was formed and becoming a proto free-city of genuine international import. Shanghai had no overarching government, no constitution and no universal legal system or judiciary. The absence of such institutions was not only constitutionally peculiar, it also had a significant impact on the city socially and developmentally: the impunity that the city's separate territories sanctioned fuelled rampant malcontent, criminally and politically; insufficient financial regulations encouraged economic laxity; and the absence of immigration controls that permitted free entry furnished the city with one of the most cosmopolitan populations in the world. For architecture, these conditions gave rise to very particular outcomes.

The world in a city: the transition of Shanghai's architecture and architects

Shanghai's status as a free port with no restriction on population movement and assorted political and economic administrations shaped the form and layout of the city's physical composition. Having accommodated successive waves of migrants since the 1840s, from exuberant tax exiles to humble vagabonds, Shanghai's openness combined with improving international travel and communications caused an upsurge of immigration in the early twentieth century. The First World War and the revolutions that followed accelerated this process, driving large numbers of Europeans and Russians into exile, many of whom ended up in China. Of all the potential sites of western arrival in China, Shanghai was the pre-eminent destination for the displaced and dispossessed, their presence boosting Shanghai's population by tens of thousands and contributing significantly to the city's genuinely international character.

Modernism's origins coincided with Shanghai's swift ascendance. The city became a processor and a barometer of modernism, a locus for contact and experimentation with modernity in all artistic milieus largely separated from the broader national context in which it was sited. By the 1920s Shanghai had become truly conscious of its own modernity and wilfully sought it in its various forms. In architectural terms, this process reached its climax in the few years from the late 1920s.

By the 1930s, Shanghai had more Chinese architects, professional practices, trade journals and professional societies than any other city in China and than the rest of China put together – excluding Manchuria, of course. Both the Chinese Society of Architects and the foreign Shanghai Society of Engineers and Architects were based in Shanghai. Among foreign architects and related professionals, who designed and built some of the largest buildings in Asia, Shanghai's autonomy and unique multiculturalism was its chief lure. Though comparatively young, Shanghai had an enduring commercial spirit that stemmed from its ancient core, the old circular-walled city. The old city of Shanghai, Nantao, was a microcosm of what the future city would become: an incomparable trading hub that eschewed imperial formalities, densely populated, and religiously, ethnically and culturally diverse. With over 30 guilds[7] representing different ethnic communities and over 100 representing different trades, from pig slaughtering to hat manufacturing, few cities in China matched Shanghai for the variety of such institutions. In the early twentieth century, 25 of China's 28 provinces[8] were represented in the city's Chinese population. Exceeding 3 million, the Chinese far outnumbered the foreign population of 50,000, which came from over 50 different countries, from Lithuania to Peru and Egypt to Tonkin.[9]

Shanghai's demographics do not make it possible to see it in conventional colonial terms, nor did it correspond to any western city. In the census of 1930, representing over 38 per cent of Shanghai's foreign population, the Japanese (18,796) were the largest single foreign community, followed by the British 17 per cent (8,449) and then the Russians 15 per cent (7,366).[10] Collectively, remaining Asian countries[11] represented 7 per cent of the foreign population. American (3,149), Portuguese (1,599), German (1,430) and French (1,406) were the only other western groups with populations exceeding 1,000.

In the 1939 essay, 'The China Sea', the modern Japanese writer, Yokomitsu Riichi, succinctly describes Shanghai's multinational character and its relation to the city's unique sense of modernity:

> The problem of the International Settlement is one of the most perplexing in the world. At the same time this location also represents the problem of the future. To some extent it is a very simple thing, but there is no other place on earth that so manifests the quality that constitutes the modern. What is more, there exists nowhere in the world except the Settlement a site where all nations have created a common city. To think about this place is to think about the world in microcosm.[12]

If Shanghai was the most 'modern' city in the world, it was on account of properties that were entirely unique to it. It was modern on its own terms, not those received from foreign individuals and institutions that had made it their home. Architecturally, a similarly unique situation prevailed where, despite the few iconic buildings and numerous foreign-styled residences, the predominant appearance was Chinese. The number of building permits issued by the Municipal Council at the start of the 1920s was 3,542. By 1925 it had risen to 8,966 and both 1930 and 1931 were above 8,000. The total number of foreign residences built throughout this period was just 1.5–2 per cent of the total number of Chinese houses,[13] resulting in an extremely high-density,[14] low-rise city blanketed in *lilong* terraced courtyard housing.

Figure 9.1
Paul Veysseyre (1896–1963), graduate of the École Nationale des Beaux-Arts in Paris.

Figure 9.2
Josef Alois Hammerschmidt (1891–?), graduate of Vienna's Polytechnic University, then Adolf Loos's (1870–1933) Free School of Architecture.

As Britain's authority and representation declined, European architects from other nationalities gained a foothold and undeniably made their mark on the built environment. The early twentieth century saw the arrival of some of the most prolific foreign architects to ever live in Shanghai: the Hungarian–Slovak, László Hudec (1893–1958);[15] the French pair, Paul Veysseyre (1896–1963) (see Figure 9.1)[16] and Alexander Léonard (1890–1946); the Austrian, Josef Alois Hammerschmidt (1891–?) (see Figure 9.2);[17] the Swiss, René Minutti (1887–?) (see Figure 9.3);[18] and the Austrian, Charles Gonda (1886–?). The Japanese, as has already been discussed, were also represented in the city, concentrated in the northern district of Hongkou.

Western architects went to China for reasons either of professional opportunism, political exile or, in some cases, disillusionment with the west after the First World War. Hudec had been a soldier in the Hungarian Army and, captured by the Russians, was a prisoner-of-war in Siberia, from where he, like the thousands of White Russians, eventually escaped to China. The Austrian architect Hammerschmidt was also a Russian prisoner-of-war in Siberia. Captured in the Carpathian Mountains in late 1914, he was incarcerated for three years before being released and travelled to China where, in 1921, he settled in Tianjin. Veysseyre had been a soldier in the French Army and was seriously wounded twice. After the war he travelled to Poland, then on to Shanghai in 1921 where he met his professional partner Léonard in Shanghai's French Volunteer Corps' Armoured Car Company. Bright Fraser (1894–?),[19] one of the few British architects later based in Shanghai who espoused modernism, had joined the Artists' Rifles in 1915 and was taken prisoner-of-war in France in 1917 (see Figure 9.4). After the Armistice, he studied in Italy before making his way to Shanghai in 1923.

Unlike Shanghai's previous generation of foreign architects, the generation that arrived after the First World War was more progressive. Much like the intermediary generation of Chinese scholars nurtured on Confucianism but willing to explore the opportunity presented by the modern world in which they were fully immersed, or like the second generation of Japanese architects, this generation of foreign architects had received a traditional training but they were conscious of the conditions and potential of modernity, particularly in the rapidly evolving setting of Shanghai. Hudec had attended the Beaux-Arts-oriented Royal Technical University of Budapest in 1914. Veysseyre, after studying architecture under Maître G. Chedanne from 1912, spent two years at the École Nationale des Beaux-Arts in Paris, where his professional partners Léonard and Arthur Kruze also studied from 1908 and 1918 respectively.[20] Fraser was articled in Liverpool and later became a student at London's first atelier of architecture. Minutti attended the Polytechnic School of Zurich. Hammerschmidt received among the most progressive educations by attending Vienna's Polytechnic University, then Adolf Loos's (1870–1933) Free School of Architecture.

The early work by Shanghai's progressive generation of architects was mostly unremarkable. Practically all were affiliated to established practices and undertook jobs that, set against their later work, appeared staid. Hudec worked for the American

Figure 9.3
René Minutti (1887–?), graduate of the Polytechnic School of Zurich.

Figure 9.4
Bright Fraser (1894–?), graduate of Liverpool University.

architect R.A. Curry, with whom he designed the French-owned International Savings Society building on Avenue Joffre (1919), the American colonial-style American Club on Fuzhou Road (1924), and the McGregor Hall of the McTyeire School on Edinburgh Road, before establishing his own firm in 1925. Hammerschmidt, who had worked for Vienna's Public Works Department during the war, undertook private work in Tianjin from 1924, designing industrial facilities, commercial properties and residences,[21] but he travelled to Shanghai in 1931 to work for the Shanghai Municipal Council's Public Works Department from where he moved to the large property developer, Asia Realty Company. In 1933, he established his own firm, where he pursued his particular interest 'in architecture of the present modern continental type', having already built in Shanghai 'a large number of buildings of various categories'.[22] Fraser worked for Atkinson & Dallas before joining Shanghai Land Investment Company in 1926, where he became Chief Architect. Léonard, having arrived in Shanghai to assume the post of Professor at the Institut Franco-Chinoise in 1921, formed a firm with Veysseyre in 1922, and was joined in 1934 by Arthur Kruze[23] who arrived in China from his post as Professor of Architecture and Director of the Ecole Superieure des Beaux-Arts de l'Indochine in Vietnam.[24] Also arriving in Shanghai

Figure 9.5 Broadway Mansions (1934), Shanghai, designed by Bright Fraser and Palmer & Turner.

Shanghai: multiple modernities' exemplar 263

Figure 9.7
Chinese-style interior of the Shanghai home of George Wilson, Head of Palmer & Turner's Shanghai office.

Figure 9.6
George Leopold Wilson (1880–1967), Head of Palmer & Turner's Shanghai office.

from Asia was Minutti, who had worked as a civil engineer in Europe, South America and Asia before settling in Shanghai in 1920 and establishing a firm of civil engineers and general contractors, Ledreux, Minutti & Co. He remained with the jointly owned firm, which specialised in structural engineering and industrial installations, including the Canidrome dog track and the French Waterworks, until 1930, when he established his own engineering and architectural firm, Minutti & Co.

Bridging this younger generation of architects and Shanghai's early twentieth-century architects was the historically and architecturally important figure, George Leopold Wilson (1880–1967)[25] of Palmer & Turner (see Figure 9.6). Wilson joined the large Hong Kong-based firm in 1908 and moved to Shanghai in 1914 to open their regional office. Although the firm did not adhere to any one architectural doctrine (they willingly swayed with the client's demands, producing anything from mock-Tudor to austere modernism), Wilson was an intelligent and thoughtful architect who contributed to the design of many of Shanghai's most important buildings and wrote extensively about architecture (see Figure 9.7).

Palmer & Turner's size and commercial orientation might have made them disinclined to champion any one style of architecture, but their prominence invariably ensured their participation in the design and construction of many of Shanghai's landmark buildings and they consistently pushed the boundaries of what was technically possible when building on Shanghai's infamously boggy terrain.[26] Most of Palmer & Turner's work was undertaken exclusively by the firm, but there were occasional and often notable collaborations with independent or in-house architects, such as

Fraser, in the design of the 22-storey Broadway Mansions (1935) (see Figure 9.5); the Canadian architect, Albert Edmund Algar, on Grosvenor House (1934) (see Plate 27); and the Chinese architect and AA graduate, Luke Him Sau, on the Bank of China Headquarters (1939) (see Plate 28). All were comparatively large structures and all helped to frame Shanghai's high-rise modernist image, despite the sea of low-rise dwellings that covered the city. Grosvenor House and Broadway Mansions shared similarly concave plans[27] and both claimed to be the city's largest apartment building. The latter was 'a sturdy link in the conception of modernity in the east'[28] containing 'the most alluring conveniences and comforts which modern ingenuity has thus far devised'.[29] The 16-storey Bank of China building, originally intended to be 34-storeys, was the 'largest and tallest bank building in the Far East'.[30] The Bank of China headquarters was more than merely the pre-eminent banking office in Asia, it was evidence of something much more profound in the shifting geopolitical conditions that had hitherto fashioned this city. It was a deliberate and conspicuous monument to the aspirations of Chinese banking and the financial potential of the Chinese customer. Luke's collaborative design was antithetical to its foreign neighbours and counterparts housed in their imperious neoclassical temples. The writer Harold Acton, who lived in Beijing from 1932 to 1937, railed at this architectural landscape forged from foreign exploitation of China, describing Shanghai's Bund as:

> a long line of pompous toadstools sprung up from the mud, raised by anonymous banks, trusts and commercial firms. They have little connexion with the people of China.... No court or government had designed them and given them life. There they stand trying to give materialism importance, but they fail.[31]

Luke's Bank of China was the sole exception.

The unprecedented transformations taking place in Shanghai's built environment from the 1920s and the increasing diversity of Shanghai's architectural styles, types and practitioners, compared to the city's earlier architectural landscape, was a symptom of the shifting socioeconomic and geopolitical order. It reflected too the way the increasing movement of people, resources and ideas into and out of the city facilitated technical and aesthetic innovations.

Architecture and technology

In terms of technological innovation, Shanghai was a leader in China. Shanghai had the first factory to implement mass production (Jiangnan Arsenal, 1864), which was said at the time to represent 'the highest development of Chinese technical industry';[32] it was the first to process gas (1866);[33] it was the first to have gas street lighting (1865); it was the first to operate a railway (1863); it was the first to install a telegraph (1866); it was the first municipality to generate electricity commercially and consequently the first to install electrical street lighting (1882); it was the first to provide a municipal power supply (1893); it was the first to have installed a modern waterworks (1893), and it was the first to host modern cotton manufacturing facilities, thus becoming a world centre for cotton manufacturing before the Second World War.[34]

Technology was not only critical to Shanghai's experience of modernity, as occurred in cities all over the world, but Shanghai was also where China first encountered

Shanghai: multiple modernities' exemplar 265

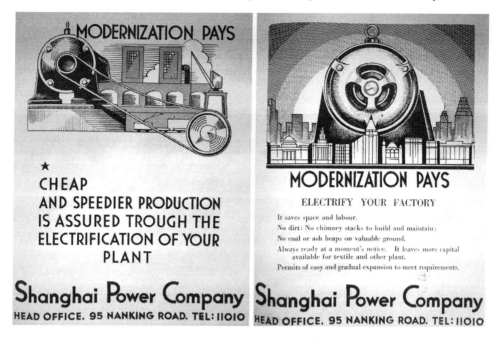

Figure 9.8 Designs from advertisements for the Shanghai Power Company utilising architectural and industrial imagery to emphasise the need to modernise.

mass technology, which in turn became an important thematic device exploited by a wide range of Chinese artists (see Plate 29). Shanghai was thus formative in creating and controlling people's urban experiences, imagined or otherwise. Traditionally, the Chinese public had treated western technology suspiciously: China's first telegraph in 1866 was deemed to upset the *feng shui* of the local residents after a man had died in the shadow of a telegraph pole and was prohibited as a result; China's first railway, built in 1877, was dismantled when a man was killed on the newly laid tracks outside Shanghai; and electricity was banned following its first demonstration in Shanghai's Public Gardens in 1882. But as with these and all the other technological innovations introduced to China through Shanghai, suspicion was short-lived and, once overcome, was embraced enthusiastically.[35] It is no coincidence that this same spirit persists today with Shanghai boasting of having more high-rises than any other city in China, the tallest building in Asia, the fastest passenger train in the world, and the largest electrical light display in the world.

As in the west, industrial and technological advances made possible the development of modern architecture, in so far as it was dependent on the novel use of new materials (typically, steel, glass and concrete) and the employment of mechanical inventions such as elevators, escalators and air-conditioning. The architectural landscape of Shanghai, which by the twentieth century was China's industrial powerhouse, went from being dominated by stout stone and brick offices, meagre commercial outlets, and the residences of wealthy merchants before the late nineteenth century to a site where 'modern buildings rear their great black smokestacks into the air [with] acres of buildings of reinforced concrete with walls and roofs of glass'.[36]

266 *Architecture and modernity*

'Against the skyline of Shanghai, unlike other cities of China which are noted for their pagodas and temples, [were] outlined hundreds of smoke-stacks and chimneys, the marks of modern industry'.[37] The dystopian scene, according to one Russian resident was 'an industrial city with sprawling factories rearing their ugly, plain walls over wide areas' (see Figure 9.9 and Plate 30).[38]

Industrialisation, as occurred in Manchuria, had a profound social impact, as subsistence farmers migrated to the cities to seek paid employment, and the concentration of men, women and children in factories 'led to the disruption of age-old family traditions [as] customs centuries in age went by the board'.[39] It was in this modernist landscape of social upheaval and mechanised dystopia that the seeds of modern architecture took root and out of which they flourished, turning Shanghai into a 'vast and heterogeneous city' (see Figure 9.10).[40]

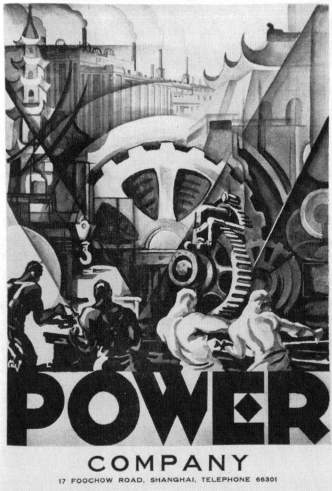

Figure 9.9 Advertisement for the Shanghai Power Company, combining the imagery of modern industry and Chinese architecture.

Figure 9.10 Montage titled 'The Future Shanghai Race Course' showing the march of modernity, praising the spirit of the urban poor whose dwellings were demolished to make way for Shanghai's high-rise buildings.

Just as China's modernist writers tended to identify themselves with western counterparts[41] and witnesses to Manchurian cities compared them with western *others*, Shanghai was frequently coupled with other global cities, such as London, Paris and New York. Such associations were made by foreign commentators as much as by their Chinese counterparts and were often self-fulfilling, whether in fashion, literature, art or architecture. Claims to being the 'Paris of the East' were largely in reference to the French Concession, greatly expanded in 1914 and brought to life by the massive influx of White Russian migrants a few years later. Associations with London were born out of the two cities being centres of trade and finance in their respective continental regions, the conceited neoclassical appearance of their institutions reflecting the imperiousness of their occupants. Architecturally, New York was the preferred and justifiable comparison, with Shanghai labelled the 'Manhattan of the Far East'.[42] In 1931, one journal exclaimed that 'Despite the Depression one finds in Shanghai gigantic new buildings going up',[43] creating a 'miniature Manhattan skyline'.[44] Architecturally, New York was a model for Shanghai and the two cities shared many parallels. Both were major international ports and genuinely global cities with largely immigrant populations. Both were essentially new cities, unburdened by architectural, historical or political precedent (especially in relation to the national capitals with whom they often had competitive and comparative relations). The commercial decorative style that characterised New York's pre-war architecture (later in the century coined 'art deco') also proliferated in Shanghai from the late 1920s. Although

268 *Architecture and modernity*

before 1927 it was correct to say that 'relatively speaking, with regard to other cities, there are no real skyscrapers in Shanghai, no fifty and sixty story (*sic*) buildings rearing to heaven',[45] in the years immediately afterwards, Shanghai joined New York in high-rise construction, though not on the same scale.

The first recorded 'high-rise' building in Shanghai, a ten-storey apartment block, was erected in 1924. Between 1926 and 1934, 59 apartment buildings were constructed, the yearly rate peaking at 13 in 1933. At the time, these were the biggest residential buildings in China and some were the largest in Asia. In 1928, *The China Architects' and Builders' Compendium* explained succinctly the situation surrounding these developments:

> A feature in building development during the last year has been in the number of modern apartment houses on the American plan that have been erected, and are still on the course of construction. Whereas formerly there was a tendency to build private residences on the outlying roads of Shanghai, insecurity has encouraged concentration within the settlement boundaries, where safety is more assured. Another point of interest to the architect and builder during recent years is the higher standard of comfort demanded in very (*sic*) direction both by foreigners and Chinese. Houses and self-contained flats fitted with the latest heating, sanitary and cooking arrangements are now the rule, and residences that a decade ago were considered modern are now being torn down to make way for buildings that contain every convenience obtainable in Britain or America.[46]

By the 1930s, the large merchant villa, that residential leviathan of yesteryear, had become impractical and financially burdensome. Shanghai was no longer the expansive suburbia it had been shortly after the settlement extensions of 1899 and 1914; extensive gardens were sold and subdivided, causing the city to become a dense, teeming metropolis, with extremely high land values and an increasingly transient population. Fewer foreign families settled in the city for life, and of those that did, fewer still needed or could afford the spacious residences that once packed the city's leafy western suburbs. Foreign residents were content to live in smaller purpose-built villas in planned residential developments beyond the settlement boundaries or in larger purpose-built apartments, along with the growing number of single men and women who were in Shanghai for the short term. For this generation of urbanites, the apartment was the perfect solution – fully furnished and replete with expressly modern conveniences, sometimes serviced, simply decorated and comfortable but not too capacious. In a relatively short space of time 'the foreign residents of Shanghai [had] become flat dwellers'.[47] The modern apartment finished with modern fittings became a pillar of Shanghai's modern metropolitan lifestyle – it contained modern furniture to create a modern setting; modern wardrobes to house modern fashions; modern bathrooms to facilitate modern sanitary habits; modern kitchens in which to prepare modern dishes; and modern gizmos to flaunt the arrival of modernity (see Figure 9.11). As always, such expressions of modernity in China could never be disassociated from wider events. By the late 1930s, China's perennial problem of civil instability, this time precipitated by Japan's increasing belligerence, increased the appeal of the high-rise apartment, which provided a vital means of accommodation for foreigners seeking the sanctuary of foreign settlements (see Figure 9.12).

The potency of Shanghai's tall buildings lay in their inherent modernist iconography, derived from and symbolic of the new technological age. However, they were

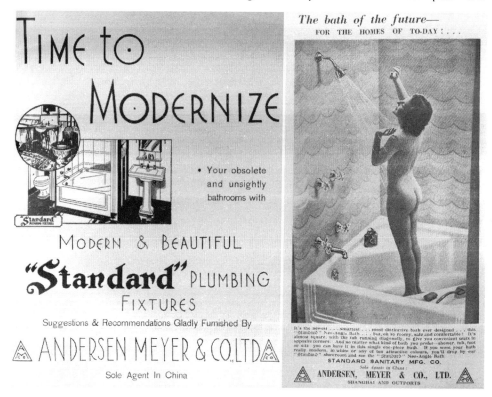

Figure 9.11 Advertisements for Andersen, Meyer & Co. drawing heavily on the theme of modernity in their designs for interior fixtures and fittings for Shanghai's residences.

relatively few in number, so they had less impact on the general fabric of the city than their low-rise residential counterpart, the *lilong*, wherein the true soul of Shanghai's urban environment could be found (see Figure 9.13). References to high-rises or 'huge monsters' as the writer Mao Dun describes them, appeared repeatedly in modern literature and art, and provided a figurative foundation on which the city constructed its modernist persona in part as an oppositional response to the ubiquity of the *lilong*, but it was the *lilong*, accommodating everything from cottage industries to political congresses, that housed the writers that lauded the high-rises. Located halfway up the stairs at the rear of the *lilong* was the box-room called the *ting zi jian*. Rented for a pittance, the *ting zi jian* was so popular among impoverished writers and artists that its name became a literary label.

The romanticism of *ting zi jian* writers attracted criticism from some Shanghai writers. Echoing Le Corbusier or Marinetti, Mao Dun appeals to his colleagues to 'sing the praise of the machine' instead of harking on about '*urban life*, [and] the romances of young men and women in coffee shops, the sadness and grievances of the unemployed intellectuals in ting zi jian, the endless love words on a park bench under the tree' in all of which 'there is no machine, the artery of the urban!'[48] The modernist writer Liu Na'ou painted a very different picture in *The Scenery*, where the convergence of modern architectural form and technological apparatus made

270 *Architecture and modernity*

Figure 9.12 Cartoon by the famous Shanghai artist, Sapajou, in 1937 following the Japanese invasion of China, depicting the plight of residents living outside the foreign settlements, which had a major impact on property inside the foreign settlements.

explicit reference to buildings as machines for living: 'Straight lines and angles form all the architecture and objects: wires, water pipes, gas pipes, radiators, rooms with a square roof – aren't people living in the middle of machines?'[49]

One of the essential components of the machinery of Shanghai's buildings – on which the city's high-rises depended and which became a potent literary symbol of modernity – was the elevator. By the 1930s, when Shanghai's oldest elevators in Astor House and the Palace Hotel were over three decades old,[50] Shanghai's 1,000 elevators were carrying over 300,000 people 4,000 miles per day. Hudec's 21-storey Joint Savings Society Building (1934), which housed 'the fastest and highest climbing elevators in the Far East', propelled guests from the ground to the seventeenth floor (66m) in 20 seconds.[51] The same experience and pace was evoked by Mu Shiying in *Shanghai Foxtrot*, where the elevator in the adjacent Race Club travelled at 'the speed of one every 15 seconds, throwing people to the roof garden like goods'.[52] The scene created by the figurative convergence of Shanghai's architects and writers appeared like a science fiction set in which modernist experiences were so varied and concentrated as to have created an entirely new world – forged by technology, satiated by consumption and overshadowed by war.

Shanghai's largest passenger elevators, accommodating 24 people,[53] could be found in the Sun Department Store (1932–33), 'undoubtedly the most modernised retail establishment of its kind in China' (see Plate 31).[54] Designed by the Chinese

Figure 9.13 Aerial photograph of Shanghai in the 1930s showing dense urban grain created almost entirely by *lilong* terraces, with comparatively few tall buildings casting their shadows over the generally low-rise landscape. Note the total absence of planning by the foreigners that administered the city.

architectural firm, Kwan, Chu & Yang, the Sun was also the first building in Shanghai to install an escalator (1934), on which 'thousands upon thousands crammed this ascending staircase, enjoying the unique ride for the first time in their lives'.[55] The dizzying scene belied a more profound experience that mirrored Kracauer's observations in the department stores of Berlin, a city whose experience throughout the twentieth century closely resembled Shanghai's. In the Sun, the escalator's role can be compared to those in Berlin, where Kracauer noted the functions of the 'moving staircase ... presumably include symbolizing the easy ascent to the higher social strata'.[56]

Shanghai's skyward trend from the late 1920s might have been a consequence of modernity and a setting in which it could be experienced and imagined, but the driving force of the city's architectural ascent was fuelled not only by technological advances, but also by financial conditions. Economically, a currency crisis caused by the decreasing value of silver caused investors to plough savings into land and property, resulting in 1,000 per cent increases in values and accelerating construction. Furthermore, the decision by foreign and Chinese banks to start issuing mortgages to Chinese customers precipitated a credit frenzy that coincided with the Great Depression, wherein 'investors generally [seemed] confident that real estate values [offered] the best possible security in these unsettled days'.[57]

Technologically, advances in materials and construction, particularly in the use of the steel frame and reinforced concrete, enabled the efficient, easier and swifter erection of taller structures than had ever been deemed possible on Shanghai's alluvial soil. Technology was also a key factor in precipitating a quiet revolution in the appearance of Shanghai's buildings. 'Simplicity in expression of modern technical achievements', not 'superfluous ornaments taken from a bygone building period', noted George Wilson, was what made Gonda's Shahmoon Building (1926–8) housing the Capitol Theatre an early 'example of ultra modern architecture'.[58] It was with Shahmoon that Gonda began honing his distinctive style characterised by strong vertical lines that appear on the Sun Sun Department Store (1926–7), the Cathay Theatre (1932) and the Transport Bank (1937–48) (see Plate 32).

The perpendicular transformation in Shanghai's architecture that has since become an essential characteristic of the cityscape was noted by Wilson in 1930: 'Instead of horizontal lines being the governing factor in design, vertical lines become the natural development.'[59] A few years earlier, a foreign resident of Beijing had noted that:

> the aesthetic wisdom of the Chinese is expressed in the horizontal line. They know how hideous, how self-debasing the vertical line can be ... one wonders if the Chinese will forget their love of beauty and allow geometric monstrosities to hurl themselves upward in the amber city.[60]

Beijing remained untouched by the high-rise, while modernism's perpendicularity prospered in Shanghai, in the reinforced concrete and plasterwork detailing of increasingly vertiginous modern buildings as well as on the printed page, where Mu Shiying wrote in *Shanghai Foxtrot* of the 'lovely man's face, straight lined, MODERN',[61] where both the terminology and the typeface were employed to emphasise the point. A similar technique was used by the writer Liu Na'ou in *The Scenery* where a modern Chinese woman exalted: 'You think I am thin? Thin, only a thin body can be straight lined. A straight line is the important quality of modern life!'[62]

Although it was celebrated by most, modernity's allure was also refuted and resisted in Shanghai, especially among the more established figures in the foreign community. Such sentiments were sometimes explicit, as in the repeated and often-published polemics of Arthur de Carle Sowerby, Editor of the *China Journal* who, in the article 'Modern Art Described as Rubbish' described ' "modernism," [as] anathema to any one with a genuine love of truth and beauty'.[63] Sometimes it was implicit, as in the case of an article in the *Far Eastern Review* about the restrictive impact on construction of Shanghai's malleable soil 'Has Shanghai Outgrown Itself?' which drew the conclusion that Shanghai would 'escape what has been called the greatest mistake of modern architecture, the skyscraper'.[64] Wilson was also among the sceptics, claiming in 1930 that 'Very few of what may be termed "modern designs" have made their appearance, and it is doubtful whether the extreme modernism of Courbesier (*sic*), for instance, will find much favour with Shanghai residents'.[65]

Shanghai's modernism might not have corresponded to that of Le Corbusier's, but many foreign and Chinese architects, responding to the city's conditions and qualities, produced some notable works with unquestionably modern characteristics. Léonard & Veysseyre[66] 'designed and supervised the construction of a large number of the finest modern buildings in Shanghai',[67] including Bearn (1930), Midget (1931), Willow Court, Magy (1936) (see Plate 33), Gascogne (1935) and Dauphine (1935) apartments, as well as Rémi (1930), Chapsal and Lagrene schools, Chung Wei Bank, the headquarters of the French Police (1935) and Musée Heude.

Minutti too designed some of the city's largest apartment and office buildings, including Picardie Apartments (1935), the new buildings at Aurora University (1936) and the tallest structure on the French Bund, the Messageries Maritimes building (1936–39).[68] The tallest building in Shanghai (even until the 1980s), which was also the 'the tallest building in the Far East',[69] was Hudec's Joint Savings Society (a Chinese-owned consortium) Building, containing the Park Hotel, 'one of the finest hotels in the world'.[70] Inspired by Raymond Hood's Radiator Building, which Hudec had witnessed on a trip to New York, the Joint Savings Society Building was rightly said to display 'the best of modern architecture'[71] and represents the apogee of Shanghai's modern architecture (see Plate 34). Contributing to this title was its physical and symbolic prominence, its technological distinction, its advanced construction, its multinational organisation and its representation as the zenith of Hudec's professional development, having evolved directly from his Expressionist phase characterised by the China Baptist Publishing Society (1930) (see Plate 35), the Christian Literature Society Building (1930) and the German Evangelical Church (1931).

Hudec was Shanghai's most prolific modern architect whose career evolved through a range of distinct stylistic stages. He spent his last years in China designing some of the most celebrated modern architecture in Asia, including the Grand Theatre (1933), Hubertus Court (1935–7), the Union Brewery (1936), Dr Wu's villa (1938) and Aurora University's Women's Institute (1939). He also drafted some of the city's most ambitious unrealised plans: the 12-storey Ambassador Apartments (1931), the Chao Tai Fire and Marine Insurance Company, and the massive Nisshin Navigation Company (NYK) offices on the Bund, which were among many fanciful projects by hopeful architects that were postponed following the economic crisis in 1932 and terminated after Japan's invasion of the Chinese areas of Shanghai in 1937.

Architecture of decadence

Shanghai's modernity could not escape being tarnished by the city's infamous licentiousness. Culturally, this became something of an addiction. Modernity, for Shanghai's cultural mediators, was equated to speed, style, sin and spending, 'a heaven built above hell!'[72] evidenced in the array of epithets: 'Paris of the East'; 'Queen of Eastern Settlements'; 'Manhattan of the Far East'; 'Whore of the Orient'; 'Sink of Iniquity'; 'Yellow Babylon of the Far East'; 'Paradise of Adventurers'; and 'City of Palaces' (see Plate 36). Architecture was inescapably implicated in infamy.

Decadence set Shanghai apart from China's other cities, where the 'lust for pleasure' became a 'hallmark of modernity' (see Plate 37).[73] However, *Haipai*, the term that encapsulated Shanghai's unique strain of modernity, conceals a debt to China's former cultural heart and reveals much about Shanghai's prodigious leisure industry, which became the envy of many of China's cultured and commercial classes alike. A letter from Jing Yuelin (Beijing resident and friend of Liang Sicheng and Lin Huiyin), to their mutual friends, John and Wilma Fairbank, typifies this transition by framing his yearning for Shanghai in the context of lamenting Beijing's decline:

> We are doomed. We are informed by L.K. Tao fresh from Nanking, that Peiping is dead. It is dead, even from the point of view of having a good time. Take for instance dancing. There are scores and scores of places where peoples dance in Shanghai ... that great commercial metropolis. And then take love-making. There are in Shanghai again hundreds and hundreds of young ladies either on the threshold of thirty and not far distant from forty, modern, sophisticated, married and divorced or widowed who are not particularly resentful towards either dashing advances or else cautious and slow approaches on the part of the emotionally unemployed young men. There is nothing in Peiping that compares with the life down south. You can easily see that it is the poor souls left in Peiping whose life should be vitalized by intellectual reorientations [and] social upheavals.[74]

Haipai originated in the 1920s with Shanghai's reinvention and adaptation of Beijing Opera[75] in what was one of the opening salvos in a cultural exchange that would see, in just a few years, Beijing's cultural capitulation to Shanghai, reinforced by succeeding literary migrations in which 'most of the modern writers who congregated in Shanghai in the early 1930s were newcomers escaping warlord-torn Beijing or sought refuge from Chiang Kai Shek's coup'.[76] One of these writers, Lu Xun, described the physical character of China's former capital when he returned in November 1932 to visit his family. He found that 'except for empty shops and general disrepair, not much had changed since his departure in 1926'.[77] His letters to Xu Guangping and other friends reveal how he 'was struck by the city's pervasive stillness, which stood in sharp contrast to the sound and fury of urban life in Shanghai'.[78]

Of the arts that benefited particularly from the migration of artists from Beijing was cinema, the second novel art form to enjoy a place in Feng Zikai's *Garden of Art*. Indebted to the ancient art of Beijing Opera, cinema was perfected in Shanghai, where it was swiftly assimilated and became a pillar of China's modern popular culture. The Chinese, like the Japanese in the context of Manchuria, knew the power of cinema and this novel typology was feverishly embraced by architects. Although Chinese cinema was born in Beijing, it made its home in Shanghai. The year in which Beijing hosted the first screening of a motion picture in China (1896) was the same year the first film was shown in Shanghai.[79] The first Chinese film, *Dingjunshan* (*Conquering Jun Mountain*), was made in Beijing in 1905 by Qingtai Ren (1850–1932),[80] and was a cinematic rendition of Beijing Opera screened in a Beijing tea-house,[81] but it came seven years after Thomas Edison's company's documentary, *Shanghai Police*.

Venues for early film screenings were invariably theatres and tea-houses, as well as public gardens and similar open spaces (or both). Not until 1907 did Beijing boast the first western-style cinema,[82] one year before the first purpose-built facility for screening films opened in Shanghai. The following year an American businessman, Benjamin Brasky, established China's first production studio, Asia Film, which produced China's first feature-length movie, *The Difficult Couple* (1912).[83] By the 1920s, with cinema's popularity in China assured, Shanghai became the 'cradle of China's film industry'.[84]

A glimpse into the proliferation of China's film industry can be gained from Mao Dun's *A Day in China*, which lists the number of different films screened across China on a day in 1936 (below in brackets). The tale reveals as much about the state of China's entertainment industry as it does about China's enthusiasm for cinema, as well as indicating Shanghai's dominance, Beijing's relative decline and the contributions of Japan to the genre in Manchuria: Shanghai (29), Guangzhou (17), Tianjing (12), Beijing (9), Changchun (8, including 2 Japanese), Nanjing (8), Hankou (5), Chengdu (4), Guiyang (3), Hangzhou (3), Zhenjiang (3), Qingdao (3), Xi'an (2), Kunming (1) and Changsha (1).[85]

The cinema, like the recreational facilities in Nanjing and Shanghai's Civic Centre, was a building type without precedent, offering unique opportunities for creative innovation. Shanghai had more cinemas than any other Chinese city, including the Lyric, Metropol, Ritz and Towa.[86] The popularity of this new art form invigorated the careers of many of Shanghai architects. Gonda (Cathay, 1932 and Capitol, 1928), 'who has given Shanghai so many theatres',[87] as well as Hudec (Grand, 1933), Fan (Majestic, 1941) and Zhao Shen (Nanking, 1928 and Metropol, 1934) all designed iconic modern cinemas in Shanghai from the late 1920s.

Cinema design invariably took its cue from theatre, together often serving a dual purpose – 'movie theatre'. Theatre underwent a quiet revolution in China paralleling the reinvigoration of Beijing Opera in Shanghai. Since traditional Chinese opera 'had undergone no major changes in the preceding two hundred years',[88] the construction in Shanghai of China's first modern theatre, the Xin Wutai (New Stage, 1908), constituted a major milestone. Fusing the traditional tea-house environment with modern semi-circular stage and technical facilities, the Xin Wutai with its 'astonishing set designs, fantastic scenes and lighting', according to the film historian Laikwan Pang, 'soon became the city's symbol of modernity, and tourists from all over China would rush to this theatre to experience what Shanghai, and modernity, meant'.[89]

The Xin Wutai's popularity caused it to outgrow its premises by 1913 and in 1915 the owner, Huang Chujiu, built a new theatre, the Xin Xin Wu Tai (the New New Stage). A radical departure from the singular entertainment venue, the Xin Xin Wu Tai was housed in a larger building constructed in reinforced concrete and glass that was China's first all-in-one entertainment complex,[90] housing a theatre, tea-house, a roof-top garden and an open-air cinema. In 1932, 'the largest Chinese theatre in Shanghai',[91] the 2,500-seater New Da Wu Tai (Grand Stage), was built. Designed by a Chinese engineer, Wang Jinshan, from the office of the British architect, Percy Tilley, every detail was said 'to suit the modern trend'.[92]

Huang sold the Xin Xin Wu Tai to build the New World on a major intersection overlooking the heart of Shanghai's leisure scene for westerners – the racecourse. Designed by Atkinson & Dallas, the New World's two wings (completed in 1914 and 1916) contained 'an amazing agglomeration of halls, theatres, menageries, distorting glasses, refreshment rooms ... roof gardens on different levels where hundreds of people drink tea and eat and there is always something new'.[93] 'Changing China', observed Darwent, 'is indeed seen here'.[94]

In 1917, Huang sold the New World to build, on an adjacent corner of the racecourse, the Great World, which became a Shanghai institution. The New World epitomised the city's uniqueness within the Chinese context. Whereas many new building types in Shanghai, such as factories, cinemas, department stores, ballrooms and night clubs, were western imports recast in a Chinese context, the Great World, designed by Zhou Huinan,[95] was entirely specific to the city and a product of its hedonism. Mu Shiying, in *Shanghai Foxtrot*, depicts the Great World's soaring needle tower emitting its 'rings and rings of light' as refusing confession from the nearby Moore Memorial Church with its 'men and women going to the hell'.[96] The Great World housed commercial stalls, a miniature racecourse, roller-skating rink, aviary, big wheel, aerial-runway, free cinema, Chinese garden and goldfish pond, newspaper press, a 5,000-seat theatre (the largest capacity in Shanghai), and a resident tiger – a true materialisation of Benjamin's phantasmagoria.[97] Every weekday, 8,000 people would visit the Great World, with 10,000 at the weekend and over 40,000 on public holidays.

The pursuit of public entertainment presents further parallels between Kracauer's Berlin and 1930s Shanghai. The customers of New and Great Worlds mirror Kracauer's 'have-nots' who pursued life through the eroticism that dance halls and other forms of entertainment offered.[98] In Shanghai, the haves invented for the have-nots China's largest shopping malls, chicest dance halls, nattiest night clubs, trendiest bars and coolest cafés, 'summoned forth', as Kracauer puts it, 'by an unerring instinct, in order to calm a metropolitan population's hunger for glamour and distraction'.[99] 'Perhaps in no other city', remarked one American journalist, 'does so much human energy go into the search for amusement'.[100] It was the golden age of Shanghai's jazz clubs and dance halls, which since 1927 had fuelled an addiction for dancing among Chinese clientele. Shanghai's iconic entertainment venues were consequently an essential part of urban life, and became vital cues in its art and literature, providing the backdrop to the city's modern portrayal and fiction, as well as characterising its cultural diversity. The titles of the city's myriad dance halls, cafés and clubs more than hint at its international variety: Federal Café (German); the Russian establishments of Ladow's Casanova, Café Renaissance, Constantine's, D.D's Café and the Balkan Milk Store; Ciro's;[101] St Anna Ballroom; Palais Café; and Vienna Ballroom.

The two pre-eminent department stores, or 'special shelters for the homeless'[102] as Kracauer described the European variety, were the world-famous Wing On and Sincere. These two retail outlets were said to mark 'the fuller modernisation of the Chinese element in Shanghai'.[103] Sincere (1917) was designed by Lester, Johnson &

Morris. Comprising four individual buildings up to five storeys high connected by overhead bridges, Sincere was much more than merely the most lavish and up-to-date department store in Asia. It contained foreign shops, tea-houses, a roof garden, an open-air cinema, staff accommodation and the Oriental Hotel.

Not to be outdone, the following year and immediately across Nanjing Road, the Great Eastern Hotel and the Wing On Department Store opened. The six-storey building was designed by Palmer & Turner and constructed in reinforced concrete topped with a roof garden and boasted every modern feature, including internal fire escapes, public elevators, flush toilets, copper shop fronts and doors, and thousands of electric bulbs illuminating the entire façade. Keen to keep up with the pace of modernity, Wing On built an extension in 1934 in the form of a 21-storey tower designed by Elliot Hazzard (1879–?) and Edward Phillips overlooking the intersection with Sincere and causing it to be dubbed Shanghai's 'Times Square' (see Figure 9.14).

Figure 9.14
The 21-storey extension to Wing On department store (1934), designed by Elliot Hazzard and Edward Phillips overlooking the intersection with Sincere and causing it to be dubbed Shanghai's 'Times Square'.

278 *Architecture and modernity*

Indulging Republican sensibilities in the period between the New Culture and May Fourth Movements, Sincere and Wing On were deliberately western, both in appearance and service. Both were classical in style. Of their respective hotels, Sincere's was said to be Shanghai's premier hotel for Chinese 'accustomed to foreign manners and customs'[104] and Wing On's was intended to 'cater for Chinese exclusively and have every modern convenience and equipment throughout' with the intention of meeting 'the demands of the Chinese accustomed to Occidental manners and customs'.[105]

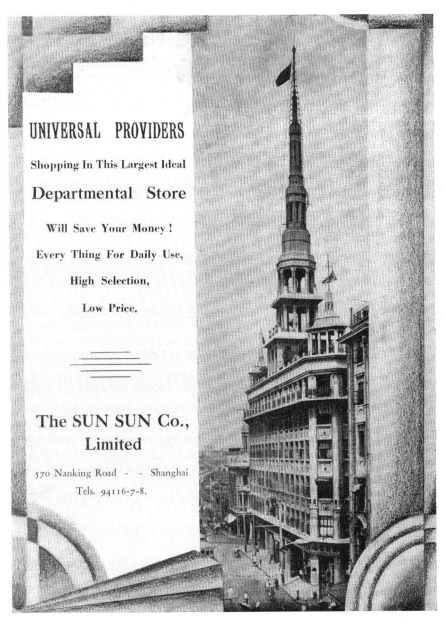

Figure 9.15 Sun Sun department store (1926), designed by Charles Gonda.

In 1926, the Sun Sun department store, 'The Store With The Needle Tower', designed by Gonda was constructed nearby (see Figure 9.15). Collectively, this trio of modern department stores on Shanghai's legendary commercial street, Nanjing Road, set the scene for Shi Zhecun in *Hua Meng (Flower Dream)*, in which he encapsulates Shanghai's internationalism, exclusivity and commercial verve:

> This is just Saturday afternoon. The three big department stores are breathing many men and women ... in the display window, the silver woman is wearing the Paris fashion ... a paper cutting of the King of the Ball holding a newly arrived football ... the American old man full of bubbles on the chin is always happily shaving with the Gillette razor. The brocade from Damascus is shining a mixed hue.[106]

In 1932 the Continental Emporium, the first large multi-purpose building on Nanjing Road designed by a Chinese architect, Zhuang Jun, was opened. Zhuang completed his Master's in Architecture in the mid-1920s in New York and his design for the Continental, like many of Shanghai's commercial buildings and entertainment venues from this era, drew strongly from New York's contemporaneous deportment.

In arguing the case for Shanghai's multiple modernities, the interconnectedness of the built environment and the sociopolitical and economic environments are inviolable. The multiplicity of experiences available in Shanghai led to the complete reconstitution of cultural norms in the city and a changed expectation of artistic activity. As Shi Zhecun wrote of the city's modern poets:

> The so-called modern life contains all kinds of unique forms: the harbour gathering large ships, the factories' thunderous noise, the mines burrowing holes deep under the earth, the dance halls with jazz music, the high-rise department stores, the airplanes in dog-fights, the vast racecourse ... even the natural scenery is different from previous times. The feelings that this type of life gives to our poets, how can it possibly be the same as what poets experienced in the past?[107]

Architecture and the imagined city

The production and interpretation of architecture in Shanghai were central to the construction and evocation of Chinese modernity throughout the 1930s. Both relied on modern art practices. The art of architecture was essential to Shanghai's modernist writers and artists, who in turn relied on contemporary buildings and novel urban settings to engage with and read modern urban life, and to distinguish their work from traditional forms of artistic expression that conformed to ancient formulae or were bound to rural imagery. Without architecture, modern Chinese literature would have been virtually meaningless. As Lee states: 'without [Shanghai's] physical environment and facilities it would have been impossible for Shi and his Shanghai "contemporaries" to create – or even imagine – a modern literature of their own'.[108] Architecture did not merely provide the backdrop to literary modernism and other manifestations of Chinese modernity – it provided the basis for it.

Architecture's centrality to the way in which Shanghai was imagined by other artists makes it all the more surprising that analyses of China's encounter with modernity before 1949 rarely incorporate architecture with other art practices, and that so little attention has been paid to the built environment's influence on these practices. Architecture is seldom given more than a peripheral acknowledgement as a factor in modernity's encounter, despite having been responsible for the very structures and spaces that shaped the environment in which Shanghai's modern artists so famously operated. Scholars of the various art practices that feature in Feng's *Garden of Art* seldom analyse the impact of architecture in any detail, while the concentrated gaze of architectural scholars on the built environment evades the wider role it had in China's broader encounter with modernity. Such dissonance may be the result of established academic specialisations, but in an increasingly multidisciplinary and globalised world characterised by multiple modernities a clearer picture of a more complex past is emerging. Indeed, a cross-disciplinarily mindset was a facet of modernity for art practitioners at the time, when artists like Feng Zikai freely wrote about and engaged in wider artistic discourses, including modern architecture.[109]

Another facet of Shanghai's architectural modernity that complicated architecture's interpretation by Shanghai's modern writers, artists and contemporary scholars was the ambiguous connection between modernity and architectural style. Aesthetic modernity, which was vital in art, for example, was not seen by artists and writers as critical to modern architecture. Architectural modernity was interpreted by those outside architecture, as well as by some architects, more in terms of function (cinemas, dance halls, factories and power stations), technology (e.g. elevators, escalators, central-heating, lighting and other technological facilities), scale (e.g. height, mass and volume), and mood (e.g. sensation and experience), than appearance or cultural reference. Zhao Shen's Nanking Theatre (1928), renowned for its conservative classical style and designed when he was working in the offices of Fan Wenzhao before producing his more progressive work with Allied Architects (such as Metropol Theatre), was lauded in Shi Zhecun's short story, *In the Paris Theatre*. In contrast to the Paris Theatre, where the 'air is so bad, there are so many people, small seats, and you cannot get tickets', Shi portrayed the Nanking Theatre as the only place to watch films because of its modern air-conditioning that produces that 'exquisite' sensation caused by 'the hot air when coming outside'.[110]

The creative potency of Shanghai's physical realm invariably relied on combined ensembles than on singular structures, whose cachet was measured by conspicuous details (e.g. the clock, the tower and the doorway) or interiors (e.g. fixtures, fittings, furnishings and colour). Lee rightly observes that Shanghai's modern writers tended to focus 'not so much [on] the exterior magnificence of the building as the lush interiors'.[111] Eileen Chang,[112] author of *Lust, Caution*, used Hudec's Grand Theatre (see Figure 9.16) for precisely this purpose. Although the architectural press reviewed Hudec's modernist masterpiece as 'an experiment which may not please everyone, but is undoubtedly an interesting and striking building',[113] Chang's depiction, in her 1947 short story *Duoshao Hen* (*How Much Sorrow!*), was far more vivid:

> the cheapest palace [where] everything is a magnificent structure of glass, velvet, and imitation marble. . . . The floor is a pale yellow as soon as you walk in. The whole place looks like a yellow chalice magnified a thousand times, possessing that shining magic beauty and purity (see Plate 38).[114]

Few literary depictions of Shanghai's modernity that relied on the architectural realm surpass the famous scene in Mao Dun's *Midnight*, where the author describes

Figure 9.16
The illuminated tower of the Grand Theatre (1933) designed by László Hudec.

with extraordinary exuberance the final moments of the main character's peasant father's life. The passage is quoted at length, from the moments following the arrival into Shanghai from the countryside of a wealthy landlord, Mr Wu, who was collected by his industrialist son in a car and driven through the city on a journey that would end in Mr Wu's untimely death from a heart attack:

> The car is racing forwards madly ... hundreds of windows lit up like hundreds of strange eyes, high-rise buildings jumping towards Wu's eye like falling mountains and roaring seas. Suddenly they disappear. Empty land, straight lamp posts, endlessly, one after another, rushing towards his face. Suddenly they disappear too. A snake-like string of black monsters, a big eye on each head, sending dizzy lights, screaming, rushing like lightening, rushing towards the little box Wu is sitting in! Closer! Closer! Wu closed his eyes, shaking all over, but nothing happened. He opened his eyes again in surprise, still the black monster with big eyes, is screaming, rushing towards him ... he feels his head spinning on his neck. In front of his eyes, red, yellow, green, black, shining, square, round

282 *Architecture and modernity*

Figure 9.17 Advertisement (1937) for Ford by Chang Ching-huei combining a sense of speed, light, the machine and technology that made Shanghai such an inspiration to modernists.

– chaos, jumping, jumping, his ears full of loud and noisy waves of sound, causing his heart to pound out of his chest!. . . . He saw her dress . . . pale blue chiffon tightly wrapped around her fit body, a pair of full breasts pointing out conspicuously, sleeves shrunk above the elbow, showing a snow white forearm. An indescribably disgusting feeling, suddenly filled his heart, he turned his face . . . another young woman wearing chiffon sitting on a rickshaw . . . a sea of all kinds of cars, rushing through the sea of red and green human bodies of men and women . . . machine noise, the stench of car exhausts and women's perfume, red neon lights – all the souls of a city just like a nightmare, crashed onto Wu's weak heart without compassion, until he is dizzy, until his ears are whizzing, until his head is splitting![115]

Employing a multitude of metaphors to convey Shanghai's unique version of urban modernity, the author creates a scene so shocking in its juxtaposition of international urban modernity and domestic 'other' that could not have occurred anywhere else in the world at that moment in time. Cultural collisions and modernity's acceptance and rejection occur at international, national and filial levels. Architecture, technology, the machine, sex and fashion – all important devices exploited in popular art to sell anything from cigarettes to homes – clash in a sensory overload that parallels the urban pandemonium they attempt to describe: technology, threatening by its peculiarity, breathes hideous life into skyscrapers and lamp-posts, while the modern motor car serves as the machine rushing the characters around this nightmarish landscape in which sex is portrayed both explicitly and implicitly, with reference to the lady's breasts and pale skin revealed beneath the seductive *qi pao* (Shanghai's uniquely modernist adaptation of the traditional Chinese dress and fashion's architectural equivalent to Shanghai's entertainment venues) (see Plate 39). Senses are overloaded by the sights, sounds and smell of Shanghai's unique and pulsating urbanity until the heart of the rural visitor can take no more. Death is both literal and symbolic: modernity's triumph.

As Mao Dun's narrative demonstrates, modernity's artistic interpretation was dependent on the viewer, eliciting anything from rousing euphoria to mortal despair, and, given Shanghai's multicultural populace and international influence, these interpretations were eminently varied. Towering architecture, neon lighting, metal automobiles, billowing smokestacks, silk dresses, pungent perfume and human flesh (both collectively impersonal and privately erotic) were all evocations of modernity whose impact transcended social, artistic and ethnic lines: rural and urban;[116] traditional and progressive; and foreign and Chinese.

The same attributes were employed by the modern Chinese poet, Shao Xunmei, who, in *The Soul of Shanghai*, used architecture to provide an appropriate vantage point from which to observe the city:

> Ah, I stand atop this seven-story building,
> Above are the unreachable heavens,
> Below are cars, electric wires, racecourse,
> The front of the stage, the back of the prostitute,
> Ah, these are the spirits of the metropolis,
> These are the soul of Shanghai.[117]

It was this soul of Shanghai, the 'dynamism' and 'bustling' city' that Clarke wrote about, that featured time and again in artistic depictions of the city locally and globally.[118] For the American artist, Mark Tobey, it was the 'terrific din' created by the 'human energy [that] spills itself into multiple forms, writhes, sweats, and strains every muscle towards the day's bowl of rice'[119] that inspired *Broadway Norm* (1935). As a global example of inverted modernist influence, this work heralded Tobey's calligraphic 'white writing' technique. Similarly, it was this pulsating, futuristic, technological, metropolitan dystopia – in war and in peace – that nurtured a young J.G. Ballard (see Plate 40 and Plate 41).

Architects also indulged in their own imaginings, which invariably pandered to the aspirational lure of the high-rise. In the late 1930s, when ambitious construction was increasingly improbable, plans were realised on the printed page, where published proposals by some of Shanghai's foreign architects assumed increasingly fantastical forms that occasionally exceeded in height and scale anything that had ever been built in Shanghai.

However, China's growing political and economic strength by the 1930s could be read in the city's boldest architectural statements. The Chinese-owned Joint Savings Society commissioned Hudec to design the city's tallest building in 1934 (see Figure 1.1 and Plate 34) and the young Bank of China constructed their towering Shanghai offices on the riverfront in 1939, designed by Luke (see Plate 28). Under these conditions, the proposal by the China Merchants Steam Navigation Company (CMSNC) to build a huge new head office on the Bund did not seem entirely

Figure 9.18 Proposal for the headquarters of the China Merchants Steam Navigation Company (1939) on Shanghai's Bund.

implausible (see Figure 9.18).[120] Demonstrating China's ascendance, the proposal was a 29-storey structure, the front slab of which evokes Le Corbusier's Quartier de la Marine in Algiers or an undersized version of Harrison and Abramovitz's United Nations Headquarters in New York. More symbolic of China's growing confidence than the domineering stature of the proposed building was its location in the centre of the Bund, the embodiment of foreign dominance for a century. Illustrating the speed and extent of change that China (and Shanghai in particular) was experiencing from the mid-1920s, the CMSNC proposal, although never built, demonstrated China's intent, just as the neighbouring HSBC offices had done over a decade earlier when the company's manager instructed the architect George Wilson to 'spare no expense, but dominate the Bund'.[121]

Far more ambitious than the CMSNC's office was a proposal by the Japanese during the war to raze the entire International Settlement and construct vast parallel boulevards from the Huangpu River westwards, as well as develop Pudong. The plan was not realised, but it would take a further half a century before Pudong was allowed to develop in what has become the ultimate contemporary expression of the imagined city of Shanghai – a science fiction set of soaring skyscrapers carefully choreographed by a Communist government in the late-capitalist age (see Plate 42). It is no coincidence that the roots, literally and figuratively, of this twenty-first century metropolis lie firmly in the heady years leading up to the Second World War when the 'Billion Dollar Skyline' was mere braggadocio rather than understatement – imagination rather than reality.

For critics of Shanghai's version of modernity, Shanghai's famous riverfront, rather than attracting praise and adulation, epitomised China's problem. If any architectural ensemble contrasted with the city's vivacious character, it was this staid row of mostly neoclassical structures built predominantly by British firms. It is not surprising, then, that it was a British writer, Arthur Ransome, when visiting Shanghai in 1928, two years before he published *Swallows and Amazons*, who saw through the architecture and witnessed the precariousness of Shanghai's condition:

> They [foreigners] seem to have lived in a hermetically sealed and isolated glass case since 1901. They look round on their magnificent buildings and are surprised that China is not grateful to them for these gifts, forgetting that the money to build them came out of China ... they prosper upon it coming and going and forget that it is the trade that is valuable to England and not the magnificent buildings which big profits and low taxes have allowed them to erect.... Extremely conservative, like most business communities in foreign countries, they are prepared to have their country go to war for them rather than to adjust themselves to inevitably changing conditions.[122]

Sympathetic though many foreign writers were to China, they were especially critical of their own country's contribution to its version of modernity. One of the sharpest critiques was written by one such foreigner, but not a westerner. In the novel *Shanghai*, by Yokomitsu Riichi, the Japanese writer upends the modernising aspirations of architecture when one of his characters abandons the profession to become a body collector because 'it's the best way to make money'. In typical Shanghai style, ethics are disoriented as the former architect declares that 'For what it costs for one corpse you can keep seven Russian mistresses'.[123] Taking to new heights the depiction of the foreigner in Shanghai as a selfish individual in a self-interested system, Riichi writes:

> each respective race of people [make] their living here as suckers on the tentacles of a giant octopus, pulling in a huge amount of wealth for their home countries. ... This was true for just about anyone of any nationality who had gathered in this colony in China. If they went back to their homeland they would have absolutely no way of making a living.[124]

Shanghai's demise

Modernity in China, as this study has attempted to demonstrate, was consequent on unique engagements between different cultures and alternative versions of the modern, a phenomenon that reached its apogee in Shanghai (and in a very different sense, in Manchuria) in a comparatively fleeting moment before the Second World War. Both sites represent inimitable urban landscapes at a specific moment in time in which multiple modernities were imagined and actualised. What set Shanghai apart from other sites in China (and outside China) was the extent of its permeability to outside influences, without any one of them emerging as dominant. Modernity in Shanghai was not static, but was being constantly renegotiated between internal and external pressures.

The first major blow to this period of multiple modernities was Japan's invasion of China in 1937. Standing at the intersection of Nanjing Road and the Bund, where Asia's most famous shopping street met Asia's most famous river-frontage, was Sassoon House, accommodating one of the most luxurious hotels in the world, the Cathay, where guests could order opium on room service while wallowing in marble baths filled with mineral water dispensed from solid silver faucets. It was here in

286 *Architecture and modernity*

Figure 9.19 The 'Ultra-Modern' suite inside the Cathay Hotel.

January 1930 that Noël Coward wrote *Private Lives* in a few days while recovering from flu. Shanghai made a strong impression on Coward. He regarded it 'tremendously modern', describing it as 'a very strange mixture ... a cross between Brussels and Huddersfield. Every nation is represented in it and the poor Chinese have to struggle with *so* many languages.'[125] The city's cosmopolitan character was reflected in the Cathay's rooms which were fitted out in a variety of styles, from 'Hindoo' to 'Ultra-Modern' (see Figure 9.19).

On the morning of 14 August 1937, or 'Bloody Saturday',[126] in what was later described as 'the worst single calamity outside Hiroshima',[127] the body parts of over 1,500 killed and wounded were sprayed over the Cathay. Two misdirected bombs had been dropped by the Chinese Air Force attempting to attack the Japanese cruiser *Idzumo*, moored in front of the Japanese Consulate nearby. At the Great World, where up to 10,000 people would normally be amusing themselves amid the phantasmagoria on a Saturday (see Figure 9.20), another 1,500 people were killed and wounded by a third bomb that landed directly outside.

A week later, another bomb landed between China's two principal department stores, Sincere and Wing On, killing over 600. As bombs, shrapnel from anti-aircraft fire, incendiary devices and faulty aircraft petrol tanks rained on Shanghai, a curfew was imposed on the foreign settlements between 10pm and 5am, extinguishing the city's nightlife. As the Japanese advanced through Shanghai's northern suburbs, their deliberate destruction of Shanghai's Civic Centre evoked the time-honoured Chinese custom of the victor razing the buildings of the defeated. Many of Shanghai's foreign residents evacuated to Hong Kong, while others retreated to Nationalist-controlled territory and the proxy capital of Chongqing in what was the start of an exodus lasting eight years: 'All possibilities for a normal artistic life in Shanghai were now

Figure 9.20 The devastating scenes outside Shanghai's Great World on 14 August 1937, in which thousands of people died when the Chinese Air Force tried to bomb Japanese ships in the Huangpu River.

lost, and the more immediate question of survival came to fore.'[128] In a city that had achieved so much in cultivating a unique form of modernity in China, the experience was destroyed, along with much of the material and artistic evidence of this era, never to return.

Notes

1 Laurence, 2003, p. 390.
2 The author has written extensively about Shanghai, including the publications: *Building Shanghai – The Story of China's Gateway* (Wiley, 2006) and *Modernism in China – Architectural Visions and Revolutions* (Wiley, 2008). The purpose of this chapter is not to duplicate the contents of these publications, but to build on their findings so as to offer new insights and a better understanding of China's encounter with architectural modernity before 1949.
3 Laurence, 2003, p. 390.
4 Speech by Admiral Freemantle given on Friday 17 November in 'The Jubilee of Shanghai 1843–1893, Shanghai: Past and Present', and a full account of the proceedings on 17 and 18 November, 1893, *North China Daily News*, Shanghai, 1893.
5 Esherick, 2000, p. 13.
6 Hsia, 1929, Preface.
7 Known as *huiguan* or *gongsuo*.
8 As they were then calculated.
9 According to an article in the *Far Eastern Review*, 'Building a New Shanghai' (June 1931, p. 348), a census in early 1931 declared Shanghai's population to be 3,156,141 (3,096,856 Chinese, 59,285 foreign), slightly higher than figures from the official census recorded the previous year and published in the *Feetham Report*, 1931.
10 The British and Russians represented 17 per cent and 15 per cent of the foreign population respectively (*Feetham Report*, 1931).
11 1,842 Indians, 941 Vietnamese, 381 Filipinos, 151 Koreans and 2 Malaysians, (*Feetham Report*, 1931).
12 Yokomitsu Riichi, 'Shinakai' ('The China Sea'), 1939, in Riichi, 1956, p. 197.

288 Architecture and modernity

13 With the exception of 1929–30 and 1932–4, where it rose to above 4 per cent but never exceeded 8 per cent (*Shanghai Municipal Council Reports*).
14 In the 1930s, overcrowded *lilong* developments enabled population densities of 600 people per acre, comparable to the most densely populated metropolitan area in the world at the time, the Eleventh Ward of New York City (696 people per acre). (Denison and Ren, 2006, pp. 160–1).
15 Hudec was born in Banskabystrica, then in Hungary (now in Slovakia). (*Men of Shanghai and North China*, 1935, p. 269.)
16 Veysseyre was born in Auvergne, France (*Men of Shanghai and North China*, 1935, p. 562).
17 Hammerschmidt was born in Vienna, Austria (*Men of Shanghai and North China*, 1935, p. 207).
18 Minutti was born in Geneva, Switzerland (*Men of Shanghai and North China*, 1935, p. 408).
19 Fraser was born in Liverpool, England (*Men of Shanghai and North China*, 1935, p. 182).
20 Alexander Léonard graduated in 1919 and Arthur Kruze in 1930.
21 Hammerschmidt designed the Tianjin residence of the former Emperor, Pu Yi (*Men of Shanghai and North China*, 1935, p. 208).
22 *Men of Shanghai and North China*, 1935, p. 208.
23 Kruze was born on 20 June 1920 at Roubaix, France (*Men of Shanghai and North China*, 1935, p. 314).
24 From March 1930 to March 1933 (*Men of Shanghai and North China*, 1935, p. 314).
25 Wilson was born in London (*Men of Shanghai and North China*, 1935, p. 605).
26 HSBC Offices, Custom House, Chartered Bank of India, Australia & China, Yokohama Specie Bank, Yangtze Insurance Building, Glen Line Building, Cathay Hotel and Sassoon House, Cathay Mansions, International Recreation Building, Wing On Department Store, Metropole Hotel, Hamilton House, Embankment Building, Royal Asiatic Society, Wayfoong House, Samarkand Apartments, Cavendish Court, Grosvenor House, and many cotton mills and factories.
27 It has been suggested that this plan is a deliberate reference to the Chinese character for the auspicious number eight.
28 Kuonin, 1938, p. 252.
29 Kuonin, 1938, p. 128.
30 Kroker, 1939, p. 315.
31 Acton, 1948, p. 292.
32 Thomson, 1875, p. 166.
33 In 1866 Shanghai's gas works produced 5,318m. cubic feet of gas for 58 consumers through 4.8 miles of mains. By 1928, it was the biggest gas works in China, producing 567,581m. cubic feet of gas for 10,035 consumers through 160 miles of mains (*Far Eastern Review*, April 1929, p. 172).
34 In 1894 there were just two cotton mills in the whole of China, at Wuchang (near Hankou) and in Shanghai. Modern cotton manufacturing in China was introduced in Shanghai in 1890, with the British cotton manufacturer Ewo (owned by Jardine, Matheson & Co.) being the first cotton mill furnished with modern machinery imported from Britain in Shanghai on 10 May 1897. A German mill, Jui Chi, and an American mill, Hung Yuan, opened in consecutive years. The Japanese adopted a different strategy by purchasing Chinese mills, two of the largest of which, Ta Shun and San Tai, were bought in 1902 and changed their names to No. 1 and No. 2. By 1934 China had 70 cotton mills, 59 of which were in Shanghai, employing over 100,000 workers and valued at $226m. Japan's stake was $180m. in 32 mills, while Britain had just three mills, the largest being Ewo with a $5m. stake. China owned the rest ('The Cotton Industry in Shanghai,' *The China Journal*, May 1930, p. 268).
35 The engagement with and modification of technology in Shanghai's context can be seen at the time in the fantastical employment of electric light, the use of trams, the high-rise buildings and even in the planes that dropped bombs on the city, all of which became symbols in various ways of Shanghai's distinction with other cities, either by emulating other international cities or being at China's frontier with the outside world.

36 Carpenter, 1934, p. 72.
37 Hsia, 1929, p. 118.
38 Kuonin, 1938, p. 41.
39 Kuonin, 1938, p. 144.
40 Wright, 1908, p. 62.
41 Ling Shuhua, for example, is often quoted as being the 'Chinese Katherine Mansfield'.
42 Kuonin, 1938, p. 172.
43 *Far Eastern Review*, June 1931, p. 348.
44 Kuonin, 1938, p. 74.
45 'Has Shanghai Outgrown Itself?', *Far Eastern Review*, October 1927, p. 448.
46 Brooke and Davis, 1928, Preface.
47 Brooke and Davis, 1935, p. 126.
48 Mao Dun, 'Ji Qi De Song Zan' ('The Praise of the Machine') in *Shen Bao Yue Kan*, Vol. 2, No. 4, Shanghai, 1933.
49 Liu Na'ou, *Du Shi Feng Jing Xian* (*The Scenery of the Metropolis*), Shui Mo Shu Dian, April 1930, p. 21.
50 The first elevator had been in the German Club, demolished in the mid-1930s ('Modern Elevators in the Far East', *Far Eastern Review*, June 1936, p. 262).
51 'Modern Elevators in the Far East', *Far Eastern Review*, June 1936, p. 262.
52 Mu, 2004, p. 163.
53 *Far Eastern Review*, June 1936, p. 262.
54 *Far Eastern Review*, June 1936, p. 264.
55 *Far Eastern Review*, June 1936, p. 262.
56 Kracauer, 1998, p. 92.
57 Brooke and Davis, 1931, Preface.
58 Wilson, 1930, p. 251.
59 Wilson, 1930, p. 251.
60 Baronti, 1925, p. 648.
61 Mu, 2004, p. 11.
62 Liu Na'ou, 'Feng Jing' ('The Scenery') in *Du Shi Feng Jing Xian* (*The Scenery of the Metropolis*), Shui Mo Shu Dian, April 1930, p. 45.
63 Sowerby, 1932, pp. 213–14.
64 *Far Eastern Review*, October 1927, p. 448.
65 Wilson, 1930, p. 251.
66 Léonard & Veysseyre became Léonard, Veysseyre & Kruze from 1934 (*Men of Shanghai and North China*, 1935, p. 314).
67 *Men of Shanghai and North China*, 1935, p. 208.
68 The Hai-Alai Building designed by Minutti & Co. and containing the 'largest and most comfortable bar in Shanghai' (*The Builder*, Vol. 1, 1934, p. 6).
69 *Far Eastern Review*, October 1935, p. 396.
70 *Far Eastern Review*, October 1935, p. 396.
71 Kuonin, 1938, p. 252.
72 Mu, 2004, p. 152.
73 George Sokolsky, an American journalist, quoted in Stella Dong, 2001, p. 229.
74 Letter from Lao Ching to John and Wilma Fairbank, 2 February 1936, Peabody Essex Museum, Salem, Massachusetts.
75 This form of opera was known as *haipai jingju* (Shanghai school, Beijing Opera). Pang (2007, p. 149) asserts that the British-born Luo Yiqing, who built Mantingfang (House of Full Fragrance), was chiefly responsible for this, inviting Beijing opera troupes to perform in Shanghai.
76 Lee, 1999, p. 34.
77 Lu Xun's letters to Xu Guangping, 15, 23 and 26 November 1932; letters to Xu Shouchang (2 December 1932) and to Cao Jinghua (12 December 1932), all in 'Lu Xun Quan Ji' ('The complete collection of Lu Xun's work'), 12, pp. 119–20, 126–31, in Tang Xiaobing, 2008, p. 140.
78 Tang Xiaobing, 2008, p. 140.

290 Architecture and modernity

79 In Tiantong Road, according to Zheng Dongtian, 'Films and Shanghai' in Danzker et al., 2004, p. 298.
80 Ren Qingtai had studied photography in Japan from 1874 and opened the first Chinese-owned photo studio, Fengtai Photographic Studio, in Beijing in 1892 (Pang, 2007, p. 143).
81 Dahengxuan/Bigwig Parlour (Pang, 2007, p. 143).
82 The Arcade (Ping'an Dianying Gongsi), in the same year as Hong Kong's Bizhao Dianying Yuan (Bizhao Theatre) (Pang, 2007, p. 167).
83 Also known as *The Wedding Night* with Zheng Zhengqiu and Zhang Shichuan.
84 Zheng Dongtian, 'Films and Shanghai' in Danzker et al., 2004, p. 298, which also states that from the 1920s–40s, at least half of all China's films were produced in Shanghai (where over 650 films were produced from 1921 to 1931) and by 1927 the city hosted 141 of China's 175 film companies (ibid., p. 300).
85 Mao Dun (ed.), *A Day in China*, Sheng Huo Shu Dian, Hong Kong, Ming Guo 25 (1936).
86 Others included: Cathay, Capitol, Carlton, Embassy, Grand, Isis, New Lyceum, Nanking, Odeon, Paris, Peking, Strand and Uptown.
87 Kroker, 1939, p. 316.
88 Pang, 2007, p. 150.
89 Pang, 2007, p. 150.
90 This building was called the 'Lou Wai Lou' or 'Building Beyond the Buildings'.
91 'New Dah Wu Dai Theatre', *The Builder*, Vol. 5, 1933, p. 15.
92 'New Dah Wu Dai Theatre', *The Builder*, Vol. 5, 1933, p. 15.
93 Darwent, 1920, p. 29.
94 Darwent, 1920, p. 29.
95 Zhou Hui Nan claimed to be an architect though he was never formally trained. He arrived in Shanghai in 1884 from Jiangsu province and later worked for the Asia Realty Company where he gained architectural experience and was self-taught. He also worked for the Shanghai Railway Bureau, South Shanghai Engineering Bureau and Zhejiang Xingye Bank's real-estate division where he was head of architecture. In the 1910s he established China's earliest Engineering and Architectural firm, Zhou Hui Nan Da Yang Jian (Zhou Hui Nan Drafting Studio). (Zhang Fuhe, 1999.)
96 Mu, 2004, p. 158.
97 Lee would dispute this association, as he sees Shanghai's department stores and Great World as no substitute for the arcades where Benjamin's flâneur felt at home (see Lee, 2001, p. 109). However, adopting Benjamin's interpretation (see Walter Benjamin, *Charles Baudelaire: A Lyric Poet in the Era of High Capitalism*, trans. Harry Zhon, London, NLB, 1973), which regards the department store (which made use of *flânerie* itself in order to sell goods) as 'the *flâneur's* final coup', I seek only to highlight the exemplar of urban distractions in the context of Shanghai.
98 Kracauer, 1995, p. 296.
99 Kracauer, 1998, p. 91.
100 George Sokolsky, in Stella Dong, 2001, p. 229.
101 Ciro's was designed by the architectural firm Graham & Painter for the International Realty Company and opened in 1935 (*The Builder*, Vol. 4, No. 8, pp. 1–2).
102 Kracauer, 1998, p. 91.
103 Kuonin, 1938, p. 158.
104 *Far Eastern Review*, Vol. 12, No. 7, 1916, p. 255.
105 *Far Eastern Review*, Vol. 12, No. 4, 1916, p. 152.
106 Shi Zhecun, 'Hua Meng' ('Flower Dream'), in *Ji Wai*, 1933, and in *Shi Nian Chuang Zuo Ji (Collection of 10 years of Creative Work)*, Hua Dong Shi Fan Da Xue Chu Ban She, Shanghai, 1996, p. 672.
107 Shi Zhecun, 'You Guan Yu Ben Kan De Shi' ('About the Poems of this Magazine'), *Xian Dai (Les Contemporains)*, Vol. 4, No. 1, Shanghai, 1933, Preface.
108 Lee, 1999, p. 144.
109 Feng Zi Kai, 'Xian Dai Jian Zhu De Xing Shi Mei,' ('The Beauty and Form of Modern Architecture,') in Feng Zikai, Feng Yiyin, and Feng Yuancao, *Feng Zi Kai Wen Ji -1920.4-*

1930.3 Yi Shu Juan (The Writings of Feng Zikai -1920.4-1930.3 Volume of Art), Zhe Jiang Wen Yi Chu Ban She (Zhe Jiang Literature and Art Publisher), Hangzhou, 1990.
110 Shi Zhecun, 'Zai Ba Li Da Xi Yuan' ('In the Paris Theatre'), *Xiao Shuo Yue Bao* (*Literary Monthly*), Shanghai, Vol. 22, No. 8, 10 August 1931, p. 1009.
111 Lee, 1999, p. 276.
112 Chang was born and schooled in Shanghai, and was accepted into London University to study literature in 1939. War prevented her passage, so she went to Hong Kong University instead (Yu, 1993).
113 Brooke and Davis, 1933, p. 108.
114 Eileen Chang, *Duo Shao Hen* (*How Much Sorrow!*), Shanghai, 1947, p. 8.
115 Mao, 1977, pp. 8–10.
116 Shi Zhecun explained in an interview in 1990 that 'Writers raised in the countryside that come to Shanghai cannot accept the urban life; although he is in Shanghai what he writes about is still rural life'. Shi Zhezun, 'Zhong Guo Xian Dai Zhu Yi De Shu Guang' ('The Dawn of the Chinese Modernism'), interview with Zheng Min Li and Lin Yao De in *Lian He Wen Xue* (*United Literature*), Vol. 6, No. 9, Taipei, 1990, pp. 130–41.
117 Shao Xunmei, 'Shangai De Ling Hun' ('The Soul of Shanghai'), in Lin Lang (ed.), *Xian Dai Chuang Zuo Xin Shi Xuan* (*Selected Modern New Poems*), Shanghai Zhong Yang Shu Dian, Vol. 4, September 1936.
118 Clarke, 2004, pp. 97–8.
119 Tobey, 1951, p. 230.
120 The CMSNC was a direct descendent of China's *Self-Strengthening Movement* that had grown to become one of the largest shipping companies in the world.
121 King, 1988, p. 132.
122 Ransome, 1927, p. 28.
123 Riichi, 2001, p. 15.
124 Riichi, 2001, p. 44.
125 Noël Coward, *The Letters of Noël Coward*, Bloomsbury, 2014, p. 170.
126 Journalist and eye-witness Percy Finch calls it 'Bloody Saturday', though other later sources call it 'Black Saturday'.
127 Finch, 1953, p. 252.
128 Clarke, 2004, p. 101.

10 Curtailed modernities

As an exploration of China's encounter with modernity, this study has attempted to move beyond merely identifying and describing the characteristics and material evidence of this encounter, to exploring new ways of reading and understanding it. The entry of western practices and values into China's built environment, whichever route they took, was a process without precedent in China's history. Hereafter, emerged an experience of architectural modernity quite distinct from that which occurred elsewhere in the world.

The speed of modernity's rise throughout the first half of the twentieth century was matched by the swiftness of its demise after 1949. The fall-out can still be felt societally and architecturally. For China's architects and other art practitioners, it was clear that change was permanent and regressive. As war approached and the world departed China, the words of Lin Huiyin in 1936 describe the sense of desperation among China's modernists: 'I have a sensation to scream or jump up or run barefooted out in the *middle* of *New York* and yell "oh, oh don't leave me behind, I want to be there too, I will do anything anything there, I *belong*".'[1]

Nobody could have foreseen that eight years of global conflict would merely preface four years of civil war, but the consequence for China's architectural development was, ultimately, the complete structural and theoretical reorganisation of the profession and its membership, and the cessation of the types of progressivism and creativity that had characterised China's architectural development throughout the first half of the twentieth century. In 1949, the Communist victory and the Nationalist exile to Taiwan shrank China's architectural community. Japanese architects were expelled from Manchuria in 1945 though had ceased being productive long before. Foreign architects had left the former treaty ports during the war and few came back. Those who did return had to promptly leave again in 1949. Joining the exodus were Chinese architects unconvinced by Communism. Only Communist sympathisers remained. From 1949, China's architectural community, greatly diminished in size and experience, entered a new and uncertain era.

For China's modern architecture and its portrayal in modern history nationally and internationally, the events of the 1940s were decisive. China's architectural history, like that of modernism globally, was the victor's narrative. China's absence in modernist histories internationally is proof, if more proof was needed, of the west's subsequent supremacy. Nationally, the architects who stayed under Communism became the pillars of the profession, and much of their work before 1949 has since been promoted and protected while those who left for Hong Kong, Taiwan or further afield receded into the shadows, their presence obscured and their contributions largely overlooked. The learned Liang Sicheng and his flamboyant wife Lin Huiyin, the distinguished Yang Tingbao, the vivacious Chen Zhi, the literary Tong Jun, and the scholarly Liu Dunzhen are among those that remained in China after 1949 whose names have become synonymous with early modern Chinese architecture. For Fan Wenzhao, Luke Him Sau, Liu Jipiao and many others who had participated equally in China's encounter with architectural modernity with these friends and former colleagues, their names and reputations have been marginalised – China's missing moderns, non-persons, erased from history until a softening of political attitudes and settling of old scores in the twenty-first century.

From multiple to minimal modernities

Another way of examining China's multiple modernities other than through their rise in the early twentieth century is to examine their descent from the late 1930s. Although there were many achievements in modern architecture in China and other art practices throughout the 1930s, retreat from artistic modernism can be traced back to 1932. The dual impact of the Great Depression reaching China and Japan's first bombing of Shanghai foreshadowed modernism's historical erasure through the destruction of its physical evidence and the cessation of its creative impetus, destroying artworks and properties. The Japanese-trained modernist painter, Chen Baoyi, lost 'all his paintings [and his] lovely suburban studio'.[2] For architects, it left the construction industry 'practically dead'.[3]

Nationally, modernism in China was dismantled deliberately and destructively. The two generations of Chinese who had encountered and attempted to negotiate modernity had to accept that the project was postponed, as Lin Huiyin said in 1935 of her own generation: 'If we are educated for a golden age and settled state of things, we have to recognize that this is no golden age or settled state'.[4] While the curtailment of China's encounter with modernity might be seen as a failed first attempt at modernisation, Harootunian offers an alternative view, taken from China's neighbour, modernist mentor, and nemesis, wherein 'the very incompleteness that thinkers discerned in Japan's modern history was, in fact, a sign of modernity itself'.[5]

That modernism was cut short in China is a further factor distinguishing China from other sites outside the west and problematising its critique. Multiple encounters with modernity occurred in China earlier than in most 'others' (with the obvious exception of Japan), but the situation was reversed from the mid-twentieth century, after which the retreat of European imperialism elsewhere, the growth of nationalism and the spread of global capital were accompanied by the widespread diffusion of architectural and urban modernism[6] that contrast starkly with China's relative isolation from the 1950s to the 1980s.

The point that marked modernity's suspension in China was Japan's invasion in 1937. In Manchuria architectural pursuits peaked and throughout the rest of China modern art practices, including architecture, stalled completely. In Shanghai, the epicentre of modernity, 'the entire modernist establishment was wiped out'.[7] 'If there was no anti-Japanese war', explained the modernist writer Shi Zhecun, in an interview in 1990, 'Shanghai would have continued to develop stably and maintain the tendency of being international, and Mu Shiying and I would have continued to write. But time and circumstances changed; the whole literary environment went wrong'.[8] The same was true of architecture.

Mu Shiying returned to Shanghai to be with his friend and fellow Japanese-educated writer Liu Na'ou who was collaborating with the Japanese. Both were assassinated (Mu in 1940 and Liu in 1939). The innocent early deaths of the pioneering architect Lü Yanzhi (1929) and the writers Xu Zhimo (1931) and Lu Xun (1936) denied China some of its best minds in their respective fields just as modernism was gaining momentum, but many politically motivated deaths and personal upheavals during the world war and civil war that followed robbed China of much of its remaining modernist spirit and vital talent, as well as severing its many global connections.

Shih describes Liu's short life as mirroring 'the literary movement which he created and which died with him'.[9] In 1945, Yu Dafu, the co-founder of *The Creation Society*, 'was assassinated by the Japanese police for his patriotic activities'.[10] The writer and Cambridge graduate Xiao Qian 'had planned to write a book for China about E.M. Forster and Virginia Woolf, but it was never written'.[11] Virginia Woolf's suicide terminated the correspondence with Ling Shuhua, though she did eventually produce her autobiography with Bloomsbury's former publishing house, Hogarth Press.[12] Collectively, 'many artists suffered [the] destruction of artwork and biographical documents' during the war, compounding their omission from subsequent historiography.[13]

The experience of China's modern writers and artists mirrored that of its modern architects. During the Second World War, many architects fled Japanese-occupied China and spent the war in the proxy capital Chongqing or Kunming. It was in Chongqing that China's exiled architectural academic community assembled in the humble surroundings of the National Central University. Here, some of China's leading architectural figures such as Luke Him Sau, Tong Jun and Yang Tingbao continued to teach a new generation of architects while participating in the war effort by designing air-raid shelters and other vital facilities.

In Manchuria, Japanese architects continued to arrive, but Japan's military machine engaged more vigorously in destruction rather than construction. The worsening conditions dragged on for over eight years until being brought to a swift and ultimately horrific end on 9 August 1945. At one minute past midnight, over a million soldiers in the Soviet army entered Manchukuo, and hours later Fat Man, America's second atomic bomb, fell on Nagasaki. The combined effect of the Soviet invasion and two atomic bombs in four days brought an end to the global war and an end to Japan's empire and ultra-modernist dream. Manchukuo, which had played such a central role in initiating this catastrophe, was returned to China. Within five years, its neighbour, Korea, returned to war and China turned to Communism. Manchukuo's fleeting tryst with modernity was swiftly overtaken by history and plunged into obscurity with the official account of modernism being penned by the victor, the west.

For the rest of China, the years between the end of the Second World War and the Communists' victory in 1949, despite the chaos, witnessed a fleeting period of architectural recovery. A new generation of Chinese architects, mirroring their Japanese counterparts at least two decades earlier, were returning home having gained professional experience with leading international modernists. The PhD student of Sir Patrick Abercrombie, Chen Zhanxiang, eventually joined Liang Sicheng on the new plan for Beijing. Wang Tan of Tsinghua University was an apprentice of Frank Lloyd Wright for much of 1948 before returning to China, where he spent his career in academia.[14] AA graduate Huang Zuoshen returned to China in 1942 and established a modernist course at St John's University where he assembled around him other friends and colleagues including fellow AA graduates AJ Brandt, Luke Him Sau and Eric Cumine. Luke was also Board Member of the Shanghai City Planning Board and put in charge of the Greater Shanghai Master Planning Department after the war, advancing Shanghai's Chinese municipal authority's earlier experience of urban planning. During the war, Cumine had been incarcerated by the Japanese at Lunghua camp on the southern outskirts of Shanghai, where he befriended the young J.G. Ballard, with whom he played chess. With the war's end in sight, he cautioned presciently, 'Jamie, you'll miss Lunghua when you leave'.[15] Luke and Cumine remained friends and architectural colleagues in Hong Kong in later years.

From 1943 to 1945, Yang Tingbao, the most celebrated Chinese architectural student from the University of Pennsylvania and partner of the firm Kwan, Chu & Yang, toured Europe, America and Canada to study the influence of industrialisation on architecture and to learn more about the Modern Movement.[16] Ever since his design for Shenyang railway station in the early 1920s, Yang was associated with the Beaux-Arts, but he had wanted to produce something modern – it was the client who demanded a classical design, and so, according to official history, 'suddenly Yang Tingbao became a young Beaux-Arts master'.[17] Years later, during the Second World War, Yang visited Wright at Taliesin, whom he respected because of his appreciation for Chinese spatial philosophy.[18] Upon his return to China, Yang designed the China Merchants Steam Navigation Company offices (1947) and a villa for Sun Yat Sen's son, Sun Ke (1948), both in Nanjing. Both were explicitly modern in their use of materials, their construction and their appearance. Importantly, they also possessed fundamental Chinese characteristics. The design for Sun Ke's villa was, according the client's request, more internationally modern, though it possessed certain Chinese features, particularly in the way *feng shui* informed the building's south-east orientation, the placement of a screen wall immediately inside the entrance and consideration of light and shade.

The China Merchants Steam Navigation Company was inspired as much by traditional Chinese building as it was by international modernism. Unlike other 'Chinese Renaissance' buildings, with their emotive surface decoration and Chinese roofs, Yang's design draws on Chinese forms in abstraction. The façade was broad, symmetrical and tapered to its peak, echoing a conventional hipped roofline. Concrete columns formed a regular frame that defined the bays by protruding from the semi-solid, semi-transparent, screen walls. The continuous balconies created deep eaves around the building, which climaxed at their corners where the protruding rounded ends evoked upturned eaves. The square plan formed by a grid of 36 rounded columns created 25 equal portions in a manner identical to the *jian*, the basic spatial unit created by the time-honoured wooden frame of traditional Chinese buildings.

Like many of his colleagues who chose to stay in China after 1949, Yang assumed a senior academic position as Head of the Architecture Department of Nanjing University and remained in education throughout the rest of his career. Liang Sicheng became Head of the newly established Department of Architecture at Tsinghua University in Beijing in 1945. His colleague Liu Dunzhen became Head of the Department of Architecture at Central University in Nanjing. AA graduate Huang Zuoshen taught at Tongji University's Architectural Department.

296 *Architecture and modernity*

For those architects who remained in practice under the new Communist regime, most joined the national body for architects and engineers, United. China's architectural profession went from being a multinational community operating in an intra-national setting under multiple and relatively weak administrations to an exclusively monocultural community operating in a national setting under a single and strong political authority.

Members of United included the founders of Allied Architects, Zhao Shen and Chen Zhi. Zhao joined in 1951 before becoming Chief Engineer of the China Eastern Architectural Design Company.[19] His former partner, Chen, also remained in the Shanghai region, working with China Eastern Architectural Design Company, then the Shanghai Urban Planning Bureau and the Shanghai Domestic Architectural Design Institute. Allied Architects' third partner, Tong Jun, also joined United, before becoming a Professor in the Architectural Department of Nanjing's Technical University. The German graduate, Xi Fuquan, also joined United, later becoming Senior Engineer in the Design Institute of the Ministry of Light Industry. Yang Xiliu, the architect of Paramount Ballroom, also joined United before being appointed Chief Architect of Beijing's Urban Planning Management Bureau Design Institute. Dong Dayou became Chief Engineer in various government positions in northern China before returning south later in his career to be Chief Engineer to Zhejiang province's Industrial Architecture Design Institute.[20]

While many architects stayed in China after 1949, many settled in Hong Kong along with other artists and writers.[21] Colonial Hong Kong was the first and, in many cases, final destination for many of China's migrant modernists. The modernist writer Mu Shiying 'joked about this cultural backwater'[22] that China's modernists now called home. Their arrival caused what Lee describes as the 'Shanghainization' of Hong Kong[23] and was part of a mass migration from mainland China that caused Hong Kong's population to double in size from 1 to 2 million from 1945 to 1950. By 1961 it reached 3.1m.[24] Shanghai's loss was Hong Kong's gain, although in modernist terms Hong Kong always 'remained a poor copy of the fabled metropolis'.[25]

Nearly sixty Chinese architects migrated to Hong Kong around 1949.[26] The sudden and massive increase transformed the colony's architectural fraternity from a professional community dominated by western practitioners to one in which Chinese architects became the majority almost overnight. Many of Hong Kong's émigré architects who had been actively involved in the constitution of China's architectural community over the preceding decades found themselves at the vanguard of its reconstitution in their new home.

Fan Wenzhao, the first Chinese architectural graduate of the University of Pennsylvania, had registered in Hong Kong in 1938 and left China in 1949 to set up a private practice with his two sons. Chen Rongzhi, the architect of Guangzhou's tallest building, crossed the border to Hong Kong after 1949. Zhu Bin, the first Chinese architectural student to have enrolled at the University of Pennsylvania and partner of Kwan, Chu & Yang, registered in Hong Kong in 1949, where he re-established the old firm and ran their Hong Kong office. His other partner, Guan Songsheng, graduate of MIT, went to Taiwan after 1949 and continued to run the firm's offices in Taipei.

The experiences of Kwan, Chu & Yang mirrored those of Five United (see Figure 7.17), whose fate was a microcosm of China's architectural community and the nation's intelligentsia more broadly. Political persuasion, patriotism and pragmatism, or a combination of all three, determined their destination as China's architects, artists, writers and scholars were scattered to the corners of the globe. Huang Zuoshen and Chen Zhanxiang chose to stay in China, while Wang Dahong, Zhen Guanxuan and Luke Him Sau went to Hong Kong. Wang later moved to Taiwan.

Luke Him Sau had registered in Hong Kong in 1948, but he had been persuaded by his old friend and colleague, Liang Sicheng (who by now was working in Beijing with Chen), to give Communism a try, as the new government had appeared receptive to his ideas about architectural research and preservation. Luke returned to China in late 1949 after the official inauguration of the Communist Party on 1 October, but after six months another old friend convinced him to leave. For the fifth time in his life Luke had to make a complete break with the past and start anew, returning to Hong Kong in 1950 where he established his own practice, PAPRO (Progressive Architecture, Planning & Research Organisation).

In 1956, Luke was among a founding group of 27 colleagues who established the Hong Kong Society of Architects. The first President was the Chinese émigré, Xu Jingzhi (1906–?), a graduate of Michigan University (1927–31) and Cranbrook Academy of Art who was apprenticed to Eliel Saarinen. After 1949, he continued a very successful career and wrote *Chinese Architecture – Past and Contemporary* (1964).

One architect whose fate exemplified China's encounter with modernity more than any other was Liang Sicheng. Most of China's early architects were internationally experienced, proud, patriotic and professionally adept. What makes Liang's case exceptional is that he not only excelled in his field, but his career illustrates the entire range of experiences that China's aspiring modern architects confronted in their lifetime and, owing to the unique circumstances of that epoch, would distinguish them from their successors.

In 1946, Liang was sent to America by the Ministry of Education 'to study the latest trends in architecture and city planning and the teaching methods on architecture in American universities'.[27] On 12 February 1947, during his six-month appointment as Visiting Professor of Fine Arts at Yale, the Permanent Headquarters Committee overseeing the planning and design of the new United Nations Headquarters in New York confirmed the nomination of a Chinese representative on the architectural advisory group. Liang's appointment placed him in an esteemed group with Le Corbusier, Niemeyer and the Director, Wallace Harrison, whose consent he sought, albeit unsuccessfully, in his promotion of Chinese principles of design and planning for the scheme (see Figure 10.1).[28] Later, upon being awarded Doctor of Letters by Princeton University, Liang humbly claimed it was 'an honour I hardly deserve. It is a reward much too high for one who did nothing more than spending a disproportionately large part of his time and energy in pursuit of perhaps the mere satisfaction of his idle curiosity'.[29]

But Liang's endeavours were no idle curiosity. Now regarded as the founder of Chinese architectural history and a champion of traditional architecture and its preservation, these labels mask the fundamental modernist in him. For Liang, research was a means to an end, not an end in itself. Without truly understanding China's traditional building methods (which he achieved through his extensive fieldwork and his decoding of the *Ying Zao Fa Shi*), there could be no basis on which to formulate a sound modern architecture that employed scientific methods and principles, espoused modern materials and constructional techniques, and that could also be considered Chinese.

298 *Architecture and modernity*

Figure 10.1 Liang Sicheng (front row third from left) with other members of the UN Permanent Headquarters Committee including Le Corbusier, Niemeyer and the Director, Wallace Harrison, in 1947.

Liang was not a prolific architect, but it is instructive to note that his two most significant designs, clearly modernist in intent, form and appearance, have received little attention (Beijing University's Geological Department (1934) and Women's Dormitory (1935)). Commenting on Liang's education at the University of Pennsylvania, Fairbank observed that a few years after his graduation:

> the Beaux Arts tradition would be supplanted by the Bauhaus-International-Style curriculum, with Walter Gropius, Mies van der Rohe and others as the influential leaders. At times in the 1930s and '40s I heard Sicheng express a wistful regret that he had just missed this induction into contemporary movements of architecture.[30]

Liang's deeper modernist sensibilities reveal themselves in his private and previously unpublished observations during his American trip. In 1946, Liang attended the bicentennial conference at Princeton University titled 'Planning Man's Built Environment', attended by an all-star all-white and (virtually) all-male cast of western modernism including Aalto, Chermayeff, Giedion, Gropius, Johnson, Neutra, Wornum and Lloyd Wright (see Figure 10.2). Besides his acquaintances with the world's great modernists at this conference and on the UN project, during which he befriended Niemeyer whom he visited in Brazil in the 1960s, one site visit caused delight and despair in equal measure. After seeing the Tennessee Valley Authority (TVA) dams, Liang wrote:

> I was able to see 3 dams and their housings in 3 days. The TVA is wonderful. Socially, economically, and architecturally. We shall need hundreds of TVA's in China. But God knows we wont get any for a long time to come[31]. . . . [The] TVA is wonderful – inspiring and enviable. But I can never be objective when

Figure 10.2 Liang Sicheng is the only non-westerner among an all-star cast of western professionals attending the bicentennial conference titled Planning Man's Built Environment, at Princeton University in 1946. Liang's peripheral cultural status is reflected in his marginal position at the end of the second row (*far left*), just as Catherine Bauer's gender might be read as the cause of her being literally sidelined at the end of the third row (*far right*), the only female among the 59 attendees.

> I look at these modern advancements. They always make me sad for I just wish that China would be some day like that. But that day is remote, perhaps a century or more away.[32]

Liang's words encapsulate the predicament confronting his intermediary generation. Liberated from the ancient traditions and Confucian codes of his reformist father's generation and able to taste modernity's promise, they were ultimately denied the chance to fully realise its potential. Parallels can be made with their Japanese counterparts, like Tange and Maekawa, whose own modernist trajectories were similarly curtailed by war and political resistance, but, unlike Liang and his Chinese colleagues, they were able to re-engage with its agenda after the war and advance its possibilities.

The freedom to pursue personal design philosophies and actively engage in related discourses lasted only a few years under Communist rule. An increasingly doctrinaire political environment extinguished independent creativity and progressive attitudes. Modernism, along with European classicism, was branded imperialist and prohibited. Even the short-lived solution of 'Chinese Renaissance', the sole-survivor of an earlier age of architectural plurality, was labelled profligate and proscribed. Independent creativity for any art practitioner was impossible, but particularly so for architects, whose work, as Feng points out in his *Garden of Art*, was distinguished from other art practices because it was 'limited by the conditions of living and therefore cannot freely create the form of beauty'.[33] The multiple fractures that modernity faced in China are summarised by Clarke in the context of the artist, Teng Baiye, whose experience paralleled that of China's architects after 1949:

Tragically, the Japanese invasion and the subsequent civil war thwarted his artistic efforts just as they were starting to come to fruition . . . the unsympathetic cultural environment of the years that followed never let him renew his artistic endeavours. . . . When celebrating the possibilities of this present era of globalisation, it is perhaps not without value to recognise how globalised cultural connections could already be in a much earlier era . . . those connections [in Teng Baiye's case] were furthermore a two-way affair.[34]

The contraction and eventual demise of China's multifaceted modernities can be seen both internally in the way it impacted upon the Chinese and externally in the way it impacted on relationships between China and the rest of the world. Despite his extraordinary devotion to his profession and to his country, Liang's professional experiences, beliefs and affiliations caused him great suffering during the Great Proletarian Cultural Revolution along with many other modernists of his generation, many of whom, out of fear of persecution, destroyed their work.

The poet, dramatist and author of the Chinese National Anthem, *March of the Volunteers*, Tian Han, was imprisoned and died in the Cultural Revolution. Teng Baiye, owing to 'his association with the Nationalist government . . . suffer[ed] quite severely'.[35] Lao She, the writer who had been in London and penned *Er Ma*, committed suicide on 24 August 1966 at the height of the Cultural Revolution by drowning himself in a lake in Beijing aged 67 following prolonged humiliation by the Red Guards. UCL graduate Chen Zhanxiang, who had worked with Liang on the Beijing Plan, had bought flight tickets to Hong Kong but the night before he was due to leave witnessed the People's Liberation Army's arrival in Nanjing and was so impressed by their conduct he tore up the tickets and stayed. In 1957, when the Communist Party set about purging its ranks in the Party Rectification campaign, Chen was singled out for criticism. On 24 July, as the 'Anti-Rightest Campaign' got underway, a headline in the *Beijing Daily* announced: 'Hit back the evil attack towards the Party by the architectural right wing – condemn the anti-socialist words and behaviour of Chen Zhanxiang.' It was the start of a long nightmare for Chen. He was forced to confess his alleged crimes and the following year was sent to the countryside for re-education. Burdened by endless labour and criticism, he frequently contemplated suicide. Throughout their ordeals, Chen and Liang never contacted one another until just weeks before Liang's death. Huang Zuoshen, Chen's fellow partner from Five United, faced re-education and such harsh criticism that Tongji University, for whom he worked, officially apologised to his family in 1978. Huang had died in June 1975.

Some architects fared better. The jazz-loving founder of Allied Architects, Chen Zhi, remained in the Shanghai region working in the Urban Planning Bureau and other government institutions. When out sketching one day, his partner at Allied Architects, Tong Jun, is alleged to have been detained by the authorities in Beijing on suspicion of spying. Tong Jun never designed another building, but became a highly respected Professor in the Architectural Department of Nanjing's Institute of Technology (later Southeast University), where he was joined by the Japanese-trained Liu Dunzhen and fellow University of Pennsylvania graduate, Yang Tingbao. Yang was not only an exceptional architect, but also a skilled politician, becoming Vice Governor of Jiangsu Province.

Liang Sicheng and his wife, Lin Huiyin, remained in Beijing where they designed the Monument for the People's Heroes in Tiananmen Square and the national emblem featuring Tiananmen Gate within a gold wreath on a red background and the five stars that feature on the national flag. Having dedicated his life to architectural research, Liang's Plan for Beijing with Chen Zhanxiang was among his boldest and bravest achievements. But his architectural ideals and passion for traditional Chinese building attracted widespread criticism in the 1950s 'Antis' campaigns. Liang was accused of promoting architectural waste and decadence and by 1955 was admitted to hospital with exhaustion. His wife, Lin Huiyin, by then very sick with tuberculosis, joined him in an adjacent room. Lin died on 1 April 1955.

Liang later returned to teaching at Tsinghua University's Architecture Department and even remarried. Throughout the late 1950s he represented China at UIA conferences in Poland, Czechoslovakia, East Germany, Moscow, Cuba, Mexico and Brazil. His final overseas trip was to Paris in 1965, after which he faced more criticisms in the Great Proletarian Cultural Revolution. In a letter from Liang and Lin's close friend Wilma Fairbank to Chen Zhi years later, she quotes Liang's second wife, Lin Zhu, as saying that 'despite the attacks and Cultural Revolution miseries SC [Sicheng] suffered he never lost faith in the New China'.[36] Chen viewed things less rosily, claiming that Liang died on 9 January 1972 'a disillusioned man, bewildered by "accusations" piled upon him', confiding in Chen on his death-bed, 'I am now notorious all over China'.[37] In 1986, as Tsinghua's Architecture Department jointly celebrated its 40th anniversary and Liang's 85th birthday, the President acknowledged the criticisms and suffering that Liang had endured during the Cultural Revolution and that these had 'worsened his physical condition and wrecked his health'.[38]

Having declared their allegiance to China, the consolation for China's architects that were stripped of their dignity during the political convulsions that rocked their country throughout the 1950s and 1960s was a place in official history. In contrast, the work of their exiled friends and former colleagues has been comparatively obscured by history's march. In Chinese literature, Laurence recognises this in the context of China's relationship with England and the way in which 'the cultural and aesthetic movement of modernism . . . have been neglected in literary and cultural studies because of complicated cultural and sexual politics'.[39] And western appreciation of the activities of Chinese artists has suffered also. When Liang died, his obituary in *The Times* newspaper summarised his extraordinary life in just two sentences. Despite all he had achieved domestically and internationally (and in the face of such adversity), his contribution amounted to less than a footnote in history, remembered merely as 'well-known as a writer on architectural matters'.[40] If, as has been previous stated, multiple modernities make us 'aware of how narrow many of our perspectives on the past have been',[41] few examples better support its case than the inaccuracy and enormity of this understatement.

Reconstructing China's encounter with modernity is uniquely complicated because so many characters have been omitted, neglected or overlooked. Identifying the 'missing actors and their various feats',[42] as Jencks describes in relation to modernism's peripheral protagonists, is part of the problem; but in China's case the bigger problem once they have been found is to locate them within a wider and unfamiliar landscape outside the west.

302 Architecture and modernity

Eileen Chang, despite being considered one of the most outstanding modernist writers of her generation, lived out the rest of her life in obscurity in America. Only in death after Ang Lee turned *Lust Caution* into a Hollywood blockbuster has due regard been paid to her talent internationally. Chang Yu (aka Sanyu), the able painter who befriended Picasso, spent the rest of his life in poverty in America, yet today his paintings are highly prized.[43] Teng Baiye, despite the significant impact he had on the father of American abstract art, Mark Tobey, is largely ignored not only in China but also in the west, where it remains 'little more than a name in the English language art history record' and even this is 'difficult to pin down with certainty' since, as Clarke highlights, there are up to eight different ways of spelling it in English.[44] Liu Jipiao, the architect and artist who designed the Chinese Section of the 1925 Paris Exposition, fled China for America with his family in 1947, leaving behind his three homes, his wealth and his possessions, including his artwork. Unable to practise architecture, Liu opened a laundry, suffered depression and went bankrupt, though he later managed to salvage an artistic and architectural career, which is at last receiving due recognition due to the efforts of surviving family members.[45]

The predicament of China's first modernist art practitioners, a small and elite bunch though they were, is summed up by Julia Andrews when citing the example of the modernist artist, Sanyu, whose life experience mirrors those of his contemporaries in architecture:

> History played countless cruel jokes on Chinese artists of the twentieth century, and the fate of Sanyu and his art was that of his tragic, if talented, generation ... [the] bureaucratic policies of the early People's Republic of China declared artists of both modernist and traditionalist orientation to be taboo, and purged them from the canon of contemporary art. In the Maoist era, the histories of art were written as though these artists, many of them China's most innovative, had never existed. And finally, many paintings and documents that survived the perils of the 1930s, 40s, and 50s were destroyed during the Cultural Revolution, and anyone tainted by foreign experiences marked as a traitor. China's cosmopolitan artistic period, the era of Sanyu's greatest success, was ripped out of the record.[46]

The meaning of modern

The question of modernism's curtailment in China is predicated on an assumption that modernism in China even existed. To assume the western interpretation of 'modernism' is to accept that modernism did not exist in China or, if it did, it was diluted and inferior, and terminated when all foreign influence was extinguished after 1949. Such a view would demonstrate ' "the winner's story" of the history of modernity',[47] as Harding describes it, which has become entrenched after more than a century of western hegemony. If we make China's encounter with architectural modernity the subject of Eisenstadt's question: 'Are the concepts developed in western social science, and above all in the social-scientific literature on modernity and modernization, adequate for the analysis of these historical experiences?' the answer must be 'no'.[48] China's experience denies the notion of a singular expression of modernism and the modernisation theories and cultural programs of modernity on which it relies, as well as (to a lesser extent) the application of post-colonial theories precisely because these theories fail to provide an adequate or accurate means of examining or understanding the three central and interrelated topics of *architecture, modernity* and *China*. In China's context, historical facts have been omitted and distorted to fit the theory, rather than the theory being constructed around all the facts.

The inadequacy of established westerncentric theories in tackling subjects outside established western contexts is increasingly recognised, as more and more attention is concentrated on such topics. Hosagrahar's work on Delhi offers one example, where westerncentricity has motivated him 'to reclaim a history of a city that has been denied modernity'.[49] Harding's intellectual engagements in the context of science, feminism and modernity provide another example, where endemic Eurocentricism in the west 'has obscured these histories even from the sight of the most progressive scholars in the west'.[50] O'Connor identified similar shortcomings in the 1980s in the context of urban studies in Asia, where he saw that 'while urban life [was] embedded in indigenous meanings, urban studies [were] imbedded in western meanings'.[51] In the context of India, Chakrabarty's effort to 'provincialize Europe'[52] is another pioneering example. All are kindred themes in an emergent intellectual landscape encapsulated by the theory of multiple modernities, which contends 'the best way to understand the contemporary world, indeed the history of modernity, is to see it as a story of continual development and formation, constitution, and reconstitution of multiple, changing and often contested and conflicting modernities'.[53]

Just as multiple modernities challenges conventional notions of how the world has changed in the twentieth century, this study seeks to challenge conventional interpretations of how China's architecture developed during the early twentieth century. Framed this way, modernism in China not only becomes a legitimate object of study, but opens up multiple lines of enquiry, most of which are yet to be fully explored or reframed. This study has drawn attention to aspects of China's architectural history that would once have been regarded as peripheral, nationally and internationally, but, on the contrary, turn out to be critical in understanding what constitutes architectural modernism in the most populous and urbanised society (numerically) in history: the notion of quasi-colonialism, the role of Japan, the nationalist discourse, Shanghai's singularity and architecture's relationship with other modern art practices.

Multidisciplinarity, complexity and heterogeneity – all inevitable facets of a multiple modernities approach – are less daunting for many scholars outside the west (and, increasingly, in the west) who live with the evidence of plurality and who have instinctively questioned theories of modernisation promoted by western intellectuals 'who typically know nothing of non-European thought'.[54] China's modernist art practitioners, such as Liang Sicheng, Chen Zhi, Yang Tingbao, Tong Jun, Luke Him Sau, Liu Jipiao, Lin Huiyin, Ling Shuhua, Teng Baiye, Sanyu, Eileen Chang and many others who are too numerous to name or detail, were more than accustomed to this cultural bias, or, as Chakrabarty describes it, 'asymmetric ignorance',[55] since their encounters with modernity required them to become fully acquainted with western language and culture. In contrast, their western colleagues seldom, if ever, made any equivalent effort to acquaint themselves with the Chinese language and culture. Those who did, through graft or good fortune, such as the British architect Wells Coates, born and raised in Japan, bear testimony to the benefits of being able to see 'both sides'. Coates quoted someone as saying 'The man whose eyes have been trained in the east will only rarely want to open them in the west',[56] and later in life claimed 'the background of Japanese culture and my early "eastern" training had been sufficiently dove-tailed ... into my "western" scientific training', which finds expression in his modernist designs, especially his furniture.[57] Although modernity was mediated on strictly western terms, it was those outside the west in being able to see and comprehend different cultural perspectives that ultimately enjoyed the richer experience. The same holds true today.

As the territories formerly appropriated by the west have mostly regained political, if not economic, independence, the intellectual and creative processes of this appropriation are also yielding ground. Evidence of China's architectural encounter with modernity serves as one example of how European ideas of modernism are being forced to give way to notions that place it not wholly within Europe's sphere of influence. This might seem a grandiose ambition, but the process is well underway in settings outside the west and, as yet, mostly outside architecture.[58] The aim, therefore, is not, as Sarkar observes, to contribute to the 'decline of the subaltern from *Subaltern studies*'[59] or, as Hosagrahar puts it, 'to celebrate and give voice to minority discourses and knowledges in order to include them in their subordinate positions into existing privileged accounts of modernity, *but to question the very master narrative*' (author's italics).[60] Rather than interpreting China's distinction as a form of 'alternative modernity', as others have sought to do, this study views it as part of a reconceptualisation of the same phenomenon: not seeing something different, but seeing the same thing differently.

Since multiple modernities enable us to see that 'western patterns of modernity are not the only "authentic" modernities',[61] China's example allows us to see further still, something that was understood by Chinese intellectuals in the early twentieth century. Liang Qichao consistently separated modernisation from westernisation, as did many Chinese reformers who identified a role for Confucianism in modern China that even the pro-western May Fourth Movement was not able to eliminate. For most outside the west, the assumption that modernisation equates to westernisation has always been questionable, but it is increasingly seen as theoretically and intellectually bankrupt. *Eating Rice* (*Chi Fan*) by Zhang Youluan and published in 1933 in the final edition of the journal by the modern Shanghai-based literary group, *The Creation Society*, is one example of China's resistance to capitulate to outright westernisation in its search for modernity:

> Westerners persuade me to go to the west. They say, when you get to the west you will change, because you will be westernised. But I don't believe the west will change me and I will be changed permanently and become the same as the west! Today I sit by the table; the tools I use to eat bread are chopsticks.[62]

Resisting the reconceptualisation of global encounters with modernity is not merely unsustainable; it denies the greater rewards that come with adopting a wider view of history. Historians therefore need to 'become far more sensitive to the culturally specific character of historical phenomena and societal processes' to avoid 'the grand narratives in history' that tend to construct simplistic depictions of historical processes.[63] Stepping outside the comfort of the west into an *other*, just like China's modern architects did in reverse, rather than undermining or diluting the experience, enriches and augments it. As westerncentric perspectives recede from their high-water mark in the second half of the twentieth century, the intellectual landscape that is revealed is one made rich from contributions beyond the west. Exploration of this intellectually abundant terrain, in China's context, has been most evident in the realms of art and literature, since the 1970s. The same cannot be said in architecture, but things are changing.

Architecture did not influence western modernism in the way some other Chinese art practices did in their respective fields, and it still lags behind studies of other practices where China encountered modernity, for two reasons in particular. First, unlike art and literature, architecture can be said to be a 'slow' art, protracted in its materialisation and thus belated in its critique. Second, architecture especially in China was rarely associated with other cultural pursuits. Feng Zikai's magnanimity in accepting architecture's admission in his *Garden of Art* at all went against a general reluctance in China to regard architecture as an art form, not least because of its craft-based traditions and its formulaic role in ordering society.

Architecture's relative neglect in twentieth-century Chinese culture can be seen as both a blessing and a curse. Architecture's late development in China meant that the generation of Chinese architects who first encountered modernism from the late 1920s, unlike other artists (whose own encounters occurred at least one decade earlier), were disconnected from a formal Confucian education and had all received overseas training, liberating them from cultural and artistic precedent to a greater degree than their colleagues in other art practices. This also meant that they were not able to benefit from a phase of development in their own profession that, for example, their Japanese counterparts had enjoyed. Isozaki explains that Japan's architectural community, having already divided in the early twentieth century, experienced further splits in the 1920s fuelled by modernist sympathies where young architects 'loudly attacked the prevailing use of historical styles . . . as superficial and dishonest'.[64] The 'first generation' of Chinese architects, small in number and versed primarily in engineering, was neither numerically nor professionally sufficient to provide a foundation from which to cultivate a comparably mature modern architectural discourse before the Second World War. Critical discourses in Chinese architecture only started to emerge in the 1930s, when they were aired in local and national publications such as *The Chinese Architect* and *The Builder*, leaving the historian with comparatively little to work with, while China's subsequent experiences that have scattered evidence across the world have produced a maze of distorting mirrors that make the piecing together of an accurate historical record particularly challenging.

Architecturally, although modernity's physical and theoretical components, and their accompanying terminology, were prescribed by foreigners, for the Chinese this only ever represented a temporary phase in the realisation of a true Chinese modernity, whereby, as one architect writing in 1935 put it, the 'gradual education of the less experienced or inappropriate ones [architects] would finally wash off the "western" and "popular" smell' that lingered in their work.[65] The sentiment is echoed by Yang Tingbao's architect son, Yang Shixuan: 'we have to digest it [the profession of architecture] very carefully and better understand its value, finally absorbing it to form our own modern architecture. This is the real Chinese modernity.'[66] Seventy years early, Tong Jun of Allied Architects put it most succinctly: 'in all the great epochs of Chinese architecture, the spirit remained distinctly Chinese, no matter how much foreign influence it had assimilated'.[67]

Marshall Berman famously stated:

> To be modern is to find ourselves in an environment that promises us adventure, power, joy, growth, transformation of ourselves and the world – and, at the same time, that threatens to destroy everything we have, everything we know, everything we are.

Such was the experience of China's modern architects, the first in China's history to experience the exhilarating rush of modernity's promise, but also aware of the likely annihilation of ancient building traditions. Like their literary and artistic colleagues, they found themselves, as Gaonkar describes, 'carried in the intoxicating rush of an epochal change and yet fixed and formulated by a disciplinary system of social roles and functions'.[68]

In this context, they join the ranks of Gaonkar's century-long list of modernist combatants: Marx's 'revolutionary', Baudelaire's 'dandy', Nietzsche's 'superman', Weber's 'social scientist', Simmel's 'stranger', Musil's 'man without qualities' and Benjamin's 'flaneur'.[69]

As agents of change in a modernist landscape defined less by the west than by multiple global characteristics, the architectural solutions that China's early modern architects arrived at, such as the 'Chinese Renaissance' style, regardless of their actual architectural merit, can be seen as manifestations of modernity just as much as Hudec's Joint Savings Society building or any other structure evincing the modernist aesthetic prescribed by the west. As Hosagrahar observes in the case of Delhi, 'the emergent built forms, their use and meanings, though not identical to the ones idealized in western Europe, were nevertheless modern'.[70] Modernism in Chinese architecture did not mean that it had to become like the west. As manufactured tradition, the 'Chinese Renaissance' style was part of 'an intellectual search and emotional yearning'[71] that was a hallmark of modernity because it was an invention of modernity – proof of what Baudelaire refers to as the 'thrilling originality' resulting from nature and the 'tyranny of circumstance'.[72]

Supplementing these indigenous deliberations were the more numerous architectural outputs by both foreign and Chinese architects that were often more adroit in negotiating and articulating modernity, functionally and aesthetically. Notable examples include the works of Allied Architects, Fan Wenzhao, Fraser, Hudec, Léonard & Veysseyre, Luke Him Sau, Palmer & Turner, and Yang Tingbao, as well as the considerable Japanese outputs in the imperial context of Manchuria.

As evidence of China's first modern architectural encounters, the buildings erected throughout China were a constant reminder that 'modernity does not dissolve traditions, but rather that they serve as resources for modernity's perceptual constitution and reconstitution'.[73] The architectural legacies of China's former foreign settlements and colonial cities have impacted on the subsequent evolution of architecture and urban planning of these urban settings, not only by constituting the historic cores of many of China's twenty-first-century cities, but in other ways too – such as in Harbin's continued referencing of art nouveau; Shanghai's fondness of the high-rise and geometric ornament; Changchun's adherence to low-density urbanism combining the picturesque; Qingdao's Teutonic classicism; and Beijing's loyalty to the Chinese 'style' are all examples of modernity's continuous constitution and reconstitution.

These developments might have started out as western constructs, but they have become part of a tradition that informs China's contemporary encounters with modernity, encounters that are now informed by local characteristics and traditions that prevent their interpretation merely as part of a homogenised western or global phenomenon. Many of these traits, such as urban planning, spatial arrangements, symbolic meaning, construction techniques, were all encountered and grappled with by China's first architects but historical amnesia has caused China's rapid growth since the late twentieth century to be depicted largely as western, novel and unprecedented, and the interventions of foreign architects represented as pioneering. Nothing could be further from the truth.

Behind China's recent developments lie not only a century of modernist encounters (albeit interrupted and only now slowly being rediscovered), but also four millennia of continuous building traditions that are among the richest sources for modernist reconstitution available to any architectural community anywhere, or, as Xu Jinzhi wrote, 'the only one that has retained its oldest form with little modification and has enjoyed the longest continuous historical prestige'.[74] It is in this respect that China once again demonstrates its distinction. The sheer weight of cultural precedent imposed by this constructional longevity dominated China's first encounter with architectural modernity in the early twentieth century and continues to do so in the twenty-first century. The issue will likely remain the most contentious and unresolved element of modern Chinese architecture.

An unpublished dialogue between Wilma Fairbank and one of China's leading early modern architects and partner of Allied Architects, Chen Zhi, on the subject of China's most famous architect and modernist icon, I.M. Pei, offers an apt conclusion. The relevance of this exchange lies in the protagonists' representativeness of the critical themes dominating this study. Chen represents those Chinese architects who first encountered the problem of reconciling the country's building traditions with the modern discipline of architecture. Fairbank represents the foreign element so critical to China's first encounter with modernity. Pei is the exemplar that links China's pre-1949 architects with a truly international modernity. Collectively, they encapsulate *architecture*, *modernity* and *China*.

In a letter to Fairbank written in 1985 referring to Pei's receipt of an Honorary Professorship at Shanghai's Tongji University, Chen remarked of Pei's work, internationally celebrated for apparently successfully marrying Chinese tradition with modernity:

> the hotel he designed in Fragrant Hill, Peking, has spoiled the scenic spot (the hotel simply *sprawls* over the hill). The high-rise he designed for the Bank of China in Hongkong does not bear the slightest trace of Chinese architectural characteristic which the Bank of China building rightfully demands. I say all this not to underrate him. He is universally recognised as one of the most eminent architects of today and is the pride of America and China alike. But prominent people are not immune from faults.[75]

Chen's views encapsulate the unresolved issues surrounding China's encounter with architectural modernity and in its ongoing interpretation. They also prove that their resolution has eluded even the most accomplished practitioners, but perhaps not for much longer.

Notes

1. Letter from Lin Huiyin to Wilma Fairbank, 10 February 1936 upon receiving a copy of the American journal, *Theatre Arts Monthly*, Peabody Essex Museum, Salem, Massachusetts.
2. Andrews and Shen, 1998, p. 173.
3. Brooke and Davis, 1932, p. 107.
4. Letter from Lin Huiyin to Wilma Fairbank, November/December 1935, Peabody Essex Museum, Salem, Massachusetts.
5. Harootunian, 2000, p. 112.
6. These were part of the global phenomenon of urbanisation that saw urban populations rise from 313m. to 655m. in the 1950s (McGee, 1967, p. 15) and fundamentally new urban types through design or scale – e.g. Brasilia, Chandigarh, Mexico, Hong Kong, Tokyo and Singapore.
7. Shih, 2001, p. 150.
8. Shi, 1990, p. 139. Interestingly, he goes on to say that 'At the beginning I thought this only happens in China, then I discovered it is the same everywhere', citing also the Soviet Union.
9. Shih, 2001, p. 276.
10. Shih, 2001, pp. 145–6.
11. Laurence, 2003, p. 209.
12. Ling Shuhua, *Ancient Melodies*, Hogarth Press, London, 1953.
13. Andrews, 2004 (unpaginated). See: http://asianart.com/exhibitions/sanyu/andrews.html, accessed 9 July 2010
14. Wang Tan was one of the principal Chinese partners in the Japanese survey of historical architecture sponsored by Toyota (*Zhong Guo Jin Dai Jian Zhu Zong Lan* (*Overview of Modern (pre-1949) Architecture in China*), 1992), which remains the most comprehensive survey of early modern Chinese architecture.
15. Ballard, 2008, p. 81.
16. This was revealed in an email from Yang Tingbao's son, Yang Shixuan, to the author, 1 January 2010, 12.08am.
17. Email from Yang Shixuan to the author, 22 December 2009, 04.01am.
18. Scholars often cite Wright's acknowledgement of the Chinese philosopher, Laotse's, description of the vacuum in Okakura's *Book of Tea* as a metaphor for defining space as proof of his knowledge of and debt to Japanese design, but Isozaki claims this to be erroneous: 'Wright misinterpreted this key issue not as omnipresent emptiness, but as a teleologically constructed internal space' (Isozaki, 2006, p. 3).
19. Zhao later moved to the Central Design Institute and then to the Shanghai Industrial Architectural Design Institute.
20. Lai, 2006.
21. Dai Wangshu had arrived in Hong Kong in 1936, followed by Guo Moruo, Mao Dun, Shi Zhecun, Yu Dafu, and Xiao Qian. In 1938, following his eviction from the League of Left-wing Writers, Ye Lingfeng arrived, the same year as the poet Xu Chi, who was best man at Dai's wedding (Lee, 1999, pp. 328–30).
22. Lee, 1999, p. 328.
23. Lee, 1999, p. 328.
24. D.J. Dwyer, 'The Problem of In-Migration and Squatter Settlement in Asian Cities: Two Case Studies, Manila and Victoria-Kowloon' in Yeung and Lo, 1976, p. 135.
25. Lee, 1999, p. 328.
26. Haoyu Wang, 'Mainland Architects in Hong Kong after 1949: A Bifurcated History of Modern Chinese Architecture', PhD Thesis, University of Hong Kong, 2008. Wang states that although architects began leaving for Hong Kong in the 1930s, the vast majority departed between around 1949 with 52 leaving China for Hong Kong from 1945 to 1950.
27. Letter from Liang Sicheng to Prof. George Rowley (of Princeton University), 11 July 1946 (Fairbank family archive).

28 The war had taken its toll on the 45-year-old Liang, who is described by Harrison's biographer as 'a frail-looking professor of architecture' (Newhouse, 1989, p. 116).
29 Quoted in Wilma Fairbank's typed notes (Fairbank family archive).
30 Fairbank, 1994, p. 26.
31 Letter from Liang Sicheng to Wilma Fairbank from Fort Wayne, 5 July 1947, Peabody Essex Museum, Salem, Massachusetts.
32 Letter from Liang Sicheng to Wilma Fairbank from Ann Arbor, 6 July 1947, Peabody Essex Museum, Salem, Massachusetts.
33 Feng, 1990, p. 37.
34 Clarke, 2004, p. 103.
35 Clarke, 2004, p. 102.
36 Letter from Wilma Fairbank to Chen Zhi, 11 December 1987, Fairbank Family Archive.
37 Letter from Chen Zhi to Wilma Fairbank, 22 June 1988.
38 Letter from Chen Zhi to Wilma Fairbank, 23 November 1986, Fairbank Family Archive. Chen was surprised that the President 'openly declared that the criticism in 1957 . . . and the sufferings he [Liang] endured during the Cultural Revolution', in the President's words, 'worsened his physical condition and wrecked his health'.
39 Laurence, 2003, p. 388.
40 *The Times*, 10 January 1972.
41 'Preface', *Dædalus*, Winter 2000, p. vii.
42 Jencks, 1980, p. 11.
43 The most recent sale of one of Sanyu's paintings, in a Hong Kong auction house in October 2009, sold for $4.7m., 'considered cheap' by the gallery owner.
44 Clarke, 2004, p. 84. The Frye Art Museum in Seattle held an exhibition on Mark Tobey and Teng Baiye from 22 February to 25 May 2014 curated by Jo-Anne Birnie Danzker and Scott Lawrimore. Available at: http://fryemuseum.org/exhibition/5450, accessed 13 May 2010.
45 For more details, see: http://liujipiao.com
46 Andrews, 2004 (unpaginated). See: http://asianart.com/exhibitions/sanyu/andrews.html, accessed 9 July 2010.
47 Harding, 2008, p. 188.
48 Eisenstadt and Schluchter, 'Introduction: Paths to Early Modernities – A Comparative View' in *Dædalus*, Summer 1998, p. 7.
49 Hosagrahar, 2005, p. 1.
50 Harding, 2008, p. 188.
51 O'Connor, 1983, p. 2.
52 Chakrabarty, 2000.
53 Sachsenmaier and Riedel, 2002, pp. 2–3.
54 Maeda and Fujii, 2004, pp. 4–5.
55 Chakrabarty, 2000, p. 28.
56 Cantacuzino, 1978, p. 11.
57 Cantacuzino, 1978, p. 14. See also Darling, 2012.
58 For example, Harding, 2008; Sadria, 2007; Scriver and Prakash, 2007; Hosagrahar, 2005; Eisenstadt, 2003; Lau, 2003; Sachsenmaier and Riedel, 2002; Tu, 2000; Gaonkar, 2001; and Harootunian, 2000.
59 Sumit Sarkar, in Chakrabarty, 2000, p. xv.
60 Hosagrahar, 2005, p. 5.
61 Eisenstadt, 'Some Observations on Multiple Modernities' in Sachsenmaier and Riedel, 2002, p. 27.
62 Zhang Youluan, 'Chi Fan' ('Eating Rice') in *Chuang Zao Ri Hui Kan* (*Collective Works of the Creation Day*), *Chuang Zao She* (*The Creation Society*), Guang Hua Shu Ju, Shanghai, 1933, pp. 40–1.
63 Eisenstadt *et al.*, 'The Context of the Multiple Modernities Paradigm' in Sachsenmaier and Riedel, 2002, p. 7.
64 Isozaki, 2006, p. 4.
65 Du, 1935, p. 26.

66 Author's email correspondence with Yang Shixuan, 26 February 2010, 11.11pm.
67 Tong, 1938, p. 410.
68 Berman, 1982, p. 15.
69 Gaonkar, 2001, p. 3.
70 Hosagrahar, 2005, p. 2.
71 Sachsenmaier, 'Multiple Modernities – The Concept and its Potential' in Sachsenmaier and Riedel, 2002, p. 46.
72 Baudelaire, 1964, p. 15.
73 Eisenstadt *et al.*, 'The Context of the Multiple Modernities Paradigm' in Sachsenmaier and Riedel, 2002, p. 10.
74 Su, 1964, p. 1.
75 Letter from Chen Zhi to Wilma Fairbank, 18 October 1985, Fairbank family archive.

Bibliography

Acton, Harold, *Memoirs of an Aesthete*, Methuen, London, 1948.
Alexander, William, *Picturesque Representations of the Dress and Manners of the Chinese*, W. Bulmer & Co., London, 1814.
Alofsin, Anthony, ed., *Frank Lloyd Wright: Europe and Beyond*, University of California Press, Berkeley, CA, 1999.
Andersen, Meyer & Co. Ltd of China – March 1906 to March 1931, Kelly & Walsh, Shanghai, 1931.
Anderson, Benedict, *Imagined Communities: Reflections on the Origin and Spread of Nationalism*, Verso Editions, New York and London, 1983.
Andrews, Julia, 'Sanyu and the Shanghai Modernists', essay accompanying the exhibition *Sanyu l'écriture du corps* in *Les étés de la modernity*, 16 June to 13 September 2004.
Andrews, Julia F. and Shen Kuiyi, *A Century in Crisis: Modernity and Tradition in the Art of Twentieth Century China*, Guggenheim Museum, New York, 1998.
Appadurai, Arjun, *Modernity at Large: Cultural Dimensions of Globalization*, University of Minnesota Press, Minneapolis, MN, 1996.
Appleton, William W., *A Cycle of Cathay: The Chinese Vogue in England during the Seventeenth and Eighteenth Centuries*, Columbia University Press, New York, 1951.
Arkush, David and Leo Ou-fan Lee, trans. and eds, *Land Without Ghosts: Chinese Impressions of America from the mid-Nineteenth Century to the Present*, University of California Press, Berkeley, CA, 1989.
Attiret, Jean Denis, *A Letter from a French Missionary in China*, Beijing, 1 November 1743.
Au, David, 'Shanghai Department Stores Have a Unique History of their Founding', *China Weekly Review*, Millard Publishing House, Shanghai, 17 November 1934.
Bakich, Olga, 'Emigré Identity: The Case of Harbin', *South Atlantic Quarterly*, Vol. 99, No. 1, 2000.
Ballard, J.G., *Miracles of Life: Shanghai to Shepperton*, 4th Estate, London, 2008.
Baronti, Gerve, 'Peking, A Memory', *The China Journal*, Vol. 3, No. 12, China Society of Arts and Science, Shanghai, December 1925.
Basu, Dilip K., ed., *The Rise and Growth of the Colonial Port Cities in Asia*, University Press of America, Lanham, MD, 1985.
Baudelaire, Charles, *The Painter in Modern Life and Other Essays*, Jonathan Mayne, trans. and ed., Phaidon Press, London, 1964.
Bayly, Chrisopher, *Imperial Meridian: The British Empire and the World, 1780–1830*, Longman, London, 1989.
Benjamin, Walter, *Charles Baudelaire: A Lyric Poet in the Era of High Capitalism*, Harry Zhon, trans., NLB, London, 1973.
Ben-Rafael, Eliezer and Yitzhak Sternberg, eds, *Comparing Modernities: Pluralism Versus Homogenity*, Brill, Leiden, 2005.

312 Bibliography

Bergamini, J. Van Wie, 'Architectural Meditations', *The Chinese Recorder*, American Presbyterian Mission Press, Shanghai, October 1924.

Berman, Marshall, *All that is Solid Melts into Air: The Experience of Modernity*, Simon & Schuster, New York, 1982.

Bigelow, Jacob, *Elements of Technology*, Hilliard, Gray, Little & Wilkins, Boston, MA, 1831.

Binyon, Laurence, *Painting in the Far East*, Edward Arnold, London, 1908.

Birnbaum, Phyllis, *Glory in a Line: A Life of Foujita, the Artist Caught Between East & West*, Faber & Faber, New York, 2006.

Bland, J.O.P., *Houseboat Days in China*, Edward Arnold, London, 1909.

Boerschmann, Ernst, *Chinese Architecture and its Relation to Chinese Culture*, United States Government, Smithsonian Report, Washington, DC, 1912.

Boerschmann, Ernst, *China: Architecture and Landscape: A Journey Through Twelve Provinces*, Atlantis-Verlag, Berlin, 1925.

Boorman, Howard, *Biographical Dictionary of Republican China*, Vol. 1, Columbia University Press, New York, 1967.

Boyd, Andrew, *Chinese Architecture and Town Planning: 1500B.C.–A.D.1911*, Alec Tiranti, London, 1962.

Bradbury, Malcolm and James McFarlane, eds, *Modernism: 1890–1930*, Penguin Books, Harmondsworth, 1976.

Breckenridge, Carol A. and Peter van der Veer, eds, *Orientalism and the Postcolonial Predicament: Perspectives on South Asia*, University of Pennsylvania Press, Philadelphia, PA, 1993.

Brooke, T.W. and R.W. Davis, *The China Architect's and Builder's Compendium*, North China Daily News and Herald, Shanghai (an annual publication from 1924 to 1935).

Bruno, Giuliana, *Streetwalking on a Ruined Map: Cultural Theory and the City Films of Elvira Notari*, Princeton University Press, Princeton, NJ, 1993.

Buck, David D., 'Railway City and National Capital: Two Faces of the Modern in Changchun', in Joseph W. Esherick (ed.), *Remaking the Chinese City: Modernity and National Identity, 1900–1950*, University of Hawaii Press, Honolulu, 2000.

Bury, Thomas Talbot, *Rudimentary Architecture: For the Use of Beginners and Students*, John Weale, London, 1853.

Bush, Christopher, *Ideographic Modernism: China, Writing, Media*, Oxford University Press, Oxford, 2010.

Bushell, Stephen, *Chinese Art*, Victoria and Albert Museum, London, 1904.

Calinescu, Matei, *Five Faces of Modernity: Modernism, Avant-Garde, Decadence, Kitsch, Postmodernism*, Indiana University Press, Bloomington, IN, 1977.

Cantacuzino, Sherban, *Wells Coates: A Monograph*, Gordon Fraser Gallery, 1978.

Carles, W.R., *Some Pages in the History of Shanghai, 1842–1856*, East & West, London, 1916.

Carpenter, Frank, *Carpenter's World Travels – China*, Doubleday, Doran & Company, New York, 1934.

Cawthorn, James, 'Of Taste: An Essay' (1756), in *The Literary Register*, D. Hymers, Newcastle, 1771.

Chakrabarty, Dipesh, *Provincializing Europe: Postcolonial Thought and Historical Difference*, Princeton University Press, Princeton, NJ, 2000.

Chakrabarty, Dipesh, *Habitations of Modernity: Essays in the Wake of Subaltern Studies*, University of Chicago Press, Chicago, 2002.

Chambers, Sir William, *Designs of Chinese Buildings, Furniture, Dresses, Machines, and Utensils*, London, (published by the author), 1757.

Chambers, Sir William, *A Dissertation on Oriental Gardening*, W. Griffin, London, 1772.

Chang, Chao-Kang, *China: Tao in Architecture*, D.Q. Stephenson, trans., Basel and Boston, MA, 1987.

Chang, Eileen, *Duo Shao Hen* (*How Much Sorrow!*), Shanghai, May 1947.

Chang, Hao, *Chinese Intellectuals in Crisis: Search for Order and Meaning, 1890–1911*, University of California Press, Berkeley, CA, 1987.
Chaund, William, 'Architectural Effort and Chinese Nationalism – Being a Radical Interpretation of Modern Architecture as a Potent Factor in Civilisation', *Far Eastern Review*, Shanghai, Peking & Manila, August 1919.
Chen, Zhanxiang (Charles Chen), 'Chinese Architectural Theory', Special China Issue, *Architectural Review*, London, July 1947a, pp. 15–25.
Chen, Zhanxiang, 'Recent Architecture in China', Special China Issue, *Architectural Review*, London, July 1947b, pp. 26–8.
Chen, Zhanxiang, *White Book*, Lei Xi, trans., December 198? (exact date unknown), Fairbank archive.
Chen Duxiu, 'Year 1916', 15 January 1916, in *Duxiu Wen Cun (Collection of Duxiu's Works)*, *Ya Dong Tu Shu Guan*, Shanghai, Vol. 1, 1922.
Chow, Rey, *Woman and Chinese Modernity: The Politics of Reading Between West and East*, University of Minnesota Press, Minneapolis, MN, 1991.
Chow, Rey, *Primitive Passions: Visuality, Sexuality, Ethnography and Contemporary Chinese Cinema*, Columbia University Press, New York, 1995.
Chu, Qi'en, *Zhong Guo Bi Hua Shi (History of Chinese Murals)*, Beijing Gong Yi Mei Shu Chu Ban She, Beijing, 2000.
Clark, J.D., *Sketches in and around Shanghai, etc.*, Shanghai Mercury, Shanghai, 1894.
Clarke, David, *Modern Chinese Art*, Oxford University Press, Oxford, 2000.
Clarke, David, 'Cross-Cultural Dialogue and Artistic Innovation: Teng Baiye and Mark Tobey', in Jo-Ann Birnie Danzker, Ken Lum and Zheng Shengtian (eds), *Shanghai Modern 1919–1945*, Hatje Cantze, Ostfildern, 2004.
Clunas, Craig, 'Chinese Art and Chinese Artists in France 1924–1925', *Arts Asiatiques*, Tome 44, 1989.
Cochran, Sherman and David Strand, eds, *Cities in Motion: Interior, Coast, and Diaspora in Transnational China*, Institute of East Asian Studies, University of California, Berkeley, CA, 2007.
Cody, Jeffrey, *Building in China – Henry K Murphy's "Adaptive Architecture", 1914–1935*, The Chinese University Press, Hong Kong, 2001.
Cody, Jeffrey, *Exporting American Architecture, 1870–2000*, Routledge, London, 2003.
Cohen, Paul, *Discovering History in China*, Columbia University Press, New York, 1984.
Cohen, Paul and Merle Goldman, eds, *Ideas Across Cultures: Essays in Honor of Benjamin Schwartz*, Harvard East Asian Monographs, Cambridge, 1990.
Cohen, Warren I., ed., 'Reflections on Orientalism', *South Asia Series*, No. 33, Asian Studies Centre, Michigan State University, Michigan, MI, 1983.
Cohn, David, 'The Search for National Forms and Modern Techniques', *Architecture, the AIA Journal*, Vol. 74, New York, September 1985.
Collier, D. and C. L'E. Malone, *Manchoukuo: Jewel of Asia*, George Allen & Unwin, London, 1936.
Collins, Peter, *Changing Ideas in Modern Architecture*, Faber & Faber, London, 1965.
Colquhoun, A.R., *China in Transformation*, Harper & Bros, London, 1898.
Colquhoun, Alan, *Modern Architecture*, Oxford University Press, Oxford, 2002.
Confucius, *Chun Qiu* (undated).
Conrads, Ulrich, *Programs and Manifestoes on 20th Century Architecture*, MIT Press, Cambridge, MA, 1990.
Cook's Tourist's Handbook to Peking, Tientsin, Shan-hai-Kwan, Mukden, Dalny, Port Arthur, and Seoul, Thomas Cook & Son, London, 1910.
Coward, Noël, *The Letters of Noël Coward*, Bloomsbury Publishing, London, 2014.
Cret, Paul Philippe, 'The Question of Education – Evolution or Revolution', *AIA Journal*, Vol. 12, The Octagon, New York, 1924.

314   Bibliography

Cret, Paul Philippe, 'Modernists and Conservatives', speech delivered to the T Square Club, Philadelphia, PA, 19 November 1927.
Cret, Paul Philippe, 'Ten Years of Modernism', *The Historical Chronicle*, University of Pennsylvania, PA, July 1933.
Cret, Paul Philippe, 'Modern Movements in Architecture', May 1933, *The Architectural Forum*, August 1933.
Croizier, Ralph, *Art and Revolution in Modern China: The Lingnan (Cantonese) School of Painting, 1906–1951*, University of California Press, Berkeley, CA, 1988.
Curtis, William, *Modern Architecture Since 1900*, 3rd edn, Phaidon, London, 1996.
Dan, Tohmasu, 'Reminiscences of Hsinking', *Manchuria*, 15 December 1936.
Danzker, Jo-Ann Birnie, Ken Lum and Zheng Shengtian, eds, *Shanghai Modern 1919–1945*, Hatje Cantze, Ostfildern, 2004.
Darling, Elizabeth, *Wells Coates*, RIBA Publishing, London, 2012.
Daruvala, Susan, *Zhou Zuoren and an Alternative Chinese Response to Modernity*, Harvard University Press, Cambridge, MA, 2000.
Darwent, C.E., *Shanghai: A Handbook for Travellers and Residents to the Chief Objects of Interests in and around the Foreign Settlements and Native City*, 2nd edn, Kelly & Walsh, Shanghai, 1920.
Davis, Sir John Francis, *The Chinese: A General Description of the Empire of China and its Inhabitants*, M. Natalli, London, 1836.
Decker, Paul, *Chinese Architecture, Civil and Ornamental*, Henry Parker & Elirabeth Bakewell, London, 1759.
Denison, Edward and Guang Yu Ren, *Building Shanghai – The Story of China's Gateway*, Wiley, London, 2006.
Denison, Edward and Guang Yu Ren, *Modernism in China: Architectural Visions and Revolutions*, Wiley, London, 2008.
Denison, Edward and Guang Yu Ren, *Luke Him Sau, Architect – China's Missing Modern*, Wiley, London, 2014.
Denison, Edward and Guang Yu Ren, 'Chinoiserie – An Unrequited Architectural Affair', *Modernism and British Chinoiserie*, Edinburgh University Press, Edinburgh, 2014.
Denison, Edward and Guang Yu Ren, *Ultra-Modernism – Architecture and Modernity in Manchuria*, Hong Kong University Press, Hong Kong, 2017.
d'Entreves, Maurizio Passerin and Seyla Benhabib, eds, *Habermas and the Unfinished Project of Modernity: Critical Essays on the Philosophical Discourse of Modernity*, MIT Press, Cambridge, MA, 1996.
Di, Hongbo, 'The Incorporation of Features of Traditional Chinese Architecture in Modern Buildings in the People's Republic of China', PhD thesis, Sheffield University, 1997.
Dirlik, Arif, *Anarchism in the Chinese Revolution*, University of California Press, Berkeley, CA, 1991.
Dong, Dayou, 'New Shanghai', *The China Quarterly*, China Quarterly Co., Shanghai, December 1935.
Dong, Dayou, 'Architecture Chronicle', *T'ien Hsia*, Vol. 3, No. 4, Shanghai, November 1936.
Dong, Stella, *Shanghai: The Rise and Fall of a Decadent City, 1842–1949*, Harper Perennial, New York, 2001.
Doremus, Thomas, *Frank Lloyd Wright and Le Corbusier: The Great Dialogue*, Van Nostrand Reinhold Company, New York, 1985.
Douyau, Jean, 'Impressions on Manchoukuo', *Contemporary Manchuria*, Vol. 2, No. 3, May 1938.
Doyle, Michael, *Empires*, Cornell University Press, New York, 1986.
Drexler, Arthur, *The Architecture of Japan*, MOMA, New York, 1955.
Du, Yangeng, 'The Consciousness that Architects Should Have', *The Builder*, Vol. 3, No. 6, Shanghai Architects Association, Shanghai, 1935.

Duara, Prasenjit, *Rescuing History from Nation*, University of Chicago Press, Chicago, 1995.
du Halde, Jean Baptiste, *The General History of China, Containing a Geographical, Historical, Chronological, Political and Physical Description of the Empire of China, Chinese-Tartary, Corea and Thibet*, John Watts, London, 1736.
Duus, Peter, Ramon Myers and Mark R. Peattie, *The Japanese Informal Empire in China, 1895–1937*, Princeton University Press, Princeton, NJ, 1989.
Dyce, C.M., *Personal Reminiscences of Thirty Years' Residence in the Model Settlement, Shanghai, 1870–1900*, Chapman & Hall, London, 1906.
'Early Modernities', *Dædalus*, Journal of the American Academy of Arts and Sciences, Vol. 127, Harvard University, Cambridge, Summer 1998.
Edkins, Joseph, 'Chinese Architecture', *Journal of the China Branch of the Royal Asiatic Society*, Kelly and Walsh, Shanghai, 1890.
Eigner, Julius, 'The Rise and Fall of Nanjing', *The National Geographic*, Vol. 73, No. 2, Washington, DC, February 1938.
Eisenstadt, Shmuel N., 'The Context of the Multiple Modernities Paradigm', in Dominic Sachsenmaier and Jens Riedel (eds), with Shmuel N. Eisenstadt, *Reflections on Multiple Modernities: European, Chinese and Other Interpretations*, Brill, Leiden, 2002.
Eisenstadt, Shmuel N., *Comparative Civilizations and Multiple Modernities*, Brill, Leiden, 2003.
Eisenstadt, Shmuel N. and Wolfgang Schluchter, 'Introduction: Paths to Early Modernities – A Comparative View', in *Dædalus*, Summer 1998.
Elman, Benjamin, *A Cultural History of Modern Science in China*, Harvard University Press, Cambridge, MA, 2006.
Esherick, Joseph W., ed., *Remaking the Chinese City: Modernity and National Identity, 1900–1950*, University of Hawaii Press, Honolulu, 2000.
Evers, Hans-Dieter and Rüdiger Korff, *Southeast Asian Urbanism: The Meaning and Power of Social Space*, Institute of Southeast Asian Studies, Singapore, 2000.
Exhibition Catalogue, Palais du Rhin, Strasbourg, 1924.
Eysteinsson, Astradur, *The Concept of Modernism*, Cornell University Press, New York, 1990.
Fairbank, John and Merle Goldman, *China: A New History*, Harvard University Press, Cambridge, MA, 2006.
Fairbank, John and Denis Twitchett, *The Cambridge History of China: Volume 12, Republican China 1912–1949, Part 1*, Cambridge University Press, Cambridge, 1983.
Fairbank, Wilma, *Liang and Lin: Partners in Exploring China's Architectural Past*, University of Pennsylvania Press, Philadelphia, PA, 1994.
Faure, David and Taotao Liu, *Town and Country in China*, Palgrave, Basingstoke, 2002.
Feetham, Richard, 'Feetham Report', *North China Daily News and Herald*, Shanghai, 1931.
Feng Zi Kai, 'Xian Dai Jian Zhu De Xing Shi Mei,' ('The Beauty and Form of Modern Architecture,') in Feng Zikai, Feng Yiyin, and Feng Yuancao, *Feng Zi Kai Wen Ji -1920.4-1930.3 Yi Shu Juan (The Writings of Feng Zikai -1920.4-1930.3 Volume of Art)*, Zhe Jiang Wen Yi Chu Ban She (Zhe Jiang Literature and Art Publisher), Hangzhou, 1990.
Feng, Zi Kai, 'Yi Shu De Yuan Di' ('The Garden of Art'), in Feng Zikai, Feng Yiyin, and Feng Yuancao, *Feng Zi Kai Wen Ji -1920.4–1930.3 Yi Shu Juan (The Writings of Feng Zikai -1920.4–1930.3, Volume of Art)*, Zhe Jiang Wen Yi Chu Ban She (Zhe Jiang Literature and Art Publisher), Hangzhou, 1990.
Ferguson, John, 'Painters Among Catholic Missionaries and their Helpers in Peking', *Journal of the North China Branch of the Royal Asiatic Society*, Vol. LXV, Shanghai, 1934.
Finch, P. *Shanghai and Beyond*, Charles Scribner's Sons, New York, 1953.
Finn, Dallas, *Meiji Revisited – The Sites of Victorian Japan*, Weatherhill, New York, 1995.
Fletcher, Banister, *A History of Architecture on the Comparative Method*, Routledge (12th edn), 1996.
Fogel, J., *Life Along the South Manchuria Railway: The Memoirs of Itō Takeo*, M.E. Sharpe, New York, 1988.

Fogel, Joshua, *The Cultural Dimension of Sino-Japanese Relations: Essays on the Nineteenth and Twentieth Centuries*, M.E. Sharpe, New York, 1995.
Fogel, Joshua, *The Literature of Travel in the Japanese Rediscovery of China, 1862–1945*, Stanford University Press, Stanford, CA, 1996.
Forbes, Dean, *Asian Metropolis: Urbanisation and the Southeast Asian City*, Oxford University Press, Melbourne, 1996.
Frampton, Kenneth, *Modern Architecture: A Critical History*, Thames & Hudson, London, 2002.
Frisby, David, *Cityscapes of Modernity: Critical Explorations*, Polity Press, Cambridge, 2001.
Fukuyama, Francis, *The End of History and the Last Man*, Penguin, New York, 1992.
Gandelsonas, Mario, ed., *Shanghai Reflections, Architecture, Urbanism, and the Search for an Alternative Modernity*, Princeton Architectural Press, Princeton, NJ, 2002.
Gaonkar, Dilip Parameshwar, ed., *Alternative Modernities*, 2nd edn, Duke University Press, Durham, NC, 2001.
General Description of Shanghae and its Environs, The Mission Press, Shanghai, 1850.
Giddens, Anthony, *The Consequences of Modernity*, Cambridge University Press, Cambridge, 1997.
Gilchrist, T.V., 'Hsinking,' *Manchuria*, 15 September 1939.
Gillespie, Rev. William M., *The Land of Sinim, Or, China and Chinese Missions*, Myles MacPhail, Edinburgh, 1854.
Ginsberg, Norton S., 'The Great City in South-East Asia' in Y.M. Yueng and C.P. Lo (eds), *Changing South-East Asian Cities: Readings on Urbanization*, Oxford University Press, Singapore, 1976.
Goldman, Merle and Leo Ou-fan Lee, *An Intellectual History of Modern China*, Cambridge University Press, Cambridge, 2001.
Gongyang, Gao, *Gong Yang Zhuan* (date unknown).
Graham, Edward D., 'The "Imaginative Geography" of China', in Warren I. Cohen (ed.), *Reflections on Orientalism*, Asian Studies Centre, South Asia Series, No. 33, Winter 1983, Michigan State University, Michigan, MI, 1983.
Grieder, Jerome B., *Hu Shih and the Chinese Renaissance*, Harvard University Press, Cambridge, MA, 1970.
Gu, Hongming, 'The Spirit of the Chinese People', a paper read before the Oriental Society of Peking, 1915.
Gunn, C.A., 'Mission Policy in Mission Architecture', *The Chinese Recorder*, American Presbyterian Mission Press, Shanghai, October 1924.
Gunn, Edward Mansfield, *Chinese Literature in Shanghai and Peking 1937–1945*, Columbia University, New York, 1978.
Guo, Jianyin, 'Qiou Yu Shanghai De Shi Jie Shang (Seeking on the Streets of Shanghai)', *Fu Ren Hua Bao*, Vol. 17, Shanghai, April 1934.
Guo, Qinghua, 'Changchun: Unfinished Capital Planning of Manzhouguo, 1932–42', *Urban History*, Vol. 31, No. 1, Cambridge University Press, Cambridge, 2004.
Guo, Qinghua, *Chinese Architecture and Planning: Ideas, Methods and Techniques*, Axel Menges, Stuttgart, London, 2005.
Habermas, Jürgen, *The Theory of Communicative Action*, T. McCarthy, trans., Beacon Press, Boston, MA, 1984.
Habermas, Jürgen, *The Philosophical Discourse of Modernity*, Frederick Lawrence, trans., Basil Blackwell, Cambridge, 1987.
Habermas, Jürgen, 'Modernity: An Unfinished Project', in Maurizio Passerin d'Entreves and Seyla Benhabib (eds), *Habermas and the Unfinished Project of Modernity: Critical Essays on the Philisophical Discourse of Modernity*, MIT Press, Cambridge, MA, 1996.
Hahn, Emily, *China to Me*, Doubleday, Doran & Co, New York, 1944.
Hakewill, George, *An Apologie or Declaration of the Power and Providence of God in the Government of the World*, W. Turner, Oxford, 1635.

Halfpenny, William, *New Designs for Chinese Temples, Triumphal Arches, Garden Seats, Palings, etc.*, R. Sayer, London, 1750.

Harding, Sandra, *Sciences from Below: Feminisms, Postcolonialities, and Modernities*, Duke University Press, Durham, NC, 2008.

Harootunian, Harry, *History's Disquiet: Modernity, Cultural Practice and the Question of Everyday Life*, Columbia University Press, New York, 2000.

Hay, Jonathan, *Shitao – Painting and Modernity in Early Qing China*, Cambridge University Press, New York, 2001.

Hay, Jonathan, *Sensuous Surfaces – the Decorative Object in Early Modern China*, Reaktion, London, 2008.

Hayot, Eric, *Chinese Dreams: Pound, Brecht, Tel quel*, The University of Michigan Press, Ann Arbor, MI, 2004.

He, Ping, *China's Search for Modernity: Cultural Discourses in the late 20th Century*, Palgrave Macmillan, Basingstoke, 2002.

He, Yeju, *Zhong Gui Gu Dai Gui Hua Shi (History of Ancient Chinese Planning)*, Zhong Guo Jian Zhu Gong Ye Chu Ban She, Beijing, 1996.

Herz, Manuel, ed., *African Modernism: The Architecture of Independence*, Park Books, Zurich, 2015.

Heynen, Hilde, *Architecture and Modernity*, MIT Press, Cambridge, MA, 1999.

Hideo, Fuegi, 'The Building Industry and Architectural Profession Past and Present', *Journal of the Manchurian Architectural Association*, Vol. 22, No. 10, November 1942.

Higachi, Shinobu, 'Manchoukuo Progress, Racial Harmony Impress Visiting Canadian Team', *Manchuria*, 1 August 1939.

Hines, Thomas S. and Richard Joseph Neutra, *Richard Neutra and the Search for Modern Architecture: A Biography and History*, Oxford University Press, Oxford, 1982.

Hirdina, Heinz, Neues Bauen and Neues Gestalten, *Das neue Frankfurt/Die neue Stadt. Eine Zeitschrift zwischen 1926 und 1933*, Elefanten Press, Berlin, 1984.

Hosagrahar, Jyoti, *Indigenous Modernities: Negotiating Architecture and Urbanism*, Routledge, London, 2005.

Hsia, Ching-Lin, *The Status of Shanghai – A Historical Review of the International Settlement – Its Future Development and Possibilities Through Sino-Foreign Co-operation*, Kelly & Walsh, Shanghai, 1929.

Hsu, Kai-yu, *Twentieth Century Chinese Poetry: An Anthology*, Doubleday, New York, 1963.

Huai Nan Zi, Han Dynasty (202BC–8AD).

Huang, Guiyou, *Whitmanism, Imagism, and Modernism in China and America*, Susquehanna University Press, Selinsgrove, PA, 1997.

Hume, Edward, 'Yale in China', *Far Eastern Review*, Shanghai, Peking & Manila, July 1914.

Huntington, Samuel, *The Clash of Civilizations?: The Debate*, Foreign Affairs, New York, 1993.

Hussey, Harry, *My Pleasures and Palaces – An Informal Memoir of Forty Years in Modern China*, Doubleday, New York, 1968.

Ino, Dan, 'Reconstruction of Tokyo and Aesthetic Problems of Architecture', in *Far Eastern Review*, Shanghai, Peking & Manila, Vol. 28, January 1932.

Institute of the History of Natural Sciences (Chinese Academy of Sciences), *History and Development of Ancient Chinese Architecture*, Science Press, Beijing, 1986.

Isaacs, Harold, *Re-encounters in China: Notes of a Journey in a Time Capsule*, M.E. Sharpe, New York, 1985.

Isozaki, Arata, *Japan-ness in Architecture*, MIT Press, Cambridge, MA, 2006.

Iyenaga, Toyokichi, ed., *Japan's Real Attitude Toward America: A Reply to Mr. George Bronson Rea's "Japan's Place in the Sun – The Menace to America"*, Putnam's, New York, 1916.

Jacques, Martin, *When China Rules the World*, Penguin, London, 2009.

Bibliography

Jameson, Frederic, 'Modernism and Imperialism', *Field Day pamphlet*, No. 14, Field Day, Ireland, 1988.
Jansen, Marius, ed., *The Emergence of Meiji Japan*, Cambridge University Press, Cambridge, 1995.
Jencks, Charles, *Modern Movements in Architecture*, 3rd edn, Penguin Books, Harmondsworth, 1980.
Jencks, Charles, *Preface: A Refolution in Five Parts* (electronic document), November 2006.
Jia, Jun, ed., *Jian Zhu Shi (Architectural History)*, Qin Hua Da Xue Chu Ban She, Beijing, 2005.
Ka Fei Zuo Tan (Café Forum), Zhen Mei Shan Shu Dian, Shanghai, 1929.
Kang, Laixin and Xu Qinqin, eds, *The Complete Collection of Liu Na'ou*, Literature Volume, Tai Nan Xian Wen Hua Ju, Taiwan, 2001.
Kao, Mayching, 'The Beginning of the Western-style Painting Movement in Relationship to Reforms in Education in Early Twentieth Century China', *New Asia Academic Bulletin*, Hong Kong, Vol. 4, 1983.
Katsumasa, H., *Mantetsu (South Manchuria Railway)*, Iwanami Shoten, Tokyo, 1981.
Kawakami, K.K., *Manchukuo: Child of Conflict*, Macmillan, New York, 1933.
Kensuke, Aiga, 'Thoughts Before and After the Establishment of Manchukuo', *Journal of the Manchurian Architectural Association*, Vol. 22, No. 10, October 1942.
Kim, Won Bae, Mike Douglass, Sang-Chuel Choe and Kong Chong Ho, eds, *Culture and the City in East Asia*, Clarendon Press, Oxford, 1997.
King, Anthony D., *Colonial Urban Development: Culture, Social Power and Environment*, Routledge & Kegan Paul, London, 1976.
King, F., *The History of the Hongkong and Shanghai Banking Corporation, Volume III: The Hongkong Bank between the Wars and the Bank Interned*, Cambridge University Press, Cambridge, 1988.
King, Gerald, 'The Utilisation of Chinese Architecture Design in Modern Building – the Rockefeller Foundation's Hospital Plant at Peking', *Far Eastern Review*, Shanghai, Peking & Manila, Vol. 15, August 1919.
Kingsmill, Thomas, 'Early Architecture in Shanghai', 'The Jubilee of Shanghai 1843–1893. Shanghai: Past and Present, and a full account of the proceedings on the 17th and 18th November, 1893', *North China Daily News*, Shanghai, 1893.
Kingsmill, Thomas, 'Early Architecture in Shanghai', *Social Shanghai*, Vol. XII, North-China News and Herald, Shanghai, July–December 1911.
Kinney, H., *Modern Manchuria and the South Manchuria Railway Company*, Japan Advertiser Press, Dalian, 1928.
Kinney, Henry, *Modern Manchuria*, Dalian, March 1929.
Kinney, Henry, *Manchuria Today*, Hamada, Osaka, 1930.
Kinnosuke, A., *Manchuria: A Survey*, Robert McBride & Co., New York, 1925.
Knapp, Ronald, *China's Traditional Rural Architecture: A Cultural Geography of the Common House*, University of Hawaii Press, Honolulu, 1986.
Knollys, Henry, *English Life in China*, Smith, Elder & Co, London, 1885.
Kon, Wajiro, *Modernologio*, Shunyodo, Tokyo, 1930.
Kracauer, Siegfried, *The Mass Ornament: Weimar Essays*, Thomas Levin, trans., Harvard University Press, Cambridge, 1995.
Kracauer, Siegfried, *The Salaried Masses*, Quintin Hoare, trans., Verso, London, 1998.
Kroker, Bruno, 'The Building Industry in Shanghai', *The China Journal*, Vol. 30, No. 5, China Society of Arts and Science, Shanghai, May 1939.
Kuklin, I.A., 'Japanese Development of Hailar', *Manchuria*, 15 November 1936.
Kuonin, I.I., *The Diamond Jubilee of the International Settlement of Shanghai*, Shanghai, 1938.
Kwata, T., ed., *Glimpses of the East*, Nippon Yusen Kaisya Official Guide, Tokyo, 1939–40.
Lai, Delin, ed., *Who's Who in Modern Chinese Architecture*, China Shui Li Shui Dan Press, Beijing, 2006.

Lanning, G. and S. Couling, *The History of Shanghai*, Kelly & Walsh, Shanghai, 1921.
Lao, She, 'Er Ma', *Xiao Shuo Yue Bao (Novel Monthly)*, Vol. 20, Nos 5–12, Beijing, 1929.
Larson, Neil, *Modernism and Hegemony: A Materialist Critique of Aesthetic Agencies*, University of Minnesota Press, Minneapolis, MN, 1989.
Lau, Jenny Kwok Wah, ed., *Multiple Modernities: Cinemas and Popular Media in Transcultural East Asia*, Temple University Press, Philadelphia, PA, 2003.
Lau, Joseph S.M., C.T. Hsia and Leo Ou-fan Lee, eds, *Modern Chinese Stories and Novellas 1919–1949*, Columbia University Press, New York, 1981.
Laurence, Patricia Ondek, *Lily Briscoe's Chinese Eyes: Bloomsbury, Modernism and China*, University of South Calorina Press, Columbia, 2003.
Lee, Edward Bing-Shuey, *Modern Canton*, The Mercury Press, Shanghai, 1936.
Lee, Gregory, *Troubadours, Trumpeters, Troubled Makers: Lyricism, Nationalism and Hybridity in China and its Others*, C. Hurst, London, 1996.
Lee, Leo Ou-fan, *The Romantic Generation of Modern Chinese Writers*, student dissertation, Harvard University, Cambridge, MA, 1973.
Lee, Leo Ou-fan, ed., *Lu Xun and His Legacy*, University of California Press, Berkeley, CA, 1985.
Lee, Leo Ou-fan, *Voices from the Iron House: A Study of Lu Xun*, Indiana University Press, Bloomington, IN, 1987.
Lee, Leo Ou-fan, *Shanghai Modern: The Flowering of a New Urban Culture in China, 1930–1945*, Harvard University Press, Cambridge, 1999.
Lee, Leo Ou-fan, 'The Cultural Construction of Modernity in Urban Shanghai: Some Preliminary Explorations', in Yeh Wen-hsin (ed.), *Becoming Chinese: Passages to Modernity and Beyond*, University of California Press, Berkeley, CA, 2000.
Lee, Leo Ou-fan, 'Shanghai Modern: Reflections on Urban Culture in China in the 1930s', in Dilip Parameshwar Gaonkar (ed.), *Alternative Modernities*, 2nd edn, Duke University Press, Durham, NC, 2001.
Lee, Thomas H.C., ed., *China and Europe: Images and Influences in Sixteenth to Eighteenth Centuries*, Chinese University Press, Hong Kong, 1991.
Lee, Y.L., 'The Port Towns of British Borneo', in Y.M. Yueng and C.P. Lo (eds), *Changing South-East Asian Cities: Readings on Urbanization*, Oxford University Press, Singapore, 1976.
Leveneon, Joseph Richmond, *Liang Ch'i-ch'ao and the Mind of Modern China*, Harvard University Press, Cambridge, MA, 1953.
Levine, Marilyn, *The Found Generation – Chinese Communists in Europe during the Twenties*, University of Washington Press, Seattle, WA, 1993.
Lewis, W.S., *The Yale Edition of Horace Walpole's Correspondence*, Yale University Press, New Haven, CT, 1937.
Leyda, Jay, *Dianying: An Account of Films and the Film Audience in China*, MIT Press, Cambridge, MA, 1972.
Li Ji (The Book of Rites), Zhou Dynasty (475–221 BC).
Li, Lincoln, *The China Factor in Modern Japanese Thought: The Case of Tachibana Shiraki, 1881–1945*, State University of New York Press, Albany, NY, 1996.
Li, Shiqiao, 'Writing a Modern Chinese Architectural History: Liang Sicheng and Liang Qichao', *Journal of Architectural Education*, Vol. 56, Association of Collegiate Schools of Architecture, 2002.
Liang, Qichao, *Qing Yi Bao*, December 1898.
Liang, Qichao, *On the Trend of the Competition between People of Nations in Current Times and the Future of China*, Qing Yi Bao, 15 October 1899.
Liang, Qichao, 'Wu Shi Nian Zhong Guo Jin Hua Lun (The Evolution of China in the Last 50 Years)', written in April 1922 and published in February 1923 for Shen Bao's 50th Anniversary Special Edition.

Liang, Sicheng, *Chou Kung's Tower – An Ancient Observatory* (unpublished), in the Fairbank family archive.
Liang, Sicheng (originally published as Ssu-ch'eng), *Open Spandrel Bridges of Ancient China – Part 1: The An-Ch'iao at Chan-chou, Hopei*, Pencil Points, Princeton, NJ, January 1938.
Liang, Sicheng (originally published as Ssu-ch'eng), *Open Spandrel Bridges of Ancient China – Part 2: The Yung-t'ung Ch'iao at Chan-chou, Hopei*, Pencil Points, Princeton, NJ, March 1938.
Liang, Sicheng (originally published as Ssu-ch'eng), 'China's Oldest Wooden Structure', *Asia: Journal of the American Asiatic Association*, Asia Publishing Co., New York, July 1941.
Liang, Sicheng (originally published as Ssu-ch'eng), 'Five Early Chinese Pagodas', *Asia: Journal of the American Asiatic Association*, Asia Publishing Co., New York, August 1941.
Liang, Sicheng, 'Wei Shen Me Yan Jiu Zhong Guo Jian Zhu' ('Why Study Chinese Architecture?') *Zhong Guo Ying Zao Xue She Hui Kan*, Vol. 7, No. 1, Beijing, October 1944.
Liang, Sicheng, *A Pictorial History of Chinese Architecture*, MIT Press, Cambridge, 1984.
Liang, Sicheng, 'Jian Zhu She Ji Can Kao Tu Ji Xu' ('Foreword of the Reference Pattern of Architectural Design'), in *Liang Sicheng Wen Ji (Collection of Liang Sicheng's Writing)*, Vol. 2, China Architectural Industry Publisher, Beijing, 1984.
Liang, Sicheng, *Liang Sicheng Wen Ji (Collection of Liang Sicheng's Writing)*, Vols 1–4, China Architectural Industry Publisher, Beijing, 1984–6.
Liang, Sicheng, 'Guan Yu Zhong Yang Ren Min Zheng Fu Xing Zheng Zhong Xin Qu Wei Zhi De Jian Yi' ('Suggestions on the Location of the Administrative Centre of the Central People's Government'), February 1950, with Chen Zhanxiang, in *Liang Sicheng Wen Ji (Collection of Liang Sicheng's Writing)*, Vol. 4, China Architectural Industry Publisher, Beijing, 1986.
Liang, Sicheng, *Liang Sicheng Quan Ji (Collection of Liang Sicheng's Writing)*, Vols 1–9, China Architectural Industry Publisher, Beijing, 2001.
Liang, Sicheng, *Jian Zhu Wen Cui (Window to China)*, San Lian Shu Dian, Beijing, 2006.
Lieberthal, Kenneth, ed., *Perspectives on Modern China: Four Anniversaries*, M.E. Sharpe, New York, 1991.
Lim, William and Jiat-Hwee Chang, *Non-West Modernist Past: On Architecture and Modernities*, World Scientific Publishing Co., Singapore, 2012.
Lin, Shan, *Lin Huiyin zhuan (Biography of Lin Huiyin)*, Shi Jie Shu Ju, Taipei, 1993.
Ling, Shuhua, *Ancient Melodies*, Hogarth Press, London, 1953.
Liu, Laurence G., *Chinese Architecture*, Academy Editions, London, 1989.
Liu, Na'ou, 'Liang Ge Shi Jian De Bu Gan Zheng Zhe' ('Two Who Do Not Feel The Time'), *Jin Dai Fu Nü*, Shanghai, No. 11, 1929.
Liu, Na'ou, *Du Shi Feng Jing Xian (The Scenery of the Metropolis)*, Shui Mo Shu Dian, April 1930.
Liu, Wenhua, 'Brief History of the Development of Motion Pictures in Manchuria', *Manchuria Special Number*, 20 July 1939.
Liu, Yishi, *Other Modernity: The Rise of a Japanese Colonial Capital City, 1932–1937*, Conference Paper, International Association for the Study of Traditional Environments, Interrogating Tradition, Oxford Brookes, 12–15 December 2008.
Ljungstedt, Andrew, *An Historical Sketch of The Portuguese Settlements in China: And of the Roman Catholic Church and Mission in China*, J. Munroe, Boston, MA, 1836.
Lü, Buwei, *Lü Shi Chun Qiu (Lü's Spring and Autumn)*, End of the Warring State (239BC).
Lu, Duanfang, ed., *Third World Modernism: Architecture, Development and Identity*, Routledge, London, 2010.
Lu Xun Quan Ji (The Complete Works of Lu Xun), Ren Min Wen Xue Chu Ban She, Beijing, 1956.

Lum, Ken, 'Aesthetic Education in Republican China: A Convergence of Ideals', in Jo-Ann Birnie Danzker, Ken Lum and Zheng Shengtian (eds), *Shanghai Modern 1919–1945*, Hatje Cantze, Ostfildern, 2004.

Lung, Bingyi, *Xiang Gang Gu Jin Jian Zhu (Hong Kong Architecture, Ancient and Modern)*, San Lian Shu Dian, Hong Kong, 1992.

Lunt, Carroll, *The China Who's Who 1927 (Foreign)*, Union Printing, Shanghai, 1927.

Macfarlane, Alan, *The Making of the Modern World: Visions from the West and East*, Palgrave, Basingstoke, 2002.

Maclellan, J.W., 'The Story of Shanghai from the Opening of the Port to Foreign Trade', *The North China Herald*, Shanghai, 1889.

Macmillan, Allister, ed., *Seaports of the Far East*, 2nd edn, W.H. & L. Collingridge, London, 1925.

MacPherson, Kerrie L., 'Designing China's Urban Future: The Greater Shanghai Plan, 1927–1937', *Planning Perspectives*, Vol. 5, No.1, Taylor & Francis, Abingdon, January 1990.

Maeda, Ai and James A. Fujii, *Text and the City: Essays on Japanese Modernity*, Duke University Press, Durham, NC, 2004.

Manchuria: Treaties and Agreements, Carnegie Endowment for International Peace, Division of International Law, Pamphlet 44, Byron S. Adams, Washington, DC, 1921.

'Manifesto', Special Edition for the establishment of the Shanghai Architects Association, Shanghai, February 1931.

Mao, Dun, 'Chun Lai Le (Spring Has Come)', *Liang You Hua Bao (The Young Companian)*, Vol. 76, Liang You Publishing Co., Shanghai, May 1933.

Mao, Dun, ed., *A Day in China*, Sheng Huo Shu Dian, Shanghai, Ming Guo, 25, 1936.

Mao, Dun, *Zi Ye (Midnight)*, Nan Guo Chu Ban She, Hong Kong, 1977.

Masami, Makino, 'Architecture of the Ten Years of Manchukuo', *Journal of the Manchurian Architectural Association*, Vol. 22, No. 10, October 1942.

Matsuoka, Yosuke, 'Speaking For Nippon', *Manchuria*, 1 November 1937.

Matsusaka, Yoshihisa, *The Making of Japanese Manchuria 1904–1932*, Harvard University Asia Centre, Cambridge, MA, 2001.

McCallum, Donald F., Book Review of Jonathan Reynolds, 'Maekawa Kunio and the Emergence of Japanese Modernist Architecture', *Journal of Japanese Studies*, The Society of Japanese Studies, Vol. 28, No. 1, Seattle, WA, 2002.

McGee, Terry, *The Southeast Asian City: A Geography of the Primate Cities of Southeast Asia*, G. Bell & Sons, London, 1967.

McNeil, Peter, 'Myths of Modernism: Japanese Architecture, Interior Design and the West, c.1920–1940', *Journal of Design History*, Oxford University Press, Vol. 5, No. 4, Oxford, 1992.

Medhurst, Walter H., *Foreigner in Far Cathay*, Edward Stanford, London, 1872.

Meech, Julia, *Japonisme Comes to America: The Japanese Impact on the Graphic Arts, 1876–1925*, H.N. Abrams, New York, 1990.

Meech, Julia, *Frank Lloyd Wright and the Art of Japan: The Architect's Other Passion*, Harry N. Abrams, New York, 2001.

Meehan, Patrick J., ed., *Truth Against the World: Frank Lloyd Wright Speaks for Organic Architecture*, Wiley, Chichester, 1987.

Men of Shanghai and North China, 2nd edn, The University Press, Shanghai, 1935.

Metcalf, Thomas R., *An Imperial Vision: Indian Architecture and Britain's Raj*, University of California Press, Berkeley, CA, 1989.

Minichiello, Shaorn, ed., *Japan's Competing Modernities: Issues in Culture and Democracy, 1900–1930*, University of Hawaii Press, Manoa, 1998.

Mirams, D.G., *A Brief History of Chinese Architecture*, Kelly & Walsh, Shanghai, 1940.

Mitchell, W.J.T., *Landscape and Power*, University of Chicago Press, Chicago, 1994.

Mojzisova, Iva, 'Avant-garde Repercussions and the School of Applied Arts in Bratislava, 1928–1939', *Journal of Design History*, Vol. 4/5, Oxford University Press, Oxford, 1992.

Mommsen, Wolfgang and Jurgen Osterhammel (eds), *Imperialism and After: Continuities and Discontinuities*, German Historical Institute, London, 1986.

Morse, Hosea Ballou, *The International Relations of the Chinese Empire, Vol. 3*, Longmans, Green & Co., London, New York, 1910–1918.

Mu, Shiying, *Shanghai De Hu Bu Wu (The Shanghai Foxtrot)*, Zhong Guo Wen Lian Chu Ban She, Beijing, 2004.

'Multiple Modernities', *Dædalus*, Journal of the American Academy of Arts and Sciences, Vol. 129, No. 1, Harvard University, Cambridge, Winter 2000.

Mungello, David, *The Great Encounter of China and the West, 1500–1800*, Rowman & Littlefield, New York, 1999.

Murotsu, 'Japan-Manchoukuo Solidarity Strengthened', *Manchuria*, 1 January 1939.

Murphey, Rhoads, *Shanghai: Key to Modern China*, Harvard University Press, Cambridge, MA, 1953.

Murphey, Rhoads, *The Treaty Ports and China's Modernization: What Went Wrong?*, University of Michigan, Ann Arbor, MI, 1970.

Murphey, Rhoads, 'What Remains to be Done', in Dilip K. Basu (ed.), *The Rise and Growth of the Colonial Port Cities in Asia*, University Press of America, Lanham, MD, 1985.

Musgrove, Charles D., 'Building a Dream: Constructing a National Capital in Nanjing, 1927–1937', in Joseph W. Esherick (ed.), *Remaking the Chinese City: Modernity and National Identity, 1900–1950*, University of Hawaii Press, Honolulu, 2000.

Narsimhan, Sushila, *Japanese Perceptions of China in the Nineteenth Century: Influence of Fukuzawa Yukichi*, Phoenix Publishing House, New Delhi, 1999.

Newhouse, Victoria, *Wallace K. Harrison, Architect*, Rizzoli, New York, 1989.

Nicolson, Nigel and Joanne Trautmann (eds), *The Letters of Virginia Woolf: 1936–1941*, Harcourt Brace Jovanovich, New York, London, 1980.

Norman, H., *All the Russias*, Heinemann, London, 1902.

O'Connor, Richard A., *A Theory of Indigenous Southeast Asian Urbanism*, Institute of Southeast Asian Studies, Singapore, 1983.

O'Malley, John, ed., *The Jesuits II: Cultures, Sciences, and the Arts, 1540–1773*, University of Toronto Press, Toronto, 2006.

Oxford, Wayne, *The Speeches of Fukuzawa: A Translation and Critical Study*, The Hokuseido Press, Tokyo, 1973.

Pang, Laikwan, *The Distorting Mirror – Visual Modernity in China*, University of Hawaii Press, Honolulu, 2007.

Pan, Lynn, *Shanghai Style: Art and Design Between the Wars*, Long River Press, 2008.

Penlington, J.N., 'Manchoukuo and Engineering Developments', *Far Eastern Review*, June 1933.

Pincus, Leslie, *Authenticating Culture in Imperial Japan: Kuki Shūzō and the Rise of National Aesthetics*, University of California Press, Berkeley, CA, 1996.

Pound, Ezra, *Selected Poems*, Faber & Gwyer, London, 1928.

Powell, John B., *My Twenty Five Years in China*, Macmillan, New York, 1945.

Průšek, Jaroslav and Leo Ou-fan Lee, *The Lyrical and the Epic: Studies in Modern Chinese Literature*, Indiana University Press, Bloomington, IN, 1980.

Pu, Ji, *Wu Deng Hui Yuan*, Vol. 7, 1252.

Pu, Yi and Eric Kramer, *The Last Manchu*, Barker, London, 1967.

Pusey, James, *China and Charles Darwin*, Council on East Asian Studies, Harvard University, Cambridge, 1983.

Qian, Zhaoming, *Orientalism and Modernism*, Duke University Press, Durham, NC, 1995.

Qian, Zhaoming, ed., *Ezra Pound and China*, University of Michigan Press, Ann Arbor, MI, 2006.

Qiu, Tongyi, in *Special Publication for the Architectural Design Exhibition of the Guangdong Provincial Rangqin University Engineering Department*, Rangqin University, Guangdong, 1935.

Quan, Ren, 'Modeng', *Zhong Hua Zhou Bao*, No. 104, 29 November, Shanghai, 1933.

Ransome, Arthur, *The Chinese Puzzle*, George Allen & Unwin, London, 1927.

Raymond, Antonin, *An Autobiography*, C.E. Tuttle, Rutland, 1973.

Rea, George Bronson, *Manchukuo: Back to First Principles!*, Kundig, Genève, 1932.

Rea, George Bronson, *The Case for Manchoukuo*, D. Appleton-Century Co., New York, 1935.

Reinhold, Christiane I., *Studying the Enemy: Japan Hands in Republican China and their Quest for National Identity*, Routledge, New York, 2001.

Remer, Charles, *A Study of Chinese Boycotts with Special Reference to their Economic Effectiveness*, The Johns Hopkins University Press, Baltimore, MD, 1933.

Reynolds, Jonathan M., 'Japan's Imperial Diet Building: Debate over Construction of a National Identity', *Art Journal*, Vol. 55, No. 3, College Art Association of America, New York, Autumn 1996.

Reynolds, Jonathan, *Maekawa Kunio and the Emergence of Japanese Modernist Architecture*, University of California Press, Berkeley, CA, 2001.

Riichi, Yokomitsu, *Shanghai: A Novel*, Dennis Washburn, trans., University of Michigan Press, Ann Arbor, MI, 2001.

Roberts, John, 'Shipping at Shanghai', in 'The Jubilee of Shanghai 1843–1893. Shanghai: Past and Present, and a Full Account of the Proceedings on the 17th and 18th November, 1893', *North China Daily News*, Shanghai, 1893.

Ross, Robert and Gerald J. Telkamp (eds), *Colonial Cities: Essays on Urbanism in a Colonial Context*, Martinus Nijhoff, Dordrecht, 1985.

Rowe, Peter and Seng Kuan, *Architectural Encounters with Essence and Form in Modern China*, MIT Press, Cambridge, MA, 2002.

Rujivacharakul, Vimalin, 'Architects and Cultural Heroes', in Sherman Cochran and David Strand (eds), *Cities in Motion: Interior, Coast, and Diaspora in Transnational China*, Institute of East Asian Studies, University of California, Berkeley, CA, 2007.

Russell, Bertrand, *The Problem of China*, Allen & Unwin, London, 1922.

Rutt, Richard, *The Book of Changes (Zhouyi): A Bronze Age Document*, Routledge Curzon, London, 2002.

Sachsenmaier, Dominic and Jens Riedel (eds), *Reflections on Multiple Modernities: European, Chinese and Other Interpretations*, Brill, Leiden, 2002.

Sadria, Modjtaba, ed., *Multiple Modernities in Muslim Societies*, Aga Khan Award for Architecture, Geneva, 2007.

Sagharchi, Alireza and Lucien Steil, *New Palladians: Modernity and Sustainability for 21st Century Architecture*, Artmedia Press, London, 2010.

Said, Edward, *Orientalism*, Routledge & Kegan Paul, London, 1978.

Said, Edward, *Culture and Imperialism*, Chatto & Windus, London, 1993.

Scherer, J.A.B., *Manchukuo: A Bird's Eye View*, Hokuseido Press, Tokyo, 1933.

Schmidt, Lewis, 'American Student Delegation', *Manchuria*, 1 September 1938.

Schmidt, Volker H., 'Multiple Modernities or Varieties of Modernity?', *Working Paper Series*, No. 170, Faculty of Social Sciences, Department of Sociology, National University of Singapore, Singapore, 2004.

Schwarcz, Vera, *The Chinese Enlightenment: Intellectuals and the Legacy of the May Fourth Movement*, University of California Press, Berkeley, CA, 1986.

Scriver, Peter and Vikramaditya Prakash, *Colonial Modernities: Building, Dwelling and Architecture in British India and Ceylon*, Routledge, London, 2007.

Sewell, William, 'Japanese Imperialism and Civic Construction in Manchuria: Changchun 1905–45' (PhD thesis), University of British Columbia, 2000.

324 Bibliography

Shanghai – 1843–1893, The Model Settlement: Its Birth, its Youth, its Jubilee, Shanghai Mercury Office, Shanghai, 1893.

Shanghai Special City Public Works Department, Tender Document for the Designs of Buildings, Shanghai, June, Year 18.

Shao, Qin, *Culturing Modernity – The Nantong Model, 1890–1930*, Stanford University Press, Palo, CA, 2004.

Shao, Xunmei, 'Shangai De Ling Hun' ('The Soul of Shanghai'), in Lin Lang (ed.), *Xian Dai Chuang Zuo Xin Shi Xuan (Selected Modern New Poems)*, Shanghai Zhong Yang Shu Dian, Vol. 4, September 1936.

Shen, Kuiyi, 'The Lure of the West: Modern Chinese Oil Painting', in Julia F. Andrews and Shen Kuiyi, *A Century in Crisis: Modernity and Tradition in the Art of Twentieth Century China*, Guggenheim Museum, New York, 1998.

Shen, Kuiyi, 'Traditional Painting in a Transitional Era, 1900–1950', in Julia F. Andrews and Shen Kuiyi, *A Century in Crisis: Modernity and Tradition in the Art of Twentieth Century China*, Guggenheim Museum, New York, 1998.

Shen, Kuiyi, 'The Modernist Woodcut Movement in the 1930s China', in Jo-Ann Birnie Danzker, Ken Lum and Zheng Shengtian (eds), *Shanghai Modern 1919–1945*, Hatje Cantze, Ostfildern, 2004.

Shi Jing (Book of Songs), Zhou Dynasty to Spring and Autumn (1000–700BC).

Shi, Zhecun, 'Zai Ba Li Da Xi Yuan' ('In the Paris Theatre'), *Xiao Shuo Yue Bao (Literary Monthly)*, Shanghai, Vol. 22, No. 8, 10 August 1931.

Shi, Zhecun, 'Mo Dao' ('Devil's Way'), *Xiao Shuo Yue Bao (Literary Monthly)*, Shanghai, Vol. 22, No. 9, 20 October 1931.

Shi, Zhecun, *Mei Yu Zhi Xi*, Zhong Guo Shu Ju, Shanghai, 1933.

Shi, Zhecun, 'You Guan Yu Ben Kan De Shi' ('About the Poems of this Magazine'), *Xian Dai (Les Contemporains)*, Vol. 4, No. 1, Shanghai, 1933.

Shi, Zhecun, 'Shi Zi Zuo Liu Xing' ('Shooting Star of Leo'), *Shan Nü Ren Xing Pin*, Shanghai Liang You Tu Shu Yin Shua Gong Si (Shanghai Liang You Book Publishing Company, November 1933.

Shi, Zhecun, 'Zhong Guo Xian Dai Zhu Yi De Shu Guang' ('The Dawn of the Chinese Modernism'), interview with Zheng Min Li and Lin Yao De in *Lian He Wen Xue (United Literature)*, Vol. 6, No. 9, Taipei, 1990.

Shi, Zhecun, *Shi Nian Chuang Zuo Ji (Collection of 10 Years of Creative Work)*, Hua Dong Shi Fan Da Xue Chu Ban She, Shanghai, 1996.

Shih, Shu-Mei, *The Lure of the Modern – Writing Modernism in Semicolonial China, 1917–1937*, University of California Press, Berkeley, CA, 2001.

Shin, Muramatsu, *Shanhai toshi to kenchiku, 1842–1949 (The Metropolitan Architecture of Shanghai 1842–1949)*, Parco, Tokyo, 1991.

Shinsaku, Tsutsui, 'Construction and Architecture of Manchoukuo', *Manchuria – Special Manchoukuo Economic Number*, 25 May 1938.

Shu, Xincheng, *Jin Dai Zhong Guo Liu Xue Shi (The Modern History of Chinese Overseas Study)*, Zhong Hua He Zhong Shu Ju, Shanghai, 1927.

Sickman, Laurence and Alexander Soper, *The Art and Architecture of China*, Penguin Books, Harmondsworth, 1956.

Sirén, Osvald, *A History of Chinese Art: Architecture*, Ernest Benn, London, 1929.

SMR, The, *South Manchuria Railway: The Pioneer on the Continent*, Herald Press, Tokyo, 1939.

Song, Qilin and Cai Lili, *Zhong Guo Wen Hua Yu Zhong Guo Cheng Shi*, Hubei Jiao Yu Chu Ban She, Wuhan, 2004.

Sowerby, Arthur de Carle, 'Modern Art Described as Rubbish', *The China Journal*, Vol. 17, No. 5, China Society of Arts and Science, Shanghai, November 1932.

Speidel, Manfred, *Japanische Architektur: Geschichte and Gegenwart*, Hatje, Berlin, 1983.

Spence, Jonathan, 'China's Modern Worlds', in Julia F. Andrews and Shen Kuiyi, *A Century in Crisis: Modernity and Tradition in the Art of Twentieth Century China*, Guggenheim Museum, New York, 1998.
St John's 1879–1919 – A Booklet of Information about the University at the end of Forty Years, Oriental Press, Shanghai, 1919.
Steinhardt, Nancy, ed., *Chinese Architecture*, Yale University Press, New Haven, CT, 2002.
Stewart, David, *The Making of a Modern Japanese Architecture: 1868 to the Present*, Kodansha International, Tokyo, 1987.
Stewart, J.L., 'West China Union University', *The Chinese Recorder*, Vol. 48, American Presbyterian Mission Press, Shanghai, September 1917.
Stipe, Margo, 'Wright and Japan', in Anthony Alofsin (ed.), Frank Llloyd Wright: Europe and Beyond, University of California Press, Berkeley, CA, 1999.
Strand, D., 'New Chinese Cities', in Joseph W. Esherick (ed.), *Remaking the Chinese City: Modernity and National Identity, 1900–1950*, University of Hawaii Press, Honolulu, 2000.
Stuart, John A. and Jewel Stern, *Ely Jacques Kahn, Architect: Beaux-Arts to Modernism in New York*, W.W. Norton, New York, 2006.
Su, Gin-Djih, *Chinese Architecture – Past and Contemporary*, The Sin Poh Amalgamated, Hong Kong, 1964.
Sullivan, Michael, *The Meeting of Eastern and Western Art from the Sixteenth Century to the Present Day*, University of California Press, Berkeley, CA, 1989.
Sullivan, Michael, *Art and Artists of Twentieth Century China*, University of California Press, Berkeley, CA, 1996.
Sun, Lung-kee, 'Chinese Intellectuals' Notion of "Epoch" in the Post-May Fourth Era', *Chinese Studies in History*, Vol. 20, No. 2, M.E. Sharpe, New York, Winter 1986/87.
Sun, Yat Sen, *Fundamentals of National Reconstruction*, China Cultural Service, Taipei, 1953.
Suzuki, Hiroyuki, Reyner Banham and Katsuhiro Kobayashi, *Contemporary Architecture of Japan 1958–1984*, Rizzoli, New York, 1985.
Tahara, Kaname, 'Harbin and Environs', *Manchuria*, 1 August 1940.
Takeuchi, Melinda, *The Artist as Professional in Japan*, Stanford University Press, Stanford, CA, 2004.
Tanaka, Stefan, *Japan's Orient*, University of California Press, Berkeley, CA, 1993.
Tanaka, Stefan, *New Times in Modern Japan*, Princeton University Press, Princeton, NJ, 2004.
Tang, Jingxian, *Other Words on the Establishment of the Association*, Special Edition for the establishment of the Shanghai Architecture Association, Shanghai, February 1931.
Tang, Xiaobing, *Origins of the Chinese Avant-Garde: The Modern Woodcut Movement*, University of California Press, Palo Alto, CA, 2008.
Taut, Bruno, *Fundamentals of Japanese Architecture*, Tokyo, 1937.
Taylor, Dave, 'Springtime in Manchuria', *Manchuria*, 1 August 1940.
Taylor, Walter, 'Chinese Architecture in Modern Buildings', *The Chinese Recorder*, American Presbyterian Mission Press, Shanghai, October 1924.
Thomson, John, *Ten Years' Travels: Adventures and Residence Abroad*, Low & Searle, London, 1875.
Thorne, Nancy, *Register of the Paul Philippe Cret Papers, 1876–1945*, University of Pennsylvania, Philadelphia, PA, 1999.
Throop, M.H., 'The China Field', *The Chinese Recorder*, American Presbyterian Mission Press, Shanghai, January 1924.
Tian, Han, *San Ge Modeng Nu Xing Yu Ruan Lin Yu (Three Modern Women and Ruan Lin Yu)*, Tian Han Wen Ji (Collection of Tian Han's writings), Vol. 11, Zhong Guo Xi Ju Chu Ban She, 1984.

Bibliography

Ting, V.K., ed., *Chronicle Biography of Liang Ch'i-ch'ao*, World Publishing Company, Taipei, 1958.

Tobey, Mark, 'Reminiscences and Reveries', *Magazine of Art*, Vol. 44, American Federation of Arts, New York, October 1951.

Tong, Jun, 'Architecture Chronicle', *T'ien Hsia*, Vol. 5, No. 3, Shanghai, October 1937.

Tong, Jun, 'Foreign Influence in Chinese Architecture', *T'ien Hsia*, Vol. 6, No. 5, Shanghai, May 1938.

Tong, Jun, *Su Lian Jian Zhu – Jian Shu Dong Ou Xian Dai Jian Zhu (Soviet Architecture – A Brief Description of Modern Architecture in Eastern Europe)*, Zhong Guo Jian Zhu Gong Ye Chu Ban She, Beijing, 1982.

Tong, Jun, *Ri Ben Jin Xian Dai Jian Zhu (Modern Architecture in Japan)*, Zhong Guo Jian Zhu Gong Ye Chu Ban She, Beijing, 1983.

Tong, Jun, *Jin Bai Nian Xi Fang Jian Zhu Shi (A Century of Western Architecture)*, Nan Jing Gong Xue Yuan Chu Ban She, Nanjing, 1986.

Towhata, Ikuo, *Geotechnical Earthquake Engineering*, Springer, Berlin, 2008.

Triggs, Inigo, *Town Planning: Past, Present and Possible*, Methuen, London, 1909.

Tu, Weiming, 'Implications of the Rise of "Confucian" East Asia', in 'Multiple Modernities', *Dædalus*, Journal of the American Academy of Arts and Sciences, Vol. 129, No. 1, Harvard University, Cambridge, Winter 2000.

Upshinsky, A.V., 'Harbin Sees Many Improvements', *Manchuria*, 1 July 1936.

Victoir, Laura and Victor Zatsepine, eds, *Harbin to Hanoi: The Colonial Built Environment in Asia, 1840 to 1940*, Hong Kong University Press, Hong Kong, 2013.

Vidler, Anthony, *The Architectural Uncanny: Essays in the Modern Unhomely*, MIT Press, Cambridge, MA, 1992.

Vines, Sherard, *Georgian Satirists*, Wishart & Co., London, 1934.

Voltaire, *Philosophical Dictionary*, Section 1, 'China', 1764.

Wakeman, Frederick, 'Boundaries of the Public Sphere in Ming and Qing China Early Modernities', in *Dædalus*, Summer 1998.

'Walpole to William Mason', 25 May 1772, in W.S. Lewis, *The Yale Edition of Horace Walpole's Correspondence*, Vol. 28, Yale University Press, New Haven, CT, 1937.

Wang, Fanzhi, *Lü Shi Chun Qiu Xuan Zhu*, Zhong Hua Shu Ju, Beijing, 1981.

Wang, Yichu, *Chinese Intellectuals and the West 1872–1949*, University of North Carolina Press, Chapel Hill, NC, 1966.

Warner, Torsten, *German Architecture in China*, Ernst & Sohn, Berlin, 1994.

Washburn, Dennis, trans., *Shanghai: A Novel* by Yokomitsu Riichi, University of Michigan Press, Ann Arbor, MI, 2001.

Waters, Dan, 'Hong Kong Hongs with Long Histories and British Connections', *Journal of the Royal Asiatic Society Hong Kong Branch*, Vol. 30, Hong Kong, 1990.

Wei Shu (Book of Wei), Northern Wei Dynasty (AD400–600).

Weisenfeld, Gennifer, *Mavo, Japanese Artists and the Avant-garde 1905–1931*, University of California Press, Berkeley, CA, 2002.

Wendelken, Cherie, 'The Tectonics of Japanese Style: Architect and Carpenter in the Late Meiji Period', *Art Journal*, Vol. 55, No. 3, College Art Association of America, New York, Fall, 1996.

Whigham, H.J., *Manchuria and Korea*, Isbister & Co., London, 1904.

'Who's Who in China – Biographies of Chinese', *The China Weekly Review*, Millard Publishing House, Shanghai, 1933.

Widmer, Ellen and David Der-Wei Wang, *From May Fourth to June Fourth: Fiction and Film in Twentieth Century China*, Harvard University Press, Cambridge, MA, 1993.

Wilson, George, 'Architecture, Interior Decoration and Building in Shanghai Twenty Years Ago and Today', *The China Journal*, Vol. 12, No. 5, China Society of Arts and Science, Shanghai, May 1930.

Witchard, Anne, ed., *Modernism and British Chinoiserie*, Edinburgh University Press, Edinburgh, 2014.

Wittrock, Björn, 'Early Modernities: Varieties and Transitions', Early Modernities, *Dædalus*, Vol. 127, Harvard University, Cambridge, MA, Summer 1998.

Wong, Rita, *Sanyu Catalogue Raisonné: Oil Paintings*, Yageo Foundation and Lin & Keng Publications, Taipei, 2001.

Wright, Arnold, *Twentieth Century Impressions of Hong Kong, Shanghai and other Treaty Ports of China*, Lloyds Greater Britain Publishing Company, London, 1908.

Wright, Frank Lloyd, *An Autobiography*, Longmans, Green & Co., New York, 1932.

Xiao, Qian, *The Dragonbeard versus the Blueprints: Meditations on Post-war Culture*, The Pilot Press, 1944.

Xu, Jinzhi (see Su, Gin-Djih).

Yeats, William Butler, *Four Plays for Dancers*, Macmillan, London, 1921.

Yeh, Wen-hsin, ed., *Becoming Chinese: Passages to Modernity and Beyond*, University of California Press, Berkeley, CA, 2000.

Yeoh, Brenda S.A., *Contesting Space in Colonial Singapore: Power Relations and the Urban Built Environment*, Singapore University Press, Singapore, 2003.

Yetts, Perceval, 'Writings on Chinese Architecture', *Burlington Magazine*, London, March 1927.

Yetts, Perceval, 'A Chinese Treatise on Architecture', *The Bulletin of the School of Oriental Studies*, Vol. 4, Issue 3, London, 1927.

Yokomitsu Riichi Zenshū (Collection of Yokomitsu Riichi's Works), Vol. 12, Kawade Shobō, Tokyo, 1956.

Young, Louise, *Japan's Total Empire: Manchuria and the Culture of Wartime Imperialism*, University of California Press, Berkeley, CA, 1998.

Yu, Qing, *Zhang Zi Ling Zhuan*, Shi Jie Shu Ju, Taiwan, 1993.

Yueng, Y.M. and C.P. Lo (eds.), *Changing South-East Asian Cities: Readings on Urbanization*, Oxford University Press, Singapore, 1976.

Yukichi, Fukuzawa, *The Autobiography of Fukuzawa Yukichi with Preface to the Collected Works of Fukuzawa*, Eiichi Kiyooka, trans., The Hokuseido Press, Tokyo, 1981.

Zhang, Fuhe, ed., *Zhong Guo Jin Dai Jian Zhu Bao Hu Yu Yan Jiu* (*The Research and Protection of Chinese Modern Architecture*), Qing Hua University Press, Beijing, 1999.

Zhang, Longxi, *Mighty Opposites: From Dichotomies to Differences in the Comparative Study of China*, Stanford University Press, Stanford, CA, 1998.

Zhang, Longxi, *Unexpected Affinities: Reading Across Cultures*, University of Toronto Press, Toronto, 2007.

Zhang, Tianyi, *Cong Kong Xu Dao Chong Shi* (*From Emptiness to Fulfilling*), San Xiong Di (Three Brothers), Wen Guang Shu Ju, Shanghai, 1937.

Zhang, Yanyuan, *Li Dai Ming Hua Ji* (*Records of Famous Painting throughout History*) (AD847), Tai Wan Shang Wu Chu Ban She, Taipei, 1965.

Zheng, Shengtian, 'Waves Lashed the Bund from the West – Shanghai's Art Scene in the 1930s', in Jo-Ann Birnie Danzker, Ken Lum and Zheng Shengtian (eds), *Shanghai Modern 1919–1945*, Hatje Cantze, Ostfildern, 2004.

Zhong Guo Jin Dai Jian Zhu Zong Lan (*Overview of Modern (pre-1949) Architecture in China*), Zhong Guo Jian Zhu Gong Ye Chu Ban She, 15 volumes, Beijing, January 1992.

Zhong, Yuanzhao and Chen Yangzheng (eds), *History and Development of Ancient Chinese Architecture*, Science Press, Beijing, 1986.

Zhou, Boxang and Zheng Xuan, *Zhou Li Zhu Shu Dong Gong Kao Gong Ji*, Tai Wan Shu Fang Chu Ban You Xian Gong Si, Taipei, 2001.

Zhou Li (*Rites of Zhou*), Zhou Dynasty (200–300BC).

Zhou, Yiliang, *Zhong Ri Wen Hua Jiao Liu Shi Da Xi*, Wen Xue Juan, Zhe Jiang Ren Min Chu Ban She, Hangzhou, 1996.

Zhu, Jianfei, *Architecture of Modern China – A Historical Critique*, Routledge, London, 2009.

328 Bibliography

Journals

Asia – Journal of the American Asiatic Association, Asia Publishing Co., New York.
The Builder, Shanghai Architects Association, Shanghai.
The China Architect's and Builder's Compendium, North China Daily News & Herald, Shanghai.
China Critic, The China Critic Publishing Company, Shanghai.
The China Journal, China Society of Arts and Science, North China Daily News and Herald, Shanghai.
The China Quarterly, China Quarterly Co., Shanghai.
The China Weekly Review, Millard Publishing House, Shanghai.
The Chinese Architect, Chinese Society of Architects, Shanghai.
The Chinese Recorder, American Presbyterian Mission Press, Shanghai.
Contemporary Manchuria, South Manchuria Railway Company, Japan.
Dædalus, Journal of the American Academy of Arts and Sciences, Harvard University, Cambridge, MA.
The East of Asia Magazine, The North China Herald, Shanghai.
Far East Magazine, Shanghai.
Far Eastern Review – Engineering, Finance, Commerce, Shanghai, Peking & Manila.
Fu Ren Hua Bao (*Women's Pictorial*), Shanghai.
Jin Dai Nu Xin (*The Modern Lady*), Shanghai.
Journal of the China Branch of the Royal Asiatic Society, Kelly & Walsh, Shanghai.
Journal of the Manchurian Architectural Association, Dalien.
Liang You Hua Bao (*The Young Companian*), Liang You Publishing Co., Shanghai.
The National Geographic, Washington, DC.
North China Herald, North China Daily News & Herald, Shanghai.
Shanghai Municipal Council Annual Report, Kelly & Walsh, Shanghai.
Shen Bao Yue Kan (*Monthly Magazine of Shen Bao*), Shanghai.
Social Shanghai, North China News & Herald, Shanghai.
T'ien Hsia, Shanghai.

Index

AA (Architectural Association) 107, 156–7, 159, 161, 165, 195
Abercrombie, Sir Patrick 158, 294
Adachi, H. 201
Adamson, Arthur Quintin 107–8, 110
adaptive Chinese Renaissance 168, 171
advertising/advertisements 52, 57–8, 74, 78–9, 219–20, 265–6, 269, 282
agriculture 45, 48, 252, 255
Algar, Albert Edmund 264
Allied Architects 144, 146, 176, 280, 296, 300, 305–6
amateurs 102
America 43–6, 70–1, 138–40, 143–6, 149–50, 152–3, 294–5, 302
American architects 170, 188, 261
Andersen, Meyer & Co 172, 197, 253, 269
Andrews, J.F. 24, 67, 195, 302
Ang Lee 302
Anshan steel foundry 6
anti-air raid design 215
architects *see Introductory Note*
Architectural Association *see* AA
architectural education 15, 17, 24, 44, 139, 143–4, 152, 161–5
architectural historians 15, 92, 144
architectural history xv, 4, 8, 14–16, 91–3, 150, 292, 297
Architectural Institute of Japan 206
architectural modernism 21–2, 72, 144, 163, 165, 208–9, 298, 302–3
architectural modernity xv–xvi, 27, 91–3, 200, 213–15, 280, 292–3, 307
architectural practices 105, 109, 139–40, 156–7, 162, 206
Architectural Review 13
architectural students 140, 150, 152–3, 295–6
architectural styles *see* styles

architecture: advent 91–8; national 137–8; *see also Introductory Note*
art 67–77, 79–80, 91, 93, 95, 144–5, 274, 305; Chinese 12, 21, 67–85, 91, 153, 185, 202, 301–2; Japanese 76, 203, 205; teachers 72; Western 68–9, 72, 75
art deco 74, 267
art education 71–2, 193
art nouveau 111, 119–20, 129, 153, 223, 225, 306
artists 67, 69, 75, 82, 279–80, 294, 296–7, 302
Asia Express 218–20
Astor House Hotel 107
Atkinson & Dallas 106–7, 166–7, 185, 262, 276
Atkinson, Brenan 107
atrocities 31, 111
Attiret, Father Jean Denis 11, 20, 101
authenticity 202, 223

Baedecker, C. 107–8
Bai'e Huahui 73
Bank of China, headquarters 158–9, 264, 307
Baudelaire, C. 49, 74, 306
beauty 53, 79, 91, 94, 102, 187, 189, 272–3
Becker & Baedecker 107–8
Becker, H. 107–8, 113–14
Beijing 100–2, 107–9, 137–8, 158–9, 162, 194–7, 274–5, 300–1
Beijing Opera 274–5
Beijing School 64, 80–1, 187
Beijing Union Medical College 167
Bell: Julian 38, 81; Vanessa 73
Benoist, Michel 101
Berlin 72, 75, 193, 220, 244, 257, 272
Berman, M. 17, 306

Binyon, L. 28
Bloomsbury Group 73, 81–2
Boerschmann, E. 12, 14, 25, 94
bomb-proofing 215
bombs 195, 249, 286–7
Boxer Indemnity 44–5, 47, 138–40, 168
Boyd, A. 14, 25, 191, 199
Bradbury, Malcolm 19
Brandt, A.J. 165, 295
bridges 54, 130–1, 222
Briscoe, L. 24
Britain 28–9, 35, 61, 64, 102, 104, 156–7, 159
British architects 105, 261, 276
Broadway Mansions 262, 264
Bubbling Well Road 107, 113
Buck, D.D. 17, 251–2
building in China 3, 11–13, 15, 93, 95–6, 168, 188, 236
building practices 68, 178
Building Shanghai 9
building traditions 165, 200–1
Bund, Shanghai 106, 111, 113, 156, 264, 273, 283–5
Burges, William 205
Burton, C.W. 109
Bush, C. 19, 21, 24, 26, 84
Bushell, S. 12
Butterfield and Swire 106

Cai Fangyin 162
Cai Yuanpei 44–6, 69, 72, 139, 153, 156, 193
calligraphy 68, 70, 91
Cambridge, UK 81, 104, 149
Canton 61, 101, 113, 197
Capital Construction Bureau *see* CCB
cartoons 18, 53, 59, 246, 270
carving 68, 116
Cary, Clarence 121, 125
Cassini Convention 116
Castiglione, Giuseppe 69, 101
Cathay Hotel 286
CCB (Capital Construction Bureau) 218, 234, 237, 247
Central Agricultural Laboratory 176–7
Central Police Station, Shanghai 104, 106
Central University 161, 196, 295
CER (China Eastern Railway) 116–21, 126, 151, 219, 222–4, 226, 232
Chakrabarty, D. 26, 177, 197, 303
Chambers, Sir William 11, 20, 26, 203

Chang, Eileen 280, 302–3
Chang Ching-huei 282
Chang Chun 101, 179
Chang Yu 72, 84, 302–3
Changchun 7, 9–10, 15–17, 128–30, 218–19, 232–47, 251–3, 255–6; *see also* Chang Chun
Charrey & Conversy 109
Chaund, W. 13, 25, 142, 193
Chen, H.S. 157, 195
Chen Baichen 53
Chen Bo Qi 152, 157, 159, 162
Chen Duxiu 33, 50, 60, 65–6
Chen Yuan 81
Chen Zhanxiang 157, 160–1, 175, 197–9, 294, 297, 300–1
Chen Zhi 14, 16, 25, 146–7, 194–6, 198, 256, 300–1
Chiang Kai Shek *see* Jiang Jieshi
children 29, 43–4, 266
China Aviation Association building 182–4
China Building Bureau 110
China Eastern Architectural Design Company 296
China Eastern Railway *see* CER
China Merchants Steam Navigation Company (CMSNC) 283–4, 295
China Mutual Life Assurance Company Building 107
China Sea 115, 118
Chinatowns 42, 110
Chinese architecture 11–16, 150–1, 171–2, 180, 182, 185–6, 188–92, 305–6; development 92–8, 172; *see also* Introductory Note
Chinese art 12, 21, 67–85, 91, 153, 185, 202, 301–2
Chinese brushwork 21, 70
Chinese colleges in Japan 32
Chinese Communist Party 33, 64
Chinese culture 3, 12, 28, 41, 56, 73, 81, 226
Chinese design 20, 96, 202
Chinese language 38, 47, 49–50, 54, 60, 251, 303
Chinese literature 38, 80, 83–4, 301
Chinese Renaissance 168, 171, 209, 295, 299
Chinese Renaissance style 186, 306
Chinese roof 188, 190, 295
Chinese Society of Architects 186–7, 198, 259

Chinese style 69, 165–7, 169–70, 172, 175, 188, 197, 202
Chineseness 49, 184
chinoiserie 20, 83, 96, 153, 202, 204
Christie, James 106
Chu & Yang 140, 144, 177, 272, 295–6
Chuo-dori 236
Church of Sao Paulo 101
Church of the Immaculate Conception 101
churches 100–1, 104, 112, 166
Ci Xi, Empress 32
CIAM (Congrès Internationaux d'Architecture Moderne) 208
cinemas 8, 22, 78–80, 229–30, 236, 238, 274–6, 280
cities cosmopolitan 113, 222; global 267; largest 108, 117, 136, 223, 232, 257; Manchurian 267; neo-Japanese 233; old 128, 182, 259; primate 80; *see also* colonial cities
Civic Centre, Shanghai 8, 152, 157, 179–84, 186, 188–9, 275, 286
civil engineers 156, 193, 195, 263
Clarke, D. 71, 283, 299
Classical Chinese 47, 63, 65
clocks 56–8, 280
Club Concordia 108
CMSNC *see* China Merchants Steam Navigation Company
Coates, Wells 107, 303
Cody, Jeffrey 16, 168
Collins, Peter 96
colonial cities 233, 258, 306
colonialism 17, 24, 27, 34, 36–8, 60, 107, 115
colonies 35, 103, 107, 120, 244, 285, 296
commercial art 67, 74, 79
commoditisation 74, 80
Communist Party 26, 33, 54, 64, 78, 297, 300
Communist period 13–15
competition 36, 174, 180, 197, 206, 208, 216
compradoric architecture 102, 186
concessions 35, 38, 109, 112, 167, 172
Conder, Josiah 129, 205
Confucius 40–2, 48, 56, 95
Congrès Internationaux d'Architecture Moderne (CIAM) 208
continuity 13–14, 49
Convention of Kanagawa 28

Cory, John Myrie 104–5
Creation Society 33, 294, 304
Cret, P.P. 143–5, 193–4
Cultural Revolution 15–16, 57, 61, 300–2
culture 21–2, 77, 82, 173, 175, 187, 191, 303
Cumine & Co 107
Cumine, E. 107, 165, 295
curtailed modernities 292–307
Curtis, William 19
customs 96, 184, 188, 214–15, 278

Dædalus 21, 25–6
Dai Wangshu 78–9
Dairen 129, 226, 229, 232, 249, 255; *see also* Dalian
Dalian 117–18, 121–3, 125, 127–31, 219–20, 226–30, 232, 251–2; plan of 9, 221, 227
Dallas, Arthur 106
Dalny *see* Dalian
Dana, Richard Henry 109, 140–1, 152, 168–9
dance halls 80, 276, 279–80
Danzker, J.B. 24, 69
Darwin, Charles 56–7, 61
Dashiqiao 117
Davies & Thomas 106, 113
Davies, Gilbert 106
Decker, Paul 11
democracy 42, 47, 54, 177
Deng Xiaoping 45
Department of Communications 7, 221
design 143–6, 166–75, 182–4, 202–3, 210–12, 230–1, 263–5, 297–8; principles 175–6
Dewey, John 38, 47, 77, 83
Dong Dayou 91, 95, 152, 179–80, 182–3, 185, 188–9, 196–9
Doyle, M. 39, 63
Du Halde, Jean-Baptiste 11, 20
Duan Qirui 48

Eastern China 13, 39
École Nationale des Beaux-Arts 143, 261
Edkins, Joseph 12
education 31, 43–4, 46, 138–9, 149–50, 161–3, 295, 297; architectural 15, 17, 24, 44, 139, 143–4, 152, 161–5; art 71–2, 193; Japanese 31–2
Eisenstadt, S.N. 11, 18, 21–2, 26
elevators 218, 265, 270, 280

empire 126, 129, 207, 212–13, 216–17, 220, 247, 249
employees 180, 211, 243
engineering 103, 105, 139–40, 156, 161, 163, 193, 196; graduates 45, 139–40
engineers 45–6, 104–7, 109, 113, 115, 162, 180, 206
Esherick, J. 16, 25
Europe 64, 69–71, 73, 92–3, 117–19, 151, 153, 208
European cities 122, 245
Exposition Internationale des Arts Décoratifs et Industriels Modernes 153–4
Eysteinsson, Astradur 19

factories 5, 102, 118, 122, 128, 266, 276, 279–80
Fairbank: John 10, 47, 70, 193, 198; Wilma 14, 62–3, 147, 194–6, 198–9, 249, 256, 307
Fan, Robert *see* Fan Wenzhao
Fan Wenzhao 140–1, 143–4, 146, 171, 177, 186, 293, 296
Far Eastern Review 13, 25, 141, 193, 197–8, 250, 252–6, 273
Feng Le 236, 238
Feng Zikai 67–8, 74, 76, 80, 91, 98, 274, 280
Fengtian Army 195
First World War 45, 47, 72, 77, 143, 258, 260–1
Five United 157, 159–60, 165, 296, 300
Foo Fong Flour Mills 107
foreign buildings 11, 101–2, 109, 112, 188
foreign communities 27, 36–7, 70, 273
foreign merchants 12, 101–3
foreign powers 35–6, 41, 62–4, 100, 121, 127–8, 193
foreign settlements 27–8, 35–8, 100–1, 103–5, 109–13, 119–23, 179, 270; before 1912 100–31
foreigners 12, 37–8, 101, 103–6, 112, 165–7, 268, 285
Forster, E.M. 83, 294
France 35, 38, 44–5, 63–4, 72, 151, 153, 156
Fraser, Bright 260–2
Free School of Architecture 260–1
French Concession, Shanghai 73, 79, 109, 112, 120, 193, 267
French programme 45
Fuchiatien 119, 224, 226

Fujimori, Terunobu 15
Fukuzawa, Y. 28–9, 61
Fushun 5–6, 128, 252
Fuzhou 5, 43, 61–2, 196

Gaonkar, D.P. 26, 306
Garden of Art 67, 74, 76, 80, 91, 98, 299, 305
gardens 20, 67–8, 76, 80, 91, 95, 97, 181
Gauntlett, G.E.L. 107
Germany 35, 44–5, 47, 63–4, 151, 153, 208, 210
Gibbings, R. 75
Gilbert Scott, Sir George 104–5
Gilchrist, T.V. 245, 252, 255–6
Gonda, C.H. 260, 272, 275, 278–9
Gong Chan Dang *see* Communist Party
Gratton, Frederick Montague 105
Great Pagoda, Kew, 20, 97
Great Wall 115, 194
Great World, Shanghai 74, 276, 286–7
Greater Shanghai 179–81
Greater Shanghai Plan 179–84
Gregorian calendar 55, 57
Grunsky, C.E. 180
Guandong Army 195, 211, 213, 234, 236, 248
Guangzhou 61–2, 73, 75, 101–4, 163, 167, 172, 174
Guo Moruo 33, 175, 197
Guo Yangmo 140, 176

Habermas, J. 17, 65
Hahn, Emily 79
Haipai 80, 187, 257, 274
Hajek, H.J. 164–5
Hakutei, Ishii 72
Halfpenny, William 11
Halse, Sidney 105
Hammerschmidt, Josef Alois 260–2
Hangzhou 53, 74–5, 139, 148, 152, 156, 196, 210
Hankou 108–9, 111, 180, 211, 254, 275
Harbin 8, 117–20, 122, 125–6, 219, 222–6, 251–2, 254; hotel Moderne 120; Kitaiskaya Street 7, 225; New Town 119, 224, 254
harbours 121, 130, 231
Harding, S. 26, 302–3
Harootunian, H. 26, 34, 57, 66, 126, 200, 250, 293
Harrison, Wallace 297–8

Hayot, E. 21, 24, 26, 84
Hazzard, Elliot 277
Hemmings & Berkley 109
Hemmings, R.E. 109
Hewitt, R.N. 109
Heynen, H. 49–50, 65
hierarchy 94–5
history 15–16, 19, 92–3, 118–19, 201, 226, 293–4, 301–4; modernist 92, 233, 292
Hong Kong 12, 14, 61–2, 103–5, 109, 112, 156, 295–7
Hong Kong and Shanghai Banking Corporation (HSBC) offices 6, 105
Hongkou 73, 157, 209–10, 260
Horta, Victor 119
Hosagrahar, J. 25–6, 69, 201, 250, 303–4, 306
hotel Moderne, Harbin 120
hotels 83, 118–19, 203, 215, 307
Hsinking *see* Changchun
Huang Chujiu 74, 275
Huang Fu 179
Huang Guiyou 24
Huang Xiling 140
Huang Yüyü 175–6
Huang Zumiao 161
Hudec, László 5, 260–1, 270, 273, 275, 280–1, 306
Hunan 45, 196
Huntington, S. 41, 61, 63
Hussey, Harry 167, 169, 182, 188, 196

identity, national 16, 77, 136–7, 175, 178–9, 202, 205, 257
Imperial College of Engineering (ICE), Tokyo 129, 205, 250
Imperial Hotel 203, 251
imperialism 33–4, 38–9, 212; from the East 38–9; European 293
Incorporated Institute of Architects in China 106
India 19, 21, 23, 97–8, 100, 102, 105–6, 111
individualism 47–8, 96
Institute for Research in Chinese Architecture 14, 16, 182
institutions 109, 139, 157, 161, 163, 166, 223, 258–9
intellectuals 30, 47–8, 137, 186
interior design 152–3, 165, 218
International Architectural Association of Japan 207

international modernism 82, 295
international modernity 74, 307
International Settlement 35, 65, 112, 259, 284
International Style 92, 140, 192, 207, 236
Ise Jingū 202–3
Isozaki, A. 201–4, 250, 305
Italian Renaissance 170, 185

Japan 27–33, 71–7, 125–31, 191–3, 200–9, 211–19, 231–3, 247–56; annexation of Manchuria 22; building traditions shared with China 201–4; colonial policy 30; emerging architectural profession 205–9; government 13, 32, 205, 242; imperial project 211, 218; Imperialism 31, 33, 39, 136, 251; as mirror to modernism 200–49; as modernity's mediator 28–31; traditions 28, 204–5
'Japan hands' 32–3
Japanese architects, in Manchukuo 244, 248
Japanese architecture 28, 200, 202–5, 255; in China 209–11
Japanese art 76, 203, 205
Japanese Consulate 108, 210, 286
Japanese education 31–2
Japanese garden 209–10
Japanese language 54, 75, 249
Japanese police 209, 294
Japanese residents 125, 222, 242
Japanese scholars 15, 28, 30, 211, 249
Japanese styles 206, 244
Jesuits 11, 56, 101, 138
Jian Zhu Yue Kan 13, 93, 165, 186
Jiang Jieshi 32–3, 48, 195, 274
Jiang Ren 95
jianzhu 51–2
Jiat-Hwee Chang 23
jidai 50
jindai 50–1, 60
jindai lishi 51
Jingpai 64, 80–1, 187
Jiujiang 111
Joint Savings Society Building, Shanghai 5, 157, 270
Jun, Tosaka 74

Kanagawa, Convention of 28
Kang Youwei 32, 46, 56–7, 62, 109
Kanzō, Uchiyama 75
Kaspe, Iosif 120
Katsura Imperial Villa 202–3

334   Index

Kerbech 121, 123–4
Kew Gardens 20, 97, 101
Kharbin *see* Harbin
Kidner, William 104–5
King, A. 23
Kingsmill, T. 102, 104, 106
Kitaiskaya Street 7, 225
Kollwitz, K. 75
Kon, Wajirō 74, 207
Korea 30, 61, 98, 115, 125, 168, 211, 256
Koshizawa, Akira 15, 17, 252
Kotoku Kaikan 236–7
Kracauer, S. 74, 80, 272, 276
Kryzhanovsky, D.A. 119
Kuomintang 48, 62, 75
Kuonin, I.I. 61
Kwan, Chu & Yang 140, 144–5, 177, 272, 295–6
Kwantung Leased Territory 117, 125, 127, 129

Lai Delin 15
Lao She 97, 181, 300
Laurence, P.O. 21, 24
Le Corbusier 159, 161, 208, 233, 242–3, 269, 273, 297–8
League of Left-wing Writers 75, 78
Lee, Leo Ou-fan 24–6, 34, 36, 38, 42, 62–3, 65, 78–9
Léonard & Veysseyre 273, 306
Lester Institute of Technical Education 157, 160, 195
Levine, M. 45, 64
Li Dazhao 33
Li Hongzhang 43, 63, 115–16
Li Jipiao 107
Li Shutong 68, 72, 74
Li Weihan 45
Liang Qichao 32, 34, 40, 56–7, 63, 81, 83, 148–51
Liang Sicheng 25, 61–2, 145–51, 162, 182, 190–6, 198–9, 297–301
Liao style 177–8
Liaodong Peninsula 115–16, 125
Li–Lobanov Treaty 116
lilong 259, 269
Lim, William 23
Lin Fengmian 72, 153, 156, 195
Lin Huiyin 68, 70, 72, 81–4, 146–8, 198, 292–3, 301
lineal time 57–8, 60, 93

Ling Shuhua 81–4, 294, 303
Lingnan School 73
linguistic integrity 38
literary modernism 19, 24, 84, 97, 279
literary modernity 19, 24, 76–84
Liu, Laurence 15
Liu Dunzhen 151, 162, 293, 300
Liu Haisu 72
Liu Jipiao 152–5, 161, 174, 195, 293, 302–3
Liu Na'ou 49, 53, 58, 65, 78–9, 269, 294
Liu Shiying 139, 161, 195
Luke, Him Sau 9, 156–9, 161, 195, 293–5, 297, 303, 306
Lu Qianshou *see* Him Sau, Luke
Lu Xun 33, 47–8, 65, 75, 78, 274, 294
Lü Yanzhi 109, 171, 174, 176, 182, 186, 193, 195
Lum, Ken 24, 72
Lunghua 106–7, 295
Lüshun 116

Macau 35, 61, 101–3
MacDonnell Mitchell Dowdall 105, 112
Maclellan, J.W. 12
Malcolm, D.A. 109
Manchu 115, 190, 211–12, 237–8, 240, 252, 254–5
Manchukuo *see* Manchuria
Manchuria 115–19, 125–9, 211–19, 221–7, 229–34, 243–5, 247–9, 251–6; Japanese architects in 244, 248; Japanese-occupied 9, 13, 127, 170, 221, 252; North 118, 254; railways in 105, 253; role in Japan's post-war developments 216; ultra-modernism 211–49
Manchuria Motion Picture Producing and Distributing Corporation 237, 255
Manchurian Architectural Association 198, 214, 245
Mao Dun 53, 58, 65, 275, 283
Mao Tse-tung 57, 61
Martyrs' Shrine 174
Marx, K. 17–18, 306
Massa, Father Nicholas 112
materialism 52, 264
May Fourth Movement 33, 46–7, 49, 56–7, 60–1, 63, 74, 77–8
Mayor's Office, Shanghai 8, 182, 189
McBain Building 105
McGee, T. 23
Meiji Restoration 28, 31, 39, 54, 73, 205

merchants 36, 80, 100–2, 104, 119–20, 128
Middle Kingdom 30, 34, 56, 94
Middle Way 69
Ming (Dynasty) 21, 56
Minutti & Co 263
Minutti, René 260–1, 263, 273
Mirams, D.G. 13
missionary schools 43, 46, 71
Mitsutani Kunishirō 72
modeng 50–3
Modeng Po Huai Tuan 53
modernisation 28–30, 47, 49–50, 200–1, 205, 230, 233, 303–4
modernism 17–22, 24, 77–9, 144, 203–5, 207–9, 257–8, 298–304; international 82, 295; Japanese 200–56; literary 19, 24, 84, 97, 279; and nationalism 136–93; Western 4, 21, 28, 33, 70, 76, 83, 97
Modernism in China 9, 24, 173, 251
modernist encounters 79, 83, 165, 307
modernist historiography xv, 92, 233, 258, 292
modernist writers 33, 73–4, 83, 302; China's 9, 267
modernity: appraisal in other art practices in China 24–5; architectural xv–xvi, 27, 91–3, 200, 213–15, 280, 292–3, 307; contemporary theories of 17; curtailed modernities 292–307; from the East 126–31; etymology of 27, 49–50; experience of 22, 76, 93, 227, 247; heterogeneous origins of xvi; international 74, 307; literary 19, 24, 76–84; measuring 17–18; multifaceted 22, 80, 215, 300; multiple expressions of 60–1; multiple modernities *see* multiple modernities; in other regional or cultural contexts 23; privileged accounts of 25, 304; Shanghai 257–8, 274, 280; and time 27, 55–60; and visual artists 67–71; *see also Introductory Note*
Montesquieu, Charles de 20
Moorhead, Robert 105
Morrison: Gabriel James 105; Gratton & Scott 106
Morrison & Gratton 105–6
Mu Shiying 49, 58, 78–9, 270, 272, 276, 293–4, 296
Mukden *see* Shenyang
Mukden Incident 162, 211, 249

multiple modernities 17–19, 21–4, 41–3, 49–51, 53–5, 69–71, 75–7, 81–3; and Chinese art 67–84; Shanghai as exemplar of 257–87
multiple moderns 54–5
Munakata Architectural Office 230
Municipal Council, Shanghai 35, 109, 113, 185, 195, 259
Murphey, R. 4, 34
Murphy: Henry 16, 109–10, 168–71, 173–5, 180, 182, 186, 188; McGill & Hamlin 109, 168
Murphy & Dana 109, 140–1, 152, 168–9
Musgrove, C.D. 17, 197

Nanjing 17, 102, 156–7, 161, 170–5, 177–80, 196–7, 295; as new capital 173–8; Treaty of 28, 35, 102, 112, 179, 205
Nanjing Road, Shanghai 104, 106, 277, 279, 285
Nanyang College 163, 196
National Academy of Art 72, 156
National Anthem 62, 300
national architecture 137–8
National Capital Construction Committee 174–5
National Central Museum 177–8
National Diet Building 206, 208, 241
national identity 16, 77, 136–7, 175, 178–9, 202, 205, 257
national projects 170–84, 208–9
national salvation 46, 48, 53
national style 9, 176–7
national style of architecture 137, 173, 189, 206
national unity 136
nationalism 13, 17, 23, 27, 39–49, 60, 84, 136–93; modern 42; and modernism 136–93
Nationalist government 136, 142, 170, 175, 177, 179, 186, 202
Nationalist Party 48, 75, 112, 157
nation-building 25, 27, 39–46, 49, 77
nationhood 27, 39–42, 78, 92, 186
nation-states 34–5, 41, 136
New Culture Movement 44, 46–7, 50, 57
New Life Movement 48, 53, 145
New Territories 35
New World 23, 107, 255–6, 276
New York 197, 203, 244, 267, 279, 284, 292, 297

New Yorker 74, 79, 110
New Youth 33, 47, 50, 60, 65, 79
Ni Yide 72–3
Nie Rongzhen 45
Nielsen & Malcolm 109
Nielsen, H.R. 109
Ningbo 61–2, 104, 157
non-West 23, 27, 92, 200, 203
North Manchuria 118, 254
north-east China 30, 100, 202
North-Eastern University 146, 151, 162
northern China 104, 116, 186, 193, 244, 296
northern district, Shanghai 210

Occidentalism 46, 80
Orientalism 19, 21
Oskolkov, Mikhail Matveevich 224

pagodas 96, 100, 173, 181, 266
painting 67–9, 73–4, 76–7, 91, 95, 97, 293, 302; European 69
Palmer & Turner 6, 105, 113, 156, 158–9, 195, 263, 277
Palmer, Clement 105
Pang Laikwan 24, 275
Paramount Ballroom 163, 296
Park Hotel, Shanghai 5, 273
Parkin, W.G. 109
parks, public 123–4, 236
Paulick, Richard 83, 163, 165
Pei, I.M. 156, 160, 307
Pei Zuyi 156
Peiping Art College 162–3
Peking University 33–4, 46, 81, 83, 196
People's Republic of China 13, 62
Pére Robert Apartment 164
Philadelphia 122, 141, 143–6
Phillips, Edward 180, 277
planned cities 122, 179
planners, urban 173, 222
planning 14, 118–26, 128–9, 169–70, 180, 242, 246–7, 297; urban 125, 165, 173, 211, 216, 222, 233, 306–7
poets 33, 78, 81–2, 193, 279, 300
Pollock, Jackson 70
Port Arthur 117, 125
ports 111, 121–3, 125, 128, 180, 227, 229, 232
Portsmouth, Treaty of 125
Portugal 35, 102
post-modernity 21

Pound, Ezra 24, 83
Poy Gum Lee 110, 171, 180
Pristan 119, 224–5, 254
Pu Luo Yi Shu Yun Dong 74
Pu Yi 35, 211, 234
Public Market, Shanghai 106, 113
publishing industry 13, 74
Pusey, J. 57, 61–2, 66

qi meng 48
Qian Juntao 74
Qian Zhaoming 24, 83
Qing Dynasty 21, 32, 48, 57, 115, 136
qing gong jian xue 45
Qing style 177–8
Qing Yi Bao 32
Qiu Tongyi 52, 65
Quan Ren 53, 65
quasi-colonial condition 37, 102–3, 111, 142, 209
quasi-colonial settlements 37, 112, 185
quasi-Japanese design 7
Quesnay, François 20

racecourses 60, 157, 243, 276, 279, 283
railway stations 41, 118, 122, 124, 128, 222, 230–2, 236
railways 115–19, 121–3, 125–6, 128–30, 180, 221–2, 224, 252–4
Ranelagh House 20
Ransome, A. 37, 63, 136, 193, 284
Raymond, A. 203–4, 250
Rea, G.B. 13, 25
reforms 39–40, 43, 47, 205
Reinhold, C.I. 28, 31, 33, 61–2
Reisner, J.H. 45
Renaissance: Chinese 168, 171, 209, 295, 299; Italian 170, 185
Republic of China 33, 42, 62, 100, 142
residences 104, 108, 119–20, 156, 160, 262, 265, 268
resistance 38, 54, 76, 93, 304
revivalism 165–70, 188
RIBA *see* Royal Institute of British Architects
Ricci, Matteo 56
Riedel, J. 22, 26, 66
Riichi, Y. 22, 30, 259, 285
roads 113, 119, 124, 229, 232, 234, 236–7, 242
Ross, R. 23
Rou Shi 75

Rowe, Peter 16
Royal Institute of British Architects (RIBA) 104
Royal Pavilion 101
Ruo Shi 75
Russell, B. 34, 38, 62, 77, 83, 111, 149
Russia 35, 115–18, 121, 123, 125–6, 129, 222–3, 226–7; China Eastern Railway 120
Russians 9–10, 111, 117–22, 125, 221, 223–6, 254, 258–60
Russo-China Convention 116
Russo-Chinese bank 113–14
Russo-Japanese War 125–6, 129, 223, 225

Sachsenmaier, Dominic 22, 26, 66
Saharoff 121, 123–4
Said, E. 19–20, 38–9, 63, 96–7
St Francis Xavier Cathedral 112
St Ignatius Cathedral 112
St John's University, Shanghai 37, 140–1, 159, 163, 165–6, 196, 295
St Petersburg 116, 118–19, 226, 232
Saint-John Perse 21
Salway, William 105
san shih 56
Sanyu *see* Chang Yu
Sapajou 270
Satō, Tomiko 33
schools 80, 143–4, 146, 148, 150, 161–2, 195–6, 215
Schwarcz, V. 48, 65
Scott, Walter 106
second generation of architects 138–9, 142–61, 207
Second World War 14, 75, 81–2, 84, 156–7, 235–6, 284–5, 294–5
Self-Strengthening Movement 29, 39–40, 43, 46
Seng Kuan 16
settlements 35, 37–8, 61–2, 65, 103–4, 109, 111–12, 221–4; quasi-colonial 37, 112, 185
Shanghai 65–6, 73–5, 78–80, 102–8, 112–15, 156–66, 195–8, 209–11; architects 258, 270, 275; Bubbling Well Road 107, 113; Central Police Station 104, 106; Civic Centre 8, 152, 157, 179–84, 186, 188–9, 275, 286; as exemplar of multiple modernities 257–87; French Concession 73, 79, 109, 112, 120, 193, 267; Great World 74, 276, 286–7; Greater 179–81; Japanese garden 209–10; Joint Savings Society Building 5, 157, 270; Mayor's Office 8, 182, 189; modernity 257–8, 274, 280; Municipal Council 35, 109, 113, 185, 195, 259; Nanjing Road 104, 106, 277, 279, 285; northern district 210; Public Market 106, 113; region 296, 300; St John's University 37, 140–1, 159, 163, 165–6, 196, 295; writers 78, 80, 269
Shanghai Domestic Architectural Design Institute 296
Shanghai Foxtrot 53, 270, 272, 276
Shanghai Land Investment Company 107
Shanghai Mutual Telephone Company Ltd 106, 113
Shanghai Power Company 265–6
Shanghai Society of Engineers and Architects 106, 113, 186, 198, 206, 259
Shen Kuiyi 24, 67, 72–3, 139–40, 145–6, 193–5
Shen Liyuan 139–40, 180
Shenyang 115, 117, 126, 128–9, 150–1, 162, 221–2, 251–3
Shi Dai Mei Shu She 73
Shi Zhecun 31, 33–4, 37–8, 51, 58, 62, 66, 279–80
shidai 50, 60, 65
Shidrovski 117
Shih Shu-Mei 26–7, 30–1, 33–4, 36–8, 61–3, 76–8, 81–3, 88
Shi-Hui Cloth Mill 105
shimao 50–3
Shimonoseki, Treaty of 29, 115
Shōmu, Noboru 34
shops 7, 9, 53, 71, 119, 215, 230, 245
Shōzan, Sakuma 29
Shu Xincheng 37
Shuntian Highway 241
Sichuan 45, 82
Sickman, Laurence 13
Singapore 23, 102, 105, 179
Sino-Japanese War 29, 31, 44, 83, 116, 128, 209
Sirén, O. 12, 14
SMR (South Manchuria Railway) 127–30, 211–12, 219, 221, 225–7, 229–32, 234, 247–8
social order 94–5, 188
Song Dynasty 12, 95
Soper, Alexander 13, 93
South Lake Complex 241–3

South Manchuria Railway *see* SMR
South Manchuria Railway's Asia Express 220
southern China 39, 101, 156, 163
space 4, 22, 40, 54–5, 95, 233, 241, 250; and time 55–7
Spain 19, 21, 35, 151
standardisation 94–5, 192, 201
stations 104, 116, 128, 215, 232, 236, 251
steel 113, 140, 172, 182, 190–1, 265; frames 113, 232, 272
Steel, R. 113–14
Steinhardt, N. 15, 25
Stewart, J.L. 102, 196, 203–5, 207, 250
stone 101–2, 172, 236, 241
Strachan, A.F. 104
students 31–2, 43–7, 62–3, 75, 141, 143–4, 198, 205–6
styles 68, 70, 101–3, 165–7, 188–91, 206, 214–15, 263–4; Chinese 69, 165–7, 169–70, 172, 175, 188, 197, 202; compradoric 102; international 92, 140, 192, 207, 236; Japanese 206, 244; Liao 177–8; Qing 177–8; Western 102, 205–6
Sü, Yang & Lei 177
subjects 3–4, 11, 13–15, 17–18, 22–3, 44–5, 62–4, 302–3
summer 25–6, 69, 107, 149–50, 162, 225
Sun Ke 175, 295
Sun Sun department store 278–9
Sun Yat Sen 33, 42, 63, 146, 173, 175, 186, 295
Sun Yat Sen Mausoleum 170–2, 177, 186
Sun Yat Sen Memorial Auditorium and Monument 172
Sun Yat Sen Memorial Pagoda 180
Sungari River 225–6
Sviridov, Petr Sergeevich 224
synagogues 100

Tabusa 220
Tahara, Kaname 226, 254
Taipei 296
Taiwan 23, 30, 35, 112, 115, 126, 292, 296–7
Takaoka Building Contractors 231–2
Takeji, Fujishima 72
tallest building 5, 157, 265, 273
Tang Dynasty 192, 200, 202
Taoism 12, 55
Tatsuno, Kingo 129, 205–6, 234
Tatung Boulevard 236–8, 241

Tatung Circle 235, 237, 240–1
Taut, Bruno 192, 203–5, 207, 250
Taylor, Walter 170, 196–8, 254
teaching 65, 73–4, 144, 161, 251, 301
tea-houses 275, 277
technology 127, 193, 196, 264, 270, 272, 280, 282
Teijō, Eguchi 212
telephones 118, 218, 221, 227, 237–8, 243
Telkamp, G. 23
temporal linearity 58, 60
Teng Baiye 70–1, 82, 84, 299–300, 302–3
Tennessee Valley Authority (TVA) 298
theatres 33, 67, 78, 80, 217, 275–6
Tian Han 33, 51–3, 65, 78–80, 300
Tian Ma Hui 73
Tiananmen Square 47–8, 301
Tianjin 35, 43, 104, 108–9, 139–41, 254, 260, 262
Tientsin, Treaty of 104, 112, 115
time 14–17, 47–50, 53–8, 60, 93–7, 126–7, 171–3, 177–9; cyclical 55; lineal 57–8, 60, 93; manifested 57–60; and modernity 27, 55–60; and space 55–7; terminology 60–1
Tobey, M. 21, 26, 38, 70–1, 283, 302
Tokiwa Cinema 230
Tokyo 72, 127, 203, 205–6, 225, 230, 252–3, 255
Tokyo Higher Technical School 139, 153, 161
Tokyo Imperial Household Museum 208
Tokyo Imperial University 33, 191, 203, 210, 234, 251
Tokyo School of Fine Arts 72, 74
Tong & Cai Architects 162
Tong Jun 13, 146, 161–2, 293–4, 296, 300, 303, 305
towns 118–19, 122, 124–5, 128–9, 213, 215, 220–2, 253
trade 34, 36, 38, 91, 95, 102–4, 121–2, 202
traditional Japanese architecture 201, 204
traditions 49–50, 68, 93, 95–6, 144, 190, 244–5, 306–7
Trans-Siberian Railway 115, 117–19, 151, 208
Treaty of Nanjing 28, 35, 102, 112, 179, 205
Treaty of Portsmouth 125
Treaty of Shimonoseki 29, 115
Treaty of Tientsin 104, 112, 115

treaty ports 29, 32, 35–6, 100, 103, 108–9, 120–1, 170
Triggs, Inigo 123
Trinity Cathedral 105
Tsinghua 37, 44–5, 64, 141, 151, 194, 196, 295
Tsinghua Xue Tang 44–5, 140–1, 145–7, 152, 168, 193
Tsuguharu, Fujita 72
Turner, Arthur 105
TVA (Tennessee Valley Authority) 298
Twenty One Demands 47, 64

Uchiyama Bookstore 75
UCL (University College London) 104, 106, 129, 140, 157–8, 160, 205
ultra-modernism 9, 200, 251; in Manchuria 211–49
ultra-modernity 235, 245, 249
United Kingdom *see* Britain
University College London *see* UCL
University of Pennsylvania 137, 139–41, 143–7, 149–50, 162, 191, 193–4, 196
urban planning 125, 165, 173, 211, 216, 222, 233, 306–7
urbanisation xv, 3, 16

Valéry, Paul 69
Vanity Fair 74
Vensan, Sergei 121
Vernacular Chinese 47, 67, 93
Versailles 47
Veysseyre, Paul 260–2, 273, 306
Virginia Woolf 38, 81–2, 294
visual artists and modernity 67–71
Vitruvius 55
Voltaire 20, 26
von Bell, Schall 101

Wakeman, F. 21, 26, 55, 66
wakon yōsai 29
Walpole, Horace 20
Wang Dahong 157, 159, 161, 297
Wang Tan 15, 294
Wang Yichu 43, 45–6, 62, 64, 157, 159, 297
war 34, 125–6, 159, 247–8, 283–5, 292, 294–5, 299
West China Union University 167
Western art 68–9, 72, 75
Western modernism 4, 21, 28, 33, 70, 76, 83, 97

Western powers xvi, 28–30, 115, 127, 209
Western styles 102, 205–6
Westerners 30, 56–7, 68, 258, 276, 285, 304
Westernisation 18, 28, 47, 60, 76, 80, 205, 304; Movement 29, 39, 60
West Lake Expo 153, 155
White Russians 120, 128, 221, 223, 226, 260, 267
Wilson, George 6, 263, 272–3, 284
Wing On 277–8, 286
Wolff, Christian 20
women 29, 53, 57, 75, 266, 268–9, 279, 282
woodcuts 74–5
Woolf, Virginia 38, 81–2, 294
Wright: Arnold 12; Frank Lloyd 40, 107, 145, 176, 192, 203, 230, 240
writers 30, 47–8, 67–9, 78–81, 129–31, 269–70, 296–7, 300–1; modernist 33, 73–4, 83, 302

Xi Fuquan 156, 296
Xiamen 61–2, 209
xiandai 34, 50–3, 55, 60
xiandai shenghuo 34
xiandai wenming 34
xiandai xing 50–1
xiandai zhuyi 50
Xiang Qin University 52, 65, 162–3, 165, 196
Xiao Qian 48, 83, 294
xin 50, 60, 65
Xin Jian Zhu 163
Xin Min 60
Xin Min Cong Bao 32
Xin Wutai 275
Xin Xin Wu Tai 275–6
xin zheng 60
Xu Beihong 72
Xu Jinzhi 14, 16, 25, 176, 178, 190–1, 307
Xu Ruifang 180

Yale 43, 139, 150, 168–9, 194, 196–7, 297
Yamato Hotel 129, 131, 218–19, 221, 225, 229, 236
Yang Jin 53, 65, 163
Yang Shenxiu 32
Yang Shixuan 305
Yang Tingbao 144–6, 161–2, 194, 196, 198, 293–5, 303, 305–6
Yang Xiliu 163, 296

Yeats, W.B. 21
Yenching 37, 70, 189
Yetts, Perceval 13
Ying Zao Fa Shi 14, 93–5, 190, 192, 206, 297
Yingkou 111, 115, 117–18, 121, 129, 253
YMCAs 108–10, 180, 229
Yu Dafu 33, 49, 65, 78–80, 294
Yuan Ming Yuan 101

Zhang Ruogu 79–80, 195
Zhang Tianyi 53, 55, 66
Zhang Xueliang 195
Zhang Youluan 304
Zhang Zhidong 31, 40, 63
Zhang Zuolin 194–5
Zhao Minyi 53
Zhao Shen 109, 144–6, 162, 180, 275, 296
Zhao Shiyan 45
Zhen Guanxuan 157, 161, 165, 297
Zheng Mantuo 74
Zhinatong writers 30
Zhong Guo see Middle Kingdom
Zhong Guo Jian Zhu 13, 186, 189
Zhong Hua bookstore 7
Zhou Enlai 45
Zhou Zuoren 31, 48, 51
Zhu Jianfe 16
Zhu Shigui 161, 195
Zhuang Jun 109, 141, 152, 193, 279